Principles of Macroeconomics 1.1

By
Libby Rittenberg and Timothy Tregarthen

For additional learning supplements created just for this textbook, visit www.FlatWorldStudents.com.

Gain access to:

Quizzes
Flash Cards
Audio Study Guides
Audiobook
Flyx

You'll get **FREE** Chapter 1 digital supplements when you register online.

Simply find your class at
www.FlatWorldStudents.com
to get started!

flatworld
KNOWLEDGE

fwk-412910

Principles of Macroeconomics 1.1
Libby Rittenberg and Timothy Tregarthen

Published by:

Flat World Knowledge, Inc.
One Bridge Street
Irvington, NY 10533

Printed in the United States of America

Brief Contents

About the Authors

Acknowledgments

Preface

Chapter 1   Economics: The Study of Choice

Chapter 2   Confronting Scarcity: Choices in Production

Chapter 3   Demand and Supply

Chapter 4   Applications of Demand and Supply

Chapter 5   Macroeconomics: The Big Picture

Chapter 6   Measuring Total Output and Income

Chapter 7   Aggregate Demand and Aggregate Supply

Chapter 8   Economic Growth

Chapter 9   The Nature and Creation of Money

Chapter 10   Financial Markets and the Economy

Chapter 11   Monetary Policy and the Fed

Chapter 12   Government and Fiscal Policy

Chapter 13   Consumption and the Aggregate Expenditures Model

Chapter 14   Investment and Economic Activity

Chapter 15   Net Exports and International Finance

Chapter 16   Inflation and Unemployment

Chapter 17   A Brief History of Macroeconomic Thought and Policy

Chapter 18   Inequality, Poverty, and Discrimination

Chapter 19   Economic Development

Chapter 20   Socialist Economies in Transition

Chapter 21   Appendix A: Graphs in Economics

Chapter 22   Appendix B: Extensions of the Aggregate Expenditures Model

Index

Contents

About the Authors   1

Acknowledgments   2

Preface   4

Chapter 1   **Economics: The Study of Choice**   7

Start Up: Economics in the News   7
Defining Economics   8
The Field of Economics   12
The Economists' Tool Kit   17
Review and Practice   21
Endnotes   23

Chapter 2   **Confronting Scarcity: Choices in Production**   25

Start Up: Tightening Security at the World's Airports   25
Factors of Production   26
The Production Possibilities Curve   30
Applications of the Production Possibilities Model   40
Review and Practice   49
Endnotes   55

Chapter 3   **Demand and Supply**   57

Start Up: Crazy for Coffee   57
Demand   58
Supply   65
Demand, Supply, and Equilibrium   72
Review and Practice   83
Endnotes   88

Chapter 4   **Applications of Demand and Supply**   89

Start Up: A Composer Logs On   89
Putting Demand and Supply to Work   90
Government Intervention in Market Prices: Price Floors and Price Ceilings   97
The Market for Health-Care Services   102
Review and Practice   107
Endnotes   110

Chapter 5   **Macroeconomics: The Big Picture**   111

Start Up: Financial Crisis Batters Economy   111
Growth of Real GDP and Business Cycles   113
Price-Level Changes   118

Unemployment 126

Review and Practice 132

Endnotes 136

Chapter 6   Measuring Total Output and Income   137

Start Up: The Lockup 137

Measuring Total Output 138

Measuring Total Income 146

GDP and Economic Well-Being 151

Review and Practice 156

Endnotes 160

Chapter 7   Aggregate Demand and Aggregate Supply   161

Start Up: The Great Warning 161

Aggregate Demand 162

Aggregate Demand and Aggregate Supply: The Long Run and the Short Run 168

Recessionary and Inflationary Gaps and Long-Run Macroeconomic Equilibrium 177

Review and Practice 185

Endnotes 189

Chapter 8   Economic Growth   191

Start Up: How Important Is Economic Growth? 191

The Significance of Economic Growth 192

Growth and the Long-Run Aggregate Supply Curve 197

Determinants of Economic Growth 204

Review and Practice 208

Endnotes 212

Chapter 9   The Nature and Creation of Money   213

Start Up: How Many Macks Does It Cost? 213

What Is Money? 214

The Banking System and Money Creation 219

The Federal Reserve System 228

Review and Practice 233

Endnotes 236

Chapter 10   Financial Markets and the Economy   237

Start Up: Clamping Down on Money Growth 237

The Bond and Foreign Exchange Markets 238

Demand, Supply, and Equilibrium in the Money Market 244

Review and Practice 254

Endnotes 257

Chapter 11   **Monetary Policy and the Fed**   **259**

Start Up: The Fed's Extraordinary Challenges in 2008   259
Monetary Policy in the United States   260
Problems and Controversies of Monetary Policy   267
Monetary Policy and the Equation of Exchange   273
Review and Practice   279
Endnotes   284

Chapter 12   **Government and Fiscal Policy**   **285**

Start Up: A Massive Stimulus   285
Government and the Economy   286
The Use of Fiscal Policy to Stabilize the Economy   293
Issues in Fiscal Policy   298
Review and Practice   302
Endnotes   306

Chapter 13   **Consumption and the Aggregate Expenditures Model**   **307**

Start Up: A Dismal 2008 for Retailers   307
Determining the Level of Consumption   307
The Aggregate Expenditures Model   314
Aggregate Expenditures and Aggregate Demand   329
Review and Practice   333
Endnotes   337

Chapter 14   **Investment and Economic Activity**   **339**

Start Up: Jittery Firms Slash Investment   339
The Role and Nature of Investment   340
Determinants of Investment   346
Investment and the Economy   351
Review and Practice   354
Endnotes   357

Chapter 15   **Net Exports and International Finance**   **359**

Start Up: Currency Crises Shake the World   359
The International Sector: An Introduction   360
International Finance   367
Exchange Rate Systems   374
Review and Practice   379
Endnotes   383

Chapter 16   **Inflation and Unemployment**   **385**

Start Up: The Inflation/Unemployment Conundrum   385
Relating Inflation and Unemployment   386
Explaining Inflation–Unemployment Relationships   391
Inflation and Unemployment in the Long Run   397

Review and Practice 404

Endnotes 407

Chapter 17   A Brief History of Macroeconomic Thought and Policy   409

Start Up: Three Revolutions in Macroeconomic Thought 409

The Great Depression and Keynesian Economics 410

Keynesian Economics in the 1960s and 1970s 416

An Emerging Consensus: Macroeconomics for the Twenty-First Century 424

Review and Practice 430

Endnotes 433

Chapter 18   Inequality, Poverty, and Discrimination   435

Start Up: Poverty in the United States 435

Income Inequality 437

The Economics of Poverty 442

The Economics of Discrimination 452

Review and Practice 457

Endnotes 461

Chapter 19   Economic Development   463

Start Up: Being Poor in a Poor Country 463

The Nature and Challenge of Economic Development 464

Population Growth and Economic Development 472

Keys to Economic Development 478

Review and Practice 483

Endnotes 485

Chapter 20   Socialist Economies in Transition   487

Start Up: The Collapse of Socialism 487

The Theory and Practice of Socialism 488

Socialist Systems in Action 492

Economies in Transition: China and Russia 496

Review and Practice 502

Endnotes 504

Chapter 21   Appendix A: Graphs in Economics   505

How to Construct and Interpret Graphs 505

Nonlinear Relationships and Graphs without Numbers 515

Using Graphs and Charts to Show Values of Variables 521

Chapter 22   Appendix B: Extensions of the Aggregate Expenditures Model   531

The Algebra of Equilibrium 531

The Aggregate Expenditures Model and Fiscal Policy 533

Review and Practice 537

Index   539

About the Authors

LIBBY RITTENBERG

Libby Rittenberg has been a Professor of Economics at Colorado College in Colorado Springs since 1989. She teaches principles of economics, intermediate macroeconomic theory, comparative economic systems, and international political economy. She received her B. A. in economics-mathematics and Spanish from Simmons College and her Ph.D. in economics from Rutgers University.

Prior to joining the faculty at Colorado College, she taught at Lafayette College and at the Rutgers University Graduate School of Management. She served as a Fulbright Scholar in Istanbul, Turkey, and as a research economist at Mathematica, Inc. in Princeton, New Jersey.

Dr. Rittenberg specializes in the internationally oriented areas of economics, with numerous articles in journals and books on comparative and development economics. Much of her work focuses on transition issues and on the Turkish economy.

She has been very involved in study abroad education and has directed programs in central Europe and Turkey.

TIM TREGARTHEN

There is one word that captures the essence of Dr. Timothy Tregarthen—inspiring. Tim was first diagnosed with multiple sclerosis (MS) in 1975. Yet, he continued a remarkable academic career of teaching and research. In 1996, he published the first edition of his principles of economics textbook to great acclaim, and it became widely used in colleges around the country. That same year, MS made him wheelchair-bound. The disease forced his retirement from teaching at the University of Colorado at Colorado Springs in 1998. He lost the use of his arms in 2001 and has been quadriplegic ever since. In 2002, Tim's doctor expected him to die.

He was placed in the Pikes Peak Hospice program and was twice given his last rites by his priest. UCCS Chancellor Shockley-Zalabak says, "I really thought that Tim would die in hospice. That's what the doctors told me, and I really believed that. I remember one day they called me and told me to try to come see him. They didn't expect him to live through the night."

Not only did he live through the night, but he eventually recovered to the point that he moved from hospice to a long-term care facility. There, he never let his disease get him down. In fact, he turned back to his love of writing and teaching for inspiration. He obtained a voice-activated computer, recruited a coauthor, Libby Rittenberg of Colorado College, and turned his attention to revising his principles of economics book. Flat World Knowledge is honored to publish a new, first edition relaunch of this wonderful book, and proud to bring Tim's incredible talents as a teacher back to life for future generations of students to learn from.

In addition to completing the rewrite of his textbook, Tim recently completed an autobiography about the thirty-two years he has had MS, titled *Suffering, Faith, and Wildflowers*. He is nearing completion of a novel, *Cool Luck*, based on the life of a friend. It is the story of a young couple facing the husband's diagnosis of ALS—Lou Gehrig's disease. Remarkably, in 2007, he was able to return to the classroom at UCCS, where he had taught economics for twenty-seven years. In January of 2009, Tim married Dinora Montenegro (now Dinora Tregarthen); the couple lives in San Gabriel, California.

Perhaps Tim's approach to life is best summed up by an observation by UCCS English Professor Thomas Naperierkowski: "One of the remarkable things is, heck, I can wake up with a headache and be a pretty grouchy character, but given his physical trials, which he faces every minute of his life these days, I've never seen him grouchy, I've never seen him cranky." Carry on, Tim.

Acknowledgments

The authors would like to thank to the following individuals who reviewed the text and whose contributions were invaluable in shaping the final product:

Carlos Aguilar	El Paso Community College
Jeff Ankrom	Wittenberg University
Lee Ash	Skagit Valley Community College
Randall Bennett	Gonzaga University
Joseph Calhoun	Florida State University
Richard Cantrell	Western Kentucky University
Gregg Davis	Flathead Valley Community College
Kevin Dunagan	Oakton Community College
Mona El Shazly	Columbia College
Jose Esteban	Palomar College
Maurita Fawls	Portland Community College
Fred Foldvary	Santa Clara University
Richard Fowles	University of Utah
Doris Geide-Stevenson	Weber State University
Sarmila Ghosh	University of Scranton, Kania School of Management
David Gordon	Illinois Valley Community College
Clinton Greene	University of Missouri-St. Louis
James Holcomb	University of Texas at El Paso
Phil Holleran	Mitchell Community College
Yu Hsing	Southeastern Louisiana University
Thomas Hyclak	Lehigh University
Bruce Johnson	Centre College
James Kahiga	Georgia Perimeter College
Andrew Kohen	James Madison University
Monaco Kristen	California State University–Long Beach
Mark Maier	Glendale Community College
David McClough	Bowling Green State University
Ann McPherren	Huntington University
John Min	Northern Virginia Community College
Shahriar Mostashari	Campbell University, Lundy-Fetterman School of Business
Francis Mummery	Fullerton College
Robert Murphy	Boston College
Kathryn Nantz	Fairfield University
Paul Okello	Tarrant County College-South Campus
Nicholas Peppes	St. Louis Community College
Ramoo Ratha	Diablo Valley College
Teresa Riley	Youngstown State University
Michael Robinson	Mount Holyoke College
Anirban Sengupta	Texas A&M University

John Solow	The University of Iowa
John Somers	Portland Community College
Charles Staelin	Smith College
Richard Stratton	The University of Akron
Kay E. Strong	Bowling Green State University–Firelands
Della Sue	Marist College
John Vahaly	University of Louisville
Robert Whaples	Wake Forest University
Mark Wheeler	Western Michigan University
Leslie Wolfson	The Pingry School
Sourushe Zandvakili	University of Cincinnati

We would like to extend a special thank you to the following instructors who class tested the text in their courses:

Johnathan Millman	University of Massachusetts–Boston
John Min	Northern Virginia Community College
Kristen Monaco	California State University–Long Beach
Steve Skinner	Western Connecticut State University
Richard Stratton	University of Akron

Preface

Greek philosopher Heraclitis said over 2500 years ago that "Nothing endures but change." Forecasting is a tricky business, but this sentiment strikes us as being as safe a bet as one can make. Change—rapid change—underlies all our lives. As we were completing this textbook, the world entered a period of marked economic uncertainty that led many students, and indeed people from all walks of life, to tune into economic events as never before to try to understand the economic world around them. So, while we as economists have the public's attention, we see an opportunity to share economics principles and the economic way of thinking in a way that emphasizes their relevance to today's world. We use applications from sports, politics, campus life, current events, and other familiar settings to illustrate the links between theoretical principles and common experiences. Because of the increasingly global nature of economic activity, we also recognize the need for a clear and consistent international focus throughout an economics text. In addition, we have tried to provide a sense of the intellectual excitement of the field and an appreciation for the gains it has made, as well as an awareness of the challenges that lie ahead.

To ensure students realize that economics is a unified discipline and not a bewildering array of seemingly unrelated topics, we develop the presentation of microeconomics and of macroeconomics around integrating themes.

The integrating theme for microeconomics is the marginal decision rule, a simple approach to choices that maximize the value of some objective. Following its presentation in an early microeconomics chapter, the marginal decision rule becomes an integrating device throughout the discussion of microeconomics. Instead of a hodgepodge of rules for different market conditions, we give a single rule that can be applied within any market setting.

The integrating theme for macroeconomics is the model of aggregate demand and aggregate supply. Following its presentation in an early macroeconomics chapter, this model allows us to look at both short-run and long-run concepts and to address a variety of policy issues and debates.

Recognizing that a course in economics may seem daunting to some students, we have tried to make the writing clear and engaging. Clarity comes in part from the intuitive presentation style, but we have also integrated a number of pedagogical features that we believe make learning economic concepts and principles easier and more fun. These features are very student-focused.

The chapters themselves are written using a "modular" format. In particular, chapters generally consist of three main content sections that break down a particular topic into manageable parts. Each content section contains not only an exposition of the material at hand but also learning objectives, summaries, examples, and problems. Each chapter is introduced with a story to motivate the material and each chapter ends with a wrap-up and additional problems. Our goal is to encourage active learning by including many examples and many problems of different types.

A tour of the features available for each chapter may give a better sense of what we mean:

- Start Up—Chapter introductions set the stage for each chapter with an example that we hope will motivate readers to study the material that follows. These essays, on topics such as the value of a college degree in the labor market or how policy makers reacted to a particular economic recession, lend themselves to the type of analysis explained in the chapter. We often refer to these examples later in the text to demonstrate the link between theory and reality.

- Learning Objectives—These succinct statements are guides to the content of each section. Instructors can use them as a snapshot of the important points of the section. After completing the section, students can return to the learning objectives to check if they have mastered the material.

- Heads Up!—These notes throughout the text warn of common errors and explain how to avoid making them. After our combined teaching experience of more than fifty years, we have seen the same mistakes made by many students. This feature provides additional clarification and shows students how to navigate possibly treacherous waters.

- Key Takeaways—These statements review the main points covered in each content section.

- Key Terms—Defined within the text, students can review them in context, a process that enhances learning.

- Try It! questions—These problems, which appear at the end of each content section and which are answered completely in the text, give students the opportunity to be active learners. They are designed to give students a clear signal as to whether they understand the material before they go on to the next topic.

- Cases in Point—These essays included at the end of each content section illustrate the influence of economic forces on real issues and real people. Unlike other texts that use boxed features to present interesting new material or newspaper articles, we have written each case ourselves to integrate them more clearly with the rest of the text.

- Summary—In a few paragraphs, the information presented in the chapter is pulled together in a way that allows for a quick review of the material.

- End-of-chapter concept and numerical problems—These are bountiful and are intended to check understanding, to promote discussion of the issues raised in the chapter, and to engage students in critical thinking about the material. Included are not only general review questions to test basic understanding but also examples drawn from the news and from results of economics research. Some have students working with real-world data.

- Chapter quizzes—Each chapter also includes online, supplementary multiple choice questions that provide students with feedback on both correct and incorrect responses. These provide yet another way for students to test themselves on the material.

ADDITIONAL MATERIAL FOR INSTRUCTORS

The authors have been personally involved in the generation of a huge *Test Bank* that includes multiple choice, true/false, and short essays questions. These questions are scored in terms of level of difficulty and include multiple ways of testing the material.

The *Solutions Manual*, with which the authors were also involved, contains answers for all concept and numerical problems found at the end of each text chapter.

The *PowerPoint Slides* include all the exhibits contained in the text to allow ease of use in class.

We hope that users will find this text an engaging and enjoyable way of becoming acquainted with economics principles and that mastery of the material will lead to looking at the world in a deeper and more meaningful way. We welcome all feedback.

Libby Rittenberg

Timothy Tregarthen

CHAPTER 1
Economics: The Study of Choice

START UP: ECONOMICS IN THE NEWS

2008 seemed to be the year of economic news. From the worst financial crisis since the Great Depression to the possibility of a global recession, to gyrating gasoline and food prices, and to plunging housing prices, economic questions were the primary factors in the presidential campaign of 2008 and dominated the news generally.

What causes the prices of some good to rise while the prices of some other goods fall? Price determination is one of the things that we will study in this book. We will also consider factors that lead an economy to fall into a recession—and the attempts to limit it.

While the investigation of these problems surely falls within the province of economics, economics encompasses a far broader range of issues. Ultimately, economics is the study of choice. Because choices range over every imaginable aspect of human experience, so does economics. Economists have investigated the nature of family life, the arts, education, crime, sports, job creation—the list is virtually endless because so much of our lives involves making choices.

How do individuals make choices: Would you like better grades? More time to relax? More time watching movies? Getting better grades probably requires more time studying, and perhaps less relaxation and entertainment. Not only must we make choices as individuals, we must make choices as a society. Do we want a cleaner environment? Faster economic growth? Both may be desirable, but efforts to clean up the environment may conflict with faster economic growth. Society must make choices.

Economics is defined less by the subjects economists investigate than by the way in which economists investigate them. Economists have a way of looking at the world that differs from the way scholars in other disciplines look at the world. It is the *economic way of thinking*; this chapter introduces that way of thinking.

1.   DEFINING ECONOMICS

Economics is a social science that examines how people choose among the alternatives available to them. It is social because it involves people and their behavior. It is a science because it uses, as much as possible, a scientific approach in its investigation of choices.

1.1   Scarcity, Choice, and Cost

All choices mean that one alternative is selected over another. Selecting among alternatives involves three ideas central to economics: scarcity, choice, and opportunity cost.

Scarcity

Our resources are limited. At any one time, we have only so much land, so many factories, so much oil, so many people. But our wants, our desires for the things that we can produce with those resources, are unlimited. We would always like more and better housing, more and better education—more and better of practically everything.

If our resources were also unlimited, we could say yes to each of our wants—and there would be no economics. Because our resources are limited, we cannot say yes to everything. To say yes to one thing requires that we say no to another. Whether we like it or not, we must make choices.

Our unlimited wants are continually colliding with the limits of our resources, forcing us to pick some activities and to reject others. **Scarcity** is the condition of having to choose among alternatives. A **scarce good** is one for which the choice of one alternative requires that another be given up.

Consider a parcel of land. The parcel presents us with several alternative uses. We could build a house on it. We could put a gas station on it. We could create a small park on it. We could leave the land undeveloped in order to be able to make a decision later as to how it should be used.

Suppose we have decided the land should be used for housing. Should it be a large and expensive house or several modest ones? Suppose it is to be a large and expensive house. Who should live in the house? If the Lees live in it, the Nguyens cannot. There are alternative uses of the land both in the sense of the type of use and also in the sense of who gets to use it. The fact that land is scarce means that society must make choices concerning its use.

Virtually everything is scarce. Consider the air we breathe, which is available in huge quantity at no charge to us. Could it possibly be scarce?

The test of whether air is scarce is whether it has alternative uses. What uses can we make of the air? We breathe it. We pollute it when we drive our cars, heat our houses, or operate our factories. In effect, one use of the air is as a garbage dump. We certainly need the air to breathe. But just as certainly, we choose to dump garbage in it. Those two uses are clearly alternatives to each other. The more garbage we dump in the air, the less desirable—and healthy—it will be to breathe. If we decide we want to breathe cleaner air, we must limit the activities that generate pollution. Air is a scarce good because it has alternative uses.

Not all goods, however, confront us with such choices. A **free good** is one for which the choice of one use does not require that we give up another. One example of a free good is gravity. The fact that gravity is holding you to the earth does not mean that your neighbor is forced to drift up into space! One person's use of gravity is not an alternative to another person's use.

There are not many free goods. Outer space, for example, was a free good when the only use we made of it was to gaze at it. But now, our use of space has reached the point where one use can be an alternative to another. Conflicts have already arisen over the allocation of orbital slots for communications satellites. Thus, even parts of outer space are scarce. Space will surely become more scarce as we find new ways to use it. Scarcity characterizes virtually everything. Consequently, the scope of economics is wide indeed.

economics

A social science that examines how people choose among the alternatives available to them.

scarcity

The condition of having to choose among alternatives.

scarce good

A good for which the choice of one alternative requires that another be given up.

free good

A good for which the choice of one use does not require that another be given up.

Scarcity and the Fundamental Economic Questions

The choices we confront as a result of scarcity raise three sets of issues. Every economy must answer the following questions:

1. **What should be produced?** Using the economy's scarce resources to produce one thing requires giving up another. Producing better education, for example, may require cutting back on other services, such as health care. A decision to preserve a wilderness area requires giving up other uses of the land. Every society must decide what it will produce with its scarce resources.

2. **How should goods and services be produced?** There are all sorts of choices to be made in determining how goods and services should be produced. Should a firm employ a few skilled or a lot of unskilled workers? Should it produce in its own country or should it use foreign plants? Should manufacturing firms use new or recycled raw materials to make their products?

3. **For whom should goods and services be produced?** If a good or service is produced, a decision must be made about who will get it. A decision to have one person or group receive a good or service usually means it will not be available to someone else. For example, representatives of the poorest nations on earth often complain that energy consumption per person in the United States is 17 *times* greater than energy consumption per person in the world's 62 poorest countries. Critics argue that the world's energy should be more evenly allocated. Should it? That is a "for whom" question.

Every economy must determine what should be produced, how it should be produced, and for whom it should be produced. We shall return to these questions again and again.

Opportunity Cost

It is within the context of scarcity that economists define what is perhaps the most important concept in all of economics, the concept of opportunity cost. **Opportunity cost** is the value of the best alternative forgone in making any choice.

The opportunity cost to you of reading the remainder of this chapter will be the value of the best other use to which you could have put your time. If you choose to spend $20 on a potted plant, you have simultaneously chosen to give up the benefits of spending the $20 on pizzas or a paperback book or a night at the movies. If the book is the most valuable of those alternatives, then the opportunity cost of the plant is the value of the enjoyment you otherwise expected to receive from the book.

The concept of opportunity cost must not be confused with the purchase price of an item. Consider the cost of a college or university education. That includes the value of the best alternative use of money spent for tuition, fees, and books. But the most important cost of a college education is the value of the forgone alternative uses of time spent studying and attending class instead of using the time in some other endeavor. Students sacrifice that time in hopes of even greater earnings in the future or because they place a value on the opportunity to learn. Or consider the cost of going to the doctor. Part of that cost is the value of the best alternative use of the money required to see the doctor. But, the cost also includes the value of the best alternative use of the time required to see the doctor. The essential thing to see in the concept of opportunity cost is found in the name of the concept. Opportunity cost is the value of the best opportunity forgone in a particular choice. It is not simply the amount spent on that choice.

The concepts of scarcity, choice, and opportunity cost are at the heart of economics. A good is scarce if the choice of one alternative requires that another be given up. The existence of alternative uses forces us to make choices. The opportunity cost of any choice is the value of the best alternative forgone in making it.

opportunity cost

The value of the best alternative forgone in making any choice.

KEY TAKEAWAYS

- Economics is a social science that examines how people choose among the alternatives available to them.
- Scarcity implies that we must give up one alternative in selecting another. A good that is not scarce is a free good.
- The three fundamental economic questions are: What should be produced? How should goods and services be produced? For whom should goods and services be produced?
- Every choice has an opportunity cost and opportunity costs affect the choices people make. The opportunity cost of any choice is the value of the best alternative that had to be forgone in making that choice.

TRY IT!

Identify the elements of scarcity, choice, and opportunity cost in each of the following:

1. The Environmental Protection Agency is considering an order that a 500-acre area on the outskirts of a large city be preserved in its natural state, because the area is home to a rodent that is considered an endangered species. Developers had planned to build a housing development on the land.

2. The manager of an automobile assembly plant is considering whether to produce cars or sport utility vehicles (SUVs) next month. Assume that the quantities of labor and other materials required would be the same for either type of production.

3. A young man who went to work as a nurses' aide after graduating from high school leaves his job to go to college, where he will obtain training as a registered nurse.

Case in Point: The Rising Cost of Energy

© 2010 Jupiterimages Corporation

Oil is an exhaustible resource. The oil we burn today will not be available for use in the future. Part of the opportunity cost of our consumption of goods such as gasoline that are produced from oil includes the value people in the future might have placed on oil we use today.

It appears that the cost of our use of oil may be rising. We have been using "light crude," the oil found in the ground in deposits that can be readily tapped. As light crude becomes more scarce, the world may need to turn to so-called "heavy crude," the crude oil that is found in the sandy soil of places such as Canada and Venezuela. That oil exists in such abundance that it propels Venezuela to the top of the world list of available oil. Saudi Arabia moves to the second position; Canada is third.

The difficulty with the oil mixed in the sand is that extracting it is far more costly than light crude, both in terms of the expenditures required and in terms of the environmental damage that mining it creates. Northern Alberta, in Canada, boasts a Florida-sized area whose sandy soils are rich in crude oil. Some of that oil is 1,200 feet underground. Extracting it requires pumping steam into the oily sand and then pumping up the resultant oily syrup. That syrup is then placed into huge, industrial-sized washing machines that separate crude oil. What is left over is toxic and will be placed in huge lakes that are being created by digging pits in the ground 200 feet deep. The oil produced from these sands has become important—Alberta is the largest foreign supplier of oil to the United States.

Sands that are closer to the surface are removed by bulldozers and giant cranes; the forest over it is cleared away. The oily sand is then hauled off in two-story dump trucks which, when filled, weigh more than a Boeing 747. Total SA, a French company, is leading the race to develop Canada's oil. Jean Luc-Guiziou, the president of Total SA's Canadian operations, says that the extraordinarily costly process of extracting heavy crude is something the world is going to have to get used to. "The light crude undiscovered today is getting scarcer and scarcer," he told *The Wall Street Journal*. "We have to accept the reality of geoscience, which is that the next generation of oil resources will be heavier."

Already, Total SA has clear-cut thousands of acres of forest land in order to gain access to the oily sand below. The process of extracting heavy crude oil costs the company $25 a barrel—compared to the $6 per barrel cost of extracting and refining light crude. Extracting heavy crude generates three times as much greenhouse gas per barrel as does light crude. By 2015, Fort McMurray, the small (population 61,000) town that has become the headquarters of Northern Alberta's crude oil boom, will emit more greenhouse gas than the entire country of Denmark (population 5.4 million). Canada will exceed its greenhouse gas quota set by the Kyoto Accords—an international treaty aimed at limiting global warming—largely as a result of developing its heavy crude deposits.

No one even considered the extraction of heavy crude when light crude was cheap. In the late 1990s, oil cost just $12 per barrel, and deposits of heavy crude such as those in Canada attracted little attention. By mid-2006, oil sold for more than $70 per barrel, and Canada's heavy crude was suddenly a hot commodity. "It moved from being just an interesting experiment in northern Canada to really this is the future source of oil supply," Greg Stringham of the Canadian Association of Petroleum Producers told Al Jazeera.

Alberta's energy minister, Greg Melchin, defends the province's decision to proceed with the exploitation of its oily sand. "There is a cost to it, but the benefits are substantially greater," he insists.

Not everyone agrees. George Poitras, a member of the Mikisew Cree tribe, lives downstream from the oil sands development. "You see a lot of the land dug up, a lot of the boreal forest struck down and it's upsetting, it fills me with rage," he says. Diana Gibson of the Parkland Institute, an environmental advocacy group, says that you can see the environmental damage generated by the extraction of oil sands around Fort McMurray from the moon. "What we are going to be having is destruction of very, very valuable ecosystems, and permanent pollution," she says.

Sources: "Alberta's Heavy Oil Burden," Al Jazeera English, March 17, 2008 (see english.aljazeera.net); and Russell Gold, "As Prices Surge, Oil Giants Turn Sludge into Gold," The Wall Street Journal Online, March 27, 2006, A1.

ANSWERS TO TRY IT! PROBLEMS

1. The 500-acre area is scarce because it has alternative uses: preservation in its natural state or a site for homes. A choice must be made between these uses. The opportunity cost of preserving the land in its natural state is the forgone value of the land as a housing development. The opportunity cost of using the land as a housing development is the forgone value of preserving the land.

2. The scarce resources are the plant and the labor at the plant. The manager must choose between producing cars and producing SUVs. The opportunity cost of producing cars is the profit that could be earned from producing SUVs; the opportunity cost of producing SUVs is the profit that could be earned from producing cars.

3. The man can devote his time to his current career or to an education; his time is a scarce resource. He must choose between these alternatives. The opportunity cost of continuing as a nurses' aide is the forgone benefit he expects from training as a registered nurse; the opportunity cost of going to college is the forgone income he could have earned working full-time as a nurses' aide.

2. THE FIELD OF ECONOMICS

LEARNING OBJECTIVES

1. Explain the distinguishing characteristics of the economic way of thinking.
2. Distinguish between microeconomics and macroeconomics.

We have examined the basic concepts of scarcity, choice, and opportunity cost in economics. In this section, we will look at economics as a field of study. We begin with the characteristics that distinguish economics from other social sciences.

2.1 The Economic Way of Thinking

Economists study choices that scarcity requires us to make. This fact is not what distinguishes economics from other social sciences; all social scientists are interested in choices. An anthropologist might study the choices of ancient peoples; a political scientist might study the choices of legislatures; a psychologist might study how people choose a mate; a sociologist might study the factors that have led to a rise in single-parent households. Economists study such questions as well. What is it about the study of choices by economists that makes economics different from these other social sciences?

Three features distinguish the economic approach to choice from the approaches taken in other social sciences:

1. Economists give special emphasis to the role of opportunity costs in their analysis of choices.
2. Economists assume that individuals make choices that seek to maximize the value of some objective, and that they define their objectives in terms of their own self-interest.
3. Individuals maximize by deciding whether to do a little more or a little less of something. Economists argue that individuals pay attention to the consequences of small changes in the levels of the activities they pursue.

The emphasis economists place on opportunity cost, the idea that people make choices that maximize the value of objectives that serve their self-interest, and a focus on the effects of small changes are ideas of great power. They constitute the core of economic thinking. The next three sections examine these ideas in greater detail.

Opportunity Costs Are Important

If doing one thing requires giving up another, then the expected benefits of the alternatives we face will affect the ones we choose. Economists argue that an understanding of opportunity cost is crucial to the examination of choices.

As the set of available alternatives changes, we expect that the choices individuals make will change. A rainy day could change the opportunity cost of reading a good book; we might expect more reading to get done in bad than in good weather. A high income can make it very costly to take a day off; we might expect highly paid individuals to work more hours than those who are not paid as well. If individuals are maximizing their level of satisfaction and firms are maximizing profits, then a change in the set of alternatives they face may affect their choices in a predictable way.

The emphasis on opportunity costs is an emphasis on the examination of alternatives. One benefit of the economic way of thinking is that it pushes us to think about the value of alternatives in each problem involving choice.

Individuals Maximize in Pursuing Self-Interest

What motivates people as they make choices? Perhaps more than anything else, it is the economist's answer to this question that distinguishes economics from other fields.

Economists assume that individuals make choices that they expect will create the maximum value of some objective, given the constraints they face. Furthermore, economists assume that people's objectives will be those that serve their own self-interest.

Economists assume, for example, that the owners of business firms seek to maximize profit. Given the assumed goal of profit maximization, economists can predict how firms in an industry will respond to changes in the markets in which they operate. As labor costs in the United States rise, for example, economists are not surprised to see firms moving some of their manufacturing operations overseas.

Similarly, economists assume that maximizing behavior is at work when they examine the behavior of consumers. In studying consumers, economists assume that individual consumers make choices aimed at maximizing their level of satisfaction. In the next chapter, we will look at the results of the shift from skiing to snowboarding; that is a shift that reflects the pursuit of self-interest by consumers and by manufacturers.

In assuming that people pursue their self-interest, economists are not assuming people are selfish. People clearly gain satisfaction by helping others, as suggested by the large charitable contributions people make. Pursuing one's own self-interest means pursuing the things that give one satisfaction. It need not imply greed or selfishness.

Choices Are Made at the Margin

Economists argue that most choices are made "at the margin." The **margin** is the current level of an activity. Think of it as the edge from which a choice is to be made. A **choice at the margin** is a decision to do a little more or a little less of something.

Assessing choices at the margin can lead to extremely useful insights. Consider, for example, the problem of curtailing water consumption when the amount of water available falls short of the amount people now use. Economists argue that one way to induce people to conserve water is to raise its price. A common response to this recommendation is that a higher price would have no effect on water consumption, because water is a necessity. Many people assert that prices do not affect water consumption because people "need" water.

But choices in water consumption, like virtually all choices, are made at the margin. Individuals do not make choices about whether they should or should not consume water. Rather, they decide whether to consume a little more or a little less water. Household water consumption in the United States totals about 105 gallons per person per day. Think of that starting point as the edge from which a choice at the margin in water consumption is made. Could a higher price cause you to use less water brushing your teeth, take shorter showers, or water your lawn less? Could a higher price cause people to reduce their use, say, to 104 gallons per person per day? To 103? When we examine the choice to consume water at the margin, the notion that a higher price would reduce consumption seems much more plausible. Prices affect our consumption of water because choices in water consumption, like other choices, are made at the margin.

The elements of opportunity cost, maximization, and choices at the margin can be found in each of two broad areas of economic analysis: microeconomics and macroeconomics. Your economics course, for example, may be designated as a "micro" or as a "macro" course. We will look at these two areas of economic thought in the next section.

2.2 Microeconomics and Macroeconomics

The field of economics is typically divided into two broad realms: microeconomics and macroeconomics. It is important to see the distinctions between these broad areas of study.

Microeconomics is the branch of economics that focuses on the choices made by individual decision-making units in the economy—typically consumers and firms—and the impacts those choices have on individual markets. **Macroeconomics** is the branch of economics that focuses on the impact of choices on the total, or aggregate, level of economic activity.

Why do tickets to the best concerts cost so much? How does the threat of global warming affect real estate prices in coastal areas? Why do women end up doing most of the housework? Why do senior citizens get discounts on public transit systems? These questions are generally regarded as microeconomic because they focus on individual units or markets in the economy.

Is the total level of economic activity rising or falling? Is the rate of inflation increasing or decreasing? What is happening to the unemployment rate? These are questions that deal with aggregates, or totals, in the economy; they are problems of macroeconomics. The question about the level of economic activity, for example, refers to the total value of all goods and services produced in the economy. Inflation is a measure of the rate of change in the average price level for the entire economy; it is a macroeconomic problem. The total levels of employment and unemployment in the economy represent the aggregate of all labor markets; unemployment is also a topic of macroeconomics.

Both microeconomics and macroeconomics give attention to individual markets. But in microeconomics that attention is an end in itself; in macroeconomics it is aimed at explaining the movement of major economic aggregates—the level of total output, the level of employment, and the price level.

We have now examined the characteristics that define the economic way of thinking and the two branches of this way of thinking: microeconomics and macroeconomics. In the next section, we will have a look at what one can do with training in economics.

---

margin

The current level of an activity.

choice at the margin

A decision to do a little more or a little less of something.

microeconomics

The branch of economics that focuses on the choices made by consumers and firms and the impacts those choices have on individual markets.

macroeconomics

The branch of economics that focuses on the impact of choices on the total, or aggregate, level of economic activity.

2.3 Putting Economics to Work

Economics is one way of looking at the world. Because the economic way of thinking has proven quite useful, training in economics can be put to work in a wide range of fields. One, of course, is in work as an economist. Undergraduate work in economics can be applied to other careers as well.

Careers in Economics

Economists work in three types of organizations. About 58% of economists work for government agencies.[1] The remainder work for business firms or in colleges and universities.

Economists working for business firms and government agencies sometimes forecast economic activity to assist their employers in planning. They also apply economic analysis to the activities of the firms or agencies for which they work or consult. Economists employed at colleges and universities teach and conduct research.

Peruse the website of your college or university's economics department. Chances are the department will discuss the wide variety of occupations that their economics majors enter. Unlike engineering and accounting majors, economics and other social science majors tend to be distributed over a broad range of occupations.

Applying Economics to Other Fields

Suppose that you are considering something other than a career in economics. Would choosing to study economics help you?

The evidence suggests it may. Suppose, for example, that you are considering law school. The study of law requires keen analytical skills; studying economics sharpens such skills. Economists have traditionally argued that undergraduate work in economics serves as excellent preparation for law school. Economist Michael Nieswiadomy of the University of North Texas collected data on Law School Admittance Test (LSAT) scores for undergraduate majors listed by 2,200 or more students taking the test in 2003. Table 1.1 gives the scores, as well as the ranking for each of these majors, in 2003 and in two previous years in which the rankings were compiled. In rankings for all three years, economics majors recorded the highest scores.

TABLE 1.1 LSAT Scores and Undergraduate Majors

Here are the average LSAT scores and rankings for the 12 undergraduate majors with more than 2200 students taking the test to enter law school in the 2003–2004 academic year.

Major field	LSAT average 2003–2004	2003–2004 Rank	1994–1995 Rank	1991–1992 Rank
Economics	156.6	1	1	1
Engineering	155.4	2	4	2
History	155.0	3	2	3
English	154.3	4	3	4
Finance	152.6	5	6	5
Political science	152.1	6	9	9
Psychology	152.1	7	7	8
Accounting	151.1	8	8	6
Communications	150.5	9	10	10
Sociology	150.2	10	12	13
Bus. Administration	149.6	11	13	12
Criminal Justice	144.7	12	14	14

Source: Michael Nieswiadomy, "LSAT Scores of Economics Majors: 2003–2004 Class Update," Journal of Economic Education, 37(2) (Spring 2006): 244–247 and Michael Nieswiadomy, "LSAT Scores of Economics Majors" Journal of Economic Education, 29(4) (Fall 1998): 377–379.

Did the strong performance by economics, engineering, and history majors mean that training in those fields sharpens analytical skills tested in the LSAT, or that students with good analytical skills are more likely to major in them? Both factors were probably at work. Economics clearly attracts students with good analytical skills—and studying economics helps develop those skills.

Economics majors shine in other areas as well. According to the Bureau of Labor Statistics *Occupational Outlook Handbook*, a strong background in economic theory, mathematics, and statistics provides the basis for competing for the best job opportunities, particularly research assistant positions, in a broad range of fields. Many graduates with bachelor's degrees will find good jobs in industry and business as management or sales trainees or as administrative assistants. Because economists are concerned with understanding and interpreting financial matters, among other subjects, they will also be attracted to and qualified for jobs as financial managers, financial analysts, underwriters, actuaries, securities and financial services sales workers, credit analysts, loan and budget officers, and urban and regional planners.

Table 1.2 shows average yearly salary offers for bachelor degree candidates for May 2006 and the outlook for related occupations to 2014.

TABLE 1.2 Average Yearly Salary Offers, May 2006 and Occupational Outlook 2004–2014, Selected Majors/Occupations

Undergraduate major	Average $ Offer May, 2006	Projected % Change in Total Employment in Occupation 2004–2014
Computer Engineering	$54,200	10.1
Electrical/Electronic Engineering	54,053	11.8
Computer Science	50,892	25.6
Accounting	46,188	22.4
Economics and Finance	45,058	12.4
Management Information Systems	44,755	25.9
Logistics and Materials Management	43,426	13.2
Business Administration	40,976	17.0
Environmental Sciences (including forestry and conservation science)	39,750	6.3
Other Business Majors (e.g., Marketing)	37,446	20.8
Human Resources (incl. Labor Relations)	36,256	15.9
Geology and Geological Sciences	35,034	8.3
Sociology	33,752	4.7
Political Science/Government	33,151	7.3
Liberal Arts & Sciences (general studies)	32,627	na
Public Relations	32,623	21.7
Special Education	31,817	23.3
Elementary Education	31,778	18.2
Foreign Languages	31,364	na
Letters (incl. English)	31,204	20.4
Other Social Sciences (Including Criminal Justice and History)	30,788	12.3
Psychology	30,308	9.9
Pre-elementary Education	27,550	22.4
Social Work	25,865	19.6
Visual and Performing Arts	21,726	15.2

Sources: National Association of Colleges and Employers, Salary Survey, Spring 2006 http://naceweb.org; Bureau of Labor Statistics, 2006–2007 edition of the Occupational Outlook Handbook; Occupational Employment, Training, and Earnings: Educational Level Report (May, 2006) URL: http://data.bls.gov/oep/noeted/empoptd.jsp (note: na = not reported; that is, no specific occupation was reported in BLS report; Other business majors, Other social sciences, Social work (including Sociology), and Environmental Sciences are weighted averages of various disciplines, calculated by authors.)

One's choice of a major, or minor, is not likely to be based solely on considerations of potential earnings or the prospect of landing a spot in law school. You will also consider your interests and abilities in making a decision about whether to pursue further study in economics. And, of course, you will consider the expected benefits of alternative courses of study. What is *your* opportunity cost of pursuing study of economics? Does studying more economics serve your interests and will doing so maximize your satisfaction level? These considerations may be on your mind as you begin to study economics at the college level and obviously students will make many different choices. But, should you decide to pursue a major or minor in economics, you should know that a background in this field is likely to serve you well in a wide range of careers.

KEY TAKEAWAYS

- Economists focus on the opportunity costs of choices, they assume that individuals make choices in a way that maximizes the value of an objective defined in terms of their own self-interest, and they assume that individuals make those choices at the margin.
- Economics is divided into two broad areas: microeconomics and macroeconomics.
- A wide range of career opportunities is open to economics majors. Empirical evidence suggests that students who enter the job market with a major in economics tend to earn more than do students in most other majors. Further, economics majors do particularly well on the LSAT.

TRY IT!

The Department of Agriculture estimated that the expenditures a middle-income, husband–wife family of three would incur to raise one additional child from birth in 2005 to age 17 would be $250,530. In what way does this estimate illustrate the economic way of thinking? Would the Department's estimate be an example of microeconomic or of macroeconomic analysis? Why?

Case in Point: The Financial Payoff to Studying Economics

© 2010 Jupiterimages Corporation

College economics professors have long argued that studying economics is good preparation for a variety of careers. A recent study suggests they are right and that studying economics is even likely to make students more prosperous. Students who major in economics but did not pursue graduate work are likely to earn more than students in virtually every other college major. Students who major in economics and then go on to law school or an MBA program are likely to earn more than students who approach those areas of study having majored in most other areas.

Economists Dan A. Black, Seth Sanders, and Lowell Taylor used the 1993 National Survey of College Graduates, which included more than 86,000 college-educated workers between the ages of 25 and 55 that asked what field they had majored in. They then controlled for variables such as gender, race, and ethnicity. They found that students who had not done graduate work and had majored in economics earned more than students in any other major except engineering. Specifically, economics majors earned about 13% more than other social sciences majors, 11% more than business administration majors, and about the same as natural science and accounting majors. The economics majors in their survey, like those who majored in other social sciences and business administration and unlike those who majored in engineering or accounting, were spread out over a wide range of occupations but with many in management positions.

Based on the survey they used, over 40% of economics majors went on to earn graduate degrees, many in law and business. Economics majors ranked first in terms of wages, as compared to other law school graduates with the 12 most common pre-law majors (including such majors as business administration, finance, English, history, psychology, and political science). MBA graduates who had majored in economics earned more than those who had majored in any other field except chemical engineering. Specifically, undergraduate economics majors with MBAs earned about 15% more than those who had majored in other disciplines represented in the survey, including business-related majors.

It is remarkable that all of the business-related majors generated salaries much lower than those earned by economics majors with an MBA. One could argue that this reflects self-selection; that students who major in economics are simply brighter. But, students who major in physics have high SAT scores, yet they, too, earned wages that were about 20% lower than MBA students who had majored in economics. This finding lends some credence to the notion that the marketplace rewards training in the economic way of thinking.

Source: Dan A. Black, Seth Sanders, and Lowell Taylor, "The Economic Reward for Studying Economics," Economic Inquiry, 41(3), July 2003, 365–377.

ANSWER TO TRY IT! PROBLEM

The information given suggests one element of the economic way of thinking: assessing the choice at the margin. The estimate reflects the cost of one more child for a family that already has one. It is not clear from the information given how close the estimate of cost comes to the economic concept of opportunity cost. The Department of Agriculture's estimate included such costs as housing, food, transportation, clothing, health care, child care, and education. An economist would add the value of the best alternative use of the additional time that will be required for the child. If the couple is looking far ahead, it may want to consider the opportunity cost of sending a child to college. And, if it is looking *very* far ahead, it may want to consider the fact that nearly half of all parents over the age of 50 support at least one child over the age of 21. This is a problem in microeconomic analysis, because it focuses on the choices of individual households.

3.   THE ECONOMISTS' TOOL KIT

LEARNING OBJECTIVES

1. Explain how economists test hypotheses, develop economic theories, and use models in their analyses.
2. Explain how the all-other-things unchanged (ceteris paribus) problem and the fallacy of false cause affect the testing of economic hypotheses and how economists try to overcome these problems.
3. Distinguish between normative and positive statements.

Economics differs from other social sciences because of its emphasis on opportunity cost, the assumption of maximization in terms of one's own self-interest, and the analysis of choices at the margin. But certainly much of the basic methodology of economics and many of its difficulties are common to every social science—indeed, to every science. This section explores the application of the scientific method to economics.

Researchers often examine relationships between variables. A **variable** is something whose value can change. By contrast, a **constant** is something whose value does not change. The speed at which a car is traveling is an example of a variable. The number of minutes in an hour is an example of a constant.

variable

Something whose value can change.

constant

Something whose value does not change.

scientific method

A systematic set of procedures through which knowledge is created.

hypothesis

An assertion of a relationship between two or more variables that could be proven to be false.

Research is generally conducted within a framework called the **scientific method**, a systematic set of procedures through which knowledge is created. In the scientific method, hypotheses are suggested and then tested. A **hypothesis** is an assertion of a relationship between two or more variables that could be proven to be false. A statement is not a hypothesis if no conceivable test could show it to be false. The statement "Plants like sunshine" is not a hypothesis; there is no way to test whether plants like sunshine or not, so it is impossible to prove the statement false. The statement "Increased solar radiation increases the rate of plant growth" is a hypothesis; experiments could be done to show the relationship between solar radiation and plant growth. If solar radiation were shown to be unrelated to plant growth or to retard plant growth, then the hypothesis would be demonstrated to be false.

If a test reveals that a particular hypothesis is false, then the hypothesis is rejected or modified. In the case of the hypothesis about solar radiation and plant growth, we would probably find that more sunlight increases plant growth over some range but that too much can actually retard plant growth. Such results would lead us to modify our hypothesis about the relationship between solar radiation and plant growth.

theory

A hypothesis that has not been rejected after widespread testing and that wins general acceptance.

law

A theory that has been subjected to even more testing and that has won virtually universal acceptance.

If the tests of a hypothesis yield results consistent with it, then further tests are conducted. A hypothesis that has not been rejected after widespread testing and that wins general acceptance is commonly called a **theory**. A theory that has been subjected to even more testing and that has won virtually universal acceptance becomes a **law**. We will examine two economic laws in the next two chapters.

Even a hypothesis that has achieved the status of a law cannot be proven true. There is always a possibility that someone may find a case that invalidates the hypothesis. That possibility means that nothing in economics, or in any other social science, or in any science, can ever be *proven* true. We can have great confidence in a particular proposition, but it is always a mistake to assert that it is "proven."

3.1   Models in Economics

model

A set of simplifying assumptions about some aspect of the real world.

All scientific thought involves simplifications of reality. The real world is far too complex for the human mind—or the most powerful computer—to consider. Scientists use models instead. A **model** is a set of simplifying assumptions about some aspect of the real world. Models are always based on assumed conditions that are simpler than those of the real world, assumptions that are necessarily false. A model of the real world cannot *be* the real world.

We will encounter our first economic model in Chapter 21. For that model, we will assume that an economy can produce only two goods. Then we will explore the model of demand and supply. One of the assumptions we will make there is that all the goods produced by firms in a particular market are identical. Of course, real economies and real markets are not that simple. Reality is never as simple as a model; one point of a model is to simplify the world to improve our understanding of it.

Economists often use graphs to represent economic models. The appendix to this chapter provides a quick, refresher course, if you think you need one, on understanding, building, and using graphs.

Models in economics also help us to generate hypotheses about the real world. In the next section, we will examine some of the problems we encounter in testing those hypotheses.

3.2   Testing Hypotheses in Economics

Here is a hypothesis suggested by the model of demand and supply: an increase in the price of gasoline will reduce the quantity of gasoline consumers demand. How might we test such a hypothesis?

Economists try to test hypotheses such as this one by observing actual behavior and using empirical (that is, real-world) data. The average retail price of gasoline in the United States rose from an average of $2.12 per gallon on May 22, 2005 to $2.88 per gallon on May 22, 2006. The number of gallons of gasoline consumed by U.S. motorists rose 0.3% during that period.

The small increase in the quantity of gasoline consumed by motorists as its price rose is inconsistent with the hypothesis that an increased price will lead to an reduction in the quantity demanded. Does that mean that we should dismiss the original hypothesis? On the contrary, we must be cautious in assessing this evidence. Several problems exist in interpreting any set of economic data. One problem is that several things may be changing at once; another is that the initial event may be unrelated to the event that follows. The next two sections examine these problems in detail.

The All-Other-Things-Unchanged Problem

ceteris paribus

A Latin phrase that means, "all other things unchanged."

The hypothesis that an increase in the price of gasoline produces a reduction in the quantity demanded by consumers carries with it the assumption that there are no other changes that might also affect consumer demand. A better statement of the hypothesis would be: An increase in the price of gasoline will reduce the quantity consumers demand, ceteris paribus. **Ceteris paribus** is a Latin phrase that means "all other things unchanged."

But things changed between May 2005 and May 2006. Economic activity and incomes rose both in the United States and in many other countries, particularly China, and people with higher incomes are likely to buy more gasoline. Employment rose as well, and people with jobs use more gasoline as they drive to work. Population in the United States grew during the period. In short, many things happened during the period, all of which tended to increase the quantity of gasoline people purchased.

Our observation of the gasoline market between May 2005 and May 2006 did not offer a conclusive test of the hypothesis that an increase in the price of gasoline would lead to a reduction in the quantity demanded by consumers. Other things changed and affected gasoline consumption. Such problems are likely to affect any analysis of economic events. We cannot ask the world to stand still while we conduct experiments in economic phenomena. Economists employ a variety of statistical methods to allow them to isolate the impact of single events such as price changes, but they can never be certain that they have accurately isolated the impact of a single event in a world in which virtually everything is changing all the time.

In laboratory sciences such as chemistry and biology, it is relatively easy to conduct experiments in which only selected things change and all other factors are held constant. The economists' laboratory is the real world; thus, economists do not generally have the luxury of conducting controlled experiments.

The Fallacy of False Cause

Hypotheses in economics typically specify a relationship in which a change in one variable causes another to change. We call the variable that responds to the change the **dependent variable**; the variable that induces a change is called the **independent variable**. Sometimes the fact that two variables move together can suggest the false conclusion that one of the variables has acted as an independent variable that has caused the change we observe in the dependent variable.

Consider the following hypothesis: People wearing shorts cause warm weather. Certainly, we observe that more people wear shorts when the weather is warm. Presumably, though, it is the warm weather that causes people to wear shorts rather than the wearing of shorts that causes warm weather; it would be incorrect to infer from this that people cause warm weather by wearing shorts.

Reaching the incorrect conclusion that one event causes another because the two events tend to occur together is called the **fallacy of false cause**. The accompanying essay on baldness and heart disease suggests an example of this fallacy.

Because of the danger of the fallacy of false cause, economists use special statistical tests that are designed to determine whether changes in one thing actually do cause changes observed in another. Given the inability to perform controlled experiments, however, these tests do not always offer convincing evidence that persuades all economists that one thing does, in fact, cause changes in another.

In the case of gasoline prices and consumption between May 2005 and May 2006, there is good theoretical reason to believe the price increase should lead to a reduction in the quantity consumers demand. And economists have tested the hypothesis about price and the quantity demanded quite extensively. They have developed elaborate statistical tests aimed at ruling out problems of the fallacy of false cause. While we cannot prove that an increase in price will, ceteris paribus, lead to a reduction in the quantity consumers demand, we can have considerable confidence in the proposition.

Normative and Positive Statements

Two kinds of assertions in economics can be subjected to testing. We have already examined one, the hypothesis. Another testable assertion is a statement of fact, such as "It is raining outside" or "Microsoft is the largest producer of operating systems for personal computers in the world." Like hypotheses, such assertions can be demonstrated to be false. Unlike hypotheses, they can also be shown to be correct. A statement of fact or a hypothesis is a **positive statement**.

Although people often disagree about positive statements, such disagreements can ultimately be resolved through investigation. There is another category of assertions, however, for which investigation can never resolve differences. A **normative statement** is one that makes a value judgment. Such a judgment is the opinion of the speaker; no one can "prove" that the statement is or is not correct. Here are some examples of normative statements in economics: "We ought to do more to help the poor." "People in the United States should save more." "Corporate profits are too high." The statements are based on the values of the person who makes them. They cannot be proven false.

Because people have different values, normative statements often provoke disagreement. An economist whose values lead him or her to conclude that we should provide more help for the poor will disagree with one whose values lead to a conclusion that we should not. Because no test exists for these values, these two economists will continue to disagree, unless one persuades the other to adopt a different set of values. Many of the disagreements among economists are based on such differences in values and therefore are unlikely to be resolved.

dependent variable

A variable that responds to change.

independent variable

A variable that induces a change.

fallacy of false cause

The incorrect assumption that one event causes another because the two events tend to occur together.

positive statement

A statement of fact or a hypothesis.

normative statement

A statement that makes a value judgment.

KEY TAKEAWAYS

- Economists try to employ the scientific method in their research.
- Scientists cannot prove a hypothesis to be true; they can only fail to prove it false.
- Economists, like other social scientists and scientists, use models to assist them in their analyses.
- Two problems inherent in tests of hypotheses in economics are the all-other-things-unchanged problem and the fallacy of false cause.
- Positive statements are factual and can be tested. Normative statements are value judgments that cannot be tested. Many of the disagreements among economists stem from differences in values.

TRY IT!

Look again at the data in Table 1.1. Now consider the hypothesis: "Majoring in economics will result in a higher LSAT score." Are the data given consistent with this hypothesis? Do the data prove that this hypothesis is correct? What fallacy might be involved in accepting the hypothesis?

Case in Point: Does Baldness Cause Heart Disease?

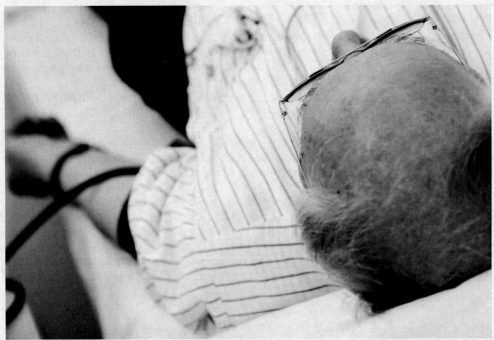

© 2010 Jupiterimages Corporation

A website called embarrassingproblems.com received the following email:

"Dear Dr. Margaret,

"I seem to be going bald. According to your website, this means I'm more likely to have a heart attack. If I take a drug to prevent hair loss, will it reduce my risk of a heart attack?"

What did Dr. Margaret answer? Most importantly, she did not recommend that the questioner take drugs to treat his baldness, because doctors do not think that the baldness causes the heart disease. A more likely explanation for the association between baldness and heart disease is that both conditions are affected by an underlying factor. While noting that more research needs to be done, one hypothesis that Dr. Margaret offers is that higher testosterone levels might be triggering both the hair loss and the heart disease. The good news for people with early balding (which is really where the association with increased risk of heart disease has been observed) is that they have a signal that might lead them to be checked early on for heart disease.

Source: http://www.embarrassingproblems.com/problems/problempage230701.htm.

ANSWER TO TRY IT! PROBLEM

The data are consistent with the hypothesis, but it is never possible to prove that a hypothesis is correct. Accepting the hypothesis could involve the fallacy of false cause; students who major in economics may already have the analytical skills needed to do well on the exam.

4. REVIEW AND PRACTICE

Summary

Choices are forced on us by scarcity; economists study the choices that people make. Scarce goods are those for which the choice of one alternative requires giving up another. The opportunity cost of any choice is the value of the best alternative forgone in making that choice.

Some key choices assessed by economists include what to produce, how to produce it, and for whom it should be produced. Economics is distinguished from other academic disciplines that also study choices by an emphasis on the central importance of opportunity costs in evaluating choices, the assumption of maximizing behavior that serves the interests of individual decision makers, and a focus on evaluating choices at the margin.

Economic analyses may be aimed at explaining individual choice or choices in an individual market; such investigations are largely the focus of microeconomics. The analysis of the impact of those individual choices on such aggregates as total output, the level of employment, and the price level is the concern of macroeconomics.

Working within the framework of the scientific method, economists formulate hypotheses and then test them. These tests can only refute a hypothesis; hypotheses in science cannot be proved. A hypothesis that has been widely tested often comes to be regarded as a theory; one that has won virtually universal acceptance is a law. Because of the complexity of the real world, economists rely on models that rest on a series of simplifying assumptions. The models are used to generate hypotheses about the economy that can be tested using real-world data.

Statements of fact and hypotheses are positive statements. Normative statements, unlike positive statements, cannot be tested and provide a source for potential disagreement.

PROBLEMS

1. Why does the fact that something is scarce require that we make choices?

2. Does the fact that something is abundant mean it is not scarce in the economic sense? Why or why not?

3. In some countries, such as Cuba and North Korea, the government makes most of the decisions about what will be produced, how it will be produced, and for whom. Does the fact that these choices are made by the government eliminate scarcity in these countries? Why or why not?

4. Explain what is meant by the opportunity cost of a choice.

5. What is the approximate dollar cost of the tuition and other fees associated with the economics course you are taking? Does this dollar cost fully reflect the opportunity cost to you of taking the course?

6. In the Case in Point essay "The Rising Cost of Energy," what would be some of the things that would be included in an estimate of the opportunity cost of preserving part of northern Alberta Canada by prohibiting heavy crude oil extraction? Do you think that the increased extraction represents the best use of the land? Why or why not?

7. Indicate whether each of the following is a topic of microeconomics or macroeconomics:

    a. The impact of higher oil prices on the production of steel

    b. The increased demand in the last 15 years for exotic dietary supplements

    c. The surge in aggregate economic activity that hit much of Asia late in the early 2000s

    d. The sharp increases in U.S. employment and total output that occurred between 2003 and 2007

    e. The impact of preservation of wilderness areas on the logging industry and on the price of lumber

8. Determine whether each of the following raises a "what," "how," or "for whom" issue. Are the statements normative or positive?

    a. A requirement that aluminum used in cars be made from recycled materials will raise the price of automobiles.

    b. The federal government does not spend enough for children.

    c. An increase in police resources provided to the inner city will lower the crime rate.

    d. Automation destroys jobs.

    e. Efforts to improve the environment tend to reduce production and employment.

    f. Japanese firms should be more willing to hire additional workers when production rises and to lay off workers when production falls.

    g. Access to health care should not be limited by income.

9. Your time is a scarce resource. What if the quantity of time were increased, say to 48 hours per day, and everyone still lived as many days as before. Would time still be scarce?

10. Most college students are under age 25. Give two explanations for this—one based on the benefits people of different ages are likely to receive from higher education and one based on the opportunity costs of a college education to students of different ages.

11. Some municipal water companies charge customers a flat fee each month, regardless of the amount of water they consume. Others meter water use and charge according to the quantity of water customers use. Compare the way the two systems affect the cost of water use at the margin.

12. How might you test each of the following hypotheses? Suggest some problems that might arise in each test due to the ceteris paribus (all-other-things-unchanged) problem and the fallacy of false cause.

    a. Reducing the quantity of heroin available will increase total spending on heroin and increase the crime rate.

    b. Higher incomes make people happier.

    c. Higher incomes make people live longer.

13. Many models in physics and in chemistry assume the existence of a perfect vacuum (that is, a space entirely empty of matter). Yet we know that a perfect vacuum cannot exist. Are such models valid? Why are models based on assumptions that are essentially incorrect?

14. Suppose you were asked to test the proposition that publishing students' teacher evaluations causes grade inflation. What evidence might you want to consider? How would the inability to carry out controlled experiments make your analysis more difficult?

15. Referring to the Case in Point "Baldness and Heart Disease," explain the possible fallacy of false cause in concluding that baldness makes a person more likely to have heart disease.

16. In 2005 the Food and Drug Administration ordered that Vioxx and other popular drugs for treating the pain of arthritis be withdrawn from the market. The order resulted from a finding that people taking the drugs had an increased risk of cardiovascular problems. Some researchers criticized the government's action, arguing that concluding that the drugs caused the cardiovascular problems represented an example of the fallacy of false cause. Can you think of any reason why this might be the case?

ENDNOTES

1. Bureau of Labor Statistics *Occupational Outlook* at http://www.bls.gov/oco/.

CHAPTER 2
Confronting Scarcity: Choices in Production

START UP: TIGHTENING SECURITY AT THE WORLD'S AIRPORTS

Do you want safer air travel or not? While that question is seldom asked so bluntly, any person who travels by air can tell you that our collective answer has been "yes," and it has been accompanied by increases in security and its associated costs at airports all over the world. Why? In short, "9/11." Terrorists hijacked four U.S. commercial airliners on September 11, 2001, and the tragic results that followed led to a sharp tightening in airport security.

In an effort to prevent similar disasters, airport security officials scrutinize luggage and passengers more carefully than ever before. In the months following 9/11, delays of as much as three hours were common as agents tried to assure that no weapons or bombs could be smuggled onto another plane.

"What to produce?" is a fundamental economic question. Every economy must answer this question. Should it produce more education, better health care, improved transportation, a cleaner environment? There are limits to what a nation can produce; deciding to produce more of one thing inevitably means producing less of something else. Individuals in much of the world, after the tragedy of 9/11, clearly were willing to give up time, and a fair amount of individual privacy, in an effort to obtain greater security. Nations and individual cities also devoted additional resources to police and other forms of protection in an effort to prevent tragedies such as 9/11. People all over the world chose to produce less of other goods in order to devote more resources to the production of greater security. And, as of early 2009, the choice to devote more resources to security had paid off; there had been no similar hijackings in the United States.

In this chapter we use our first model, the production possibilities model, to examine the nature of choices to produce more of some goods and less of others. As its name suggests, the **production possibilities model** shows the goods and services that an economy is capable of producing—its possibilities—given the factors of production and the technology it has available. The model specifies what it means to use resources fully and efficiently and suggests some important implications for international trade. We can also use the model to illustrate economic growth, a process that expands the set of production possibilities available to an economy.

We then turn to an examination of the type of economic system in which choices are made. An **economic system** is the set of rules that define how an economy's resources are to be owned and how decisions about their use are to be made. We will see that economic systems differ in terms of how they answer the fundamental economic questions. Many of the world's economic systems, including the systems that prevail in North America, Europe, and much of Asia and Central and South America, rely on individuals operating in a market economy to make those choices. Other economic systems, including those of Cuba and North Korea today and historically

production possibilities model

Model that shows the goods and services that an economy is capable of producing—its possibilities—given the factors of production and the technology it has available.

economic system

The set of rules that define how an economy's resources are to be owned and how decisions about their use are to be made.

those of the former Soviet Union, Soviet bloc countries, and China, rely—or relied—on government to make these choices. Different economic systems result in different sets of choices and thus different outcomes; the fact that market economies generally outperform the others when it comes to providing more of the things that people want helps to explain the dramatic shift from government-dominated toward market-dominated economic systems that has occurred throughout the world in the past 25 years. The chapter concludes with an examination of the role of government in an economy that relies chiefly on markets to allocate goods and services.

1. FACTORS OF PRODUCTION

LEARNING OBJECTIVES

1. Define the three factors of production—labor, capital, and natural resources.
2. Explain the role of technology and entrepreneurs in the utilization of the economy's factors of production.

factors of production

The resources available to the economy for the production of goods and services.

utility

The value, or satisfaction, that people derive from the goods and services they consume and the activities they pursue.

labor

The human effort that can be applied to the production of goods and services.

capital

A factor of production that has been produced for use in the production of other goods and services.

natural resources

The resources of nature that can be used for the production of goods and services.

human capital

The skills a worker has as a result of education, training, or experience that can be used in production.

Choices concerning what goods and services to produce are choices about an economy's use of its **factors of production**, the resources available to it for the production of goods and services. The value, or satisfaction, that people derive from the goods and services they consume and the activities they pursue is called **utility**. Ultimately, then, an economy's factors of production create utility; they serve the interests of people.

The factors of production in an economy are its labor, capital, and natural resources. **Labor** is the human effort that can be applied to the production of goods and services. People who are employed or would like to be are considered part of the labor available to the economy. **Capital** is a factor of production that has been produced for use in the production of other goods and services. Office buildings, machinery, and tools are examples of capital. **Natural resources** are the resources of nature that can be used for the production of goods and services.

In the next three sections, we will take a closer look at the factors of production we use to produce the goods and services we consume. The three basic building blocks of labor, capital, and natural resources may be used in different ways to produce different goods and services, but they still lie at the core of production. We will then look at the roles played by technology and entrepreneurs in putting these factors of production to work. As economists began to grapple with the problems of scarcity, choice, and opportunity cost two centuries ago, they focused on these concepts, just as they are likely to do two centuries hence.

1.1 Labor

Labor is human effort that can be applied to production. People who work to repair tires, pilot airplanes, teach children, or enforce laws are all part of the economy's labor. People who would like to work but have not found employment—who are unemployed—are also considered part of the labor available to the economy.

In some contexts, it is useful to distinguish two forms of labor. The first is the human equivalent of a natural resource. It is the natural ability an untrained, uneducated person brings to a particular production process. But most workers bring far more. The skills a worker has as a result of education, training, or experience that can be used in production are called **human capital**. Students who are attending a college or university are acquiring human capital. Workers who are gaining skills through experience or through training are acquiring human capital. Children who are learning to read are acquiring human capital.

The amount of labor available to an economy can be increased in two ways. One is to increase the total quantity of labor, either by increasing the number of people available to work or by increasing the average number of hours of work per week. The other is to increase the amount of human capital possessed by workers.

1.2 Capital

Long ago, when the first human beings walked the earth, they produced food by picking leaves or fruit off a plant or by catching an animal and eating it. We know that very early on, however, they began shaping stones into tools, apparently for use in butchering animals. Those tools were the first capital because they were produced for use in producing other goods—food and clothing.

Modern versions of the first stone tools include saws, meat cleavers, hooks, and grinders; all are used in butchering animals. Tools such as hammers, screwdrivers, and wrenches are also capital. Transportation equipment, such as cars and trucks, is capital. Facilities such as roads, bridges, ports, and airports are capital. Buildings, too, are capital; they help us to produce goods and services.

Capital does not consist solely of physical objects. The score for a new symphony is capital because it will be used to produce concerts. Computer software used by business firms or government agencies to produce goods and services is capital. Capital may thus include physical goods and intellectual discoveries. Any resource is capital if it satisfies two criteria:

1. The resource must have been produced.
2. The resource can be used to produce other goods and services.

One thing that is not considered capital is money. A firm cannot use money directly to produce other goods, so money does not satisfy the second criterion for capital. Firms can, however, use money to acquire capital. Money is a form of financial capital. **Financial capital** includes money and other "paper" assets (such as stocks and bonds) that represent claims on future payments. These financial assets are not capital, but they can be used directly or indirectly to purchase factors of production or goods and services.

financial capital

Includes money and other "paper" assets (such as stocks and bonds) that represent claims on future payments.

1.3 Natural Resources

There are two essential characteristics of natural resources. The first is that they are found in nature—that no human effort has been used to make or alter them. The second is that they can be used for the production of goods and services. That requires knowledge; we must know how to use the things we find in nature before they become resources.

Consider oil. Oil in the ground is a natural resource because it is found (not manufactured) and can be used to produce goods and services. However, 250 years ago oil was a nuisance, not a natural resource. Pennsylvania farmers in the eighteenth century who found oil oozing up through their soil were dismayed, not delighted. No one knew what could be done with the oil. It was not until the mid-nineteenth century that a method was found for refining oil into kerosene that could be used to generate energy, transforming oil into a natural resource. Oil is now used to make all sorts of things, including clothing, drugs, gasoline, and plastic. It became a natural resource because people discovered and implemented a way to use it.

Defining something as a natural resource only if it can be used to produce goods and services does not mean that a tree has value only for its wood or that a mountain has value only for its minerals. If people gain utility from the existence of a beautiful wilderness area, then that wilderness provides a service. The wilderness is thus a natural resource.

The natural resources available to us can be expanded in three ways. One is the discovery of new natural resources, such as the discovery of a deposit of ore containing titanium. The second is the discovery of new uses for resources, as happened when new techniques allowed oil to be put to productive use or sand to be used in manufacturing computer chips. The third is the discovery of new ways to extract natural resources in order to use them. New methods of discovering and mapping oil deposits have increased the world's supply of this important natural resource.

1.4 Technology and the Entrepreneur

technology

The knowledge that can be applied to the production of goods and services.

entrepreneur

A person who, operating within the context of a market economy, seeks to earn profits by finding new ways to organize factors of production.

Goods and services are produced using the factors of production available to the economy. Two things play a crucial role in putting these factors of production to work. The first is **technology**, the knowledge that can be applied to the production of goods and services. The second is an individual who plays a key role in a market economy: the entrepreneur. An **entrepreneur** is a person who, operating within the context of a market economy, seeks to earn profits by finding new ways to organize factors of production. In non-market economies the role of the entrepreneur is played by bureaucrats and other decision makers who respond to incentives other than profit to guide their choices about resource allocation decisions.

The interplay of entrepreneurs and technology affects all our lives. Entrepreneurs put new technologies to work every day, changing the way factors of production are used. Farmers and factory workers, engineers and electricians, technicians and teachers all work differently than they did just a few years ago, using new technologies introduced by entrepreneurs. The music you enjoy, the books you read, the athletic equipment with which you play are produced differently than they were five years ago. The book you are reading was written and manufactured using technologies that did not exist ten years ago. We can dispute whether all the changes have made our lives better. What we cannot dispute is that they have made our lives different.

KEY TAKEAWAYS

- Factors of production are the resources the economy has available to produce goods and services.
- Labor is the human effort that can be applied to the production of goods and services. Labor's contribution to an economy's output of goods and services can be increased either by increasing the quantity of labor or by increasing human capital.
- Capital is a factor of production that has been produced for use in the production of other goods and services.
- Natural resources are those things found in nature that can be used for the production of goods and services.
- Two keys to the utilization of an economy's factors of production are technology and, in the case of a market economic system, the efforts of entrepreneurs.

TRY IT!

Explain whether each of the following is labor, capital, or a natural resource.

1. An unemployed factory worker
2. A college professor
3. The library building on your campus
4. Yellowstone National Park
5. An untapped deposit of natural gas
6. The White House
7. The local power plant

Case in Point: Technology Cuts Costs, Boosts Productivity and Profits

© 2010 Jupiterimages Corporation

Technology can seem an abstract force in the economy—important, but invisible.

It is not invisible to the 130 people who work on a Shell Oil Company oil rig called Mars, located in the deep waters of the Gulf of Mexico, about 160 miles southwest of Pensacola, Florida. The name Mars reflects its otherworld appearance—it extends 300 feet above the water's surface and has steel tendons that reach 3,000 feet to the floor of the gulf. This facility would not exist if it were not for the development of better oil discovery methods that include three-dimensional seismic mapping techniques, satellites that locate oil from space, and drills that can make turns as drilling foremen steer them by monitoring them on computer screens from the comfort of Mars. "We don't hit as many dry holes," commented Shell manager Miles Barrett. As a result of these new technologies, over the past two decades, the cost of discovering a barrel of oil dropped from $20 to under $5. And the technologies continue to improve. Three-dimensional surveys are being replaced with four-dimensional ones that allow geologists to see how the oil fields change over time.

The Mars project was destroyed by Hurricane Katrina in 2005. Royal Dutch Shell completed repairs in 2006—at a cost of $200 million. But, the facility is again pumping 130,000 barrels of oil per day and 150 million cubic feet of natural gas—the energy equivalent of an additional 26,000 barrels of oil.

Technology is doing more than helping energy companies track oil deposits. It is changing the way soft drinks and other grocery items are delivered to retail stores. For example, when a PepsiCo delivery driver arrives at a 7-Eleven, the driver keys into a handheld computer the inventory of soft drinks, chips, and other PepsiCo products. The information is transmitted to a main computer at the warehouse that begins processing the next order for that store. The result is that the driver can visit more stores in a day and PepsiCo can cover a given territory with fewer drivers and trucks.

New technology is even helping to produce more milk from cows. Ed Larsen, who owns a 1,200-cow dairy farm in Wisconsin, never gets up before dawn to milk the cows, the way he did as a boy. Rather, the cows are hooked up to electronic milkers. Computers measure each cow's output, and cows producing little milk are sent to a "hospital wing" for treatment. With the help of such technology, as well as better feed, today's dairy cows produce 50% more milk than did cows 20 years ago. Even though the number of dairy cows in the United States in the last 20 years has fallen 17%, milk output has increased 25%.

Who benefits from technological progress? Consumers gain from lower prices and better service. Workers gain: Their greater ability to produce goods and services translates into higher wages. And firms gain: Lower production costs mean higher profits. Of course, some people lose as technology advances. Some jobs are eliminated, and some firms find their services are no longer needed. One can argue about whether particular technological changes have improved our lives, but they have clearly made—and will continue to make—them far different.

Sources: David Ballingrud, "Drilling in the Gulf: Life on Mars," St. Petersburg Times (Florida), August 5, 2001, p. 1A; Barbara Hagenbaugh, "Dairy Farms Evolve to Survive," USA Today, August 7, 2003, p. 1B; Del Jones and Barbara Hansen, "Special Report: A Who's Who of Productivity," USA Today, August 30, 2001, p. 1B; and Christopher Helman, Shell Shocked, Forbes Online, July 27, 2006.

ANSWERS TO TRY IT! PROBLEMS

1. An unemployed factory worker could be put to work; he or she counts as labor.
2. A college professor is labor.
3. The library building on your campus is part of capital.
4. Yellowstone National Park. Those areas of the park left in their natural state are a natural resource. Facilities such as visitors' centers, roads, and campgrounds are capital.
5. An untapped deposit of natural gas is a natural resource. Once extracted and put in a storage tank, natural gas is capital.
6. The White House is capital.
7. The local power plant is capital.

---

2. THE PRODUCTION POSSIBILITIES CURVE

LEARNING OBJECTIVES

1. **Explain the concept of the production possibilities curve and understand the implications of its downward slope and bowed-out shape.**
2. **Use the production possibilities model to distinguish between full employment and situations of idle factors of production and between efficient and inefficient production.**
3. **Understand specialization and its relationship to the production possibilities model and comparative advantage.**

production possibilities curve

A graphical representation of the alternative combinations of goods and services an economy can produce.

An economy's factors of production are scarce; they cannot produce an unlimited quantity of goods and services. A **production possibilities curve** is a graphical representation of the alternative combinations of goods and services an economy can produce. It illustrates the production possibilities model. In drawing the production possibilities curve, we shall assume that the economy can produce only two goods and that the quantities of factors of production and the technology available to the economy are fixed.

2.1 Constructing a Production Possibilities Curve

To construct a production possibilities curve, we will begin with the case of a hypothetical firm, Alpine Sports, Inc., a specialized sports equipment manufacturer. Christie Ryder began the business 15 years ago with a single ski production facility near Killington ski resort in central Vermont. Ski sales grew, and she also saw demand for snowboards rising—particularly after snowboard competition events were included in the 2002 Winter Olympics in Salt Lake City. She added a second plant in a nearby town. The second plant, while smaller than the first, was designed to produce snowboards as well as skis. She also modified the first plant so that it could produce both snowboards and skis. Two years later she added a third plant in another town. While even smaller than the second plant, the third was primarily designed for snowboard production but could also produce skis.

We can think of each of Ms. Ryder's three plants as a miniature economy and analyze them using the production possibilities model. We assume that the factors of production and technology available to each of the plants operated by Alpine Sports are unchanged.

Suppose the first plant, Plant 1, can produce 200 pairs of skis per month when it produces only skis. When devoted solely to snowboards, it produces 100 snowboards per month. It can produce skis and snowboards simultaneously as well.

The table in Figure 2.2 gives three combinations of skis and snowboards that Plant 1 can produce each month. Combination A involves devoting the plant entirely to ski production; combination C means shifting all of the plant's resources to snowboard production; combination B involves the production of both goods. These values are plotted in a production possibilities curve for Plant 1. The curve is a downward-sloping straight line, indicating that there is a linear, negative relationship between the production of the two goods.

Neither skis nor snowboards is an independent or a dependent variable in the production possibilities model; we can assign either one to the vertical or to the horizontal axis. Here, we have placed the number of pairs of skis produced per month on the vertical axis and the number of snowboards produced per month on the horizontal axis.

The negative slope of the production possibilities curve reflects the scarcity of the plant's capital and labor. Producing more snowboards requires shifting resources out of ski production and thus producing fewer skis. Producing more skis requires shifting resources out of snowboard production and thus producing fewer snowboards.

The slope of Plant 1's production possibilities curve measures the rate at which Alpine Sports must give up ski production to produce additional snowboards. Because the production possibilities curve for Plant 1 is linear, we can compute the slope between any two points on the curve and get the same result. Between points A and B, for example, the slope equals −2 pairs of skis/snowboard (equals −100 pairs of skis/50 snowboards). (Many students are helped when told to read this result as "−2 pairs of skis *per* snowboard.") We get the same value between points B and C, and between points A and C.

FIGURE 2.2   A Production Possibilities Curve

The table shows the combinations of pairs of skis and snowboards that Plant 1 is capable of producing each month. These are also illustrated with a production possibilities curve. Notice that this curve is linear.

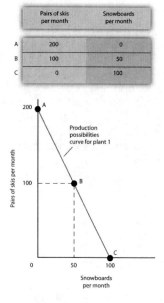

	Pairs of skis per month	Snowboards per month
A	200	0
B	100	50
C	0	100

To see this relationship more clearly, examine Figure 2.3. Suppose Plant 1 is producing 100 pairs of skis and 50 snowboards per month at point B. Now consider what would happen if Ms. Ryder decided to produce 1 more snowboard per month. The segment of the curve around point B is magnified in Figure 2.3. The slope between points B and B′ is −2 pairs of skis/snowboard. Producing 1 additional snowboard at point B′ requires giving up 2 pairs of skis. We can think of this as the opportunity cost of producing an additional snowboard at Plant 1. This opportunity cost equals the absolute value of the slope of the production possibilities curve.

FIGURE 2.3 The Slope of a Production Possibilities Curve

The slope of the linear production possibilities curve in Figure 2.2 is constant; it is −2 pairs of skis/snowboard. In the section of the curve shown here, the slope can be calculated between points B and B′. Expanding snowboard production to 51 snowboards per month from 50 snowboards per month requires a reduction in ski production to 98 pairs of skis per month from 100 pairs. The slope equals −2 pairs of skis/snowboard (that is, it must give up two pairs of skis to free up the resources necessary to produce one additional snowboard). To shift from B′ to B″, Alpine Sports must give up two more pairs of skis per snowboard. The absolute value of the slope of a production possibilities curve measures the opportunity cost of an additional unit of the good on the horizontal axis measured in terms of the quantity of the good on the vertical axis that must be forgone.

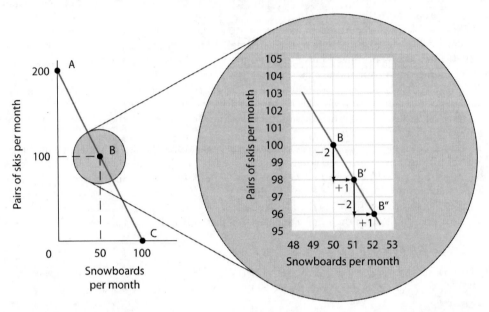

The absolute value of the slope of any production possibilities curve equals the opportunity cost of an additional unit of the good on the horizontal axis. It is the amount of the good on the vertical axis that must be given up in order to free up the resources required to produce one more unit of the good on the horizontal axis. We will make use of this important fact as we continue our investigation of the production possibilities curve.

Figure 2.4 shows production possibilities curves for each of the firm's three plants. Each of the plants, if devoted entirely to snowboards, could produce 100 snowboards. Plants 2 and 3, if devoted exclusively to ski production, can produce 100 and 50 pairs of skis per month, respectively. The exhibit gives the slopes of the production possibilities curves for each plant. The opportunity cost of an additional snowboard at each plant equals the absolute values of these slopes (that is, the number of pairs of skis that must be given up per snowboard).

FIGURE 2.4 Production Possibilities at Three Plants

The slopes of the production possibilities curves for each plant differ. The steeper the curve, the greater the opportunity cost of an additional snowboard. Here, the opportunity cost is lowest at Plant 3 and greatest at Plant 1.

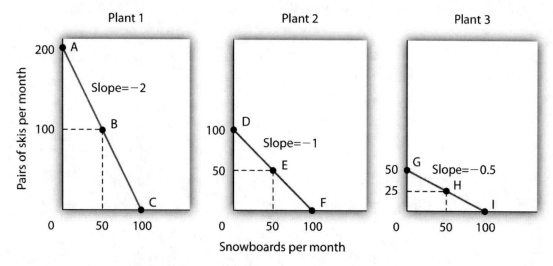

The exhibit gives the slopes of the production possibilities curves for each of the firm's three plants. The opportunity cost of an additional snowboard at each plant equals the absolute values of these slopes. More generally, the absolute value of the slope of any production possibilities curve at any point gives the opportunity cost of an additional unit of the good on the horizontal axis, measured in terms of the number of units of the good on the vertical axis that must be forgone.

The greater the absolute value of the slope of the production possibilities curve, the greater the opportunity cost will be. The plant for which the opportunity cost of an additional snowboard is greatest is the plant with the steepest production possibilities curve; the plant for which the opportunity cost is lowest is the plant with the flattest production possibilities curve. The plant with the lowest opportunity cost of producing snowboards is Plant 3; its slope of −0.5 means that Ms. Ryder must give up half a pair of skis in that plant to produce an additional snowboard. In Plant 2, she must give up one pair of skis to gain one more snowboard. We have already seen that an additional snowboard requires giving up two pairs of skis in Plant 1.

2.2 Comparative Advantage and the Production Possibilities Curve

To construct a combined production possibilities curve for all three plants, we can begin by asking how many pairs of skis Alpine Sports could produce if it were producing only skis. To find this quantity, we add up the values at the vertical intercepts of each of the production possibilities curves in Figure 2.4. These intercepts tell us the maximum number of pairs of skis each plant can produce. Plant 1 can produce 200 pairs of skis per month, Plant 2 can produce 100 pairs of skis at per month, and Plant 3 can produce 50 pairs. Alpine Sports can thus produce 350 pairs of skis per month if it devotes its resources exclusively to ski production. In that case, it produces no snowboards.

Now suppose the firm decides to produce 100 snowboards. That will require shifting one of its plants out of ski production. Which one will it choose to shift? The sensible thing for it to do is to choose the plant in which snowboards have the lowest opportunity cost—Plant 3. It has an advantage not because it can produce more snowboards than the other plants (all the plants in this example are capable of producing up to 100 snowboards per month) but because it is the least productive plant for making skis. Producing a snowboard in Plant 3 requires giving up just half a pair of skis.

Economists say that an economy has a **comparative advantage** in producing a good or service if the opportunity cost of producing that good or service is lower for that economy than for any other. Plant 3 has a comparative advantage in snowboard production because it is the plant for which the opportunity cost of additional snowboards is lowest. To put this in terms of the production possibilities curve, Plant 3 has a comparative advantage in snowboard production (the good on the horizontal axis) because its production possibilities curve is the flattest of the three curves.

comparative advantage

In producing a good or service, the situation that occurs if the opportunity cost of producing that good or service is lower for that economy than for any other.

FIGURE 2.5   The Combined Production Possibilities Curve for Alpine Sports

The curve shown combines the production possibilities curves for each plant. At point A, Alpine Sports produces 350 pairs of skis per month and no snowboards. If the firm wishes to increase snowboard production, it will first use Plant 3, which has a comparative advantage in snowboards.

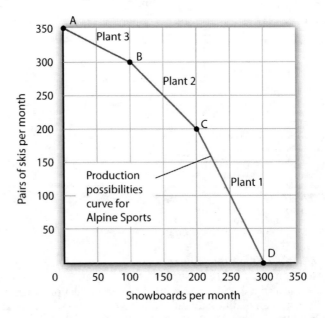

Plant 3's comparative advantage in snowboard production makes a crucial point about the nature of comparative advantage. It need not imply that a particular plant is especially good at an activity. In our example, all three plants are equally good at snowboard production. Plant 3, though, is the least efficient of the three in ski production. Alpine thus gives up fewer skis when it produces snowboards in Plant 3. Comparative advantage thus can stem from a lack of efficiency in the production of an alternative good rather than a special proficiency in the production of the first good.

The combined production possibilities curve for the firm's three plants is shown in Figure 2.5. We begin at point A, with all three plants producing only skis. Production totals 350 pairs of skis per month and zero snowboards. If the firm were to produce 100 snowboards at Plant 3, ski production would fall by 50 pairs per month (recall that the opportunity cost per snowboard at Plant 3 is half a pair of skis). That would bring ski production to 300 pairs, at point B. If Alpine Sports were to produce still more snowboards in a single month, it would shift production to Plant 2, the facility with the next-lowest opportunity cost. Producing 100 snowboards at Plant 2 would leave Alpine Sports producing 200 snowboards and 200 pairs of skis per month, at point C. If the firm were to switch entirely to snowboard production, Plant 1 would be the last to switch because the cost of each snowboard there is 2 pairs of skis. With all three plants producing only snowboards, the firm is at point D on the combined production possibilities curve, producing 300 snowboards per month and no skis.

Notice that this production possibilities curve, which is made up of linear segments from each assembly plant, has a bowed-out shape; the absolute value of its slope increases as Alpine Sports produces more and more snowboards. This is a result of transferring resources from the production of one good to another according to comparative advantage. We shall examine the significance of the bowed-out shape of the curve in the next section.

2.3   The Law of Increasing Opportunity Cost

We see in Figure 2.5 that, beginning at point A and producing only skis, Alpine Sports experiences higher and higher opportunity costs as it produces more snowboards. The fact that the opportunity cost of additional snowboards increases as the firm produces more of them is a reflection of an important economic law. The **law of increasing opportunity cost** holds that as an economy moves along its production possibilities curve in the direction of producing more of a particular good, the opportunity cost of additional units of that good will increase.

We have seen the law of increasing opportunity cost at work traveling from point A toward point D on the production possibilities curve in Figure 2.5. The opportunity cost of each of the first 100 snowboards equals half a pair of skis; each of the next 100 snowboards has an opportunity cost of 1 pair of skis, and each of the last 100 snowboards has an opportunity cost of 2 pairs of skis. The law also applies as the firm shifts from snowboards to skis. Suppose it begins at point D, producing 300 snowboards per month and no skis. It can shift to ski production at a relatively low cost at first. The

law of increasing opportunity cost

As an economy moves along its production possibilities curve in the direction of producing more of a particular good, the opportunity cost of additional units of that good will increase.

opportunity cost of the first 200 pairs of skis is just 100 snowboards at Plant 1, a movement from point D to point C, or 0.5 snowboards per pair of skis. We would say that Plant 1 has a comparative advantage in ski production. The next 100 pairs of skis would be produced at Plant 2, where snowboard production would fall by 100 snowboards per month. The opportunity cost of skis at Plant 2 is 1 snowboard per pair of skis. Plant 3 would be the last plant converted to ski production. There, 50 pairs of skis could be produced per month at a cost of 100 snowboards, or an opportunity cost of 2 snowboards per pair of skis.

The bowed-out production possibilities curve for Alpine Sports illustrates the law of increasing opportunity cost. Scarcity implies that a production possibilities curve is downward sloping; the law of increasing opportunity cost implies that it will be bowed out, or concave, in shape.

The bowed-out curve of Figure 2.5 becomes smoother as we include more production facilities. Suppose Alpine Sports expands to 10 plants, each with a linear production possibilities curve. Panel (a) of Figure 2.6 shows the combined curve for the expanded firm, constructed as we did in Figure 2.5. This production possibilities curve includes 10 linear segments and is almost a smooth curve. As we include more and more production units, the curve will become smoother and smoother. In an actual economy, with a tremendous number of firms and workers, it is easy to see that the production possibilities curve will be smooth. We will generally draw production possibilities curves for the economy as smooth, bowed-out curves, like the one in Panel (b). This production possibilities curve shows an economy that produces only skis and snowboards. Notice the curve still has a bowed-out shape; it still has a negative slope. Notice also that this curve has no numbers. Economists often use models such as the production possibilities model with graphs that show the general shapes of curves but that do not include specific numbers.

FIGURE 2.6 Production Possibilities for the Economy

As we combine the production possibilities curves for more and more units, the curve becomes smoother. It retains its negative slope and bowed-out shape. In Panel (a) we have a combined production possibilities curve for Alpine Sports, assuming that it now has 10 plants producing skis and snowboards. Even though each of the plants has a linear curve, combining them according to comparative advantage, as we did with 3 plants in Figure 2.5, produces what appears to be a smooth, nonlinear curve, even though it is made up of linear segments. In drawing production possibilities curves for the economy, we shall generally assume they are smooth and "bowed out," as in Panel (b). This curve depicts an entire economy that produces only skis and snowboards.

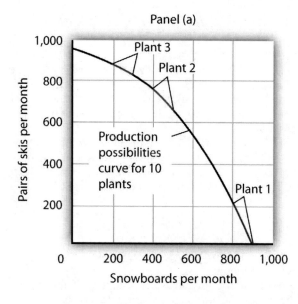

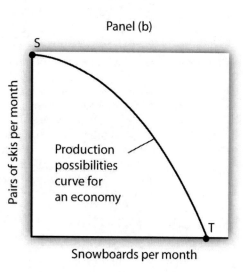

2.4 Movements Along the Production Possibilities Curve

We can use the production possibilities model to examine choices in the production of goods and services. In applying the model, we assume that the economy can produce two goods, and we assume that technology and the factors of production available to the economy remain unchanged. In this section, we shall assume that the economy operates on its production possibilities curve so that an increase in the production of one good in the model implies a reduction in the production of the other.

We shall consider two goods and services: national security and a category we shall call "all other goods and services." This second category includes the entire range of goods and services the economy can produce, aside from national defense and security. Clearly, the transfer of resources to the effort to enhance national security reduces the quantity of other goods and services that can be produced. In the wake of the 9/11 attacks in 2001, nations throughout the world increased their spending for national security. This spending took a variety of forms. One, of course, was increased defense spending. Local and state governments also increased spending in an effort to prevent terrorist attacks. Airports around the world hired additional agents to inspect luggage and passengers.

The increase in resources devoted to security meant fewer "other goods and services" could be produced. In terms of the production possibilities curve in Figure 2.7, the choice to produce more security and less of other goods and services means a movement from A to B. Of course, an economy cannot really *produce* security; it can only attempt to provide it. The attempt to provide it requires resources; it is in that sense that we shall speak of the economy as "producing" security.

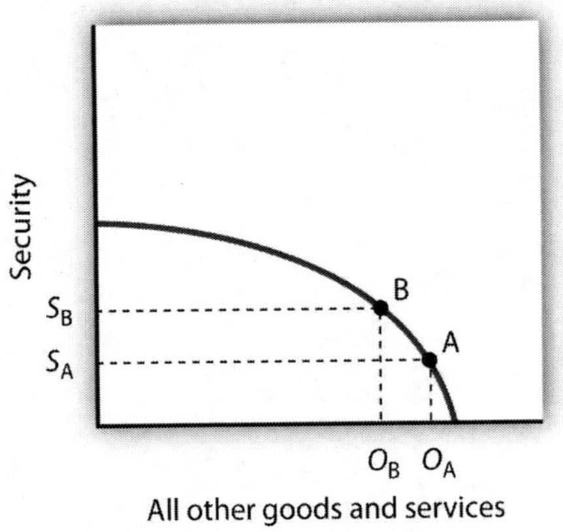

At point A, the economy was producing S_A units of security on the vertical axis—defense services and various forms of police protection—and O_A units of other goods and services on the horizontal axis. The decision to devote more resources to security and less to other goods and services represents the choice we discussed in the chapter introduction. In this case we have categories of goods rather than specific goods. Thus, the economy chose to increase spending on security in the effort to defeat terrorism. Since we have assumed that the economy has a fixed quantity of available resources, the increased use of resources for security and national defense necessarily reduces the number of resources available for the production of other goods and services.

The law of increasing opportunity cost tells us that, as the economy moves along the production possibilities curve in the direction of more of one good, its opportunity cost will increase. We may conclude that, as the economy moved along this curve in the direction of greater production of security, the opportunity cost of the additional security began to increase. That is because the resources transferred from the production of other goods and services to the production of security had a greater and greater comparative advantage in producing things other than security.

The production possibilities model does not tell us where on the curve a particular economy will operate. Instead, it lays out the possibilities facing the economy. Many countries, for example, chose to move along their respective production possibilities curves to produce more security and national defense and less of all other goods in the wake of 9/11. We will see in the chapter on demand and supply how choices about what to produce are made in the marketplace.

FIGURE 2.7 Spending More for Security

Here, an economy that can produce two categories of goods, security and "all other goods and services," begins at point A on its production possibilities curve. The economy produces S_A units of security and O_A units of all other goods and services per period. A movement from A to B requires shifting resources out of the production of all other goods and services and into spending on security. The increase in spending on security, to S_A units of security per period, has an opportunity cost of reduced production of all other goods and services. Production of all other goods and services falls by O_A - O_B units per period.

All other goods and services

2.5 Producing on Versus Producing Inside the Production Possibilities Curve

An economy that is operating inside its production possibilities curve could, by moving onto it, produce more of all the goods and services that people value, such as food, housing, education, medical care, and music. Increasing the availability of these goods would improve the standard of living. Economists conclude that it is better to be on the production possibilities curve than inside it.

Two things could leave an economy operating at a point inside its production possibilities curve. First, the economy might fail to use fully the resources available to it. Second, it might not allocate resources on the basis of comparative advantage. In either case, production within the production possibilities curve implies the economy could improve its performance.

Idle Factors of Production

Suppose an economy fails to put all its factors of production to work. Some workers are without jobs, some buildings are without occupants, some fields are without crops. Because an economy's production possibilities curve assumes the full use of the factors of production available to it, the failure to use some factors results in a level of production that lies inside the production possibilities curve.

If all the factors of production that are available for use under current market conditions are being utilized, the economy has achieved **full employment**. An economy cannot operate on its production possibilities curve unless it has full employment.

full employment

Situation in which all the factors of production that are available for use under current market conditions are being utilized.

FIGURE 2.8 Idle Factors and Production

The production possibilities curve shown suggests an economy that can produce two goods, food and clothing. As a result of a failure to achieve full employment, the economy operates at a point such as B, producing F_B units of food and C_B units of clothing per period. Putting its factors of production to work allows a move to the production possibilities curve, to a point such as A. The production of both goods rises.

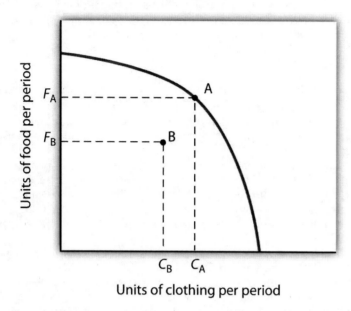

Units of clothing per period

Figure 2.8 shows an economy that can produce food and clothing. If it chooses to produce at point A, for example, it can produce F_A units of food and C_A units of clothing. Now suppose that a large fraction of the economy's workers lose their jobs, so the economy no longer makes full use of one factor of production: labor. In this example, production moves to point B, where the economy produces less food (F_B) and less clothing (C_B) than at point A. We often think of the loss of jobs in terms of the workers; they have lost a chance to work and to earn income. But the production possibilities model points to another loss: goods and services the economy could have produced that are not being produced.

Inefficient Production

Now suppose Alpine Sports is fully employing its factors of production. Could it still operate inside its production possibilities curve? Could an economy that is using all its factors of production still produce less than it could? The answer is "Yes," and the key lies in comparative advantage. An economy achieves a point on its production possibilities curve only if it allocates its factors of production on the basis of comparative advantage. If it fails to do that, it will operate inside the curve.

Suppose that, as before, Alpine Sports has been producing only skis. With all three of its plants producing skis, it can produce 350 pairs of skis per month (and no snowboards). The firm then starts producing snowboards. This time, however, imagine that Alpine Sports switches plants from skis to snowboards in numerical order: Plant 1 first, Plant 2 second, and then Plant 3. Figure 2.9 illustrates the result. Instead of the bowed-out production possibilities curve ABCD, we get a bowed-in curve, AB′C′D. Suppose that Alpine Sports is producing 100 snowboards and 150 pairs of skis at point B′. Had the firm based its production choices on comparative advantage, it would have switched Plant 3 to snowboards and then Plant 2, so it could have operated at a point such as C. It would be producing more snowboards and more pairs of skis—and using the same quantities of factors of production it was using at B′. Had the firm based its production choices on comparative advantage, it would have switched Plant 3 to snowboards and then Plant 2, so it would have operated at point C. It would be producing more snowboards and more pairs of skis—and using the same quantities of factors of production it was using at B′. When an economy is operating on its production possibilities curve, we say that it is engaging in **efficient production**. If it is using the same quantities of factors of production but is operating inside its production possibilities curve, it is engaging in **inefficient production**. Inefficient production implies that the economy could be producing more goods without using any additional labor, capital, or natural resources.

efficient production

When an economy is operating on its production possibilities curve.

inefficient production

Situation in which the economy is using the same quantities of factors of production but is operating inside its production possibilities curve.

FIGURE 2.9 Efficient Versus Inefficient Production

When factors of production are allocated on a basis other than comparative advantage, the result is inefficient production. Suppose Alpine Sports operates the three plants we examined in Figure 2.4. Suppose further that all three plants are devoted exclusively to ski production; the firm operates at A. Now suppose that, to increase snowboard production, it transfers plants in numerical order: Plant 1 first, then Plant 2, and finally Plant 3. The result is the bowed-in curve AB'C'D. Production on the production possibilities curve ABCD requires that factors of production be transferred according to comparative advantage.

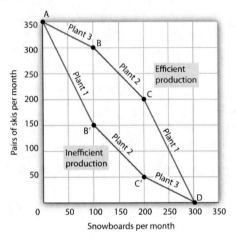

Points on the production possibilities curve thus satisfy two conditions: the economy is making full use of its factors of production, and it is making efficient use of its factors of production. If there are idle or inefficiently allocated factors of production, the economy will operate inside the production possibilities curve. Thus, the production possibilities curve not only shows what can be produced; it provides insight into how goods and services should be produced. It suggests that to obtain efficiency in production, factors of production should be allocated on the basis of comparative advantage. Further, the economy must make full use of its factors of production if it is to produce the goods and services it is capable of producing.

Specialization

The production possibilities model suggests that specialization will occur. **Specialization** implies that an economy is producing the goods and services in which it has a comparative advantage. If Alpine Sports selects point C in Figure 2.9, for example, it will assign Plant 1 exclusively to ski production and Plants 2 and 3 exclusively to snowboard production.

Such specialization is typical in an economic system. Workers, for example, specialize in particular fields in which they have a comparative advantage. People work and use the income they earn to buy—perhaps import—goods and services from people who have a comparative advantage in doing other things. The result is a far greater quantity of goods and services than would be available without this specialization.

Think about what life would be like without specialization. Imagine that you are suddenly completely cut off from the rest of the economy. You must produce everything you consume; you obtain nothing from anyone else. Would you be able to consume what you consume now? Clearly not. It is hard to imagine that most of us could even survive in such a setting. The gains we achieve through specialization are enormous.

Nations specialize as well. Much of the land in the United States has a comparative advantage in agricultural production and is devoted to that activity. Hong Kong, with its huge population and tiny endowment of land, allocates virtually none of its land to agricultural use; that option would be too costly. Its land is devoted largely to nonagricultural use.

specialization

Situation in which an economy is producing the goods and services in which it has a comparative advantage.

KEY TAKEAWAYS

- A production possibilities curve shows the combinations of two goods an economy is capable of producing.
- The downward slope of the production possibilities curve is an implication of scarcity.
- The bowed-out shape of the production possibilities curve results from allocating resources based on comparative advantage. Such an allocation implies that the law of increasing opportunity cost will hold.
- An economy that fails to make full and efficient use of its factors of production will operate inside its production possibilities curve.
- Specialization means that an economy is producing the goods and services in which it has a comparative advantage.

TRY IT!

Suppose a manufacturing firm is equipped to produce radios or calculators. It has two plants, Plant R and Plant S, at which it can produce these goods. Given the labor and the capital available at both plants, it can produce the combinations of the two goods at the two plants shown.

Output per day, Plant R

Combination	Calculators	Radios
A	100	0
B	50	25
C	0	50

Output per day, Plant S

Combination	Calculators	Radios
D	50	0
E	25	50
F	0	100

Put calculators on the vertical axis and radios on the horizontal axis. Draw the production possibilities curve for Plant R. On a separate graph, draw the production possibilities curve for Plant S. Which plant has a comparative advantage in calculators? In radios? Now draw the combined curves for the two plants. Suppose the firm decides to produce 100 radios. Where will it produce them? How many calculators will it be able to produce? Where will it produce the calculators?

Case in Point: The Cost of the Great Depression

© 2010 Jupiterimages Corporation

The U.S. economy looked very healthy in the beginning of 1929. It had enjoyed seven years of dramatic growth and unprecedented prosperity. Its resources were fully employed; it was operating quite close to its production possibilities curve.

In the summer of 1929, however, things started going wrong. Production and employment fell. They continued to fall for several years. By 1933, more than 25% of the nation's workers had lost their jobs. Production had plummeted by almost 30%. The economy had moved well within its production possibilities curve.

Output began to grow after 1933, but the economy continued to have vast numbers of idle workers, idle factories, and idle farms. These resources were not put back to work fully until 1942, after the U.S. entry into World War II demanded mobilization of the economy's factors of production.

Between 1929 and 1942, the economy produced 25% fewer goods and services than it would have if its resources had been fully employed. That was a loss, measured in today's dollars, of well over $3 trillion. In material terms, the forgone output represented a greater cost than the United States would ultimately spend in World War II. The Great Depression was a costly experience indeed.

ANSWER TO TRY IT! PROBLEM

The production possibilities curves for the two plants are shown, along with the combined curve for both plants. Plant R has a comparative advantage in producing calculators. Plant S has a comparative advantage in producing radios, so, if the firm goes from producing 150 calculators and no radios to producing 100 radios, it will produce them at Plant S. In the production possibilities curve for both plants, the firm would be at M, producing 100 calculators at Plant R.

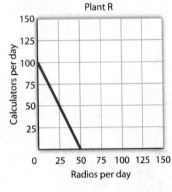
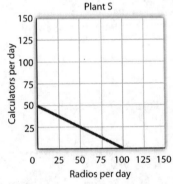
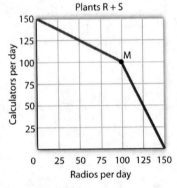

3. APPLICATIONS OF THE PRODUCTION POSSIBILITIES MODEL

LEARNING OBJECTIVES

1. Understand the argument for unrestricted international trade in terms of economic specialization and comparative advantage.
2. Define economic growth in terms of the production possibilities model and discuss factors that make such growth possible.
3. Explain the classification of economic systems, the role of government in different economic systems, and the strengths and weaknesses of different systems.

The production possibilities curve gives us a model of an economy. The model provides powerful insights about the real world, insights that help us to answer some important questions: How does trade between two countries affect the quantities of goods available to people? What determines the rate at which production will increase over time? What is the role of economic freedom in the economy? In this section we explore applications of the model to questions of international trade, economic growth, and the choice of an economic system.

3.1   Comparative Advantage and International Trade

One of the most important implications of the concepts of comparative advantage and the production possibilities curve relates to international trade. We can think of different nations as being equivalent to Christie Ryder's plants. Each will have a comparative advantage in certain activities, and efficient world production requires that each nation specialize in those activities in which it has a comparative advantage. A failure to allocate resources in this way means that world production falls inside the production possibilities curve; more of each good could be produced by relying on comparative advantage.

If nations specialize, then they must rely on each other. They will sell the goods in which they specialize and purchase other goods from other nations. Suppose, for example, that the world consists of two continents that can each produce two goods: South America and Europe can produce food and computers. Suppose they can produce the two goods according to the tables in Panels (a) and (b) of Figure 2.12. We have simplified this example by assuming that each continent has a linear production possibilities curve; the curves are plotted below the tables in Panels (a) and (b). Each continent has a separate production possibilities curve; the two have been combined to illustrate a world production possibilities curve in Panel (c) of the exhibit.

FIGURE 2.12   Production Possibilities Curves and Trade

Suppose the world consists of two continents: South America and Europe. They can each produce two goods: food and computers. In this example, we assume that each continent has a linear production possibilities curve, as shown in Panels (a) and (b). South America has a comparative advantage in food production and Europe has a comparative advantage in computer production. With free trade, the world can operate on the bowed-out curve GHI, shown in Panel (c). If the continents refuse to trade, the world will operate inside its production possibilities curve. If, for example, each continent were to produce at the midpoint of its production possibilities curve, the world would produce 300 computers and 300 units of food per period at point Q. If each continent were to specialize in the good in which it has a comparative advantage, world production could move to a point such as H, with more of both goods produced.

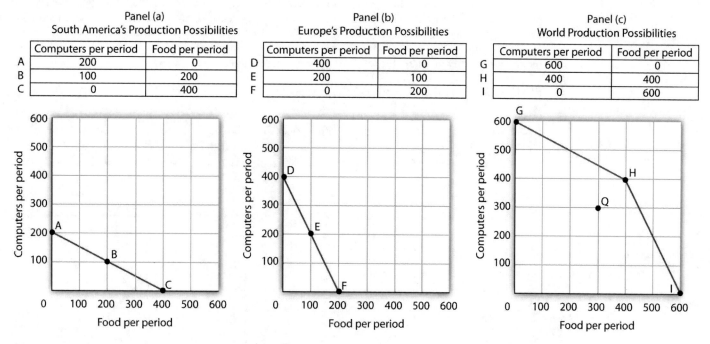

	Panel (a) South America's Production Possibilities	
	Computers per period	Food per period
A	200	0
B	100	200
C	0	400

	Panel (b) Europe's Production Possibilities	
	Computers per period	Food per period
D	400	0
E	200	100
F	0	200

	Panel (c) World Production Possibilities	
	Computers per period	Food per period
G	600	0
H	400	400
I	0	600

The world production possibilities curve assumes that resources are allocated between computer and food production based on comparative advantage. Notice that, even with only two economies and the assumption of linear production possibilities curves for each, the combined curve still has a bowed-out shape. At point H, for example, South America specializes in food, while Europe produces only computers. World production equals 400 units of each good. In this situation, we would expect South America to export food to Europe while Europe exports computers to South America.

But suppose the regions refuse to trade; each insists on producing its own food and computers. Suppose further that each chooses to produce at the midpoint of its own production possibilities curve. South America produces 100 units of computers and 200 units of food per period, while Europe produces 200 units of computers and 100 units of food per period. World production thus totals 300 units of each good per period; the world operates at point Q in Figure 2.12. If the two continents were willing to move from isolation to trade, the world could achieve an increase in the production of both goods. Producing at point H requires no more resources, no more effort than production at Q. It does, however, require that the world's resources be allocated on the basis of comparative advantage.

The implications of our model for trade are powerful indeed. First, we see that trade allows the production of more of all goods and services. Restrictions on trade thus reduce production of goods and services. Second, we see a lesson often missed in discussions of trade: a nation's trade policy has nothing to do with its level of employment of its factors of production. In our example, when South America and Europe do not engage in trade and produce at the midpoints of each of their respective production possibilities curves, *they each have full employment*. With trade, the two nations still operate on their respective production possibilities curves: *they each have full employment*. Trade certainly redistributes employment in the two continents. In South America, employment shifts from computer production to food production. In Europe, it shifts from food production to computer production. Once the shift is made, though, there is no effect on employment in either continent.

Of course, this idealized example would have all of South America's computer experts becoming farmers while all of Europe's farmers become computer geeks! That is a bit much to swallow, but it is merely the result of assuming linear production possibilities curves and complete specialization. In the real world, production possibilities curves are concave, and the reallocation of resources required by trade is not nearly as dramatic. Still, free trade can require shifts in resources from one activity to another. These shifts produce enormous benefits, but they do not come without costs.

Nearly all economists agree that largely unrestricted trade between countries is desirable; restrictions on trade generally force the world to operate inside its production possibilities curve. In some cases restrictions on trade could be desirable, but in the main, free trade promotes greater production of goods and services for the world's people. The role of international trade is explored in greater detail in subsequent chapters of this book.

3.2 Economic Growth

economic growth

The process through which an economy achieves an outward shift in its production possibilities curve.

An increase in the physical quantity or in the quality of factors of production available to an economy or a technological gain will allow the economy to produce more goods and services; it will shift the economy's production possibilities curve outward. The process through which an economy achieves an outward shift in its production possibilities curve is called **economic growth**. An outward shift in a production possibilities curve is illustrated in Figure 2.13. In Panel (a), a point such as N is not attainable; it lies outside the production possibilities curve. Growth shifts the curve outward, as in Panel (b), making previously unattainable levels of production possible.

FIGURE 2.13 Economic Growth and the Production Possibilities Curve

An economy capable of producing two goods, A and B, is initially operating at point M on production possibilities curve OMR in Panel (a). Given this production possibilities curve, the economy could not produce a combination such as shown by point N, which lies outside the curve. An increase in the factors of production available to the economy would shift the curve outward to SNT, allowing the choice of a point such as N, at which more of both goods will be produced.

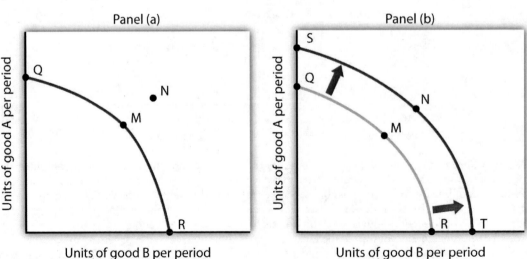

The Sources of Economic Growth

Economic growth implies an outward shift in an economy's production possibilities curve. Recall that when we draw such a curve, we assume that the quantity and quality of the economy's factors of production and its technology are unchanged. Changing these will shift the curve. Anything that increases the quantity or quality of the factors of production available to the economy or that improves the technology available to the economy contributes to economic growth.

Consider, for example, the dramatic gains in human capital that have occurred in the United States since the beginning of the past century. In 1900, about 3.5% of U.S. workers had completed a high school education. By 2006, that percentage rose almost to 92. Fewer than 1% of the workers in 1900 had graduated from college; as late as 1940 only 3.5% had graduated from college. By 2006, nearly 32% had graduated from college. In addition to being better educated, today's workers have received more and better training on the job. They bring far more economically useful knowledge and skills to their work than did workers a century ago.

Moreover, the technological changes that have occurred within the past 100 years have greatly reduced the time and effort required to produce most goods and services. Automated production has become commonplace. Innovations in transportation (automobiles, trucks, and airplanes) have made the movement of goods and people cheaper and faster. A dizzying array of new materials is available for manufacturing. And the development of modern information technology—including computers, software, and communications equipment—that seemed to proceed at breathtaking pace especially during the final years of the last century and continuing to the present has transformed the way we live and work.

Look again at the technological changes of the last few years described in the Case in Point on advances in technology. Those examples of technological progress through applications of computer technology—from new ways of mapping oil deposits to new methods of milking cows—helped propel the United States and other economies to dramatic gains in the ability to produce goods and services. They have helped shift the countries' production possibilities curve outward. They have helped fuel economic growth.

Table 2.1 summarizes the factors that have contributed to U.S. economic growth in the past half century. When looking at the period of 1948–2002 as a whole we see that about 60% of economic growth stems from increases in the quantities of capital and labor and 40% from increases in the qualities of the factors of production and improvements in technology. In the most recent period, 1995–2002, however, these percentages are essentially reversed, with a little less than 30% explained by increases in quantities of the factors of production and a whopping 70% explained by improvements in factor quality and technology.

TABLE 2.1 Sources of U.S. Economic Growth, 1948–2002

Total output during the period shown increased sixfold. The chart shows the percentage of this increase accounted for by increases in the quantity of labor and of capital and by increases in the quality of labor and of capital and improvements in technology. In the 1995–2002 period, the incorporation of information technology led to improvements in the quality of capital and technology that greatly contributed to growth.

Year	Percentage contribution to growth	Period growth rate
Years 1948–2002		**3.46%**
Increase in quantity of labor	21%	
Increase in quantity of capital	41%	
Increase in quality of labor	10%	
Increase in quality of capital	20%	
Improved technology	25%	
Years 1948–1973		**3.99%**
Increase in quantity of labor	15%	
Increase in quantity of capital	44%	
Increase in quality of labor	11%	
Increase in quality of capital	5%	
Improved technology	25%	
Years 1973–1989		**2.97%**
Increase in quantity of labor	31%	
Increase in quantity of capital	39%	
Increase in quality of labor	7%	
Increase in quality of capital	12%	
Improved technology	10%	
Years 1989–1995		**2.43%**
Increase in quantity of labor	26%	
Increase in quantity of capital	33%	
Increase in quality of labor	15%	
Increase in quality of capital	17%	
Improved technology	11%	
Years 1995–2002		**3.59%**
Increase in quantity of labor	19%	
Increase in quantity of capital	8%	
Increase in quality of labor	5%	
Increase in quality of capital	47%	
Improved technology	20%	

Source: Based on Dale W. Jorgenson, "Accounting for Growth in the Information Age," Handbook of Economic Growth, Phillipe Aghion and Steven Durlauf, eds. Amsterdam: North Holland, 2005.

Another way of looking at these data for the most recent period is to notice that the increase in the rate of economic growth between the 1989 to 1995 period and the 1995 to 2002 period of more than one percentage point per year is largely explained by better-quality capital and better technology. The study by economist Dale Jorgenson on which the data shown in Table 2.1 are derived notes that these two main contributors to higher economic growth can be largely attributed to the development of information technology and its incorporation in the workplace.

Waiting for Growth

One key to growth is, in effect, the willingness to wait, to postpone current consumption in order to enhance future productive capability. When Stone Age people fashioned the first tools, they were spending time building capital rather than engaging in consumption. They delayed current consumption to enhance their future consumption; the tools they made would make them more productive in the future.

Resources society could have used to produce consumer goods are being used to produce new capital goods and new knowledge for production instead—all to enhance future production. An even more important source of growth in many nations has been increased human capital. Increases in human capital often require the postponement of consumption. If you are a college student, you are engaged in precisely this effort. You are devoting time to study that could have been spent working, earning income, and thus engaging in a higher level of consumption. If you are like most students, you are making this choice to postpone consumption because you expect it will allow you to earn more income, and thus enjoy greater consumption, in the future.

Think of an economy as being able to produce two goods, capital and consumer goods (those destined for immediate use by consumers). By focusing on the production of consumer goods, the people in the economy will be able to enjoy a higher standard of living today. If they reduce their consumption—and their standard of living—today to enhance their ability to produce goods and services in the future, they will be able to shift their production possibilities curve outward. That may allow them to produce even more consumer goods. A decision for greater growth typically involves the sacrifice of present consumption.

3.3   Arenas for Choice: A Comparison of Economic Systems

Under what circumstances will a nation achieve efficiency in the use of its factors of production? The discussion above suggested that Christie Ryder would have an incentive to allocate her plants efficiently because by doing so she could achieve greater output of skis and snowboards than would be possible from inefficient production. But why would she want to produce more of these two goods—or of any goods? Why would decision makers throughout the economy want to achieve such efficiency?

Economists assume that privately owned firms seek to maximize their profits. The drive to maximize profits will lead firms such as Alpine Sports to allocate resources efficiently to gain as much production as possible from their factors of production. But whether firms will seek to maximize profits depends on the nature of the economic system within which they operate.

Classifying Economic Systems

Each of the world's economies can be viewed as operating somewhere on a spectrum between market capitalism and command socialism. In a **market capitalist economy**, resources are generally owned by private individuals who have the power to make decisions about their use. A market capitalist system is often referred to as a free enterprise economic system. In a **command socialist economy**, the government is the primary owner of capital and natural resources and has broad power to allocate the use of factors of production. Between these two categories lie **mixed economies** that combine elements of market capitalist and of command socialist economic systems.

No economy represents a pure case of either market capitalism or command socialism. To determine where an economy lies between these two types of systems, we evaluate the extent of government ownership of capital and natural resources and the degree to which government is involved in decisions about the use of factors of production.

Figure 2.14 suggests the spectrum of economic systems. Market capitalist economies lie toward the left end of this spectrum; command socialist economies appear toward the right. Mixed economies lie in between. The market capitalist end of the spectrum includes countries such as the United States, the United Kingdom, and Chile. Hong Kong, though now part of China, has a long history as a market capitalist economy and is generally regarded as operating at the market capitalist end of the spectrum. Countries at the command socialist end of the spectrum include North Korea and Cuba.

FIGURE 2.14 Economic Systems

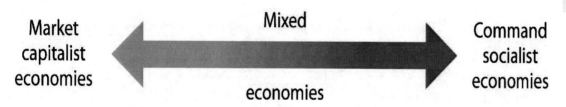

Some European economies, such as France, Germany, and Sweden, have a sufficiently high degree of regulation that we consider them as operating more toward the center of the spectrum. Russia and China, which long operated at the command socialist end of the spectrum, can now be considered mixed economies. Most economies in Latin America once operated toward the right end of the spectrum. While their governments did not exercise the extensive ownership of capital and natural resources that are one characteristic of command socialist systems, their governments did impose extensive

market capitalist economy

Economy in which resources are generally owned by private individuals who have the power to make decisions about their use.

command socialist economy

Economy in which government is the primary owner of capital and natural resources and has broad power to allocate the use of factors of production.

mixed economies

Economy that combine elements of market capitalist and of command socialist economic systems.

regulations. Many of these nations are in the process of carrying out economic reforms that will move them further in the direction of market capitalism.

The global shift toward market capitalist economic systems that occurred in the 1980s and 1990s was in large part the result of three important features of such economies. First, the emphasis on individual ownership and decision-making power has generally yielded greater individual freedom than has been available under command socialist or some more heavily regulated mixed economic systems that lie toward the command socialist end of the spectrum. People seeking political, religious, and economic freedom have thus gravitated toward market capitalism. Second, market economies are more likely than other systems to allocate resources on the basis of comparative advantage. They thus tend to generate higher levels of production and income than do other economic systems. Third, market capitalist-type systems appear to be the most conducive to entrepreneurial activity.

Suppose Christie Ryder had the same three plants we considered earlier in this chapter but was operating in a mixed economic system with extensive government regulation. In such a system, she might be prohibited from transferring resources from one use to another to achieve the gains possible from comparative advantage. If she were operating under a command socialist system, she would not be the owner of the plants and thus would be unlikely to profit from their efficient use. If that were the case, there is no reason to believe she would make any effort to assure the efficient use of the three plants. Generally speaking, it is economies toward the market capitalist end of the spectrum that offer the greatest inducement to allocate resources on the basis of comparative advantage. They tend to be more productive and to deliver higher material standards of living than do economies that operate at or near the command socialist end of the spectrum.

FIGURE 2.15 Economic Freedom and Income

The horizontal axis shows the degree of economic freedom—"free," "mostly free," "mostly unfree," and "repressed"—according to the measures used by the Heritage Foundation and *The Wall Street Journal*. The graph shows the relationship between economic freedom and per capita income. Countries with higher degrees of economic freedom tended to have higher per capita incomes.

Economic Freedom and Per Capita Income

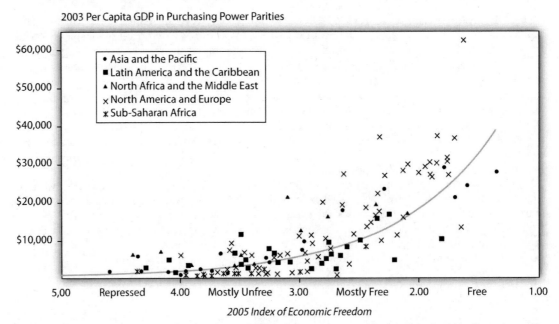

Source: World Bank, World Development Indicators Online, available by subscription at www.worldbank.org/data; Central Intelligence Agency, The World Factbook 2004, available at http://www.cia.gov/cia/publications/factbook/index.html for the following countries: Bahamas, Burma, Cuba, Cyprus, Equatorial Guinea, North Korea, Libya, Qatar, Suriname, Taiwan, Zimbabwe; Marc A. Miles, Edwin J. Feulner, and Mary Anastasia O'Grady, 2005 Index of Economic Freedom (Washington, D.C.: The Heritage Foundation and Dow Jones & Company, Inc., 2005), at www.heritage.org/index.

Market capitalist economies rely on economic freedom. Indeed, one way we can assess the degree to which a country can be considered market capitalist is by the degree of economic freedom it permits. Several organizations have attempted to compare economic freedom in various countries. One of the most extensive comparisons is a joint annual effort by the Heritage Foundation and *The Wall Street Journal*. The 2008 rating was based on policies in effect in 162 nations early that year. The report ranks these nations on the basis of such things as the degree of regulation of firms, tax levels, and restrictions on international trade. Hong Kong ranked as the freest economy in the world. North Korea received the dubious distinction of being the least free.

It seems reasonable to expect that the greater the degree of economic freedom a country permits, the greater the amount of income per person it will generate. This proposition is illustrated in Figure 2.15. The group of countries categorized as "free" generated the highest incomes in the Heritage Foundation/*Wall Street Journal* study; those rated as "repressed" had the lowest. The study also found that countries that over the last decade have done the most to improve their positions in the economic freedom rankings have also had the highest rates of growth. We must be wary of slipping into the fallacy of false cause by concluding from this evidence that economic freedom generates higher incomes. It could be that higher incomes lead nations to opt for greater economic freedom. But in this case, it seems reasonable to conclude that, in general, economic freedom does lead to higher incomes.

3.4 Government in a Market Economy

The production possibilities model provides a menu of choices among alternative combinations of goods and services. Given those choices, which combinations will be produced?

In a market economy, this question is answered in large part through the interaction of individual buyers and sellers. As we have already seen, government plays a role as well. It may seek to encourage greater consumption of some goods and discourage consumption of others. In the United States, for example, taxes imposed on cigarettes discourage smoking, while special treatment of property taxes and mortgage interest in the federal income tax encourages home ownership. Government may try to stop the production and consumption of some goods altogether, as many governments do with drugs such as heroin and cocaine. Government may supplement the private consumption of some goods by producing more of them itself, as many U.S. cities do with golf courses and tennis courts. In other cases, there may be no private market for a good or service at all. In the choice between security and defense versus all other goods and services outlined at the beginning of this chapter, government agencies are virtually the sole providers of security and national defense.

All nations also rely on government to provide defense, enforce laws, and redistribute income. Even market economies rely on government to regulate the activities of private firms, to protect the environment, to provide education, and to produce a wide range of other goods and services. Government's role may be limited in a market economy, but it remains fundamentally important.

KEY TAKEAWAYS

- The ideas of comparative advantage and specialization suggest that restrictions on international trade are likely to reduce production of goods and services.
- Economic growth is the result of increasing the quantity or quality of an economy's factors of production and of advances in technology.
- Policies to encourage growth generally involve postponing consumption to increase capital and human capital.
- Market capitalist economies have generally proved more productive than mixed or command socialist economies.
- Government plays a crucial role in any market economy.

TRY IT!

Draw a production possibilities curve for an economy that can produce two goods, CD players and jackets. You do not have numbers for this one—just draw a curve with the usual bowed-out shape. Put the quantity of CD players per period on the vertical axis and the quantity of jackets per period on the horizontal axis. Now mark a point A on the curve you have drawn; extend dotted lines from this point to the horizontal and vertical axes. Mark the initial quantities of the two goods as CD_A and J_A, respectively. Explain why, in the absence of economic growth, an increase in jacket production requires a reduction in the production of CD players. Now show how economic growth could lead to an increase in the production of both goods.

Case in Point: The European Union and the Production Possibilities Curve

© 2010 Jupiterimages Corporation

Formed by the Maastricht Treaty of 1993, The European Union represents one of the boldest efforts of our time to exploit the theory of comparative advantage. The Treaty sought to eliminate all trade barriers between the European Union's members. It established a European Parliament and a European Central Bank. The Bank introduced the euro in 1999, a currency that replaced national currencies such as the German deutsche mark and the French franc. At first, the euro was used only for transactions between banks. 320 million people in 15 EU nations (Austria, Belgium, Cyprus, Finland, France, Germany, Greece, Ireland, Italy, Luxembourg, Malta, the Netherlands, Portugal, Slovenia, and Spain) used the euro by 2008. While the dollar continues to be more widely used, the total value of euros in circulation exceeds that of dollars.

The movement toward European integration can be dated back more than half a century. In 1950, just five years after a war that had devastated much of the world, Robert Schuman, the French Minister of Foreign Affairs, proposed a union between France and Germany to cooperate in the production of iron and steel. In the context of the time, Schuman's proposal was a radical one. World War II had begun with Germany's attempt to seize control of Europe—and ultimately the world. Japan and Italy joined Germany in this effort. Germany had captured France; France had been liberated in 1944 by the Allied invasion in Normandy. The proposal for cooperation between two countries that had been the most bitter of enemies was a revolutionary one. Schuman's speech, delivered on May 9, 1950, is celebrated throughout Europe as "Europe Day."

In effect, the European Union has created an entity very much like the United States. Countries within the European Union retain their own languages and cultural differences, but they have ceded a remarkable degree of sovereignty to the Union. Members of the European Union can trade as freely with each other as can states within the United States. Just as the U.S. Constitution prohibits states from restricting trade with other states, the European Union has dismantled all forms of restrictions that countries within the Union used to impose on one another. Just as restrictions on specialization among Ms. Ryder's plants in Alpine Sports would have forced it to operate inside its production possibilities curve, restrictions that had existed among members of the European Union once put the members of the Union inside their collective production possibilities curve.

The experiment appears to have been a success. Trade among member nations has expanded sharply. A study by Carmen Diaz Mora, an economist at the University of Castilla-La Mancha in Spain, found that the bulk of the expanded trade within the Union was trade within industries and that it was driven by comparative advantage. In particular, she found that countries in the northern part of the Union, such as France and Germany, tended to specialize in relatively high-valued goods—office equipment and electrical goods—while countries in the southern part of the Union specialized in relatively low-valued goods such as food and textile products. In trade within the clothing industry, countries such as Italy tend to specialize in the production of higher-valued clothing, while lower-income countries such as Portugal specialize in the production of cheaper clothing. In sparkling wines, France specializes in the higher-quality end of the spectrum, while Spain specializes in the low-quality end. Similarly, Germany specializes in the production of higher-quality cars while Spain specializes in lower-quality vehicles. Similar exchanges occur across a wide range of goods and services.

Diaz Mora found that comparative advantage tended to correspond to income levels. Countries in the northern part of the European Union tend to have high per capita incomes and high levels of human capital and technology—these countries gained by specializing in the production of high-valued goods. Countries in the southern part of the Union also gained by specialization—in the production of low-valued goods. This specialization has increased the welfare of people throughout the Union.

Sources: Carmen Diaz Mora, "The Role of Comparative Advantage in Trade Within Industries: A Panel Data Approach for the European Union," Weltwirtschaftliches Archiv 138:2 (2002), 291–316.

ANSWER TO TRY IT! PROBLEM

Your first production possibilities curve should resemble the one in Panel (a). Starting at point A, an increase in jacket production requires a move down and to the right along the curve, as shown by the arrow, and thus a reduction in the production of CD players. Alternatively, if there is economic growth, it shifts the production possibilities curve outward, as in Panel (b). This shift allows an increase in production of both goods, as suggested by the arrow.

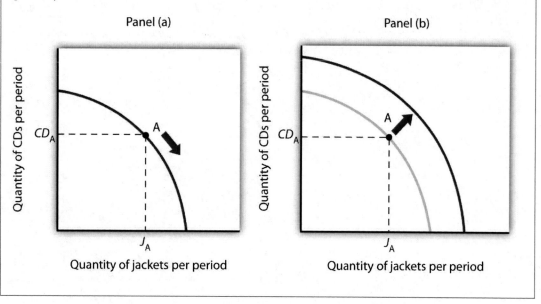

4.   REVIEW AND PRACTICE

Summary

Economics deals with choices. In this chapter we have examined more carefully the range of choices in production that must be made in any economy. In particular, we looked at choices involving the allocation of an economy's factors of production: labor, capital, and natural resources.

In addition, in any economy, the level of technology plays a key role in determining how productive the factors of production will be. In a market economy, entrepreneurs organize factors of production and act to introduce technological change.

The production possibilities model is a device that assists us in thinking about many of the choices about resource allocation in an economy. The model assumes that the economy has factors of production that are fixed in both quantity and quality. When illustrated graphically, the production possibilities model typically limits our analysis to two goods. Given the economy's factors of production and technology, the economy can produce various combinations of the two goods. If it uses its factors of production efficiently and has full employment, it will be operating on the production possibilities curve.

Two characteristics of the production possibilities curve are particularly important. First, it is downward sloping. This reflects the scarcity of the factors of production available to the economy; producing more of one good requires giving up some of the other. Second, the curve is bowed out. Another way of saying this is to say that the curve gets steeper as we move from left to right; the absolute value of its slope is increasing. Producing each additional unit of the good on the horizontal axis requires a greater sacrifice of the good on the vertical axis than did the previous units produced. This fact, called the law of increasing opportunity cost, is the inevitable result of efficient choices in production—choices based on comparative advantage.

The production possibilities model has important implications for international trade. It suggests that free trade will allow countries to specialize in the production of goods and services in which they have a comparative advantage. This specialization increases the production of all goods and services.

Increasing the quantity or quality of factors of production and/or improving technology will shift the production possibilities curve outward. This process is called economic growth. In the last 50 years, economic growth in the United States has resulted chiefly from increases in human capital and from technological advance.

Choices concerning the use of scarce resources take place within the context of a set of institutional arrangements that define an economic system. The principal distinctions between systems lie in the degree to which ownership of capital and natural resources and decision making authority over scarce resources are held by government or by private individuals. Economic systems include market capitalist, mixed, and command socialist economies. An increasing body of evidence suggests that market capitalist economies tend to be most productive; many command socialist and mixed economies are moving in the direction of market capitalist systems.

The presumption in favor of market-based systems does not preclude a role for government. Government is necessary to provide the system of laws on which market systems are founded. It may also be used to provide certain goods and services, to help individuals in need, and to regulate the actions of individuals and firms.

CONCEPT PROBLEMS

1. How does a college education increase one's human capital?

2. Why does the downward-sloping production possibilities curve imply that factors of production are scarce?

3. In what ways are the bowed-out shape of the production possibilities curve and the law of increasing opportunity cost related?

4. What is the relationship between the concept of comparative advantage and the law of increasing opportunity cost?

5. Suppose an economy can produce two goods, A and B. It is now operating at point E on production possibilities curve RT. An improvement in the technology available to produce good A shifts the curve to ST, and the economy selects point E'. How does this change affect the opportunity cost of producing an additional unit of good B?

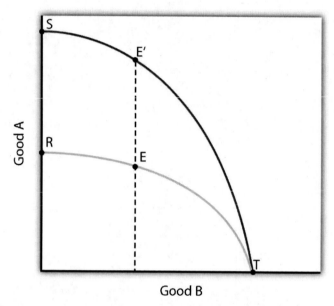

6. Could a nation's production possibilities curve ever shift inward? Explain what such a shift would mean, and discuss events that might cause such a shift to occur.

7. Suppose blue-eyed people were banned from working. How would this affect a nation's production possibilities curve?

8. Evaluate this statement: "The U.S. economy could achieve greater growth by devoting fewer resources to consumption and more to investment; it follows that such a shift would be desirable."

9. Two countries, Sportsland and Foodland, have similar total quantities of labor, capital, and natural resources. Both can produce two goods, figs and footballs. Sportsland's resources are particularly well suited to the production of footballs but are not very productive in producing figs. Foodland's resources are very productive when used for figs but are not capable of producing many footballs. In which country is the cost of additional footballs generally greater? Explain.

10. Suppose a country is committed to using its resources based on the reverse of comparative advantage doctrine: it first transfers those resources for which the cost is greatest, not lowest. Describe this country's production possibilities curve.

11. The U.S. Constitution bans states from restricting imports of goods and services from other states. Suppose this restriction did not exist and that states were allowed to limit imports of goods and services produced in other states. How do you think this would affect U.S. output? Explain.

12. By 1993, nations in the European Union (EU) had eliminated all barriers to the flow of goods, services, labor, and capital across their borders. Even such things as consumer protection laws and the types of plugs required to plug in appliances have been standardized to ensure that there will be no barriers to trade. How do you think this elimination of trade barriers affected EU output?

13. How did the technological changes described in the Case in Point "Technology Cuts Costs, Boosts Productivity and Profits" affect the production possibilities curve for the United States?

NUMERICAL PROBLEMS

1. Nathan can mow four lawns in a day or plant 20 trees in a day.

    a. Draw Nathan's production possibilities curve for mowing lawns and planting trees. Assume the production possibilities curve is linear and put the quantity of lawns mowed per day on the horizontal axis and the quantity of trees planted per day on the vertical axis.

    b. What is Nathan's opportunity cost of planting trees?

    c. What is Nathan's opportunity cost of mowing lawns?

2. David can mow four lawns in a day or plant four trees in a day.

    a. Draw David's production possibilities curve for mowing lawns and planting trees. Again, assume a linear production possibilities curve and put the quantity of lawns mowed per day on the horizontal axis.

    b. What is David's opportunity cost of planting trees?

    c. What is David's opportunity cost of mowing lawns?

3. Given the production information in problems 1 and 2 above, who has the comparative advantage in planting trees? Mowing lawns?

4. The exhibits below describe the production possibilities for Germany and Turkey.

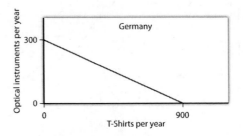

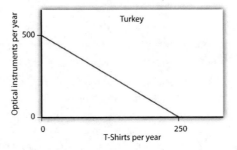

    a. What is the slope of Germany's production possibilities curve?

    b. What is the slope of Turkey's production possibilities curve?

    c. What is the opportunity cost of producing T-shirts in Germany?

    d. What is the opportunity cost of producing T-shirts in Turkey?

    e. What is the opportunity cost of producing optical instruments in Germany?

    f. What is the opportunity cost of producing optical instruments in Turkey?

    g. In which good does Germany have a comparative advantage?

    h. In which good does Turkey have a comparative advantage?

5. The nation of Leisureland can produce two goods, bicycles and bowling balls. The western region of Leisureland can, if it devotes all its resources to bicycle production, produce 100 bicycles per month. Alternatively, it could devote all its resources to bowling balls and produce 400 per month—or it could produce any combination of bicycles and bowling balls lying on a straight line between these two extremes.

    a. Draw a production possibilities curve for western Leisureland (with bicycles on the vertical axis).

    b. What it is the opportunity cost of producing an additional bowling ball measured in terms of forgone bicycles in western Leisureland?

    c. Suppose that eastern Leisureland can, if it devotes all its resources to the production of bicycles, produce 400. If it devotes all its resources to bowling ball production, though, it can produce only 100. Draw the production possibilities curve for eastern Leisureland (again, assume it is linear and put bicycles on the vertical axis).

d. What is the opportunity cost of producing an additional bowling ball measured in terms of forgone bicycles in eastern Leisureland?

e. Explain the difference in opportunity cost between western and eastern Leisureland. Which region has a comparative advantage in producing bowling balls? Bicycles?

f. Draw the production possibilities curve for Leisureland, one that combines the curves for western and eastern Leisureland.

g. Suppose it is determined that 400 bicycles must be produced. How many bowling balls can be produced?

h. Where will these goods be produced?

6. The table below shows the production possibilities schedule for an economy.

Production Alternatives	Capital goods per period	Consumer goods per period
A	0	40
B	1	36
C	2	28
D	3	16
E	4	0

a. Putting capital goods per period on the horizontal axis and consumer goods per period on the vertical axis, graph the production possibilities curve for the economy.

b. If the economy is producing at alternative B, what is the opportunity cost to it of producing at alternative C instead?

c. If the economy is producing at alternative C, what is the opportunity cost to it of producing at alternative D instead?

d. Is it possible for this economy to produce 30 units of consumer goods per period while producing 1 unit of capital goods? Would this combination of goods represent efficient or inefficient production? Explain.

e. Which point, B or C, would lead to higher economic growth? Explain your answer.

7. The exhibit below shows the sources of growth in the United States between 1909 and 1929 and between 1950 and 1979, according to a study by Edward Denison.[1] (Note: The sources of economic growth are cumulative and, taken collectively, explain 100% of total growth over the period.)

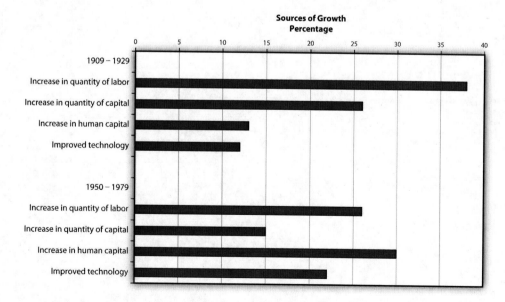

a. Approximately what percentage of U.S. growth between 1909 and 1929 was due to increases in quantities of factors of production?

b. Approximately what percentage of U.S. growth between 1909 and 1929 was due to increases in quality of factors of production and technological improvement?

c. Approximately what percentage of U.S. growth between 1950 and 1979 was due to increases in quantities of factors of production?

d. Approximately what percentage of U.S. growth between 1950 and 1979 was due to increases in quality of factors of production and technological improvement?

ENDNOTES

1. Edward Denison, *The Sources of Economic Growth in the United States* (New York: Committee for Economic Development, 1962) and Edward Denison, *Trends in American Growth 1929–1982* (Washington, D.C.: Brookings Institutions, 1985).

CHAPTER 3
Demand and Supply

START UP: CRAZY FOR COFFEE

Starbucks Coffee Company revolutionized the coffee-drinking habits of millions of Americans. Starbucks, whose bright green-and-white logo is almost as familiar as the golden arches of McDonald's, began in Seattle in 1971. Fifteen years later it had grown into a chain of four stores in the Seattle area. Then in 1987 Howard Schultz, a former Starbucks employee, who had become enamored with the culture of Italian coffee bars during a trip to Italy, bought the company from its founders for $3.8 million. In 2008, Americans were willingly paying $3 or more for a cappuccino or a latté, and Starbuck's had grown to become an international chain, with over 16,000 stores around the world.

The change in American consumers' taste for coffee and the profits raked in by Starbucks lured other companies to get into the game. Retailers such as Seattle's Best Coffee and Gloria Jean's Coffees entered the market, and today there are thousands of coffee bars, carts, drive-throughs, and kiosks in downtowns, malls, and airports all around the country. Even McDonald's began selling specialty coffees.

But over the last decade the price of coffee beans has been quite volatile. Just as consumers were growing accustomed to their cappuccinos and lattés, in 1997, the price of coffee beans shot up. Excessive rain and labor strikes in coffee-growing areas of South America had reduced the supply of coffee, leading to a rise in its price. In the early 2000s, Vietnam flooded the market with coffee, and the price of coffee beans plummeted. More recently, weather conditions in various coffee-growing countries reduced supply, and the price of coffee beans went back up.

Markets, the institutions that bring together buyers and sellers, are always responding to events, such as bad harvests and changing consumer tastes that affect the prices and quantities of particular goods. The demand for some goods increases, while the demand for others decreases. The supply of some goods rises, while the supply of others falls. As such events unfold, prices adjust to keep markets in balance. This chapter explains how the market forces of demand and supply interact to determine equilibrium prices and equilibrium quantities of goods and services. We will see how prices and quantities adjust to changes in demand and supply and how changes in prices serve as signals to buyers and sellers.

The model of demand and supply that we shall develop in this chapter is one of the most powerful tools in all of economic analysis. You will be using it throughout your study of economics. We will first look at the variables that influence demand. Then we will turn to supply, and finally we will put demand and supply together to explore how the model of demand and supply operates. As we examine the model, bear in mind that demand is a representation of the behavior of buyers and that supply is a representation of the behavior of sellers. Buyers may be consumers purchasing groceries or producers purchasing iron ore to make steel. Sellers may be firms selling cars or households selling their labor services. We shall see that the ideas of demand and supply apply, whatever the identity of the buyers or sellers and whatever the good or service being exchanged in the market. In this chapter, we shall focus on buyers and sellers of goods and services.

markets

The institutions that bring together buyers and sellers.

1. DEMAND

LEARNING OBJECTIVES

1. Define the quantity demanded of a good or service and illustrate it using a demand schedule and a demand curve.
2. Distinguish between the following pairs of concepts: demand and quantity demanded, demand schedule and demand curve, movement along and shift in a demand curve.
3. Identify demand shifters and determine whether a change in a demand shifter causes the demand curve to shift to the right or to the left.

How many pizzas will people eat this year? How many doctor visits will people make? How many houses will people buy?

Each good or service has its own special characteristics that determine the quantity people are willing and able to consume. One is the price of the good or service itself. Other independent variables that are important determinants of demand include consumer preferences, prices of related goods and services, income, demographic characteristics such as population size, and buyer expectations. The number of pizzas people will purchase, for example, depends very much on whether they like pizza. It also depends on the prices for alternatives such as hamburgers or spaghetti. The number of doctor visits is likely to vary with income—people with higher incomes are likely to see a doctor more often than people with lower incomes. The demands for pizza, for doctor visits, and for housing are certainly affected by the age distribution of the population and its size.

While different variables play different roles in influencing the demands for different goods and services, economists pay special attention to one: the price of the good or service. Given the values of all the other variables that affect demand, a higher price tends to reduce the quantity people demand, and a lower price tends to increase it. A medium pizza typically sells for $5 to $10. Suppose the price were $30. Chances are, you would buy fewer pizzas at that price than you do now. Suppose pizzas typically sold for $2 each. At that price, people would be likely to buy more pizzas than they do now.

We will discuss first how price affects the quantity demanded of a good or service and then how other variables affect demand.

1.1 Price and the Demand Curve

Because people will purchase different quantities of a good or service at different prices, economists must be careful when speaking of the "demand" for something. They have therefore developed some specific terms for expressing the general concept of demand.

The **quantity demanded** of a good or service is the quantity buyers are willing and able to buy at a particular price during a particular period, all other things unchanged. (As we learned, we can substitute the Latin phrase "ceteris paribus" for "all other things unchanged.") Suppose, for example, that 100,000 movie tickets are sold each month in a particular town at a price of $8 per ticket. That quantity—100,000—is the quantity of movie admissions demanded per month at a price of $8. If the price were $12, we would expect the quantity demanded to be less. If it were $4, we would expect the quantity demanded to be greater. The quantity demanded at each price would be different if other things that might affect it, such as the population of the town, were to change. That is why we add the qualifier that other things have not changed to the definition of quantity demanded.

A **demand schedule** is a table that shows the quantities of a good or service demanded at different prices during a particular period, all other things unchanged. To introduce the concept of a demand schedule, let us consider the demand for coffee in the United States. We will ignore differences among types of coffee beans and roasts, and speak simply of coffee. The table in Figure 3.1 shows quantities of coffee that will be demanded each month at prices ranging from $9 to $4 per pound; the table is a demand schedule. We see that the higher the price, the lower the quantity demanded.

quantity demanded

The quantity buyers are willing and able to buy of a good or service at a particular price during a particular period, all other things unchanged.

demand schedule

A table that shows the quantities of a good or service demanded at different prices during a particular period, all other things unchanged.

FIGURE 3.1 A Demand Schedule and a Demand Curve

The table is a demand schedule; it shows quantities of coffee demanded per month in the United States at particular prices, all other things unchanged. These data are then plotted on the demand curve. At point A on the curve, 25 million pounds of coffee per month are demanded at a price of $6 per pound. At point B, 30 million pounds of coffee per month are demanded at a price of $5 per pound.

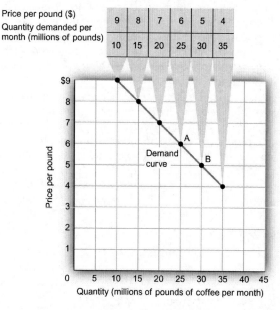

The information given in a demand schedule can be presented with a **demand curve**, which is a graphical representation of a demand schedule. A demand curve thus shows the relationship between the price and quantity demanded of a good or service during a particular period, all other things unchanged. The demand curve in Figure 3.1 shows the prices and quantities of coffee demanded that are given in the demand schedule. At point A, for example, we see that 25 million pounds of coffee per month are demanded at a price of $6 per pound. By convention, economists graph price on the vertical axis and quantity on the horizontal axis.

Price alone does not determine the quantity of coffee or any other good that people buy. To isolate the effect of changes in price on the quantity of a good or service demanded, however, we show the quantity demanded at each price, assuming that those other variables remain unchanged. We do the same thing in drawing a graph of the relationship between any two variables; we assume that the values of other variables that may affect the variables shown in the graph (such as income or population) remain unchanged for the period under consideration.

A change in price, with no change in any of the other variables that affect demand, results in a movement *along* the demand curve. For example, if the price of coffee falls from $6 to $5 per pound, consumption rises from 25 million pounds to 30 million pounds per month. That is a movement from point A to point B along the demand curve in Figure 3.1. A movement along a demand curve that results from a change in price is called a **change in quantity demanded**. Note that a change in quantity demanded is not a change or shift in the demand curve; it is a movement *along* the demand curve.

The negative slope of the demand curve in Figure 3.1 suggests a key behavioral relationship of economics. All other things unchanged, the **law of demand** holds that, for virtually all goods and services, a higher price leads to a reduction in quantity demanded and a lower price leads to an increase in quantity demanded.

The law of demand is called a law because the results of countless studies are consistent with it. Undoubtedly, you have observed one manifestation of the law. When a store finds itself with an overstock of some item, such as running shoes or tomatoes, and needs to sell these items quickly, what does it do? It typically has a sale, expecting that a lower price will increase the quantity demanded. In general, we expect the law of demand to hold. Given the values of other variables that influence demand, a higher price reduces the quantity demanded. A lower price increases the quantity demanded. Demand curves, in short, slope downward.

demand curve

A graphical representation of a demand schedule.

change in quantity demanded

A movement along a demand curve that results from a change in price.

law of demand

For virtually all goods and services, a higher price leads to a reduction in quantity demanded and a lower price leads to an increase in quantity demanded.

1.2   Changes in Demand

Of course, price alone does not determine the quantity of a good or service that people consume. Coffee consumption, for example, will be affected by such variables as income and population. Preferences also play a role. The story at the beginning of the chapter illustrates as much. Starbucks "turned people on" to coffee. We also expect other prices to affect coffee consumption. People often eat doughnuts or bagels with their coffee, so a reduction in the price of doughnuts or bagels might induce people to drink more coffee. An alternative to coffee is tea, so a reduction in the price of tea might result in the consumption of more tea and less coffee. Thus, a change in any one of the variables held constant in constructing a demand schedule will change the quantities demanded at each price. The result will be a *shift* in the entire demand curve rather than a movement along the demand curve. A *shift* in a demand curve is called a **change in demand**.

Suppose, for example, that something happens to increase the quantity of coffee demanded at each price. Several events could produce such a change: an increase in incomes, an increase in population, or an increase in the price of tea would each be likely to increase the quantity of coffee demanded at each price. Any such change produces a new demand schedule. Figure 3.2 shows such a change in the demand schedule for coffee. We see that the quantity of coffee demanded per month is greater at each price than before. We show that graphically as a shift in the demand curve. The original curve, labeled D_1, shifts to the right to D_2. At a price of $6 per pound, for example, the quantity demanded rises from 25 million pounds per month (point A) to 35 million pounds per month (point A').

FIGURE 3.2   An Increase in Demand

An increase in the quantity of a good or service demanded at each price is shown as an increase in demand. Here, the original demand curve D_1 shifts to D_2. Point A on D_1 corresponds to a price of $6 per pound and a quantity demanded of 25 million pounds of coffee per month. On the new demand curve D_2, the quantity demanded at this price rises to 35 million pounds of coffee per month (point A').

Price	Old quantity demanded	New quantity demanded
$9	10	20
8	15	25
7	20	30
6	25	35
5	30	40
4	35	45

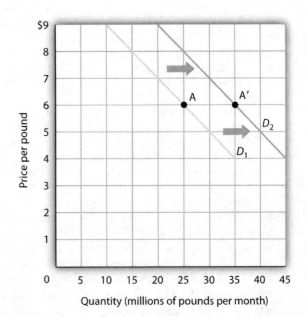

Just as demand can increase, it can decrease. In the case of coffee, demand might fall as a result of events such as a reduction in population, a reduction in the price of tea, or a change in preferences. For example, a definitive finding that the caffeine in coffee contributes to heart disease, which is currently being debated in the scientific community, could change preferences and reduce the demand for coffee.

A reduction in the demand for coffee is illustrated in Figure 3.3. The demand schedule shows that less coffee is demanded at each price than in Figure 3.1. The result is a shift in demand from the original curve D_1 to D_3. The quantity of coffee demanded at a price of $6 per pound falls from 25 million pounds per month (point A) to 15 million pounds per month (point A''). Note, again, that a change in quantity demanded, ceteris paribus, refers to a movement *along* the demand curve, while a change in demand refers to a *shift* in the demand curve.

FIGURE 3.3 A Reduction in Demand

A reduction in demand occurs when the quantities of a good or service demanded fall at each price. Here, the demand schedule shows a lower quantity of coffee demanded at each price than we had in Figure 3.1. The reduction shifts the demand curve for coffee to D_3 from D_1. The quantity demanded at a price of $6 per pound, for example, falls from 25 million pounds per month (point A) to 15 million pounds of coffee per month (point A″).

Price	Old quantity demanded	New quantity demanded
$9	10	0
8	15	5
7	20	10
6	25	15
5	30	20
4	35	25

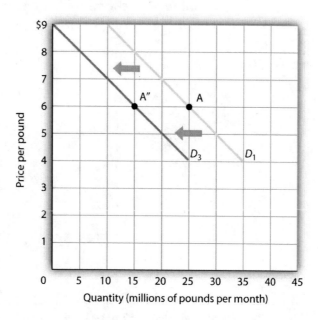

A variable that can change the quantity of a good or service demanded at each price is called a **demand shifter**. When these other variables change, the all-other-things-unchanged conditions behind the original demand curve no longer hold. Although different goods and services will have different demand shifters, the demand shifters are likely to include (1) consumer preferences, (2) the prices of related goods and services, (3) income, (4) demographic characteristics, and (5) buyer expectations. Next we look at each of these.

Preferences

Changes in preferences of buyers can have important consequences for demand. We have already seen how Starbucks supposedly increased the demand for coffee. Another example is reduced demand for cigarettes caused by concern about the effect of smoking on health. A change in preferences that makes one good or service more popular will shift the demand curve to the right. A change that makes it less popular will shift the demand curve to the left.

Prices of Related Goods and Services

Suppose the price of doughnuts were to fall. Many people who drink coffee enjoy dunking doughnuts in their coffee; the lower price of doughnuts might therefore increase the demand for coffee, shifting the demand curve for coffee to the right. A lower price for tea, however, would be likely to reduce coffee demand, shifting the demand curve for coffee to the left.

In general, if a reduction in the price of one good increases the demand for another, the two goods are called **complements**. If a reduction in the price of one good reduces the demand for another, the two goods are called **substitutes**. These definitions hold in reverse as well: two goods are complements if an increase in the price of one reduces the demand for the other, and they are substitutes if an increase in the price of one increases the demand for the other. Doughnuts and coffee are complements; tea and coffee are substitutes.

Complementary goods are goods used in conjunction with one another. Tennis rackets and tennis balls, eggs and bacon, and stationery and postage stamps are complementary goods. Substitute goods are goods used instead of one another. iPODs, for example, are likely to be substitutes for CD players. Breakfast cereal is a substitute for eggs. A file attachment to an e-mail is a substitute for both a fax machine and postage stamps.

demand shifter

A variable that can change the quantity of a good or service demanded at each price.

complements

Two goods for which an increase in price of one reduces the demand for the other.

substitutes

Two goods for which an increase in price of one increases the demand for the other.

FIGURE 3.4

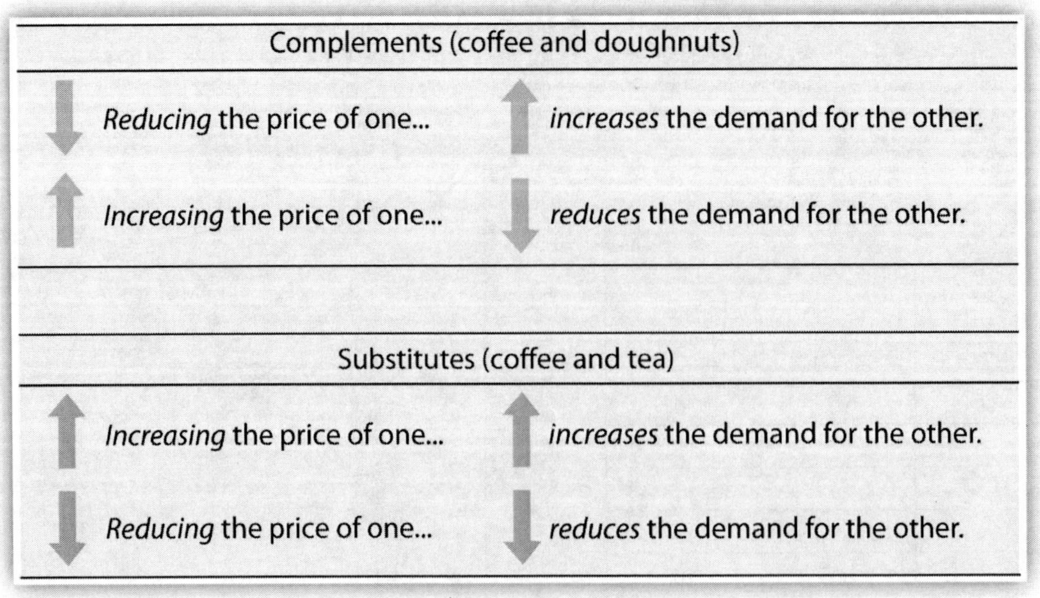

Income

As incomes rise, people increase their consumption of many goods and services, and as incomes fall, their consumption of these goods and services falls. For example, an increase in income is likely to raise the demand for gasoline, ski trips, new cars, and jewelry. There are, however, goods and services for which consumption falls as income rises—and rises as income falls. As incomes rise, for example, people tend to consume more fresh fruit but less canned fruit.

A good for which demand increases when income increases is called a **normal good**. A good for which demand decreases when income increases is called an **inferior good**. An increase in income shifts the demand curve for fresh fruit (a normal good) to the right; it shifts the demand curve for canned fruit (an inferior good) to the left.

Demographic Characteristics

The number of buyers affects the total quantity of a good or service that will be bought; in general, the greater the population, the greater the demand. Other demographic characteristics can affect demand as well. As the share of the population over age 65 increases, the demand for medical services, ocean cruises, and motor homes increases. The birth rate in the United States fell sharply between 1955 and 1975 but has gradually increased since then. That increase has raised the demand for such things as infant supplies, elementary school teachers, soccer coaches, in-line skates, and college education. Demand can thus shift as a result of changes in both the number and characteristics of buyers.

Buyer Expectations

The consumption of goods that can be easily stored, or whose consumption can be postponed, is strongly affected by buyer expectations. The expectation of newer TV technologies, such as high-definition TV, could slow down sales of regular TVs. If people expect gasoline prices to rise tomorrow, they will fill up their tanks today to try to beat the price increase. The same will be true for goods such as automobiles and washing machines: an expectation of higher prices in the future will lead to more purchases today. If the price of a good is expected to fall, however, people are likely to reduce their purchases today and await tomorrow's lower prices. The expectation that computer prices will fall, for example, can reduce current demand.

normal good

A good for which demand increases when income increases.

inferior good

A good for which demand decreases when income increases.

Heads Up!

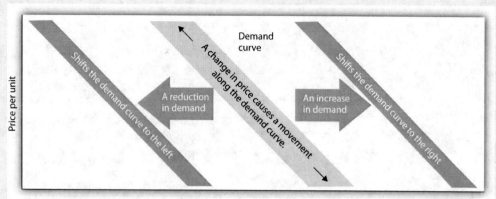

It is crucial to distinguish between a change in quantity demanded, which is a movement along the demand curve caused by a change in price, and a change in demand, which implies a shift of the demand curve itself. A change in demand is caused by a change in a demand shifter. An increase in demand is a shift of the demand curve to the right. A decrease in demand is a shift in the demand curve to the left. This drawing of a demand curve highlights the difference.

KEY TAKEAWAYS

- The quantity demanded of a good or service is the quantity buyers are willing and able to buy at a particular price during a particular period, all other things unchanged.
- A demand schedule is a table that shows the quantities of a good or service demanded at different prices during a particular period, all other things unchanged.
- A demand curve shows graphically the quantities of a good or service demanded at different prices during a particular period, all other things unchanged.
- All other things unchanged, the law of demand holds that, for virtually all goods and services, a higher price induces a reduction in quantity demanded and a lower price induces an increase in quantity demanded.
- A change in the price of a good or service causes a change in the quantity demanded—a movement *along* the demand curve.
- A change in a demand shifter causes a change in demand, which is shown as a *shift* of the demand curve. Demand shifters include preferences, the prices of related goods and services, income, demographic characteristics, and buyer expectations.
- Two goods are substitutes if an increase in the price of one causes an increase in the demand for the other. Two goods are complements if an increase in the price of one causes a decrease in the demand for the other.
- A good is a normal good if an increase in income causes an increase in demand. A good is an inferior good if an increase in income causes a decrease in demand.

TRY IT!

All other things unchanged, what happens to the demand curve for DVD rentals if there is (a) an increase in the price of movie theater tickets, (b) a decrease in family income, or (c) an increase in the price of DVD rentals? In answering this and other "Try It!" problems in this chapter, draw and carefully label a set of axes. On the horizontal axis of your graph, show the quantity of DVD rentals. It is necessary to specify the time period to which your quantity pertains (e.g., "per period," "per week," or "per year"). On the vertical axis show the price per DVD rental. Since you do not have specific data on prices and quantities demanded, make a "free-hand" drawing of the curve or curves you are asked to examine. Focus on the general shape and position of the curve(s) before and after events occur. Draw new curve(s) to show what happens in each of the circumstances given. The curves could shift to the left or to the right, or stay where they are.

Case in Point: Solving Campus Parking Problems Without Adding More Parking Spaces

© 2010 Jupiterimages Corporation

Unless you attend a "virtual" campus, chances are you have engaged in more than one conversation about how hard it is to find a place to park on campus. Indeed, according to Clark Kerr, a former president of the University of California system, a university is best understood as a group of people "held together by a common grievance over parking."

Clearly, the demand for campus parking spaces has grown substantially over the past few decades. In surveys conducted by Daniel Kenney, Ricardo Dumont, and Ginger Kenney, who work for the campus design company Sasaki and Associates, it was found that 7 out of 10 students own their own cars. They have interviewed "many students who confessed to driving from their dormitories to classes that were a five-minute walk away," and they argue that the deterioration of college environments is largely attributable to the increased use of cars on campus and that colleges could better service their missions by not adding more parking spaces.

Since few universities charge enough for parking to even cover the cost of building and maintaining parking lots, the rest is paid for by all students as part of tuition. Their research shows that "for every 1,000 parking spaces, the median institution loses almost $400,000 a year for surface parking, and more than $1,200,000 for structural parking." Fear of a backlash from students and their parents, as well as from faculty and staff, seems to explain why campus administrators do not simply raise the price of parking on campus.

While Kenney and his colleagues do advocate raising parking fees, if not all at once then over time, they also suggest some subtler, and perhaps politically more palatable, measures—in particular, shifting the demand for parking spaces to the left by lowering the prices of substitutes.

Two examples they noted were at the University of Washington and the University of Colorado at Boulder. At the University of Washington, car poolers may park for free. This innovation has reduced purchases of single-occupancy parking permits by 32% over a decade. According to University of Washington assistant director of transportation services Peter Dewey, "Without vigorously managing our parking and providing commuter alternatives, the university would have been faced with adding approximately 3,600 parking spaces, at a cost of over $100 million…The university has created opportunities to make capital investments in buildings supporting education instead of structures for cars." At the University of Colorado, free public transit has increased use of buses and light rail from 300,000 to 2 million trips per year over the last decade. The increased use of mass transit has allowed the university to avoid constructing nearly 2,000 parking spaces, which has saved about $3.6 million annually.

Sources: Daniel R. Kenney, "How to Solve Campus Parking Problems Without Adding More Parking," The Chronicle of Higher Education, March 26, 2004, Section B, pp. B22-B23.

Since going to the movies is a substitute for watching a DVD at home, an increase in the price of going to the movies should cause more people to switch from going to the movies to staying at home and renting DVDs. Thus, the demand curve for DVD rentals will shift to the right when the price of movie theater tickets increases [Panel (a)].

A decrease in family income will cause the demand curve to shift to the left if DVD rentals are a normal good but to the right if DVD rentals are an inferior good. The latter may be the case for some families, since staying at home and watching DVDs is a cheaper form of entertainment than taking the family to the movies. For most others, however, DVD rentals are probably a normal good [Panel (b)].

An increase in the price of DVD rentals does not shift the demand curve for DVD rentals at all; rather, an increase in price, say from P_1 to P_2, is a movement upward to the left along the demand curve. At a higher price, people will rent fewer DVDs, say Q_2 instead of Q_1, ceteris paribus [Panel (c)].

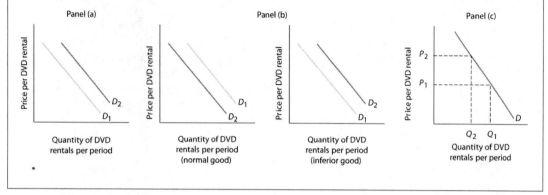

2. SUPPLY

LEARNING OBJECTIVES

1. Define the quantity supplied of a good or service and illustrate it using a supply schedule and a supply curve.
2. Distinguish between the following pairs of concepts: supply and quantity supplied, supply schedule and supply curve, movement along and shift in a supply curve.
3. Identify supply shifters and determine whether a change in a supply shifter causes the supply curve to shift to the right or to the left.

What determines the quantity of a good or service sellers are willing to offer for sale? Price is one factor; ceteris paribus, a higher price is likely to induce sellers to offer a greater quantity of a good or service. Production cost is another determinant of supply. Variables that affect production cost include the prices of factors used to produce the good or service, returns from alternative activities, technology, the expectations of sellers, and natural events such as weather changes. Still another factor affecting the quantity of a good that will be offered for sale is the number of sellers—the greater the number of sellers of a particular good or service, the greater will be the quantity offered at any price per time period.

2.1 Price and the Supply Curve

The **quantity supplied** of a good or service is the quantity sellers are willing to sell at a particular price during a particular period, all other things unchanged. Ceteris paribus, the receipt of a higher price increases profits and induces sellers to increase the quantity they supply.

In general, when there are many sellers of a good, an increase in price results in an increase in quantity supplied, and this relationship is often referred to as the law of supply. We will see, though, through our exploration of microeconomics, that there are a number of exceptions to this relationship. There are cases in which a higher price will not induce an increase in quantity supplied. Goods that cannot be produced, such as additional land on the corner of Park Avenue and 56th Street in Manhattan, are fixed in supply—a higher price cannot induce an increase in the quantity supplied. There are

quantity supplied

The quantity sellers are willing to sell of a good or service at a particular price during a particular period, all other things unchanged.

even cases, which we investigate in microeconomic analysis, in which a higher price induces a reduction in the quantity supplied.

Generally speaking, however, when there are many sellers of a good, an increase in price results in a greater quantity supplied. The relationship between price and quantity supplied is suggested in a **supply schedule**, a table that shows quantities supplied at different prices during a particular period, all other things unchanged. Figure 3.8 gives a supply schedule for the quantities of coffee that will be supplied per month at various prices, ceteris paribus. At a price of $4 per pound, for example, producers are willing to supply 15 million pounds of coffee per month. A higher price, say $6 per pound, induces sellers to supply a greater quantity—25 million pounds of coffee per month.

supply schedule

A table that shows quantities supplied at different prices during a particular period, all other things unchanged.

FIGURE 3.8 A Supply Schedule and a Supply Curve

The supply schedule shows the quantity of coffee that will be supplied in the United States each month at particular prices, all other things unchanged. The same information is given graphically in the supply curve. The values given here suggest a positive relationship between price and quantity supplied.

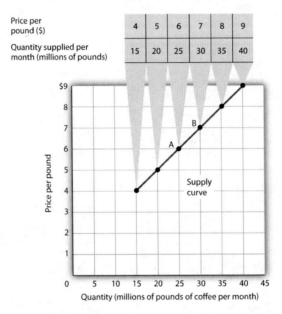

Price per pound ($)	4	5	6	7	8	9
Quantity supplied per month (millions of pounds)	15	20	25	30	35	40

A **supply curve** is a graphical representation of a supply schedule. It shows the relationship between price and quantity supplied during a particular period, all other things unchanged. Because the relationship between price and quantity supplied is generally positive, supply curves are generally upward sloping. The supply curve for coffee in Figure 3.8 shows graphically the values given in the supply schedule.

supply curve

A graphical representation of a supply schedule.

change in quantity supplied

Movement along the supply curve caused by a change in price.

A change in price causes a movement *along* the supply curve; such a movement is called a **change in quantity supplied**. As is the case with a change in quantity demanded, a change in quantity supplied does not shift the supply curve. By definition, it is a movement along the supply curve. For example, if the price rises from $6 per pound to $7 per pound, the quantity supplied rises from 25 million pounds per month to 30 million pounds per month. That's a movement from point A to point B along the supply curve in Figure 3.8.

2.2 Changes in Supply

change in supply

A shift in the supply curve.

When we draw a supply curve, we assume that other variables that affect the willingness of sellers to supply a good or service are unchanged. It follows that a change in any of those variables will cause a **change in supply**, which is a shift in the supply curve. A change that increases the quantity of a good or service supplied at each price shifts the supply curve to the right. Suppose, for example, that the price of fertilizer falls. That will reduce the cost of producing coffee and thus increase the quantity of coffee producers will offer for sale at each price. The supply schedule in Figure 3.9 shows an increase in the quantity of coffee supplied at each price. We show that increase graphically as a shift in the supply curve from S_1 to S_2. We see that the quantity supplied at each price increases by 10 million pounds of coffee per month. At point A on the original supply curve S_1, for example, 25 million pounds of coffee per month are supplied at a price of $6 per pound. After the increase in supply, 35 million pounds per month are supplied at the same price (point A' on curve S_2).

FIGURE 3.9 An Increase in Supply

If there is a change in supply that increases the quantity supplied at each price, as is the case in the supply schedule here, the supply curve shifts to the right. At a price of $6 per pound, for example, the quantity supplied rises from the previous level of 25 million pounds per month on supply curve S_1 (point A) to 35 million pounds per month on supply curve S_2 (point A').

Price	Old quantity supplied	New quantity supplied
$4	15	25
5	20	30
6	25	35
7	30	40
8	35	45
9	40	50

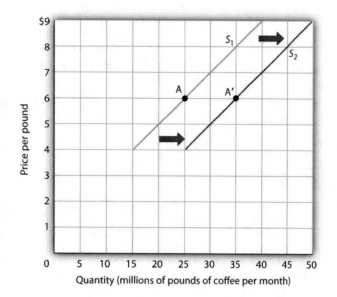

An event that reduces the quantity supplied at each price shifts the supply curve to the left. An increase in production costs and excessive rain that reduces the yields from coffee plants are examples of events that might reduce supply. Figure 3.10 shows a reduction in the supply of coffee. We see in the supply schedule that the quantity of coffee supplied falls by 10 million pounds of coffee per month at each price. The supply curve thus shifts from S_1 to S_3.

FIGURE 3.10 A Reduction in Supply

A change in supply that reduces the quantity supplied at each price shifts the supply curve to the left. At a price of $6 per pound, for example, the original quantity supplied was 25 million pounds of coffee per month (point A). With a new supply curve S_3, the quantity supplied at that price falls to 15 million pounds of coffee per month (point A").

Price	Old quantity supplied	New quantity supplied
$4	15	5
5	20	10
6	25	15
7	30	20
8	35	25
9	40	30

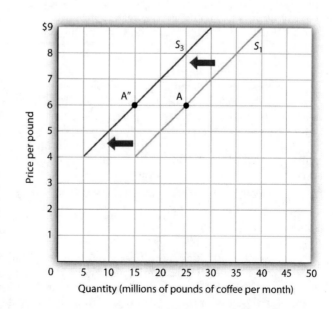

supply shifter

A variable that can change the quantity of a good or service supplied at each price.

A variable that can change the quantity of a good or service supplied at each price is called a **supply shifter**. Supply shifters include (1) prices of factors of production, (2) returns from alternative activities, (3) technology, (4) seller expectations, (5) natural events, and (6) the number of sellers. When these other variables change, the all-other-things-unchanged conditions behind the original supply curve no longer hold. Let us look at each of the supply shifters.

Prices of Factors of Production

A change in the price of labor or some other factor of production will change the cost of producing any given quantity of the good or service. This change in the cost of production will change the quantity that suppliers are willing to offer at any price. An increase in factor prices should decrease the quantity suppliers will offer at any price, shifting the supply curve to the left. A reduction in factor prices increases the quantity suppliers will offer at any price, shifting the supply curve to the right.

Suppose coffee growers must pay a higher wage to the workers they hire to harvest coffee or must pay more for fertilizer. Such increases in production cost will cause them to produce a smaller quantity at each price, shifting the supply curve for coffee to the left. A reduction in any of these costs increases supply, shifting the supply curve to the right.

Returns from Alternative Activities

To produce one good or service means forgoing the production of another. The concept of opportunity cost in economics suggests that the value of the activity forgone is the opportunity cost of the activity chosen; this cost should affect supply. For example, one opportunity cost of producing eggs is not selling chickens. An increase in the price people are willing to pay for fresh chicken would make it more profitable to sell chickens and would thus increase the opportunity cost of producing eggs. It would shift the supply curve for eggs to the left, reflecting a decrease in supply.

Technology

A change in technology alters the combinations of inputs or the types of inputs required in the production process. An improvement in technology usually means that fewer and/or less costly inputs are needed. If the cost of production is lower, the profits available at a given price will increase, and producers will produce more. With more produced at every price, the supply curve will shift to the right, meaning an increase in supply.

Impressive technological changes have occurred in the computer industry in recent years. Computers are much smaller and are far more powerful than they were only a few years ago—and they are much cheaper to produce. The result has been a huge increase in the supply of computers, shifting the supply curve to the right.

While we usually think of technology as enhancing production, declines in production due to problems in technology are also possible. Outlawing the use of certain equipment without pollution-control devices has increased the cost of production for many goods and services, thereby reducing profits available at any price and shifting these supply curves to the left.

Seller Expectations

All supply curves are based in part on seller expectations about future market conditions. Many decisions about production and selling are typically made long before a product is ready for sale. Those decisions necessarily depend on expectations. Changes in seller expectations can have important effects on price and quantity.

Consider, for example, the owners of oil deposits. Oil pumped out of the ground and used today will be unavailable in the future. If a change in the international political climate leads many owners to expect that oil prices will rise in the future, they may decide to leave their oil in the ground, planning to sell it later when the price is higher. Thus, there will be a decrease in supply; the supply curve for oil will shift to the left.

Natural Events

Storms, insect infestations, and drought affect agricultural production and thus the supply of agricultural goods. If something destroys a substantial part of an agricultural crop, the supply curve will shift to the left. The terrible cyclone that killed more than 50,000 people in Myanmar in 2008 also destroyed some of the country's prime rice growing land. That shifted the supply curve for rice to the left. If there is an unusually good harvest, the supply curve will shift to the right.

The Number of Sellers

The supply curve for an industry, such as coffee, includes all the sellers in the industry. A change in the number of sellers in an industry changes the quantity available at each price and thus changes supply. An increase in the number of sellers supplying a good or service shifts the supply curve to the right; a reduction in the number of sellers shifts the supply curve to the left.

The market for cellular phone service has been affected by an increase in the number of firms offering the service. Over the past decade, new cellular phone companies emerged, shifting the supply curve for cellular phone service to the right.

Heads Up!

There are two special things to note about supply curves. The first is similar to the Heads Up! on demand curves: it is important to distinguish carefully between changes in supply and changes in quantity supplied. A change in supply results from a change in a supply shifter and implies a shift of the supply curve to the right or left. A change in price produces a change in quantity supplied and induces a movement along the supply curve. A change in price does not shift the supply curve.

The second caution relates to the interpretation of increases and decreases in supply. Notice that in Figure 3.9 an increase in supply is shown as a shift of the supply curve to the right; the curve shifts in the direction of increasing quantity with respect to the horizontal axis. In Figure 3.10 a reduction in supply is shown as a shift of the supply curve to the left; the curve shifts in the direction of decreasing quantity with respect to the horizontal axis.

Because the supply curve is upward sloping, a shift to the right produces a new curve that in a sense lies "below" the original curve. Students sometimes make the mistake of thinking of such a shift as a shift "down" and therefore as a reduction in supply. Similarly, it is easy to make the mistake of showing an increase in supply with a new curve that lies "above" the original curve. But that is a reduction in supply!

To avoid such errors, focus on the fact that an increase in supply is an increase in the quantity supplied at each price and shifts the supply curve in the direction of increased quantity on the horizontal axis. Similarly, a reduction in supply is a reduction in the quantity supplied at each price and shifts the supply curve in the direction of a lower quantity on the horizontal axis.

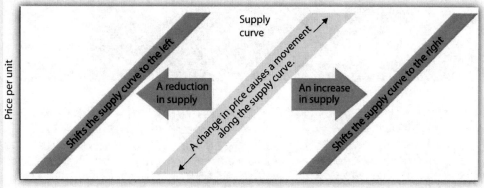

KEY TAKEAWAYS

- The quantity supplied of a good or service is the quantity sellers are willing to sell at a particular price during a particular period, all other things unchanged.
- A supply schedule shows the quantities supplied at different prices during a particular period, all other things unchanged. A supply curve shows this same information graphically.
- A change in the price of a good or service causes a change in the quantity supplied—a movement *along* the supply curve.
- A change in a supply shifter causes a change in supply, which is shown as a *shift* of the supply curve. Supply shifters include prices of factors of production, returns from alternative activities, technology, seller expectations, natural events, and the number of sellers.
- An increase in supply is shown as a shift to the right of a supply curve; a decrease in supply is shown as a shift to the left.

If all other things are unchanged, what happens to the supply curve for DVD rentals if there is (a) an increase in wages paid to DVD rental store clerks, (b) an increase in the price of DVD rentals, or (c) an increase in the number of DVD rental stores? Draw a graph that shows what happens to the supply curve in each circumstance. The supply curve can shift to the left or to the right, or stay where it is. Remember to label the axes and curves, and remember to specify the time period (e.g., "DVDs rented per week").

Case in Point: The Monks of St. Benedict's Get Out of the Egg Business

© 2010 Jupiterimages Corporation

It was cookies that lured the monks of St. Benedict's out of the egg business, and now private retreat sponsorship is luring them away from cookies.

St. Benedict's is a Benedictine monastery, nestled on a ranch high in the Colorado Rockies, about 20 miles down the road from Aspen. The monastery's 15 monks operate the ranch to support themselves and to provide help for poor people in the area. They lease out about 3,500 acres of their land to cattle and sheep grazers, produce cookies, and sponsor private retreats. They used to produce eggs.

Attracted by potential profits and the peaceful nature of the work, the monks went into the egg business in 1967. They had 10,000 chickens producing their Monastery Eggs brand. For a while, business was good. Very good. Then, in the late 1970s, the price of chicken feed started to rise rapidly.

"When we started in the business, we were paying $60 to $80 a ton for feed—delivered," recalls the monastery's abbot, Father Joseph Boyle. "By the late 1970s, our cost had more than doubled. We were paying $160 to $200 a ton. That really hurt, because feed represents a large part of the cost of producing eggs."

The monks adjusted to the blow. "When grain prices were lower, we'd pull a hen off for a few weeks to molt, then return her to laying. After grain prices went up, it was 12 months of laying and into the soup pot," Father Joseph says.

Grain prices continued to rise in the 1980s and increased the costs of production for all egg producers. It caused the supply of eggs to fall. Demand fell at the same time, as Americans worried about the cholesterol in eggs. Times got tougher in the egg business.

"We were still making money in the financial sense," Father Joseph says. "But we tried an experiment in 1985 producing cookies, and it was a success. We finally decided that devoting our time and energy to the cookies would pay off better than the egg business, so we quit the egg business in 1986."

The mail-order cookie business was good to the monks. They sold 200,000 ounces of Monastery Cookies in 1987.

By 1998, however, they had limited their production of cookies, selling only locally and to gift shops. Since 2000, they have switched to "providing private retreats for individuals and groups—about 40 people per month," according to Brother Charles.

The monks' calculation of their opportunity costs revealed that they would earn a higher return through sponsorship of private retreats than in either cookies or eggs. This projection has proved correct.

And there is another advantage as well.

"The chickens didn't stop laying eggs on Sunday," Father Joseph chuckles. "When we shifted to cookies we could take Sundays off. We weren't hemmed in the way we were with the chickens." The move to providing retreats is even better in this regard. Since guests provide their own meals, most of the monastery's effort goes into planning and scheduling, which frees up even more of their time for other worldly as well as spiritual pursuits.

Source: Personal interviews.

ANSWER TO TRY IT! PROBLEM

DVD rental store clerks are a factor of production in the DVD rental market. An increase in their wages raises the cost of production, thereby causing the supply curve of DVD rentals to shift to the left [Panel (a)]. (*Caution*: It is possible that you thought of the wage increase as an increase in income, a demand shifter, that would lead to an increase in demand, but this would be incorrect. The question refers only to wages of DVD rental store clerks. They may rent some DVD, but their impact on total demand would be negligible. Besides, we have no information on what has happened overall to incomes of people who rent DVDs. We do know, however, that the cost of a factor of production, which is a supply shifter, increased.)

An increase in the price of DVD rentals does not shift the supply curve at all; rather, it corresponds to a movement upward to the right along the supply curve. At a higher price of P_2 instead of P_1, a greater quantity of DVD rentals, say Q_2 instead of Q_1, will be supplied [Panel (b)].

An increase in the number of stores renting DVDs will cause the supply curve to shift to the right [Panel (c)].

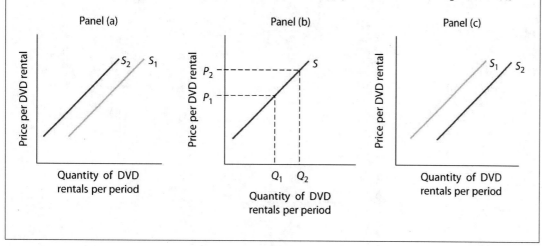

3. DEMAND, SUPPLY, AND EQUILIBRIUM

LEARNING OBJECTIVES

1. Use demand and supply to explain how equilibrium price and quantity are determined in a market.
2. Understand the concepts of surpluses and shortages and the pressures on price they generate.
3. Explain the impact of a change in demand or supply on equilibrium price and quantity.
4. Explain how the circular flow model provides an overview of demand and supply in product and factor markets and how the model suggests ways in which these markets are linked.

model of demand and supply

Model that uses demand and supply curves to explain the determination of price and quantity in a market.

In this section we combine the demand and supply curves we have just studied into a new model. The **model of demand and supply** uses demand and supply curves to explain the determination of price and quantity in a market.

3.1 The Determination of Price and Quantity

The logic of the model of demand and supply is simple. The demand curve shows the quantities of a particular good or service that buyers will be willing and able to purchase at each price during a specified period. The supply curve shows the quantities that sellers will offer for sale at each price during that same period. By putting the two curves together, we should be able to find a price at which the quantity buyers are willing and able to purchase equals the quantity sellers will offer for sale.

equilibrium price

The price at which quantity demanded equals quantity supplied.

equilibrium quantity

The quantity demanded and supplied at the equilibrium price.

Figure 3.14 combines the demand and supply data introduced in Figure 3.1 and Figure 3.8 Notice that the two curves intersect at a price of $6 per pound—at this price the quantities demanded and supplied are equal. Buyers want to purchase, and sellers are willing to offer for sale, 25 million pounds of coffee per month. The market for coffee is in equilibrium. Unless the demand or supply curve shifts, there will be no tendency for price to change. The **equilibrium price** in any market is the price at which quantity demanded equals quantity supplied. The equilibrium price in the market for coffee is thus $6 per pound. The **equilibrium quantity** is the quantity demanded and supplied at the equilibrium price.

FIGURE 3.14 The Determination of Equilibrium Price and Quantity

When we combine the demand and supply curves for a good in a single graph, the point at which they intersect identifies the equilibrium price and equilibrium quantity. Here, the equilibrium price is $6 per pound. Consumers demand, and suppliers supply, 25 million pounds of coffee per month at this price.

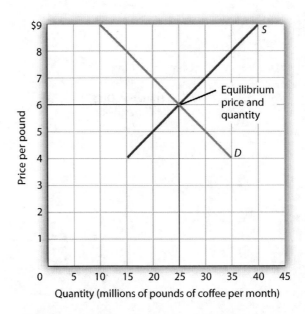

With an upward-sloping supply curve and a downward-sloping demand curve, there is only a single price at which the two curves intersect. This means there is only one price at which equilibrium is

achieved. It follows that at any price other than the equilibrium price, the market will not be in equilibrium. We next examine what happens at prices other than the equilibrium price.

Surpluses

Figure 3.15 shows the same demand and supply curves we have just examined, but this time the initial price is $8 per pound of coffee. Because we no longer have a balance between quantity demanded and quantity supplied, this price is not the equilibrium price. At a price of $8, we read over to the demand curve to determine the quantity of coffee consumers will be willing to buy—15 million pounds per month. The supply curve tells us what sellers will offer for sale—35 million pounds per month. The difference, 20 million pounds of coffee per month, is called a surplus. More generally, a **surplus** is the amount by which the quantity supplied exceeds the quantity demanded at the current price. There is, of course, no surplus at the equilibrium price; a surplus occurs only if the current price exceeds the equilibrium price.

> **surplus**
>
> The amount by which the quantity supplied exceeds the quantity demanded at the current price.

FIGURE 3.15   A Surplus in the Market for Coffee

At a price of $8, the quantity supplied is 35 million pounds of coffee per month and the quantity demanded is 15 million pounds per month; there is a surplus of 20 million pounds of coffee per month. Given a surplus, the price will fall quickly toward the equilibrium level of $6.

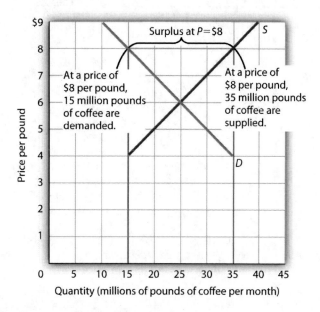

A surplus in the market for coffee will not last long. With unsold coffee on the market, sellers will begin to reduce their prices to clear out unsold coffee. As the price of coffee begins to fall, the quantity of coffee supplied begins to decline. At the same time, the quantity of coffee demanded begins to rise. Remember that the reduction in quantity supplied is a movement *along* the supply curve—the curve itself does not shift in response to a reduction in price. Similarly, the increase in quantity demanded is a movement *along* the demand curve—the demand curve does not shift in response to a reduction in price. Price will continue to fall until it reaches its equilibrium level, at which the demand and supply curves intersect. At that point, there will be no tendency for price to fall further. In general, surpluses in the marketplace are short-lived. The prices of most goods and services adjust quickly, eliminating the surplus. Later on, we will discuss some markets in which adjustment of price to equilibrium may occur only very slowly or not at all.

Shortages

Just as a price above the equilibrium price will cause a surplus, a price below equilibrium will cause a shortage. A **shortage** is the amount by which the quantity demanded exceeds the quantity supplied at the current price.

Figure 3.16 shows a shortage in the market for coffee. Suppose the price is $4 per pound. At that price, 15 million pounds of coffee would be supplied per month, and 35 million pounds would be demanded per month. When more coffee is demanded than supplied, there is a shortage.

FIGURE 3.16 A Shortage in the Market for Coffee

At a price of $4 per pound, the quantity of coffee demanded is 35 million pounds per month and the quantity supplied is 15 million pounds per month. The result is a shortage of 20 million pounds of coffee per month.

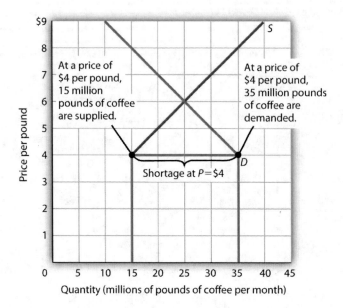

In the face of a shortage, sellers are likely to begin to raise their prices. As the price rises, there will be an increase in the quantity supplied (but not a change in supply) and a reduction in the quantity demanded (but not a change in demand) until the equilibrium price is achieved.

3.2 Shifts in Demand and Supply

FIGURE 3.17 Changes in Demand and Supply

A change in demand or in supply changes the equilibrium solution in the model. Panels (a) and (b) show an increase and a decrease in demand, respectively; Panels (c) and (d) show an increase and a decrease in supply, respectively.

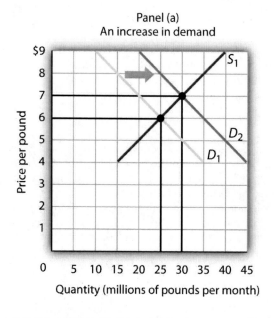

Panel (a)
An increase in demand

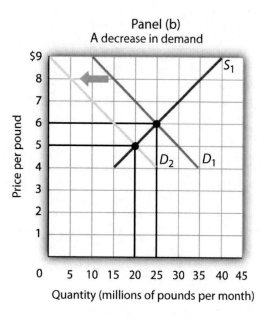

Panel (b)
A decrease in demand

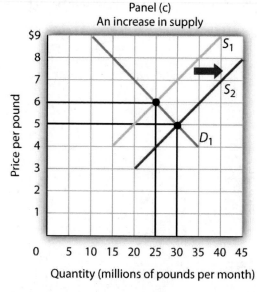

Panel (c)
An increase in supply

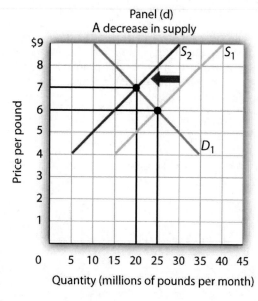

Panel (d)
A decrease in supply

A change in one of the variables (shifters) held constant in any model of demand and supply will create a change in demand or supply. A shift in a demand or supply curve changes the equilibrium price and equilibrium quantity for a good or service. Figure 3.17 combines the information about changes in the demand and supply of coffee presented in Figure 3.2 Figure 3.3 Figure 3.9 and Figure 3.10 In each case, the original equilibrium price is $6 per pound, and the corresponding equilibrium quantity is 25 million pounds of coffee per month. Figure 3.17 shows what happens with an increase in demand, a reduction in demand, an increase in supply, and a reduction in supply. We then look at what happens if both curves shift simultaneously. Each of these possibilities is discussed in turn below.

An Increase in Demand

An increase in demand for coffee shifts the demand curve to the right, as shown in Panel (a) of Figure 3.17. The equilibrium price rises to $7 per pound. As the price rises to the new equilibrium level, the quantity supplied increases to 30 million pounds of coffee per month. Notice that the supply curve does not shift; rather, there is a movement along the supply curve.

Demand shifters that could cause an increase in demand include a shift in preferences that leads to greater coffee consumption; a lower price for a complement to coffee, such as doughnuts; a higher price for a substitute for coffee, such as tea; an increase in income; and an increase in population. A change in buyer expectations, perhaps due to predictions of bad weather lowering expected yields on coffee plants and increasing future coffee prices, could also increase current demand.

A Decrease in Demand

Panel (b) of Figure 3.17 shows that a decrease in demand shifts the demand curve to the left. The equilibrium price falls to $5 per pound. As the price falls to the new equilibrium level, the quantity supplied decreases to 20 million pounds of coffee per month.

Demand shifters that could reduce the demand for coffee include a shift in preferences that makes people want to consume less coffee; an increase in the price of a complement, such as doughnuts; a reduction in the price of a substitute, such as tea; a reduction in income; a reduction in population; and a change in buyer expectations that leads people to expect lower prices for coffee in the future.

An Increase in Supply

An increase in the supply of coffee shifts the supply curve to the right, as shown in Panel (c) of Figure 3.17. The equilibrium price falls to $5 per pound. As the price falls to the new equilibrium level, the quantity of coffee demanded increases to 30 million pounds of coffee per month. Notice that the demand curve does not shift; rather, there is movement along the demand curve.

Possible supply shifters that could increase supply include a reduction in the price of an input such as labor, a decline in the returns available from alternative uses of the inputs that produce coffee, an improvement in the technology of coffee production, good weather, and an increase in the number of coffee-producing firms.

A Decrease in Supply

Panel (d) of Figure 3.17 shows that a decrease in supply shifts the supply curve to the left. The equilibrium price rises to $7 per pound. As the price rises to the new equilibrium level, the quantity demanded decreases to 20 million pounds of coffee per month.

Possible supply shifters that could reduce supply include an increase in the prices of inputs used in the production of coffee, an increase in the returns available from alternative uses of these inputs, a decline in production because of problems in technology (perhaps caused by a restriction on pesticides used to protect coffee beans), a reduction in the number of coffee-producing firms, or a natural event, such as excessive rain.

Heads Up!

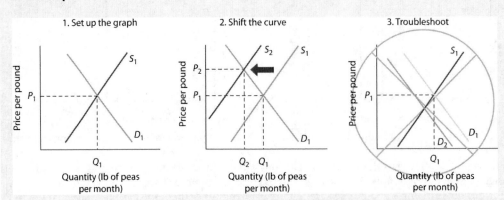

You are likely to be given problems in which you will have to shift a demand or supply curve.

Suppose you are told that an invasion of pod-crunching insects has gobbled up half the crop of fresh peas, and you are asked to use demand and supply analysis to predict what will happen to the price and quantity of peas demanded and supplied. Here are some suggestions.

Put the quantity of the good you are asked to analyze on the horizontal axis and its price on the vertical axis. Draw a downward-sloping line for demand and an upward-sloping line for supply. The initial equilibrium price is determined by the intersection of the two curves. Label the equilibrium solution. You may find it helpful to use a number for the equilibrium price instead of the letter "P." Pick a price that seems plausible, say, 79¢ per pound. Do not worry about the precise positions of the demand and supply curves; you cannot be expected to know what they are.

Step 2 can be the most difficult step; the problem is to decide which curve to shift. The key is to remember the difference between a change in demand or supply and a change in quantity demanded or supplied. At each price, ask yourself whether the given event would change the quantity demanded. Would the fact that a bug has attacked the pea crop change the quantity demanded at a price of, say, 79¢ per pound? Clearly not; none of the demand shifters have changed. The event would, however, reduce the quantity supplied at this price, and the supply curve would shift to the left. There is a change in supply and a reduction in the quantity demanded. There is no change in demand.

Next check to see whether the result you have obtained makes sense. The graph in Step 2 makes sense; it shows price rising and quantity demanded falling.

It is easy to make a mistake such as the one shown in the third figure of this Heads Up! One might, for example, reason that when fewer peas are available, fewer will be demanded, and therefore the demand curve will shift to the left. This suggests the price of peas will fall—but that does not make sense. If only half as many fresh peas were available, their price would surely rise. The error here lies in confusing a change in quantity demanded with a change in demand. Yes, buyers will end up buying fewer peas. But no, they will not demand fewer peas at each price than before; the demand curve does not shift.

Simultaneous Shifts

As we have seen, when *either* the demand or the supply curve shifts, the results are unambiguous; that is, we know what will happen to both equilibrium price and equilibrium quantity, so long as we know whether demand or supply increased or decreased. However, in practice, several events may occur at around the same time that cause *both* the demand and supply curves to shift. To figure out what happens to equilibrium price and equilibrium quantity, we must know not only in which direction the demand and supply curves have shifted but also the relative amount by which each curve shifts. Of course, the demand and supply curves could shift in the same direction or in opposite directions, depending on the specific events causing them to shift.

For example, all three panels of Figure 3.19 show a decrease in demand for coffee (caused perhaps by a decrease in the price of a substitute good, such as tea) and a simultaneous decrease in the supply of coffee (caused perhaps by bad weather). Since reductions in demand and supply, considered separately, each cause the equilibrium quantity to fall, the impact of both curves shifting simultaneously to the left means that the new equilibrium quantity of coffee is less than the old equilibrium quantity. The effect on the equilibrium price, though, is ambiguous. Whether the equilibrium price is higher, lower, or unchanged depends on the extent to which each curve shifts.

FIGURE 3.19 Simultaneous Decreases in Demand and Supply

Both the demand and the supply of coffee decrease. Since decreases in demand and supply, considered separately, each cause equilibrium quantity to fall, the impact of both decreasing simultaneously means that a new equilibrium quantity of coffee must be less than the old equilibrium quantity. In Panel (a), the demand curve shifts farther to the left than does the supply curve, so equilibrium price falls. In Panel (b), the supply curve shifts farther to the left than does the demand curve, so the equilibrium price rises. In Panel (c), both curves shift to the left by the same amount, so equilibrium price stays the same.

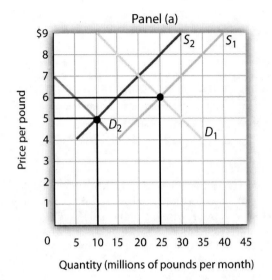

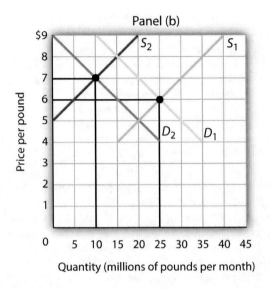

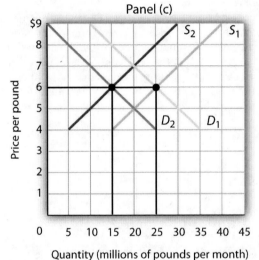

If the demand curve shifts farther to the left than does the supply curve, as shown in Panel (a) of Figure 3.19, then the equilibrium price will be lower than it was before the curves shifted. In this case the new equilibrium price falls from $6 per pound to $5 per pound. If the shift to the left of the supply curve is greater than that of the demand curve, the equilibrium price will be higher than it was before, as shown in Panel (b). In this case, the new equilibrium price rises to $7 per pound. In Panel (c), since both curves shift to the left by the same amount, equilibrium price does not change; it remains $6 per pound.

Regardless of the scenario, changes in equilibrium price and equilibrium quantity resulting from two different events need to be considered separately. If both events cause equilibrium price or quantity to move in the same direction, then clearly price or quantity can be expected to move in that direction. If one event causes price or quantity to rise while the other causes it to fall, the extent by which each curve shifts is critical to figuring out what happens. Figure 3.20 summarizes what may happen to equilibrium price and quantity when demand and supply both shift.

FIGURE 3.20 Simultaneous Shifts in Demand and Supply

If simultaneous shifts in demand and supply cause equilibrium price or quantity to move in the same direction, then equilibrium price or quantity clearly moves in that direction. If the shift in one of the curves causes equilibrium price or quantity to rise while the shift in the other curve causes equilibrium price or quantity to fall, then the relative amount by which each curve shifts is critical to figuring out what happens to that variable.

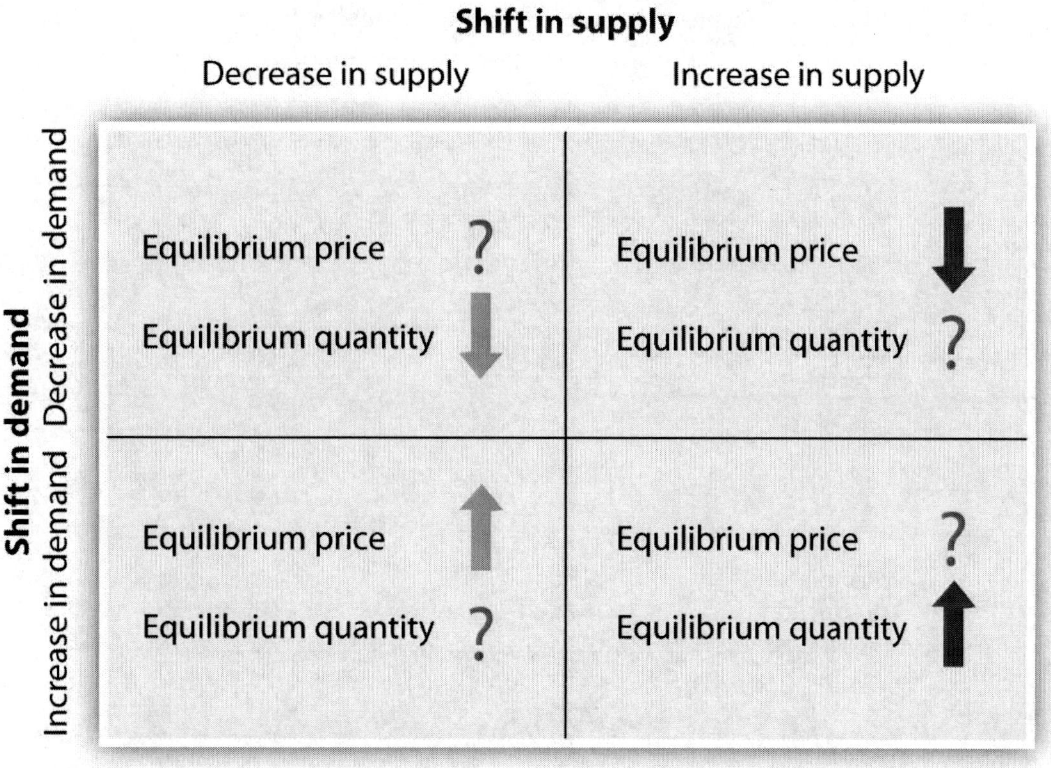

As demand and supply curves shift, prices adjust to maintain a balance between the quantity of a good demanded and the quantity supplied. If prices did not adjust, this balance could not be maintained.

Notice that the demand and supply curves that we have examined in this chapter have all been drawn as linear. This simplification of the real world makes the graphs a bit easier to read without sacrificing the essential point: whether the curves are linear or nonlinear, demand curves are downward sloping and supply curves are generally upward sloping. As circumstances that shift the demand curve or the supply curve change, we can analyze what will happen to price and what will happen to quantity.

3.3 An Overview of Demand and Supply: The Circular Flow Model

Implicit in the concepts of demand and supply is a constant interaction and adjustment that economists illustrate with the circular flow model. The **circular flow model** provides a look at how markets work and how they are related to each other. It shows flows of spending and income through the economy.

A great deal of economic activity can be thought of as a process of exchange between households and firms. Firms supply goods and services to households. Households buy these goods and services from firms. Households supply factors of production—labor, capital, and natural resources—that firms require. The payments firms make in exchange for these factors represent the incomes households earn.

The flow of goods and services, factors of production, and the payments they generate is illustrated in Figure 3.21. This circular flow model of the economy shows the interaction of households and firms as they exchange goods and services and factors of production. For simplicity, the model here shows only the private domestic economy; it omits the government and foreign sectors.

circular flow model

Model that provides a look at how markets work and how they are related to each other.

FIGURE 3.21 The Circular Flow of Economic Activity

This simplified circular flow model shows flows of spending between households and firms through product and factor markets. The inner arrows show goods and services flowing from firms to households and factors of production flowing from households to firms. The outer flows show the payments for goods, services, and factors of production. These flows, in turn, represent millions of individual markets for products and factors of production.

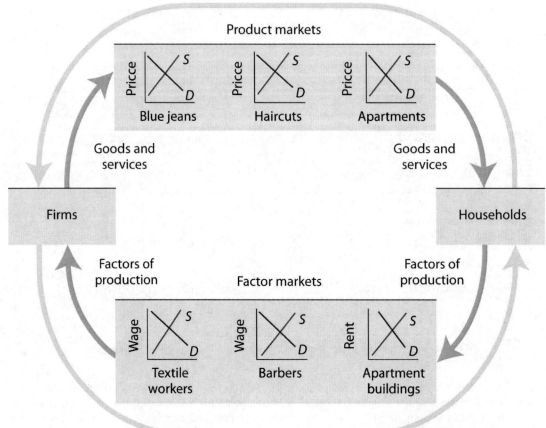

The circular flow model shows that goods and services that households demand are supplied by firms in **product markets**. The exchange for goods and services is shown in the top half of Figure 3.21. The bottom half of the exhibit illustrates the exchanges that take place in factor markets. **factor markets** are markets in which households supply factors of production—labor, capital, and natural resources—demanded by firms.

Our model is called a circular flow model because households use the income they receive from their supply of factors of production to buy goods and services from firms. Firms, in turn, use the payments they receive from households to pay for their factors of production.

The demand and supply model developed in this chapter gives us a basic tool for understanding what is happening in each of these product or factor markets and also allows us to see how these markets are interrelated. In Figure 3.21, markets for three goods and services that households want—blue jeans, haircuts, and apartments—create demands by firms for textile workers, barbers, and apartment buildings. The equilibrium of supply and demand in each market determines the price and quantity of that item. Moreover, a change in equilibrium in one market will affect equilibrium in related markets. For example, an increase in the demand for haircuts would lead to an increase in demand for barbers. Equilibrium price and quantity could rise in both markets. For some purposes, it will be adequate to simply look at a single market, whereas at other times we will want to look at what happens in related markets as well.

In either case, the model of demand and supply is one of the most widely used tools of economic analysis. That widespread use is no accident. The model yields results that are, in fact, broadly consistent with what we observe in the marketplace. Your mastery of this model will pay big dividends in your study of economics.

product markets

Markets in which firms supply goods and services demanded by households.

factor markets

Markets in which households supply factors of production—labor, capital, and natural resources—demanded by firms.

KEY TAKEAWAYS

- The equilibrium price is the price at which the quantity demanded equals the quantity supplied. It is determined by the intersection of the demand and supply curves.

- A surplus exists if the quantity of a good or service supplied exceeds the quantity demanded at the current price; it causes downward pressure on price. A shortage exists if the quantity of a good or service demanded exceeds the quantity supplied at the current price; it causes upward pressure on price.

- An increase in demand, all other things unchanged, will cause the equilibrium price to rise; quantity supplied will increase. A decrease in demand will cause the equilibrium price to fall; quantity supplied will decrease.

- An increase in supply, all other things unchanged, will cause the equilibrium price to fall; quantity demanded will increase. A decrease in supply will cause the equilibrium price to rise; quantity demanded will decrease.

- To determine what happens to equilibrium price and equilibrium quantity when both the supply and demand curves shift, you must know in which direction each of the curves shifts and the extent to which each curve shifts.

- The circular flow model provides an overview of demand and supply in product and factor markets and suggests how these markets are linked to one another.

TRY IT!

What happens to the equilibrium price and the equilibrium quantity of DVD rentals if the price of movie theater tickets increases and wages paid to DVD rental store clerks increase, all other things unchanged? Be sure to show all possible scenarios, as was done in Figure 3.19. Again, you do not need actual numbers to arrive at an answer. Just focus on the general position of the curve(s) before and after events occurred.

Case in Point: Demand, Supply, and Obesity

© 2010 Jupiterimages Corporation

Why are so many Americans fat? Put so crudely, the question may seem rude, but, indeed, the number of obese Americans has increased by more than 50% over the last generation, and obesity may now be the nation's number one health problem. According to Sturm Roland in a recent RAND Corporation study, "Obesity appears to have a stronger association with the occurrence of chronic medical conditions, reduced physical health-related quality of life and increased health care and medication expenditures than smoking or problem drinking."

Many explanations of rising obesity suggest higher demand for food. What more apt picture of our sedentary life style is there than spending the afternoon watching a ballgame on TV, while eating chips and salsa, followed by a dinner of a lavishly topped, take-out pizza? Higher income has also undoubtedly contributed to a rightward shift in the demand curve for food. Plus, any additional food intake translates into more weight increase because we spend so few calories preparing it, either directly or in the process of earning the income to buy it. A study by economists Darius Lakdawalla and Tomas Philipson suggests that about 60% of the recent growth in weight may be explained in this way—that is, demand has shifted to the right, leading to an increase in the equilibrium quantity of food consumed and, given our less strenuous life styles, even more weight gain than can be explained simply by the increased amount we are eating.

What accounts for the remaining 40% of the weight gain? Lakdawalla and Philipson further reason that a rightward shift in demand would by itself lead to an increase in the quantity of food as well as an increase in the price of food. The problem they have with this explanation is that over the post-World War II period, the relative price of food has declined by an average of 0.2 percentage points per year. They explain the fall in the price of food by arguing that agricultural innovation has led to a substantial rightward shift in the supply curve of food. As shown, lower food prices and a higher equilibrium quantity of food have resulted from simultaneous rightward shifts in demand and supply and that the rightward shift in the supply of food from S_1 to S_2 has been substantially larger than the rightward shift in the demand curve from D_1 to D_2.

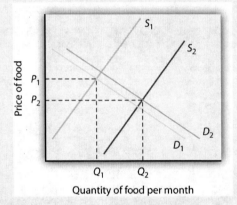

Sources: Roland, Sturm, "The Effects of Obesity, Smoking, and Problem Drinking on Chronic Medical Problems and Health Care Costs," Health Affairs, 2002; 21(2): 245–253. Lakdawalla, Darius and Tomas Philipson, "The Growth of Obesity and Technological Change: A Theoretical and Empirical Examination," National Bureau of Economic Research Working Paper no. w8946, May 2002.

ANSWER TO TRY IT! PROBLEM

An increase in the price of movie theater tickets (a substitute for DVD rentals) will cause the demand curve for DVD rentals to shift to the right. An increase in the wages paid to DVD rental store clerks (an increase in the cost of a factor of production) shifts the supply curve to the left. Each event taken separately causes equilibrium price to rise. Whether equilibrium quantity will be higher or lower depends on which curve shifted more.

If the demand curve shifted more, then the equilibrium quantity of DVD rentals will rise [Panel (a)].

If the supply curve shifted more, then the equilibrium quantity of DVD rentals will fall [Panel (b)].

If the curves shifted by the same amount, then the equilibrium quantity of DVD rentals would not change [Panel (c)].

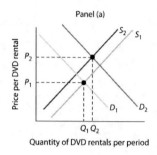

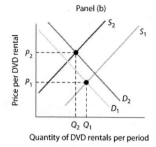

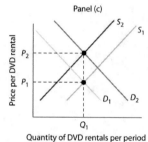

4. REVIEW AND PRACTICE

Summary

In this chapter we have examined the model of demand and supply. We found that a demand curve shows the quantity demanded at each price, all other things unchanged. The law of demand asserts that an increase in price reduces the quantity demanded and a decrease in price increases the quantity demanded, all other things unchanged. The supply curve shows the quantity of a good or service that sellers will offer at various prices, all other things unchanged. Supply curves are generally upward sloping: an increase in price generally increases the quantity supplied, all other things unchanged.

The equilibrium price occurs where the demand and supply curves intersect. At this price, the quantity demanded equals the quantity supplied. A price higher than the equilibrium price increases the quantity supplied and reduces the quantity demanded, causing a surplus. A price lower than the equilibrium price increases the quantity demanded and reduces the quantity supplied, causing a shortage. Usually, market surpluses and shortages are short-lived. Changes in demand or supply, caused by changes in the determinants of demand and supply otherwise held constant in the analysis, change the equilibrium price and output. The circular flow model allows us to see how demand and supply in various markets are related to one another.

CONCEPT PROBLEMS

1. What do you think happens to the demand for pizzas during the Super Bowl? Why?

2. Which of the following goods are likely to be classified as normal goods or services? Inferior? Defend your answer.

   a. Beans
   b. Tuxedos
   c. Used cars
   d. Used clothing
   e. Computers
   f. Books reviewed in *The New York Times*
   g. Macaroni and cheese
   h. Calculators
   i. Cigarettes
   j. Caviar
   k. Legal services

3. Which of the following pairs of goods are likely to be classified as substitutes? Complements? Defend your answer.

   a. Peanut butter and jelly
   b. Eggs and ham
   c. Nike brand and Reebok brand sneakers
   d. IBM and Apple Macintosh brand computers
   e. Dress shirts and ties
   f. Airline tickets and hotels
   g. Gasoline and tires
   h. Beer and wine
   i. Faxes and first-class mail
   j. Cereal and milk
   k. Cereal and eggs

4. A study found that lower airfares led some people to substitute flying for driving to their vacation destinations. This reduced the demand for car travel and led to reduced traffic fatalities, since air travel is safer per passenger mile than car travel. Using the logic suggested by that study, suggest how each of the following events would affect the number of highway fatalities in any one year.

   a. An increase in the price of gasoline
   b. A large reduction in rental rates for passenger vans
   c. An increase in airfares

5. Children under age 2 are now allowed to fly free on U.S. airlines; they usually sit in their parents' laps. Some safety advocates have urged that they be required to be strapped in infant seats, which would mean their parents would have to purchase tickets for them. Some economists have argued that such a measure would actually increase infant fatalities. Can you say why?

6. The graphs below show four possible shifts in demand or in supply that could occur in particular markets. Relate each of the events described below to one of them.

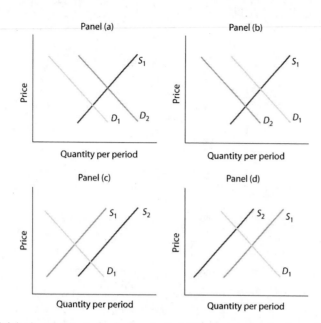

a. How did the heavy rains in South America in 1997 affect the market for coffee?

b. The Surgeon General decides french fries are not bad for your health after all and issues a report endorsing their use. What happens to the market for french fries?

c. How do you think rising incomes affect the market for ski vacations?

d. A new technique is discovered for manufacturing computers that greatly lowers their production cost. What happens to the market for computers?

e. How would a ban on smoking in public affect the market for cigarettes?

7. As low-carb diets increased in popularity, egg prices rose sharply. How might this affect the monks' supply of cookies or private retreats? (See the Case in Point on the Monks of St. Benedict's.)

8. Gasoline prices typically rise during the summer, a time of heavy tourist traffic. A "street talk" feature on a radio station sought tourist reaction to higher gasoline prices. Here was one response: "I don't like 'em [the higher prices] much. I think the gas companies just use any excuse to jack up prices, and they're doing it again now." How does this tourist's perspective differ from that of economists who use the model of demand and supply?

9. The introduction to the chapter argues that preferences for coffee changed in the 1990s and that excessive rain hurt yields from coffee plants. Show and explain the effects of these two circumstances on the coffee market.

10. With preferences for coffee remaining strong in the early part of the century, Vietnam entered the market as a major exporter of coffee. Show and explain the effects of these two circumstances on the coffee market.

11. The study on the economics of obesity discussed in the Case in Point in this chapter on that topic also noted that another factor behind rising obesity is the decline in cigarette smoking as the price of cigarettes has risen. Show and explain the effect of higher cigarette prices on the market for food. What does this finding imply about the relationship between cigarettes and food?

12. In 2004, *The New York Times* reported that India might be losing its outsourcing edge due to rising wages[1] The reporter noted that a recent report "projected that if India continued to produce college graduates at the current rate, demand would exceed supply by 20% in the main outsourcing markets by 2008." Using the terminology you learned in this chapter, explain what he meant to say was happening in the market for Indian workers in outsourcing jobs. In particular, is demand for Indian workers increasing or decreasing? Is the supply of Indian workers increasing or decreasing? Which is shifting faster? How do you know?

13. For more than a century, milk producers have produced skim milk, which contains virtually no fat, along with regular milk, which contains 4% fat. But a century ago, skim milk accounted for only about 1% of total production, and much of it was fed to hogs. Today, skim and other reduced-fat milks make up the bulk of milk sales. What curve shifted, and what factor shifted it?

14. Suppose firms in the economy were to produce fewer goods and services. How do you think this would affect household spending on goods and services? (*Hint:* Use the circular flow model to analyze this question.)

NUMERICAL PROBLEMS

Problems 1–5 are based on the graph below.

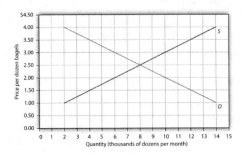

1. At a price of $1.50 per dozen, how many bagels are demanded per month?
2. At a price of $1.50 per dozen, how many bagels are supplied per month?
3. At a price of $3.00 per dozen, how many bagels are demanded per month?
4. At a price of $3.00 per dozen, how many bagels are supplied per month?
5. What is the equilibrium price of bagels? What is the equilibrium quantity per month?

Problems 6–9 are based on the model of demand and supply for coffee as shown in Figure 3.17 You can graph the initial demand and supply curves by using the following values, with all quantities in millions of pounds of coffee per month:

Price	Quantity demanded	Quantity supplied
$3	40	10
4	35	15
5	30	20
6	25	25
7	20	30
8	15	35
9	10	40

6. Suppose the quantity demanded rises by 20 million pounds of coffee per month at each price. Draw the initial demand and supply curves based on the values given in the table above. Then draw the new demand curve given by this change, and show the new equilibrium price and quantity.

7. Suppose the quantity demanded falls, relative to the values given in the above table, by 20 million pounds per month at prices between $4 and $6 per pound; at prices between $7 and $9 per pound, the quantity demanded becomes zero. Draw the new demand curve and show the new equilibrium price and quantity.

8. Suppose the quantity supplied rises by 20 million pounds per month at each price, while the quantities demanded retain the values shown in the table above. Draw the new supply curve and show the new equilibrium price and quantity.

9. Suppose the quantity supplied falls, relative to the values given in the table above, by 20 million pounds per month at prices above $5; at a price of $5 or less per pound, the quantity supplied becomes zero. Draw the new supply curve and show the new equilibrium price and quantity.

Problems 10–15 are based on the demand and supply schedules for gasoline below (all quantities are in thousands of gallons per week):

Price per gallon	Quantity demanded	Quantity supplied
$1	8	0
2	7	1
3	6	2
4	5	3
5	4	4
6	3	5
7	2	6
8	1	7

10. Graph the demand and supply curves and show the equilibrium price and quantity.

11. At a price of $3 per gallon, would there be a surplus or shortage of gasoline? How much would the surplus or shortage be? Indicate the surplus or shortage on the graph.

12. At a price of $6 per gallon, would there be a surplus or shortage of gasoline? How much would the surplus or shortage be? Show the surplus or shortage on the graph.

13. Suppose the quantity demanded increased by 2,000 gallons per month at each price. At a price of $3 per gallon, how much would the surplus or shortage be? Graph the demand and supply curves and show the surplus or shortage.

14. Suppose the quantity supplied decreased by 2,000 gallons per month at each price for prices between $4 and $8 per gallon. At prices less than $4 per gallon the quantity supplied becomes zero, while the quantities demanded retain the values shown in the table. At a price of $4 per gallon, how much would the surplus or shortage be? Graph the demand and supply curves and show the surplus or shortage.

15. If the demand curve shifts as in problem 13 and the supply curve shifts as in problem 14, without drawing a graph or consulting the data, can you predict whether equilibrium price increases or decreases? What about equilibrium quantity? Now draw a graph that shows what the new equilibrium price and quantity are.

ENDNOTES

1. Noam Scheiber, "As a Center for Outsourcing, India Could Be Losing Its Edge," *New York Times*, May 9, 2004, p. BU3.

CHAPTER 4
Applications of Demand and Supply

START UP: A COMPOSER LOGS ON

"Since the age of seven, I knew that I would be a musician. And from age fourteen, I knew that I would be a composer," says Israeli-born Ofer Ben-Amots. What he did not know was that he would use computers to carry out his work. He is now a professor of music at Colorado College, and Dr. Ben-Amots's compositions and operas have been performed in the United States, Europe, and Japan.

For over 15 years, he has used musical notation software to help in composing music. "The output is extremely elegant. Performers enjoy looking at such a clear and clean score. The creation of parts out of a full score is as easy as pressing the <ENTER> key on the keyboard." Changes can easily be inserted into the notation file, which eliminates the need for recopying. In addition, Dr. Ben-Amots uses computers for playback. "I can listen to a relatively accurate 'digital performance' of the score at any given point, with any tempo or instrumentation I choose. The sound quality has improved so much that digital files sound almost identical to real performance." He can also produce CDs on his own and create Podcasts so that anyone in the world can hear his music. He engages in self-publication of scores and self-marketing. "In my case, I get to keep the copyrights on all of my music. This would have been impossible ten to twelve years ago when composers transferred their rights to publishers. Home pages on the World Wide Web allow me to promote my own work." Professor Ben-Amots also changed the way he teaches music composition. New application software, such as GarageBand, has opened the way for anyone interested to try to compose music. Whereas his music composition classes used to have music theory prerequisites, today his classes are open to all.

Dr. Ben-Amots started out in 1989 with a Macintosh SE30 that had 4 megabytes of random access memory (RAM) and an 80-megabyte hard drive. It cost him about $3,000. Today, he uses a Macintosh Powerbook G4 laptop with 1.5 gigabytes of memory, built-in DVD/CD burner, and wireless Internet connections. His new computer cost about $2,000. How personal computers rose so dramatically in power as they fell so steeply in price is just one of the stories about markets we will tell in this chapter, which aims to help you understand how the model of demand and supply applies to the real world.

In the first section of this chapter, we will look at several markets that you are likely to have participated in or be familiar with—the market for personal computers, the markets for crude oil and for gasoline, and the stock market. You probably own or have access to a computer. Each of us was affected by the sharp rise in crude oil and gasoline prices from 2004 to mid-2008. The performance of the stock market is always a major news item and may affect you personally, if not now, then in the future. The concepts of demand and supply go a long way in explaining the behavior of equilibrium prices and quantities in all of these markets. The purpose of this section is to allow you to practice using the model of demand and supply and get you to start thinking about the myriad ways the model of demand and supply can be applied.

In the second part of the chapter we will look at markets in which the government has historically played a large role in regulating prices. By legislating maximum or minimum prices, the government has kept the prices of certain goods below or above equilibrium. We will look at the arguments for direct government intervention in controlling prices as well as the consequences of such policies. As we shall see, preventing the price of a good from finding its own equilibrium often has consequences that may be at odds with the intentions of the policy makers who put the regulations in place.

In the third section of the chapter we will look at the market for health care. This market is interesting because how well (or poorly) it works can be a matter of life and death and because it has special characteristics. In particular, markets in which participants do not pay for goods directly, but rather pay insurers who then pay the suppliers of the goods, operate somewhat differently from those in which participants pay directly for their purchases. This extension of demand and supply analysis reveals much about how such markets operate.

1. PUTTING DEMAND AND SUPPLY TO WORK

LEARNING OBJECTIVES

1. Learn how to apply the model of demand and supply to explaining the behavior of equilibrium prices and quantities in a variety of markets.
2. Explain how technological change can be represented using the model of demand and supply.
3. Explain how the model of demand and supply can be used to explain changes in prices of shares of stock.

A shift in either demand or supply, or in both, leads to a change in equilibrium price and equilibrium quantity. We begin this chapter by examining markets in which prices adjust quickly to changes in demand or supply: the market for personal computers, the markets for crude oil and gasoline, and the stock market. These markets are thus direct applications of the model of demand and supply.

1.1 The Personal Computer Market

In the 1960s, to speak of computers was to speak of IBM, the dominant maker of large mainframe computers used by business and government agencies. Then between 1976, when Apple Computer introduced its first desktop computer, and 1981, when IBM produced its first personal computers (PCs), the old world was turned upside down. In 1984, just 8.2% of U.S. households owned a personal computer. By 2007, Google estimates that 78% did. The tools of demand and supply tell the story from an economic perspective.

Technological change has been breathtakingly swift in the computer industry. Because personal computers have changed so dramatically in performance and in the range of the functions they perform, we shall speak of "quality-adjusted" personal computers. The price per unit of quality-adjusted desktop computers fell by about half every 50 months during the period 1976–1989. In the first half of the 1990s, those prices fell by half every 28 months. In the second half of the 1990s, the "halving time" fell to every 24 months.[1]

Consider another indicator of the phenomenal change in computers. Between 1993 and 1998, the Bureau of Labor Statistics estimates that central processing unit (CPU) speed rose 1,263%, system memory increased 1,500%, hard drive capacity soared by 3,700%, and monitor size went up 13%. It seems safe to say that the dizzying pace of change recorded in the 1990s has increased in this century. A "computer" today is not the same good as a "computer" even five years ago. To make them comparable, we must adjust for these changes in quality.

Initially, most personal computers were manufactured by Apple or Compaq; both companies were very profitable. The potential for profits attracted IBM and other firms to the industry. Unlike large mainframe computers, personal computer clones turned out to be fairly easy things to manufacture. As shown in Table 4.1, the top five personal computer manufacturers produced only 48% of the personal computers sold in the world in 2005, and the largest manufacturer, Dell, sold only about 19% of the total in that year. This is a far cry from the more than 90% of the mainframe computer market that IBM once held. The market has become far more competitive.

TABLE 4.1 Personal Computer Shipments, Market Percentage Shares by Vendors, World and United States

Company	% of World Shipments	Company	% of U.S. Shipments
Dell	18.9	Dell	34
Hewlett-Packard	15.4	Hewlett-Packard	18.2
IBM	5.1	Gateway	5.7
Fujitsu Seimens	4.6	IBM	4.3
Acer	4	Apple	3.9
Others	52	Others	34
Total	**100.0**	**Total**	**100.0**

Source: IDC—Press Release 15 Apr 2005 "PC Market Approaches 11% Growth as International Demand Remains Strong, According to IDC"

(http://www.idc.com/getdoc.jsp?containerId=pr2005_04_14_17070722) (Totals may not add due to rounding)

Figure 4.1 illustrates the changes that have occurred in the computer market. The horizontal axis shows the quantity of quality-adjusted personal computers. Thus, the quantity axis can be thought of as a unit of computing power. Similarly, the price axis shows the price per unit of computing power. The rapid increase in the number of firms, together with dramatic technological improvements, led to an increase in supply, shifting the supply curve in Figure 4.1 to the right from S_1 to S_2.

FIGURE 4.1 The Personal Computer Market

The supply curve for quality-adjusted personal computers has shifted markedly to the right, reducing the equilibrium price from P_1 to P_2 and increasing the equilibrium quantity from Q_1 to Q_2 in 2005.

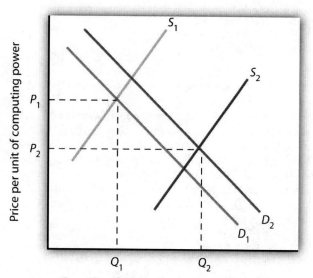

Demand also shifted to the right from D_1 to D_2, as incomes rose and new uses for computers, from e-mail and social networking to Voice over Internet Protocol (VoIP) and Radio Frequency ID (RFID) tags (which allow wireless tracking of commercial shipments via desktop computers), altered the preferences of consumer and business users. Because we observe a fall in equilibrium price and an increase in equilibrium quantity, we conclude that the rightward shift in supply has outweighed the rightward shift in demand. The power of market forces has profoundly affected the way we live and work.

1.2 The Markets for Crude Oil and for Gasoline

The market for crude oil took a radical turn in 1973. The price per barrel of crude oil quadrupled in 1973 and 1974. Price remained high until the early 1980s but then fell back drastically and remained low for about two decades. In 2004, the price of oil began to move upward and by 2008 had reached $147 per barrel.

What caused the dramatic increase in gasoline and oil prices in 2008? It appeared to be increasing worldwide demand outpacing producers' ability—or willingness—to increase production much. This increase in demand is illustrated in Figure 4.2.

FIGURE 4.2 The Increasing Demand for Crude Oil

The price of oil was $35 per barrel at the beginning of 2004, as determined by the intersection of world demand, D_1, and world supply, S_1. Increasing world demand, prompted largely by increasing demand from China as well as from other countries, shifted world demand to D_2, pushing the price as high as $140 per barrel by the middle of 2008.

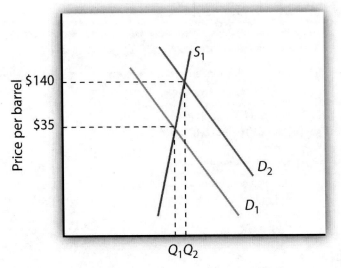

Higher oil prices also increase the cost of producing virtually every good or service, as at a minimum, the production of most goods requires transportation. These costs inevitably translate into higher prices for nearly all goods and services. Supply curves of the goods and services thus affected shift to the left, putting downward pressure on output and upward pressure on prices.

Graphically, the impact of higher gasoline prices on businesses that use gasoline is illustrated in Figure 4.3. Because higher gasoline prices increase the cost of doing business, they shift the supply curves for nearly all businesses to the left, putting upward pressure on prices and downward pressure on output. In the case shown here, the supply curve in a typical industry shifts from S_1 to S_2. This increases the equilibrium price from P_1 to P_2 and reduces the equilibrium quantity from Q_1 to Q_2.

FIGURE 4.3   The Impact of Higher Gasoline Prices

Higher gasoline prices increase the cost of producing virtually every good or service. In the case shown here, the supply curve in a typical industry shifts from S_1 to S_2. This increases the equilibrium price from P_1 to P_2 and reduces equilibrium quantity from Q_1 to Q_2.

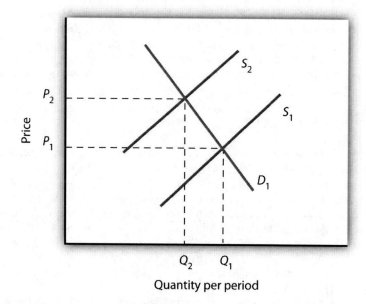

Then, as the world economy slowed dramatically in the second half of 2008, the demand curve for oil shifted back to the left. By November 2008, the price per barrel had dropped back to below $60 per barrel. As gas prices also subsided, so did the threat of higher prices in other industries.

1.3   The Stock Market

The circular flow model suggests that capital, like other factors of production, is supplied by households to firms. Firms, in turn, pay income to those households for the use of their capital. Generally speaking, however, capital is actually owned by firms themselves. General Motors owns its assembly plants, and Wal-Mart owns its stores; these firms therefore own their capital. But firms, in turn, are owned by people—and those people, of course, live in households. It is through their ownership of firms that households own capital.

A firm may be owned by one individual (a **sole proprietorship**), by several individuals (a **partnership**), or by shareholders who own stock in the firm (a **corporation**). Although most firms in the United States are sole proprietorships or partnerships, the bulk of the nation's total output (about 90%) is produced by corporations. Corporations also own most of the capital (machines, plants, buildings, and the like).

This section describes how the prices of shares of **corporate stock**, shares in the ownership of a corporation, are determined by the interaction of demand and supply. Ultimately, the same forces that determine the value of a firm's stock determine the value of a sole proprietorship or partnership.

When a corporation needs funds to increase its capital or for other reasons, one means at its disposal is to issue new stock in the corporation. (Other means include borrowing funds or using past profits.) Once the new shares have been sold in what is called an initial public offering (IPO), the corporation receives no further funding as shares of its stock are bought and sold on the secondary market. The secondary market is the market for stocks that have been issued in the past, and the daily news reports about stock prices almost always refer to activity in the secondary market. Generally, the corporations whose shares are traded are not involved in these transactions.

The **stock market** is the set of institutions in which shares of stock are bought and sold. The New York Stock Exchange (NYSE) is one such institution. There are many others all over the world, such as the DAX in Germany and the Bolsa in Mexico. To buy or sell a share of stock, one places an order with a stockbroker who relays the order to one of the traders at the NYSE or at some other exchange.

The process through which shares of stock are bought and sold can seem chaotic. At many exchanges, traders with orders from customers who want to buy stock shout out the prices those customers are willing to pay. Traders with orders from customers who want to sell shout out offers of prices at which their customers are willing to sell. Some exchanges use electronic trading, but the principle is the same: if the price someone is willing to pay matches the price at which someone else is willing to sell,

sole proprietorship

A firm owned by one individual.

partnership

A firm owned by several individuals.

corporation

A firm owned by shareholders who own stock in the firm.

corporate stock

Shares in the ownership of a corporation.

stock market

The set of institutions in which shares of stock are bought and sold.

the trade is made. The most recent price at which a stock has traded is reported almost instantaneously throughout the world.

Figure 4.4 applies the model of demand and supply to the determination of stock prices. Suppose the demand curve for shares in Intel Corporation is given by D_1 and the supply by S_1. (Even though the total number of shares outstanding is fixed at any point in time, the supply curve is not vertical. Rather, the supply curve is upward sloping because it represents how many shares current owners are prepared to sell at each price, and that number will be greater at higher prices.) Suppose that these curves intersect at a price of $25, at which Q_1 shares are traded each day. If the price were higher, more shares would be offered for sale than would be demanded, and the price would quickly fall. If the price were lower, more shares would be demanded than would be supplied, and the price would quickly rise. In general, we can expect the prices of shares of stock to move quickly to their equilibrium levels.

FIGURE 4.4 Demand and Supply in the Stock Market

The equilibrium price of stock shares in Intel Corporation is initially $25, determined by the intersection of demand and supply curves D_1 and S_1, at which Q_1 million shares are traded each day.

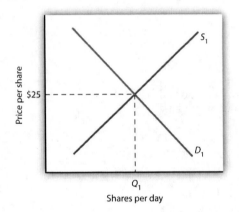

The intersection of the demand and supply curves for shares of stock in a particular company determines the equilibrium price for a share of stock. But what determines the demand and supply for shares of a company's stock?

The owner of a share of a company's stock owns a share of the company, and, hence, a share of its profits; typically, a corporation will retain and reinvest some of its profits to increase its future profitability. The profits kept by a company are called **retained earnings**. Profits distributed to shareholders are called **dividends**. Because a share of stock gives its owner a claim on part of a company's future profits, it follows that the expected level of future profits plays a role in determining the value of its stock.

Of course, those future profits cannot be known with certainty; investors can only predict what they might be, based on information about future demand for the company's products, future costs of production, information about the soundness of a company's management, and so on. Stock prices in the real world thus reflect estimates of a company's profits projected into the future.

The downward slope of the demand curve suggests that at lower prices for the stock, more people calculate that the firm's future earnings will justify the stock's purchase. The upward slope of the supply curve tells us that as the price of the stock rises, more people conclude that the firm's future earnings do not justify holding the stock and therefore offer to sell it. At the equilibrium price, the number of shares supplied by people who think holding the stock no longer makes sense just balances the number of shares demanded by people who think it does.

retained earnings

Profits kept by a company.

dividends

Profits distributed to shareholders.

What factors, then, cause the demand or supply curves for shares of stocks to shift? The most important factor is a change in the expectations of a company's future profits. Suppose Intel announces a new generation of computer chips that will lead to faster computers with larger memories. Current owners of Intel stock would adjust upward their estimates of what the value of a share of Intel stock should be. At the old equilibrium price of $25 fewer owners of Intel stock would be willing to sell. Since this would be true at every possible share price, the supply curve for Intel stock would shift to the left, as shown in Figure 4.5. Just as the expectation that a company will be more profitable shifts the supply curve for its stock to the left, that same change in expectations will cause more people to want to purchase the stock, shifting the demand curve to the right. In Figure 4.5, we see the supply curve shifting to the left, from S_1 to S_2, while the demand curve shifts to the right, from D_1 to D_2.

Other factors may alter the price of an individual corporation's share of stock or the level of stock prices in general. For example, demographic change and rising incomes have affected the demand for stocks in recent years. For example, with a large proportion of the U.S. population nearing retirement age and beginning to think about and plan for their lives during retirement, the demand for stocks has risen.

Information on the economy as a whole is also likely to affect stock prices. If the economy overall is doing well and people expect that to continue, they may become more optimistic about how profitable companies will be in general, and thus the prices of stocks will rise. Conversely, expectations of a sluggish economy, as happened in the fall of 2008, could cause stock prices in general to fall.

The stock market is bombarded with new information every minute of every day. Firms announce their profits of the previous quarter. They announce that they plan to move into a new product line or sell their goods in another country. We learn that the price of Company A's good, which is a substitute for one sold by Company B, has risen. We learn that countries sign trade agreements, launch wars, or make peace. All of this information may affect stock prices because any information can affect how buyers and sellers value companies.

FIGURE 4.5 A Change in Expectations Affects the Price of Corporate Stock

If financial investors decide that a company is likely to be more profitable, then the supply of the stock shifts to the left (in this case, from S_1 to S_2), and the demand for the stock shifts to the right (in this case, from D_1 to D_2), resulting in an increase in price from P_1 to P_2.

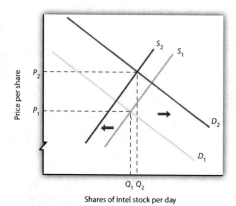

Shares of Intel stock per day

KEY TAKEAWAYS

- Technological change, which has caused the supply curve for computing power to shift to the right, is the main reason for the rapid increase in equilibrium quantity and decrease in equilibrium price of personal computers.

- The increase in crude oil and gasoline prices in 2008 was driven primarily by increased demand for crude oil, an increase that was created by economic growth throughout the world. Crude oil and gas prices fell markedly as world economic growth subsided later in the year.

- Higher gasoline prices increased the cost of producing virtually every good and service, shifting supply curves for most goods and services to the left. This tended to push prices up and output down.

- Demand and supply determine prices of shares of corporate stock. The equilibrium price of a share of stock strikes a balance between those who think the stock is worth more and those who think it is worth less than the current price.

- If a company's profits are expected to increase, the demand curve for its stock shifts to the right and the supply curve shifts to the left, causing equilibrium price to rise. The opposite would occur if a company's profits were expected to decrease.

- Other factors that influence the price of corporate stock include demographic and income changes and the overall health of the economy.

TRY IT!

Suppose an airline announces that its earnings this year are lower than expected due to reduced ticket sales. The airline spokesperson gives no information on how the company plans to turn things around. Use the model of demand and supply to show and explain what is likely to happen to the price of the airline's stock.

Case in Point: 9/11 and the Stock Market

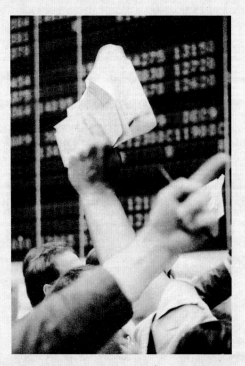

© 2010 Jupiterimages Corporation

The hijacking of four airplanes and the steering of them into buildings is perhaps the only disaster that has become universally known by its date: September 11, 2001—hence, 9/11. "9/11" will remain etched in our collective memory for a great many generations.

Disasters such as 9/11 represent the kind of complete surprises that dramatically affect stock prices, if only temporarily. The New York Stock Exchange was closed on the day of the attack and remained closed for six days. On the day the market opened, the Dow Jones Industrial Average (the "DOW", a widely used gauge of stock prices) fell nearly 685 points to 8,920. It was one of the biggest one-day decline in U.S. history.

Why did the attacks on September 11, 2001, have such a dramatic short-term impact on the stock market? The attacks of 9/11 plunged the United States and much of the rest of the world into a very frightening war against terrorism. The realization that terrorists could strike anytime and in any place sapped consumer and business confidence alike and affected both the demand and supply of most stocks. The attacks on 9/11 provoked fear and uncertainty—two things that are certain to bring stock prices down, at least until other events and more information cause expectations to change again in this very responsive market.

The information given in the problem suggests that the airline's profits are likely to fall below expectations. Current owners of the airline's stock and potential buyers of the stock would adjust downward their estimates of what the value of the corporation's stock should be. As a result the supply curve for the stock would increase, shifting it to the right, while the demand curve for the stock would decrease, shifting it to the left. As a result, equilibrium price of the stock falls from P_1 to P_2. What happens to equilibrium quantity depends on the extent to which each curve shifts. In the diagram, equilibrium quantity is shown to decrease from Q_1 to Q_2.

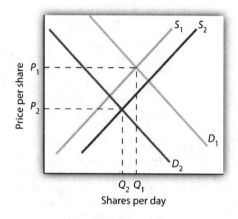

2. GOVERNMENT INTERVENTION IN MARKET PRICES: PRICE FLOORS AND PRICE CEILINGS

LEARNING OBJECTIVES

1. Use the model of demand and supply to explain what happens when the government imposes price floors or price ceilings.
2. Discuss the reasons why governments sometimes choose to control prices and the consequences of price control policies.

So far in this chapter and in the previous chapter, we have learned that markets tend to move toward their equilibrium prices and quantities. Surpluses and shortages of goods are short-lived as prices adjust to equate quantity demanded with quantity supplied.

In some markets, however, governments have been called on by groups of citizens to intervene to keep prices of certain items higher or lower than what would result from the market finding its own equilibrium price. In this section we will examine agricultural markets and apartment rental markets—two markets that have often been subject to price controls. Through these examples, we will identify the effects of controlling prices. In each case, we will look at reasons why governments have chosen to control prices in these markets and the consequences of these policies.

2.1 Agricultural Price Floors

Governments often seek to assist farmers by setting price floors in agricultural markets. A minimum allowable price set above the equilibrium price is a **price floor**. With a price floor, the government forbids a price below the minimum. (Notice that, if the price floor were for whatever reason set below the equilibrium price, it would be irrelevant to the determination of the price in the market since nothing would prohibit the price from rising to equilibrium.) A price floor that is set above the equilibrium price creates a surplus.

Figure 4.8 shows the market for wheat. Suppose the government sets the price of wheat at P_F. Notice that P_F is above the equilibrium price of P_E. At P_F, we read over to the demand curve to find that the quantity of wheat that buyers will be willing and able to purchase is W_1 bushels. Reading over to the supply curve, we find that sellers will offer W_2 bushels of wheat at the price floor of P_F. Because

price floor

A minimum allowable price set above the equilibrium price.

P_F is above the equilibrium price, there is a surplus of wheat equal to ($W_2 - W_1$) bushels. The surplus persists because the government does not allow the price to fall.

FIGURE 4.8 Price Floors in Wheat Markets

A price floor for wheat creates a surplus of wheat equal to ($W_2 - W_1$) bushels.

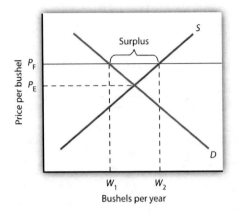

FIGURE 4.9 Supply and Demand Shifts for Agricultural Products

A relatively large increase in the supply of agricultural products, accompanied by a relatively small increase in demand, has reduced the price received by farmers and increased the quantity of agricultural goods.

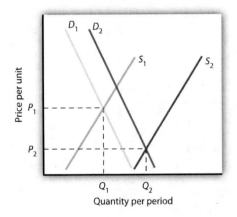

Why have many governments around the world set price floors in agricultural markets? Farming has changed dramatically over the past two centuries. Technological improvements in the form of new equipment, fertilizers, pesticides, and new varieties of crops have led to dramatic increases in crop output per acre. Worldwide production capacity has expanded markedly. As we have learned, technological improvements cause the supply curve to shift to the right, reducing the price of food. While such price reductions have been celebrated in computer markets, farmers have successfully lobbied for government programs aimed at keeping their prices from falling.

While the supply curve for agricultural goods has shifted to the right, the demand has increased with rising population and with rising income. But as incomes rise, people spend a smaller and smaller fraction of their incomes on food. While the demand for food has increased, that increase has not been nearly as great as the increase in supply. Figure 4.9 shows that the supply curve has shifted much farther to the right, from S_1 to S_2, than the demand curve has, from D_1 to D_2. As a result, equilibrium quantity has risen dramatically, from Q_1 to Q_2, and equilibrium price has fallen, from P_1 to P_2.

On top of this long-term historical trend in agriculture, agricultural prices are subject to wide swings over shorter periods. Droughts or freezes can sharply reduce supplies of particular crops, causing sudden increases in prices. Demand for agricultural goods of one country can suddenly dry up if the government of another country imposes trade restrictions against its products, and prices can fall. Such dramatic shifts in prices and quantities make incomes of farmers unstable.

The Great Depression of the 1930s led to a major federal role in agriculture. The Depression affected the entire economy, but it hit farmers particularly hard. Prices received by farmers plunged nearly two-thirds from 1930 to 1933. Many farmers had a tough time keeping up mortgage payments. By 1932, more than half of all farm loans were in default.

Farm legislation passed during the Great Depression has been modified many times, but the federal government has continued its direct involvement in agricultural markets. This has meant a variety of government programs that guarantee a minimum price for some types of agricultural products. These programs have been accompanied by government purchases of any surplus, by requirements to restrict acreage in order to limit those surpluses, by crop or production restrictions, and the like.

To see how such policies work, look back at Figure 4.8. At P_F, W_2 bushels of wheat will be supplied. With that much wheat on the market, there is market pressure on the price of wheat to fall. To prevent price from falling, the government buys the surplus of ($W_2 - W_1$) bushels of wheat, so that only W_1 bushels are actually available to private consumers for purchase on the market. The government can store the surpluses or find special uses for them. For example, surpluses generated in the United States have been shipped to developing countries as grants-in-aid or distributed to local school lunch programs. As a variation on this program, the government can require farmers who want to participate in the price support program to reduce acreage in order to limit the size of the surpluses.

After 1973, the government stopped buying the surpluses (with some exceptions) and simply guaranteed farmers a "target price." If the average market price for a crop fell below the crop's target price, the government paid the difference. If, for example, a crop had a market price of $3 per unit and a target price of $4 per unit, the government would give farmers a payment of $1 for each unit sold. Farmers would thus receive the market price of $3 plus a government payment of $1 per unit. For farmers to receive these payments, they had to agree to remove acres from production and to comply with certain conservation provisions. These restrictions sought to reduce the size of the surplus generated by the target price, which acted as a kind of price floor.

What are the effects of such farm support programs? The intention is to boost and stabilize farm incomes. But, with price floors, consumers pay more for food than they would otherwise, and governments spend heavily to finance the programs. With the target price approach, consumers pay less, but government financing of the program continues. U.S. federal spending for agriculture averaged well over $22 billion per year between 2003 and 2007, roughly $70 per person.

Help to farmers has sometimes been justified on the grounds that it boosts incomes of "small" farmers. However, since farm aid has generally been allotted on the basis of how much farms produce rather than on a per-farm basis, most federal farm support has gone to the largest farms. If the goal is to eliminate poverty among farmers, farm aid could be redesigned to supplement the incomes of small or poor farmers rather than to undermine the functioning of agricultural markets.

In 1996, the U.S. Congress passed the Federal Agriculture Improvement and Reform Act of 1996, or FAIR. The thrust of the new legislation was to do away with the various programs of price support for most crops and hence provide incentives for farmers to respond to market price signals. To protect farmers through a transition period, the act provided for continued payments that were scheduled to decline over a seven-year period. However, with prices for many crops falling in 1998, the U.S. Congress passed an emergency aid package that increased payments to farmers. In 2008, as farm prices reached record highs, Congress passed a farm bill that increased subsidy payments to $40 billion. It did, however, for the first time limit payments to the wealthiest farmers. Individual farmers whose farm incomes exceed $750,000 (or $1.5 million for couples) would be ineligible for some subsidy programs.

2.2   Rental Price Ceilings

The purpose of rent control is to make rental units cheaper for tenants than they would otherwise be. Unlike agricultural price controls, rent control in the United States has been largely a local phenomenon, although there were national rent controls in effect during World War II. Currently, about 200 cities and counties have some type of rent control provisions, and about 10% of rental units in the United States are now subject to price controls. New York City's rent control program, which began in 1943, is among the oldest in the country. Many other cities in the United States adopted some form of rent control in the 1970s. Rent controls have been pervasive in Europe since World War I, and many large cities in poorer countries have also adopted rent controls.

Rent controls in different cities differ in terms of their flexibility. Some cities allow rent increases for specified reasons, such as to make improvements in apartments or to allow rents to keep pace with price increases elsewhere in the economy. Often, rental housing constructed after the imposition of the rent control ordinances is exempted. Apartments that are vacated may also be decontrolled. For simplicity, the model presented here assumes that apartment rents are controlled at a price that does not change.

Figure 4.10 shows the market for rental apartments. Notice that the demand and supply curves are drawn to look like all the other demand and supply curves you have encountered so far in this text: the demand curve is downward-sloping and the supply curve is upward-sloping.

The demand curve shows that a higher price (rent) reduces the quantity of apartments demanded. For example, with higher rents, more young people will choose to live at home with their parents. With lower rents, more will choose to live in apartments. Higher rents may encourage more apartment sharing; lower rents would induce more people to live alone.

The supply curve is drawn to show that as rent increases, property owners will be encouraged to offer more apartments to rent. Even though an aerial photograph of a city would show apartments to be fixed at a point in time, owners of those properties will decide how many to rent depending on the amount of rent they anticipate. Higher rents may also induce some homeowners to rent out apartment space. In addition, renting out apartments implies a certain level of service to renters, so that low rents may lead some property owners to keep some apartments vacant.

Rent control is an example of a **price ceiling**, a maximum allowable price. With a price ceiling, the government forbids a price above the maximum. A price ceiling that is set below the equilibrium price creates a shortage that will persist.

Suppose the government sets the price of an apartment at P_C in Figure 4.10. Notice that P_C is below the equilibrium price of P_E. At P_C, we read over to the supply curve to find that sellers are willing to offer A_1 apartments. Reading over to the demand curve, we find that consumers would like to rent A_2 apartments at the price ceiling of P_C. Because P_C is below the equilibrium price, there is a shortage of apartments equal to $(A_2 - A_1)$. (Notice that if the price ceiling were set above the equilibrium price it would have no effect on the market since the law would not prohibit the price from settling at an equilibrium price that is lower than the price ceiling.)

FIGURE 4.10 Effect of a Price Ceiling on the Market for Apartments

A price ceiling on apartment rents that is set below the equilibrium rent creates a shortage of apartments equal to $(A_2 - A_1)$ apartments.

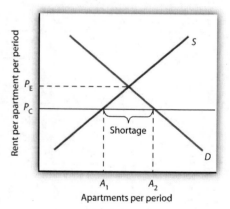

price ceiling

A maximum allowable price.

FIGURE 4.11 The Unintended Consequences of Rent Control

Controlling apartment rents at P_C creates a shortage of $(A_2 - A_1)$ apartments. For A_1 apartments, consumers are willing and able to pay P_B, which leads to various "backdoor" payments to apartment owners.

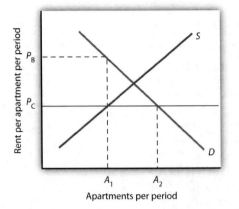

If rent control creates a shortage of apartments, why do some citizens nonetheless clamor for rent control and why do governments often give in to the demands? The reason generally given for rent control is to keep apartments affordable for low- and middle-income tenants.

But the reduced quantity of apartments supplied must be rationed in some way, since, at the price ceiling, the quantity demanded would exceed the quantity supplied. Current occupants may be reluctant to leave their dwellings because finding other apartments will be difficult. As apartments do become available, there will be a line of potential renters waiting to fill them, any of whom is willing to pay the controlled price of P_C or more. In fact, reading up to the demand curve in Figure 4.11 from A_1 apartments, the quantity available at P_C, you can see that for A_1 apartments, there are potential renters willing and able to pay P_B. This often leads to various "backdoor" payments to apartment owners, such as large security deposits, payments for things renters may not want (such as furniture), so-called "key" payments ("The monthly rent is $500 and the key price is $3,000"), or simple bribes.

In the end, rent controls and other price ceilings often end up hurting some of the people they are intended to help. Many people will have trouble finding apartments to rent. Ironically, some of those who do find apartments may actually end up paying more than they would have paid in the absence of rent control. And many of the people that the rent controls do help (primarily current occupants, regardless of their income, and those lucky enough to find apartments) are not those they are intended to help (the poor). There are also costs in government administration and enforcement.

Because New York City has the longest history of rent controls of any city in the United States, its program has been widely studied. There is general agreement that the rent control program has reduced tenant mobility, led to a substantial gap between rents on controlled and uncontrolled units, and favored long-term residents at the expense of newcomers to the city.[2] These distortions have grown over time, another frequent consequence of price controls.

A more direct means of helping poor tenants, one that would avoid interfering with the functioning of the market, would be to subsidize their incomes. As with price floors, interfering with the market mechanism may solve one problem, but it creates many others at the same time.

KEY TAKEAWAYS

- Price floors create surpluses by fixing the price above the equilibrium price. At the price set by the floor, the quantity supplied exceeds the quantity demanded.
- In agriculture, price floors have created persistent surpluses of a wide range of agricultural commodities. Governments typically purchase the amount of the surplus or impose production restrictions in an attempt to reduce the surplus.
- Price ceilings create shortages by setting the price below the equilibrium. At the ceiling price, the quantity demanded exceeds the quantity supplied.
- Rent controls are an example of a price ceiling, and thus they create shortages of rental housing.
- It is sometimes the case that rent controls create "backdoor" arrangements, ranging from requirements that tenants rent items that they do not want to outright bribes, that result in rents higher than would exist in the absence of the ceiling.

TRY IT!

A minimum wage law is another example of a price floor. Draw demand and supply curves for unskilled labor. The horizontal axis will show the quantity of unskilled labor per period and the vertical axis will show the hourly wage rate for unskilled workers, which is the price of unskilled labor. Show and explain the effect of a minimum wage that is above the equilibrium wage.

Case in Point: Corn: It Is Not Just Food Any More

© 2010 Jupiterimages Corporation

Government support for corn dates back to the Agricultural Act of 1938 and, in one form or another, has been part of agricultural legislation ever since. Types of supports have ranged from government purchases of surpluses to target pricing, land set asides, and loan guarantees. According to one estimate, the U.S. government spent nearly $42 billion to support corn between 1995 and 2004.

Then, during the period of rising oil prices of the late 1970s and mounting concerns about dependence on foreign oil from volatile regions in the world, support for corn, not as a food, but rather as an input into the production of ethanol—an alternative to oil-based fuel—began. Ethanol tax credits were part of the Energy Act of 1978. Since 1980, a tariff of 50¢ per gallon against imported ethanol, even higher today, has served to protect domestic corn-based ethanol from imported ethanol, in particular from sugar-cane-based ethanol from Brazil.

The Energy Policy Act of 2005 was another milestone in ethanol legislation. Through loan guarantees, support for research and development, and tax credits, it mandated that 4 billion gallons of ethanol be used by 2006 and 7.5 billion gallons by 2012. Ethanol production had already reached 6.5 billion gallons by 2007, so new legislation in 2007 upped the ante to 15 billion gallons by 2015.

Beyond the increased amount the government is spending to support corn and corn-based ethanol, criticism of the policy has three major prongs:

1. Corn-based ethanol does little to reduce U.S. dependence on foreign oil because the energy required to produce a gallon of corn-based ethanol is quite high. A 2006 National Academy of Sciences paper estimated that one gallon of ethanol is needed to bring 1.25 gallons of it to market. Other studies show an even less favorable ratio.

2. Biofuels, such as corn-based ethanol, are having detrimental effects on the environment, with increased deforestation, stemming from more land being used to grow fuel inputs, contributing to global warming.

3. The diversion of corn and other crops from food to fuel is contributing to rising food prices and an increase in world hunger. C. Ford Runge and Benjamin Senauer wrote in *Foreign Affairs* that even small increases in prices of food staples have severe consequences on the very poor of the world, and "Filling the 25-gallon tank of an SUV with pure ethanol requires over 450 pounds of corn—which contains enough calories to feed one person for a year."

Some of these criticisms may be contested as exaggerated: Will the ratio of energy-in to energy-out improve as new technologies emerge for producing ethanol? Did not other factors, such as weather and rising food demand worldwide, contribute to higher grain prices? Nonetheless, it is clear that corn-based ethanol is no free lunch. It is also clear that the end of government support for corn is nowhere to be seen.

Sources: Alexei Barrionuevo, "Mountains of Corn and a Sea of Farm Subsidies," New York Times, November 9, 2005, online version; David Freddoso, "Children of the Corn," National Review Online, May 6, 2008; C. Ford Runge and Benjamin Senauer, "How Biofuels Could Starve the Poor," Foreign Affairs, May/June 2007, online version; Michael Grunwald, "The Clean Energy Scam," Time 171:14 (April 7, 2008): 40–45.

ANSWER TO TRY IT! PROBLEM

A minimum wage (W_{min}) that is set above the equilibrium wage would create a surplus of unskilled labor equal to ($L_2 - L_1$). That is, L_2 units of unskilled labor are offered at the minimum wage, but companies only want to use L_1 units at that wage. Because unskilled workers are a substitute for a skilled workers, forcing the price of unskilled workers higher would increase the demand for skilled labor and thus increase their wages.

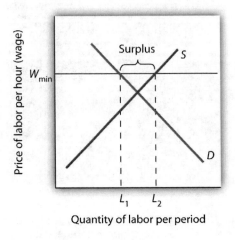

3. THE MARKET FOR HEALTH-CARE SERVICES

LEARNING OBJECTIVE

1. Use the model of demand and supply to explain the effects of third-party payers on the health-care market and on health-care spending.

There has been much discussion over the past three decades about the health-care problem in the United States. Much of this discussion has focused on rising spending for health care. In this section, we will apply the model of demand and supply to health care to see what we can learn about some of the reasons behind rising spending in this important sector of the economy.

Figure 4.14 shows the share of U.S. output devoted to health care since 1960. In 1960, about 5% of total output was devoted to health care; by 2004 this share had risen to 15.4%. That has meant that we are devoting more of our spending to health care, and less to other goods and services, than we would be had health-care spending not risen so much.

FIGURE 4.14 Health-Care Spending as a Percentage of U.S. Output, 1960–2003

Health care's share of total U.S. output rose from about 5% in 1960 to 15.3% in 2003.

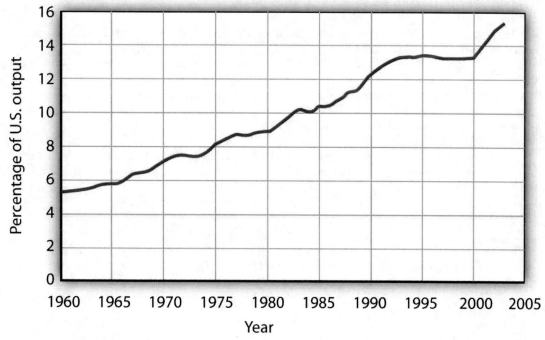

Data for period 1960–1992 from Health Care Finance Association (which was the predecessor to the Centers for Medicare and Medicaid Services);

Data for period 1993–2003 from Centers for Medicare and Medicaid Services, Office of the Actuary: National Health Statistics Group

http://www.cms.hhs.gov/statistics/nhe/historical/t1.asp.

Why were Americans willing to increase their spending on health care so dramatically? The model of demand and supply gives us part of the answer. As we apply the model to this problem, we will also gain a better understanding of the role of prices in a market economy.

3.1 The Demand and Supply for Health Care

When we speak of "health care," we are speaking of the entire health-care industry. This industry produces services ranging from heart transplant operations to therapeutic massages; it produces goods ranging from X-ray machines to aspirin tablets. Clearly each of these goods and services is exchanged in a particular market. To assess the market forces affecting health care, we will focus first on just one of these markets: the market for physician office visits. When you go to the doctor, you are part of the demand for these visits. Your doctor, by seeing you, is part of the supply.

Figure 4.15 shows the market, assuming that it operates in a fashion similar to other markets. The demand curve D_1 and the supply curve S_1 intersect at point E, with an equilibrium price of $30 per office visit. The equilibrium quantity of office visits per week is 1,000,000.

We can use the demand and supply graph to show total spending, which equals the price per unit (in this case, $30 per visit) times the quantity consumed (in this case, 1,000,000 visits per week). Total spending for physician office visits thus equals $30,000,000 per week ($30 times 1,000,000 visits). We show total spending as the area of a rectangle bounded by the price and the quantity. It is the shaded region in Figure 4.15.

The picture in Figure 4.15 misses a crucial feature of the market. Most people in the United States have health insurance, provided either by private firms, by private purchases, or by the government. With health insurance, people agree to pay a fixed amount to the insurer in exchange for the insurer's agreement to pay for most of the health-care expenses they incur. While insurance plans differ in their specific provisions, let us suppose that all individuals have plans that require them to pay $10 for an office visit; the insurance company will pay the rest.

How will this insurance affect the market for physician office visits? If it costs only $10 for a visit instead of $30, people will visit their doctors more often. The quantity of office visits demanded will

FIGURE 4.15 Total Spending for Physician Office Visits

Total spending on physician office visits is $30 per visit multiplied by 1,000,000 visits per week, which equals $30,000,000. It is the shaded area bounded by price and quantity.

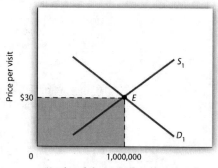

increase. In Figure 4.16, this is shown as a movement along the demand curve. Think about your own choices. When you get a cold, do you go to the doctor? Probably not, if it is a minor cold. But if you feel like you are dying, or wish you were, you probably head for the doctor. Clearly, there are lots of colds in between these two extremes. Whether you drag yourself to the doctor will depend on the severity of your cold and what you will pay for a visit. At a lower price, you are more likely to go to the doctor; at a higher price, you are less likely to go.

In the case shown, the quantity of office visits rises to 1,500,000 per week. But that suggests a potential problem. The quantity of visits supplied at a price of $30 per visit was 1,000,000. According to supply curve S_1, it will take a price of $50 per visit to increase the quantity supplied to 1,500,000 visits (Point F on S_1). But consumers—patients—pay only $10.

third-party payer

An agent other than the seller or the buyer who pays part of the price of a good or service.

Insurers make up the difference between the fees doctors receive and the price patients pay. In our example, insurers pay $40 per visit of insured patients to supplement the $10 that patients pay. When an agent other than the seller or the buyer pays part of the price of a good or service, we say that the agent is a **third-party payer**.

Notice how the presence of a third-party payer affects total spending on office visits. When people paid for their own visits, and the price equaled $30 per visit, total spending equaled $30 million per week. Now doctors receive $50 per visit and provide 1,500,000 visits per week. Total spending has risen to $75 million per week ($50 times 1,500,000 visits, shown by the darkly shaded region plus the lightly shaded region).

FIGURE 4.16 Total Spending for Physician Office Visits Covered by Insurance

With insurance, the quantity of physician office visits demanded rises to 1,500,000. The supply curve shows that it takes a price of $50 per visit to increase the quantity supplied to 1,500,000 visits. Patients pay $10 per visit and insurance pays $40 per visit. Total spending rises to $75,000,000 per week, shown by the darkly shaded region plus the lightly shaded region.

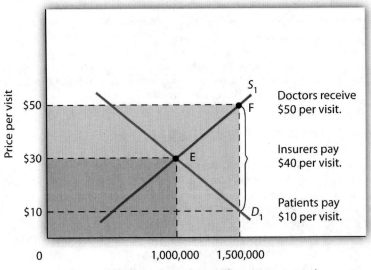

The response described in Figure 4.16 holds for many different types of goods and services covered by insurance or otherwise paid for by third-party payers. For example, the availability of scholarships and subsidized tuition at public and private universities increases the quantity of education demanded and the total expenditures on higher education. In markets with third-party payers, an equilibrium is achieved, but it is not at the intersection of the demand and supply curves. The effect of third-party payers is to decrease the price that consumers directly pay for the goods and services they consume and to increase the price that suppliers receive. Consumers use more than they would in the absence of third-party payers, and providers are encouraged to supply more than they otherwise would. The result is increased total spending.

KEY TAKEAWAYS

- The rising share of the output of the United States devoted to health care represents a rising opportunity cost. More spending on health care means less spending on other goods and services, compared to what would have transpired had health-care spending not risen so much.
- The model of demand and supply can be used to show the effect of third-party payers on total spending. With third-party payers (for example, health insurers), the quantity of services consumed rises, as does spending.

TRY IT!

The provision of university education through taxpayer-supported state universities is another example of a market with a third-party payer. Use the model of demand and supply to discuss the impact this has on the higher education market. Specifically, draw a graph similar to Figure 4.16. How would you label the axes? Show the equilibrium price and quantity in the absence of a third-party payer and indicate total spending on education. Now show the impact of lower tuition As a result of state support for education. How much education do students demand at the lower tuition? How much tuition must educational institutions receive to produce that much education? How much spending on education will occur? Compare total spending before and after a third-party payer enters this market.

Case in Point: The Oregon Plan

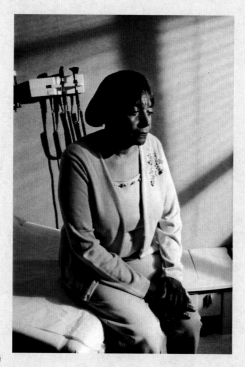

© 2010 Jupiterimages Corporation

The health-care industry presents us with a dilemma. Clearly, it makes sense for people to have health insurance. Just as clearly, health insurance generates a substantial increase in spending for health care. If that spending is to be limited, some mechanism must be chosen to do it. One mechanism would be to require patients to pay a larger share of their own health-care consumption directly, reducing the payments made by third-party payers. Allowing people to accumulate tax-free private medical savings accounts is one way to do this. Another option is to continue the current trend to use insurance companies as the agents that limit spending. A third option is government regulation; this Case in Point describes how the state of Oregon tried to limit health-care spending by essentially refusing to be a third-party payer for certain services.

Like all other states, Oregon has wrestled with the problem of soaring Medicaid costs. Its solution to the problem illustrates some of the choices society might make in seeking to reduce health-care costs.

Oregon used to have a plan similar to plans in many other states. Households whose incomes were lower than 50% of the poverty line qualified for Medicaid. In 1987, the state began an effort to manage its Medicaid costs. It decided that it would no longer fund organ transplants and that it would use the money saved to give better care to pregnant women. The decision turned out to be a painful one; the first year, a seven-year-old boy with leukemia, who might have been saved with a bone marrow transplant, died. But state officials argued that the shift of expenditures to pregnant women would ultimately save more lives.

The state gradually expanded its concept of determining what services to fund and what services not to fund. It collapsed a list of 10,000 different diagnoses that had been submitted to its Medicaid program in the past into a list of more than 700 condition-treatment pairs. One such pair, for example, is appendicitis-appendectomy. Health-care officials then ranked these pairs in order of priority. The rankings were based on such factors as the seriousness of a particular condition and the cost and efficacy of treatments. The state announced that it would provide Medicaid to all households below the poverty line, but that it would not fund any procedure ranked below a certain level, initially number 588 on its list. The plan also set a budget limit for any one year; if spending rose above that limit, the legislature must appropriate additional money or drop additional procedures from the list of those covered by the plan. The Oregon Health Plan officially began operation in 1994.

While the Oregon plan has been applied only to households below the poverty line that are not covered by other programs, it suggests a means of reducing health-care spending. Clearly, if part of the health-care problem is excessive provision of services, a system designed to cut services must determine what treatments not to fund.

Professors Jonathan Oberlander, Theodore Marmor, and Lawrence Jacobs studied the impact of this plan in practice through the year 2000 and found that, in contrast to initial expectations, excluded procedures were generally ones of marginal medical value, so the "line in the sand" had little practical significance. In addition, they found that patients were often able to receive supposedly excluded services when physicians, for example, treated an uncovered illness in conjunction with a covered one. During the period of the study, the number of people covered by the plan expanded substantially and yet rationing of services essentially did not occur. How do they explain this seeming contradiction? Quite simply: state government increased revenues from various sources to support the plan. Indeed, they argue that, because treatments that might not be included were explicitly stated, political pressure made excluding them even more difficult and may have inadvertently increased the cost of the program.

In the early 2000s, Oregon, like many other states, confronted severe budgetary pressures. To limit spending, it chose the perhaps less visible strategy of reducing the number of people covered through the plan. Once serving more than 100,000 people, budget cuts reduced the number served to about 17,000. Whereas in 1996, 11% of Oregonians lacked health insurance, in 2008 16% did.

Trailblazing again, in 2008 Oregon realized that its budget allowed room for coverage for a few thousand additional people. But how to choose among the 130,000 eligibles? The solution: to hold a lottery. More than 90,000 people queued up, hoping to be lucky winners.

Sources: Jonathan Oberlander, Theodore Marmor, and Lawrence Jacobs, "Rationing Medical Care: Rhetoric and Reality in the Oregon Health Plan," Canadian Medical Association Journal 164: 11 (May 29, 2001): 1583–1587; William Yardley, "Drawing Lots for Health Care," The New York Times, March 13, 2008: p. A12.

ANSWER TO TRY IT! PROBLEM

Without a third-party payer for education, the graph shows equilibrium tuition of P_1 and equilibrium quantity of education of Q_1. State support for education lowers tuition that students pay to P_2. As a result, students demand Q_2 courses per year. To provide that amount of education, educational institutions require tuition per course of P_3. Without a third-party payer, spending on education is $0P_1EQ_1$. With a third-party payer, spending rises to $0P_3FQ_2$.

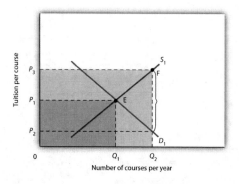

4. REVIEW AND PRACTICE

Summary

In this chapter we used the tools of demand and supply to understand a wide variety of market outcomes. We learned that technological change and the entry of new sellers has caused the supply curve of personal computers to shift markedly to the right, thereby reducing equilibrium price and increasing equilibrium quantity. Market forces have made personal computers a common item in offices and homes.

Crude oil and gasoline prices soared in 2008 and then fell back. We looked at the causes of these increases as well as their impacts. Crude oil prices rose in large part As a result of increased demand, particularly from China. Higher prices for crude oil led to higher prices for gasoline. Those higher prices not only hurt consumers of gasoline, they also put upward pressure on the prices of a wide range of goods and services. Crude oil and gasoline prices then decreased dramatically in the last part of 2008, as world growth declined.

The model of demand and supply also explains the determination of stock prices. The price per share of corporate stock reflects the market's estimate of the expected profitability of the firm. Any information about the firm that causes potential buyers or current owners of corporate stock to reevaluate how profitable they think the firm is, or will be, will cause the equilibrium price of the stock to change.

We then examined markets in which some form of government price control keeps price permanently above or below equilibrium. A price floor leads to persistent surpluses because it is set above the equilibrium price, whereas a price ceiling, because it is set below the equilibrium price, leads to persistent shortages. We saw that interfering with the market mechanism may solve one problem but often creates other problems at the same time. We discussed what some of these unintended consequences might be. For example, agricultural price floors aimed at boosting farm income have also raised prices for consumers and cost taxpayers dearly, and the bulk of government payments have gone to large farms. Rent controls have lowered rents, but they have also reduced the quantity of rental housing supplied, created shortages, and sometimes led to various forms of "backdoor" payments, which sometimes force the price of rental housing above what would exist in the absence of controls.

Finally, we looked at the market for health care and a special feature behind demand and supply in this market that helps to explain why the share of output of the United States that is devoted to health care has risen. Health care is an example of a market in which there are third-party payers (primarily private insurers and the government). With third-party payers the quantity of health-care services consumed rises, as does health-care spending.

CONCEPT PROBLEMS

1. Like personal computers, digital cameras have become a common household item. Digital camera prices have plunged in the last 10 years. Use the model of demand and supply to explain the fall in price and increase in quantity.

2. Enron Corp. was one of several corporations convicted of fraud in its accounting practices during the early part of this decade. It had created dummy corporations to hide massive borrowing and to give it the appearance of extraordinary profitability. Use the model of demand and supply to explain the likely impact of such convictions on the stocks of other corporations.

3. During World War II there was a freeze on wages, and corporations found they could evade the freeze by providing other fringe benefits such as retirement funds for their employees. The Office of Price Administration, which administered the wage freeze, ruled that the offer of retirement funds was not a violation of the freeze. The Internal Revenue Service went along with this and ruled that employer-financed retirement plans were not taxable income. Was the wage freeze an example of a price floor or a price ceiling? Use the model of demand and supply to explain why employers began to offer such benefits to their employees.

4. The text argues that political instability in potential suppliers of oil such as Iraq and Venezuela accounts for a relatively steep supply curve for crude oil such as the one shown in Figure 4.2 Suppose that this instability eases considerably and that the world supply curve for crude oil becomes much flatter. Draw such a curve, and explain its implications for the world economy and for typical consumers.

5. Suppose that technological change affects the dairy industry in the same way it has affected the computer industry. However, suppose that dairy price supports remain in place. How would this affect government spending on the dairy program? Use the model of demand and supply to support your answer.

6. People often argue that there is a "shortage" of child care. Using the model of demand and supply, evaluate whether this argument is likely to be correct.

7. "During most of the past 50 years the United States has had a surplus of farmers, and this has been the root of the farm problem." Comment.

8. Suppose the Department of Agriculture ordered all farmers to reduce the acreage they plant by 10%. Would you expect a 10% reduction in food production? Why or why not?

9. The text argues that the increase in gasoline prices had a particularly strong impact on low-income people. Name some other goods and services for which a sharp increase in price would have a similar impact on people with low incomes.

10. Suppose that the United States and the European Union impose a price ceiling on crude oil of $25 per barrel. Explain, and illustrate graphically, how this would affect the markets for crude oil and for gasoline in the United States and in the European Union.

11. Given that rent controls can actually hurt low-income people, devise a housing strategy that would provide affordable housing for those whose incomes fall below the poverty line (in 2004, this was about $19,000 for a family of four).

12. Using the model of demand and supply, show and explain how an increase in the share individuals must pay directly for medical care affects the quantity they consume. Explain how this would address the total amount of spending on health care.

13. Given that people pay premiums for their health insurance, how can we say that insurance lowers the prices people pay for health-care services?

14. Suppose that physicians now charge $30 for an office visit and insurance policies require patients to pay 33 1/3% of the amount they pay the physicians, so the out-of-pocket cost to consumers is $10 per visit. In an effort to control costs, the government imposes a price ceiling of $27 per office visit. Using a demand and supply model, show how this policy would affect the market for health care.

15. Do you think the U.S. health-care system requires reform? Why or why not? If you think reform is in order, explain the approach to reform you advocate.

NUMERICAL PROBLEMS

Problems 1–4 are based on the following demand and supply schedules for corn (all quantities are in millions of bushels per year).

Price per bushel	Quantity demanded	Quantity supplied
$0	6	0
1	5	1
2	4	2
3	3	3
4	2	4
5	1	5
6	0	6

1. Draw the demand and supply curves for corn. What is the equilibrium price? The equilibrium quantity?
2. Suppose the government now imposes a price floor at $4 per bushel. Show the effect of this program graphically. How large is the surplus of corn?
3. With the price floor, how much do farmers receive for their corn? How much would they have received if there were no price floor?
4. If the government buys all the surplus wheat, how much will it spend?

Problems 5–9 are based on the following hypothetical demand and supply curves for apartments

Rent/Month	Number of Apts. Demanded/Month	Number of Apts. Supplied/Month
$0	120,000	0
200	100,000	20,000
400	80,000	40,000
600	60,000	60,000
800	40,000	80,000
1000	20,000	100,000
1200	0	120,000

5. Draw the demand and supply curves for apartments.
6. What is the equilibrium rent per month? At this rent, what is the number of apartments demanded and supplied per month?
7. Suppose a ceiling on rents is set at $400 per month. Characterize the situation that results from this policy.
8. At the rent ceiling, how many apartments are demanded? How many are supplied?
9. How much are people willing to pay for the number of apartments supplied at the ceiling? Describe the arrangements to which this situation might lead.

ENDNOTES

1. Ilkka Tuomi, "The Lives and Death of Moore's Law." http://www.firstmonday.org/issues/issue7_11/tuomi/index. *First Monday* (http://www.firstmonday.org) is a peer-reviewed journal on the Internet.

2. Richard Arnott, "Time for Revisionism on Rent Control," *Journal of Economic Perspectives* 9(1) (Winter, 1995): 99–120.

CHAPTER 5
Macroeconomics: The Big Picture

START UP: FINANCIAL CRISIS BATTERS ECONOMY

The U.S. economy seemed to be doing well overall after the recession of 2001. Growth had been fairly rapid, unemployment had stayed low, and inflation seemed to be under control. The economy began to unravel at the end of 2007—total output fell in the fourth quarter. It recovered—barely—in the first quarter, and picked up substantially in the second. Then things went sour…very sour. The economies of the United States and those of much of the world were rocked by the worst financial crisis in nearly 80 years. That crisis plunged the economy into a downturn in total output and employment that seemed likely to last a long time.

A good deal of the economy's momentum when things were going well had been fueled by rising house prices. Between 1995 and 2007, housing prices in the United States more than doubled. As house prices rose, consumers who owned houses grew richer and increased their consumption purchases. That helped fuel economic growth. The boom in housing prices had been encouraged by policies of the nation's monetary authority, the Federal Reserve, which had shifted to an expansionary monetary policy that held short-term interest rates below the inflation rate. Another development, subprime mortgages—mortgage loans to buyers whose credit or income would not ordinarily qualify for mortgage loans—helped bring on the ultimate collapse. When they were first developed, subprime mortgage loans seemed a hugely profitable investment for banks and a good deal for home buyers. Financial institutions developed a wide range of instruments based on "mortgage-backed securities." As long as house prices kept rising, the system worked and was profitable for virtually all players in the mortgage market. Many firms undertook investments in mortgage-backed securities that assumed house prices would keep rising. Large investment banks bet heavily that house prices would continue rising. Powerful members of Congress pressured two government-sponsored enterprises, Fannie Mae (the Federal National Mortgage Association) and Freddie Mac (the Federal Home Loan Mortgage Corporation), to be even more aggressive in encouraging banks to make mortgage loans to low-income families. The pressure came from the executive branch of government as well—under both Democratic and Republican administrations. In 1996, the Department of Housing and Urban Development (under Bill Clinton, a Democrat) required that 12% of mortgages purchased by Fannie Mae and Freddie Mac be for households with incomes less than 60% of the median income in their region. That target was increased to 20% in 2000, 22% in 2005 (now under George W. Bush, a Republican), and was to have increased to 28% in 2008.[1] But that final target would not be reached, as both Fannie Mae and Freddie Mac were seized by the government in 2008. To top things off, a loosening in bank and investment bank regulations gave financial institutions greater leeway in going overboard with purchases of mortgage-backed securities. As house prices began falling in 2007, a system based on the assumption they would continue rising began to unravel very fast. The investment bank Bear Stearns and insurance company American International Group (AIG) required massive infusions of federal money to keep them afloat. In September of 2008, firm after firm with assets tied to mortgage-backed securities began to fail. In some cases, the government rescued them; in other cases, such as Lehman Brothers, they were allowed to fail.

The financial crisis had dramatic and immediate effects on the economy. The economy's total output, which had been growing through the first half of 2008, fell at an annual rate of 0.5% in the third quarter, according to advance estimates by the Bureau of Economic Analysis. Consumers, having weathered higher gasoline prices and higher food prices for most of the year, reduced their consumption expenditures as the value of their houses and the stocks they held plunged—consumption fell at an annual rate of 3.7% in the third quarter. As cold fear gripped financial markets and expectations of further slowdown ensued, firms cut down on investment spending, which includes spending on plant and equipment used in production. While this nonresidential investment component of output fell at an annual rate of 1.5%, the residential component fell even faster as housing investment sank at an annual rate of 17.6%. Government purchases and net exports rose, but not enough to offset reductions in consumption and private investment.[2] As output shrank, unemployment rose. Through the first nine months of 2008 there was concern that price levels in the United States and in most of the world economies were rising rapidly, but toward the end of the year the concern shifted to whether or not the price level might fall.

This recession, which officially began in December 2007 and ended in June 2009, was brutal: At 18 months in length, it was the longest U.S. recession since World War II. The nation's output fell over 4%. The unemployment rate rose dramatically, hitting 10% at the end of 2009, and remaining above 9% throughout 2010. In 2010, to many people it certainly did not feel that the so-called Great Recession had really ended.

Output, employment, and the price level are the key variables in the study of macroeconomics, which is the analysis of aggregate values of economic variables. What determines a country's output, and why does output in some economies expand while in others it contracts? Why do some economies grow faster than others? What causes prices throughout an economy to fluctuate, and how do such fluctuations affect people? What causes employment and unemployment? Why does a country's unemployment rate fluctuate? Why do different countries have different unemployment rates?

We would pronounce an economy "healthy" if its annual output of goods and services were growing at a rate it can sustain, its price level stable, and its unemployment rate low. What would constitute "good" numbers for each of these variables depends on time and place, but those are the outcomes that most people would agree are desirable for the aggregate economy. When the economy deviates from what is considered good performance, there are often calls for the government to "do something" to improve performance. How government policies affect economic performance is a major topic of macroeconomics. When the financial and economic crises struck throughout the world in 2008, there was massive intervention from world central banks and from governments throughout the world in an effort to stimulate their economies.

This chapter provides a preliminary sketch of the most important macroeconomic issues: growth of total output and the business cycle, changes in the price level, and unemployment. Grappling with these issues will be important to you not only in your exploration of macroeconomics but throughout your life.

1.   GROWTH OF REAL GDP AND BUSINESS CYCLES

LEARNING OBJECTIVES

1. Define real gross domestic product and explain how its calculation avoids both double-counting and the effects of changes in the price level.
2. Identify the phases of a business cycle.
3. Relate business cycles to the overall long-run trend in real GDP in the United States.

To determine whether the economy of a nation is growing or shrinking in size, economists use a measure of total output called real GDP. **Real GDP**, short for real gross domestic product, is the total value of all final goods and services produced during a particular year or period, adjusted to eliminate the effects of changes in prices. Let us break that definition up into parts.

Notice that only "final" goods and services are included in GDP. Many goods and services are purchased for use as inputs in producing something else. For example, a pizza parlor buys flour to make pizzas. If we counted the value of the flour and the value of the pizza, we would end up counting the flour twice and thus overstating the value of total production. Including only final goods avoids double-counting. If the flour is produced during a particular period but has not been sold, then it is a "final good" for that period and is counted.

We want to determine whether the economy's output is growing or shrinking. If each final good or service produced, from hammers to haircuts, were valued at its current market price, and then we were to add the values of all such items produced, we would not know if the total had changed because output changed or because prices changed or both. The market value of all final goods and services produced can rise even if total output falls. To isolate the behavior of total output only, we must hold prices constant at some level. For example, if we measure the value of basketball output over time using a fixed price for valuing the basketballs, then only an increase in the number of basketballs produced could increase the value of the contribution made by basketballs to total output. By making such an adjustment for basketballs and all other goods and services, we obtain a value for real GDP. In contrast, **nominal GDP**, usually just referred to as gross domestic product (GDP), is the total value of final goods and services for a particular period valued in terms of prices for that period. For example, real GDP fell in the third quarter of 2008. But, because the price level in the United States was rising, nominal GDP rose 3.6%.

We will save a detailed discussion of the computation of GDP for another chapter. In this section, our goal is to use the concept of real GDP to look at the **business cycle**—the economy's pattern of expansion, then contraction, then expansion again—and at growth of real GDP.

1.1   Phases of the Business Cycle

Figure 5.1 shows a stylized picture of a typical business cycle. It shows that economies go through periods of increasing and decreasing real GDP, but that over time they generally move in the direction of increasing levels of real GDP. A sustained period in which real GDP is rising is an **expansion**; a sustained period in which real GDP is falling is a **recession**. Typically, an economy is said to be in a recession when real GDP drops for two consecutive quarters, but in the United States, the responsibility of defining precisely when the economy is in recession is left to the Business Cycle Dating Committee of the National Bureau of Economic Research (NBER). The Committee defines a recession as a "significant decline in economic activity spread across the economy, lasting more than a few months, normally visible in real GDP, real income, employment, industrial production, and wholesale-retail sales."[3]

real GDP

The total value of all final goods and services produced during a particular year or period, adjusted to eliminate the effects of changes in prices.

nominal GDP

The total value of final goods and services for a particular period valued in terms of prices for that period.

business cycle

The economy's pattern of expansion, then contraction, then expansion again.

expansion

A sustained period in which real GDP is rising.

recession

A sustained period in which real GDP is falling.

FIGURE 5.1 Phases of the Business Cycle

The business cycle is a series of expansions and contractions in real GDP. The cycle begins at a peak and continues through a recession, a trough, and an expansion. A new cycle begins at the next peak. Here, the first peak occurs at time t_1, the trough at time t_2, and the next peak at time t_3. Notice that there is a tendency for real GDP to rise over time.

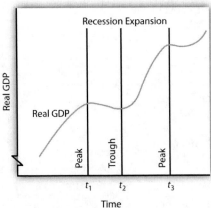

peak

The point of the business cycle at which an expansion ends and a recession begins.

trough

The point of the business cycle at which a recession ends and an expansion begins.

At time t_1 in Figure 5.1, an expansion ends and real GDP turns downward. The point at which an expansion ends and a recession begins is called the **peak** of the business cycle. Real GDP then falls during a period of recession. Eventually it starts upward again (at time t_2). The point at which a recession ends and an expansion begins is called the **trough** of the business cycle. The expansion continues until another peak is reached at time t_3.[4] A complete business cycle is defined by the passage from one peak to the next.

Because the Business Cycle Dating Committee dates peaks and troughs by specific months, and because real GDP is estimated only on a quarterly basis by the Bureau of Economic Analysis, the committee relies on a variety of other indicators that are published monthly, including real personal income, employment, industrial production, and real wholesale and retail sales. The committee typically determines that a recession has happened long after it has actually begun and sometimes ended! In large part, that avoids problems when data released about the economy are revised, and the committee avoids having to reverse itself on its determination of when a recession begins or ends, something it has never done. In December 2008, the Committee announced that a recession in the United States had begun in December 2007. Interestingly, real GDP fell in the fourth quarter of 2007, grew in the first and second quarters of 2008, and shrank in the third quarter of 2008, so clearly the Committee was not using the two consecutive quarters of declining GDP rule-of-thumb. Rather, it was taking into account the behavior of a variety of other variables, such as employment and personal income.

1.2 Business Cycles and the Growth of Real GDP in the United States

Figure 5.2 shows movements in real GDP in the United States from 1960 to 2010. Over those years, the economy experienced eight recessions (including the current one), shown by the shaded areas in the chart. Although periods of expansion have been more prolonged than periods of recession, we see the cycle of economic activity that characterizes economic life.

FIGURE 5.2 Expansions and Recessions, 1960–2010

The chart shows movements in real GDP since 1960. Recessions—periods of falling real GDP—are shown as shaded areas. On average, the annual rate of growth of real GDP over the period was 3.2% per year.

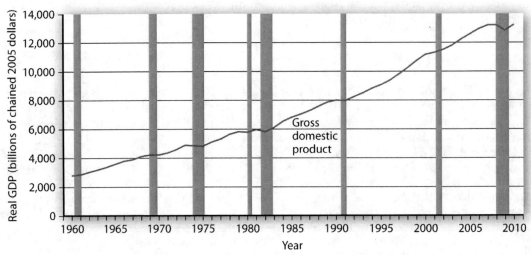

Source: Bureau of Economic Analysis, NIPA Table 1.1.6. Real Gross Domestic Product, Chained Dollars [Billions of chained (2005) dollars]. Seasonally adjusted at annual rates. Data for 2010 is through 3rd quarter.

Real GDP clearly grew between 1960 and 2010. While the economy experienced expansions and recessions, its general trend during the period was one of rising real GDP. The average annual rate of growth of real GDP was about 3.2%.

During the post–World War II period, the average expansion has lasted 58 months, and the average recession has lasted about 11 months. The 2001 recession, which lasted eight months, was thus slightly shorter than the average. The 2007-2009 recession lasted 18 months; it was the longest of the post-World War II period.

Economists have sought for centuries to explain the forces at work in a business cycle. Not only are the currents that move the economy up or down intellectually fascinating but also an understanding of them is of tremendous practical importance. A business cycle is not just a movement along a curve in a textbook. It is new jobs for people, or the loss of them. It is new income, or the loss of it. It is the funds to build new schools or to provide better health care—or the lack of funds to do all those things. The story of the business cycle is the story of progress and plenty, of failure and sacrifice.

During the recent recession, the job outlook for college graduates deteriorated. According to a National Association of Colleges and Employers study, 20% of college graduates seeking jobs had one waiting after graduation in 2009. In 2010, that percent rose to 24% but the average salary had slipped 1.7% from the previous year. The unemployment rate for college graduates under age 25 rose from 3.7% in April 2007 to 8% in April 2010. The unemployment rate for high school graduates who never enrolled in college went from 11.4% to 24.5% over the same two-year period.[5]

The effects of recessions extend beyond the purely economic realm and influence the social fabric of society as well. Suicide rates and property crimes—burglary, larceny, and motor vehicle theft tend to rise during recessions. Even popular music appears to be affected. Terry F. Pettijohn II, a psychologist at Coastal Carolina University, has studied Billboard No. 1 songs from 1955–2003. He finds that during recessions, popular songs tend to be longer and slower, and to have more serious lyrics. "It's 'Bridge over Troubled Water' or 'That's What Friends Are For'," he says. During expansions, songs tend to be faster, shorter, and somewhat sillier, such as "At the Hop" or "My Sharona."[6]

In our study of macroeconomics, we will gain an understanding of the forces at work in the business cycle. We will also explore policies through which the public sector might act to make recessions less severe and, perhaps, to prolong expansions. We turn next to an examination of price-level changes and unemployment.

KEY TAKEAWAYS

- Real gross domestic product (real GDP) is a measure of the value of all final goods and services produced during a particular year or period, adjusted to eliminate the effects of price changes.
- The economy follows a path of expansion, then contraction, then expansion again. These fluctuations make up the business cycle.
- The point at which an expansion becomes a recession is called the peak of a business cycle; the point at which a recession becomes an expansion is called the trough.
- Over time, the general trend for most economies is one of rising real GDP. On average, real GDP in the United States has grown at a rate of over 3% per year since 1960.

TRY IT!

The data below show the behavior of real GDP in Turkey from the first quarter of 2001 through the third quarter of 2002. Use the data to plot real GDP in Turkey and indicate the phases of the business cycle.

Period	Real GDP (billions of New Turkish lira, 1987 prices)
First quarter, 2001	24.1
Second quarter, 2001	26.0
Third quarter, 2001	33.1
Fourth quarter, 2001	27.1
First quarter, 2002	24.6
Second quarter, 2002	28.3
Third quarter, 2002	35.7

Case in Point: The Art of Predicting Recessions

People who make a living tracking the economy and trying to predict its future do not do a very good job at predicting turning points in economic activity. The 52 economists surveyed by the *Wall Street Journal* each month did predict that the economy would slip into a recession in the third quarter of 2008. They made that prediction, however, in October—after the third quarter had ended. In September, the last month of the third quarter, the average forecast among the 52 economists had the economy continuing to grow through the third and fourth quarters of 2008. That September survey was taken before the financial crisis hit, a crisis that took virtually everyone by surprise. Of course, as we have already noted, the third-quarter downturn had not been identified as a recession by the NBER's Business Cycle Dating Committee as of November of 2008.

Predicting business cycle turning points has always been a tricky business. The experience of the recession of 2001 illustrates this. As the accompanying table shows, even as late as September 10, 2001, only 13 out of the 100 Blue Chip forecasters had answered in the affirmative to the question, "Has the United States slipped into a recession?" even though we now know the recession had begun the previous March. Comparing the data that were originally released by the U.S. Bureau of Economic Analysis shortly after the end of each quarter with the revised data that were released after July 2002 provides an important insight into explaining why the forecasters seem to have done so badly. As the graph on pre-revision and post-revision estimates of real GDP growth shows, the data released shortly after the end of each quarter showed an economy expanding through the second quarter of 2001, whereas the revised data show the economy contracting modestly in the first quarter of 2001 and then more forcefully in the second quarter. Only after the attacks on the World Trade Center in New York City and the Pentagon in Washington, D.C., on September 11, 2001, did most of the Blue Chip forecasters realize the economy was in recession.

The National Bureau of Economic Research (NBER) Business Cycle Dating Committee in November 2001 released a press announcement dating the onset of the recession as March 2001. The committee argued that "before the attacks of September 11, it is possible that the decline in the economy would have been too mild to qualify as a recession. The attacks clearly deepened the contraction and may have been an important factor in turning the episode into a recession." While surprising at the time, the revised data suggest that the committee made a good call.

This episode in economic history also points out the difference between the common definition of a recession as two consecutive quarters of declining real GDP and the NBER Dating Committee's continued insistence that it does not define a recession in this way. Rather the committee looks not only at real GDP but also at employment, income, and other factors. The behavior of employment during 2001 seems to have been an important factor in the November 2001 decision to proclaim March 2001 as the peak despite the misleading information on real GDP coming out of the Bureau of Economic Analysis at the time. The slow pickup in employment may also, though, have made it hesitate to call November 2001 the trough until July 2003.

Question posed: "Has the United States slipped into a recession?"		
Date	Percent of Blue Chip responders answering "Yes"	Percent of Blue Chip responders answering "No"
February 2001	5	95
June 2001	7	93
July 2001	13	87
August 2001	5	85
September 10, 2001	13	87
September 19, 2001	82	18

Real GDP Growth: Pre- and Post-July, 2002

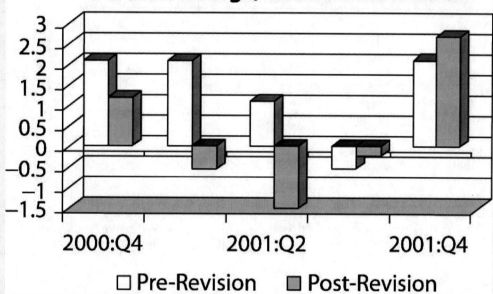

Sources: Phil Izzo, "Economists Expect Crisis to Deepen," Wall Street Journal Online, October 10, 2008; Kevin L. Kliesen, "The 2001 Recession: How Was It Different and What Developments May Have Caused It?" Federal Reserve Bank of St. Louis Review, September/October 2003: 23–37; http://www.nber.org/cycles/; "Press Release," Business Cycle Dating Committee, National Bureau of Economic Research, press release, Cambridge, Massachusetts, July 17, 2002.

ANSWER TO TRY IT! PROBLEM

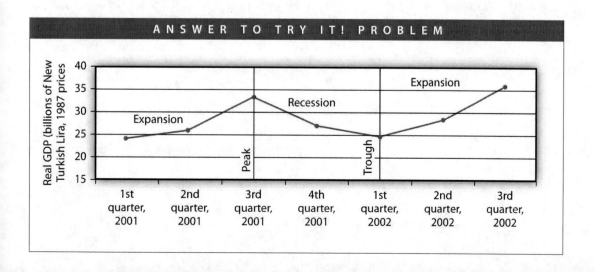

2. PRICE-LEVEL CHANGES

Concern about changes in the price level has always dominated economic discussion. With inflation in the United States generally averaging only between 2% and 3% each year since 1990, it may seem surprising how much attention the behavior of the price level still commands. Yet inflation was a concern in 2004 when there was fear that the rising price of oil could trigger higher prices in other areas. Just the year before, when inflation fell below 2%, there was talk about the risk of deflation. That did not happen; prices continued rising. Inflation rose substantially in the first half of 2008, renewing fears about subsequent further increases. 2010 brought on renewed concern of possible deflation. Just what are inflation and deflation? How are they measured? And most important, why do we care? These are some of the questions we will explore in this section.

Inflation is an increase in the average level of prices, and **deflation** is a decrease in the average level of prices. In an economy experiencing inflation, most prices are likely to be rising, whereas in an economy experiencing deflation, most prices are likely to be falling.

There are two key points in these definitions:

1. Inflation and deflation refer to changes in the average level of prices, not to changes in particular prices. An increase in medical costs is not inflation. A decrease in gasoline prices is not deflation. Inflation means the average level of prices is rising, and deflation means the average level of prices is falling.

2. Inflation and deflation refer to *rising* prices and *falling* prices, respectively; therefore, they do not have anything to do with the *level* of prices at any one time. "High" prices do not imply the presence of inflation, nor do "low" prices imply deflation. Inflation means a positive *rate of change* in average prices, and deflation means a negative *rate of change* in average prices.

inflation

An increase in the average level of prices.

deflation

A decrease in the average level of prices.

2.1 Why Do We Care?

What difference does it make if the average level of prices changes? First, consider the impact of inflation.

Inflation is measured as the annual rate of increase in the average level of prices. Figure 5.6 shows how volatile inflation has been in the United States over the past four decades. In the 1960s the inflation rate rose, and it became dramatically worse in the 1970s. The inflation rate plunged in the 1980s and continued to ease downward in the 1990s. It remained low in the early 2000s and began to accelerate in 2007 and has remained low since.

FIGURE 5.6 Inflation, 1960–2010

The U.S. inflation rate, measured as the annual rate of change in the average level of prices paid by consumers, varied considerably over the 1960–2010 period.

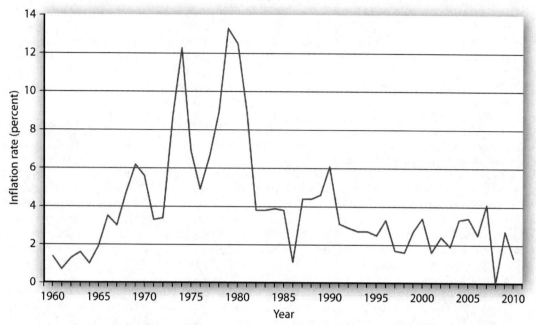

Source: Bureau of Labor Statistics, All Urban Consumers CPI-U, 1982–84 = 100, Dec.–Dec. inflation rate. Data for 2010 is through October.

Whether one regards inflation as a "good" thing or a "bad" thing depends very much on one's economic situation. If you are a borrower, unexpected inflation is a good thing—it reduces the value of money that you must repay. If you are a lender, it is a bad thing because it reduces the value of future payments you will receive. Whatever any particular person's situation may be, inflation always produces the following effects on the economy: it reduces the value of money and it reduces the value of future monetary obligations. It can also create uncertainty about the future.

Suppose that you have just found a $10 bill you stashed away in 1990. Prices have increased by about 50% since then; your money will buy less than what it would have purchased when you put it away. Your money has thus lost value.

Money loses value when its purchasing power falls. Since inflation is a rise in the level of prices, the amount of goods and services a given amount of money can buy falls with inflation.

Just as inflation reduces the value of money, it reduces the value of future claims on money. Suppose you have borrowed $100 from a friend and have agreed to pay it back in one year. During the year, however, prices double. That means that when you pay the money back, it will buy only half as much as it could have bought when you borrowed it. That is good for you but tough on the person who lent you the money. Of course, if you and your friend had anticipated such rapid inflation, you might have agreed to pay back a larger sum to adjust for it. When people anticipate inflation, they can adjust for its consequences in determining future obligations. But *unanticipated* inflation helps borrowers and hurts lenders.

Inflation's impact on future claims can be particularly hard on people who must live on a fixed income, that is, on an income that is predetermined through some contractual arrangement and does not change with economic conditions. An annuity, for example, typically provides a fixed stream of money payments. Retirement pensions sometimes generate fixed income. Inflation erodes the value of such payments.

Given the danger posed by inflation for people on fixed incomes, many retirement plans provide for indexed payments. An indexed payment is one whose dollar amount changes with the rate of change in the price level. If a payment changes at the same rate as the rate of change in the price level, the purchasing power of the payment remains constant. Social Security payments, for example, are indexed to maintain their purchasing power.

Because inflation reduces the purchasing power of money, the threat of future inflation can make people reluctant to lend for long periods. From a lender's point of view, the danger of a long-term commitment of funds is that future inflation will wipe out the value of the amount that will eventually be paid back. Lenders are reluctant to make such commitments.

hyperinflation

An inflation rate in excess of 200% per year.

Uncertainty can be particularly pronounced in countries where extremely high inflation is a threat. **Hyperinflation** is generally defined as an inflation rate in excess of 200% per year. Inflation of that magnitude erodes the value of money very quickly. Hyperinflations occurred in Germany in the 1920s and in Yugoslavia in the early 1990s. There are stories about how people in Germany during the hyperinflation brought wheelbarrows full of money to stores to pay for ordinary items. In Yugoslavia in 1993 there was a report of a shop owner barring the entrance to his store with a mop while he changed his prices.

The inflation rate rose to an astronomical rate in 2008 in Zimbabwe. As the government printed more money and put it in circulation, prices rose. When inflation began to accelerate, the government found it "necessary" to print more and more money, causing prices to rise very fast. The inflation rate in Zimbabwe reached an astonishing 11.2 million percent in July of 2008, according to Zimbabwe's Central Statistics Office. A loaf of bread cost 200,000 Zimbabwe dollars in February 2008. That same loaf cost 1.6 trillion Zimbabwe dollars by August.[7]

Do the problems associated with inflation imply that deflation would be a good thing? The answer is simple: no. Like inflation, deflation changes the value of money and the value of future obligations. It also creates uncertainty about the future.

If there is deflation, the real value of a given amount of money rises. In other words, if there had been deflation since 2000, a $10 bill you had stashed away in 2000 would buy more goods and services today. That sounds good, but should you buy $10 worth of goods and services now when you would be able to buy even more for your $10 in the future if the deflation continues? When Japan experienced deflation in the late 1990s and early 2000s, Japanese consumers seemed to be doing just that—waiting to see if prices would fall further. They were spending less per person and, as we will see throughout our study of macroeconomics, less consumption often meant less output, fewer jobs, and the prospect of a recurring recessions.

And, if you had to use the $10 to pay back a debt you owed, the purchasing power of your money would be higher than when you borrowed the money. The lender would feel good about being able to buy more with the $10 than you were able to, but you would feel like you had gotten a raw deal.

Unanticipated deflation hurts borrowers and helps lenders. If the parties anticipate the deflation, a loan agreement can be written to reflect expected changes in the price level.

The threat of deflation can make people reluctant to borrow for long periods. Borrowers become reluctant to enter into long-term contracts because they fear that deflation will raise the value of the money they must pay back in the future. In such an environment, firms may be reluctant to borrow to build new factories, for example. This is because they fear that the prices at which they can sell their output will drop, making it difficult for them to repay their loans.

Deflation was common in the United States in the latter third of the 19th century. In the 20th century, there was a period of deflation after World War I and again during the Great Depression in the 1930s.

2.2 Price Indexes

How do we actually measure inflation and deflation (that is, changes in the price level)? Price-level change is measured as the percentage rate of change in the level of prices. But how do we find a price level?

Economists measure the price level with a price index. A **price index** is a number whose movement reflects movement in the average level of prices. If a price index rises 10%, it means the average level of prices has risen 10%.

price index

A number whose movement reflects movement in the average level of prices.

base period

A time period against which costs of the market basket in other periods will be compared in computing a price index.

There are four steps one must take in computing a price index:

1. Select the kinds and quantities of goods and services to be included in the index. A list of these goods and services, and the quantities of each, is the "market basket" for the index.

2. Determine what it would cost to buy the goods and services in the market basket in some period that is the base period for the index. A **base period** is a time period against which costs of the market basket in other periods will be compared in computing a price index. Most often, the base period for an index is a single year. If, for example, a price index had a base period of 1990, costs of the basket in other periods would be compared to the cost of the basket in 1990. We will encounter one index, however, whose base period stretches over three years.

3. Compute the cost of the market basket in the current period.

4. Compute the price index. It equals the current cost divided by the base-period cost of the market basket.

EQUATION 5.1

Price index = current cost of basket / base-period cost of basket

(While published price indexes are typically reported with this number multiplied by 100, our work with indexes will be simplified by omitting this step.)

Suppose that we want to compute a price index for movie fans, and a survey of movie watchers tells us that a typical fan rents 4 movies on DVD and sees 3 movies in theaters each month. At the theater, this viewer consumes a medium-sized soft drink and a medium-sized box of popcorn. Our market basket thus might include 4 DVD rentals, 3 movie admissions, 3 medium soft drinks, and 3 medium servings of popcorn.

Our next step in computing the movie price index is to determine the cost of the market basket. Suppose we surveyed movie theaters and DVD-rental stores in 2007 to determine the average prices of these items, finding the values given in Table 5.1. At those prices, the total monthly cost of our movie market basket in 2007 was $48. Now suppose that in 2008 the prices of movie admissions and DVD rentals rise, soft-drink prices at movies fall, and popcorn prices remain unchanged. The combined effect of these changes pushes the 2008 cost of the basket to $50.88.

TABLE 5.1 Pricing a Market Basket

To compute a price index, we need to define a market basket and determine its price. The table gives the composition of the movie market basket and prices for 2007 and 2008. The cost of the entire basket rises from $48 in 2007 to $50.88 in 2008.

Item	Quantity in Basket	2007 Price	Cost in 2007 Basket	2008 Price	Cost in 2008 Basket
DVD rental	4	$2.25	$9.00	$2.97	$11.88
Movie admission	3	7.75	23.25	8.00	24.00
Popcorn	3	2.25	6.75	2.25	6.75
Soft drink	3	3.00	9.00	2.75	8.25
Total cost of basket		**2007**	$48.00	**2008**	$50.88

Using the data in Table 5.1, we could compute price indexes for each year. Recall that a price index is the ratio of the current cost of the basket to the base-period cost. We can select any year we wish as the base year; take 2007. The 2008 movie price index (MPI) is thus

$$\text{MPI}_{2008} = \$50.88 / \$48 = 1.06$$

The value of any price index in the base period is always 1. In the case of our movie price index, the 2007 index would be the current (2007) cost of the basket, $48, divided by the base-period cost, which is the same thing: $48/$48 = 1.

The Consumer Price Index (CPI)

One widely used price index in the United States is the **consumer price index (CPI)**, a price index whose movement reflects changes in the prices of goods and services typically purchased by consumers. When the media report the U.S. inflation rate, the number cited is usually a rate computed using the CPI. The CPI is also used to determine whether people's incomes are keeping up with the costs of the things they buy. The CPI is often used to measure changes in the cost of living, though as we shall see, there are problems in using it for this purpose.

The market basket for the CPI contains thousands of goods and services. The composition of the basket is determined by the Bureau of Labor Statistics (BLS), an agency of the Department of Labor, based on Census Bureau surveys of household buying behavior. Surveyors tally the prices of the goods and services in the basket each month in cities all over the United States to determine the current cost of the basket. The major categories of items in the CPI are food and beverages, housing, apparel, transportation, medical care, recreation, education and communication, and other goods and services.

The current cost of the basket of consumer goods and services is then compared to the base-period cost of that same basket. The base period for the CPI is 1982–1984; the base-period cost of the basket is its average cost over this period. Each month's CPI thus reflects the ratio of the current cost of the basket divided by its base-period cost.

consumer price index (CPI)

A price index whose movement reflects changes in the prices of goods and services typically purchased by consumers.

EQUATION 5.2

$$\text{CPI} = \text{current cost of basket} / 1982\text{–}1984 \text{ cost of basket}$$

Like many other price indexes, the CPI is computed with a fixed market basket. The composition of the basket generally remains unchanged from one period to the next. Because buying patterns change, however, the basket is revised accordingly. The data in Table 5.1, for example, are based on 2005–2006 expenditure weights. The base period, though, was still 1982–1984.

The Implicit Price Deflator

implicit price deflator

A price index for all final goods and services produced; it is the ratio of nominal GDP to real GDP.

Values for nominal and real GDP, described earlier in this chapter, provide us with the information to calculate the most broad-based price index available. The **implicit price deflator**, a price index for all final goods and services produced, is the ratio of nominal GDP to real GDP.

In computing the implicit price deflator for a particular period, economists define the market basket quite simply: it includes all the final goods and services produced during that period. The nominal GDP gives the current cost of that basket; the real GDP adjusts the nominal GDP for changes in prices. The implicit price deflator is thus given by

EQUATION 5.3

$$\text{Implicit price deflator} = \text{nominal GDP} / \text{real GDP}$$

For example, in 2007, nominal GDP in the United States was $13,807.5 billion, and real GDP was $11,523.9 billion. Thus, the implicit price deflator was 1.198. Following the convention of multiplying price indexes by 100, the published number for the implicit price deflator was 119.8.

In our analysis of the determination of output and the price level in subsequent chapters, we will use the implicit price deflator as the measure of the price level in the economy.

The PCE Price Index

personal consumption expenditures price index

A price index that includes durable goods, nondurable goods, and services and is provided along with estimates for prices of each component of consumption spending.

The Bureau of Economic Analysis also produces price index information for each of the components of GDP (that is, a separate price index for consumer prices, prices for different components of gross private domestic investment, and government spending). The **personal consumption expenditures price index**, or PCE price index, includes durable goods, nondurable goods, and services and is provided along with estimates for prices of each component of consumption spending. Because prices for food and energy can be volatile, the price measure that excludes food and energy is often used as a measure of underlying, or "core," inflation. Note that the PCE price index differs substantially from the consumer price index, primarily because it is not a "fixed basket" index.[8] The PCE price index has become a politically important measure of inflation since the Federal Reserve (discussed in detail in later chapters) uses it as its primary measure of price levels in the United States.

2.3 Computing the Rate of Inflation or Deflation

The rate of inflation or deflation is the percentage rate of change in a price index between two periods. Given price-index values for two periods, we can calculate the rate of inflation or deflation as the change in the index divided by the initial value of the index, stated as a percentage:

EQUATION 5.4

$$\text{Rate of inflation or deflation} = \text{percentage change in index} / \text{initial value of index}$$

To calculate inflation in movie prices over the 2007–2008 period, for example, we could apply Equation 5.4 to the price indexes we computed for those two years as follows:

$$\text{Movie inflation rate in 2008} = (1.06 - 1.00) / 1.00 = 0.06 = 6\%$$

The CPI is often used for calculating price-level change for the economy. For example, the rate of inflation in 2007 can be computed from the December 2006 price level (2.016) and the December 2007 level (2.073):

$$\text{Inflation rate} = (2.073 - 2.016) / 2.016 = 0.028 = 2.8\%$$

2.4 Computing Real Values Using Price Indexes

Suppose your uncle started college in 1998 and had a job busing dishes that paid $5 per hour. In 2008 you had the same job; it paid $6 per hour. Which job paid more?

At first glance, the answer is straightforward: $6 is a higher wage than $5. But $1 had greater purchasing power in 1998 than in 2008 because prices were lower in 1998 than in 2008. To obtain a valid comparison of the two wages, we must use dollars of equivalent purchasing power. A value expressed in units of constant purchasing power is a **real value**. A value expressed in dollars of the current period is called a **nominal value**. The $5 wage in 1998 and the $6 wage in 2008 are nominal wages.

To convert nominal values to real values, we divide by a price index. The real value for a given period is the nominal value for that period divided by the price index for that period. This procedure gives us a value in dollars that have the purchasing power of the base period for the price index used. Using the CPI, for example, yields values expressed in dollars of 1982–1984 purchasing power, the base period for the CPI. The real value of a nominal amount X at time t, X_t, is found using the price index for time t:

EQUATION 5.5

$$\text{Real value of } X_t = X_t / \text{price index at time } t$$

Let us compute the real value of the $6 wage for busing dishes in 2008 versus the $5 wage paid to your uncle in 1998. The CPI in 1998 was 163.0; in 2008 it was 216.5. Real wages for the two years were thus

$$\text{Real wage in 1998} = \$5 / 1.630 = \$3.07$$

$$\text{Real wage in 2008} = \$6 / 2.165 = \$2.77$$

Given the nominal wages in our example, you earned about 10% less in real terms in 2008 than your uncle did in 1998.

Price indexes are useful. They allow us to see how the general level of prices has changed. They allow us to estimate the rate of change in prices, which we report as the rate of inflation or deflation. And they give us a tool for converting nominal values to real values so we can make better comparisons of economic performance across time.

Are Price Indexes Accurate Measures of Price-Level Changes?

Price indexes that employ fixed market baskets are likely to overstate inflation (and understate deflation) for four reasons:

1. Because the components of the market basket are fixed, the index does not incorporate consumer responses to changing relative prices.
2. A fixed basket excludes new goods and services.
3. Quality changes may not be completely accounted for in computing price-level changes.
4. The type of store in which consumers choose to shop can affect the prices they pay, and the price indexes do not reflect changes consumers have made in where they shop.

To see how these factors can lead to inaccurate measures of price-level changes, suppose the price of chicken rises and the price of beef falls. The law of demand tells us that people will respond by consuming less chicken and more beef. But if we use a fixed market basket of goods and services in computing a price index, we will not be able to make these adjustments. The market basket holds constant the quantities of chicken and beef consumed. The importance in consumer budgets of the higher chicken price is thus overstated, while the importance of the lower beef price is understated. More generally, a fixed market basket will overstate the importance of items that rise in price and understate the importance of items that fall in price. This source of bias is referred to as the substitution bias.

The new-product bias, a second source of bias in price indexes, occurs because it takes time for new products to be incorporated into the market basket that makes up the CPI. A good introduced to the market after the basket has been defined will not, of course, be included in it. But a new good, once successfully introduced, is likely to fall in price. When VCRs were first introduced, for example, they generally cost more than $1,000. Within a few years, an equivalent machine cost less than $200. But when VCRs were introduced, the CPI was based on a market basket that had been defined in the early 1970s. There was no VCR in the basket, so the impact of this falling price was not reflected in the index. The DVD player was introduced into the CPI within a year of its availability.

A third price index bias, the quality-change bias, comes from improvements in the quality of goods and services. Suppose, for example, that Ford introduces a new car with better safety features and a smoother ride than its previous model. Suppose the old model cost $20,000 and the new model costs $24,000, a 20% increase in price. Should economists at the Bureau of Labor Statistics (BLS) simply record the new model as being 20% more expensive than the old one? Clearly, the new model is not the same product as the old model. BLS economists faced with such changes try to adjust for quality. To

---

real value

A value expressed in units of constant purchasing power.

nominal value

A value expressed in dollars of the current period.

the extent that such adjustments understate quality change, they overstate any increase in the price level.

The fourth source of bias is called the outlet bias. Households can reduce some of the impact of rising prices by shopping at superstores or outlet stores (such as T.J. Maxx, Wal-Mart, or factory outlet stores), though this often means they get less customer service than at traditional department stores or at smaller retail stores. However, since such shopping has increased in recent years, it must be that for their customers, the reduction in prices has been more valuable to them than loss of service. Prior to 1998, the CPI did not account for a change in the number of households shopping at these newer kinds of stores in a timely manner, but the BLS now does quarterly surveys and updates its sample of stores much more frequently. Another form of this bias arises because the government data collectors do not collect price data on weekends and holidays, when many stores run sales.

Economists differ on the degree to which these biases result in inaccuracies in recording price-level changes. In late 1996, Michael Boskin, an economist at Stanford University, chaired a panel of economists appointed by the Senate Finance Committee to determine the magnitude of the problem in the United States. The panel reported that the CPI was overstating inflation in the United States by 0.8 to 1.6 percentage points per year. Their best estimate was 1.1 percentage points, as shown in Table 5.2. Since then, the Bureau of Labor Statistics has made a number of changes to correct for these sources of bias and since August 2002 has reported a new consumer price index called the Chained Consumer Price Index for all Urban Consumers (C-CPU-U) that attempts to provide a closer approximation to a "cost-of-living" index by utilizing expenditure data that reflect the substitutions that consumers make across item categories in response to changes in relative prices.[9] However, a 2006 study by Robert Gordon, a professor at Northwestern University and a member of the original 1996 Boskin Commission, estimates that the total bias is still about 0.8 percentage points per year, as also shown in Table 5.2.

TABLE 5.2 Estimates of Bias in the Consumer Price Index

The Boskin Commission reported that the CPI overstates the rate of inflation by 0.8 to 1.6 percentage points due to the biases shown, with a best-guess estimate of 1.1. A 2006 study by Robert Gordon estimates that the bias fell but is still about 0.8 percentage points.

Sources of Bias	1997 Estimate	2006 Estimate
Substitution	0.4	0.4
New products and quality change	0.6	0.3
Switching to new outlets	0.1	0.1
Total	1.1	0.8
Plausible range	0.8–1.6	—

Source: Robert J. Gordon, "The Boskin Commission Report: A Retrospective One Decade Later" (National Bureau of Economic Research Working Paper 12311, June 2006), available at http://www.nber.org/papers/w12311.

These findings of upward bias have enormous practical significance. With annual inflation running below 2% in three out of the last 10 years and averaging 2.7% over the 10 years, it means that the United States has come close to achieving price stability for almost a decade.

To the extent that the computation of price indexes overstates the rate of inflation, then the use of price indexes to correct nominal values results in an understatement of gains in real incomes. For example, average nominal hourly earnings of U.S. production workers were $13.01 in 1998 and $17.42 in 2007. Adjusting for CPI-measured inflation, the average real hourly earnings was $7.98 in 1998 and $8.40 in 2007, suggesting that real wages rose about 5.3% over the period. If inflation was overstated by 0.8% per year over that entire period, as suggested by Gordon's updating of the Boskin Commission's best estimate, then, adjusting for this overstatement, real wages should have been reported as $7.98 for 1998 and $9.01 for 2007, a gain of nearly 13%.

Also, because the CPI is used as the basis for calculating U.S. government payments for programs such as Social Security and for adjusting tax brackets, this price index affects the government's budget balance, the difference between government revenues and government expenditures. The Congressional Budget Office has estimated that correcting the biases in the index would have increased revenue by $2 billion and reduced outlays by $4 billion in 1997. By 2007, the U.S. government's budget would have had an additional $140 billion if the bias were removed.

KEY TAKEAWAYS

- Inflation is an increase in the average level of prices, and deflation is a decrease in the average level of prices. The rate of inflation or deflation is the percentage rate of change in a price index.
- The consumer price index (CPI) is the most widely used price index in the United States.
- Nominal values can be converted to real values by dividing by a price index.
- Inflation and deflation affect the real value of money, of future obligations measured in money, and of fixed incomes. Unanticipated inflation and deflation create uncertainty about the future.
- Economists generally agree that the CPI and other price indexes that employ fixed market baskets of goods and services do not accurately measure price-level changes. Biases include the substitution bias, the new-product bias, the quality-change bias, and the outlet bias.

TRY IT!

Suppose that nominal GDP is $10 trillion in 2003 and $11 trillion in 2004, and that the implicit price deflator has gone from 1.063 in 2003 to 1.091 in 2004. Compute real GDP in 2003 and 2004. Using the percentage change in the implicit price deflator as the gauge, what was the inflation rate over the period?

Case in Point: Take Me Out to the Ball Game …

The cost of a trip to the old ball game jumped 7.9% in 2008, according to *Team Marketing Report*, a Chicago-based newsletter. The report bases its estimate on its fan price index, whose market basket includes two adult average-priced tickets, two child average-priced tickets, two small draft beers, four small soft drinks, four regular-sized hot dogs, parking for one car, two game programs, and two least expensive, adult-sized adjustable baseball caps. The average price of the market basket was $191.92 in 2008.

Team Marketing compiles the cost of the basket for each of major league baseball's 30 teams. According to this compilation, the Boston Red Sox was the most expensive team to watch in 2008; the Tampa Bay Rays was the cheapest. The Rays made it to the World Series in 2008; the Red Sox did not. By that measure, the Rays were something of a bargain. The table shows the cost of the fan price index market basket for 2008.

Team	Basket Cost	Team	Basket Cost
Boston Red Sox	$320.71	San Francisco Giants	$183.74
New York Yankees	$275.10	Cincinnati Reds	$167.14
Chicago Cubs	$251.96	Minnesota Twins	$165.71
New York Mets	$251.19	Baltimore Orioles	$165.40
Toronto Blue Jays	$230.46	Florida Marlins	$164.26
Los Angeles Dodgers	$229.14	AZ Diamondbacks	$162.84
St. Louis Cardinals	$217.28	Colorado Rockies	$160.00
Houston Astros	$215.45	Atlanta Braves	$157.15
Chicago White Sox	$214.51	Kansas City Royals	$151.16
Oakland Athletics	$206.80	Texas Rangers	$148.04
San Diego Padres	$201.72	Pittsburgh Pirates	$146.32
Philadelphia Phillies	$199.56	Milwaukee Brewers	$141.52
Washington Nationals	$195.50	Los Angeles Angels	$140.42
Cleveland Indians	$192.38	Tampa Bay Rays	$136.31
Seattle Mariners	$191.16	**MLB Average**	**$191.92**
Detroit Tigers	$190.13		

Sources: Team Marketing Report, TMR's Fan Cost Index Major League Baseball 2008 at http://www.teammarketing.com and personal interview.

ANSWER TO TRY IT! PROBLEM

Rearranging Equation 5.3, real GDP = nominal GDP/implicit price deflator. Therefore,

Real GDP in 2003 = $10 trillion/1.063 = $9.4 trillion.

Real GDP in 2004 = $11 trillion/1.091 = $10.1 trillion.

Thus, in this economy in real terms, GDP has grown by $0.7 trillion.

To find the rate of inflation, we refer to Equation 5.4, and we calculate:

Inflation rate in 2004 = (1.091 − 1.063)/1.063 = 0.026 = 2.6%

Thus, the price level rose 2.6% between 2003 and 2004.

3. UNEMPLOYMENT

LEARNING OBJECTIVES

1. Explain how unemployment is measured in the United States.
2. Define three different types of unemployment.
3. Define and illustrate graphically what is meant by the natural level of employment. Relate the natural level of employment to the natural rate of unemployment.

For an economy to produce all it can and achieve a solution on its production possibilities curve, the factors of production in the economy must be fully employed. Failure to fully employ these factors leads to a solution inside the production possibilities curve in which society is not achieving the output it is capable of producing.

In thinking about the employment of society's factors of production, we place special emphasis on labor. The loss of a job can wipe out a household's entire income; it is a more compelling human problem than, say, unemployed capital, such as a vacant apartment. In measuring unemployment, we thus focus on labor rather than on capital and natural resources.

3.1 Measuring Unemployment

The Bureau of Labor Statistics defines a person as unemployed if he or she is not working but is looking for and available for work. The **labor force** is the total number of people working or unemployed. The **unemployment rate** is the percentage of the labor force that is unemployed.

To estimate the unemployment rate, government surveyors fan out across the country each month to visit roughly 60,000 households. At each of these randomly selected households, the surveyor asks about the employment status of each adult (everyone age 16 or over) who lives there. Many households include more than one adult; the survey gathers information on about roughly 100,000 adults. The surveyor asks if each adult is working. If the answer is yes, the person is counted as employed. If the answer is no, the surveyor asks if that person has looked for work at some time during the previous four weeks and is available for work at the time of the survey. If the answer to that question is yes, the person is counted as unemployed. If the answer is no, that person is not counted as a member of the labor force. Figure 5.8 shows the survey's results for the civilian (nonmilitary) population for November 2010. The unemployment rate is then computed as the number of people unemployed divided by the labor force—the sum of the number of people not working but available and looking for work plus the number of people working. In November 2010, the unemployment rate was 9.8%.

labor force

The total number of people working or unemployed.

unemployment rate

The percentage of the labor force that is unemployed.

FIGURE 5.8 Computing the Unemployment Rate

A monthly survey of households divides the civilian adult population into three groups. Those who have jobs are counted as employed; those who do not have jobs but are looking for them and are available for work are counted as unemployed; and those who are not working and are not looking for work are not counted as members of the labor force. The unemployment rate equals the number of people looking for work divided by the sum of the number of people looking for work and the number of people employed. Values are for November 2010. All numbers are in thousands.

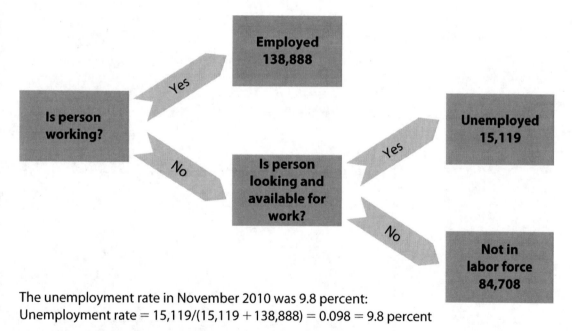

The unemployment rate in November 2010 was 9.8 percent:
Unemployment rate = 15,119/(15,119 + 138,888) = 0.098 = 9.8 percent

There are several difficulties with the survey. The old survey, designed during the 1930s, put the "Are you working?" question differently depending on whether the respondent was a man or woman. A man was asked, "Last week, did you do any work for pay or profit?" A woman was asked, "What were you doing for work last week, keeping house or something else?" Consequently, many women who were looking for paid work stated that they were "keeping house"; those women were not counted as unemployed. The BLS did not get around to fixing the survey—asking women the same question it asked men—until 1994. The first time the new survey question was used, the unemployment rate among women rose by 0.5 percentage point. More than 50 million women are in the labor force; the change added more than a quarter of a million workers to the official count of the unemployed.[10]

The problem of understating unemployment among women has been fixed, but others remain. A worker who has been cut back to part-time work still counts as employed, even if that worker would prefer to work full time. A person who is out of work, would like to work, has looked for work in the past year, and is available for work, but who has given up looking, is considered a discouraged worker. Discouraged workers are not counted as unemployed, but a tally is kept each month of the number of discouraged workers.

The official measures of employment and unemployment can yield unexpected results. For example, when firms expand output, they may be reluctant to hire additional workers until they can be sure the demand for increased output will be sustained. They may respond first by extending the hours of employees previously reduced to part-time work or by asking full-time personnel to work overtime. None of that will increase employment, because people are simply counted as "employed" if they are working, regardless of how much or how little they are working. In addition, an economic expansion may make discouraged workers more optimistic about job prospects, and they may resume their job searches. Engaging in a search makes them unemployed again—and increases unemployment. Thus, an economic expansion may have little effect initially on employment and may even increase unemployment.

3.2   Types of Unemployment

natural level of employment

The employment level at which the quantity of labor demanded equals the quantity supplied.

Workers may find themselves unemployed for different reasons. Each source of unemployment has quite different implications, not only for the workers it affects but also for public policy.

Figure 5.9 applies the demand and supply model to the labor market. The price of labor is taken as the real wage, which is the nominal wage divided by the price level; the symbol used to represent the real wage is the Greek letter omega, ω. The supply curve is drawn as upward sloping, though steep, to reflect studies showing that the quantity of labor supplied at any one time is nearly fixed. Thus, an increase in the real wage induces a relatively small increase in the quantity of labor supplied. The demand curve shows the quantity of labor demanded at each real wage. The lower the real wage, the greater the quantity of labor firms will demand. In the case shown here, the real wage, ω_e, equals the equilibrium solution defined by the intersection of the demand curve D_1 and the supply curve S_1. The quantity of labor demanded, L_e, equals the quantity supplied. The employment level at which the quantity of labor demanded equals the quantity supplied is called the **natural level of employment**. It is sometimes referred to as full employment.

FIGURE 5.9   The Natural Level of Employment

The employment level at which the quantity of labor demanded equals the quantity supplied is called the natural level of employment. Here, the natural level of employment is L_e, which is achieved at a real wage ω_e.

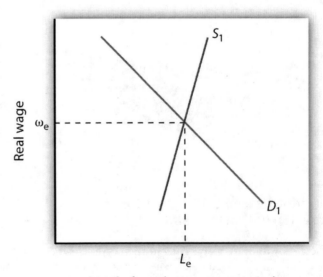

natural rate of unemployment

The rate of unemployment consistent with the natural level of employment.

Even if the economy is operating at its natural level of employment, there will still be some unemployment. The rate of unemployment consistent with the natural level of employment is called the **natural rate of unemployment**. Business cycles may generate additional unemployment. We discuss these various sources of unemployment below.

Frictional Unemployment

Even when the quantity of labor demanded equals the quantity of labor supplied, not all employers and potential workers have found each other. Some workers are looking for jobs, and some employers are looking for workers. During the time it takes to match them up, the workers are unemployed. Unemployment that occurs because it takes time for employers and workers to find each other is called **frictional unemployment**.

The case of college graduates engaged in job searches is a good example of frictional unemployment. Those who did not land a job while still in school will seek work. Most of them will find jobs, but it will take time. During that time, these new graduates will be unemployed. If information about the labor market were costless, firms and potential workers would instantly know everything they needed to know about each other and there would be no need for searches on the part of workers and firms. There would be no frictional unemployment. But information is costly. Job searches are needed to produce this information, and frictional unemployment exists while the searches continue.

The government may attempt to reduce frictional unemployment by focusing on its source: information costs. Many state agencies, for example, serve as clearinghouses for job market information. They encourage firms seeking workers and workers seeking jobs to register with them. To the extent that such efforts make labor-market information more readily available, they reduce frictional unemployment.

Structural Unemployment

Another reason there can be unemployment even if employment equals its natural level stems from potential mismatches between the skills employers seek and the skills potential workers offer. Every worker is different; every job has its special characteristics and requirements. The qualifications of job seekers may not match those that firms require. Even if the number of employees firms demand equals the number of workers available, people whose qualifications do not satisfy what firms are seeking will find themselves without work. Unemployment that results from a mismatch between worker qualifications and the characteristics employers require is called **structural unemployment**.

Structural unemployment emerges for several reasons. Technological change may make some skills obsolete or require new ones. The widespread introduction of personal computers since the 1980s, for example, has lowered demand for typists who lacked computer skills.

Structural unemployment can occur if too many or too few workers seek training or education that matches job requirements. Students cannot predict precisely how many jobs there will be in a particular category when they graduate, and they are not likely to know how many of their fellow students are training for these jobs. Structural unemployment can easily occur if students guess wrong about how many workers will be needed or how many will be supplied.

Structural unemployment can also result from geographical mismatches. Economic activity may be booming in one region and slumping in another. It will take time for unemployed workers to relocate and find new jobs. And poor or costly transportation may block some urban residents from obtaining jobs only a few miles away.

Public policy responses to structural unemployment generally focus on job training and education to equip workers with the skills firms demand. The government publishes regional labor-market information, helping to inform unemployed workers of where jobs can be found. The North American Free Trade Agreement (NAFTA), which created a free trade region encompassing Mexico, the United States, and Canada, has created some structural unemployment in the three countries. In the United States, the legislation authorizing the pact also provided for job training programs for displaced U.S. workers.

Although government programs may reduce frictional and structural unemployment, they cannot eliminate it. Information in the labor market will always have a cost, and that cost creates frictional unemployment. An economy with changing demands for goods and services, changing technology, and changing production costs will always have some sectors expanding and others contracting—structural unemployment is inevitable. An economy at its natural level of employment will therefore have frictional and structural unemployment.

Cyclical Unemployment

Of course, the economy may not be operating at its natural level of employment, so unemployment may be above or below its natural level. In a later chapter we will explore what happens when the economy generates employment greater or less than the natural level. **Cyclical unemployment** is unemployment in excess of the unemployment that exists at the natural level of employment.

Figure 5.10 shows the unemployment rate in the United States for the period from 1960 through November 2010. We see that it has fluctuated considerably. How much of it corresponds to the natural rate of unemployment varies over time with changing circumstances. For example, in a country with a demographic "bulge" of new entrants into the labor force, frictional unemployment is likely to be high,

frictional unemployment
Unemployment that occurs because it takes time for employers and workers to find each other.

structural unemployment
Unemployment that results from a mismatch between worker qualifications and the characteristics employers require.

cyclical unemployment
Unemployment in excess of the unemployment that exists at the natural level of employment.

because it takes the new entrants some time to find their first jobs. This factor alone would raise the natural rate of unemployment. A demographic shift toward more mature workers would lower the natural rate. During recessions, highlighted in Figure 5.10, the part of unemployment that is cyclical unemployment grows. The analysis of fluctuations in the unemployment rate, and the government's responses to them, will occupy center stage in much of the remainder of this book.

FIGURE 5.10 Unemployment Rate, 1960–2010

The chart shows the unemployment rate for each year from 1960 to 2010. Recessions are shown as shaded areas.

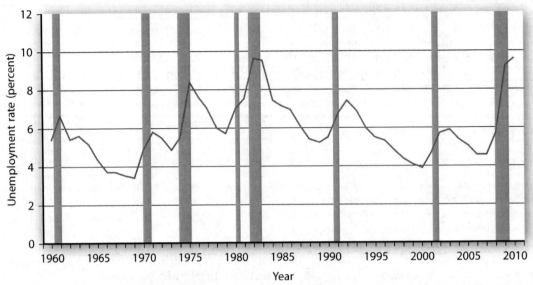

Source: Economic Report of the President, 2010, Table B-42. Data for 2010 is average of first eleven months from the Bureau of Labor Statistics home page.

KEY TAKEAWAYS

- People who are not working but are looking and available for work at any one time are considered unemployed. The unemployment rate is the percentage of the labor force that is unemployed.
- When the labor market is in equilibrium, employment is at the natural level and the unemployment rate equals the natural rate of unemployment.
- Even if employment is at the natural level, the economy will experience frictional and structural unemployment. Cyclical unemployment is unemployment in excess of that associated with the natural level of employment.

TRY IT!

Given the data in the table, compute the unemployment rate in Year 1 and in Year 2. Explain why, in this example, both the number of people employed and the unemployment rate increased.

Year	Number employed (in millions)	Number unemployed (in millions)
1	20	2
2	21	2.4

Case in Point: Might Increased Structural Unemployment Explain the "Jobless Recovery" Following the 2001 Recession?

The U.S. 2001 recession was mild by historical standards, but recovery in terms of increased employment seemed painfully slow in coming. Economists Erica Goshen and Simon Potter at the Federal Reserve Bank of New York think the reason for the slow recovery in jobs may have actually reflected structural changes in the U.S. economy. They argue that during the recession permanent rather than temporary layoffs predominated and that it takes longer for firms to hire workers into new positions than to hire them back into former jobs.

What is their evidence? When the layoff is temporary, the employer "suspends" the job, due to slack demand, and the employee expects to be recalled once demand picks up. With a permanent layoff, the employer eliminates the job. So, they looked at the contribution of temporary layoffs to the unemployment rate during the recent recession compared to the situation in the four recessions before 1990. In the earlier recessions, unemployment from temporary layoffs rose when the economy was shrinking and fell after the economy began to recover. In both the 1991 and 2001 recessions, temporary layoffs were minor. Then, the authors examined job flows in 70 industries. They classified layoffs in an industry as being cyclical in nature if the job losses during the recession were reversed during the recovery but structural if job losses for the industry continued during the recovery. Their analysis revealed that during the recession of the early 1980s, job losses were about evenly split between cyclical and structural changes. In the 1991 recession and then more strongly in the 2001 recession, structural changes dominated. "Most of the industries that lost jobs during the [2001] recession—for example, communications, electronic equipment, and securities and commodities brokers—[were] still losing jobs" in 2003. "The trend revealed . . . is one in which jobs are relocated from some industries to others, not reclaimed by the same industries that lost them earlier."

The authors suggest three possible reasons for the recent increased role of structural change: (1) The structural decline in some industries could be the result of overexpansion in those industries during the 1990s. The high tech and telecommunications industries in particular could be examples of industries that were overbuilt before the 2001 recession. (2) Improved government policies may have reduced cyclical unemployment. Examination of macroeconomic policy in future chapters will return to this issue. (3) New management strategies to reduce costs may be promoting leaner staffing. For firms adopting such strategies, a recession may provide an opportunity to reorganize the production process permanently and reduce payrolls in the process.

Goshen and Potter point out that, for workers, finding new jobs is harder than simply returning to old ones. For firms, making decisions about the nature of new jobs is time consuming at best. The uncertainty created by the war in Iraq and the imposition of new accounting standards following the "Enron"-like scandals may have further prolonged the creation of new jobs.

Source: Erica L. Goshen and Simon Potter, "Has Structural Change Contributed to a Jobless Recovery?" Federal Reserve Bank of New York Current Issues in Economics and Finance 9, no. 8 (August 2003): 1–7.

4. REVIEW AND PRACTICE

Summary

In this chapter we examined growth in real GDP and business cycles, price-level changes, and unemployment. We saw how these phenomena are defined and looked at their consequences.

Examining real GDP, rather than nominal GDP, over time tells us whether the economy is expanding or contracting. Real GDP in the United States shows a long upward trend, but with the economy going through phases of expansion and recession around that trend. These phases make up the business cycle. An expansion reaches a peak, and the economy falls into a recession. The recession reaches a trough and begins an expansion again.

Inflation is an increase in the price level and deflation is a decrease in the price level. The rate of inflation or deflation is the percentage rate of change in a price index. We looked at the calculation of the consumer price index (CPI) and the implicit price deflator. The CPI is widely used in the calculation of price-level changes. There are, however, biases in its calculation: the substitution bias, the new-product bias, the quality-change bias, and the outlet bias.

Inflation and deflation affect economic activity in several ways. They change the value of money and of claims on money. Unexpected inflation benefits borrowers and hurts lenders. Unexpected deflation benefits lenders and hurts borrowers. Both inflation and deflation create uncertainty and make it difficult for individuals and firms to enter into long-term financial commitments.

The unemployment rate is measured as the percentage of the labor force not working but seeking work. Frictional unemployment occurs because information about the labor market is costly; it takes time for firms seeking workers and workers seeking firms to find each other. Structural unemployment occurs when there is a mismatch between the skills offered by potential workers and the skills sought by firms. Both frictional and structural unemployment occur even if employment and the unemployment rate are at their natural levels. Cyclical unemployment is unemployment that is in excess of that associated with the natural level of employment.

CONCEPT PROBLEMS

1. Describe the phases of a business cycle.

2. On the basis of recent news reports, what phase of the business cycle do you think the economy is in now? What is the inflation or deflation rate? The unemployment rate?

3. Suppose you compare your income this year and last year and find that your nominal income fell but your real income rose. How could this have happened?

4. Suppose you calculate a grocery price inflation rate. Using the arguments presented in the chapter, explain possible sources of upward bias in the rate you calculate, relative to the actual trend of food prices.

5. Name three items you have purchased during the past year that have increased in quality during the year. What kind of adjustment would you make in assessing their prices for the CPI?

6. Why do some people gain and other people lose from inflation and deflation?

7. Suppose unemployed people leave a state to obtain jobs in other states. What do you predict will happen to the unemployment rate in the state experiencing the out-migration? What might happen to the unemployment rates in the states experiencing in-migration?

8. Minority teenagers have the highest unemployment rates of any group. One reason for this phenomenon is high transportation costs for many minority teens. What form of unemployment (cyclical, frictional, or structural) do high transportation costs suggest?

9. Welfare reforms enacted in 1996 put more pressure on welfare recipients to look for work. The new law mandated cutting off benefits after a certain length of time. How do you think this provision might affect the unemployment rate?

10. American workers work more hours than their European counterparts. Should Congress legislate a shorter workweek?

NUMERICAL PROBLEMS

1. Plot the quarterly data for real GDP for the last two years. (You can find the data in the *Survey of Current Business* or in *Current Economic Indicators* in the current periodicals section of your library. Alternatively, go to the White House, Economic Statistics Briefing Room at http://www.whitehouse.gov/fsbr/esbr.html. Relate recent changes in real GDP to the concept of the phases of the business cycle.)

2. Suppose that in 2009, the items in the market basket for our movie price index cost $53.40. Use the information in the chapter to compute the price index for that year. How does the rate of movie price inflation from 2008 to 2009 compare with the rate from 2007 to 2008?

3. Recompute the movie price indexes for 2007 and 2008 using 2008 as the base year. Now compute the rate of inflation for the 2007–2008 period. Compare your result to the inflation rate calculated for that same period using 2007 as the base year.

4. Here are some statistics for August 2006. Compute the unemployment rate for that month (all figures are in thousands).

Population (Civilian, noninstitutional)	229,167
Civilian Labor Force	151,698
Participation Rate	66.2%
Not in Labor Force	77,469
Employed	144,579
Unemployed	7,119

5. Suppose an economy has 10,000 people who are not working but looking and available for work and 90,000 people who are working. What is its unemployment rate? Now suppose 4,000 of the people looking for work get discouraged and give up their searches. What happens to the unemployment rate? Would you interpret this as good news for the economy or bad news? Explain.

6. The average price of going to a baseball game in 2008, based on the observations in the Case in Point, was $191.92. Using this average as the equivalent of a base year, compute fan price indexes for:

    a. The New York Yankees.

    b. The Chicago Cubs.

    c. The Boston Red Sox.

    d. The Tampa Bay Rays.

    e. The team of your choice.

7. Suppose you are given the following data for a small economy:

    Number of unemployed workers: 1,000,000.

    Labor force: 10,000,000.

    Based on this data, answer following:

    a. What is the unemployment rate?

    b. Can you determine whether the economy is operating at its full employment level?

    c. Now suppose people who had been seeking jobs become discouraged, and give up their job searches. The labor force shrinks to 900,500 workers, and unemployment falls to 500,000 workers. What is the unemployment rate now? Has the economy improved?

8. Nominal GDP for an economy is $10 trillion. Real GDP is $9 trillion. What is the value of the implicit price deflator?

9. Suppose you are given the following data for an economy:

Month	Real GDP	Employment
1	$10.0 trillion	100 million
2	$10.4 trillion	104 million
3	$10.5 trillion	105 million
4	$10.3 trillion	103 million
5	$10.2 trillion	102 million
6	$10.3 trillion	103 million
7	$10.6 trillion	106 million
8	$10.7 trillion	107 million
9	$10.6 trillion	106 million

a. Plot the data for real GDP, with the time period on the horizontal axis and real GDP on the vertical axis.

b. There are two peaks. When do they occur?

c. When does the trough occur?

10. The Consumer Price Index in Period 1 is 107.5. It is 103.8 in Period 2. Is this a situation of inflation for deflation? What is the rate?

ENDNOTES

1. Russell Roberts, "How Government Stoked the Mania," *Wall Street Journal*, October 3, 2008, p. A21.

2. Bureau of Economic Analysis, press release, November 25, 2008.

3. "The NBER's Recession Dating Procedure," National Bureau of Economic Research, January 7, 2008.

4. Some economists prefer to break the expansion phase into two parts. The recovery phase is said to be the period between the previous trough and the time when the economy achieves its previous peak level of real GDP. The "expansion" phase is from that point until the following peak.

5. Steven Greenhouse, "Job Market Gets Better for U.S. Graduates, But Only Slightly: Offers Will Increase 5% Over Last Year; Average Starting Salaries Are Down," *The International Herald Tribune*, May 26, 2010, Finance 16.

6. Tamar Lewin, "A Hemline Index, Updated," *New York Times*, October 19, 2008, Section WK, 1.

7. "Zimbabwe Inflation Hits 11,200,000%," CNN.com, August 19, 2008.

8. For a comparison of price measures, including a comparison of the PCE price index and the Consumer Price Index, see Brain C. Moyer, "Comparing Price Measures—The CPI and PCE Price Index" (lecture, National Association for Business Economics, 2006 Washington Economic Policy Conference, March 13–14, 2006), available at http://www.bea.gov/bea/papers.htm.

9. Robert Cage, John Greenlees, and Patrick Jackman, "Introducing the Chained Consumer Price Index" (paper, Seventh Meeting of the International Working Group on Price Indices, Paris, France, May 2003), available at http://stats.bls.gov/cpi/superlink.htm.

10. For a description of the new survey and other changes introduced in the method of counting unemployment, see Janet L. Norwood and Judith M. Tanur, "Unemployment Measures for the Nineties," *Public Opinion Quarterly* 58, no. 2 (Summer 1994): 277–94.

CHAPTER 6
Measuring Total Output and Income

START UP: THE LOCKUP

It is early morning when a half-dozen senior officials enter the room at the Commerce Department in Washington. Once inside, they will have no communication with the outside world until they have completed their work later that day. They will have no telephone, no computer links. They will be able to slip out to an adjoining restroom, but only in pairs. It is no wonder the room is called "the Lockup." The Lockup produces one of the most important indicators of economic activity we have: the official estimate of the value of the economy's total output, known as its gross domestic product (GDP).

When the team has finished its computations, the results will be placed in a sealed envelope. A government messenger will hand carry the envelope to the Executive Office Building and deliver it to a senior adviser to the president of the United States. The adviser will examine its contents, then carry it across the street to the White House and give it to the president.

The senior officials who meet in secret to compute GDP are not spies; they are economists. The adviser who delivers the estimate to the president is the chairman of the Council of Economic Advisers.

The elaborate precautions for secrecy do not end there. At 7:30 the next morning, journalists from all over the world will gather in an electronically sealed auditorium at the Commerce Department. There they will be given the GDP figure and related economic indicators, along with an explanation. The reporters will have an hour to prepare their reports, but they will not be able to communicate with anyone else until an official throws the switch at 8:30. At that instant their computers will connect to their news services, and they will be able to file their reports. These will be major stories on the Internet and in the next editions of the nation's newspapers; the estimate of the previous quarter's GDP will be one of the lead items on television and radio news broadcasts that day.

The clandestine preparations for the release of quarterly GDP figures reflect the importance of this indicator. The estimate of GDP provides the best available reading of macroeconomic performance. It will affect government policy, and it will influence millions of decisions in the private sector. Prior knowledge of the GDP estimate could be used to anticipate the response in the stock and bond markets, so great care is taken that only a handful of trusted officials have access to the information until it is officially released.

The GDP estimate took on huge significance in the fall of 2008 as the United States and much of the rest of the world went through the wrenching experience of the worst financial crisis since the Great Depression of the 1930s. The expectation that the financial crisis would lead to an economic collapse was widespread, and the quarterly announcements of GDP figures were more anxiously awaited than ever.

The primary measure of the ups and downs of economic activity—the business cycle—is real GDP. When an economy's output is rising, the economy creates more jobs, more income, and more opportunities for people. In the long run, an economy's output and income, relative to its population, determine the material standard of living of its people.

Clearly GDP is an important indicator of macroeconomic performance. It is the topic we will consider in this chapter. We will learn that GDP can be measured either in terms of the total value of output produced or as the total value of income generated in producing that output. We will begin with an examination of measures of GDP in terms of output. Our initial focus will be on nominal GDP: the value of total output measured in current prices. We will turn to real GDP—a measure of output that has been adjusted for price level changes—later in the chapter. We will refer to nominal GDP simply as GDP. When we discuss the real value of the measure, we will call it real GDP.

1. MEASURING TOTAL OUTPUT

LEARNING OBJECTIVES

1. Define gross domestic product and its four major spending components and illustrate the various flows using the circular flow model.
2. Distinguish between measuring GDP as the sum of the values of final goods and services and as the sum of values added at each stage of production.
3. Distinguish between gross domestic product and gross national product.

An economy produces a mind-boggling array of goods and services. In 2007, for example, Domino's Pizza produced 400 million pizzas. The United States Steel Corporation, the nation's largest steel company, produced 23.6 million tons of steel. Strong Brothers Lumber Co., a Colorado firm, produced 2.1 million board feet of lumber. The Louisiana State University football team drew 722,166 fans to its home games—and won the national championship. Leonor Montenegro, a pediatric nurse in Los Angeles, delivered 387 babies and took care of 233 additional patients. A list of all the goods and services produced in any year would be virtually endless.

So—what kind of year was 2007? We would not get very far trying to wade through a list of all the goods and services produced that year. It is helpful to have instead a single number that measures total output in the economy; that number is GDP.

1.1 The Components of GDP

We can divide the goods and services produced during any period into four broad components, based on who buys them. These components of GDP are personal consumption (C), gross private domestic investment (I), government purchases (G), and net exports (X_n). Thus

EQUATION 6.1

$$\text{GDP} = \text{consumption } (C) + \text{private investment } (I) + \text{government purchases } (G) + \text{net exports } (X_n),$$

or

$$\text{GDP} = C + I + G + X_n$$

flow variable

A variable that is measured over a specific period of time.

stock variable

A variable that is independent of time.

We will examine each of these components, and we will see how each fits into the pattern of macroeconomic activity. Before we begin, it will be helpful to distinguish between two types of variables: stocks and flows. A **flow variable** is a variable that is measured over a specific period of time. A **stock variable** is a variable that is independent of time. Income is an example of a flow variable. To say one's income is, for example, $1,000 is meaningless without a time dimension. Is it $1,000 per hour? Per day? Per week? Per month? Until we know the time period, we have no idea what the income figure means. The balance in a checking account is an example of a stock variable. When we learn that the balance in a checking account is $1,000, we know precisely what that means; we do not need a time dimension. We will see that stock and flow variables play very different roles in macroeconomic analysis.

Personal Consumption

Personal consumption is a flow variable that measures the value of goods and services purchased by households during a time period. Purchases by households of groceries, health-care services, clothing, and automobiles—all are counted as consumption.

The production of consumer goods and services accounts for about 70% of total output. Because consumption is such a large part of GDP, economists seeking to understand the determinants of GDP must pay special attention to the determinants of consumption. In a later chapter we will explore these determinants and the impact of consumption on economic activity.

Personal consumption represents a demand for goods and services placed on firms by households. In the chapter on demand and supply, we saw how this demand could be presented in a circular flow model of the economy. Figure 6.1 presents a circular flow model for an economy that produces only personal consumption goods and services. (We will add the other components of GDP to the circular flow as we discuss them.) Spending for these goods flows from households to firms; it is the arrow labeled "Personal consumption." Firms produce these goods and services using factors of production: labor, capital, and natural resources. These factors are ultimately owned by households. The production of goods and services thus generates income to households; we see this income as the flow from firms to households labeled "Factor incomes" in the exhibit.

In exchange for payments that flow from households to firms, there is a flow of consumer goods and services from firms to households. This flow is shown in Figure 6.1 as an arrow going from firms to households. When you buy a soda, for example, your payment to the store is part of the flow of personal consumption; the soda is part of the flow of consumer goods and services that goes from the store to a household—yours.

Similarly, the lower arrow in Figure 6.1 shows the flow of factors of production—labor, capital, and natural resources—from households to firms. If you work for a firm, your labor is part of this flow. The wages you receive are part of the factor incomes that flow from firms to households.

There is a key difference in our interpretation of the circular flow picture in Figure 6.1 from our analysis of the same model in the demand and supply chapter. There, our focus was microeconomics, which examines individual units of the economy. In thinking about the flow of consumption spending from households to firms, we emphasized demand and supply in particular markets—markets for such things as blue jeans, haircuts, and apartments. In thinking about the flow of income payments from firms to households, we focused on the demand and supply for particular factors of production, such as textile workers, barbers, and apartment buildings. Because our focus now is macroeconomics, the study of aggregates of economic activity, we will think in terms of the *total* of personal consumption and the *total* of payments to households.

Private Investment

Gross private domestic investment is the value of all goods produced during a period for use in the production of other goods and services. Like personal consumption, gross private domestic investment is a flow variable. It is often simply referred to as "private investment." A hammer produced for a carpenter is private investment. A printing press produced for a magazine publisher is private investment, as is a conveyor-belt system produced for a manufacturing firm. Capital includes all the goods that have been produced for use in producing other goods; it is a stock variable. Private investment is a flow variable that adds to the stock of capital during a period.

Heads Up!

The term "*investment*" can generate confusion. In everyday conversation, we use the term "*investment*" to refer to uses of money to earn income. We say we have invested in a stock or invested in a bond. Economists, however, restrict "*investment*" to activities that increase the economy's stock of capital. The purchase of a share of stock does not add to the capital stock; it is not investment in the economic meaning of the word. We refer to the exchange of financial assets, such as stocks or bonds, as financial investment to distinguish it from the creation of capital that occurs as the result of investment. Only when new capital is produced does investment occur. Confusing the economic concept of private investment with the concept of financial investment can cause misunderstanding of the way in which key components of the economy relate to one another.

Gross private domestic investment includes three flows that add to or maintain the nation's capital stock: expenditures by business firms on new buildings, plants, tools, equipment, and software that will

personal consumption

A flow variable that measures the value of goods and services purchased by households during a time period.

FIGURE 6.1 Personal Consumption in the Circular Flow

Personal consumption spending flows from households to firms. In return, consumer goods and services flow from firms to households. To produce the goods and services households demand, firms employ factors of production owned by households. There is thus a flow of factor services from households to firms, and a flow of payments of factor incomes from firms to households.

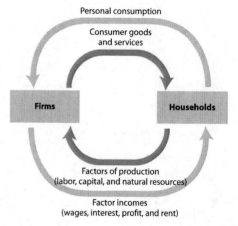

gross private domestic investment

The value of all goods produced during a period for use in the production of other goods and services.

be used in the production of goods and services; expenditures on new residential housing; and changes in business inventories. Any addition to a firm's inventories represents an addition to investment; a reduction subtracts from investment. For example, if a clothing store stocks 1,000 pairs of jeans, the jeans represent an addition to inventory and are part of gross private domestic investment. As the jeans are sold, they are subtracted from inventory and thus subtracted from investment.

By recording additions to inventories as investment and reductions from inventories as subtractions from investment, the accounting for GDP records production in the period in which it occurs. Suppose, for example, that Levi Strauss manufactures 1 million pairs of jeans late in 2007 and distributes them to stores at the end of December. The jeans will be added to inventory; they thus count as investment in 2007 and enter GDP for that year. Suppose they are sold in January 2008. They will be counted as consumption in GDP for 2008 but subtracted from inventory, and from investment. Thus, the production of the jeans will add to GDP in 2007, when they were produced. They will not count in 2008, save for any increase in the value of the jeans resulting from the services provided by the retail stores that sold them.

Private investment accounts for about 16% of GDP and at times even less. Despite its relatively small share of total economic activity, private investment plays a crucial role in the macroeconomy for two reasons:

1. Private investment represents a choice to forgo current consumption in order to add to the capital stock of the economy. Private investment therefore adds to the economy's capacity to produce and shifts its production possibilities curve outward. Investment is thus one determinant of economic growth, which is explored in another chapter.

2. Private investment is a relatively volatile component of GDP; it can change dramatically from one year to the next. Fluctuations in GDP are often driven by fluctuations in private investment. We will examine the determinants of private investment in a chapter devoted to the study of investment.

Private investment represents a demand placed on firms for the production of capital goods. While it is a demand placed on firms, it flows from firms. In the circular flow model in Figure 6.2, we see a flow of investment going from firms to firms. The production of goods and services for consumption generates factor incomes to households; the production of capital goods for investment generates income to households as well.

Figure 6.2 shows only spending flows and omits the physical flows represented by the arrows in Figure 6.1. This simplification will make our analysis of the circular flow model easier. It will also focus our attention on spending flows, which are the flows we will be studying.

Government Purchases

Government agencies at all levels purchase goods and services from firms. They purchase office equipment, vehicles, buildings, janitorial services, and so on. Many government agencies also produce goods and services. Police departments produce police protection. Public schools produce education. The National Aeronautics and Space Administration (NASA) produces space exploration.

Government purchases are the sum of purchases of goods and services from firms by government agencies plus the total value of output produced by government agencies themselves during a time period. Government purchases make up about 20% of GDP.

FIGURE 6.2 Private Investment in the Circular Flow

Private investment constitutes a demand placed on firms by other firms. It also generates factor incomes for households. To simplify the diagram, only the spending flows are shown—the corresponding flows of goods and services have been omitted.

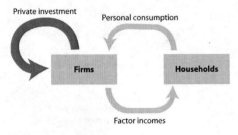

government purchases

The sum of purchases of goods and services from firms by government agencies plus the total value of output produced by government agencies themselves during a time period.

Government purchases are not the same thing as government spending. Much government spending takes the form of **transfer payments**, which are payments that do not require the recipient to produce a good or service in order to receive them. Transfer payments include Social Security and other types of assistance to retired people, welfare payments to poor people, and unemployment compensation to people who have lost their jobs. Transfer payments are certainly significant—they account for roughly half of all federal government spending in the United States. They do not count in a nation's GDP, because they do not reflect the production of a good or service.

Government purchases represent a demand placed on firms, represented by the flow shown in Figure 6.3. Like all the components of GDP, the production of goods and services for government agencies creates factor incomes for households.

Net Exports

Sales of a country's goods and services to buyers in the rest of the world during a particular time period represent its **exports**. A purchase by a Japanese buyer of a Ford Taurus produced in the United States is a U.S. export. Exports also include such transactions as the purchase of accounting services from a New York accounting firm by a shipping line based in Hong Kong or the purchase of a ticket to Disney World by a tourist from Argentina. **Imports** are purchases of foreign-produced goods and services by a country's residents during a period. United States imports include such transactions as the purchase by Americans of cars produced in Japan or tomatoes grown in Mexico or a stay in a French hotel by a tourist from the United States. Subtracting imports from exports yields **net exports**.

EQUATION 6.2

$$\text{Exports } (X) - \text{imports } (M) = \text{net exports } (X_n)$$

In the third quarter of 2010, foreign buyers purchased $1,847.0 billion worth of goods and services from the United States. In the same year, U.S. residents, firms, and government agencies purchased $2,339.1 billion worth of goods and services from foreign countries. The difference between these two figures, −$552.2 billion, represented the net exports of the U.S. economy in the third quarter of 2010. Net exports were negative because imports exceeded exports. Negative net exports constitute a **trade deficit**. The amount of the deficit is the amount by which imports exceed exports. When exports exceed imports there is a **trade surplus**. The magnitude of the surplus is the amount by which exports exceed imports.

The United States has recorded more deficits than surpluses since World War II, but the amounts have typically been relatively small, only a few billion dollars. The trade deficit began to soar, however, in the 1980s and again in the 2000s. We will examine the reasons for persistent trade deficits in another chapter. The rest of the world plays a key role in the domestic economy and, as we will see later in the book, there is nothing particularly good or bad about trade surpluses or deficits. Goods and services produced for export represent roughly 13% of GDP, and the goods and services the United States imports add significantly to our standard of living.

In the circular flow diagram in Figure 6.4, net exports are shown with an arrow connecting firms to the rest of the world. The balance between the flows of exports and imports is net exports. When there is a trade surplus, net exports are positive and add spending to the circular flow. A trade deficit implies negative net exports; spending flows from firms to the rest of the world.

transfer payments

Payments that do not require the recipient to produce a good or service in order to receive them.

FIGURE 6.3 Government Purchases in the Circular Flow

Purchases of goods and services by government agencies create demands on firms. As firms produce these goods and services, they create factor incomes for households.

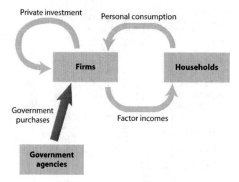

exports

Sales of a country's goods and services to buyers in the rest of the world during a particular time period.

imports

Purchases of foreign-produced goods and services by a country's residents during a period.

net exports

Exports minus imports.

trade deficit

Negative net exports.

trade surplus

Positive net exports.

FIGURE 6.4 Net Exports in the Circular Flow

Net exports represent the balance between exports and imports. Net exports can be positive or negative. If they are positive, net export spending flows from the rest of the world to firms. If they are negative, spending flows from firms to the rest of the world.

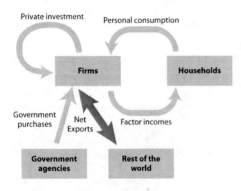

FIGURE 6.5 Spending in the Circular Flow Model

GDP equals the sum of production by firms of goods and services for personal consumption (1), private investment (2), government purchases (3), and net exports (4). The circular flow model shows these flows and shows that the production of goods and services generates factor incomes (5) to households.

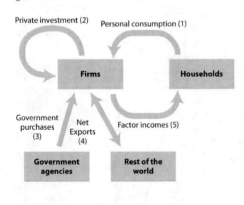

The production of goods and services for personal consumption, private investment, government purchases, and net exports makes up a nation's GDP. Firms produce these goods and services in response to demands from households (personal consumption), from other firms (private investment), from government agencies (government purchases), and from the rest of the world (net exports). All of this production creates factor income for households. Figure 6.5 shows the circular flow model for all the spending flows we have discussed. Each flow is numbered for use in the exercise at the end of this section.

The circular flow model identifies some of the forces at work in the economy, forces that we will be studying in later chapters. For example, an increase in any of the flows that place demands on firms (personal consumption, private investment, government purchases, and exports) will induce firms to expand their production. This effect is characteristic of the expansion phase of the business cycle. An increase in production will require firms to employ more factors of production, which will create more income for households. Households are likely to respond with more consumption, which will induce still more production, more income, and still more consumption. Similarly, a reduction in any of the demands placed on firms will lead to a reduction in output, a reduction in firms' use of factors of production, a reduction in household incomes, a reduction in income, and so on. This sequence of events is characteristic of the contraction phase of the business cycle. Much of our work in macroeconomics will involve an analysis of the forces that prompt such changes in demand and an examination of the economy's response to them.

Figure 6.6 shows the size of the components of GDP in 2010. We see that the production of goods and services for personal consumption accounted for about 70% of GDP. Imports exceeded exports, so net exports were negative.

FIGURE 6.6 Components of GDP, 2010 (Q3) in Billions of Dollars

Consumption makes up the largest share of GDP. Net exports were negative in 2010. Total GDP—the sum of personal consumption, private investment, government purchases, and net exports—equaled $14,750.2 billion in 2010.

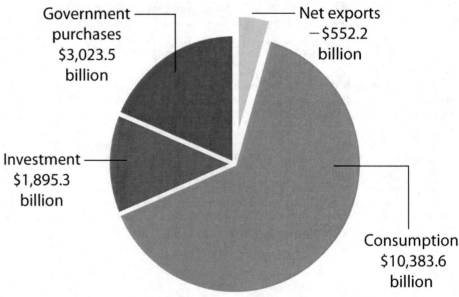

Source: Bureau of Economic Analysis, National Income and Product Accounts, Table 1.1.5 (December 2010)

1.2 Final Goods and Value Added

GDP is the total value of all *final* goods and services produced during a particular period valued at prices in that period. That is not the same as the total value of all goods and services produced during a period. This distinction gives us another method of estimating GDP in terms of output.

Suppose, for example, that a logger cuts some trees and sells the logs to a sawmill. The mill makes lumber and sells it to a construction firm, which builds a house. The market price for the lumber includes the value of the logs; the price of the house includes the value of the lumber. If we try to estimate GDP by adding the value of the logs, the lumber, and the house, we would be counting the lumber twice and the logs three times. This problem is called "double counting," and the economists who compute GDP seek to avoid it.

In the case of logs used for lumber and lumber produced for a house, GDP would include the value of the house. The lumber and the logs would not be counted as additional production because they are intermediate goods that were produced for use in building the house.

Another approach to estimating the value of final production is to estimate for each stage of production the **value added**, the amount by which the value of a firm's output exceeds the value of the goods and services the firm purchases from other firms. Table 6.1 illustrates the use of value added in the production of a house.

value added

The amount by which the value of a firm's output exceeds the value of the goods and services the firm purchases from other firms.

TABLE 6.1 Final Value and Value Added

If we sum the value added at each stage of the production of a good or service, we get the final value of the item. The example shown here involves the construction of a house, which is produced from lumber that is, in turn, produced from logs.

Good	Produced by	Purchased by	Price	Value Added
Logs	Logger	Sawmill	$12,000	$12,000
Lumber	Sawmill	Construction firm	$25,000	$13,000
House	Construction firm	Household	$125,000	$100,000
		Final Value	**$125,000**	
		Sum of Values Added		**$125,000**

Suppose the logs produced by the logger are sold for $12,000 to a mill, and that the mill sells the lumber it produces from these logs for $25,000 to a construction firm. The construction firm uses the lumber to build a house, which it sells to a household for $125,000. (To simplify the example, we will ignore inputs other than lumber that are used to build the house.) The value of the final product, the house, is $125,000. The value added at each stage of production is estimated as follows:

a. The logger adds $12,000 by cutting the logs.

b. The mill adds $13,000 ($25,000 − $12,000) by cutting the logs into lumber.

c. The construction firm adds $100,000 ($125,000 − $25,000) by using the lumber to build a house.

The sum of values added at each stage ($12,000 + $13,000 + $100,000) equals the final value of the house, $125,000.

The value of an economy's output in any period can thus be estimated in either of two ways. The values of final goods and services produced can be added directly, or the values added at each stage in the production process can be added. The Commerce Department uses both approaches in its estimate of the nation's GDP.

1.3   GNP: An Alternative Measure of Output

While GDP represents the most commonly used measure of an economy's output, economists sometimes use an alternative measure. **Gross national product (GNP)** is the total value of final goods and services produced during a particular period with factors of production owned by the residents of a particular country.

The difference between GDP and GNP is a subtle one. The GDP of a country equals the value of final output produced within the borders of that country; the GNP of a country equals the value of final output produced using factors owned by residents of the country. Most production in a country employs factors of production owned by residents of that country, so the two measures overlap. Differences between the two measures emerge when production in one country employs factors of production *owned* by residents of other countries.

Suppose, for example, that a resident of Bellingham, Washington, owns and operates a watch repair shop across the Canadian–U.S. border in Victoria, British Columbia. The value of watch repair services produced at the shop would be counted as part of Canada's GDP because they are produced in Canada. That value would not, however, be part of U.S. GDP. But, because the watch repair services were produced using capital and labor provided by a resident of the United States, they would be counted as part of GNP in the United States and not as part of GNP in Canada.

Because most production fits in both a country's GDP as well as its GNP, there is seldom much difference between the two measures. The relationship between GDP and GNP is given by

gross national product (GNP)

The total value of final goods and services produced during a particular period with factors of production owned by the residents of a particular country.

EQUATION 6.3

$$\text{GDP} + \text{net income received from abroad by residents of a nation} = \text{GNP}$$

In the third quarter of 2010, for example, GDP equaled $14,750.2 billion. We add income receipts earned by residents of the United States from the rest of the world of $706.0 billion and then subtract income payments that went from the United States to the rest of the world of $516.1 billion to get GNP of $14,940.0 billion for the third quarter of 2010. GNP is often used in international comparisons of income; we shall examine those later in this chapter.

KEY TAKEAWAYS

- GDP is the sum of final goods and services produced for consumption (C), private investment (I), government purchases (G), and net exports (X_n). Thus GDP = $C + I + G + X_n$.
- GDP can be viewed in the context of the circular flow model. Consumption goods and services are produced in response to demands from households; investment goods are produced in response to demands for new capital by firms; government purchases include goods and services purchased by government agencies; and net exports equal exports less imports.
- Total output can be measured two ways: as the sum of the values of final goods and services produced and as the sum of values added at each stage of production.
- GDP plus net income received from other countries equals GNP. GNP is the measure of output typically used to compare incomes generated by different economies.

TRY IT!

Here is a two-part exercise.

1. Suppose you are given the following data for an economy:

Personal consumption	$1,000
Home construction	100
Increase in inventories	40
Equipment purchases by firms	60
Government purchases	100
Social Security payments to households	40
Government welfare payments	100
Exports	50
Imports	150

Identify the number of the flow in Figure 6.5 to which each of these items corresponds. What is the economy's GDP?

2. Suppose a dairy farm produces raw milk, which it sells for $1,000 to a dairy. The dairy produces cream, which it sells for $3,000 to an ice cream manufacturer. The ice cream manufacturer uses the cream to make ice cream, which it sells for $7,000 to a grocery store. The grocery store sells the ice cream to consumers for $10,000. Compute the value added at each stage of production, and compare this figure to the final value of the product produced. Report your results in a table similar to that given in Table 6.1.

Case in Point: The Spread of the Value Added Tax

Outside the United States, the value added tax (VAT) has become commonplace. Governments of more than 120 countries use it as their primary means of raising revenue. While the concept of the VAT originated in France in the 1920s, no country adopted it until after World War II. In 1948, France became the first country in the world to use the VAT. In 1967, Brazil became the first country in the Western Hemisphere to do so. The VAT spread to other western European and Latin American countries in the 1970s and 1980s and then to countries in the Asia/Pacific region, central European and former Soviet Union area, and Africa in the 1990s and early 2000s.

What is the VAT? It is equivalent to a sales tax on final goods and services but is collected at each stage of production.

Take the example given in Table 6.1, which is a simplified illustration of a house built in three stages. If there were a sales tax of 10% on the house, the household buying it would pay $137,500, of which the construction firm would keep $125,000 of the total and turn $12,500 over to the government.

With a 10% VAT, the sawmill would pay the logger $13,200, of which the logger would keep $12,000 and turn $1,200 over to the government. The sawmill would sell the lumber to the construction firm for $27,500—keeping $26,200, which is the $25,000 for the lumber itself and $1,200 it already paid in tax. The government at this stage would get $1,300, the difference between the $2,500 the construction firm collected as tax and the $1,200 the sawmill already paid in tax to the logger at the previous stage. The household would pay the construction firm $137,500. Of that total, the construction firm would turn over to the government $10,000, which is the difference between the $12,500 it collected for the government in tax from the household and the $2,500 in tax that it already paid when it bought the lumber from the sawmill. The table below shows that in the end, the tax revenue generated by a 10% VAT is the same as that generated by a 10% tax on final sales.

Why bother to tax in stages instead of just on final sales? One reason is simply record keeping, since it may be difficult to determine in practice if any particular sale is the final one. In the example, the construction firm does not need to know if it is selling the house to a household or to some intermediary business.

Also, the VAT may lead to higher revenue collected. For example, even if somehow the household buying the house avoided paying the tax, the government would still have collected some tax revenue at earlier stages of production. With a tax on retail sales, it would have collected nothing. The VAT has another advantage from the point of view of government agencies. It has the appearance at each stage of taking a smaller share. The individual amounts collected are not as obvious to taxpayers as a sales tax might be.

Good	Price	Value Added	Tax Collected	− Tax Already Paid	= Value Added Tax
Logs	$12,000	$12,000	$1,200	− $0	= $1,200
Lumber	$25,000	$13,000	$2,500	− $1,200	= $1,300
House	$125,000	$100,000	$12,500	− $2,500	= $10,000
Total			**$16,200**	**−$3,700**	**= $12,500**

ANSWER TO TRY IT! PROBLEM

1. GDP equals $1,200 and is computed as follows (the numbers in parentheses correspond to the flows in Figure 6.5):

Personal consumption (1)	$1,000
Private investment (2)	200
Housing	100
Equipment and software	60
Inventory change	40
Government purchases (3)	100
Net exports (4)	−100
GDP	$1,200

Notice that neither welfare payments nor Social Security payments to households are included. These are transfer payments, which are not part of the government purchases component of GDP.

2. Here is the table of value added.

Good	Produced by	Purchased by	Price	Value Added
Raw milk	Dairy farm	Dairy	$1,000	$1,000
Cream	Dairy	Ice cream maker	3,000	2,000
Ice cream	Ice cream manufacturer	Grocery store	7,000	4,000
Retail ice cream	Grocery store	Consumer	10,000	3,000
		Final Value	**$10,000**	
		Sum of Values Added		**$10,000**

2. MEASURING TOTAL INCOME

LEARNING OBJECTIVES

1. Define gross domestic income and explain its relationship to gross domestic product.
2. Discuss the components of gross domestic income.
3. Define disposable personal income and explain how to calculate it from GDP.

gross domestic income (GDI)

The total income generated in an economy by the production of final goods and services during a particular period.

We saw in the last section that the production of goods and services generates factor incomes to households. The production of a given value of goods and services generates an equal value of total income. **Gross domestic income (GDI)** equals the total income generated in an economy by the production of final goods and services during a particular period. It is a flow variable. Because an economy's total output equals the total income generated in producing that output, GDP = GDI. We can estimate GDP either by measuring total output or by measuring total income.

Consider a $4 box of Cheerios. It is part of total output and thus is part of GDP. Who gets the $4? Part of the answer to that question can be found by looking at the cereal box. Cheerios are made from oat flour, wheat starch, sugar, salt, and a variety of vitamins and minerals. Therefore, part of the $4 goes to the farmers who grew the oats, the wheat, and the beets or cane from which the sugar was extracted. Workers and machines at General Mills combined the ingredients, crafted all those little O's, toasted them, and put them in a box. The workers were paid part of the $4 as wages. The owners of General Mills and the capital it used received part of the $4 as profit. The box containing the Cheerios was made from a tree, so a lumber company somewhere received part of the $4. The truck driver who brought the box of cereal to the grocery store got part of the $4, as did the owner of the truck itself and the owner of the oil that fueled the truck. The clerk who rang up the sale at the grocery store was paid part of the $4. And so on.

How much of the $4 was income generated in the production of the Cheerios? The answer is simple: all of it. Some of the money went to workers as wages. Some went to owners of the capital and natural resources used to produce it. Profits generated along the way went to the owners of the firms involved. All these items represent costs of producing the Cheerios and also represent income to households.

Part of the $4 cost of the Cheerios, while it makes up a portion of GDI, does not represent ordinary income actually earned by households. That part results from two other production costs: depreciation and taxes related to the production of the Cheerios. Nevertheless, they are treated as a kind of income; we will examine their role in GDI below.

As it is with Cheerios, so it is with everything else. The value of output equals the income generated as the output is produced.

2.1   The Components of GDI

Employee compensation is the largest among the components of factor income. Factor income also includes profit, rent, and interest. In addition, GDI includes charges for depreciation and taxes associated with production. Depreciation and production-related taxes, such as sales taxes, make up part of the cost of producing goods and services and must be accounted for in estimating GDI. We will discuss each of these components of GDI next.

Employee Compensation

Compensation of employees in the form of wages, salaries, and benefits makes up the largest single component of income generated in the production of GDP. In the second quarter of 2008, employee compensation represented 57% of GDI.

The structure of employee compensation has changed dramatically in the last several decades. In 1950, virtually all employee compensation—95% of it—came in the form of wages and salaries. The remainder, about 5%, came in the form of additional benefits such as employer contributions to retirement programs and health insurance. In 2008, the share of benefits was roughly 20% of total employee compensation.

Profits

The profit component of income earned by households equals total revenues of firms less costs as measured by conventional accounting. Profits amounted to about 16% of GDI, or $2,332.2 billion in 2010, down sharply from five decades earlier, when profits represented about 25% of the income generated in GDI.[1]

Profits are the reward the owners of firms receive for being in business. The opportunity to earn profits is the driving force behind production in a market economy.

Rental Income

Rental income, such as the income earned by owners of rental housing or payments for the rent of natural resources, is the smallest component of GDI (about 2%); it is the smallest of the income flows to households. The meaning of rent in the computation of GDI is the same as its meaning in conventional usage; it is a charge for the temporary use of some capital asset or natural resource.[2]

Net Interest

Businesses both receive and pay interest. GDI includes net interest, which equals interest paid less interest received by domestic businesses, plus interest received from foreigners less interest paid to foreigners. Interest payments on mortgage and home improvement loans are counted as interest paid by business, because homeowners are treated as businesses in the income accounts. In 2010 net interest accounted for 6.3% of GDI.

Depreciation

Over time the machinery and buildings that are used to produce goods and services wear out or become obsolete. A farmer's tractor, for example, wears out as it is used. A technological change may make some equipment obsolete. The introduction of personal computers, for example, made the electric typewriters used by many firms obsolete. **Depreciation** is a measure of the amount of capital that wears out or becomes obsolete during a period. Depreciation is referred to in official reports as the consumption of fixed capital.

Depreciation is a cost of production, so it represents part of the price charged for goods and services. It is therefore counted as part of the income generated in the production of those goods and services. Depreciation represented about 13% of GDI in 2008.

depreciation

A measure of the amount of capital that wears out or becomes obsolete during a period.

Indirect Taxes

The final component of the income measure of GDI is indirect business taxes.[3] **Indirect taxes** are taxes imposed on the production or sale of goods and services or on other business activity. (By contrast, a **direct tax** is a tax imposed directly on income; the personal income and corporate income taxes are direct taxes.) Indirect taxes, which include sales and excise taxes and property taxes, make up part of the cost to firms of producing goods and services. Like depreciation, they are part of the price of those goods and services and are therefore treated as part of the income generated in their production. Indirect business taxes amounted to 7.7% of GDI in 2010.

Table 6.2 shows the components of GDI in 2010. Employee compensation represented the largest share of GDI. The exhibit also shows the components of GDP for the same year.

In principle, GDP and GDI should be equal, but their estimated values never are, because the data come from different sources. Output data from a sample of firms are used to estimate GDP, while income data from a sample of households are used to estimate GDI. The difference is the statistical discrepancy shown in the right-hand column of Table 6.2. Some of the difficulties with these data are examined in the Case in Point feature on discrepancies between GDP and GDI.

TABLE 6.2 GDP and GDI, 2010

The table shows the composition of GDP and GDI in the third quarter of 2010 (in billions of dollars at an annual rate). Notice the rough equality of the two measures. (They are not quite equal because of measurement errors; the difference is due to a statistical discrepancy and is reduced significantly over time as the data are revised.)

Gross domestic product	$14,750.2	Gross Domestic Income	$14,584.8
Personal Consumption Expenditures	10,383.6	Compensation of Employees	8,040.8
Gross Private Domestic Investment	1,895.3	Profits[4]	2,332.3
Government consumption expenditures and gross investment	3,023.5	Rental income of persons	304.7
Net exports of goods and services	- 552.2	Net interest	913.9
		Taxes on production and imports[5]	1,121.0
		Consumption of fixed capital (depreciation)	1872.1
		Statistical discrepancy	165.4

Sources: Bureau of Economic Analysis National Income and Product Accounts, Tables 1.10 and 1.1.5 (December, 2010). See Brent R. Moulton and Eugene P. Seskin, "Preview of the 2003 Comprehensive Revision of the National Income and Product Accounts," Bureau of Economic Analysis, Survey of Current Business, June 2003, pp. 17–34.

2.2 Tracing Income from the Economy to Households

We have seen that the production of goods and services generates income for households. Thus, the value of total output equals the value of total income in an economy. But we have also seen that our measure of total income, GDI, includes such things as depreciation and indirect business taxes that are not actually received by households. Households also receive some income, such as transfer payments, that does not count as part of GDP or GDI. Because the income households actually receive plays an important role in determining their consumption, it is useful to examine the relationship between a nation's total output and the income households actually receive.

Table 6.3 traces the path we take in going from GDP to **disposable personal income**, which equals the income households have available to spend on goods and services. We first convert GDP to GNP and then subtract elements of GNP that do not represent income received by households and add payments such as transfer payments that households receive but do not earn in the production of GNP. Disposable personal income is either spent for personal consumption or saved by households.

TABLE 6.3 From GDP to Disposable Personal Income

GDP, a measure of total output, equals GDI, the total income generated in the production of goods and services in an economy. The chart traces the path from GDP to disposable personal income, which equals the income households actually receive. We first convert GDP to GNP. Then, we subtract depreciation to obtain net national product and subtract the statistical discrepancy to arrive at national income (i.e., gross national income [GNI] net of depreciation and the statistical discrepancy). Next, we subtract components of GNP and GNI that do not represent income actually received by households, such as taxes on production and imports, corporate profit and payroll taxes (contributions to social insurance), and corporate retained earnings. We add items such as transfer payments that are income to households but are not part of GNP and GNI. The adjustments shown are the most important adjustments in going from GNP and GNI to disposable personal income; several smaller adjustments (e.g., subsidies, business current transfer payments [net], and current surplus of government enterprises) have been omitted.

GDP + net factor earnings from abroad	= gross national product (GNP)
GNP − depreciation (consumption of fixed capital)	= net national product (NNP)
NNP − statistical discrepancy	= national income (NI)
NI − income earned but not received [e.g., taxes on production and imports, social security payroll taxes, corporate profit taxes, and retained earnings] + transfer payments and other income received but not earned in the production of GNP	= personal income (PI)
PI − personal income taxes	= disposable personal income (DPI)

KEY TAKEAWAYS

- Gross domestic product, GDP, equals gross domestic income, GDI, which includes compensation, profits, rental income, indirect taxes, and depreciation.
- We can use GDP, a measure of total output, to compute disposable personal income, a measure of income received by households and available for them to spend.

TRY IT!

The following income data refer to the same economy for which you had output data in the first part of the previous Try It! Compute GDI from the data below and confirm that your result equals the GDP figure you computed in the previous Try It! Assume that GDP = GNP for this problem (that is, assume all factor incomes are earned and paid in the domestic economy).

Employee compensation	$700
Social Security payments to households	40
Welfare payments	100
Profits	200
Rental income	50
Net interest	25
Depreciation	50
Indirect taxes	175

Case in Point: The GDP–GDI Gap

GDP equals GDI; at least, that is the way it is supposed to work. But in an enormously complex economy, the measurement of these two variables inevitably goes awry. Estimates of the two are never quite equal. In recent years, the absolute value of the gap has been quite sizable. For 2007 and 2008, for example, GDI has differed from GDP by −$81.4 and $160.5 billion per year, respectively.

Although the gap seems large, it represents a remarkably small fraction of measured activity—around 1% or less. Of course, 1% of a big number is still a big number. But it is important to remember that, relative to the size of the economy, the gap between GDI and GDP is not large. The gap is listed as a "statistical discrepancy" in the Department of Commerce reporting of the two numbers.

Why does the gap exist? From an accounting point of view, it should not. The total value of final goods and services produced must be equal to the total value of income generated in that production. But output is measured from sales and inventory figures collected from just 10% of commercial establishments. Preliminary income figures are obtained from household surveys, but these represent a tiny fraction of households. More complete income data are provided by income tax returns, but these are available to the economists who estimate GDI only after a two- to four-year delay.

The Department of Commerce issues revisions of its GDP and GDI estimates as more complete data become available. With each revision, the gap between GDP and GDI estimates is significantly reduced.

While GDP and GDI figures cannot provide precise measures of economic activity, they come remarkably close. Indeed, given that the numbers come from entirely different sources, the fact that they come as close as they do provides an impressive check of the accuracy of the department's estimates of GDP and GDI.

ANSWER TO TRY IT! PROBLEM

GDI equals $1,200. Note that this value equals the value for GDP obtained from the estimate of output in the first part of the previous Try It! Here is the computation:

Employee compensation	$700
Profits	200
Rental income	50
Net interest	25
Depreciation	50
Indirect taxes	175
GDI	$1,200

Once again, note that Social Security and welfare payments to households are transfer payments. They do not represent payments to household factors of production for current output of goods and services, and therefore are not included in GDI.

3. GDP AND ECONOMIC WELL-BEING

LEARNING OBJECTIVES

1. Discuss and give examples of measurement and conceptual problems in using real GDP as a measure of economic performance and of economic well-being.
2. Explain the use of per capita real GNP or GDP to compare economic performance across countries and discuss its limitations.

GDP is the measure most often used to assess the economic well-being of a country. Besides measuring the pulse of a country, it is the figure used to compare living standards in different countries.

Of course, to use GDP as an indicator of overall economic performance, we must convert nominal GDP to real GDP, since nominal values can rise or fall simply as a result of changes in the price level. For example, the movie *Titanic*, released in 1997, brought in $601 million—the highest amount ever in gross box office receipts, while *Gone with the Wind*, released in 1939, earned only $199 million and ranks 49th in terms of nominal receipts. But does that mean that *Titanic* actually did better than *Gone with the Wind*? After all, the average price of a movie ticket in 1939 was 25 cents. At the time of *Titanic*, the average ticket price was about $5. A better way to compare these two movies in terms of popularity is to control for the price of movie tickets—the same strategy that economists use with real GDP in order to determine whether output is rising or falling. Adjusting the nominal box-office receipts using 1998 movie prices to obtain real revenue reveals that in real terms *Gone with the Wind* continues to be the top real grosser of all time with real box-office receipts of about $1.3 billion. As illustrated by this example on revenues from popular movies, we might draw erroneous conclusions about performance if we base them on nominal values instead of on real values. In contrast, real GDP, despite the problems with price indexes that were explained in another chapter, provides a reasonable measure of the total output of an economy, and changes in real GDP provide an indication of the direction of movement in total output.

We begin this section by noting some of the drawbacks of using real GDP as a measure of the economic welfare of a country. Despite these shortcomings, we will see that it probably remains our best single indicator of macroeconomic performance.

3.1 Measurement Problems in Real GDP

There are two measurement problems, other than those associated with adjusting for price level changes, in using real GDP to assess domestic economic performance.

Revisions

The first estimate of real GDP for a calendar quarter is called the advance estimate. It is issued about a month after the quarter ends. To produce a measure so quickly, officials at the Department of Commerce must rely on information from relatively few firms and households. One month later, it issues a revised estimate, and a month after that it issues its final estimate. Often the advance estimate of GDP and the final estimate do not correspond. The recession of 2001, for example, began in March of that year. But the first estimates of real GDP for the second and third quarters of 2001 showed output continuing to rise. It was not until later revisions that it became clear that a recession had been under way.

But the revision story does not end there. Every summer, the Commerce Department issues revised figures for the previous two or three years. Once every five years, the department conducts an extensive analysis that traces flows of inputs and outputs throughout the economy. It focuses on the outputs of some firms that are inputs to other firms. In the process of conducting this analysis, the department revises real GDP estimates for the previous five years. Sometimes the revisions can paint a picture of economic activity that is quite different from the one given even by the revised estimates of GDP. For example, revisions of the data for the 1990–1991 recession issued several years later showed that the recession had been much more serious than had previously been apparent, and the recovery was more pronounced.

The Service Sector

Another problem lies in estimating production in the service sector. The output of goods in an economy is relatively easy to compute. There are so many bushels of corn, so many pounds of beef. But what is the output of a bank? Of a hospital? It is easy to record the dollar value of output to enter in nominal GDP, but estimating the quantity of output to use in real GDP is quite another matter. In some cases, the Department of Commerce estimates service sector output based on the quantity of labor used. For example, if this technique were used in the banking industry and banking used 10% more labor, the department would report that production has risen 10%. If the number of employees remains unchanged, reported output remains unchanged. In effect, this approach assumes that output per worker—productivity—in those sectors remains constant when studies have indicated that productivity has increased greatly in the service sector. Since 1990 progress has been made in measurement in this area, which allows in particular for better estimation of productivity changes and price indexes for different service sector industries, but more remains to be done in this large sector of the U.S. economy.[6]

3.2 Conceptual Problems with Real GDP

A second set of limitations of real GDP stems from problems inherent in the indicator itself. Real GDP measures market activity. Goods and services that are produced and exchanged in a market are counted; goods and services that are produced but that are not exchanged in markets are not.[7]

Household Production

Suppose you are considering whether to eat at home for dinner tonight or to eat out. You could cook dinner for yourself at a cost of $5 for the ingredients plus an hour or so of your time. Alternatively, you could buy an equivalent meal at a restaurant for perhaps $15. Your decision to eat out rather than cook would add $10 to the GDP.

But that $10 addition would be misleading. After all, if you had stayed home you might have produced an equivalent meal. The only difference is that the value of your time would not have been counted. But surely your time is not worthless; it is just not counted. Similarly, GDP does not count the value of your efforts to clean your own house, to wash your own car, or to grow your own vegetables. In general, GDP omits the entire value added by members of a household who do household work themselves.

There is reason to believe this omission is serious. Economists J. Steven Landefeld and Stephanie H. McCulla of the U.S. Bureau of Economic Analysis estimated in a 2000 paper the value of household output from 1946 to 1997. Their estimate of household output in 1946 was 50% of reported GDP. Since then, that percentage has fallen, because more women have entered the workforce, so that more production that once took place in households now occurs in the market. Households now eat out more, purchase more prepared foods at the grocery store, hire out child-care services they once performed themselves, and so on. Their estimate for 1997, for example, suggests that household production amounted to 36% of reported GDP.[8]

This problem is especially significant when GDP is used to make comparisons across countries. In low-income countries, a much greater share of goods and services is not exchanged in a market. Estimates of GDP in such countries are adjusted to reflect nonmarket production, but these adjustments are inevitably imprecise.

Underground and Illegal Production

Some production goes unreported in order to evade taxes or the law. It is not likely to be counted in GDP. Legal production for which income is unreported in order to evade taxes generally takes place in what is known as the "underground economy." For example, a carpenter might build a small addition to a dentist's house in exchange for orthodontic work for the carpenter's children. Although income has been earned and output generated in this example of bartering, the transaction is unlikely to be reported for income tax or other purposes and thus is not counted in GDP. Illegal activities are not reported for income taxes for obvious reasons and are thus difficult to include in GDP.

Leisure

Leisure is an economic good. All other things being equal, more leisure is better than less leisure.

But all other things are not likely to be equal when it comes to consuming leisure. Consuming more leisure means supplying less work effort. And that means producing less GDP. If everyone decided to work 10% fewer hours, GDP would fall. But that would not mean that people were worse off. In fact, their choice of more leisure would suggest they prefer the extra leisure to the goods and services they give up by consuming it. Consequently, a reduction in GDP would be accompanied by an increase in satisfaction, not a reduction.

The GDP Accounts Ignore "Bads"

Suppose a wave of burglaries were to break out across the United States. One would expect people to respond by buying more and louder burglar alarms, better locks, fiercer German shepherds, and more guard services than they had before. To the extent that they pay for these by dipping into savings rather than replacing other consumption, GDP increases. An epidemic might have much the same effect on GDP by driving up health-care spending. But that does not mean that crime and disease are good things; it means only that crime and disease may force an increase in the production of goods and services counted in the GDP.

Similarly, the GDP accounts ignore the impact of pollution on the environment. We might produce an additional $200 billion in goods and services but create pollution that makes us feel worse off by, say, $300 billion. The GDP accounts simply report the $200 billion in increased production. Indeed, some of the environmental degradation might itself boost GDP. Dirtier air may force us to wash clothes more often, to paint buildings more often, and to see the doctor more often, all of which will tend to increase GDP!

Conclusion: GDP and Human Happiness

More GDP cannot necessarily be equated with more human happiness. But more GDP does mean more of the goods and services we measure. It means more jobs. It means more income. And most people seem to place a high value on these things. For all its faults, GDP does measure the production of most goods and services. And goods and services get produced, for the most part, because we want them. We might thus be safe in giving two cheers for GDP—and holding back the third in recognition of the conceptual difficulties that are inherent in using a single number to summarize the output of an entire economy.

3.3   International Comparisons of Real GDP and GNP

Real GDP or GNP estimates are often used in comparing economic performance among countries. In making such comparisons, it is important to keep in mind the general limitations to these measures of economic performance that we noted earlier. Further, countries use different methodologies for collecting and compiling data.

Three other issues are important in comparing real GDP or GNP for different countries: the adjustment of these figures for population, adjusting to a common currency, and the incorporation of nonmarket production.

In international comparisons of real GNP or real GDP, economists generally make comparisons not of real GNP or GDP but of **per capita real GNP or GDP**, which equals a country's real GNP or GDP divided by its population. In 2009, for example, Japan had a real GDP of about $4,000 billion and Luxembourg had a real GDP of about $29 billion. We can conclude that Japan's economy produced far more goods and services than did Luxembourg's. But Japan had almost 300 times as many people as did Luxembourg. Japan's per capita real GDP in 2009 was $33,280; Luxembourg's was $57,640, the highest in the world that year.

Figure 6.9 compares per capita real GNP for 11 countries in 2009. It is based on data that uses a measure called "international dollars" in order to correct for differences in the purchasing power of $1 across countries. The data also attempt to adjust for nonmarket production (such as that of rural families that grow their own food, make their own clothing, and produce other household goods and services themselves).

per capita real GNP or GDP

A country's real GNP or GDP divided by its population.

FIGURE 6.9 Comparing Per Capita Real GNP, 2009

There is a huge gap between per capita income in one of the poorest countries in the world, Liberia, and wealthier nations such as the United States and Luxembourg.

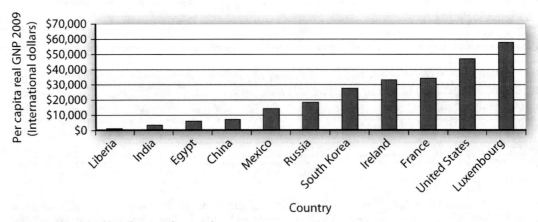

Source: World Bank, World Development Indicators Online

The disparities in income are striking; Luxembourg, the country with the highest per capita real GNP, had an income level more than 200 times greater than Liberia, the country with the lowest per capita real GNP.

What can we conclude about international comparisons in levels of GDP and GNP? Certainly we must be cautious. There are enormous difficulties in estimating any country's total output. Comparing one country's output to another presents additional challenges. But the fact that a task is difficult does not mean it is impossible. When the data suggest huge disparities in levels of GNP per capita, for example, we observe real differences in living standards.

KEY TAKEAWAYS

- Real GDP or real GNP is often used as an indicator of the economic well-being of a country.
- Problems in the measurement of real GDP, in addition to problems encountered in converting from nominal to real GDP, stem from revisions in the data and the difficulty of measuring output in some sectors, particularly the service sector.
- Conceptual problems in the use of real GDP as a measure of economic well-being include the facts that it does not include nonmarket production and that it does not properly adjust for "bads" produced in the economy.
- Per capita real GDP or GNP can be used to compare economic performance in different countries.

TRY IT!

What impact would each of the following have on real GDP? Would economic well-being increase or decrease as a result?

1. On average, people in a country decide to increase the number of hours they work by 5%.
2. Spending on homeland security increases in response to a terrorist attack.
3. The price level and nominal GDP increase by 10%.

Case in Point: Per Capita Real GDP and Olympic Medal Counts

In the popular lore, the Olympics provide an opportunity for the finest athletes in the world to compete with each other head-to-head on the basis of raw talent and hard work. And yet, contenders from Laos tend to finish last or close to it in almost any event in which they compete. One Laotian athlete garnered the unenviable record of having been the slowest entrant in the nearly half-century long history of the 20-kilometer walk. In contrast, U.S. athletes won 103 medals at the 2004 Athens Olympics and 110 medals at the 2008 Beijing Olympics. Why do Laotians fare so poorly and Americans so well, with athletes from other countries falling in between?

Economists Daniel K. N. Johnson and Ayfer Ali have been able to predict with astonishing accuracy the number of medals different countries will win on the basis of a handful of factors, including population, climate, political structure, and real per capita GDP. For example, they predicted that the United States would win 103 medals in Athens and that is precisely how many the United States won. They predicted 103 medals for the United States in Beijing; 110 were won. They did not expect the Laotians to win any medals in either Athens or Beijing, and that was indeed the outcome.

Johnson and Ali estimated that summer game participant nations average one more medal per additional $1,000 of per capita real GDP. With per capita real GDP in Laos less than the equivalent of $500 compared to per capita real GDP in the United States of about $38,000, the results for these two nations could be considered a foregone conclusion. According to Johnson and Ali, "High productive capacity or income per person displays an ability to pay the costs necessary to send athletes to the Games, and may also be associated with a higher quality of training and better equipment." For example, a Laotian swimmer at Athens, Vilayphone Vongphachanh, had never practiced in an Olympic-size pool, and a runner, Sirivanh Ketavong, had worn the same running shoes for four years.

The good news is that as the per capita real GDP in some relatively poor countries has risen, the improved living standards have led to increased Olympic medal counts. China, for instance, won 28 medals in 1988 and 63 in 2004. As the host for the 2008 games, it won an impressive total of 100 medals.

While not a perfect measure of the well-being of people in a country, per capita real GDP does tell us about the opportunities available to the average citizen in a country. Americans would surely find it hard to imagine living at the level of consumption of the average Laotian. In *The Progress Paradox: How Life Gets Better While People Feel Worse*, essayist Gregg Easterbrook notes that a higher material standard of living is not associated with higher reported happiness. But, he concludes, the problems of prosperity seem less serious than those of poverty, and prosperity gives people and nations the means to address problems. The Olympic medal count for each nation strongly reflects its average standard of living and hence the opportunities available to its citizens.

Sources: *Gregg Easterbrook, The Progress Paradox: How Life Gets Better While People Feel Worse (New York: Random House, 2003); Daniel K. N. Johnson and Ayfer Ali, "A Tale of Two Seasons: Participation and Medal Counts at the Summer and Winter Olympic Games," Social Science Quarterly 84, no. 4 (December 2004): 974–93; David Wallechinsky, "Why I'll Cheer for Laos," Parade Magazine, August 8, 2004, p. 8.*

ANSWER TO TRY IT! PROBLEM

1. Real GDP would increase. Assuming the people chose to increase their work effort and forgo the extra leisure, economic well-being would increase as well.

2. Real GDP would increase, but the extra expenditure in the economy was due to an increase in something "bad," so economic well-being would likely be lower.

3. No change in real GDP. For some people, economic well-being might increase and for others it might decrease, since inflation does not affect each person in the same way.

4. REVIEW AND PRACTICE

Summary

This chapter focused on the measurement of GDP. The total value of output (GDP) equals the total value of income generated in producing that output (GDI). We can illustrate the flows of spending and income through the economy with the circular flow model. Firms produce goods and services in response to demands from households (personal consumption), other firms (private investment), government agencies (government purchases), and the rest of the world (net exports). This production, in turn, creates a flow of factor incomes to households. Thus, GDP can be estimated using two types of data: (1) data that show the total value of output and (2) data that show the total value of income generated by that output.

In looking at GDP as a measure of output, we divide it into four components: consumption, investment, government purchases, and net exports. GDP equals the sum of final values produced in each of these areas. It can also be measured as the sum of values added at each stage of production. The components of GDP measured in terms of income (GDI) are employee compensation, profits, rental income, net interest, depreciation, and indirect taxes.

We also explained other measures of income such as GNP and disposable personal income. Disposable personal income is an important economic indicator, because it is closely related to personal consumption, the largest component of GDP.

GDP is often used as an indicator of how well off a country is. Of course, to use it for this purpose, we must be careful to use real GDP rather than nominal GDP. Still, there are problems with our estimate of real GDP. Problems encountered in converting nominal GDP to real GDP were discussed in the previous chapter. In this chapter we looked at additional measurement problems and conceptual problems.

Frequent revisions in the data sometimes change our picture of the economy considerably. Accounting for the service sector is quite difficult. Conceptual problems include the omission of nonmarket production and of underground and illegal production. GDP ignores the value of leisure and includes certain "bads."

We cannot assert with confidence that more GDP is a good thing and that less is bad. However, real GDP remains our best single indicator of economic performance. It is used not only to indicate how any one economy is performing over time but also to compare the economic performance of different countries.

CONCEPT PROBLEMS

1. GDP is used as a measure of macroeconomic performance. What, precisely, does it measure?

2. Many economists have attempted to create a set of social accounts that would come closer to measuring the economic well-being of the society than does GDP. What modifications of the current approach would you recommend to them?

3. Every good produced creates income for the owners of the factors of production that created the product or service. For a recent purchase you made, try to list all the types of factors of production involved in making the product available, and try to determine who received income as a result of your purchase.

4. Explain how the sale of used textbooks in your campus bookstore affects the GDP calculation.

5. Look again at the circular flow diagram in Figure 6.5 and assume it is drawn for the United States. State the flows in which each of the following transactions would be entered.

   a. A consumer purchases fresh fish at a local fish market.

   b. A grocery store acquires 1,000 rolls of paper towels for later resale.

   c. NASA purchases a new Saturn rocket.

   d. People in France flock to see the latest Brad Pitt movie.

   e. A construction firm builds a new house.

   f. A couple from Seattle visits Guadalajara and stays in a hotel there.

   g. The city of Dallas purchases computer paper from a local firm.

6. Suggest an argument for and an argument against counting in GDP all household-produced goods and services that are not sold, such as the value of child care or home-cooked meals.

7. Suppose a nation's firms make heavy use of factors of production owned by residents of foreign countries, while foreign firms make relatively little use of factors owned by residents of that nation. How does the nation's GDP compare to its GNP?

8. Suppose Country A has the same GDP as Country B, and that neither nation's residents own factors of production used by foreign firms, nor do either nation's firms use factors of production owned by foreign residents. Suppose that, relative to Country B, depreciation, indirect business taxes, and personal income taxes in Country A are high, while welfare and Social Security payments to households in Country A are relatively low. Which country has the higher disposable personal income? Why?

9. Suppose that virtually everyone in the United States decides to take life a little easier, and the length of the average workweek falls by 25%. How will that affect GDP? Per capita GDP? How will it affect economic welfare?

10. Comment on the following statement: "It does not matter that the value of the labor people devote to producing things for themselves is not counted in GDP; because we make the same 'mistake' every year, relative values are unaffected."

11. Name some of the services, if any, you produced at home that do get counted in GDP. Are there any goods you produce that are not counted?

12. Marijuana is sometimes estimated to be California's largest cash crop. It is not included in estimates of GDP. Should it be?

NUMERICAL PROBLEMS

1. Given the following nominal data, compute GDP. Assume net factor incomes from abroad = 0 (that is, GDP = GNP).

Nominal Data for GDP and NNP	$ Billions
Consumption	2,799.8
Depreciation	481.6
Exports	376.2
Gross private domestic investment	671.0
Indirect taxes	331.4
Government purchases	869.7
Government transfer payments	947.8
Imports	481.7

2. Find data for each of the following countries on real GDP and population. Use the data to calculate the GDP per capita for each of the following countries:

   a. Mozambique

   b. India

   c. Pakistan

   d. United States

   e. Canada

   f. Russia

   g. Brazil

   h. Iran

   i. Colombia

3. Now construct a bar graph showing your results in the previous problem, organizing the countries from the highest to the lowest GNP per capita, with countries on the horizontal axis and GNP per capita on the vertical axis.

4. Suppose Country A has a GDP of $4 trillion. Residents of this country earn $500 million from assets they own in foreign countries. Residents of foreign countries earn $300 million from assets they own in Country A. Compute:

   a. Country A's net foreign income.

   b. Country A's GNP.

5. Suppose a country's GDP equals $500 billion for a particular year. Economists in the country estimate that household production equals 40% of GDP.

   a. What is the value of the country's household production for that year?

   b. Counting both GDP and household production, what is the country's total output for the year?

6. A miner extracts iron from the earth. A steel mill converts the iron to steel beams for use in construction. A construction company uses the steel beams to make a building. Assume that the total product of these firms represents the only components of the building and that they will have no other uses. Complete the following table:

Company	Product	Total Sales	Value Added
Acme Mining	iron ore	$100,000	?
Fuller Mill	steel beams	$175,000	?
Crane Construction	building	$1,100,000	?
Total Value Added			?

7. You are given the data below for 2008 for the imaginary country of Amagre, whose currency is the G.

Consumption	350 billion G
Transfer payments	100 billion G
Investment	100 billion G
Government purchases	200 billion G
Exports	50 billion G
Imports	150 billion G
Bond purchases	200 billion G
Earnings on foreign investments	75 billion G
Foreign earnings on Amagre investment	25 billion G

    a. Compute net foreign investment.

    b. Compute net exports.

    c. Compute GDP.

    d. Compute GNP.

ENDNOTES

1. Although reported separately by the Department of Commerce, we have combined proprietors' income (typically independent business owners and farmers) with corporate profits to simplify the discussion.

2. If you have studied microeconomics, you know that the term "*rent*" in economics has a quite different meaning. The national income and product accounts use the accounting, not the economic, meaning of "*rent*."

3. The adjustment for indirect business taxes includes two other minor elements: transfer payments made by business firms and surpluses or deficits of government enterprises.

4. Profit is corporate profit ($1,274.7) plus proprietors' income ($1,057.6), both with inventory valuation and capital consumption adjustment.

5. Indirect taxes include taxes on production and imports of $1,060.6 plus business transfer payments ($133.1) less subsidies ($58.5) and current surplus of government enterprise ($14.1). Prior to the 2003 National Income and Product Accounts (NIPA) revisions, the category "taxes on production and imports" was, with some technical and other minor adjustments, referred to as "indirect business taxes." See Brent R. Moulton and Eugene P. Seskin, "Preview of the 2003 Comprehensive Revision of the National Income and Product Accounts," Bureau of Economic Analysis, *Survey of Current Business*, June 2003, pp. 17-34.

6. Jack E. Triplett and Barry P. Bosworth, "The State of Data for Services Productivity Measurement in the United States," *International Productivity Monitor* 16 (Spring 2008): 53–70.

7. There are two exceptions to this rule. The value of food produced and consumed by farm households is counted in GDP. More important, an estimate of the rental values of owner-occupied homes is included. If a family rents a house, the rental payments are included in GDP. If a family lives in a house it owns, the Department of Commerce estimates what the house would rent for and then includes that rent in the GDP estimate, even though the house's services were not exchanged in the marketplace.

8. J. Steven Landefeld and Stephanie H. McCulla, "Accounting for Nonmarket Household Production within a National Accounts Framework," *Review of Income & Wealth* 46, no. 3 (September 2000): 289–307.

CHAPTER 7
Aggregate Demand and Aggregate Supply

START UP: THE GREAT WARNING

The first warning came from the Harvard Economic Society, an association of Harvard economics professors, early in 1929. The society predicted in its weekly newsletter that the seven-year-old expansion was coming to an end. Recession was ahead. Almost no one took the warning seriously. The economy, fueled by soaring investment, had experienced stunning growth. The 1920s had seen the emergence of many entirely new industries—automobiles, public power, home appliances, synthetic fabrics, radio, and motion pictures. The decade seemed to have acquired a momentum all its own. Prosperity was not about to end, no matter what a few economists might say.

Summer came, and no recession was apparent. The Harvard economists withdrew their forecast. As it turned out, they lost their nerve too soon. Indeed, industrial production had already begun to fall. The worst downturn in our history, the Great Depression, had begun.

The collapse was swift. The stock market crashed in October 1929. Real GDP plunged nearly 10% by 1930. By the time the economy hit bottom in 1933, real GDP had fallen 30%, unemployment had increased from 3.2% in 1929 to 25% in 1933, and prices, measured by the implicit price deflator, had plunged 23% from their 1929 level. The depression held the economy in its cruel grip for more than a decade; it was not until World War II that full employment was restored.

In this chapter we go beyond explanations of the main macroeconomic variables to introduce a model of macroeconomic activity that we can use to analyze problems such as fluctuations in gross domestic product (real GDP), the price level, and employment: the model of aggregate demand and aggregate supply. We will use this model throughout our exploration of macroeconomics. In this chapter we will present the broad outlines of the model; greater detail, more examples, and more thorough explanations will follow in subsequent chapters.

We will examine the concepts of the aggregate demand curve and the short- and long-run aggregate supply curves. We will identify conditions under which an economy achieves an equilibrium level of real GDP that is consistent with full employment of labor. **Potential output** is the level of output an economy can achieve when labor is employed at its natural level. Potential output is also called the natural level of real GDP. When an economy fails to produce at its potential, there may be actions that the government or the central bank can take to push the economy toward it, and in this chapter we will begin to consider the pros and cons of doing so.

potential output

The level of output an economy can achieve when labor is employed at its natural level.

1. AGGREGATE DEMAND

LEARNING OBJECTIVES

1. Define potential output, also called the natural level of GDP.
2. Define aggregate demand, represent it using a hypothetical aggregate demand curve, and identify and explain the three effects that cause this curve to slope downward.
3. Distinguish between a change in the aggregate quantity of goods and services demanded and a change in aggregate demand.
4. Use examples to explain how each component of aggregate demand can be a possible aggregate demand shifter.
5. Explain what a multiplier is and tell how to calculate it.

aggregate demand

The relationship between the total quantity of goods and services demanded (from all the four sources of demand) and the price level, all other determinants of spending unchanged.

aggregate demand curve

A graphical representation of aggregate demand.

Firms face four sources of demand: households (personal consumption), other firms (investment), government agencies (government purchases), and foreign markets (net exports). **Aggregate demand** is the relationship between the total quantity of goods and services demanded (from all the four sources of demand) and the price level, all other determinants of spending unchanged. The **aggregate demand curve** is a graphical representation of aggregate demand.

1.1 The Slope of the Aggregate Demand Curve

We will use the implicit price deflator as our measure of the price level; the aggregate quantity of goods and services demanded is measured as real GDP. The table in Figure 7.1 gives values for each component of aggregate demand at each price level for a hypothetical economy. Various points on the aggregate demand curve are found by adding the values of these components at different price levels. The aggregate demand curve for the data given in the table is plotted on the graph in Figure 7.1. At point A, at a price level of 1.18, $11,800 billion worth of goods and services will be demanded; at point C, a reduction in the price level to 1.14 increases the quantity of goods and services demanded to $12,000 billion; and at point E, at a price level of 1.10, $12,200 billion will be demanded.

FIGURE 7.1 Aggregate Demand

An aggregate demand curve (*AD*) shows the relationship between the total quantity of output demanded (measured as real GDP) and the price level (measured as the implicit price deflator). At each price level, the total quantity of goods and services demanded is the sum of the components of real GDP, as shown in the table. There is a negative relationship between the price level and the total quantity of goods and services demanded, all other things unchanged.

Point on aggregate demand curve	Price level	$C+$	$I+$	$G+$	$X_n =$	Aggregate demand
A	1.18	8,400	1,820	2,150	−570	11,800
B	1.16	8,450	1,860	2,150	−560	11,900
C	1.14	8,500	1,900	2,150	−550	12,000
D	1.12	8,550	1,940	2,150	−540	12,100
E	1.10	8,600	1,980	2,150	−530	12,200

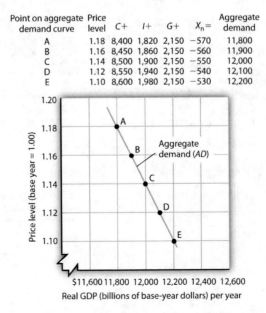

The negative slope of the aggregate demand curve suggests that it behaves in the same manner as an ordinary demand curve. But we *cannot* apply the reasoning we use to explain downward-sloping demand curves in individual markets to explain the downward-sloping aggregate demand curve. There are two reasons for a negative relationship between price and quantity demanded in individual markets. First, a lower price induces people to substitute more of the good whose price has fallen for other goods, increasing the quantity demanded. Second, the lower price creates a higher real income. This normally increases quantity demanded further.

Neither of these effects is relevant to a change in prices in the aggregate. When we are dealing with the average of all prices—the price level—we can no longer say that a fall in prices will induce a change in relative prices that will lead consumers to buy more of the goods and services whose prices have fallen and less of the goods and services whose prices have not fallen. The price of corn may have fallen, but the prices of wheat, sugar, tractors, steel, and most other goods or services produced in the economy are likely to have fallen as well.

Furthermore, a reduction in the price level means that it is not just the prices consumers pay that are falling. It means the prices people receive—their wages, the rents they may charge as landlords, the interest rates they earn—are likely to be falling as well. A falling price level means that goods and services are cheaper, but incomes are lower, too. There is no reason to expect that a change in real income will boost the quantity of goods and services demanded—indeed, no change in real income would occur. If nominal incomes and prices all fall by 10%, for example, real incomes do not change.

Why, then, does the aggregate demand curve slope downward? One reason for the downward slope of the aggregate demand curve lies in the relationship between real wealth (the stocks, bonds, and other assets that people have accumulated) and consumption (one of the four components of aggregate demand). When the price level falls, the real value of wealth increases—it packs more purchasing power. For example, if the price level falls by 25%, then $10,000 of wealth could purchase more goods and services than it would have if the price level had not fallen. An increase in wealth will induce people to increase their consumption. The consumption component of aggregate demand will thus be greater at lower price levels than at higher price levels. The tendency for a change in the price level to affect real wealth and thus alter consumption is called the **wealth effect**; it suggests a negative relationship between the price level and the real value of consumption spending.

A second reason the aggregate demand curve slopes downward lies in the relationship between interest rates and investment. A lower price level lowers the demand for money, because less money is required to buy a given quantity of goods. What economists mean by money demand will be explained in more detail in a later chapter. But, as we learned in studying demand and supply, a reduction in the demand for something, all other things unchanged, lowers its price. In this case, the "something" is money and its price is the interest rate. A lower price level thus reduces interest rates. Lower interest rates make borrowing by firms to build factories or buy equipment and other capital more attractive. A lower interest rate means lower mortgage payments, which tends to increase investment in residential houses. Investment thus rises when the price level falls. The tendency for a change in the price level to affect the interest rate and thus to affect the quantity of investment demanded is called the **interest rate effect**. John Maynard Keynes, a British economist whose analysis of the Great Depression and what to do about it led to the birth of modern macroeconomics, emphasized this effect. For this reason, the interest rate effect is sometimes called the Keynes effect.

A third reason for the rise in the total quantity of goods and services demanded as the price level falls can be found in changes in the net export component of aggregate demand. All other things unchanged, a lower price level in an economy reduces the prices of its goods and services relative to foreign-produced goods and services. A lower price level makes that economy's goods more attractive to foreign buyers, increasing exports. It will also make foreign-produced goods and services less attractive to the economy's buyers, reducing imports. The result is an increase in net exports. The **international trade effect** is the tendency for a change in the price level to affect net exports.

Taken together, then, a fall in the price level means that the quantities of consumption, investment, and net export components of aggregate demand may all rise. Since government purchases are determined through a political process, we assume there is no causal link between the price level and the real volume of government purchases. Therefore, this component of GDP does not contribute to the downward slope of the curve.

In general, a change in the price level, with all other determinants of aggregate demand unchanged, causes a movement along the aggregate demand curve. A movement along an aggregate demand curve is a **change in the aggregate quantity of goods and services demanded**. A movement from point A to point B on the aggregate demand curve in Figure 7.1 is an example. Such a change is a response to a change in the price level.

Notice that the axes of the aggregate demand curve graph are drawn with a break near the origin to remind us that the plotted values reflect a relatively narrow range of changes in real GDP and the price level. We do not know what might happen if the price level or output for an entire economy approached zero. Such a phenomenon has never been observed.

wealth effect

The tendency for a change in the price level to affect real wealth and thus alter consumption.

interest rate effect

The tendency for a change in the price level to affect the interest rate and thus to affect the quantity of investment demanded.

international trade effect

The tendency for a change in the price level to affect net exports.

change in the aggregate quantity of goods and services demanded

Movement along an aggregate demand curve.

1.2 Changes in Aggregate Demand

change in aggregate demand

Change in the aggregate quantity of goods and services demanded at every price level.

Aggregate demand changes in response to a change in any of its components. An increase in the total quantity of consumer goods and services demanded at every price level, for example, would shift the aggregate demand curve to the right. A change in the aggregate quantity of goods and services demanded at every price level is a **change in aggregate demand**, which shifts the aggregate demand curve. Increases and decreases in aggregate demand are shown in Figure 7.2.

FIGURE 7.2 Changes in Aggregate Demand

An increase in consumption, investment, government purchases, or net exports shifts the aggregate demand curve AD_1 to the right as shown in Panel (a). A reduction in one of the components of aggregate demand shifts the curve to the left, as shown in Panel (b).

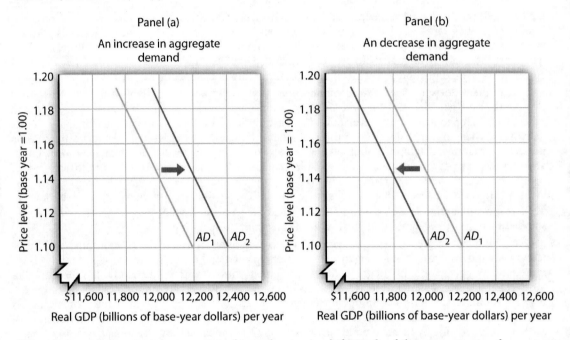

What factors might cause the aggregate demand curve to shift? Each of the components of aggregate demand is a possible aggregate demand shifter. We shall look at some of the events that can trigger changes in the components of aggregate demand and thus shift the aggregate demand curve.

Changes in Consumption

Several events could change the quantity of consumption at each price level and thus shift aggregate demand. One determinant of consumption is consumer confidence. If consumers expect good economic conditions and are optimistic about their economic prospects, they are more likely to buy major items such as cars or furniture. The result would be an increase in the real value of consumption at each price level and an increase in aggregate demand. In the second half of the 1990s, sustained economic growth and low unemployment fueled high expectations and consumer optimism. Surveys revealed consumer confidence to be very high. That consumer confidence translated into increased consumption and increased aggregate demand. In contrast, a decrease in consumption would accompany diminished consumer expectations and a decrease in consumer confidence, as happened after the stock market crash of 1929. The same problem has plagued the economies of most Western nations in 2008 as declining consumer confidence has tended to reduce consumption. A survey by the Conference Board in September of 2008 showed that just 13.5% of consumers surveyed expected economic conditions in the United States to improve in the next six months. Similarly pessimistic views prevailed in the previous two months. That contributed to the decline in consumption that occurred in the third quarter of the year.

Another factor that can change consumption and shift aggregate demand is tax policy. A cut in personal income taxes leaves people with more after-tax income, which may induce them to increase their consumption. The federal government in the United States cut taxes in 1964, 1981, 1986, 1997, and 2003; each of those tax cuts tended to increase consumption and aggregate demand at each price level.

In the United States, another government policy aimed at increasing consumption and thus aggregate demand has been the use of rebates in which taxpayers are simply sent checks in hopes that those checks will be used for consumption. Rebates have been used in 1975, 2001, and 2008. In each case the rebate was a one-time payment. Careful studies by economists of the 1975 and 2001 rebates showed little impact on consumption. Final evidence on the impact of the 2008 rebates is not yet in, but early results suggest a similar outcome. In a subsequent chapter, we will investigate arguments about whether temporary increases in income produced by rebates are likely to have a significant impact on consumption.

Transfer payments such as welfare and Social Security also affect the income people have available to spend. At any given price level, an increase in transfer payments raises consumption and aggregate demand, and a reduction lowers consumption and aggregate demand.

Changes in Investment

Investment is the production of new capital that will be used for future production of goods and services. Firms make investment choices based on what they think they will be producing in the future. The expectations of firms thus play a critical role in determining investment. If firms expect their sales to go up, they are likely to increase their investment so that they can increase production and meet consumer demand. Such an increase in investment raises the aggregate quantity of goods and services demanded at each price level; it increases aggregate demand.

Changes in interest rates also affect investment and thus affect aggregate demand. We must be careful to distinguish such changes from the interest rate effect, which causes a movement along the aggregate demand curve. A change in interest rates that results from a change in the price level affects investment in a way that is already captured in the downward slope of the aggregate demand curve; it causes a movement along the curve. A change in interest rates for some other reason shifts the curve. We examine reasons interest rates might change in another chapter.

Investment can also be affected by tax policy. One provision of the Job and Growth Tax Relief Reconciliation Act of 2003 was a reduction in the tax rate on certain capital gains. Capital gains result when the owner of an asset, such as a house or a factory, sells the asset for more than its purchase price (less any depreciation claimed in earlier years). The lower capital gains tax could stimulate investment, because the owners of such assets know that they will lose less to taxes when they sell those assets, thus making assets subject to the tax more attractive.

Changes in Government Purchases

Any change in government purchases, all other things unchanged, will affect aggregate demand. An increase in government purchases increases aggregate demand; a decrease in government purchases decreases aggregate demand.

Many economists argued that reductions in defense spending in the wake of the collapse of the Soviet Union in 1991 tended to reduce aggregate demand. Similarly, increased defense spending for the wars in Afghanistan and Iraq increased aggregate demand. Dramatic increases in defense spending to fight World War II accounted in large part for the rapid recovery from the Great Depression.

Changes in Net Exports

A change in the value of net exports at each price level shifts the aggregate demand curve. A major determinant of net exports is foreign demand for a country's goods and services; that demand will vary with foreign incomes. An increase in foreign incomes increases a country's net exports and aggregate demand; a slump in foreign incomes reduces net exports and aggregate demand. For example, several major U.S. trading partners in Asia suffered recessions in 1997 and 1998. Lower real incomes in those countries reduced U.S. exports and tended to reduce aggregate demand.

Exchange rates also influence net exports, all other things unchanged. A country's **exchange rate** is the price of its currency in terms of another currency or currencies. A rise in the U.S. exchange rate means that it takes more Japanese yen, for example, to purchase one dollar. That also means that U.S. traders get more yen per dollar. Since prices of goods produced in Japan are given in yen and prices of goods produced in the United States are given in dollars, a rise in the U.S. exchange rate increases the price to foreigners for goods and services produced in the United States, thus reducing U.S. exports; it reduces the price of foreign-produced goods and services for U.S. consumers, thus increasing imports to the United States. A higher exchange rate tends to reduce net exports, reducing aggregate demand. A lower exchange rate tends to increase net exports, increasing aggregate demand.

Foreign price levels can affect aggregate demand in the same way as exchange rates. For example, when foreign price levels fall relative to the price level in the United States, U.S. goods and services become relatively more expensive, reducing exports and boosting imports in the United States. Such a reduction in net exports reduces aggregate demand. An increase in foreign prices relative to U.S. prices has the opposite effect.

The trade policies of various countries can also affect net exports. A policy by Japan to increase its imports of goods and services from India, for example, would increase net exports in India.

exchange rate

The price of a currency in terms of another currency or currencies.

The Multiplier

A change in any component of aggregate demand shifts the aggregate demand curve. Generally, the aggregate demand curve shifts by more than the amount by which the component initially causing it to shift changes.

Suppose that net exports increase due to an increase in foreign incomes. As foreign demand for domestically made products rises, a country's firms will hire additional workers or perhaps increase the average number of hours that their employees work. In either case, incomes will rise, and higher incomes will lead to an increase in consumption. Taking into account these other increases in the components of aggregate demand, the aggregate demand curve will shift by more than the initial shift caused by the initial increase in net exports.

The **multiplier** is the ratio of the change in the quantity of real GDP demanded at each price level to the initial change in one or more components of aggregate demand that produced it:

multiplier

The ratio of the change in the quantity of real GDP demanded at each price level to the initial change in one or more components of aggregate demand that produced it.

EQUATION 7.1

$$\text{Multiplier} = \frac{\Delta \text{ (real GDP demanded at each price level)}}{\text{initial } \Delta \text{ (component of } AD)}$$

We use the capital Greek letter delta (Δ) to mean "change in." In the aggregate demand–aggregate supply model presented in this chapter, it is the number by which we multiply an initial change in aggregate demand to obtain the amount by which the aggregate demand curve shifts as a result of the initial change. In other words, we can use Equation 7.1 to solve for the change in real GDP demanded at each price level:

EQUATION 7.2

$$\Delta \text{ (real GDP demanded at each price level)} = \text{multiplier} \times \text{initial } \Delta \text{ (component of } AD)$$

Suppose that the initial increase in net exports is $100 billion and that the initial $100-billion increase generates additional consumption of $100 billion at each price level. In Panel (a) of Figure 7.3, the aggregate demand curve shifts to the right by $200 billion—the amount of the initial increase in net exports times the multiplier of 2. We obtained the value for the multiplier in this example by plugging $200 billion (the initial $100-billion increase in net exports plus the $100-billion increase that it generated in consumption) into the numerator of Equation 7.1 and $100 billion into the denominator. Similarly, a decrease in net exports of $100 billion leads to a decrease in aggregate demand of $200 billion at each price level, as shown in Panel (b).

FIGURE 7.3 The Multiplier

A change in one component of aggregate demand shifts the aggregate demand curve by more than the initial change. In Panel (a), an initial increase of $100 billion of net exports shifts the aggregate demand curve to the right by $200 billion at each price level. In Panel (b), a decrease of net exports of $100 billion shifts the aggregate demand curve to the left by $200 billion. In this example, the multiplier is 2.

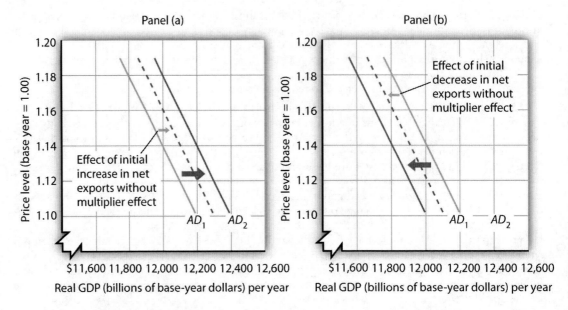

KEY TAKEAWAYS

- Potential output is the level of output an economy can achieve when labor is employed at its natural level. When an economy fails to produce at its potential, the government or the central bank may try to push the economy toward its potential.
- The aggregate demand curve represents the total of consumption, investment, government purchases, and net exports at each price level in any period. It slopes downward because of the wealth effect on consumption, the interest rate effect on investment, and the international trade effect on net exports.
- The aggregate demand curve shifts when the quantity of real GDP demanded at each price level changes.
- The multiplier is the number by which we multiply an initial change in aggregate demand to obtain the amount by which the aggregate demand curve shifts at each price level as a result of the initial change.

TRY IT!

Explain the effect of each of the following on the aggregate demand curve for the United States:

1. A decrease in consumer optimism
2. An increase in real GDP in the countries that buy U.S. exports
3. An increase in the price level
4. An increase in government spending on highways

Case in Point: The Multiplied Economic Impact of SARS on China's Economy

Severe Acute Respiratory Syndrome (SARS), an atypical pneumonia-like disease, broke onto the world scene in late 2002. In March 2003, the World Health Organization (WHO) issued its first worldwide alert and a month later its first travel advisory, which recommended that travelers avoid Hong Kong and the southern province of China, Guangdong. Over the next few months, additional travel advisories were issued for other parts of China, Taiwan, and briefly for Toronto, Canada. By the end of June, all WHO travel advisories had been removed.

To estimate the overall impact of SARS on the Chinese economy in 2003, economists Wen Hai, Zhong Zhao, and Jian Want of Peking University's China Center for Economic Research conducted a survey of Beijing's tourism industry in April 2003. Based on findings from the Beijing area, they projected the tourism sector of China as a whole would lose $16.8 billion—of which $10.8 billion came from an approximate 50% reduction in foreign tourist revenue and $6 billion from curtailed domestic tourism, as holiday celebrations were cancelled and domestic travel restrictions imposed.

To figure out the total impact of SARS on China's economy, they argued that the multiplier for tourism revenue in China is between 2 and 3. Since the SARS outbreak only began to have a major economic impact after March, they assumed a smaller multiplier of 1.5 for all of 2003. They thus predicted that the Chinese economy would be $25.3 billion smaller in 2003 as a result of SARS:

Source: *Wen Hai, Zhong Zhao, and Jian Wan, "The Short-Term Impact of SARS on the Chinese Economy," Asian Economic Papers 3, no. 1 (Winter 2004): 57–61.*

ANSWER TO TRY IT! PROBLEM

1. A decline in consumer optimism would cause the aggregate demand curve to shift to the left. If consumers are more pessimistic about the future, they are likely to cut purchases, especially of major items.
2. An increase in the real GDP of other countries would increase the demand for U.S. exports and cause the aggregate demand curve to shift to the right. Higher incomes in other countries will make consumers in those countries more willing and able to buy U.S. goods.
3. An increase in the price level corresponds to a movement up along the unchanged aggregate demand curve. At the higher price level, the consumption, investment, and net export components of aggregate demand will all fall; that is, there will be a reduction in the total quantity of goods and services demanded, but not a shift of the aggregate demand curve itself.
4. An increase in government spending on highways means an increase in government purchases. The aggregate demand curve would shift to the right.

2. AGGREGATE DEMAND AND AGGREGATE SUPPLY: THE LONG RUN AND THE SHORT RUN

LEARNING OBJECTIVES

1. Distinguish between the short run and the long run, as these terms are used in macroeconomics.
2. Draw a hypothetical long-run aggregate supply curve and explain what it shows about the natural levels of employment and output at various price levels, given changes in aggregate demand.
3. Draw a hypothetical short-run aggregate supply curve, explain why it slopes upward, and explain why it may shift; that is, distinguish between a change in the aggregate quantity of goods and services supplied and a change in short-run aggregate supply.
4. Discuss various explanations for wage and price stickiness.
5. Explain and illustrate what is meant by equilibrium in the short run and relate the equilibrium to potential output.

short run

In macroeconomic analysis, a period in which wages and some other prices are sticky and do not respond to changes in economic conditions.

sticky price

A price that is slow to adjust to its equilibrium level, creating sustained periods of shortage or surplus.

long run

In macroeconomic analysis, a period in which wages and prices are flexible.

In macroeconomics, we seek to understand two types of equilibria, one corresponding to the short run and the other corresponding to the long run. The **short run** in macroeconomic analysis is a period in which wages and some other prices do not respond to changes in economic conditions. In certain markets, as economic conditions change, prices (including wages) may not adjust quickly enough to maintain equilibrium in these markets. A **sticky price** is a price that is slow to adjust to its equilibrium level, creating sustained periods of shortage or surplus. Wage and price stickiness prevent the economy from achieving its natural level of employment and its potential output. In contrast, the **long run** in macroeconomic analysis is a period in which wages and prices are flexible. In the long run, employment will move to its natural level and real GDP to potential.

We begin with a discussion of long-run macroeconomic equilibrium, because this type of equilibrium allows us to see the macroeconomy after full market adjustment has been achieved. In contrast, in the short run, price or wage stickiness is an obstacle to full adjustment. Why these deviations from the potential level of output occur and what the implications are for the macroeconomy will be discussed in the section on short-run macroeconomic equilibrium.

2.1 The Long Run

As explained in a previous chapter, the natural level of employment occurs where the real wage adjusts so that the quantity of labor demanded equals the quantity of labor supplied. When the economy achieves its natural level of employment, it achieves its potential level of output. We will see that real GDP eventually moves to potential, because all wages and prices are assumed to be flexible in the long run.

Long-Run Aggregate Supply

The **long-run aggregate supply (LRAS) curve** relates the level of output produced by firms to the price level in the long run. In Panel (b) of Figure 7.5, the long-run aggregate supply curve is a vertical line at the economy's potential level of output. There is a single real wage at which employment reaches its natural level. In Panel (a) of Figure 7.5, only a real wage of ω_e generates natural employment L_e. The economy could, however, achieve this real wage with any of an infinitely large set of nominal wage and price-level combinations. Suppose, for example, that the equilibrium real wage (the ratio of wages to the price level) is 1.5. We could have that with a nominal wage level of 1.5 and a price level of 1.0, a nominal wage level of 1.65 and a price level of 1.1, a nominal wage level of 3.0 and a price level of 2.0, and so on.

FIGURE 7.5 Natural Employment and Long-Run Aggregate Supply

When the economy achieves its natural level of employment, as shown in Panel (a) at the intersection of the demand and supply curves for labor, it achieves its potential output, as shown in Panel (b) by the vertical long-run aggregate supply curve *LRAS* at Y_P.

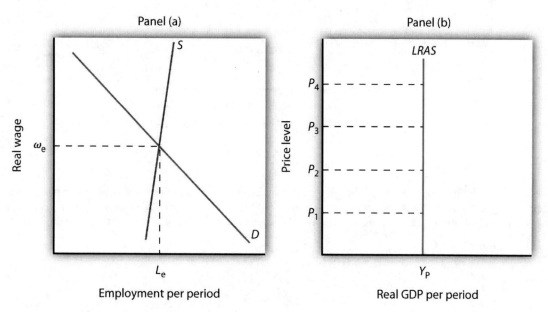

In Panel (b) we see price levels ranging from P_1 to P_4. Higher price levels would require higher nominal wages to create a real wage of ω_e, and flexible nominal wages would achieve that in the long run.

In the long run, then, the economy can achieve its natural level of employment and potential output at any price level. This conclusion gives us our long-run aggregate supply curve. With only one level of output at any price level, the long-run aggregate supply curve is a vertical line at the economy's potential level of output of Y_P.

Equilibrium Levels of Price and Output in the Long Run

The intersection of the economy's aggregate demand curve and the long-run aggregate supply curve determines its equilibrium real GDP and price level in the long run. Figure 7.6 depicts an economy in long-run equilibrium. With aggregate demand at AD_1 and the long-run aggregate supply curve as shown, real GDP is $12,000 billion per year and the price level is 1.14. If aggregate demand increases to AD_2, long-run equilibrium will be reestablished at real GDP of $12,000 billion per year, but at a higher price level of 1.18. If aggregate demand decreases to AD_3, long-run equilibrium will still be at real GDP of $12,000 billion per year, but with the now lower price level of 1.10.

FIGURE 7.6 Long-Run Equilibrium

Long-run equilibrium occurs at the intersection of the aggregate demand curve and the long-run aggregate supply curve. For the three aggregate demand curves shown, long-run equilibrium occurs at three different price levels, but always at an output level of $12,000 billion per year, which corresponds to potential output.

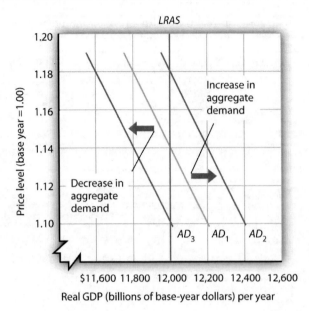

2.2 The Short Run

Analysis of the macroeconomy in the short run—a period in which stickiness of wages and prices may prevent the economy from operating at potential output—helps explain how deviations of real GDP from potential output can and do occur. We will explore the effects of changes in aggregate demand and in short-run aggregate supply in this section.

Short-Run Aggregate Supply

The model of aggregate demand and long-run aggregate supply predicts that the economy will eventually move toward its potential output. To see how nominal wage and price stickiness can cause real GDP to be either above or below potential in the short run, consider the response of the economy to a change in aggregate demand. Figure 7.7 shows an economy that has been operating at potential output of $12,000 billion and a price level of 1.14. This occurs at the intersection of AD_1 with the long-run aggregate supply curve at point B. Now suppose that the aggregate demand curve shifts to the right (to AD_2). This could occur as a result of an increase in exports. (The shift from AD_1 to AD_2 includes the multiplied effect of the increase in exports.) At the price level of 1.14, there is now excess demand and pressure on prices to rise. If all prices in the economy adjusted quickly, the economy would quickly settle at potential output of $12,000 billion, but at a higher price level (1.18 in this case).

Is it possible to expand output above potential? Yes. It may be the case, for example, that some people who were in the labor force but were frictionally or structurally unemployed find work because of the ease of getting jobs at the going nominal wage in such an environment. The result is an economy operating at point A in Figure 7.7 at a higher price level and with output temporarily above potential.

Consider next the effect of a reduction in aggregate demand (to AD_3), possibly due to a reduction in investment. As the price level starts to fall, output also falls. The economy finds itself at a price level–output combination at which real GDP is below potential, at point C. Again, price stickiness is to blame. The prices firms receive are falling with the reduction in demand. Without corresponding reductions in nominal wages, there will be an increase in the real wage. Firms will employ less labor and produce less output.

By examining what happens as aggregate demand shifts over a period when price adjustment is incomplete, we can trace out the short-run aggregate supply curve by drawing a line through points A, B, and C. The **short-run aggregate supply (SRAS) curve** is a graphical representation of the relationship between production and the price level in the short run. Among the factors held constant in drawing a short-run aggregate supply curve are the capital stock, the stock of natural resources, the level of technology, and the prices of factors of production.

A change in the price level produces a **change in the aggregate quantity of goods and services supplied** and is illustrated by the movement along the short-run aggregate supply curve. This occurs between points A, B, and C in Figure 7.7.

A change in the quantity of goods and services supplied at every price level in the short run is a **change in short-run aggregate supply**. Changes in the factors held constant in drawing the short-run aggregate supply curve shift the curve. (These factors may also shift the long-run aggregate supply curve; we will discuss them along with other determinants of long-run aggregate supply in the next chapter.)

One type of event that would shift the short-run aggregate supply curve is an increase in the price of a natural resource such as oil. An increase in the price of natural resources or any other factor of production, all other things unchanged, raises the cost of production and leads to a reduction in short-run aggregate supply. In Panel (a) of Figure 7.8, $SRAS_1$ shifts leftward to $SRAS_2$. A decrease in the price of a natural resource would lower the cost of production and, other things unchanged, would allow greater production from the economy's stock of resources and would shift the short-run aggregate supply curve to the right; such a shift is shown in Panel (b) by a shift from $SRAS_1$ to $SRAS_3$.

FIGURE 7.7 Deriving the Short-Run Aggregate Supply Curve

The economy shown here is in long-run equilibrium at the intersection of AD_1 with the long-run aggregate supply curve. If aggregate demand increases to AD_2, in the short run, both real GDP and the price level rise. If aggregate demand decreases to AD_3, in the short run, both real GDP and the price level fall. A line drawn through points A, B, and C traces out the short-run aggregate supply curve SRAS.

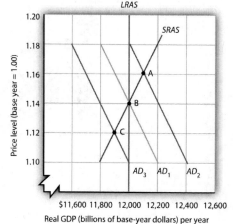

short-run aggregate supply (SRAS) curve

A graphical representation of the relationship between production and the price level in the short run.

change in the aggregate quantity of goods and services supplied

Movement along the short-run aggregate supply curve.

change in short-run aggregate supply

A change in the aggregate quantity of goods and services supplied at every price level in the short run.

FIGURE 7.8 Changes in Short-Run Aggregate Supply

A reduction in short-run aggregate supply shifts the curve from $SRAS_1$ to $SRAS_2$ in Panel (a). An increase shifts it to the right to $SRAS_3$, as shown in Panel (b).

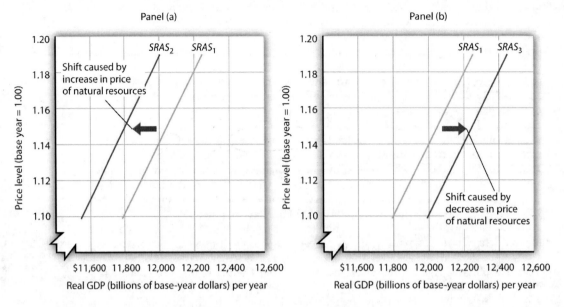

Reasons for Wage and Price Stickiness

Wage or price stickiness means that the economy may not always be operating at potential. Rather, the economy may operate either above or below potential output in the short run. Correspondingly, the overall unemployment rate will be below or above the natural level.

Many prices observed throughout the economy do adjust quickly to changes in market conditions so that equilibrium, once lost, is quickly regained. Prices for fresh food and shares of common stock are two such examples.

Other prices, though, adjust more slowly. Nominal wages, the price of labor, adjust very slowly. We will first look at why nominal wages are sticky, due to their association with the unemployment rate, a variable of great interest in macroeconomics, and then at other prices that may be sticky.

Wage Stickiness

Wage contracts fix nominal wages for the life of the contract. The length of wage contracts varies from one week or one month for temporary employees, to one year (teachers and professors often have such contracts), to three years (for most union workers employed under major collective bargaining agreements). The existence of such explicit contracts means that both workers and firms accept some wage at the time of negotiating, even though economic conditions could change while the agreement is still in force.

Think about your own job or a job you once had. Chances are you go to work each day knowing what your wage will be. Your wage does not fluctuate from one day to the next with changes in demand or supply. You may have a formal contract with your employer that specifies what your wage will be over some period. Or you may have an informal understanding that sets your wage. Whatever the nature of your agreement, your wage is "stuck" over the period of the agreement. Your wage is an example of a sticky price.

One reason workers and firms may be willing to accept long-term nominal wage contracts is that negotiating a contract is a costly process. Both parties must keep themselves adequately informed about market conditions. Where unions are involved, wage negotiations raise the possibility of a labor strike, an eventuality that firms may prepare for by accumulating additional inventories, also a costly process. Even when unions are not involved, time and energy spent discussing wages takes away from time and energy spent producing goods and services. In addition, workers may simply prefer knowing that their nominal wage will be fixed for some period of time.

Some contracts do attempt to take into account changing economic conditions, such as inflation, through cost-of-living adjustments, but even these relatively simple contingencies are not as widespread as one might think. One reason might be that a firm is concerned that while the aggregate price level is rising, the prices for the goods and services it sells might not be moving at the same rate. Also, cost-of-living or other contingencies add complexity to contracts that both sides may want to avoid.

Even markets where workers are not employed under explicit contracts seem to behave as if such contracts existed. In these cases, wage stickiness may stem from a desire to avoid the same uncertainty and adjustment costs that explicit contracts avert.

Finally, minimum wage laws prevent wages from falling below a legal minimum, even if unemployment is rising. Unskilled workers are particularly vulnerable to shifts in aggregate demand.

Price Stickiness

Rigidity of other prices becomes easier to explain in light of the arguments about nominal wage stickiness. Since wages are a major component of the overall cost of doing business, wage stickiness may lead to output price stickiness. With nominal wages stable, at least some firms can adopt a "wait and see" attitude before adjusting their prices. During this time, they can evaluate information about why sales are rising or falling (Is the change in demand temporary or permanent?) and try to assess likely reactions by consumers or competing firms in the industry to any price changes they might make (Will consumers be angered by a price increase, for example? Will competing firms match price changes?).

In the meantime, firms may prefer to adjust output and employment in response to changing market conditions, leaving product price alone. Quantity adjustments have costs, but firms may assume that the associated risks are smaller than those associated with price adjustments.

Another possible explanation for price stickiness is the notion that there are adjustment costs associated with changing prices. In some cases, firms must print new price lists and catalogs, and notify customers of price changes. Doing this too often could jeopardize customer relations.

Yet another explanation of price stickiness is that firms may have explicit long-term contracts to sell their products to other firms at specified prices. For example, electric utilities often buy their inputs of coal or oil under long-term contracts.

Taken together, these reasons for wage and price stickiness explain why aggregate price adjustment may be incomplete in the sense that the change in the price level is insufficient to maintain real GDP at its potential level. These reasons do not lead to the conclusion that no price adjustments occur. But the adjustments require some time. During this time, the economy may remain above or below its potential level of output.

Equilibrium Levels of Price and Output in the Short Run

To illustrate how we will use the model of aggregate demand and aggregate supply, let us examine the impact of two events: an increase in the cost of health care and an increase in government purchases. The first reduces short-run aggregate supply; the second increases aggregate demand. Both events change equilibrium real GDP and the price level in the short run.

A Change in the Cost of Health Care

In the United States, most people receive health insurance for themselves and their families through their employers. In fact, it is quite common for employers to pay a large percentage of employees' health insurance premiums, and this benefit is often written into labor contracts. As the cost of health care has gone up over time, firms have had to pay higher and higher health insurance premiums. With nominal wages fixed in the short run, an increase in health insurance premiums paid by firms raises the cost of employing each worker. It affects the cost of production in the same way that higher wages would. The result of higher health insurance premiums is that firms will choose to employ fewer workers.

Suppose the economy is operating initially at the short-run equilibrium at the intersection of AD_1 and $SRAS_1$, with a real GDP of Y_1 and a price level of P_1, as shown in Figure 7.9. This is the initial equilibrium price and output in the short run. The increase in labor cost shifts the short-run aggregate supply curve to $SRAS_2$. The price level rises to P_2 and real GDP falls to Y_2.

FIGURE 7.9 An Increase in Health Insurance Premiums Paid by Firms

An increase in health insurance premiums paid by firms increases labor costs, reducing short-run aggregate supply from $SRAS_1$ to $SRAS_2$. The price level rises from P_1 to P_2 and output falls from Y_1 to Y_2.

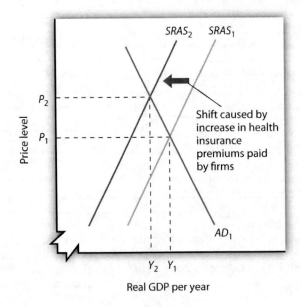

Real GDP per year

A reduction in health insurance premiums would have the opposite effect. There would be a shift to the right in the short-run aggregate supply curve with pressure on the price level to fall and real GDP to rise.

A Change in Government Purchases

Suppose the federal government increases its spending for highway construction. This circumstance leads to an increase in U.S. government purchases and an increase in aggregate demand.

Assuming no other changes affect aggregate demand, the increase in government purchases shifts the aggregate demand curve by a multiplied amount of the initial increase in government purchases to AD_2 in Figure 7.10. Real GDP rises from Y_1 to Y_2, while the price level rises from P_1 to P_2. Notice that the increase in real GDP is less than it would have been if the price level had not risen.

FIGURE 7.10 An Increase in Government Purchases

An increase in government purchases boosts aggregate demand from AD_1 to AD_2. Short-run equilibrium is at the intersection of AD_2 and the short-run aggregate supply curve $SRAS_1$. The price level rises to P_2 and real GDP rises to Y_2.

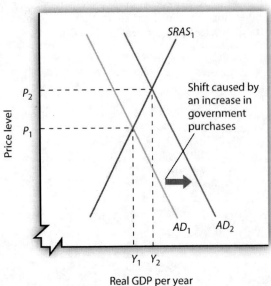

Real GDP per year

In contrast, a reduction in government purchases would reduce aggregate demand. The aggregate demand curve shifts to the left, putting pressure on both the price level and real GDP to fall.

In the short run, real GDP and the price level are determined by the intersection of the aggregate demand and short-run aggregate supply curves. Recall, however, that the short run is a period in which sticky prices may prevent the economy from reaching its natural level of employment and potential output. In the next section, we will see how the model adjusts to move the economy to long-run equilibrium and what, if anything, can be done to steer the economy toward the natural level of employment and potential output.

KEY TAKEAWAYS

- The short run in macroeconomics is a period in which wages and some other prices are sticky. The long run is a period in which full wage and price flexibility, and market adjustment, has been achieved, so that the economy is at the natural level of employment and potential output.
- The long-run aggregate supply curve is a vertical line at the potential level of output. The intersection of the economy's aggregate demand and long-run aggregate supply curves determines its equilibrium real GDP and price level in the long run.
- The short-run aggregate supply curve is an upward-sloping curve that shows the quantity of total output that will be produced at each price level in the short run. Wage and price stickiness account for the short-run aggregate supply curve's upward slope.
- Changes in prices of factors of production shift the short-run aggregate supply curve. In addition, changes in the capital stock, the stock of natural resources, and the level of technology can also cause the short-run aggregate supply curve to shift.
- In the short run, the equilibrium price level and the equilibrium level of total output are determined by the intersection of the aggregate demand and the short-run aggregate supply curves. In the short run, output can be either below or above potential output.

TRY IT!

The tools we have covered in this section can be used to understand the Great Depression of the 1930s. We know that investment and consumption began falling in late 1929. The reductions were reinforced by plunges in net exports and government purchases over the next four years. In addition, nominal wages plunged 26% between 1929 and 1933. We also know that real GDP in 1933 was 30% below real GDP in 1929. Use the tools of aggregate demand and short-run aggregate supply to graph and explain what happened to the economy between 1929 and 1933.

Case in Point: The U.S. Recession of 2001

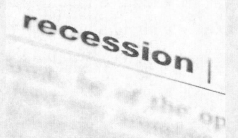

What were the causes of the U.S. recession of 2001? Economist Kevin Kliesen of the Federal Reserve Bank of St. Louis points to four factors that, taken together, shifted the aggregate demand curve to the left and kept it there for a long enough period to keep real GDP falling for about nine months. They were the fall in stock market prices, the decrease in business investment both for computers and software and in structures, the decline in the real value of exports, and the aftermath of 9/11. Notable exceptions to this list of culprits were the behavior of consumer spending during the period and new residential housing, which falls into the investment category.

During the expansion in the late 1990s, a surging stock market probably made it easier for firms to raise funding for investment in both structures and information technology. Even though the stock market bubble burst well before the actual recession, the continuation of projects already underway delayed the decline in the investment component of GDP. Also, spending for information technology was probably prolonged as firms dealt with Y2K computing issues, that is, computer problems associated with the change in the date from 1999 to 2000. Most computers used only two digits to indicate the year, and when the year changed from '99 to '00, computers did not know how to interpret the change, and extensive reprogramming of computers was required.

Real exports fell during the recession because (1) the dollar was strong during the period and (2) real GDP growth in the rest of the world fell almost 5% from 2000 to 2001.

Then, the terrorist attacks of 9/11, which literally shut down transportation and financial markets for several days, may have prolonged these negative tendencies just long enough to turn what might otherwise have been a mild decline into enough of a downtown to qualify the period as a recession.

During this period the measured price level was essentially stable—with the implicit price deflator rising by less than 1%. Thus, while the aggregate demand curve shifted left as a result of all the reasons given above, there was also a leftward shift in the short-run aggregate supply curve.

Source: *Kevin L. Kliesen, "The 2001 Recession: How Was It Different and What Developments May Have Caused It?" The Federal Reserve Bank of St. Louis Review, September/October 2003: 23–37.*

ANSWER TO TRY IT! PROBLEM

All components of aggregate demand (consumption, investment, government purchases, and net exports) declined between 1929 and 1933. Thus the aggregate demand curve shifted markedly to the left, moving from AD_{1929} to AD_{1933}. The reduction in nominal wages corresponds to an increase in short-run aggregate supply from $SRAS_{1929}$ to $SRAS_{1933}$. Since real GDP in 1933 was less than real GDP in 1929, we know that the movement in the aggregate demand curve was greater than that of the short-run aggregate supply curve.

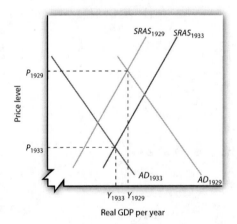

3. RECESSIONARY AND INFLATIONARY GAPS AND LONG-RUN MACROECONOMIC EQUILIBRIUM

LEARNING OBJECTIVES

1. Explain and illustrate graphically recessionary and inflationary gaps and relate these gaps to what is happening in the labor market.
2. Identify the various policy choices available when an economy experiences an inflationary or recessionary gap and discuss some of the pros and cons that make these choices controversial.

The intersection of the economy's aggregate demand and short-run aggregate supply curves determines equilibrium real GDP and price level in the short run. The intersection of aggregate demand and long-run aggregate supply determines its long-run equilibrium. In this section we will examine the process through which an economy moves from equilibrium in the short run to equilibrium in the long run.

The long run puts a nation's macroeconomic house in order: only frictional and structural unemployment remain, and the price level is stabilized. In the short run, stickiness of nominal wages and other prices can prevent the economy from achieving its potential output. Actual output may exceed or fall short of potential output. In such a situation the economy operates with a gap. When output is above potential, employment is above the natural level of employment. When output is below potential, employment is below the natural level.

3.1 Recessionary and Inflationary Gaps

At any time, real GDP and the price level are determined by the intersection of the aggregate demand and short-run aggregate supply curves. If employment is below the natural level of employment, real GDP will be below potential. The aggregate demand and short-run aggregate supply curves will intersect to the left of the long-run aggregate supply curve.

Suppose an economy's natural level of employment is L_e, shown in Panel (a) of Figure 7.13. This level of employment is achieved at a real wage of ω_e. Suppose, however, that the initial real wage ω_1 exceeds this equilibrium value. Employment at L_1 falls short of the natural level. A lower level of employment produces a lower level of output; the aggregate demand and short-run aggregate supply curves, *AD* and *SRAS*, intersect to the left of the long-run aggregate supply curve *LRAS* in Panel (b). The gap between the level of real GDP and potential output, when real GDP is less than potential, is called a **recessionary gap**.

recessionary gap

The gap between the level of real GDP and potential output, when real GDP is less than potential.

FIGURE 7.13 A Recessionary Gap

If employment is below the natural level, as shown in Panel (a), then output must be below potential. Panel (b) shows the recessionary gap $Y_P - Y_1$, which occurs when the aggregate demand curve AD and the short-run aggregate supply curve SRAS intersect to the left of the long-run aggregate supply curve LRAS.

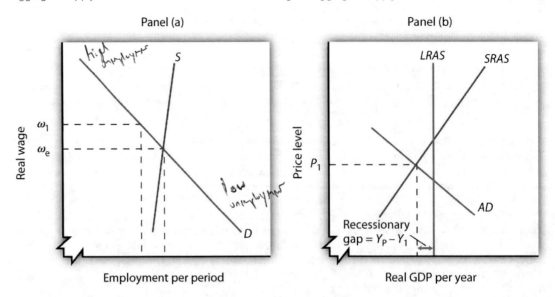

inflationary gap

The gap between the level of real GDP and potential output, when real GDP is greater than potential.

Just as employment can fall short of its natural level, it can also exceed it. If employment is greater than its natural level, real GDP will also be greater than its potential level. Figure 7.14 shows an economy with a natural level of employment of L_e in Panel (a) and potential output of Y_P in Panel (b). If the real wage ω_1 is less than the equilibrium real wage ω_e, then employment L_1 will exceed the natural level. As a result, real GDP, Y_1, exceeds potential. The gap between the level of real GDP and potential output, when real GDP is greater than potential, is called an **inflationary gap**. In Panel (b), the inflationary gap equals $Y_1 - Y_P$.

FIGURE 7.14 An Inflationary Gap

Panel (a) shows that if employment is above the natural level, then output must be above potential. The inflationary gap, shown in Panel (b), equals $Y_1 - Y_P$. The aggregate demand curve AD and the short-run aggregate supply curve SRAS intersect to the right of the long-run aggregate supply curve LRAS.

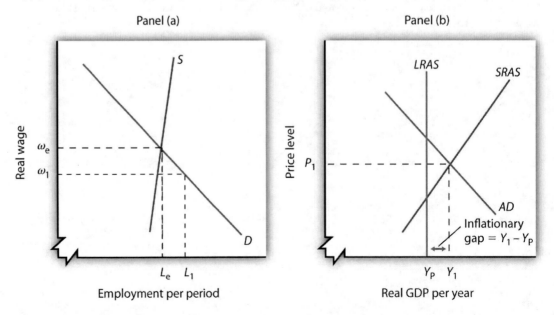

3.2   Restoring Long-Run Macroeconomic Equilibrium

We have already seen that the aggregate demand curve shifts in response to a change in consumption, investment, government purchases, or net exports. The short-run aggregate supply curve shifts in response to changes in the prices of factors of production, the quantities of factors of production available, or technology. Now we will see how the economy responds to a shift in aggregate demand or short-run aggregate supply using two examples presented earlier: a change in government purchases and a change in health-care costs. By returning to these examples, we will be able to distinguish the long-run response from the short-run response.

A Shift in Aggregate Demand: An Increase in Government Purchases

Suppose an economy is initially in equilibrium at potential output YP as in Figure 7.15. Because the economy is operating at its potential, the labor market must be in equilibrium; the quantities of labor demanded and supplied are equal.

Now suppose aggregate demand increases because one or more of its components (consumption, investment, government purchases, and net exports) has increased at each price level. For example, suppose government purchases increase. The aggregate demand curve shifts from AD_1 to AD_2 in Figure 7.15. That will increase real GDP to Y_2 and force the price level up to P_2 in the short run. The higher price level, combined with a fixed nominal wage, results in a lower real wage. Firms employ more workers to supply the increased output.

The economy's new production level Y_2 exceeds potential output. Employment exceeds its natural level. The economy with output of Y_2 and price level of P_2 is only in short-run equilibrium; there is an inflationary gap equal to the difference between Y_2 and Y_P. Because real GDP is above potential, there will be pressure on prices to rise further.

Ultimately, the nominal wage will rise as workers seek to restore their lost purchasing power. As the nominal wage rises, the short-run aggregate supply curve will begin shifting to the left. It will continue to shift as long as the nominal wage rises, and the nominal wage will rise as long as there is an inflationary gap. These shifts in short-run aggregate supply, however, will reduce real GDP and thus begin to close this gap. When the short-run aggregate supply curve reaches $SRAS_2$, the economy will have returned to its potential output, and employment will have returned to its natural level. These adjustments will close the inflationary gap.

A Shift in Short-Run Aggregate Supply: An Increase in the Cost of Health Care

Again suppose, with an aggregate demand curve at AD_1 and a short-run aggregate supply at $SRAS_1$, an economy is initially in equilibrium at its potential output Y_P, at a price level of P_1, as shown in Figure 7.16. Now suppose that the short-run aggregate supply curve shifts owing to a rise in the cost of health care. As we explained earlier, because health insurance premiums are paid primarily by firms for their workers, an increase in premiums raises the cost of production and causes a reduction in the short-run aggregate supply curve from $SRAS_1$ to $SRAS_2$.

FIGURE 7.15 Long-Run Adjustment to an Inflationary Gap

An increase in aggregate demand to AD_2 boosts real GDP to Y_2 and the price level to P_2, creating an inflationary gap of $Y_2 - Y_P$. In the long run, as price and nominal wages increase, the short-run aggregate supply curve moves to $SRAS_2$. Real GDP returns to potential.

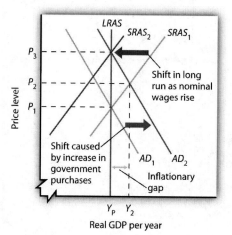

FIGURE 7.16 Long-Run Adjustment to a Recessionary Gap

A decrease in aggregate supply from $SRAS_1$ to $SRAS_2$ reduces real GDP to Y_2 and raises the price level to P_2, creating a recessionary gap of $Y_P - Y_2$. In the long run, as prices and nominal wages decrease, the short-run aggregate supply curve moves back to $SRAS_1$ and real GDP returns to potential.

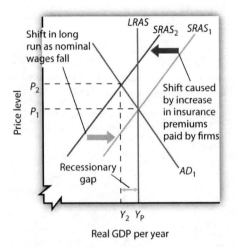

As a result, the price level rises to P_2 and real GDP falls to Y_2. The economy now has a recessionary gap equal to the difference between Y_P and Y_2. Notice that this situation is particularly disagreeable, because both unemployment and the price level rose.

With real GDP below potential, though, there will eventually be pressure on the price level to fall. Increased unemployment also puts pressure on nominal wages to fall. In the long run, the short-run aggregate supply curve shifts back to $SRAS_1$. In this case, real GDP returns to potential at Y_P, the price level falls back to P_1, and employment returns to its natural level. These adjustments will close the recessionary gap.

How sticky prices and nominal wages are will determine the time it takes for the economy to return to potential. People often expect the government or the central bank to respond in some way to try to close gaps. This issue is addressed next.

3.3 Gaps and Public Policy

If the economy faces a gap, how do we get from that situation to potential output?

Gaps present us with two alternatives. First, we can do nothing. In the long run, real wages will adjust to the equilibrium level, employment will move to its natural level, and real GDP will move to its potential. Second, we can do something. Faced with a recessionary or an inflationary gap, policy makers can undertake policies aimed at shifting the aggregate demand or short-run aggregate supply curves in a way that moves the economy to its potential. A policy choice to take no action to try to close a recessionary or an inflationary gap, but to allow the economy to adjust on its own to its potential output, is a **nonintervention policy**. A policy in which the government or central bank acts to move the economy to its potential output is called a **stabilization policy**.

Nonintervention or Expansionary Policy?

Figure 7.17 illustrates the alternatives for closing a recessionary gap. In both panels, the economy starts with a real GDP of Y_1 and a price level of P_1. There is a recessionary gap equal to $Y_P - Y_1$. In Panel (a), the economy closes the gap through a process of self-correction. Real and nominal wages will fall as long as employment remains below the natural level. Lower nominal wages shift the short-run aggregate supply curve. The process is a gradual one, however, given the stickiness of nominal wages, but after a series of shifts in the short-run aggregate supply curve, the economy moves toward equilibrium at a price level of P_2 and its potential output of Y_P.

nonintervention policy

A policy choice to take no action to try to close a recessionary or an inflationary gap, but to allow the economy to adjust on its own to its potential output.

stabilization policy

A policy in which the government or central bank acts to move the economy to its potential output.

FIGURE 7.17 Alternatives in Closing a Recessionary Gap

Panel (a) illustrates a gradual closing of a recessionary gap. Under a nonintervention policy, short-run aggregate supply shifts from $SRAS_1$ to $SRAS_2$. Panel (b) shows the effects of expansionary policy acting on aggregate demand to close the gap.

Panel (a)

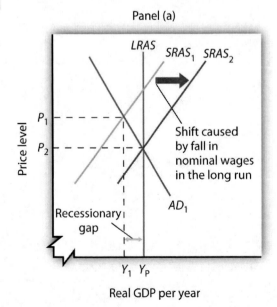

Panel (b)

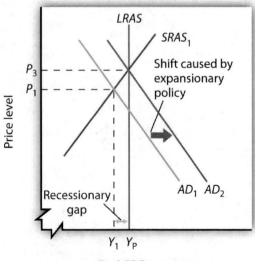

Panel (b) illustrates the stabilization alternative. Faced with an economy operating below its potential, public officials act to stimulate aggregate demand. For example, the government can increase government purchases of goods and services or cut taxes. Tax cuts leave people with more after-tax income to spend, boost their consumption, and increase aggregate demand. As AD_1 shifts to AD_2 in Panel (b) of Figure 7.17, the economy achieves output of Y_P, but at a higher price level, P_3. A stabilization policy designed to increase real GDP is known as an **expansionary policy**.

expansionary policy

A stabilization policy designed to increase real GDP.

Nonintervention or Contractionary Policy?

Figure 7.18 illustrates the alternatives for closing an inflationary gap. Employment in an economy with an inflationary gap exceeds its natural level—the quantity of labor demanded exceeds the long-run supply of labor. A nonintervention policy would rely on nominal wages to rise in response to the shortage of labor. As nominal wages rise, the short-run aggregate supply curve begins to shift, as shown in Panel (a), bringing the economy to its potential output when it reaches $SRAS_2$ and P_2.

FIGURE 7.18 Alternatives in Closing an Inflationary Gap

Panel (a) illustrates a gradual closing of an inflationary gap. Under a nonintervention policy, short-run aggregate supply shifts from $SRAS_1$ to $SRAS_2$. Panel (b) shows the effects of contractionary policy to reduce aggregate demand from AD_1 to AD_2 in order to close the gap.

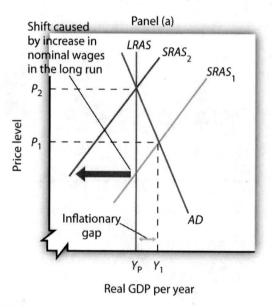
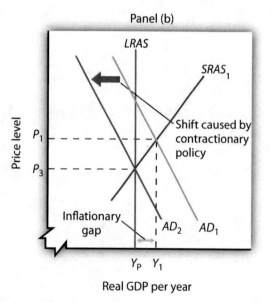

A stabilization policy that reduces the level of GDP is a **contractionary policy**. Such a policy would aim at shifting the aggregate demand curve from AD_1 to AD_2 to close the gap, as shown in Panel (b). A policy to shift the aggregate demand curve to the left would return real GDP to its potential at a price level of P_3.

contractionary policy

A stabilization policy designed to reduce real GDP.

fiscal policy

The use of government purchases, transfer payments, and taxes to influence the level of economic activity.

monetary policy

The use of central bank policies to influence the level of economic activity.

For both kinds of gaps, a combination of letting market forces in the economy close part of the gap and of using stabilization policy to close the rest of the gap is also an option. Later chapters will explain stabilization policies in more detail, but there are essentially two types of stabilization policy: fiscal policy and monetary policy. **Fiscal policy** is the use of government purchases, transfer payments, and taxes to influence the level of economic activity. **Monetary policy** is the use of central bank policies to influence the level of economic activity.

To Intervene or Not to Intervene: An Introduction to the Controversy

How large are inflationary and recessionary gaps? Panel (a) of Figure 7.19 shows potential output versus the actual level of real GDP in the United States since 1960. Real GDP appears to follow potential output quite closely, although you see some periods where there have been inflationary or recessionary gaps. Panel (b) shows the sizes of these gaps expressed as percentages of potential output. The percentage gap is positive during periods of inflationary gaps and negative during periods of recessionary gaps. The economy seldom departs by more than 5% from its potential output.

FIGURE 7.19 Real GDP and Potential Output

Panel (a) shows potential output (the blue line) and actual real GDP (the purple line) since 1960. Panel (b) shows the gap between potential and actual real GDP expressed as a percentage of potential output. Inflationary gaps are shown in green and recessionary gaps are shown in yellow.

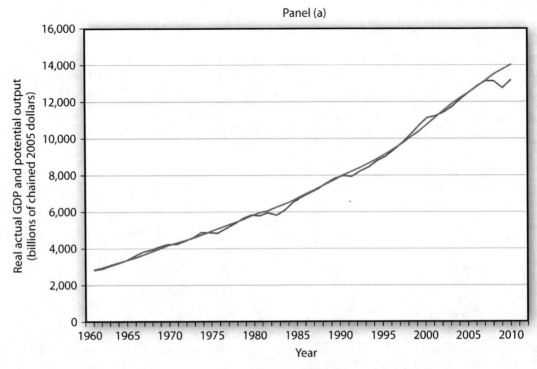

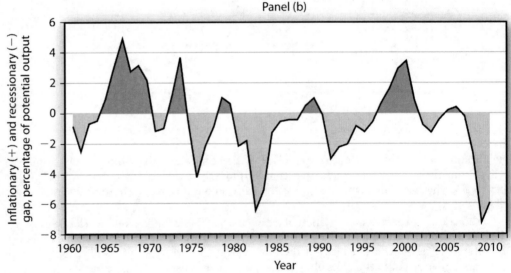

Source: Bureau of Economic Analysis, NIPA Table 1.1.6. Real Gross Domestic Product, Chained Dollars [Billions of chained (2005) dollars]. Seasonally adjusted at annual rates 2010 is through 3rd quarter; Congressional Budget Office, The Budget and Economic Outlook, August 2010.

Panel (a) gives a long-run perspective on the economy. It suggests that the economy generally operates at about potential output. In Panel (a), the gaps seem minor. Panel (b) gives a short-run perspective; the view it gives emphasizes the gaps. Both of these perspectives are important. While it is reassuring to see that the economy is often close to potential, the years in which there are substantial gaps have real effects: Inflation or unemployment can harm people.

Some economists argue that stabilization policy can and should be used when recessionary or inflationary gaps exist. Others urge reliance on the economy's own ability to correct itself. They sometimes argue that the tools available to the public sector to influence aggregate demand are not likely to shift the curve, or they argue that the tools would shift the curve in a way that could do more harm than good.

Economists who advocate stabilization policies argue that prices are sufficiently sticky that the economy's own adjustment to its potential will be a slow process—and a painful one. For an economy with a recessionary gap, unacceptably high levels of unemployment will persist for too long a time. For an economy with an inflationary gap, the increased prices that occur as the short-run aggregate supply curve shifts upward impose too high an inflation rate in the short run. These economists believe it is far preferable to use stabilization policy to shift the aggregate demand curve in an effort to shorten the time the economy is subject to a gap.

Economists who favor a nonintervention approach accept the notion that stabilization policy can shift the aggregate demand curve. They argue, however, that such efforts are not nearly as simple in the real world as they may appear on paper. For example, policies to change real GDP may not affect the economy for months or even years. By the time the impact of the stabilization policy occurs, the state of the economy might have changed. Policy makers might choose an expansionary policy when a contractionary one is needed or vice versa. Other economists who favor nonintervention also question how sticky prices really are and if gaps even exist.

The debate over how policy makers should respond to recessionary and inflationary gaps is an ongoing one. These issues of nonintervention versus stabilization policies lie at the heart of the macroeconomic policy debate. We will return to them as we continue our analysis of the determination of output and the price level.

KEY TAKEAWAYS

- When the aggregate demand and short-run aggregate supply curves intersect below potential output, the economy has a recessionary gap. When they intersect above potential output, the economy has an inflationary gap.

- Inflationary and recessionary gaps are closed as the real wage returns to equilibrium, where the quantity of labor demanded equals the quantity supplied. Because of nominal wage and price stickiness, however, such an adjustment takes time.

- When the economy has a gap, policy makers can choose to do nothing and let the economy return to potential output and the natural level of employment on its own. A policy to take no action to try to close a gap is a nonintervention policy.

- Alternatively, policy makers can choose to try to close a gap by using stabilization policy. Stabilization policy designed to increase real GDP is called expansionary policy. Stabilization policy designed to decrease real GDP is called contractionary policy.

TRY IT!

Using the scenario of the Great Depression of the 1930s, as analyzed in the previous Try It!, tell what kind of gap the U.S. economy faced in 1933, assuming the economy had been at potential output in 1929. Do you think the unemployment rate was above or below the natural rate of unemployment? How could the economy have been brought back to its potential output?

Case in Point: Survey of Economists Reveals Little Consensus on Macroeconomic Policy Issues

"An economy in short-run equilibrium at a real GDP below potential GDP has a self-correcting mechanism that will eventually return it to potential real GDP."

Of economists surveyed, 36% disagreed, 33% agreed with provisos, 25% agreed, and 5% did not respond. So, only about 60% of economists responding to the survey agreed that the economy would adjust on its own.

"Changes in aggregate demand affect real GDP in the short run but not in the long run."

On this statement, 36% disagreed, 31% agreed with provisos, 29% agreed, and 4% did not respond. Once again, about 60% of economists accepted the conclusion of the aggregate demand–aggregate supply model.

This level of disagreement on macroeconomic policy issues among economists, based on a fall 2000 survey of members of the American Economic Association, stands in sharp contrast to their more harmonious responses to questions on international economics and microeconomics. For example,

"Tariffs and import quotas usually reduce the general welfare of society."

Seventy-two percent of those surveyed agreed with this statement outright and another 21% agreed with provisos. So, 93% of economists generally agreed with the statement.

"Minimum wages increase unemployment among young and unskilled workers."

On this, 45% agreed and 29% agreed with provisos.

"Pollution taxes or marketable pollution permits are a more economically efficient approach to pollution control than emission standards."

On this environmental question, only 6% disagreed and 63% wholeheartedly agreed.

The relatively low degree of consensus on macroeconomic policy issues and the higher degrees of consensus on other economic issues found in this survey concur with results of other periodic surveys since 1976.

So, as textbook authors, we will not hide the dirty laundry from you. Fortunately, though, the model of aggregate demand–aggregate supply we present throughout the macroeconomic chapters can handle most of these disagreements. For example, economists who agree with the first proposition quoted above, that an economy operating below potential has self-correcting mechanisms to bring it back to potential, are probably assuming that wages and prices are not very sticky and hence that the short-run aggregate supply curve will shift rather easily to the right, as shown in Panel (a) of Figure 7.17. In contrast, economists who disagree with the statement are saying that the movement of the short-run aggregate supply curve is likely to be slow. This latter group of economists probably advocates expansionary policy as shown in Panel (b) of Figure 7.17. Both groups of economists can use the same model and its constructs to analyze the macroeconomy, but they may disagree on such things as the slopes of the various curves, on how fast these various curves shift, and on the size of the underlying multiplier. The model allows economists to speak the same language of analysis even though they disagree on some specifics.

Source: *Dan Fuller and Doris Geide-Stevenson, "Consensus on Economic Issues: A Survey of Republicans, Democrats and Economists," Eastern Economic Journal 33, no. 1 (Winter 2007): 81–94.*

To the graph in the previous Try It! problem we add the long-run aggregate supply curve to show that, with output below potential, the U.S. economy in 1933 was in a recessionary gap. The unemployment rate was above the natural rate of unemployment. Indeed, real GDP in 1933 was about 30% below what it had been in 1929, and the unemployment rate had increased from 3% to 25%. Note that during the period of the Great Depression, wages did fall. The notion of nominal wage and other price stickiness discussed in this section should not be construed to mean complete wage and price inflexibility. Rather, during this period, nominal wages and other prices were not flexible enough to restore the economy to the potential level of output. There are two basic choices on how to close recessionary gaps. Nonintervention would mean waiting for wages to fall further. As wages fall, the short-run aggregate supply curve would continue to shift to the right. The alternative would be to use some type of expansionary policy. This would shift the aggregate demand curve to the right. These two options were illustrated in Figure 7.18.

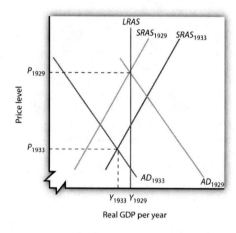

4.   REVIEW AND PRACTICE

Summary

In this chapter, we outlined the model of aggregate demand and aggregate supply. We saw that the aggregate demand curve slopes downward, reflecting the tendency for the aggregate quantity of goods and services demanded to rise as the price level falls and to fall as the price level rises. The negative relationship between the price level and the quantity of goods and services demanded results from the wealth effect for consumption, the interest rate effect for investment, and the international trade effect for net exports. We examined the factors that can shift the aggregate demand curve as well. Generally, the aggregate demand curve shifts by a multiple of the initial amount by which the component causing it to shift changes.

We distinguished between two types of equilibria in macroeconomics—one corresponding to the short run, a period of analysis in which nominal wages and some prices are sticky, and the other corresponding to the long run, a period in which full wage and price flexibility, and hence market adjustment, have been achieved. Long-run equilibrium occurs at the intersection of the aggregate demand curve with the long-run aggregate supply curve. The long-run aggregate supply curve is a vertical line at the economy's potential level of output. Short-run equilibrium occurs at the intersection of the aggregate demand curve with the short-run aggregate supply curve. The short-run aggregate supply curve relates the quantity of total output produced to the price level in the short run. It is upward sloping because of wage and price stickiness. In short-run equilibrium, output can be below or above potential.

If an economy is initially operating at its potential output, then a change in aggregate demand or short-run aggregate supply will induce a recessionary or inflationary gap. Such a gap will be closed in the long run by changes in the nominal wage, which will shift the short-run aggregate supply curve to the left (to close an inflationary gap) or to the right (to close a recessionary gap). Policy makers might respond to a recessionary or inflationary gap with a nonintervention policy, or they could use stabilization policy.

CONCEPT PROBLEMS

1. Explain how the following changes in aggregate demand or short-run aggregate supply, other things held unchanged, are likely to affect the level of total output and the price level in the short run.

    a. An increase in aggregate demand

    b. A decrease in aggregate demand

    c. An increase in short-run aggregate supply

    d. A reduction in short-run aggregate supply

2. Explain why a change in one component of aggregate demand will cause the aggregate demand curve to shift by a multiple of the initial change.

3. Use the model of aggregate demand and short-run aggregate supply to explain how each of the following would affect real GDP and the price level in the short run.

    a. An increase in government purchases

    b. A reduction in nominal wages

    c. A major improvement in technology

    d. A reduction in net exports

4. How would an increase in the supply of labor affect the natural level of employment and potential output? How would it affect the real wage, the level of real GDP, and the price level in the short run? How would it affect long-run aggregate supply? What kind of gaps would be created?

5. Give three reasons for the downward slope of the aggregate demand curve.

6. "When the price level falls, people's wealth increases. When wealth increases, the real volume of consumption increases. Therefore, a decrease in the price level will cause the aggregate demand curve to shift to the right." Do you agree? Explain.

7. Suppose the economy has a recessionary gap. We know that if we do nothing, the economy will close the gap on its own. Alternatively, we could arrange for an increase in aggregate demand (say, by increasing government spending) to close the gap. How would your views about the degree of price stickiness in the economy influence your views on whether such a policy would be desirable?

8. The cost of hiring workers includes not only payments made directly to workers, that is, wages, but payments made on behalf of workers as well, such as contributions by employers to pension plans and to health-care insurance for employees. How would a decrease in the cost of employer-provided health insurance affect the economy? Using Figure 7.9 as a guide, draw a graph to illustrate your answer.

9. Suppose nominal wages never changed. What would be the significance of such a characteristic?

10. Suppose the minimum wage were increased sharply. How would this affect the equilibrium price level and output level in the model of aggregate demand and aggregate supply in the short run? In the long run?

11. Explain the short-run impact of each of the following.

    a. A discovery that makes cold fusion a reality, greatly reducing the cost of producing energy

    b. An increase in the payroll tax

NUMERICAL PROBLEMS

1. Suppose the aggregate demand and short-run aggregate supply schedules for an economy whose potential output equals $2,700 are given by the table.

Price Level	Aggregate Quantity of Goods and Services	
	Demanded	Supplied
0.50	$3,500	$1,000
0.75	3,000	2,000
1.00	2,500	2,500
1.25	2,000	2,700
1.50	1,500	2,800

   a. Draw the aggregate demand, short-run aggregate supply, and long-run aggregate supply curves.
   b. State the short-run equilibrium level of real GDP and the price level.
   c. Characterize the current economic situation. Is there an inflationary or a recessionary gap? If so, how large is it?
   d. Now suppose aggregate demand increases by $700 at each price level; for example, the aggregate quantity of goods and services demanded at a price level of 0.50 now equals $4,200. Show the new aggregate demand curve, state the new short-run equilibrium price level and real GDP, and state whether there is an inflationary or a recessionary gap and give its size.

2. An economy is characterized by the values in the table for aggregate demand and short-run aggregate supply. Its potential output is $1,500.

Price Level	Aggregate Quantity of Goods and Services	
	Demanded	Supplied
0.50	$2,500	$1,500
0.75	2,000	2,000
1.00	1,500	2,300
1.25	1,000	2,500
1.50	500	2,600

   a. Draw the aggregate demand, short-run aggregate supply, and long-run aggregate supply curves.
   b. State the equilibrium level of real GDP and the price level.
   c. Characterize the current economic situation. Is there an inflationary or a recessionary gap? If so, how large is it?
   d. Now suppose that nominal wages rise and that the price level required to induce a particular level of total output rises by 0.50. For example, a price level of 1.00 is now required to induce producers to produce a real GDP of $1,500. Show the new short-run aggregate supply curve, state the new equilibrium price level and real GDP, and state whether there is an inflationary or a recessionary gap and give its size. Why might such a change occur?

3. Suppose the price level in a particular economy equals 1.3 and that the quantity of real GDP demanded at that price level is $1,200. An increase of 0.1 point in the price level reduces the quantity of real GDP demanded by $220, and a reduction of 0.1 point would produce an increase in the quantity of real GDP demanded of $220. Draw the aggregate demand curve and show the price level and quantity of real GDP demanded at three points.

4. Suppose an economy is described by the following aggregate demand and short-run aggregate supply curves. The potential level of output is $10 trillion.

	Aggregate Quantity of Goods and Services	
Price Level	Demanded	Supplied
3.0	$11.0 trillion	$9.0 trillion
3.4	$10.8 trillion	$9.2 trillion
3.8	$10.6 trillion	$9.4 trillion
4.2	$10.4 trillion	$9.6 trillion
4.6	$10.2 trillion	$9.8 trillion
5.0	$10.0 trillion	$10.0 trillion
5.4	$9.8 trillion	$10.2 trillion
5.8	$9.6 trillion	$10.4 trillion
6.2	$9.4 trillion	$10.6 trillion
6.6	$9.2 trillion	$10.8 trillion
7.0	$9.0 trillion	$11.0 trillion

    a. Draw the aggregate demand and short-run aggregate supply curves.

    b. What is the initial real GDP?

    c. What is the initial price level?

    d. What kind of gap, if any, exists?

    e. After the increase in health-care costs, each level of real GDP requires an increase in the price level of 0.8. For example, producing $9.0 trillion worth of goods and services now requires a price level of 3.8. What is the short-run equilibrium level of real GDP?

    f. After the health-care cost increase, what is the new equilibrium price level in the short run?

    g. What sort of gap, if any, now exists?

5. According to Alaskan state economist Mark Edwards, the multiplier effect of Alaska's trade with Japan is such that for every $1 billion exported from Alaska to Japan another $600 million is added to the state's economy.[1] Calculate the size of the export multiplier.

6. The Nottinghamshire Research Observatory in England calculated that students who attend Nottingham Technical University spend about £2,760 each in the local economy for a total of £50.45 million. In total, the impact of their spending on the local economy is £63 million.[2] Calculate the size of the student spending multiplier.

7. In Goa, India, the multiplier effect of iron ore exports is calculated to be 1.62.[3] Calculate the impact of an additional 1,000 rupees of iron ore exports on the economy of Goa.

ENDNOTES

1. Matt Volz, "Trade Officials Hopeful for Japanese Recovery," *Associated Press and Local Wire*, June 22, 2004, BC cycle.

2. "University Brings in £250m to Economy," *Nottingham Evening Post*, November 4, 2004, p. 37.

3. Vidyut Kumar Ta, "Iron Ore Mining Gives Impetus to Goa's Economy," *Times of India*, April 30, 2003.

CHAPTER 8
Economic Growth

START UP: HOW IMPORTANT IS ECONOMIC GROWTH?

How important is economic growth? The best way to answer that question is to imagine life without growth—to imagine that we did not have the gains growth brings.

For starters, divide your family's current income by six and imagine what your life would be like. Think about the kind of housing your family could afford, the size of your entertainment budget, whether you could still attend school. That will give you an idea of life a century ago in the United States, when average household incomes, adjusted for inflation, were about one-sixth what they are today. People had far smaller homes, they rarely had electricity in their homes, and only a tiny percentage of the population could even consider a college education.

To get a more recent perspective, consider how growth has changed living standards over the past half-century or so. In 1950, the United States was the world's richest nation. But if households were rich then, subsequent economic growth has made them far richer. Average per capita real disposable personal income has tripled since then. Indeed, the average household income in 1950, which must have seemed lofty then, was below what we now define as the poverty line for a household of four, even after adjusting for inflation. Economic growth during the last half-century has dramatically boosted our standard of living—and our standard of what it takes to get by.

One gauge of rising living standards is housing. A half-century ago, most families did not own homes. Today, about two-thirds do. Those homes have gotten a lot bigger: new homes built today are more than twice the size of new homes built 50 years ago. Some household appliances, such as telephones or washing machines, that we now consider basic, were luxuries a half-century ago. In 1950, less than two-thirds of housing units had complete plumbing facilities. Today, over 99% do.

Economic growth has brought gains in other areas as well. For one thing, we are able to afford more schooling. In 1950, the median number of years of school completed by adults age 25 or over was 6.8. Today, about 85% have completed 12 years of schooling and about 28% have completed four years of college. We also live longer. A baby born in 1950 had a life expectancy of 68 years. A baby born in 2004 had an expected life of nearly 10 years longer.

Of course, while economic growth can improve our material well-being, it is no panacea for all the ills of society. Americans today worry about the level of violence in society, environmental degradation, and what seems to be a loss of basic values. But while it is easy to be dismayed about many challenges of modern life, we can surely be grateful for our material wealth. Our affluence gives us the opportunity to grapple with some of our most difficult problems and to enjoy a range of choices that people only a few decades ago could not have imagined.

We learned a great deal about economic growth in the context of the production possibilities curve. Our purpose in this chapter is to relate the concept of economic growth to the model of aggregate demand and aggregate supply that we developed in the previous chapter and will use throughout our exploration of macroeconomics.

We will review the forces that determine a nation's economic growth rate and examine the prospects for growth in the future. We begin by looking at the significance of growth to the overall well-being of society.

1. THE SIGNIFICANCE OF ECONOMIC GROWTH

LEARNING OBJECTIVES

1. Define economic growth and explain it using the production possibilities model and the concept of potential output.
2. State the rule of 72 and use it to show how even small differences in growth rates can have major effects on a country's potential output over time.
3. Calculate the percentage rate of growth of output per capita.

To demonstrate the impact of economic growth on living standards of a nation, we must start with a clear definition of economic growth and then study its impact over time. We will also see how population growth affects the relationship between economic growth and the standard of living an economy is able to achieve.

1.1 Defining Economic Growth

Economic growth is a long-run process that occurs as an economy's potential output increases. Changes in real GDP from quarter to quarter or even from year to year are short-run fluctuations that occur as aggregate demand and short-run aggregate supply change. Regardless of media reports stating that the economy grew at a certain rate in the last quarter or that it is expected to grow at a particular rate during the next year, short-run changes in real GDP say little about economic growth. In the long run, economic activity moves toward its level of potential output. Increases in potential constitute economic growth.

Earlier we defined economic growth as the process through which an economy achieves an outward shift in its production possibilities curve. How does a shift in the production possibilities curve relate to a change in potential output? To produce its potential level of output, an economy must operate on its production possibilities curve. An increase in potential output thus implies an outward shift in the production possibilities curve. In the framework of the macroeconomic model of aggregate demand and aggregate supply, we show economic growth as a shift to the right in the long-run aggregate supply curve.

There are three key points about economic growth to keep in mind:

1. Growth is a process. It is not a single event; rather, it is an unfolding series of events.
2. We define growth in terms of the economy's ability to produce goods and services, as indicated by its level of potential output.
3. Growth suggests that the economy's ability to produce goods and services is rising. A discussion of economic growth is thus a discussion of the series of events that increase the economy's ability to produce goods and services.

Figure 8.1 shows the record of economic growth for the U.S. economy over the past century. The graph shows annual levels of actual real GDP and of potential output. We see that the economy has experienced dramatic growth over the past century; potential output has soared more than 30-fold. The figure also reminds us of a central theme of our analysis of macroeconomics: real GDP fluctuates about potential output. Real GDP sagged well below its potential during the Great Depression of the 1930s and rose well above its potential as the nation mobilized its resources to fight World War II. With the exception of these two periods, real GDP has remained close to the economy's potential output. Since 1950, the actual level of real GDP has deviated from potential output by an average of less than 2%.

FIGURE 8.1   A Century of Economic Growth

At the start of the 21st century, the level of potential output reached a level nearly 30 times its level a century earlier. Over the years, actual real GDP fluctuated about a rising level of potential output.

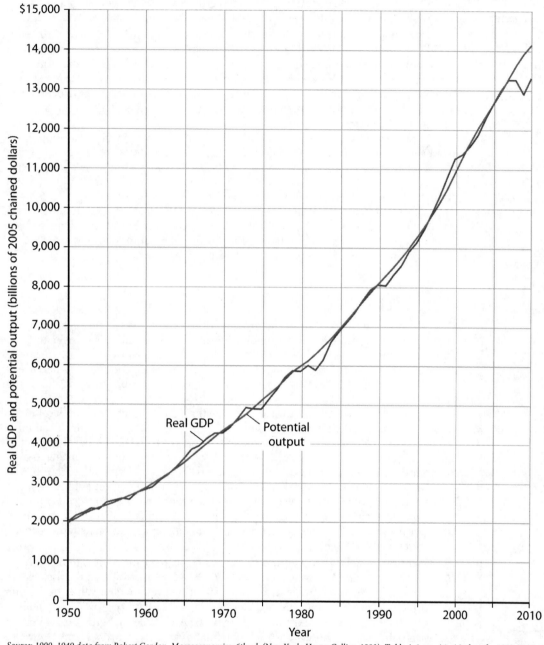

Source: 1900–1949 data from Robert Gordon, Macroeconomics, 6th ed. (New York: HarperCollins, 1993), Table A-1, pp. A1–A3; data for 1950–2010 from Congressional Budget Office, The Budget and Economic Outlook, August 2010.

We urge you to take some time with Figure 8.1. Over the course of the last century, it is economic growth that has taken center stage. Certainly, the fluctuations about potential output have been important. The recessionary gaps—periods when real GDP slipped below its potential—were often wrenching experiences in which millions of people endured great hardship. The inflationary gaps—periods when real GDP rose above its potential level—often produced dramatic increases in price levels. Those fluctuations mattered. It was the unemployment and/or the inflation that came with them that made headlines. But it was the quiet process of economic growth that pushed living standards ever higher. We must understand growth if we are to understand how we got where we are, and where we are likely to be going during the 21st century.

Figure 8.2 tells us why we use changes in potential output, rather than actual real GDP, as our measure of economic growth. Actual values of real GDP are affected not just by changes in the potential level of output, but also by the cyclical fluctuations about that level of output.

Given our definition of economic growth, we would say that the hypothetical economy depicted in Figure 8.2 grew at a 2.5% annual rate throughout the period. If we used actual values of real GDP, however, we would obtain quite different interpretations. Consider, for example, the first decade of this period: it began with a real GDP of $900 billion and a recessionary gap, and it ended in year 10 with a real GDP of $1,408 billion and an inflationary gap. If we record growth as the annual rate of change between these levels, we find an annual rate of growth of 4.6%—a rather impressive performance.

Now consider the second decade shown in Figure 8.2. It began in year 10, and it ended in year 20 with a recessionary gap. If we measure the growth rate over that period by looking at beginning and ending values of actual real GDP, we compute an annual growth rate of 0.5%. Viewed in this way, performance in the first decade is spectacular while performance in the second is rather lackluster. But these figures depend on the starting and ending points we select; the growth rate of potential output was 2.5% throughout the period.

By measuring economic growth as the rate of increase in potential output, we avoid such problems. One way to do this is to select years in which the economy was operating at the natural level of employment and then to compute the annual rate of change between those years. The result is an estimate of the rate at which potential output increased over the period in question. For the economy shown in Figure 8.2, for example, we see that real GDP equaled its potential in years 5 and 15. Real GDP in year 5 was $1,131, and real GDP in year 15 was $1,448. The annual rate of change between these two years was 2.5%. If we have estimates of potential output, of course, we can simply compute annual rates of change between any two years.

1.2 The Rule of 72 and Differences in Growth Rates

The Case in Point on presidents and growth at the end of this section suggests a startling fact: the U.S. growth rate began slowing in the 1970s, did not recover until the mid-1990s, only to slow down again in the 2000s. The question we address here is: does it matter? Does a percentage point drop in the growth rate make much difference? It does. To see why, let us investigate what happens when a variable grows at a particular percentage rate.

Suppose two economies with equal populations start out at the same level of real GDP but grow at different rates. Economy A grows at a rate of 3.5%, and Economy B grows at a rate of 2.4%. After a year, the difference in real GDP will hardly be noticeable. After a decade, however, real GDP in Economy A will be 11% greater than in Economy B. Over longer periods, the difference will be more dramatic. After 100 years, for example, income in Economy A will be nearly three times as great as in Economy B. If population growth in the two countries has been the same, the people of Economy A will have a far higher standard of living than those in Economy B. The difference in real GDP per person will be roughly equivalent to the difference that exists today between Great Britain and Mexico.

Over time, small differences in growth rates create large differences in incomes. An economy growing at a 3.5% rate increases by 3.5% of its initial value in the first year. In the second year, the economy increases by 3.5% of that new, higher value. In the third year, it increases by 3.5% of a still higher value. When a quantity grows at a given percentage rate, it experiences **exponential growth**. A variable that grows exponentially follows a path such as those shown for potential output in Figure 8.1 and Figure 8.2. These curves become steeper over time because the growth rate is applied to an ever-larger base.

A variable growing at some exponential rate doubles over fixed intervals of time. The doubling time is given by the **rule of 72**, which states that a variable's approximate doubling time equals 72 divided by the growth rate, stated as a whole number. If the level of income were increasing at a 9% rate, for example, its doubling time would be roughly 72/9, or 8 years.[1]

Let us apply this concept of a doubling time to the reduction in the U.S. growth rate. Had the U.S. economy continued to grow at a 3.5% rate after 1970, then its potential output would have doubled roughly every 20 years (72/3.5 = 20). That means potential output would have doubled by 1990, would double again by 2010, and would double again by 2030. Real GDP in 2030 would thus be eight times as great as its 1970 level. Growing at a 2.4% rate, however, potential output doubles only every 30 years (72/2.4 = 30). It would take until 2000 to double once from its 1970 level, and it would double once more by 2030. Potential output in 2030 would thus be four times its 1970 level if the economy grew at a 2.4% rate (versus eight times its 1970 level if it grew at a 3.5% rate). The 1.1% difference in growth rates produces a 100% difference in potential output by 2030. The different growth paths implied by these growth rates are illustrated in Figure 8.3.

FIGURE 8.2 Cyclical Change Versus Growth

The use of actual values of real GDP to measure growth can give misleading results. Here, an economy's potential output (shown in green) grows at a steady rate of 2.5% per year, with actual values of real GDP fluctuating about that trend. If we measure growth in the first 10 years as the annual rate of change between beginning and ending values of real GDP, we get a growth rate of 4.6%. The rate for the second decade is 0.5%. Growth estimates based on changes in real GDP are affected by cyclical changes that do not represent economic growth.

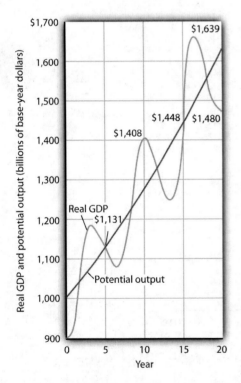

exponential growth

When a quantity grows at a given percentage rate.

rule of 72

A variable's approximate doubling time equals 72 divided by the growth rate, stated as a whole number.

FIGURE 8.3 Differences in Growth Rates

The chart suggests the significance in the long run of a small difference in the growth rate of real GDP. We begin in 1970, when real GDP equaled $2,873.9 billion. If real GDP grew at an annual rate of 3.5% from that year, it would double roughly every 20 years: in 1990, 2010, and 2030. Growth at a 2.4% rate, however, implies doubling every 30 years: in 2000 and 2030. By 2030, the 3.5% growth rate leaves real GDP at twice the level that would be achieved by 2.4% growth.

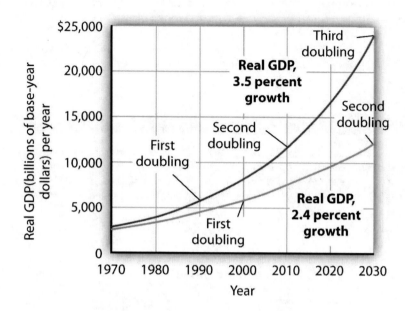

1.3 Growth in Output per Capita

Of course, it is not just how fast potential output grows that determines how fast the average person's material standard of living rises. For that purpose, we examine economic growth on a per capita basis. An economy's **output per capita** equals real GDP per person. If we let N equal population, then

output per capita

Real GDP per person.

EQUATION 8.1

$$\text{Output per capita} = \frac{\text{real GDP}}{N}$$

In the United States in the third quarter of 2010, for example, real GDP was $13,277.4 billion (annual rate). The U.S. population was 311.0 million. Real U.S. output per capita thus equaled $42,693.

We use output per capita as a gauge of an economy's material standard of living. If the economy's population is growing, then output must rise as rapidly as the population if output per capita is to remain unchanged. If, for example, population increases by 2%, then real GDP would have to rise by 2% to maintain the current level of output per capita. If real GDP rises by less than 2%, output per capita will fall. If real GDP rises by more than 2%, output per capita will rise. More generally, we can write:

EQUATION 8.2

% rate of growth of output per capita ≅ % rate of growth of output − % rate of growth of population

For economic growth to translate into a higher standard of living on average, economic growth must exceed population growth. From 1970 to 2004, for example, Sierra Leone's population grew at an annual rate of 2.1% per year, while its real GDP grew at an annual rate of 1.4%; its output per capita thus fell at a rate of 0.7% per year. Over the same period, Singapore's population grew at an annual rate of 2.1% per year, while its real GDP grew 7.4% per year. The resultant 5.3% annual growth in output per capita transformed Singapore from a relatively poor country to a country with the one of the highest per capita incomes in the world.

KEY TAKEAWAYS

- Economic growth is the process through which an economy's production possibilities curve shifts outward. We measure it as the rate at which the economy's potential level of output increases.
- Measuring economic growth as the rate of increase of the actual level of real GDP can lead to misleading results due to the business cycle.
- Growth of a quantity at a particular percentage rate implies exponential growth. When something grows exponentially, it doubles over fixed intervals of time; these intervals may be computed using the rule of 72.
- Small differences in rates of economic growth can lead to large differences in levels of potential output over long periods of time.
- To assess changes in average standards of living, we subtract the percentage rate of growth of population from the percentage rate of growth of output to get the percentage rate of growth of output per capita.

TRY IT!

Suppose an economy's potential output and real GDP is $5 million in 2000 and its rate of economic growth is 3% per year. Also suppose that its population is 5,000 in 2000, and that its population grows at a rate of 1% per year. Compute GDP per capita in 2000. Now estimate GDP and GDP per capita in 2072, using the rule of 72. At what rate does GDP per capita grow? What is its doubling time? Is this result consistent with your findings for GDP per capita in 2000 and in 2072?

Case in Point: Presidents and Economic Growth

President	Annual Increase in Real GDP (%)	Growth Rate (%)
Truman 1949–1952	5.4	4.4
Eisenhower 1953–1960	2.4	3.4
Kennedy-Johnson 1961–1968	5.1	4.3
Nixon-Ford 1969–1976	2.7	3.4
Carter 1977–1980	3.2	3.1
Reagan 1981–1988	3.5	3.1
G. H. W. Bush 1989–1992	2.4	2.7
Clinton 1992–2000	3.6	3.2
G. W. Bush 2001–2008 (Q3)	2.1	2.7

Presidents are often judged by the rate at which the economy grew while they were in office. This test is unfair on two counts. First, a president has little to do with the forces that determine growth. And second, such tests simply compute the annual rate of growth in real GDP over the course of a presidential term, which we know can be affected by cyclical factors. A president who takes office when the economy is down and goes out with the economy up will look like an economic star; a president with the bad luck to have reverse circumstances will seem like a dud. Here are annual rates of change in real GDP for each of the postwar presidents, together with rates of economic growth, measured as the annual rate of change in potential output.

The presidents' economic records are clearly affected by luck. Presidents Truman, Kennedy, Reagan, and Clinton, for example, began their terms when the economy had a recessionary gap and ended them with an inflationary gap or at about potential output. Real GDP thus rose faster than potential output during their presidencies. The Eisenhower, Nixon-Ford, H. W. Bush, and G. W. Bush administrations each started with an inflationary gap or at about potential and ended with a recessionary gap, thus recording rates of real GDP increase below the rate of gain in potential. Only Jimmy Carter, who came to office and left it with recessionary gaps, presided over a relatively equivalent rate of increase in actual GDP versus potential output.

ANSWER TO TRY IT! PROBLEM

GDP per capita in 2000 equals $1,000 ($5,000,000/5,000). If GDP rises 3% per year, it doubles every 24 years (= 72/3). Thus, GDP will be $10,000,000 in 2024, $20,000,000 in 2048, and $40,000,000 in 2072. Growing at a rate of 1% per year, population will have doubled once by 2072 to 10,000. GDP per capita will thus be $4,000 (= $40,000,000/10,000). Notice that GDP rises by eight times its original level, while the increase in GDP per capita is fourfold. The latter value represents a growth rate in output per capita of 2% per year, which implies a doubling time of 36 years. That gives two doublings in GDP per capita between 2000 and 2072 and confirms a fourfold increase.

2.   GROWTH AND THE LONG-RUN AGGREGATE SUPPLY CURVE

LEARNING OBJECTIVES

1. Explain and illustrate graphically the concept of the aggregate production function. Explain how its shape relates to the concept of diminishing marginal returns.
2. Derive the long-run aggregate supply curve from the model of the labor market and the aggregate production function.
3. Explain how the long-run aggregate supply curve shifts in responses to shifts in the aggregate production function or to shifts in the demand for or supply of labor.

Economic growth means the economy's potential output is rising. Because the long-run aggregate supply curve is a vertical line at the economy's potential, we can depict the process of economic growth as one in which the long-run aggregate supply curve shifts to the right.

FIGURE 8.5 Economic Growth and the Long-Run Aggregate Supply Curve

Because economic growth is the process through which the economy's potential output is increased, we can depict it as a series of rightward shifts in the long-run aggregate supply curve. Notice that with exponential growth, each successive shift in *LRAS* is larger and larger.

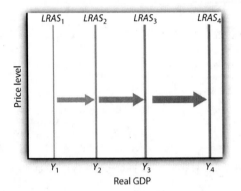

aggregate production function

Function that relates the total output of an economy to the total amount of labor employed in the economy, all other determinants of production (capital, natural resources, and technology) being unchanged.

diminishing marginal returns

Situation that occurs when additional units of a variable factor add less and less to total output, given constant quantities of other factors.

Figure 8.5 illustrates the process of economic growth. If the economy begins at potential output of Y_1, growth increases this potential. The figure shows a succession of increases in potential to Y_2, then Y_3, and Y_4. If the economy is growing at a particular percentage rate, and if the levels shown represent successive years, then the size of the increases will become larger and larger, as indicated in the figure.

Because economic growth can be considered as a process in which the long-run aggregate supply curve shifts to the right, and because output tends to remain close to this curve, it is important to gain a deeper understanding of what determines long-run aggregate supply (*LRAS*). We shall examine the derivation of *LRAS* and then see what factors shift the curve. We shall begin our work by defining an aggregate production function.

2.1 The Aggregate Production Function

An **aggregate production function** relates the total output of an economy to the total amount of labor employed in the economy, all other determinants of production (that is, capital, natural resources, and technology) being unchanged. An economy operating on its aggregate production function is producing its potential level of output.

Figure 8.6 shows an aggregate production function (*PF*). It shows output levels for a range of employment between 120 million and 140 million workers. When the level of employment is 120 million, the economy produces a real GDP of $11,500 billion (point A). A level of employment of 130 million produces a real GDP of $12,000 billion (point B), and when 140 million workers are employed, a real GDP of $12,300 billion is produced (point C). In drawing the aggregate production function, the amount of labor varies, but everything else that could affect output, specifically the quantities of other factors of production and technology, is fixed.

The shape of the aggregate production function shows that as employment increases, output increases, but at a decreasing rate. Increasing employment from 120 million to 130 million, for example, increases output by $500 billion to $12,000 billion at point B. The next 10 million workers increase production by $300 billion to $12,300 billion at point C. This example illustrates diminishing marginal returns. **Diminishing marginal returns** occur when additional units of a variable factor add less and less to total output, given constant quantities of other factors.

FIGURE 8.6 The Aggregate Production Function

An aggregate production function (*PF*) relates total output to total employment, assuming all other factors of production and technology are fixed. It shows that increases in employment lead to increases in output but at a decreasing rate.

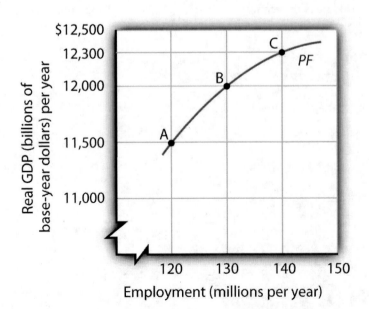

It is easy to picture the problem of diminishing marginal returns in the context of a single firm. The firm is able to increase output by adding workers. But because the firm's plant size and stock of equipment are fixed, the firm's capital per worker falls as it takes on more workers. Each additional worker adds less to output than the worker before. The firm, like the economy, experiences diminishing marginal returns.

2.2   The Aggregate Production Function, the Market for Labor, and Long-Run Aggregate Supply

To derive the long-run aggregate supply curve, we bring together the model of the labor market, introduced in the first macro chapter and the aggregate production function.

As we learned, the labor market is in equilibrium at the natural level of employment. The demand and supply curves for labor intersect at the real wage at which the economy achieves its natural level of employment. We see in Panel (a) of Figure 8.7 that the equilibrium real wage is ω_1 and the natural level of employment is L_1. Panel (b) shows that with employment of L_1, the economy can produce a real GDP of Y_P. That output equals the economy's potential output. It is that level of potential output that determines the position of the long-run aggregate supply curve in Panel (c).

FIGURE 8.7   Deriving the Long-Run Aggregate Supply Curve

Panel (a) shows that the equilibrium real wage is ω_1, and the natural level of employment is L_1. Panel (b) shows that with employment of L_1, the economy can produce a real GDP of Y_P. That output equals the economy's potential output. It is at that level of potential output that we draw the long-run aggregate supply curve in Panel (c).

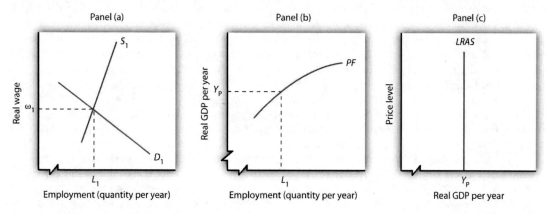

Changes in Long-Run Aggregate Supply

The position of the long-run aggregate supply curve is determined by the aggregate production function and the demand and supply curves for labor. A change in any of these will shift the long-run aggregate supply curve.

Figure 8.8 shows one possible shifter of long-run aggregate supply: a change in the production function. Suppose, for example, that an improvement in technology shifts the aggregate production function in Panel (b) from PF_1 to PF_2. Other developments that could produce an upward shift in the curve include an increase in the capital stock or in the availability of natural resources.

FIGURE 8.8 Shift in the Aggregate Production Function and the Long-Run Aggregate Supply Curve

An improvement in technology shifts the aggregate production function upward in Panel (b). Because labor is more productive, the demand for labor shifts to the right in Panel (a), and the natural level of employment increases to L_2. In Panel (c) the long-run aggregate supply curve shifts to the right to Y_2.

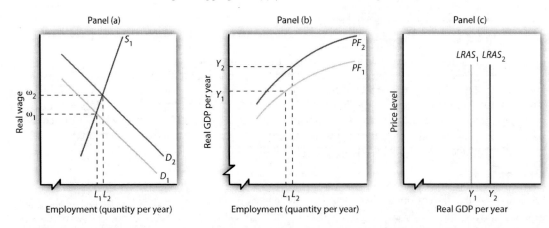

productivity

The amount of output per worker.

The shift in the production function to PF_2 means that labor is now more productive than before. This will affect the demand for labor in Panel (a). Before the technological change, firms employed L_1 workers at a real wage ω_1. If workers are more productive, firms will find it profitable to hire more of them at ω_1. The demand curve for labor thus shifts to D_2 in Panel (a). The real wage rises to ω_2, and the natural level of employment rises to L_2. The increase in the real wage reflects labor's enhanced **productivity**, the amount of output per worker. To see how potential output changes, we see in Panel (b) how much output can be produced given the new natural level of employment and the new aggregate production function. The real GDP that the economy is capable of producing rises from Y_1 to Y_2. The higher output is a reflection of a higher natural level of employment, along with the fact that labor has become more productive as a result of the technological advance. In Panel (c) the long-run aggregate supply curve shifts to the right to the vertical line at Y_2.

This analysis dispels a common misconception about the impact of improvements in technology or increases in the capital stock on employment. Some people believe that technological gains or increases in the stock of capital reduce the demand for labor, reduce employment, and reduce real wages. Certainly the experience of the United States and most other countries belies that notion. Between 1990 and 2007, for example, the U.S. capital stock and the level of technology increased dramatically. During the same period, employment and real wages rose, suggesting that the demand for labor increased by more than the supply of labor. As some firms add capital or incorporate new technologies, some workers at those firms may lose their jobs. But for the economy as a whole, new jobs become available *and* they generally offer higher wages. The demand for labor rises.

Another event that can shift the long-run aggregate supply curve is an increase in the supply of labor, as shown in Figure 8.9. An increased supply of labor could result from immigration, an increase in the population, or increased participation in the labor force by the adult population. Increased participation by women in the labor force, for example, has tended to increase the supply curve for labor during the past several decades.

FIGURE 8.9   Increase in the Supply of Labor and the Long-Run Aggregate Supply Curve

An increase in the supply of labor shifts the supply curve in Panel (a) to S_2, and the natural level of employment rises to L_2. The real wage falls to ω_2. With increased labor, the aggregate production function in Panel (b) shows that the economy is now capable of producing real GDP at Y_2. The long-run aggregate supply curve in Panel (c) shifts to $LRAS_2$.

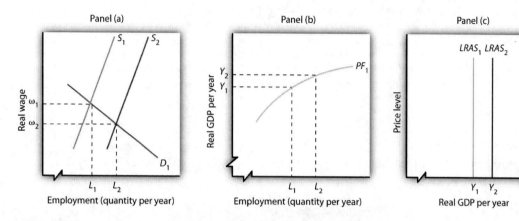

In Panel (a), an increase in the labor supply shifts the supply curve to S_2. The increase in the supply of labor does not change the stock of capital or natural resources, nor does it change technology—it therefore does not shift the aggregate production function. Because there is no change in the production function, there is no shift in the demand for labor. The real wage falls from ω_1 to ω_2 in Panel (a), and the natural level of employment rises from L_1 to L_2. To see the impact on potential output, Panel (b) shows that employment of L_2 can produce real GDP of Y_2. The long-run aggregate supply curve in Panel (c) thus shifts to $LRAS_2$. Notice, however, that this shift in the long-run aggregate supply curve to the right is associated with a reduction in the real wage to ω_2.

Of course, the aggregate production function and the supply curve of labor can shift together, producing higher real wages at the same time population rises. That has been the experience of most industrialized nations. The increase in real wages in the United States between 1990 and 2007, for example, came during a period in which an increasing population increased the supply of labor. The demand for labor increased by more than the supply, pushing the real wage up. The accompanying Case in Point looks at gains in real wages in the face of technological change, an increase in the stock of capital, and rapid population growth in the United States during the 19th century.

Our model of long-run aggregate supply tells us that in the long run, real GDP, the natural level of employment, and the real wage are determined by the economy's production function and by the demand and supply curves for labor. Unless an event shifts the aggregate production function, the demand curve for labor, or the supply curve for labor, it affects neither the natural level of employment nor potential output. Economic growth occurs only if an event shifts the economy's production function or if there is an increase in the demand for or the supply of labor.

KEY TAKEAWAYS

- The aggregate production function relates the level of employment to the level of real GDP produced per period.
- The real wage and the natural level of employment are determined by the intersection of the demand and supply curves for labor. Potential output is given by the point on the aggregate production function corresponding to the natural level of employment. This output level is the same as that shown by the long-run aggregate supply curve.
- Economic growth can be shown as a series of shifts to the right in *LRAS*. Such shifts require either upward shifts in the production function or increases in demand for or supply of labor.

TRY IT!

Suppose that the quantity of labor supplied is 50 million workers when the real wage is $20,000 per year and that potential output is $2,000 billion per year. Draw a three-panel graph similar to the one presented in Figure 8.9 to show the economy's long-run equilibrium. Panel (a) of your graph should show the demand and supply curves for labor, Panel (b) should show the aggregate production function, and Panel (c) should show the long-run aggregate supply curve. Now suppose a technological change increases the economy's output with the same quantity of labor as before to $2,200 billion, and the real wage rises to $21,500. In response, the quantity of labor supplied increases to 51 million workers. In the same three panels you have already drawn, sketch the new curves that result from this change. Explain what happens to the level of employment, the level of potential output, and the long-run aggregate supply curve. (Hint: you have information for only one point on each of the curves you draw—two for the supply of labor; simply draw curves of the appropriate shape. Do not worry about getting the scale correct.)

Case in Point: Technological Change, Employment, and Real Wages During the Industrial Revolution

Technological change and the capital investment that typically comes with it are often criticized because they replace labor with machines, reducing employment. Such changes, critics argue, hurt workers. Using the model of aggregate demand and aggregate supply, however, we arrive at a quite different conclusion. The model predicts that improved technology will increase the demand for labor and boost real wages.

The period of industrialization, generally taken to be the time between the Civil War and World War I, was a good test of these competing ideas. Technological changes were dramatic as firms shifted toward mass production and automation. Capital investment soared. Immigration increased the supply of labor. What happened to workers?

Employment more than doubled during this period, consistent with the prediction of our model. It is harder to predict, from a theoretical point of view, the consequences for real wages. The latter third of the 19th century was a period of massive immigration to the United States. Between 1865 and 1880, more than 5 million people came to the United States from abroad; most were of working age. The pace accelerated between 1880 and 1923, when more than 23 million people moved to the United States from other countries. Immigration increased the supply of labor, which should reduce the real wage. There were thus two competing forces at work: Technological change and capital investment tended to increase real wages, while immigration tended to reduce them by increasing the supply of labor.

The evidence suggests that the forces of technological change and capital investment proved far more powerful than increases in labor supply. Real wages soared 60% between 1860 and 1890. They continued to increase after that. Real wages in manufacturing, for example, rose 37% from 1890 to 1914.

Technological change and capital investment displace workers in some industries. But for the economy as a whole, they increase worker productivity, increase the demand for labor, and increase real wages.

Sources: *Wage data taken from Clarence D. Long, Wages and Earnings in the United States, 1860–1990 (Princeton, NJ: Princeton University Press, 1960), p. 109, and from Albert Rees, Wages in Manufacturing, 1890–1914 (Princeton, NJ: Princeton University Press, 1961), pp. 3–5. Immigration figures taken from Gary M. Walton and Hugh Rockoff, History of the American Economy, 6th ed. (New York: Harcourt Brace Jovanovich, 1990), p. 371.*

ANSWER TO TRY IT! PROBLEM

The production function in Panel (b) shifts up to PF_2. Because it reflects greater productivity of labor, firms will increase their demand for labor, and the demand curve for labor shifts to D_2 in Panel (a). $LRAS_1$ shifts to $LRAS_2$ in Panel (c). Employment and potential output rise. Potential output will be greater than $2,200 billion.

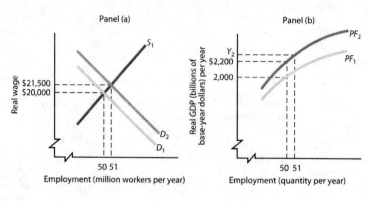

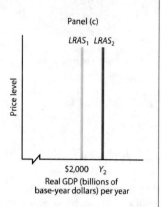

3. DETERMINANTS OF ECONOMIC GROWTH

LEARNING OBJECTIVES

1. Discuss the sources of economic growth.
2. Discuss possible reasons why countries grow at different rates.

In this section, we review the main determinants of economic growth. We also examine the reasons for the widening disparities in economic growth rates among countries in recent years.

3.1 The Sources of Economic Growth

As we have learned, there are two ways to model economic growth: (1) as an outward shift in an economy's production possibilities curve, and (2) as a shift to the right in its long-run aggregate supply curve. In drawing either one at a point in time, we assume that the economy's factors of production and its technology are unchanged. Changing these will shift both curves. Therefore, anything that increases the quantity or quality of factors of production or that improves the technology available to the economy contributes to economic growth.

The sources of growth for the U.S. economy in the 20th century were presented in the chapter on sources of production. There we learned that the main sources of growth for the United States from 1948 to 2002 were divided between increases in the quantities of labor and of physical capital (about 60%) and in improvements in the qualities of the factors of production and technology (about 40%). Since 1995, however, improvements in factor quality and technology have been the main drivers of economic growth in the United States.

In order to devote resources to increasing physical and human capital and to improving technology—activities that will enhance future production—society must forgo using them now to produce consumer goods. Even though the people in the economy would enjoy a higher standard of living today without this sacrifice, they are willing to reduce present consumption in order to have more goods and services available for the future.

As a college student, you personally made such a choice. You decided to devote time to study that you could have spent earning income. With the higher income, you could enjoy greater consumption today. You made this choice because you expect to earn higher income in the future and thus to enjoy greater consumption in the future. Because many other people in the society also choose to acquire more education, society allocates resources to produce education. The education produced today will enhance the society's human capital and thus its economic growth.

All other things equal, higher saving allows more resources to be devoted to increases in physical and human capital and technological improvement. In other words, saving, which is income not spent on consumption, promotes economic growth by making available resources that can be channeled into growth-enhancing uses.

3.2 Explaining Recent Disparities in Growth Rates

Toward the end of the 20th century, it appeared that some of the world's more affluent countries were growing robustly while others were growing more slowly or even stagnating. This observation was confirmed in a major study by the Organization for Economic Co-operation and Development (OECD),[2] whose members are listed in Table 8.1. The table shows that for the OECD countries as a whole, economic growth per capita fell from an average of 2.2% per year in the 1980s to an average of 1.9% per year in the 1990s. The higher standard deviation in the latter period confirms an increased disparity of growth rates in the more recent period. Moreover, the data on individual countries show that per capita growth in some countries (specifically, the United States, Canada, Ireland, Netherlands, Norway, and Spain) picked up, especially in the latter half of the 1990s, while it decelerated in most of the countries of continental Europe and Japan.

TABLE 8.1 Growing Disparities in Rates of Economic Growth

Variation in the growth in real GDP per capita has widened among the world's leading industrialized economies.

Trend Growth of GDP per Capita			
Country	1980–1990	1990–2000	1996–2000
United States	2.1	2.3	2.8
Japan	3.3	1.4	0.9
Germany	1.9	1.2	1.7
France	1.6	1.5	1.9
Italy	2.3	1.5	1.7
United Kingdom	2.2	2.1	2.3
Canada	1.4	1.7	2.6
Austria	2.1	1.9	2.3
Belgium	2.0	1.9	2.3
Denmark	1.9	1.9	2.3
Finland	2.2	2.1	3.9
Greece	0.5	1.8	2.7
Iceland	1.7	1.5	2.6
Ireland	3.0	6.4	7.9
Luxembourg	4.0	4.5	4.6
Netherlands	1.6	2.4	2.7
Portugal	3.1	2.8	2.7
Spain	2.3	2.7	3.2
Sweden	1.7	1.5	2.6
Switzerland	1.4	0.4	1.1
Turkey	2.1	2.1	1.9
Australia	1.6	2.4	2.8
New Zealand	1.4	1.2	1.8
Mexico	0.0	1.6	2.7
Korea	7.2	5.1	4.2
Hungary	—	2.3	3.5
Poland	—	4.2	4.8
Czech Republic	—	1.7	1.4
OECD24[3]	2.2	1.9	2.2
Standard Deviation of OECD24	0.74	1.17	1.37

Source: Excerpted from Table 1.1 Organization for Economic Co-operation and Development, Sources of Economic Growth in OECD Countries, 2003: p. 32–33.

The study goes on to try to explain the reasons for the divergent growth trends. The main findings were:

- In general, countries with accelerating per capita growth rates also experienced significant increases in employment, while those with stagnant or declining employment generally experienced reductions in per capita growth rates.

- Enhancements in human capital contributed to labor productivity and economic growth, but in slower growing countries such improvements were not enough to offset the impact of reduced or stagnant labor utilization.

- Information and communication technology has contributed to economic growth both through rapid technological progress within the information and communication technology industry itself as well as, more recently, through the use of information and communication technology equipment in other industries. This has made an important contribution to growth in several of the faster growing countries.

- Other factors associated with more growth include: investments in physical and human capital, sound macroeconomic policies (especially low inflation), private sector research and development, trade exposure, and better developed financial markets. Results concerning the impact of the size of the government and of public sector research and development on growth were more difficult to interpret.

- With qualifications, the study found that strict regulation of product markets (for example, regulations that reduce competition) and strict employment protection legislation (for example, laws that make hiring and firing of workers more difficult) had negative effects on growth.

- All countries show a large number of firms entering and exiting markets. But, a key difference between the United States and Europe is that new firms in the United States start out smaller and less productive than those of Europe but grow faster when they are successful. The report hypothesizes that lower start-up costs and less strict labor market regulations may encourage U.S. entrepreneurs to enter a market and then to expand, if warranted. European entrepreneurs may be less willing to experiment in a market in the first place.

The general concern in the second half of the 1970s and the 1980s was that economic growth was slowing down and that it might not be possible to reverse this pattern. The 1990s and early 2000s, in which growth picked up in some countries but not in others, suggested that the problem was not universal and led to a search for the reasons for the disparities in growth rates that emerged. The OECD study described above gives some possible explanations. The findings of that study practically beg countries to examine closely their economic policies at a variety of levels and to consider changes that may add flexibility to their economies.

In closing, it is worth reiterating that economic freedom and higher incomes tend to go together. Countries could not have attained high levels of income if they had not maintained the economic freedom that contributed to high incomes in the first place. Thus, it is also likely that rates of economic growth in the future will be related to the amount of economic freedom countries choose. We shall see in later chapters that monetary and fiscal policies that are used to stabilize the economy in the short run can also have an impact on long-run economic growth.

KEY TAKEAWAYS

- The main sources of growth for the United States from 1948 to 2002 were divided between increases in the quantities of labor and of physical capital (about 60%) and in improvements in the qualities of the factors of production and technology (about 40%). Since 1995, however, improvements in factor quality and technology have been the main drivers of economic growth in the United States.

- There has been a growing disparity in the rates of economic growth in industrialized countries in the last decade, which may reflect various differences in economic structures and policies.

TRY IT!

All other things unchanged, compare the position of a country's expected production possibility curve and the expected position of its long-run aggregate supply curve if:

1. Its labor force increases in size by 3% per year compared to 2% per year.

2. Its saving rate falls from 15% to 10%.

3. It passes a law making it more difficult to fire workers.

4. Its level of education rises more quickly than it has in the past.

Case in Point: Economic Growth in Poor Countries … or Lack Thereof

Economist William Easterly in his aptly named book *The Elusive Quest for Growth: Economists' Adventures and Misadventures in the Tropics* admits that after 50 years of searching for the magic formula for turning poor countries into rich ones, the quest remains elusive.

Poor countries just need more physical capital, you say? Easterly points out that between 1960 and 1985, the capital stock per work in both Gambia and Japan rose by over 500%. The result? In Gambia, output per worker over the 25-year period rose 2%; in Japan, output per worker rose 260%.

So, it must be that poor countries need more human capital? Again, he finds startling comparisons. For example, human capital expanded faster in Zambia than in Korea, but Zambia's annual growth rate is 7 percentage points below Korea's.

Too much population growth? Too little? More foreign aid? Too much? As Easterly proceeds, writing a prescription for growth seems ever more difficult: "None has delivered as promised," he concludes (p. xi).

While Easterly does not offer his own new panacea for how to move countries to a higher level of per capita GDP, where the model presented in this chapter does seem to provide some explanations of why a country's growth rate may vary over time or differ from another country's, he does argue that creating incentives for growth in poor countries is crucial. Acknowledging a role for plain luck, Easterly argues that good government policies—ones that keep low such negatives as inflation, corruption, and red tape—and quality institutions and laws—ones that, for example, honor contracts and reward merit—will help.

How to actually improve such incentives might constitute the next great quest:

> *"We have learned once and for all that there are no magical elixirs to bring a happy ending to our quest for growth. Prosperity happens when all the players in the development game have the right incentives. It happens when government incentives induce technological adaptation, high-quality investment in machines, and high-quality schooling. It happens when donors face incentives that induce them to give aid to countries with good policies where aid will have high payoffs, not to countries with poor policies where aid is wasted. It happens when the poor get good opportunities and incentives, which requires government welfare programs that reward rather than penalize earning income. It happens when politics is not polarized between antagonistic interest groups. . . . The solutions are a lot more difficult to describe than the problems. The way forward must be to create incentives for growth for the trinity of governments, donors, and individuals." (p. 289–90)*

Source: *William Easterly, The Elusive Quest for Growth: Economists' Adventures and Misadventures in the Tropics (Cambridge: MIT Press, 2002).*

ANSWER TO TRY IT! PROBLEM

Situations 1 and 4 should lead to a shift further outward in the country's production possibility curve and further to the right in its long-run aggregate supply curve. Situations 2 and 3 should lead to smaller outward shifts in the country's production possibility curve and smaller rightward shifts in its long-run aggregate supply curve.

4. REVIEW AND PRACTICE

Summary

We saw that economic growth can be measured by the rate of increase in potential output. Measuring the rate of increase in actual real GDP can confuse growth statistics by introducing elements of cyclical variation.

Growth is an exponential process. A variable increasing at a fixed percentage rate doubles over fixed intervals. The doubling time is approximated by the rule of 72. The exponential nature of growth means that small differences in growth rates have large effects over long periods of time. Per capita rates of increase in real GDP are found by subtracting the growth rate of the population from the growth rate of GDP.

Growth can be shown in the model of aggregate demand and aggregate supply as a series of rightward shifts in the long-run aggregate supply curve. The position of the *LRAS* is determined by the aggregate production function and by the demand and supply curves for labor. A rightward shift in *LRAS* results either from an upward shift in the production function, due to increases in factors of production other than labor or to improvements in technology, or from an increase in the demand for or the supply of labor.

Saving plays an important role in economic growth, because it allows for more capital to be available for future production, so the rate of economic growth can rise. Saving thus promotes growth.

In recent years, rates of growth among the world's industrialized countries have grown more disparate. Recent research suggests this may be related to differing labor and product market conditions, differences in the diffusion of information and communications technologies, as well as differences in macroeconomic and trade policies. Evidence on the role that government plays in economic growth was less conclusive.

CONCEPT PROBLEMS

1. Suppose the people in a certain economy decide to stop saving and instead use all their income for consumption. They do nothing to add to their stock of human or physical capital. Discuss the prospects for growth of such an economy.

2. Singapore has a saving rate that is roughly three times greater than that of the United States. Its greater saving rate has been one reason why the Singapore economy has grown faster than the U.S. economy. Suppose that if the United States increased its saving rate to, say, twice the Singapore level, U.S. growth would surpass the Singapore rate. Would that be a good idea?

3. Suppose an increase in air pollution causes capital to wear out more rapidly, doubling the rate of depreciation. How would this affect economic growth?

4. Some people worry that increases in the capital stock will bring about an economy in which everything is done by machines, with no jobs left for people. What does the model of economic growth presented in this chapter predict?

5. China's annual rate of population growth was 1.2% from 1975 to 2003 and is expected to be 0.6% from 2003 through 2015. How do you think this will affect the rate of increase in real GDP? How will this affect the rate of increase in per capita real GDP?

6. Suppose technology stops changing. Explain the impact on economic growth.

7. Suppose a series of terrorist attacks destroys half the capital in the United States but does not affect the population. What will happen to potential output and to the real wage?

8. "Given the rate at which scientists are making new discoveries, we will soon reach the point that no further discoveries can be made. Economic growth will come to a stop." Discuss.

9. Suppose real GDP increases during President Obama's term in office at a 5% rate. Would that imply that his policies were successful in "growing the economy"?

10. Suppose that for some country it was found that its economic growth was based almost entirely on increases in quantities of factors of production. Why might such growth be difficult to sustain?

NUMERICAL PROBLEMS

1. The population of the world in 2003 was 6.314 billion. It grew between 1975 and 2003 at an annual rate of 1.6%. Assume that it continues to grow at this rate.

   a. Compute the doubling time.

   b. Estimate the world population in 2048 and 2093 (assuming all other things remain unchanged).

2. With a world population in 2003 of 6.314 billion and a projected population growth rate of 1.1% instead (which is the United Nations' projection for the period 2003 to 2015).

   a. Compute the doubling time.

   b. State the year in which the world's population would be 12.628 billion.

3. Suppose a country's population grows at the rate of 2% per year and its output grows at the rate of 3% per year.

   a. Calculate its rate of growth of per capita output.

   b. If instead its population grows at 3% per year and its output grows at 2% per year, calculate its rate of growth of per capita output.

4. The rate of economic growth per capita in France from 1996 to 2000 was 1.9% per year, while in Korea over the same period it was 4.2%. Per capita real GDP was $28,900 in France in 2003, and $12,700 in Korea. Assume the growth rates for each country remain the same.

   a. Compute the doubling time for France's per capita real GDP.

   b. Compute the doubling time for Korea's per capita real GDP.

   c. What will France's per capita real GDP be in 2045?

   d. What will Korea's per capita real GDP be in 2045?

5. Suppose real GDPs in country A and country B are identical at $10 trillion dollars in 2005. Suppose country A's economic growth rate is 2% and country B's is 4% and both growth rates remain constant over time.

   a. On a graph, show country A's potential output until 2025.

   b. On the same graph, show country B's potential output.

   c. Calculate the percentage difference in their levels of potential output in 2025.

   Suppose country A's population grows 1% per year and country B's population grows 3% per year.

   d. On a graph, show country A's potential output per capita in 2025.

   e. On the same graph, show country B's potential output per capita in 2025.

   f. Calculate the percentage difference in their levels of potential output per capita in 2025.

6. Two countries, A and B, have identical levels of real GDP per capita. In Country A, an increase in the capital stock increases the potential output by 10%. Country B also experiences a 10% increase in its potential output, but this increase is the result of an increase in its labor force. Using aggregate production functions and labor-market analyses for the two countries, illustrate and explain how these events are likely to affect living standards in the two economies.

7. Suppose the information below characterizes an economy:

Employment (in millions)	Real GDP (in billions)
1	200
2	700
3	1,100
4	1,400
5	1,650
6	1,850
7	2,000
8	2,100
9	2,170
10	2,200

   a. Construct the aggregate production function for this economy.

   b. What kind of returns does this economy experience? How do you know?

   c. Assuming that total available employment is 7 million, draw the economy's long-run aggregate supply curve.

Suppose that improvement in technology means that real GDP at each level of employment rises by $200 billion.

    d. Construct the new aggregate production function for this economy.

    e. Construct the new long-run aggregate supply curve for the economy.

8. In Table 8.1, we can see that Japan's growth rate of per capita real GDP fell from 3.3% per year in the 1980s to 1.4% per year in the 1990s.

    a. Compare the percent increase in its per capita real GDP over the 20-year period to what it would have been if it had maintained the 3.3% per capita growth rate of the 1980s.

    b. Japan's per capita GDP in 1980 was about $24,000 (in U.S. 2000 dollars) in 1980. Calculate what it would have been if the growth rate of the 1980s had been maintained Calculate about how much it is, given the actual growth rates over the two decades.

    c. In Table 8.1, we can see that Ireland's growth rate of per capita real GDP grew from 3.0% per year in the 1980s to 6.4% per year in the 1990s.

    d. Compare the percent increase in its per capita real GDP over the 20-year period to what it would have been if it had maintained the 3.0% per capita growth rate of the 1980s.

    e. Ireland's per capita GDP in 1980 was about $10,000 (in U.S. 2000 dollars). Calculate what it would have been if the growth rate of the 1980s had been maintained. Calculate about how much it is, given the actual growth rates over the two decades.

ENDNOTES

1. Notice the use of the words *roughly* and *approximately*. The actual value of an income of $1,000 growing at rate r for a period of n years is $1,000 \times (1 + r)^n$. After 8 years of growth at a 9% rate, income would thus be $1,000 (1 + 0.09)^8 = $1,992.56.

The rule of 72 predicts that its value will be $2,000. The rule of 72 gives an approximation, not an exact measure, of the impact of exponential growth.

2. The material in this section is based on Organization for Economic Co-operation and Development, *The Sources of Economic Growth in OECD Countries*, 2003.

3. Excludes Czech Republic, Hungary, Korean, Mexico, Poland, and Slovak Republic

CHAPTER 9
The Nature and Creation of Money

START UP: HOW MANY MACKS DOES IT COST?

Larry Levine helped a client prepare divorce papers a few years ago. He was paid in mackerel.

"It's the coin of the realm," his client, Mark Bailey told the *Wall Street Journal*. The two men were prisoners at the time at the federal penitentiary at Lompoc, California.

By the time his work on the case was completed, he had accumulated "a stack of macks," Mr. Levine said. He used his fishy hoard to buy items such as haircuts at the prison barber shop, to have his laundry pressed, or to have his cell cleaned.

The somewhat unpleasant fish emerged as the currency of choice in many federal prisons in 1994 when cigarettes, the previous commodity used as currency, were banned. Plastic bags of mackerel sold for about $1 in prison commissaries. Almost no one likes them, so the prison money supply did not get eaten. Prisoners knew other prisoners would readily accept macks, so they were accepted in exchange for goods and services. Their $1 price made them convenient as a unit of account. And, as Mr. Levine's experience suggests, they acted as a store of value. As we shall see, macks served all three functions of money—they were a medium of exchange, a unit of account, and a store of value.[1]

In this chapter and the next we examine money and the way it affects the level of real GDP and the price level. In this chapter, we will focus on the nature of money and the process through which it is created.

As the experience of the prisoners in Lompoc suggests, virtually anything can serve as money. Historically, salt, horses, tobacco, cigarettes, gold, and silver have all served as money. We shall examine the characteristics that define a good as money.

We will also introduce the largest financial institution in the world, the Federal Reserve System of the United States. The Fed, as it is commonly called, plays a key role in determining the quantity of money in the United States. We will see how the Fed operates and how it attempts to control the supply of money.

1. WHAT IS MONEY?

L E A R N I N G   O B J E C T I V E S

1. Define money and discuss its three basic functions.
2. Distinguish between commodity money and fiat money, giving examples of each.
3. Define what is meant by the money supply and tell what is included in the Federal Reserve System's two definitions of it (M1 and M2).

money

Anything that serves as a medium of exchange.

medium of exchange

Anything that is widely accepted as a means of payment.

If cigarettes and mackerel can be used as money, then just what is money? **Money** is anything that serves as a medium of exchange. A **medium of exchange** is anything that is widely accepted as a means of payment. In Romania under Communist Party rule in the 1980s, for example, Kent cigarettes served as a medium of exchange; the fact that they could be exchanged for other goods and services made them money.

Money, ultimately, is defined by people and what they do. When people use something as a medium of exchange, it becomes money. If people were to begin accepting basketballs as payment for most goods and services, basketballs would be money. We will learn in this chapter that changes in the way people use money have created new types of money and changed the way money is measured in recent decades.

1.1 The Functions of Money

Money serves three basic functions. By definition, it is a medium of exchange. It also serves as a unit of account and as a store of value—as the "mack" did in Lompoc.

A Medium of Exchange

The exchange of goods and services in markets is among the most universal activities of human life. To facilitate these exchanges, people settle on something that will serve as a medium of exchange—they select something to be money.

barter

When goods are exchanged directly for other goods.

We can understand the significance of a medium of exchange by considering its absence. **Barter** occurs when goods are exchanged directly for other goods. Because no one item serves as a medium of exchange in a barter economy, potential buyers must find things that individual sellers will accept. A buyer might find a seller who will trade a pair of shoes for two chickens. Another seller might be willing to provide a haircut in exchange for a garden hose. Suppose you were visiting a grocery store in a barter economy. You would need to load up a truckful of items the grocer might accept in exchange for groceries. That would be an uncertain affair; you could not know when you headed for the store which items the grocer might agree to trade. Indeed, the complexity—and cost—of a visit to a grocery store in a barter economy would be so great that there probably would not be any grocery stores! A moment's contemplation of the difficulty of life in a barter economy will demonstrate why human societies invariably select something—sometimes more than one thing—to serve as a medium of exchange, just as prisoners in federal penitentiaries accepted mackerel.

A Unit of Account

Ask someone in the United States what he or she paid for something, and that person will respond by quoting a price stated in dollars: "I paid $75 for this radio," or "I paid $15 for this pizza." People do not say, "I paid five pizzas for this radio." That statement might, of course, be literally true in the sense of the opportunity cost of the transaction, but we do not report prices that way for two reasons. One is that people do not arrive at places like Radio Shack with five pizzas and expect to purchase a radio. The other is that the information would not be very useful. Other people may not think of values in pizza terms, so they might not know what we meant. Instead, we report the value of things in terms of money.

unit of account

A consistent means of measuring the value of things.

Money serves as a **unit of account**, which is a consistent means of measuring the value of things. We use money in this fashion because it is also a medium of exchange. When we report the value of a good or service in units of money, we are reporting what another person is likely to have to pay to obtain that good or service.

A Store of Value

The third function of money is to serve as a **store of value**, that is, an item that holds value over time. Consider a $20 bill that you accidentally left in a coat pocket a year ago. When you find it, you will be pleased. That is because you know the bill still has value. Value has, in effect, been "stored" in that little piece of paper.

Money, of course, is not the only thing that stores value. Houses, office buildings, land, works of art, and many other commodities serve as a means of storing wealth and value. Money differs from these other stores of value by being readily exchangeable for other commodities. Its role as a medium of exchange makes it a convenient store of value.

Because money acts as a store of value, it can be used as a standard for future payments. When you borrow money, for example, you typically sign a contract pledging to make a series of future payments to settle the debt. These payments will be made using money, because money acts as a store of value.

Money is not a risk-free store of value, however. We saw in the chapter that introduced the concept of inflation that inflation reduces the value of money. In periods of rapid inflation, people may not want to rely on money as a store of value, and they may turn to commodities such as land or gold instead.

1.2 Types of Money

Although money can take an extraordinary variety of forms, there are really only two types of money: money that has intrinsic value and money that does not have intrinsic value.

Commodity money is money that has value apart from its use as money. Mackerel in federal prisons is an example of commodity money. Mackerel could be used to buy services from other prisoners; they could also be eaten.

Gold and silver are the most widely used forms of commodity money. Gold and silver can be used as jewelry and for some industrial and medicinal purposes, so they have value apart from their use as money. The first known use of gold and silver coins was in the Greek city-state of Lydia in the beginning of the seventh century B.C. The coins were fashioned from electrum, a natural mixture of gold and silver.

One disadvantage of commodity money is that its quantity can fluctuate erratically. Gold, for example, was one form of money in the United States in the 19th century. Gold discoveries in California and later in Alaska sent the quantity of money soaring. Some of this nation's worst bouts of inflation were set off by increases in the quantity of gold in circulation during the 19th century. A much greater problem exists with commodity money that can be produced. In the southern part of colonial America, for example, tobacco served as money. There was a continuing problem of farmers increasing the quantity of money by growing more tobacco. The problem was sufficiently serious that vigilante squads were organized. They roamed the countryside burning tobacco fields in an effort to keep the quantity of tobacco, hence money, under control. (Remarkably, these squads sought to control the money supply by burning tobacco grown by other farmers.)

Another problem is that commodity money may vary in quality. Given that variability, there is a tendency for lower-quality commodities to drive higher-quality commodities out of circulation. Horses, for example, served as money in colonial New England. It was common for loan obligations to be stated in terms of a quantity of horses to be paid back. Given such obligations, there was a tendency to use lower-quality horses to pay back debts; higher-quality horses were kept out of circulation for other uses. Laws were passed forbidding the use of lame horses in the payment of debts. This is an example of Gresham's law: the tendency for a lower-quality commodity (bad money) to drive a higher-quality commodity (good money) out of circulation. Unless a means can be found to control the quality of commodity money, the tendency for that quality to decline can threaten its acceptability as a medium of exchange.

But something need not have intrinsic value to serve as money. **Fiat money** is money that some authority, generally a government, has ordered to be accepted as a medium of exchange. The **currency**—paper money and coins—used in the United States today is fiat money; it has no value other than its use as money. You will notice that statement printed on each bill: "This note is legal tender for all debts, public and private."

checkable deposits

Balances in checking accounts.

check

A written order to a bank to transfer ownership of a checkable deposit.

Checkable deposits, which are balances in checking accounts, and traveler's checks are other forms of money that have no intrinsic value. They can be converted to currency, but generally they are not; they simply serve as a medium of exchange. If you want to buy something, you can often pay with a check or a debit card. A **check** is a written order to a bank to transfer ownership of a checkable deposit. A debit card is the electronic equivalent of a check. Suppose, for example, that you have $100 in your checking account and you write a check to your campus bookstore for $30 or instruct the clerk to swipe your debit card and "charge" it $30. In either case, $30 will be transferred from your checking account to the bookstore's checking account. *Notice that it is the checkable deposit, not the check or debit card, that is money.* The check or debit card just tells a bank to transfer money, in this case checkable deposits, from one account to another.

What makes something money is really found in its acceptability, not in whether or not it has intrinsic value or whether or not a government has declared it as such. For example, fiat money tends to be accepted so long as too much of it is not printed too quickly. When that happens, as it did in Russia in the 1990s, people tend to look for other items to serve as money. In the case of Russia, the U.S. dollar became a popular form of money, even though the Russian government still declared the ruble to be its fiat money.

Heads Up!

The term *money*, as used by economists and throughout this book, has the very specific definition given in the text. People can hold assets in a variety of forms, from works of art to stock certificates to currency or checking account balances. Even though individuals may be very wealthy, only when they are holding their assets in a form that serves as a medium of exchange do they, according to the precise meaning of the term, have "money." To qualify as "money," something must be widely accepted as a medium of exchange.

1.3 Measuring Money

money supply

The total quantity of money in the economy at any one time.

The total quantity of money in the economy at any one time is called the **money supply**. Economists measure the money supply because it affects economic activity. What should be included in the money supply? We want to include as part of the money supply those things that serve as media of exchange. However, the items that provide this function have varied over time.

Before 1980, the basic money supply was measured as the sum of currency in circulation, traveler's checks, and checkable deposits. Currency serves the medium-of-exchange function very nicely but denies people any interest earnings. (Checking accounts did not earn interest before 1980.)

Over the last few decades, especially as a result of high interest rates and high inflation in the late 1970s, people sought and found ways of holding their financial assets in ways that earn interest and that can easily be converted to money. For example, it is now possible to transfer money from your savings account to your checking account using an automated teller machine (ATM), and then to withdraw cash from your checking account. Thus, many types of savings accounts are easily converted into currency.

liquidity

The ease with which an asset can be converted into currency.

Economists refer to the ease with which an asset can be converted into currency as the asset's **liquidity**. Currency itself is perfectly liquid; you can always change two $5 bills for a $10 bill. Checkable deposits are almost perfectly liquid; you can easily cash a check or visit an ATM. An office building, however, is highly illiquid. It can be converted to money only by selling it, a time-consuming and costly process.

As financial assets other than checkable deposits have become more liquid, economists have had to develop broader measures of money that would correspond to economic activity. In the United States, the final arbiter of what is and what is not measured as money is the Federal Reserve System. Because it is difficult to determine what (and what not) to measure as money, the Fed reports several different measures of money, including M1 and M2.

M1 is the narrowest of the Fed's money supply definitions. It includes currency in circulation, checkable deposits, and traveler's checks. **M2** is a broader measure of the money supply than M1. It includes M1 and other deposits such as small savings accounts (less than $100,000), as well as accounts such as money market mutual funds (MMMFs) that place limits on the number or the amounts of the checks that can be written in a certain period.

M2 is sometimes called the broadly defined money supply, while M1 is the narrowly defined money supply. The assets in M1 may be regarded as perfectly liquid; the assets in M2 are highly liquid, but somewhat less liquid than the assets in M1. Even broader measures of the money supply include large time-deposits, money market mutual funds held by institutions, and other assets that are somewhat less liquid than those in M2. Figure 9.1 shows the composition of M1 and M2 in October 2010.

FIGURE 9.1   The Two Ms: October 2010

M1, the narrowest definition of the money supply, includes assets that are perfectly liquid. M2 provides a broader measure of the money supply and includes somewhat less liquid assets. Amounts represent money supply data in billions of dollars for October 2010, seasonally adjusted.

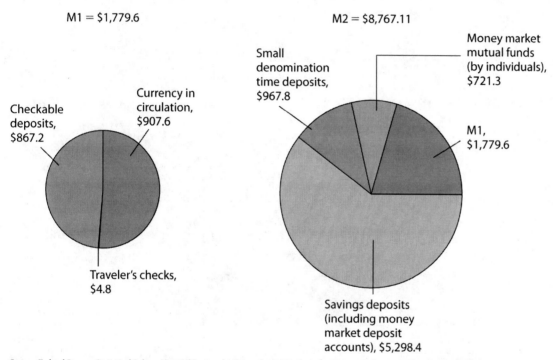

Source: Federal Reserve Statistical Release H.6, Tables 3 and 4 (December 2, 2010). Amounts are in billions of dollars for October 2010, seasonally adjusted.

Heads Up!

Credit cards are not money. A credit card identifies you as a person who has a special arrangement with the card issuer in which the issuer will lend you money and transfer the proceeds to another party whenever you want. Thus, if you present a MasterCard to a jeweler as payment for a $500 ring, the firm that issued you the card will lend you the $500 and send that money, less a service charge, to the jeweler. You, of course, will be required to repay the loan later. But a card that says you have such a relationship is not money, just as your debit card is not money.

With all the operational definitions of money available, which one should we use? Economists generally answer that question by asking another: Which measure of money is most closely related to real GDP and the price level? As that changes, so must the definition of money.

In 1980, the Fed decided that changes in the ways people were managing their money made M1 useless for policy choices. Indeed, the Fed now pays little attention to M2 either. It has largely given up tracking a particular measure of the money supply. The choice of what to measure as money remains the subject of continuing research and considerable debate.

M1

The narrowest of the Fed's money supply definitions that includes currency in circulation, checkable deposits, and traveler's checks.

M2

A broader measure of the money supply than M1 that includes M1 and other deposits.

KEY TAKEAWAYS

- Money is anything that serves as a medium of exchange. Other functions of money are to serve as a unit of account and as a store of value.
- Money may or may not have intrinsic value. Commodity money has intrinsic value because it has other uses besides being a medium of exchange. Fiat money serves only as a medium of exchange, because its use as such is authorized by the government; it has no intrinsic value.
- The Fed reports several different measures of money, including M1 and M2.

TRY IT!

Which of the following are money in the United States today and which are not? Explain your reasoning in terms of the functions of money.

1. Gold
2. A Van Gogh painting
3. A dime

Case in Point: Fiat-less Money

"We don't have a currency of our own," proclaimed Nerchivan Barzani, the Kurdish regional government's prime minister in a news interview in 2003. But, even without official recognition by the government, the so-called "Swiss" dinar certainly seemed to function as a fiat money. Here is how the Kurdish area of northern Iraq, during the period between the Gulf War in 1991 and the fall of Saddam Hussein in 2003, came to have its own currency, despite the pronouncement of its prime minister to the contrary.

After the Gulf War, the northern, mostly Kurdish area of Iraq was separated from the rest of Iraq though the enforcement of the no-fly-zone. Because of United Nations sanctions that barred the Saddam Hussein regime in the south from continuing to import currency from Switzerland, the central bank of Iraq announced it would replace the "Swiss" dinars, so named because they had been printed in Switzerland, with locally printed currency, which became known as "Saddam" dinars. Iraqi citizens in southern Iraq were given three weeks to exchange their old dinars for the new ones. In the northern part of Iraq, citizens could not exchange their notes and so they simply continued to use the old ones.

And so it was that the "Swiss" dinar for a period of about 10 years, even without government backing or any law establishing it as legal tender, served as northern Iraq's fiat money. Economists use the word "*fiat*," which in Latin means "let it be done," to describe money that has no intrinsic value. Such forms of money *usually* get their value because a government or authority has declared them to be legal tender, but, as this story shows, it does not really require much "fiat" for a convenient, in-and-of-itself worthless, medium of exchange to evolve.

What happened to both the "Swiss" and "Saddam" dinars? After the Coalition Provisional Authority (CPA) assumed control of all of Iraq, Paul Bremer, then head of the CPA, announced that a new Iraqi dinar would be exchanged for both of the existing currencies over a three-month period ending in January 2004 at a rate that implied that one "Swiss" dinar was valued at 150 "Saddam" dinars. Because Saddam Hussein's regime had printed many more "Saddam" dinars over the 10-year period, while no "Swiss" dinars had been printed, and because the cheap printing of the "Saddam" dinars made them easy to counterfeit, over the decade the "Swiss" dinars became relatively more valuable and the exchange rate that Bremer offered about equalized the purchasing power of the two currencies. For example, it took about 133 times as many "Saddam" dinars as "Swiss" dinars to buy a man's suit in Iraq at the time. The new notes, sometimes called "Bremer" dinars, were printed in Britain and elsewhere and flown into Iraq on 22 flights using Boeing 747s and other large aircraft. In both the northern and southern parts of Iraq, citizens turned in their old dinars for the new ones, suggesting at least more confidence at that moment in the "Bremer" dinar than in either the "Saddam" or "Swiss" dinars.

Sources: *Mervyn A. King, "The Institutions of Monetary Policy" (lecture, American Economics Association Annual Meeting, San Diego, January 4, 2004), available at http://www.bankofengland.co.uk/speeches/speech208.pdf. Hal R. Varian, "Paper Currency Can Have Value without Government Backing, but Such Backing Adds Substantially to Its Value," New York Times, January 15, 2004, p. C2.*

ANSWER TO TRY IT! PROBLEM

1. Gold is not money because it is not used as a medium of exchange. In addition, it does not serve as a unit of account. It may, however, serve as a store of value.

2. A Van Gogh painting is not money. It serves as a store of value. It is highly illiquid but could eventually be converted to money. It is neither a medium of exchange nor a unit of account.

3. A dime is money and serves all three functions of money. It is, of course, perfectly liquid.

2. THE BANKING SYSTEM AND MONEY CREATION

LEARNING OBJECTIVES

1. Explain what banks are, what their balance sheets look like, and what is meant by a fractional reserve banking system.
2. Describe the process of money creation (destruction), using the concept of the deposit multiplier.
3. Describe how and why banks are regulated and insured.

Where does money come from? How is its quantity increased or decreased? The answer to these questions suggests that money has an almost magical quality: *money is created by banks when they issue loans.* In effect, money is created by the stroke of a pen or the click of a computer key.

We will begin by examining the operation of banks and the banking system. We will find that, like money itself, the nature of banking is experiencing rapid change.

2.1 Banks and Other Financial Intermediaries

An institution that amasses funds from one group and makes them available to another is called a **financial intermediary**. A pension fund is an example of a financial intermediary. Workers and firms place earnings in the fund for their retirement; the fund earns income by lending money to firms or by purchasing their stock. The fund thus makes retirement saving available for other spending. Insurance companies are also financial intermediaries, because they lend some of the premiums paid by their customers to firms for investment. Mutual funds make money available to firms and other institutions by purchasing their initial offerings of stocks or bonds.

Banks play a particularly important role as financial intermediaries. Banks accept depositors' money and lend it to borrowers. With the interest they earn on their loans, banks are able to pay interest to their depositors, cover their own operating costs, and earn a profit, all the while maintaining the ability of the original depositors to spend the funds when they desire to do so. One key characteristic of banks is that they offer their customers the opportunity to open checking accounts, thus creating checkable deposits. These functions define a **bank**, which is a financial intermediary that accepts deposits, makes loans, and offers checking accounts.

Over time, some nonbank financial intermediaries have become more and more like banks. For example, some brokerage firms offer customers interest-earning accounts and make loans. They now allow their customers to write checks on their accounts.

financial intermediary

An institution that amasses funds from one group and makes them available to another.

bank

A financial intermediary that accepts deposits, makes loans, and offers checking accounts.

As nonbank financial intermediaries have grown, banks' share of the nation's credit market financial assets has diminished. In 1972, banks accounted for nearly 30% of U.S. credit market financial assets. In 2007, that share had dropped to about 15%.

The fact that banks account for a declining share of U.S. financial assets alarms some observers. We will see that banks are more tightly regulated than are other financial institutions; one reason for that regulation is to maintain control over the money supply. Other financial intermediaries do not face the same regulatory restrictions as banks. Indeed, their freedom from regulation is one reason they have grown so rapidly. As other financial intermediaries become more important, central authorities begin to lose control over the money supply.

The declining share of financial assets controlled by "banks" began to change in 2008. Many of the nation's largest investment banks—financial institutions that provided services to firms but were not regulated as commercial banks—began having serious financial difficulties as a result of their investments tied to home mortgage loans. As home prices in the United States began falling, many of those mortgage loans went into default. Investment banks that had made substantial purchases of securities whose value was ultimately based on those mortgage loans themselves began failing. Bear Stearns, one of the largest investment banks in the United States, required federal funds to remain solvent. Another large investment bank, Lehman Brothers, failed. In an effort to avoid a similar fate, several other investment banks applied for status as ordinary commercial banks subject to the stringent regulation those institutions face. One result of the terrible financial crisis that crippled the U.S. and other economies in 2008 may be greater control of the money supply by the Fed.

2.2 Bank Finance and a Fractional Reserve System

Bank finance lies at the heart of the process through which money is created. To understand money creation, we need to understand some of the basics of bank finance.

Banks accept deposits and issue checks to the owners of those deposits. Banks use the money collected from depositors to make loans. The bank's financial picture at a given time can be depicted using a simplified **balance sheet**, which is a financial statement showing assets, liabilities, and net worth. **Assets** are anything of value. **Liabilities** are obligations to other parties. **Net worth** equals assets less liabilities. All these are given dollar values in a firm's balance sheet. The sum of liabilities plus net worth therefore must equal the sum of all assets. On a balance sheet, assets are listed on the left, liabilities and net worth on the right.

The main way that banks earn profits is through issuing loans. Because their depositors do not typically all ask for the entire amount of their deposits back at the same time, banks lend out most of the deposits they have collected—to companies seeking to expand their operations, to people buying cars or homes, and so on. Banks keep only a fraction of their deposits as cash in their vaults and in deposits with the Fed. These assets are called **reserves**. Banks lend out the rest of their deposits. A system in which banks hold reserves whose value is less than the sum of claims outstanding on those reserves is called a **fractional reserve banking system**.

Table 9.1 shows a consolidated balance sheet for commercial banks in the United States for October 2010. Banks hold reserves against the liabilities represented by their checkable deposits. Notice that these reserves were a small fraction of total deposit liabilities of that month. Most bank assets are in the form of loans.

balance sheet

A financial statement showing assets, liabilities, and net worth.

assets

Anything of value.

liabilities

Obligations to other parties.

net worth

Assets less liabilities.

reserves

Bank assets held as cash in vaults and in deposits with the Federal Reserve.

fractional reserve banking system

System in which banks hold reserves whose value is less than the sum of claims outstanding on those reserves.

TABLE 9.1 The Consolidated Balance Sheet for U.S. Commercial Banks, October 2010

This balance sheet for all commercial banks in the United States shows their financial situation in billions of dollars, seasonally adjusted, on October 2010.

Assets		Liabilities and Net Worth	
Reserves	$1,040.2	Checkable deposits	$1,792.0
Other assets	1,743.7	Other deposits	6,103.6
Loans	6,788.7	Borrowings	1,927.5
Securities	2,452.6	Other liabilities	855.8
Total assets	$12,025.2	Total liabilities	10,678.9
		Net worth	1,346.4

Source: Federal Reserve Statistical Release H.8, December 3, 2010.

In the next section, we will learn that money is created when banks issue loans.

2.3 Money Creation

To understand the process of money creation today, let us create a hypothetical system of banks. We will focus on three banks in this system: Acme Bank, Bellville Bank, and Clarkston Bank. Assume that all banks are required to hold reserves equal to 10% of their checkable deposits. The quantity of reserves banks are required to hold is called **required reserves**. The reserve requirement is expressed as a **required reserve ratio**; it specifies the ratio of reserves to checkable deposits a bank must maintain. Banks may hold reserves in excess of the required level; such reserves are called **excess reserves**. Excess reserves plus required reserves equal total reserves.

Because banks earn relatively little interest on their reserves held on deposit with the Federal Reserve, we shall assume that they seek to hold no excess reserves. When a bank's excess reserves equal zero, it is **loaned up**. Finally, we shall ignore assets other than reserves and loans and deposits other than checkable deposits. To simplify the analysis further, we shall suppose that banks have no net worth; their assets are equal to their liabilities.

Let us suppose that every bank in our imaginary system begins with $1,000 in reserves, $9,000 in loans outstanding, and $10,000 in checkable deposit balances held by customers. The balance sheet for one of these banks, Acme Bank, is shown in Table 9.2. The required reserve ratio is 0.1: Each bank must have reserves equal to 10% of its checkable deposits. Because reserves equal required reserves, excess reserves equal zero. Each bank is loaned up.

required reserves

The quantity of reserves banks are required to hold.

required reserve ratio

The ratio of reserves to checkable deposits a bank must maintain.

excess reserves

Reserves in excess of the required level.

loaned up

When a bank's excess reserves equal zero.

TABLE 9.2 A Balance Sheet for Acme Bank

We assume that all banks in a hypothetical system of banks have $1,000 in reserves, $10,000 in checkable deposits, and $9,000 in loans. With a 10% reserve requirement, each bank is loaned up; it has zero excess reserves.

Acme Bank			
Assets		Liabilities	
Reserves	$1,000	Deposits	$10,000
Loans	$9,000		

Acme Bank, like every other bank in our hypothetical system, initially holds reserves equal to the level of required reserves. Now suppose one of Acme Bank's customers deposits $1,000 in cash in a checking account. The money goes into the bank's vault and thus adds to reserves. The customer now has an additional $1,000 in his or her account. Two versions of Acme's balance sheet are given here. The first shows the changes brought by the customer's deposit: reserves and checkable deposits rise by $1,000. The second shows how these changes affect Acme's balances. Reserves now equal $2,000 and checkable deposits equal $11,000. With checkable deposits of $11,000 and a 10% reserve requirement, Acme is required to hold reserves of $1,100. With reserves equaling $2,000, Acme has $900 in excess reserves.

At this stage, there has been no change in the money supply. When the customer brought in the $1,000 and Acme put the money in the vault, currency in circulation fell by $1,000. At the same time, the $1,000 was added to the customer's checking account balance, so the money supply did not change.

FIGURE 9.3

Acme Bank, Changes in Balance Sheet		Acme Bank, Balance Sheet	
Assets	Liabilities	Assets	Liabilities
Reserves +$1,000	Deposits +$1,000	Reserves $2,000 Loans $9,000	Deposits $11,000
		(Excess reserves = $900)	

Because Acme earns only a low interest rate on its excess reserves, we assume it will try to loan them out. Suppose Acme lends the $900 to one of its customers. It will make the loan by crediting the customer's checking account with $900. Acme's outstanding loans and checkable deposits rise by $900. The $900 in checkable deposits is new money; Acme created it when it issued the $900 loan. Now you know where money comes from—it is created when a bank issues a loan.

FIGURE 9.4

Acme Bank, Changes in Balance Sheet		Acme Bank, Balance Sheet	
Assets	Liabilities	Assets	Liabilities
Loans +$900	Deposits +$900	Reserves $2,000 Loans $9,900	Deposits $11,900

Presumably, the customer who borrowed the $900 did so in order to spend it. That customer will write a check to someone else, who is likely to bank at some other bank. Suppose that Acme's borrower writes a check to a firm with an account at Bellville Bank. In this set of transactions, Acme's checkable deposits fall by $900. The firm that receives the check deposits it in its account at Bellville Bank, increasing that bank's checkable deposits by $900. Bellville Bank now has a check written on an Acme account. Bellville will submit the check to the Fed, which will reduce Acme's deposits with the Fed—its reserves—by $900 and increase Bellville's reserves by $900.

FIGURE 9.5

Acme Bank, Changes in Balance Sheet		Acme Bank, Balance Sheet	
Assets	Liabilities	Assets	Liabilities
Reserves −$900	Deposits −$900	Reserves $1,100 Loans $9,900	Deposits $11,000

Bellville Bank, Changes in Balance Sheet		Bellville Bank, Balance Sheet	
Assets	Liabilities	Assets	Liabilities
Reserves +$900	Deposits +$900	Reserves $1,900 Loans $9,000 (Excess reserves = $810)	Deposits $10,900

Notice that Acme Bank emerges from this round of transactions with $11,000 in checkable deposits and $1,100 in reserves. It has eliminated its excess reserves by issuing the loan for $900; Acme is now loaned up. Notice also that from Acme's point of view, it has not created any money! It merely took in a $1,000 deposit and emerged from the process with $1,000 in additional checkable deposits.

The $900 in new money Acme created when it issued a loan has not vanished—it is now in an account in Bellville Bank. Like the magician who shows the audience that the hat from which the rabbit appeared was empty, Acme can report that it has not created any money. There is a wonderful irony in the magic of money creation: banks create money when they issue loans, but no one bank ever seems to keep the money it creates. That is because money is created within the banking system, not by a single bank.

The process of money creation will not end there. Let us go back to Bellville Bank. Its deposits and reserves rose by $900 when the Acme check was deposited in a Bellville account. The $900 deposit required an increase in required reserves of $90. Because Bellville's reserves rose by $900, it now has $810 in excess reserves. Just as Acme lent the amount of its excess reserves, we can expect Bellville to lend this $810. The next set of balance sheets shows this transaction. Bellville's loans and checkable deposits rise by $810.

FIGURE 9.6

Bellville Bank, Changes in Balance Sheet		Bellville Bank, Balance Sheet	
Assets	Liabilities	Assets	Liabilities
Loans +$810	Deposits +$810	Reserves $1,900 Loans $9,810	Deposits $11,710

The $810 that Bellville lent will be spent. Let us suppose it ends up with a customer who banks at Clarkston Bank. Bellville's checkable deposits fall by $810; Clarkston's rise by the same amount. Clarkston submits the check to the Fed, which transfers the money from Bellville's reserve account to Clarkston's. Notice that Clarkston's deposits rise by $810; Clarkston must increase its reserves by $81. But its reserves have risen by $810, so it has excess reserves of $729.

FIGURE 9.7

Bellville Bank, Changes in Balance Sheet		Bellville Bank, Balance Sheet	
Assets	Liabilities	Assets	Liabilities
Reserves −$810	Deposits −$810	Reserves $1,090 Loans $9,810	Deposits $10,900

Clarkston Bank, Changes in Balance Sheet		Clarkston Bank, Balance Sheet	
Assets	Liabilities	Assets	Liabilities
Reserves +$810	Deposits +$810	Reserves $1,810 Loans $9,000 (Excess reserves = $729)	Deposits $10,810

Notice that Bellville is now loaned up. And notice that it can report that it has not created any money either! It took in a $900 deposit, and its checkable deposits have risen by that same $900. The $810 it created when it issued a loan is now at Clarkston Bank.

The process will not end there. Clarkston will lend the $729 it now has in excess reserves, and the money that has been created will end up at some other bank, which will then have excess reserves—and create still more money. And that process will just keep going as long as there are excess reserves to pass through the banking system in the form of loans. How much will ultimately be created by the system as a whole? With a 10% reserve requirement, each dollar in reserves backs up $10 in checkable deposits. The $1,000 in cash that Acme's customer brought in adds $1,000 in reserves to the banking system. It can therefore back up an additional $10,000! In just the three banks we have shown, checkable deposits have risen by $2,710 ($1,000 at Acme, $900 at Bellville, and $810 at Clarkston). Additional banks in the system will continue to create money, up to a maximum of $7,290 among them. Subtracting the original $1,000 that had been a part of currency in circulation, we see that the money supply could rise by as much as $9,000.

Heads Up!

Notice that when the banks received new deposits, they could make new loans only up to the amount of their excess reserves, not up to the amount of their deposits and total reserve increases. For example, with the new deposit of $1,000, Acme Bank was able to make additional loans of $900. If instead it made new loans equal to its increase in total reserves, then after the customers who received new loans wrote checks to others, its reserves would be less than the required amount. In the case of Acme, had it lent out an additional $1,000, after checks were written against the new loans, it would have been left with only $1,000 in reserves against $11,000 in deposits, for a reserve ratio of only 0.09, which is less than the required reserve ratio of 0.1 in the example.

2.4 The Deposit Multiplier

deposit multiplier

The ratio of the maximum possible change in checkable deposits (ΔD) to the change in reserves (ΔR).

We can relate the potential increase in the money supply to the change in reserves that created it using the **deposit multiplier** (m_d), which equals the ratio of the maximum possible change in checkable deposits (ΔD) to the change in reserves (ΔR). In our example, the deposit multiplier was 10:

EQUATION 9.1

$$m_d = \frac{\Delta D}{\Delta R} = \frac{\$10,000}{\$1,000} = 10$$

To see how the deposit multiplier m_d is related to the required reserve ratio, we use the fact that if banks in the economy are loaned up, then reserves, R, equal the required reserve ratio (rrr) times checkable deposits, D:

EQUATION 9.2

$$R = rrrD$$

A change in reserves produces a change in loans and a change in checkable deposits. Once banks are fully loaned up, the change in reserves, ΔR, will equal the required reserve ratio times the change in deposits, ΔD:

EQUATION 9.3

$$\Delta R = rrr\Delta D$$

Solving for ΔD, we have

EQUATION 9.4

$$\frac{1}{rrr}\Delta R = \Delta D$$

Dividing both sides by ΔR, we see that the deposit multiplier, m_d, is $1/rrr$:

EQUATION 9.5

$$\frac{1}{rrr} = \frac{\Delta D}{\Delta R} = m_d$$

The deposit multiplier is thus given by the reciprocal of the required reserve ratio. With a required reserve ratio of 0.1, the deposit multiplier is 10. A required reserve ratio of 0.2 would produce a deposit multiplier of 5. The higher the required reserve ratio, the lower the deposit multiplier.

Actual increases in checkable deposits will not be nearly as great as suggested by the deposit multiplier. That is because the artificial conditions of our example are not met in the real world. Some banks hold excess reserves, customers withdraw cash, and some loan proceeds are not spent. Each of these factors reduces the degree to which checkable deposits are affected by an increase in reserves. The basic mechanism, however, is the one described in our example, and it remains the case that checkable deposits increase by a multiple of an increase in reserves.

The entire process of money creation can work in reverse. When you withdraw cash from your bank, you reduce the bank's reserves. Just as a deposit at Acme Bank increases the money supply by a multiple of the original deposit, your withdrawal reduces the money supply by a multiple of the amount you withdraw. And just as money is created when banks issue loans, it is destroyed as the loans are repaid. A loan payment reduces checkable deposits; it thus reduces the money supply.

Suppose, for example, that the Acme Bank customer who borrowed the $900 makes a $100 payment on the loan. Only part of the payment will reduce the loan balance; part will be interest. Suppose $30 of the payment is for interest, while the remaining $70 reduces the loan balance. The effect of the payment on Acme's balance sheet is shown below. Checkable deposits fall by $100, loans fall by $70, and net worth rises by the amount of the interest payment, $30.

Similar to the process of money creation, the money reduction process decreases checkable deposits by, at most, the amount of the reduction in deposits times the deposit multiplier.

2.5   The Regulation of Banks

FIGURE 9.8

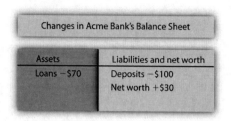

Banks are among the most heavily regulated of financial institutions. They are regulated in part to protect individual depositors against corrupt business practices. Banks are also susceptible to crises of confidence. Because their reserves equal only a fraction of their deposit liabilities, an effort by customers to get all their cash out of a bank could force it to fail. A few poorly managed banks could create such a crisis, leading people to try to withdraw their funds from well-managed banks. Another reason for the high degree of regulation is that variations in the quantity of money have important effects on the economy as a whole, and banks are the institutions through which money is created.

Deposit Insurance

From a customer's point of view, the most important form of regulation comes in the form of deposit insurance. For commercial banks, this insurance is provided by the Federal Deposit Insurance Corporation (FDIC). Insurance funds are maintained through a premium assessed on banks for every $100 of bank deposits.

If a commercial bank fails, the FDIC guarantees to reimburse depositors up to $250,000 (raised from $100,000 during the financial crisis of 2008) per insured bank, for each account ownership category. From a depositor's point of view, therefore, it is not necessary to worry about a bank's safety.

One difficulty this insurance creates, however, is that it may induce the officers of a bank to take more risks. With a federal agency on hand to bail them out if they fail, the costs of failure are reduced. Bank officers can thus be expected to take more risks than they would otherwise, which, in turn, makes failure more likely. In addition, depositors, knowing that their deposits are insured, may not scrutinize the banks' lending activities as carefully as they would if they felt that unwise loans could result in the loss of their deposits.

Thus, banks present us with a fundamental dilemma. A fractional reserve system means that banks can operate only if their customers maintain their confidence in them. If bank customers lose confidence, they are likely to try to withdraw their funds. But with a fractional reserve system, a bank actually holds funds in reserve equal to only a small fraction of its deposit liabilities. If its customers think a bank will fail and try to withdraw their cash, the bank is likely to fail. Bank panics, in which frightened customers rush to withdraw their deposits, contributed to the failure of one-third of the nation's banks between 1929 and 1933. Deposit insurance was introduced in large part to give people confidence in their banks and to prevent failure. But the deposit insurance that seeks to prevent bank failures may lead to less careful management—and thus encourage bank failure.

Regulation to Prevent Bank Failure

To reduce the number of bank failures, banks are severely limited in what they can do. They are barred from certain types of financial investments and from activities viewed as too risky. Banks are required to maintain a minimum level of net worth as a fraction of total assets. Regulators from the FDIC regularly perform audits and other checks of individual banks to ensure they are operating safely.

The FDIC has the power to close a bank whose net worth has fallen below the required level. In practice, it typically acts to close a bank when it becomes insolvent, that is, when its net worth becomes negative. Negative net worth implies that the bank's liabilities exceed its assets.

When the FDIC closes a bank, it arranges for depositors to receive their funds. When the bank's funds are insufficient to return customers' deposits, the FDIC uses money from the insurance fund for this purpose. Alternatively, the FDIC may arrange for another bank to purchase the failed bank. The FDIC, however, continues to guarantee that depositors will not lose any money.

KEY TAKEAWAYS

- Banks are financial intermediaries that accept deposits, make loans, and provide checking accounts for their customers.
- Money is created within the banking system when banks issue loans; it is destroyed when the loans are repaid.
- An increase (decrease) in reserves in the banking system can increase (decrease) the money supply. The maximum amount of the increase (decrease) is equal to the deposit multiplier times the change in reserves; the deposit multiplier equals the reciprocal of the required reserve ratio.
- Bank deposits are insured and banks are heavily regulated.

TRY IT!

1. Suppose Acme Bank initially has $10,000 in deposits, reserves of $2,000, and loans of $8,000. At a required reserve ratio of 0.2, is Acme loaned up? Show the balance sheet of Acme Bank at present.

2. Now suppose that an Acme Bank customer, planning to take cash on an extended college graduation trip to India, withdraws $1,000 from her account. Show the changes to Acme Bank's balance sheet and Acme's balance sheet after the withdrawal. By how much are its reserves now deficient?

3. Acme would probably replenish its reserves by reducing loans. This action would cause a multiplied contraction of checkable deposits as other banks lose deposits because their customers would be paying off loans to Acme. How large would the contraction be?

Case in Point: A Big Bank Goes Under

It was the darling of Wall Street—it showed rapid growth and made big profits. Washington Mutual, a savings and loan based in the state of Washington, was a relatively small institution whose CEO, Kerry K. Killinger, had big plans. He wanted to transform his little Seattle S&L into the Wal-Mart of banks.

Mr. Killinger began pursuing a relatively straightforward strategy. He acquired banks in large cities such as Chicago and Los Angeles. He acquired banks up and down the east and west coasts. He aggressively extended credit to low-income individuals and families—credit cards, car loans, and mortgages. In making mortgage loans to low-income families, WaMu, as the bank was known, quickly became very profitable. But it was exposing itself to greater and greater risk, according to the *New York Times*.

Housing prices in the United States more than doubled between 1997 and 2007. During that time, loans to even low-income households were profitable. But, as housing prices began falling in 2007, banks such as WaMu began to experience losses as homeowners began to walk away from houses whose values suddenly fell below their outstanding mortgages. WaMu began losing money in 2007 as housing prices began falling. The company had earned $3.6 billion in 2006, and swung to a loss of $67 million in 2007, according to the *Puget Sound Business Journal*. Mr. Killinger was ousted by the board early in September of 2008. The bank failed later that month. It was the biggest bank failure in the history of the United States.

The Federal Deposit Insurance Corporation (FDIC) had just rescued another bank, IndyMac, which was only a tenth the size of WaMu, and would have done the same for WaMu if it had not been able to find a company to purchase it. But in this case, JPMorgan Chase agreed to take it over—its deposits, bank branches, and its troubled asset portfolio. The government and the Fed even negotiated the deal behind WaMu's back! The then chief executive officer of the company, Alan H. Fishman, was reportedly flying from New York to Seattle when the deal was finalized.

The government was anxious to broker a deal that did not require use of the FDIC's depleted funds following IndyMac's collapse. But it would have done so if a buyer had not been found. As the FDIC reports on its Web site: "Since the FDIC's creation in 1933, no depositor has ever lost even one penny of FDIC-insured funds."

Sources: Eric Dash and Andrew Ross Sorkin, "Government Seizes WaMu and Sells Some Assets," The New York Times, September 25, 2008, p. A1; Kirsten Grind, "Insiders Detail Reasons for WaMu's Failure," Puget Sound Business Journal, January 23, 2009; and FDIC Web site at https://www.fdic.gov/edie/fdic_info.html.

ANSWER TO TRY IT! PROBLEM

1. Acme Bank is loaned up, since $2,000/$10,000 = 0.2, which is the required reserve ratio. Acme's balance sheet is:

Assets	Liabilities plus net worth
Reserves $2,000	Deposits $10,000
Loans $8,000	

2. Acme Bank's balance sheet after losing $1,000 in deposits:

Acme Bank, Changes in Balance Sheet		Acme Bank, Balance Sheet	
Assets	Liabilities	Assets	Liabilities
Reserves −$1,000	Deposits −$1,000	Reserves $1,000	Deposits $9,000
		Loans $8,000	

   Required reserves are deficient by $800. Acme must hold 20% of its deposits, in this case $1,800 (0.2 × $9,000 = $1,800), as reserves, but it has only $1,000 in reserves at the moment.

3. The contraction in checkable deposits would be

$$\Delta D = (1/0.2) \times (-\$1,000) = -\$5,000$$

3. THE FEDERAL RESERVE SYSTEM

LEARNING OBJECTIVES

1. Explain the primary functions of central banks.
2. Describe how the Federal Reserve System is structured and governed.
3. Identify and explain the tools of monetary policy.
4. Describe how the Fed creates and destroys money when it buys and sells federal government bonds.

central bank

A bank that acts as a banker to the central government, acts as a banker to banks, acts as a regulator of banks, conducts monetary policy, and supports the stability of the financial system.

The Federal Reserve System of the United States, or Fed, is the U.S. central bank. Japan's central bank is the Bank of Japan; the European Union has established the European Central Bank. Most countries have a central bank. A **central bank** performs five primary functions: (1) it acts as a banker to the central government, (2) it acts as a banker to banks, (3) it acts as a regulator of banks, (4) it conducts monetary policy, and (5) it supports the stability of the financial system.

For the first 137 years of its history, the United States did not have a true central bank. While a central bank was often proposed, there was resistance to creating an institution with such enormous power. A series of bank panics slowly increased support for the creation of a central bank. The bank panic of 1907 proved to be the final straw. Bank failures were so widespread, and depositor losses so heavy, that concerns about centralization of power gave way to a desire for an institution that would provide a stabilizing force in the banking industry. Congress passed the Federal Reserve Act in 1913, creating the Fed and giving it all the powers of a central bank.

3.1 Structure of the Fed

In creating the Fed, Congress determined that a central bank should be as independent of the government as possible. It also sought to avoid too much centralization of power in a single institution. These potentially contradictory goals of independence and decentralized power are evident in the Fed's structure and in the continuing struggles between Congress and the Fed over possible changes in that structure.

In an effort to decentralize power, Congress designed the Fed as a system of 12 regional banks, as shown in Figure 9.12. Each of these banks operates as a kind of bankers' cooperative; the regional banks are owned by the commercial banks in their districts that have chosen to be members of the Fed. The owners of each Federal Reserve bank select the board of directors of that bank; the board selects the bank's president.

FIGURE 9.12 The 12 Federal Reserve Districts and the Cities Where Each Bank Is Located

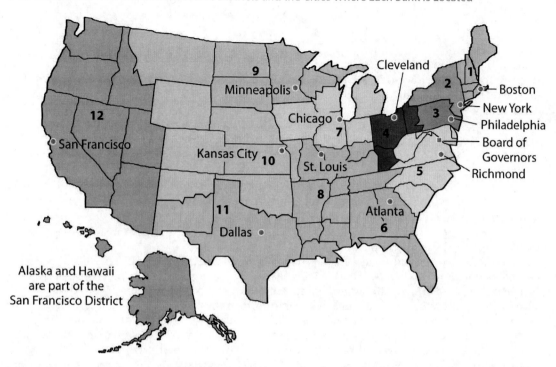

Alaska and Hawaii
are part of the
San Francisco District

Several provisions of the Federal Reserve Act seek to maintain the Fed's independence. The board of directors for the entire Federal Reserve System is called the Board of Governors. The seven members of the board are appointed by the president of the United States and confirmed by the Senate. To ensure a large measure of independence from any one president, the members of the Board of Governors have 14-year terms. One member of the board is selected by the president of the United States to serve as chairman for a four-year term.

As a further means of ensuring the independence of the Fed, Congress authorized it to buy and sell federal government bonds. This activity is a profitable one that allows the Fed to pay its own bills. The Fed is thus not dependent on a Congress that might otherwise be tempted to force a particular set of policies on it. The Fed is limited in the profits it is allowed to earn; its "excess" profits are returned to the Treasury.

It is important to recognize that the Fed is technically not part of the federal government. Members of the Board of Governors do not legally have to answer to Congress, the president, or anyone else. The president and members of Congress can certainly try to influence the Fed, but they cannot order it to do anything. Congress, however, created the Fed. It could, by passing another law, abolish the Fed's independence. The Fed can maintain its independence only by keeping the support of Congress—and that sometimes requires being responsive to the wishes of Congress.

In recent years, Congress has sought to increase its oversight of the Fed. The chairman of the Federal Reserve Board is required to report to Congress twice each year on its monetary policy, the set of policies that the central bank can use to influence economic activity.

3.2   Powers of the Fed

The Fed's principal powers stem from its authority to conduct monetary policy. It has three main policy tools: setting reserve requirements, operating the discount window and other credit facilities, and conducting open-market operations.

Reserve Requirements

The Fed sets the required ratio of reserves that banks must hold relative to their deposit liabilities. In theory, the Fed could use this power as an instrument of monetary policy. It could lower reserve requirements when it wanted to increase the money supply and raise them when it wanted to reduce the money supply. In practice, however, the Fed does not use its power to set reserve requirements in this way. The reason is that frequent manipulation of reserve requirements would make life difficult for bankers, who would have to adjust their lending policies to changing requirements.

The Fed's power to set reserve requirements was expanded by the Monetary Control Act of 1980. Before that, the Fed set reserve requirements only for commercial banks that were members of the Federal Reserve System. Most banks are not members of the Fed; the Fed's control of reserve requirements thus extended to only a minority of banks. The 1980 act required virtually all banks to satisfy the Fed's reserve requirements.

The Discount Window and Other Credit Facilities

discount rate

The interest rate charged by the Fed when it lends reserves to banks.

A major responsibility of the Fed is to act as a lender of last resort to banks. When banks fall short on reserves, they can borrow reserves from the Fed through its discount window. The **discount rate** is the interest rate charged by the Fed when it lends reserves to banks. The Board of Governors sets the discount rate.

Lowering the discount rate makes funds cheaper to banks. A lower discount rate could place downward pressure on interest rates in the economy. However, when financial markets are operating normally, banks rarely borrow from the Fed, reserving use of the discount window for emergencies. A typical bank borrows from the Fed only about once or twice per year.

federal funds market

A market in which banks lend reserves to one another.

federal funds rate

The interest rate charged when one bank lends reserves to another.

Instead of borrowing from the Fed when they need reserves, banks typically rely on the federal funds market to obtain reserves. The **federal funds market** is a market in which banks lend reserves to one another. The **federal funds rate** is the interest rate charged for such loans; it is determined by banks' demand for and supply of these reserves. The ability to set the discount rate is no longer an important tool of Federal Reserve policy.

To deal with the recent financial and economic conditions, the Fed greatly expanded its lending beyond its traditional discount window lending. As falling house prices led to foreclosures, private investment banks and other financial institutions came under increasing pressure. The Fed made credit available to a wide range of institutions in an effort to stem the crisis. In 2008, the Fed bailed out two major housing finance firms that had been established by the government to prop up the housing industry—Fannie Mae (the Federal National Mortgage Association) and Freddie Mac (the Federal Home Mortgage Corporation). Together, the two institutions backed the mortgages of half of the nation's mortgage loans.[2] It also agreed to provide $85 billion to AIG, the huge insurance firm. AIG had a subsidiary that was heavily exposed to mortgage loan losses, and that crippled the firm. The Fed determined that AIG was simply too big to be allowed to fail. Many banks had ties to the giant institution, and its failure would have been a blow to those banks. As the United States faced the worst financial crisis since the Great Depression, the Fed took center stage. Whatever its role in the financial crisis of 2007–2008, the Fed remains an important backstop for banks and other financial institutions needing liquidity. And for that, it uses the traditional discount window, supplemented with a wide range of other credit facilities. The Case in Point in this section discusses these new credit facilities.

Open-Market Operations

bond

A promise by the issuer of the bond to pay the owner of the bond a payment or a series of payments on a specific date or dates.

open-market operations

The buying and selling of federal government bonds by the Fed.

The Fed's ability to buy and sell federal government bonds has proved to be its most potent policy tool. A **bond** is a promise by the issuer of the bond (in this case the federal government) to pay the owner of the bond a payment or a series of payments on a specific date or dates. The buying and selling of federal government bonds by the Fed are called **open-market operations**. When the Fed buys or sells government bonds, it adds or subtracts reserves from the banking system. Such changes affect the money supply.

Suppose the Fed buys a government bond in the open market. It writes a check on its own account to the seller of the bond. When the seller deposits the check at a bank, the bank submits the check to the Fed for payment. The Fed "pays" the check by crediting the bank's account at the Fed, so the bank has more reserves.

The Fed's purchase of a bond can be illustrated using a balance sheet. Suppose the Fed buys a bond for $1,000 from one of Acme Bank's customers. When that customer deposits the check at Acme, checkable deposits will rise by $1,000. The check is written on the Federal Reserve System; the Fed will credit Acme's account. Acme's reserves thus rise by $1,000. With a 10% reserve requirement, that will create $900 in excess reserves and set off the same process of money expansion as did the cash deposit we have already examined. The difference is that the Fed's purchase of a bond created new reserves with the stroke of a pen, where the cash deposit created them by removing $1,000 from currency in circulation. The purchase of the $1,000 bond by the Fed could thus increase the money supply by as much as $10,000, the maximum expansion suggested by the deposit multiplier.

Where does the Fed get $1,000 to purchase the bond? It simply creates the money when it writes the check to purchase the bond. On the Fed's balance sheet, assets increase by $1,000 because the Fed now has the bond; bank deposits with the Fed, which represent a liability to the Fed, rise by $1,000 as well.

When the Fed sells a bond, it gives the buyer a federal government bond that it had previously purchased and accepts a check in exchange. The bank on which the check was written will find its deposit with the Fed reduced by the amount of the check. That bank's reserves and checkable deposits will fall by equal amounts; the reserves, in effect, disappear. The result is a reduction in the money supply. The Fed thus increases the money supply by buying bonds; it reduces the money supply by selling them.

Figure 9.14 shows how the Fed influences the flow of money in the economy. Funds flow from the public—individuals and firms—to banks as deposits. Banks use those funds to make loans to the public—to individuals and firms. The Fed can influence the volume of bank lending by buying bonds and thus injecting reserves into the system. With new reserves, banks will increase their lending, which creates still more deposits and still more lending as the deposit multiplier goes to work. Alternatively, the Fed can sell bonds. When it does, reserves flow out of the system, reducing bank lending and reducing deposits.

The Fed's purchase or sale of bonds is conducted by the Open Market Desk at the Federal Reserve Bank of New York, one of the 12 district banks. Traders at the Open Market Desk are guided by policy directives issued by the Federal Open Market Committee (FOMC). The FOMC consists of the seven members of the Board of Governors plus five regional bank presidents. The president of the New York Federal Reserve Bank serves as a member of the FOMC; the other 11 bank presidents take turns filling the remaining four seats.

The FOMC meets eight times per year to chart the Fed's monetary policies. In the past, FOMC meetings were closed, with no report of the committee's action until the release of the minutes six weeks after the meeting. Faced with pressure to open its proceedings, the Fed began in 1994 issuing a report of the decisions of the FOMC immediately after each meeting.

In practice, the Fed sets targets for the federal funds rate. To achieve a lower federal funds rate, the Fed goes into the open market buying securities and thus increasing the money supply. When the Fed raises its target rate for the federal funds rate, it sells securities and thus reduces the money supply.

Traditionally, the Fed has bought and sold short-term government securities; however, in dealing with the condition of the economy in 2009, wherein the Fed has already set the target for the federal funds rate at near zero, the Fed has announced that it will also be buying longer term government securities. In so doing, it hopes to influence longer term interest rates, such as those related to mortgages.

FIGURE 9.13

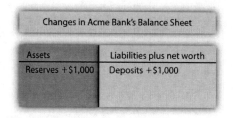

FIGURE 9.14 The Fed and the Flow of Money in the Economy

Individuals and firms (the public) make deposits in banks; banks make loans to individuals and firms. The Fed can buy bonds to inject new reserves into the system, thus increasing bank lending, which creates new deposits, creating still more lending as the deposit multiplier goes to work. Alternatively, the Fed can sell bonds, withdrawing reserves from the system, thus reducing bank lending and reducing total deposits.

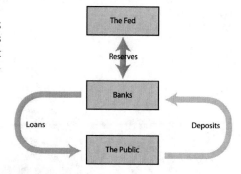

KEY TAKEAWAYS

- The Fed, the central bank of the United States, acts as a bank for other banks and for the federal government. It also regulates banks, sets monetary policy, and maintains the stability of the financial system.
- The Fed sets reserve requirements and the discount rate and conducts open-market operations. Of these tools of monetary policy, open-market operations are the most important.
- Starting in 2007, the Fed began creating additional credit facilities to help to stabilize the financial system.
- The Fed creates new reserves and new money when it purchases bonds. It destroys reserves and thus reduces the money supply when it sells bonds.

Suppose the Fed sells $8 million worth of bonds.

1. How do bank reserves change?
2. Will the money supply increase or decrease?
3. What is the maximum possible change in the money supply if the required reserve ratio is 0.2?

Case in Point: Fed Supports the Financial System by Creating New Credit Facilities

Well before most of the public became aware of the precarious state of the U.S. financial system, the Fed began to see signs of growing financial strains and to act on reducing them. In particular, the Fed saw that short-term interest rates that are often quite close to the federal funds rate began to rise markedly above it. The widening spread was alarming, because it suggested that lender confidence was declining, even for what are generally considered low-risk loans. Commercial paper, in which large companies borrow funds for a period of about a month to manage their cash flow, is an example. Even companies with high credit ratings were having to pay unusually high interest rate premiums in order to get funding, or in some cases could not get funding at all.

To deal with the drying up of credit markets, beginning in late 2007 and accelerating ever since, the Fed has created an alphabet soup of new credit facilities. Some of these are offered in conjunction with the Department of the Treasury, which has more latitude in terms of accepting some credit risk. The facilities differ in terms of collateral used, the duration of the loan, which institutions are eligible to borrow, and the cost to the borrower. For example, the Primary Dealer Credit Facility (PDCF) allows primary dealers (i.e., those financial institutions that normally handle the Fed's open market operations) to obtain overnight loans. The Term Asset-Backed Securities Loan Facility (TALF) allows a wide range of companies to borrow, using the primary dealers as conduits, based on qualified asset-backed securities related to student, auto, credit card, and small business debt, for a three-year period. Most of these new facilities are designed to be temporary, with expirations some time in 2009, but they can be extended.

What they have in common, though, is increasing liquidity that will hopefully stimulate private spending. For example, these credit facilities may encourage banks to pare down their excess reserves (which grew enormously as the financial crisis unfolded and the economy deteriorated) and to make more loans. In the words of Fed Chairman Ben Bernanke:

"Liquidity provision by the central bank reduces systemic risk by assuring market participants that, should short-term investors begin to lose confidence, financial institutions will be able to meet the resulting demands for cash without resorting to potentially destabilizing fire sales of assets. Moreover, backstopping the liquidity needs of financial institutions reduces funding stresses and, all else equal, should increase the willingness of those institutions to lend and make markets."

The legal authority for most of these new credit facilities comes from a particular section of the Federal Reserve Act that allows the Board of Governors "in unusual and exigent circumstances" to extend credit to a wide range of market players.

Sources: *Ben S. Bernanke, "The Crisis and the Policy Response" (Stemp Lecture, London School of Economics, London, England, January 13, 2009); Richard DiCecio and Charles S. Gascon, "New Monetary Policy Tools?" Federal Reserve Bank of St. Louis Monetary Trends, May 2008; Federal Reserve Board of Governors Web site at http://www.federalreserve.gov/monetarypolicy/default.htm.*

ANSWER TO TRY IT! PROBLEM

1. Bank reserves fall by $8 million.
2. The money supply decreases.
3. The maximum possible decrease is $40 million, since $\Delta D = (1/0.2) \times (-\$8 \text{ million}) = -\$40 \text{ million}$.

---

4. REVIEW AND PRACTICE

Summary

In this chapter we investigated the money supply and looked at how it is determined. Money is anything that serves as a medium of exchange. Whatever serves as money also functions as a unit of account and as a store of value. Money may or may not have intrinsic value. In the United States, the total of currency in circulation, traveler's checks, and checkable deposits equals M1. A broader measure of the money supply is M2, which includes M1 plus assets that are highly liquid, but less liquid than those in M1.

Banks create money when they issue loans. The ability of banks to issue loans is controlled by their reserves. Reserves consist of cash in bank vaults and bank deposits with the Fed. Banks operate in a fractional reserve system; that is, they maintain reserves equal to only a small fraction of their deposit liabilities. Banks are heavily regulated to protect individual depositors and to prevent crises of confidence. Deposit insurance protects individual depositors.

A central bank serves as a bank for banks, a regulator of banks, a manager of the money supply, a bank for a nation's government, and a supporter of financial markets generally. In the financial crisis that rocked the United States and much of the world in 2008, the Fed played a central role in keeping bank and nonbank institutions afloat and in keeping credit available. The Federal Reserve System (Fed) is the central bank for the United States. The Fed is governed by a Board of Governors whose members are appointed by the president of the United States, subject to confirmation by the Senate.

The Fed can lend to banks and other institutions through the discount window and other credit facilities, change reserve requirements, and engage in purchases and sales of federal government bonds in the open market. Decisions to buy or sell bonds are made by the Federal Open Market Committee (FOMC); the Fed's open-market operations represent its primary tool for influencing the money supply. Purchases of bonds by the Fed initially increase the reserves of banks. With excess reserves on hand, banks will attempt to increase their loans, and in the process the money supply will change by an amount less than or equal to the deposit multiplier times the change in reserves. Similarly, the Fed can reduce the money supply by selling bonds.

CONCEPT PROBLEMS

1. Airlines have "frequent flier" clubs in which customers accumulate miles according to the number of miles they have flown with the airline. Frequent flier miles can then be used to purchase other flights, to rent cars, or to stay in some hotels. Are frequent flier miles money?

2. Debit cards allow an individual to transfer funds directly in a checkable account to a merchant without writing a check. How is this different from the way credit cards work? Are either credit cards or debit cards money? Explain.

3. Many colleges sell special cards that students can use to purchase everything from textbooks or meals in the cafeteria to use of washing machines in the dorm. Students deposit money in their cards; as they use their cards for purchases, electronic scanners remove money from the cards. To replenish a card's money, a student makes a cash deposit that is credited to the card. Would these cards count as part of the money supply?

4. A smart card, also known as an electronic purse, is a plastic card that can be loaded with a monetary value. Its developers argue that, once widely accepted, it could replace the use of currency in vending machines, parking meters, and elsewhere. Suppose smart cards came into widespread use. Present your views on the following issues:

    a. Would you count balances in the purses as part of the money supply? If so, would they be part of M1? M2?

    b. Should any institution be permitted to issue them, or should they be restricted to banks?

    c. Should the issuers be subject to reserve requirements?

    d. Suppose they were issued by banks. How do you think the use of such purses would affect the money supply? Explain your answer carefully.

5. Which of the following items is part of M1? M2?

    a. $0.27 cents that has accumulated under a couch cushion.

    b. Your $2,000 line of credit with your Visa account.

    c. The $210 balance in your checking account.

    d. $417 in your savings account.

    e. 10 shares of stock your uncle gave you on your 18th birthday, which are now worth $520.

    f. $200 in traveler's checks you have purchased for your spring-break trip.

6. In the Middle Ages, goldsmiths took in customers' deposits (gold coins) and issued receipts that functioned much like checks do today. People used the receipts as a medium of exchange. Goldsmiths also issued loans by writing additional receipts against which they were holding no gold to borrowers. Were goldsmiths engaging in fractional reserve banking? Why do you think that customers turned their gold over to goldsmiths? Who benefited from the goldsmiths' action? Why did such a system generally work? When would it have been likely to fail?

7. A $1,000 deposit in Acme Bank has increased reserves by $1,000. A loan officer at Acme reasons as follows: "The reserve requirement is 10%. That means that the $1,000 in new reserves can back $10,000 in checkable deposits. Therefore I'll loan an additional $10,000." Is there any problem with the loan officer's reasoning? Explain.

8. When the Fed buys and sells bonds through open-market operations, the money supply changes, but there is no effect on the money supply when individuals buy and sell bonds. Explain.

NUMERICAL PROBLEMS

1. Consider the following example of bartering:

   1 10-ounce T-bone steak can be traded for 5 soft drinks.
   1 soft drink can be traded for 10 apples.
   100 apples can be traded for a T-shirt.
   5 T-shirts can be exchanged for 1 textbook.
   It takes 4 textbooks to get 1 VCR.

   a. How many 10-ounce T-bone steaks could you exchange for 1 textbook? How many soft drinks? How many apples?

   b. State the price of T-shirts in terms of apples, textbooks, and soft drinks.

   c. Why do you think we use money as a unit of account?

2. Assume that the banking system is loaned up and that any open-market purchase by the Fed directly increases reserves in the banks. If the required reserve ratio is 0.2, by how much could the money supply expand if the Fed purchased $2 billion worth of bonds?

3. Suppose the Fed sells $5 million worth of bonds to Econobank.

   a. What happens to the reserves of the bank?

   b. What happens to the money supply in the economy as a whole if the reserve requirement is 10%, all payments are made by check, and there is no net drain into currency?

   c. How would your answer in part b be affected if you knew that some people involved in the money creation process kept some of their funds as cash?

4. If half the banks in the nation borrow additional reserves totaling $10 million at the Fed discount window, and at the same time the other half of the banks reduce their excess reserves by a total of $10 million, what is likely to happen to the money supply? Explain.

5. Suppose a bank with a 10% reserve requirement has $10 million in reserves and $100 million in checkable deposits, and a major corporation makes a deposit of $1 million.

   a. Explain how the deposit affects the bank's reserves and checkable deposits.

   b. By how much can the bank increase its lending?

6. Suppose a bank with a 25% reserve requirement has $50 million in reserves and $200 million in checkable deposits, and one of the bank's depositors, a major corporation, writes a check to another corporation for $5 million. The check is deposited in another bank.

   a. Explain how the withdrawal affects the bank's reserves and checkable deposits.

   b. By how much will the bank have to reduce its lending?

7. Suppose the bank in problem 6 faces a 20% reserve requirement. The customer writes the same check. How will this affect your answers?

8. Now consider an economy in which the central bank has just purchased $8 billion worth of government bonds from banks in the economy. What would be the effect of this purchase on the money supply in the country, assuming reserve requirements of:

   a. 10%.

   b. 15%.

   c. 20%.

   d. 25%.

9. Now consider the same economy, and the central bank sells $8 billion worth of government bonds to local banks. State the likely effects on the money supply under reserve requirements of:

   a. 10%.

   b. 15%.

   c. 20%.

   d. 25%.

10. How would the purchase of $8 billion of bonds by the central bank from local banks be likely to affect interest rates? How about the effect on interest rates of the sale of $8 billion worth of bonds? Explain your answers carefully.

ENDNOTES

1. Justin Scheck, "Mackerel Economics in Prison Leads to Appreciation for Oily Fish," *Wall Street Journal*, October 2, 2008, p. A1.

2. Sam Zuckerman, "Feds Take Control of Fannie Mae, Freddie Mac," *The San Francisco Chronicle*, September 8, 2008, p. A-1.

CHAPTER 10

Financial Markets and the Economy

START UP: CLAMPING DOWN ON MONEY GROWTH

For nearly three decades, Americans have come to expect very low inflation, on the order of 2% to 3% a year. How did this expectation come to be? Was it always so? Absolutely not.

In July 1979, with inflation approaching 14% and interest rates on three-month Treasury bills soaring past 10%, a desperate President Jimmy Carter took action. He appointed Paul Volcker, the president of the New York Federal Reserve Bank, as chairman of the Fed's Board of Governors. Mr. Volcker made clear that his objective as chairman was to bring down the inflation rate—no matter what the consequences for the economy. Mr. Carter gave this effort his full support.

Mr. Volcker wasted no time in putting his policies to work. He slowed the rate of money growth immediately. The economy's response was swift; the United States slipped into a brief recession in 1980, followed by a crushing recession in 1981–1982. In terms of the goal of reducing inflation, Mr. Volcker's monetary policies were a dazzling success. Inflation plunged below a 4% rate within three years; by 1986 the inflation rate had fallen to 1.1%. The tall, bald, cigar-smoking Mr. Volcker emerged as a folk hero in the fight against inflation. Indeed he has returned 20 years later as part of President Obama's economic team to perhaps once again rescue the U.S. economy.

The Fed's seven-year fight against inflation from 1979 to 1986 made the job for Alan Greenspan, Mr. Volcker's successor, that much easier. To see how the decisions of the Federal Reserve affect key macroeconomic variables—real GDP, the price level, and unemployment—in this chapter we will explore how **financial markets**, markets in which funds accumulated by one group are made available to another group, are linked to the economy.

> **financial markets**
>
> Markets in which funds accumulated by one group are made available to another group.

This chapter provides the building blocks for understanding financial markets. Beginning with an overview of bond and foreign exchange markets, we will examine how they are related to the level of real GDP and the price level. The second section completes the model of the money market. We have learned that the Fed can change the amount of reserves in the banking system, and that when it does the money supply changes. Here we explain money demand—the quantity of money people and firms want to hold—which, together with money supply, leads to an equilibrium rate of interest.

The model of aggregate demand and supply shows how changes in the components of aggregate demand affect GDP and the price level. In this chapter, we will learn that changes in the financial markets can affect aggregate demand—and in turn can lead to changes in real GDP and the price level. Showing how the financial markets fit into the model of aggregate demand and aggregate supply we developed earlier provides a more complete picture of how the macroeconomy works.

1. THE BOND AND FOREIGN EXCHANGE MARKETS

In this section, we will look at the bond market and at the market for foreign exchange. Events in these markets can affect the price level and output for the entire economy.

1.1 The Bond Market

In their daily operations and in pursuit of new projects, institutions such as firms and governments often borrow. They may seek funds from a bank. Many institutions, however, obtain credit by selling bonds. The federal government is one institution that issues bonds. A local school district might sell bonds to finance the construction of a new school. Your college or university has probably sold bonds to finance new buildings on campus. Firms often sell bonds to finance expansion. The market for bonds is an enormously important one.

When an institution sells a bond, it obtains the price paid for the bond as a kind of loan. The institution that issues the bond is obligated to make payments on the bond in the future. The interest rate is determined by the price of the bond. To understand these relationships, let us look more closely at bond prices and interest rates.

Bond Prices and Interest Rates

Suppose the manager of a manufacturing company needs to borrow some money to expand the factory. The manager could do so in the following way: he or she prints, say, 500 pieces of paper, each bearing the company's promise to pay the bearer $1,000 in a year. These pieces of paper are bonds, and the company, as the issuer, promises to make a single payment. The manager then offers these bonds for sale, announcing that they will be sold to the buyers who offer the highest prices. Suppose the highest price offered is $950, and all the bonds are sold at that price. Each bond is, in effect, an obligation to repay buyers $1,000. The buyers of the bonds are being paid $50 for the service of lending $950 for a year.

The $1,000 printed on each bond is the **face value of the bond**; it is the amount the issuer will have to pay on the **maturity date** of the bond—the date when the loan matures, or comes due. The $950 at which they were sold is their price. The difference between the face value and the price is the amount paid for the use of the money obtained from selling the bond.

An **interest rate** is the payment made for the use of money, expressed as a percentage of the amount borrowed. Bonds you sold command an interest rate equal to the difference between the face value and the bond price, divided by the bond price, and then multiplied by 100 to form a percentage:

EQUATION 10.1

$$\frac{\text{Face value} - \text{bond price}}{\text{Bond price}} \times 100 = \text{interest rate}$$

At a price of $950, the interest rate is 5.3%

$$\frac{\$1{,}000 - \$950}{\$950} \times 100 = 5.3\ \%$$

The interest rate on any bond is determined by its price. As the price falls, the interest rate rises. Suppose, for example, that the best price the manager can get for the bonds is $900. Now the interest rate is 11.1%. A price of $800 would mean an interest rate of 25%; $750 would mean an interest rate of 33.3%; a price of $500 translates into an interest rate of 100%. The lower the price of a bond relative to its face value, the higher the interest rate.

Bonds in the real world are more complicated than the piece of paper in our example, but their structure is basically the same. They have a face value (usually an amount between $1,000 and

face value of a bond

The amount the issuer of a bond will have to pay on the maturity date.

maturity date

The date when a bond matures, or comes due.

interest rate

Payment made for the use of money, expressed as a percentage of the amount borrowed.

$100,000) and a maturity date. The maturity date might be three months from the date of issue; it might be 30 years.

Whatever the period until it matures, and whatever the face value of the bond may be, its issuer will attempt to sell the bond at the highest possible price. Buyers of bonds will seek the lowest prices they can obtain. Newly issued bonds are generally sold in auctions. Potential buyers bid for the bonds, which are sold to the highest bidders. The lower the price of the bond relative to its face value, the higher the interest rate.

Both private firms and government entities issue bonds as a way of raising funds. The original buyer need not hold the bond until maturity. Bonds can be resold at any time, but the price the bond will fetch at the time of resale will vary depending on conditions in the economy and the financial markets.

Figure 10.1 illustrates the market for bonds. Their price is determined by demand and supply. Buyers of newly issued bonds are, in effect, lenders. Sellers of newly issued bonds are borrowers—recall that corporations, the federal government, and other institutions sell bonds when they want to borrow money. Once a newly issued bond has been sold, its owner can resell it; a bond may change hands several times before it matures.

Bonds are not exactly the same sort of product as, say, broccoli or some other good or service. Can we expect bonds to have the same kind of downward-sloping demand curves and upward-sloping supply curves we encounter for ordinary goods and services? Yes. Consider demand. At lower prices, bonds pay higher interest. That makes them more attractive to buyers of bonds and thus increases the quantity demanded. On the other hand, lower prices mean higher costs to borrowers—suppliers of bonds—and should reduce the quantity supplied. Thus, the negative relationship between price and quantity demanded and the positive relationship between price and quantity supplied suggested by conventional demand and supply curves holds true in the market for bonds.

If the quantity of bonds demanded is not equal to the quantity of bonds supplied, the price will adjust almost instantaneously to balance the two. Bond prices are perfectly flexible in that they change immediately to balance demand and supply. Suppose, for example, that the initial price of bonds is $950, as shown by the intersection of the demand and supply curves in Figure 10.1. We will assume that all bonds have equal risk and a face value of $1,000 and that they mature in one year. Now suppose that borrowers increase their borrowing by offering to sell more bonds at every interest rate. This increases the supply of bonds: the supply curve shifts to the right from S_1 to S_2. That, in turn, lowers the equilibrium price of bonds—to $900 in Figure 10.1. The lower price for bonds means a higher interest rate.

The Bond Market and Macroeconomic Performance

The connection between the bond market and the economy derives from the way interest rates affect aggregate demand. For example, investment is one component of aggregate demand, and interest rates affect investment. Firms are less likely to acquire new capital (that is, plant and equipment) if interest rates are high; they're more likely to add capital if interest rates are low.[1]

If bond prices fall, interest rates go up. Higher interest rates tend to discourage investment, so aggregate demand will fall. A fall in aggregate demand, other things unchanged, will mean fewer jobs and less total output than would have been the case with lower rates of interest. In contrast, an increase in the price of bonds lowers interest rates and makes investment in new capital more attractive. That change may boost investment and thus boost aggregate demand.

Figure 10.2 shows how an event in the bond market can stimulate changes in the economy's output and price level. In Panel (a), an increase in demand for bonds raises bond prices. Interest rates thus fall. Lower interest rates increase the quantity of investment demanded, shifting the aggregate demand curve to the right, from AD_1 to AD_2 in Panel (b). Real GDP rises from Y_1 to Y_2; the price level rises from P_1 to P_2. In Panel (c), an increase in the supply of bonds pushes bond prices down. Interest rates rise. The quantity of investment is likely to fall, shifting aggregate demand to the left, from AD_1 to AD_2 in Panel (d). Output and the price level fall from Y_1 to Y_2 and from P_1 to P_2, respectively. Assuming other determinants of aggregate demand remain unchanged, higher interest rates will tend to reduce aggregate demand and lower interest rates will tend to increase aggregate demand.

FIGURE 10.1   The Bond Market

The equilibrium price for bonds is determined where the demand and supply curves intersect. The initial solution here is a price of $950, implying an interest rate of 5.3%. An increase in borrowing, all other things equal, increases the supply of bonds to S_2 and forces the price of bonds down to $900. The interest rate rises to 11.1%.

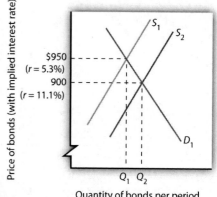

FIGURE 10.2 Bond Prices and Macroeconomic Activity

An increase in the demand for bonds to D_2 in Panel (a) raises the price of bonds to P^b_2, which lowers interest rates and boosts investment. That increases aggregate demand to AD_2 in Panel (b); real GDP rises to Y_2 and the price level rises to P_2. An increase in the supply of bonds to S_2 lowers bond prices to P^b_2 in Panel (c) and raises interest rates. The higher interest rate, taken by itself, is likely to cause a reduction in investment and aggregate demand. AD_1 falls to AD_2, real GDP falls to Y_2, and the price level falls to P_2 in Panel (d).

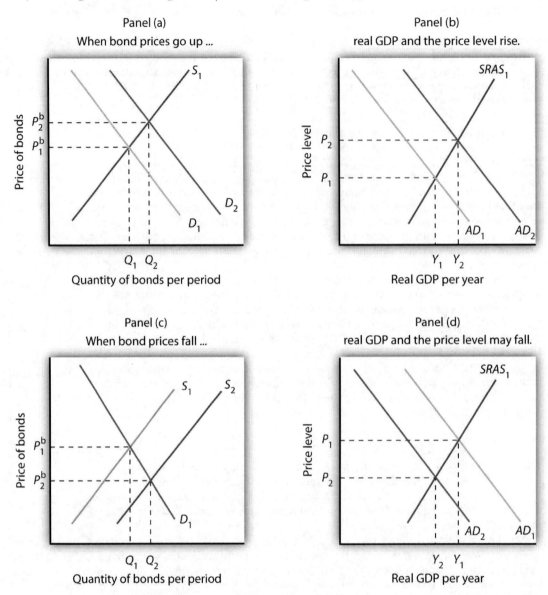

In thinking about the impact of changes in interest rates on aggregate demand, we must remember that some events that change aggregate demand can affect interest rates. We will examine those events in subsequent chapters. Our focus in this chapter is on the way in which events that originate in financial markets affect aggregate demand.

1.2 Foreign Exchange Markets

foreign exchange market

A market in which currencies of different countries are traded for one another.

Another financial market that influences macroeconomic variables is the **foreign exchange market**, a market in which currencies of different countries are traded for one another. Since changes in exports and imports affect aggregate demand and thus real GDP and the price level, the market in which currencies are traded has tremendous importance in the economy.

Foreigners who want to purchase goods and services or assets in the United States must typically pay for them with dollars. United States purchasers of foreign goods must generally make the purchase in a foreign currency. An Egyptian family, for example, exchanges Egyptian pounds for dollars in order to pay for admission to Disney World. A German financial investor purchases dollars to buy U.S.

government bonds. A family from the United States visiting India, on the other hand, needs to obtain Indian rupees in order to make purchases there. A U.S. bank wanting to purchase assets in Mexico City first purchases pesos. These transactions are accomplished in the foreign exchange market.

The foreign exchange market is not a single location in which currencies are traded. The term refers instead to the entire array of institutions through which people buy and sell currencies. It includes a hotel desk clerk who provides currency exchange as a service to hotel guests, brokers who arrange currency exchanges worth billions of dollars, and governments and central banks that exchange currencies. Major currency dealers are linked by computers so that they can track currency exchanges all over the world.

The Exchange Rate

A country's exchange rate is the price of its currency in terms of another currency or currencies. On December 12, 2008, for example, the dollar traded for 91.13 Japanese yen, 0.75 euros, 10.11 South African rands, and 13.51 Mexican pesos. There are as many exchange rates for the dollar as there are countries whose currencies exchange for the dollar—roughly 200 of them.

Economists summarize the movement of exchange rates with a **trade-weighted exchange rate**, which is an index of exchange rates. To calculate a trade-weighted exchange rate index for the U.S. dollar, we select a group of countries, weight the price of the dollar in each country's currency by the amount of trade between that country and the United States, and then report the price of the dollar based on that trade-weighted average. Because trade-weighted exchange rates are so widely used in reporting currency values, they are often referred to as exchange rates themselves. We will follow that convention in this text.

> **trade-weighted exchange rate**
>
> An index of exchange rates.

Determining Exchange Rates

The rates at which most currencies exchange for one another are determined by demand and supply. How does the model of demand and supply operate in the foreign exchange market?

The demand curve for dollars relates the number of dollars buyers want to buy in any period to the exchange rate. An increase in the exchange rate means it takes more foreign currency to buy a dollar. A higher exchange rate, in turn, makes U.S. goods and services more expensive for foreign buyers and reduces the quantity they will demand. That is likely to reduce the quantity of dollars they demand. Foreigners thus will demand fewer dollars as the price of the dollar—the exchange rate—rises. Consequently, the demand curve for dollars is downward sloping, as in Figure 10.3.

The supply curve for dollars emerges from a similar process. When people and firms in the United States purchase goods, services, or assets in foreign countries, they must purchase the currency of those countries first. They supply dollars in exchange for foreign currency. The supply of dollars on the foreign exchange market thus reflects the degree to which people in the United States are buying foreign money at various exchange rates. A higher exchange rate means that a dollar trades for more foreign currency. In effect, the higher rate makes foreign goods and services cheaper to U.S. buyers, so U.S. consumers will purchase more foreign goods and services. People will thus supply more dollars at a higher exchange rate; we expect the supply curve for dollars to be upward sloping, as suggested in Figure 10.3.

In addition to private individuals and firms that participate in the foreign exchange market, most governments participate as well. A government might seek to lower its exchange rate by selling its currency; it might seek to raise the rate by buying its currency. Although governments often participate in foreign exchange markets, they generally represent a very small share of these markets. The most important traders are private buyers and sellers of currencies.

FIGURE 10.3 Determining an Exchange Rate

The equilibrium exchange rate is the rate at which the quantity of dollars demanded equals the quantity supplied. Here, equilibrium occurs at exchange rate E, at which Q dollars are exchanged per period.

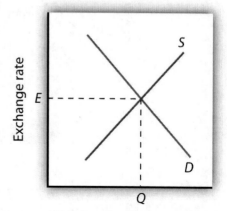

Quantity of dollars per period

Exchange Rates and Macroeconomic Performance

People purchase a country's currency for two quite different reasons: to purchase goods or services in that country, or to purchase the assets of that country—its money, its capital, its stocks, its bonds, or its real estate. Both of these motives must be considered to understand why demand and supply in the foreign exchange market may change.

One thing that can cause the price of the dollar to rise, for example, is a reduction in bond prices in American markets. Figure 10.4 illustrates the effect of this change. Suppose the supply of bonds in the U.S. bond market increases from S_1 to S_2 in Panel (a). Bond prices will drop. Lower bond prices mean higher interest rates. Foreign financial investors, attracted by the opportunity to earn higher returns in the United States, will increase their demand for dollars on the foreign exchange market in order to purchase U.S. bonds. Panel (b) shows that the demand curve for dollars shifts from D_1 to D_2. Simultaneously, U.S. financial investors, attracted by the higher interest rates at home, become less likely to make financial investments abroad and thus supply fewer dollars to exchange markets. The fall in the price of U.S. bonds shifts the supply curve for dollars on the foreign exchange market from S_1 to S_2, and the exchange rate rises from E_1 to E_2.

FIGURE 10.4 Shifts in Demand and Supply for Dollars on the Foreign Exchange Market

In Panel (a), an increase in the supply of bonds lowers bond prices to P^b_2 (and thus raises interest rates). Higher interest rates boost the demand and reduce the supply for dollars, increasing the exchange rate in Panel (b) to E_2. These developments in the bond and foreign exchange markets are likely to lead to a reduction in net exports and in investment, reducing aggregate demand from AD_1 to AD_2 in Panel (c). The price level in the economy falls to P_2, and real GDP falls from Y_1 to Y_2.

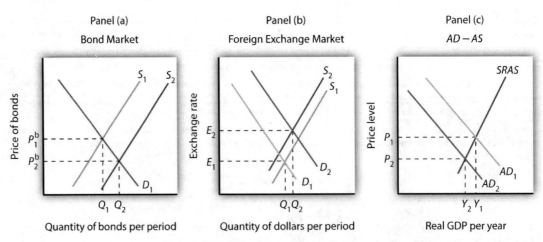

The higher exchange rate makes U.S. goods and services more expensive to foreigners, so it reduces exports. It makes foreign goods cheaper for U.S. buyers, so it increases imports. Net exports thus fall, reducing aggregate demand. Panel (c) shows that output falls from Y_1 to Y_2; the price level falls from P_1 to P_2. This development in the foreign exchange market reinforces the impact of higher interest rates we observed in Figure 10.2, Panels (c) and (d). They not only reduce investment—they reduce net exports as well.

KEY TAKEAWAYS

- A bond represents a borrower's debt; bond prices are determined by demand and supply.
- The interest rate on a bond is negatively related to the price of the bond. As the price of a bond increases, the interest rate falls.
- An increase in the interest rate tends to decrease the quantity of investment demanded and, hence, to decrease aggregate demand. A decrease in the interest rate increases the quantity of investment demanded and aggregate demand.
- The demand for dollars on foreign exchange markets represents foreign demand for U.S. goods, services, and assets. The supply of dollars on foreign exchange markets represents U.S. demand for foreign goods, services, and assets. The demand for and the supply of dollars determine the exchange rate.
- A rise in U.S. interest rates will increase the demand for dollars and decrease the supply of dollars on foreign exchange markets. As a result, the exchange rate will increase and aggregate demand will decrease. A fall in U.S. interest rates will have the opposite effect.

TRY IT!

Suppose the supply of bonds in the U.S. market decreases. Show and explain the effects on the bond and foreign exchange markets. Use the aggregate demand/aggregate supply framework to show and explain the effects on investment, net exports, real GDP, and the price level.

Case in Point: Betting on a Plunge

In 2004, a certain Thomas J. from Florida had a plan. He understood clearly the inverse relationship between bond prices and interest rates. What he did not understand was how expensive guessing incorrectly the direction of interest rates would be when he decided to buy into an "inverse bond" fund.

An "inverse bond" fund is one that performs well when bond prices fall. The fund Thomas bought into happened to trade in 30-year U.S. Treasury bonds, and Thomas guessed that interest rates on them would rise.

The only problem with the plan was that the interest rate on 30-year bonds actually fell over the next year. So, the fund Thomas bought into lost value when the prices of these bonds rose. Expenses associated with this type of fund exacerbated Thomas's loss. If only Thomas had known both the relationship between bond prices and interest rates *and* the direction of interest rates!

Perhaps another thing he did not understand was that when he heard that the Federal Reserve was raising rates in 2004 that this referred to the federal funds rates, a very short-term interest rate. While other short-term interest rates moved with the federal funds rate in 2004, long-term rates did not even blink.

Source: Chuck Jaffee, "Don't Be Stupid: He Had Little Fun with 'Inverse Bond Funds,'" Boston Herald, June 14, 2005, p. 34.

ANSWER TO TRY IT! PROBLEM

If the supply of bonds decreases from S_1 to S_2, bond prices will rise from P^b_1 to P^b_2, as shown in Panel (a). Higher bond prices mean lower interest rates. Lower interest rates in the United States will make financial investments in the United States less attractive to foreigners. As a result, their demand for dollars will decrease from D_1 to D_2, as shown in Panel (b). Similarly, U.S. financial investors will look abroad for higher returns and thus supply more dollars to foreign exchange markets, shifting the supply curve from S_1 to S_2. Thus, the exchange rate will decrease. The quantity of investment rises due to the lower interest rates. Net exports rise because the lower exchange rate makes U.S. goods and services more attractive to foreigners, thus increasing exports, and makes foreign goods less attractive to U.S. buyers, thus reducing imports. Increases in investment and net exports imply a rightward shift in the aggregate demand curve from AD_1 to AD_2. Real GDP and the price level increase.

Panel (a)

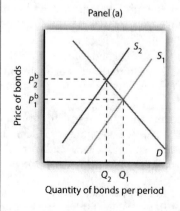

Panel (b)

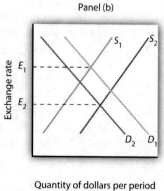

Panel (c)

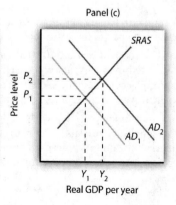

2. DEMAND, SUPPLY, AND EQUILIBRIUM IN THE MONEY MARKET

LEARNING OBJECTIVES

1. Explain the motives for holding money and relate them to the interest rate that could be earned from holding alternative assets, such as bonds.
2. Draw a money demand curve and explain how changes in other variables may lead to shifts in the money demand curve.
3. Illustrate and explain the notion of equilibrium in the money market.
4. Use graphs to explain how changes in money demand or money supply are related to changes in the bond market, in interest rates, in aggregate demand, and in real GDP and the price level.

In this section we will explore the link between money markets, bond markets, and interest rates. We first look at the demand for money. The demand curve for money is derived like any other demand curve, by examining the relationship between the "price" of money (which, we will see, is the interest rate) and the quantity demanded, holding all other determinants unchanged. We then link the demand for money to the concept of money supply developed in the last chapter, to determine the equilibrium rate of interest. In turn, we show how changes in interest rates affect the macroeconomy.

2.1 The Demand for Money

demand for money

The relationship between the quantity of money people want to hold and the factors that determine that quantity.

In deciding how much money to hold, people make a choice about how to hold their wealth. How much wealth shall be held as money and how much as other assets? For a given amount of wealth, the answer to this question will depend on the relative costs and benefits of holding money versus other assets. The **demand for money** is the relationship between the quantity of money people want to hold and the factors that determine that quantity.

To simplify our analysis, we will assume there are only two ways to hold wealth: as money in a checking account, or as funds in a bond market mutual fund that purchases long-term bonds on behalf of its subscribers. A bond fund is not money. Some money deposits earn interest, but the return on these accounts is generally lower than what could be obtained in a bond fund. The advantage of checking accounts is that they are highly liquid and can thus be spent easily. We will think of the demand for money as a curve that represents the outcomes of choices between the greater liquidity of money deposits and the higher interest rates that can be earned by holding a bond fund. The difference between the interest rates paid on money deposits and the interest return available from bonds is the cost of holding money.

Motives for Holding Money

One reason people hold their assets as money is so that they can purchase goods and services. The money held for the purchase of goods and services may be for everyday transactions such as buying groceries or paying the rent, or it may be kept on hand for contingencies such as having the funds available to pay to have the car fixed or to pay for a trip to the doctor.

transactions demand for money

Money people hold to pay for goods and services they anticipate buying.

The **transactions demand for money** is money people hold to pay for goods and services they anticipate buying. When you carry money in your purse or wallet to buy a movie ticket or maintain a checking account balance so you can purchase groceries later in the month, you are holding the money as part of your transactions demand for money.

precautionary demand for money

The money people hold for contingencies.

The money people hold for contingencies represents their **precautionary demand for money**. Money held for precautionary purposes may include checking account balances kept for possible home repairs or health-care needs. People do not know precisely when the need for such expenditures will occur, but they can prepare for them by holding money so that they'll have it available when the need arises.

People also hold money for speculative purposes. Bond prices fluctuate constantly. As a result, holders of bonds not only earn interest but experience gains or losses in the value of their assets. Bond-holders enjoy gains when bond prices rise and suffer losses when bond prices fall. Because of this, expectations play an important role as a determinant of the demand for bonds. Holding bonds is one alternative to holding money, so these same expectations can affect the demand for money.

John Maynard Keynes, who was an enormously successful speculator in bond markets himself, suggested that bondholders who anticipate a drop in bond prices will try to sell their bonds ahead of the price drop in order to avoid this loss in asset value. Selling a bond means converting it to money. Keynes referred to the **speculative demand for money** as the money held in response to concern that bond prices and the prices of other financial assets might change.

Of course, money is money. One cannot sort through someone's checking account and locate which funds are held for transactions and which funds are there because the owner of the account is worried about a drop in bond prices or is taking a precaution. We distinguish money held for different motives in order to understand how the quantity of money demanded will be affected by a key determinant of the demand for money: the interest rate.

Interest Rates and the Demand for Money

The quantity of money people hold to pay for transactions and to satisfy precautionary and speculative demand is likely to vary with the interest rates they can earn from alternative assets such as bonds. When interest rates rise relative to the rates that can be earned on money deposits, people hold less money. When interest rates fall, people hold more money. The logic of these conclusions about the money people hold and interest rates depends on the people's motives for holding money.

The quantity of money households want to hold varies according to their income and the interest rate; different average quantities of money held can satisfy their transactions and precautionary demands for money. To see why, suppose a household earns and spends $3,000 per month. It spends an equal amount of money each day. For a month with 30 days, that is $100 per day. One way the household could manage this spending would be to leave the money in a checking account, which we will assume pays zero interest. The household would thus have $3,000 in the checking account when the month begins, $2,900 at the end of the first day, $1,500 halfway through the month, and zero at the end of the last day of the month. Averaging the daily balances, we find that the quantity of money the household demands equals $1,500. This approach to money management, which we will call the "cash approach," has the virtue of simplicity, but the household will earn no interest on its funds.

Consider an alternative money management approach that permits the same pattern of spending. At the beginning of the month, the household deposits $1,000 in its checking account and the other $2,000 in a bond fund. Assume the bond fund pays 1% interest per month, or an annual interest rate of 12.7%. After 10 days, the money in the checking account is exhausted, and the household withdraws another $1,000 from the bond fund for the next 10 days. On the 20th day, the final $1,000 from the bond fund goes into the checking account. With this strategy, the household has an average daily balance of $500, which is the quantity of money it demands. Let us call this money management strategy the "bond fund approach."

Remember that both approaches allow the household to spend $3,000 per month, $100 per day. The cash approach requires a quantity of money demanded of $1,500, while the bond fund approach lowers this quantity to $500.

The bond fund approach generates some interest income. The household has $1,000 in the fund for 10 days (1/3 of a month) and $1,000 for 20 days (2/3 of a month). With an interest rate of 1% per month, the household earns $10 in interest each month ([$1,000 × 0.01 × 1/3] + [$1,000 × 0.01 × 2/3]). The disadvantage of the bond fund, of course, is that it requires more attention—$1,000 must be transferred from the fund twice each month. There may also be fees associated with the transfers.

Of course, the bond fund strategy we have examined here is just one of many. The household could begin each month with $1,500 in the checking account and $1,500 in the bond fund, transferring $1,500 to the checking account midway through the month. This strategy requires one less transfer, but it also generates less interest—$7.50 (= $1,500 × 0.01 × 1/2). With this strategy, the household demands a quantity of money of $750. The household could also maintain a much smaller average quantity of money in its checking account and keep more in its bond fund. For simplicity, we can think of any strategy that involves transferring money in and out of a bond fund or another interest-earning asset as a bond fund strategy.

Which approach should the household use? That is a choice each household must make—it is a question of weighing the interest a bond fund strategy creates against the hassle and possible fees associated with the transfers it requires. Our example does not yield a clear-cut choice for any one household, but we can make some generalizations about its implications.

First, a household is more likely to adopt a bond fund strategy when the interest rate is higher. At low interest rates, a household does not sacrifice much income by pursuing the simpler cash strategy. As the interest rate rises, a bond fund strategy becomes more attractive. That means that the higher the interest rate, the lower the quantity of money demanded.

Second, people are more likely to use a bond fund strategy when the cost of transferring funds is lower. The creation of savings plans, which began in the 1970s and 1980s, that allowed easy transfer of funds between interest-earning assets and checkable deposits tended to reduce the demand for money.

speculative demand for money

The money held in response to concern that bond prices and the prices of other financial assets might change.

Some money deposits, such as savings accounts and money market deposit accounts, pay interest. In evaluating the choice between holding assets as some form of money or in other forms such as bonds, households will look at the differential between what those funds pay and what they could earn in the bond market. A higher interest rate in the bond market is likely to increase this differential; a lower interest rate will reduce it. An increase in the spread between rates on money deposits and the interest rate in the bond market reduces the quantity of money demanded; a reduction in the spread increases the quantity of money demanded.

Firms, too, must determine how to manage their earnings and expenditures. However, instead of worrying about $3,000 per month, even a relatively small firm may be concerned about $3,000,000 per month. Rather than facing the difference of $10 versus $7.50 in interest earnings used in our household example, this small firm would face a difference of $2,500 per month ($10,000 versus $7,500). For very large firms such as Toyota or AT&T, interest rate differentials among various forms of holding their financial assets translate into millions of dollars per day.

How is the speculative demand for money related to interest rates? When financial investors believe that the prices of bonds and other assets will fall, their speculative demand for money goes up. The speculative demand for money thus depends on expectations about future changes in asset prices. Will this demand also be affected by present interest rates?

If interest rates are low, bond prices are high. It seems likely that if bond prices are high, financial investors will become concerned that bond prices might fall. That suggests that high bond prices—low interest rates—would increase the quantity of money held for speculative purposes. Conversely, if bond prices are already relatively low, it is likely that fewer financial investors will expect them to fall still further. They will hold smaller speculative balances. Economists thus expect that the quantity of money demanded for speculative reasons will vary negatively with the interest rate.

The Demand Curve for Money

demand curve for money

Curve that shows the quantity of money demanded at each interest rate, all other things unchanged.

We have seen that the transactions, precautionary, and speculative demands for money vary negatively with the interest rate. Putting those three sources of demand together, we can draw a demand curve for money to show how the interest rate affects the total quantity of money people hold. The **demand curve for money** shows the quantity of money demanded at each interest rate, all other things unchanged. Such a curve is shown in Figure 10.7. An increase in the interest rate reduces the quantity of money demanded. A reduction in the interest rate increases the quantity of money demanded.

The relationship between interest rates and the quantity of money demanded is an application of the law of demand. If we think of the alternative to holding money as holding bonds, then the interest rate—or the differential between the interest rate in the bond market and the interest paid on money deposits—represents the price of holding money. As is the case with all goods and services, an increase in price reduces the quantity demanded.

FIGURE 10.7 The Demand Curve for Money

The demand curve for money shows the quantity of money demanded at each interest rate. Its downward slope expresses the negative relationship between the quantity of money demanded and the interest rate.

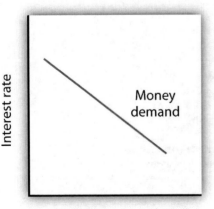

Quantity of money per period

Other Determinants of the Demand for Money

We draw the demand curve for money to show the quantity of money people will hold at each interest rate, all other determinants of money demand unchanged. A change in those "other determinants" will shift the demand for money. Among the most important variables that can shift the demand for money are the level of income and real GDP, the price level, expectations, transfer costs, and preferences.

Real GDP

A household with an income of $10,000 per month is likely to demand a larger quantity of money than a household with an income of $1,000 per month. That relationship suggests that money is a normal good: as income increases, people demand more money at each interest rate, and as income falls, they demand less.

An increase in real GDP increases incomes throughout the economy. The demand for money in the economy is therefore likely to be greater when real GDP is greater.

The Price Level

The higher the price level, the more money is required to purchase a given quantity of goods and services. All other things unchanged, the higher the price level, the greater the demand for money.

Expectations

The speculative demand for money is based on expectations about bond prices. All other things unchanged, if people expect bond prices to fall, they will increase their demand for money. If they expect bond prices to rise, they will reduce their demand for money.

The expectation that bond prices are about to change actually causes bond prices to change. If people expect bond prices to fall, for example, they will sell their bonds, exchanging them for money. That will shift the supply curve for bonds to the right, thus lowering their price. The importance of expectations in moving markets can lead to a self-fulfilling prophecy.

Expectations about future price levels also affect the demand for money. The expectation of a higher price level means that people expect the money they are holding to fall in value. Given that expectation, they are likely to hold less of it in anticipation of a jump in prices.

Expectations about future price levels play a particularly important role during periods of hyperinflation. If prices rise very rapidly and people expect them to continue rising, people are likely to try to reduce the amount of money they hold, knowing that it will fall in value as it sits in their wallets or their bank accounts. Toward the end of the great German hyperinflation of the early 1920s, prices were doubling as often as three times a day. Under those circumstances, people tried not to hold money even for a few minutes—within the space of eight hours money would lose half its value!

Transfer Costs

For a given level of expenditures, reducing the quantity of money demanded requires more frequent transfers between nonmoney and money deposits. As the cost of such transfers rises, some consumers will choose to make fewer of them. They will therefore increase the quantity of money they demand. In general, the demand for money will increase as it becomes more expensive to transfer between money and nonmoney accounts. The demand for money will fall if transfer costs decline. In recent years, transfer costs have fallen, leading to a decrease in money demand.

Preferences

Preferences also play a role in determining the demand for money. Some people place a high value on having a considerable amount of money on hand. For others, this may not be important.

Household attitudes toward risk are another aspect of preferences that affect money demand. As we have seen, bonds pay higher interest rates than money deposits, but holding bonds entails a risk that bond prices might fall. There is also a chance that the issuer of a bond will default, that is, will not pay the amount specified on the bond to bondholders; indeed, bond issuers may end up paying nothing at all. A money deposit, such as a savings deposit, might earn a lower yield, but it is a safe yield. People's attitudes about the trade-off between risk and yields affect the degree to which they hold their wealth as money. Heightened concerns about risk in the last half of 2008 led many households to increase their demand for money.

Figure 10.8 shows an increase in the demand for money. Such an increase could result from a higher real GDP, a higher price level, a change in expectations, an increase in transfer costs, or a change in preferences.

FIGURE 10.8 An Increase in Money Demand

An increase in real GDP, the price level, or transfer costs, for example, will increase the quantity of money demanded at any interest rate r, increasing the demand for money from D_1 to D_2. The quantity of money demanded at interest rate r rises from M to M'. The reverse of any such events would reduce the quantity of money demanded at every interest rate, shifting the demand curve to the left.

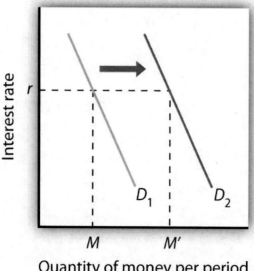

2.2   The Supply of Money

supply curve of money

Curve that shows the relationship between the quantity of money supplied and the market interest rate, all other determinants of supply unchanged.

The **supply curve of money** shows the relationship between the quantity of money supplied and the market interest rate, all other determinants of supply unchanged. We have learned that the Fed, through its open-market operations, determines the total quantity of reserves in the banking system. We shall assume that banks increase the money supply in fixed proportion to their reserves. Because the quantity of reserves is determined by Federal Reserve policy, we draw the supply curve of money in Figure 10.9 as a vertical line, determined by the Fed's monetary policies. In drawing the supply curve of money as a vertical line, we are assuming the money supply does not depend on the interest rate. Changing the quantity of reserves and hence the money supply is an example of monetary policy.

FIGURE 10.9   The Supply Curve of Money

We assume that the quantity of money supplied in the economy is determined as a fixed multiple of the quantity of bank reserves, which is determined by the Fed. The supply curve of money is a vertical line at that quantity.

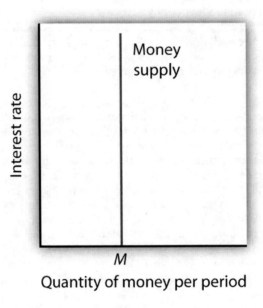

2.3   Equilibrium in the Market for Money

money market

The interaction among institutions through which money is supplied to individuals, firms, and other institutions that demand money.

money market equilibrium

The interest rate at which the quantity of money demanded is equal to the quantity of money supplied.

The **money market** is the interaction among institutions through which money is supplied to individuals, firms, and other institutions that demand money. **Money market equilibrium** occurs at the interest rate at which the quantity of money demanded is equal to the quantity of money supplied. Figure 10.10 combines demand and supply curves for money to illustrate equilibrium in the market for money. With a stock of money (M), the equilibrium interest rate is r.

FIGURE 10.10 Money Market Equilibrium

The market for money is in equilibrium if the quantity of money demanded is equal to the quantity of money supplied. Here, equilibrium occurs at interest rate r.

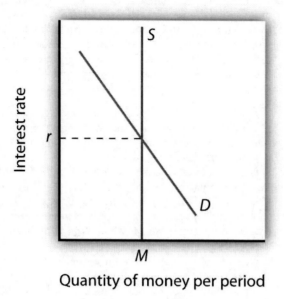

2.4 Effects of Changes in the Money Market

A shift in money demand or supply will lead to a change in the equilibrium interest rate. Let's look at the effects of such changes on the economy.

Changes in Money Demand

Suppose that the money market is initially in equilibrium at r_1 with supply curve S and a demand curve D_1 as shown in Panel (a) of Figure 10.11. Now suppose that there is a decrease in money demand, all other things unchanged. A decrease in money demand could result from a decrease in the cost of transferring between money and nonmoney deposits, from a change in expectations, or from a change in preferences.[2] Panel (a) shows that the money demand curve shifts to the left to D_2. We can see that the interest rate will fall to r_2. To see why the interest rate falls, we recall that if people want to hold less money, then they will want to hold more bonds. Thus, Panel (b) shows that the demand for bonds increases. The higher price of bonds means lower interest rates; lower interest rates restore equilibrium in the money market.

FIGURE 10.11 A Decrease in the Demand for Money

A decrease in the demand for money due to a change in transactions costs, preferences, or expectations, as shown in Panel (a), will be accompanied by an increase in the demand for bonds as shown in Panel (b), and a fall in the interest rate. The fall in the interest rate will cause a rightward shift in the aggregate demand curve from AD_1 to AD_2, as shown in Panel (c). As a result, real GDP and the price level rise.

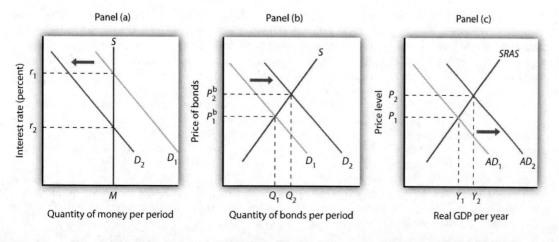

Lower interest rates in turn increase the quantity of investment. They also stimulate net exports, as lower interest rates lead to a lower exchange rate. The aggregate demand curve shifts to the right as shown in Panel (c) from AD_1 to AD_2. Given the short-run aggregate supply curve $SRAS$, the economy moves to a higher real GDP and a higher price level.

An increase in money demand due to a change in expectations, preferences, or transactions costs that make people want to hold more money at each interest rate will have the opposite effect. The money demand curve will shift to the right and the demand for bonds will shift to the left. The resulting higher interest rate will lead to a lower quantity of investment. Also, higher interest rates will lead to a higher exchange rate and depress net exports. Thus, the aggregate demand curve will shift to the left. All other things unchanged, real GDP and the price level will fall.

Changes in the Money Supply

Now suppose the market for money is in equilibrium and the Fed changes the money supply. All other things unchanged, how will this change in the money supply affect the equilibrium interest rate and aggregate demand, real GDP, and the price level?

Suppose the Fed conducts open-market operations in which it buys bonds. This is an example of expansionary monetary policy. The impact of Fed bond purchases is illustrated in Panel (a) of Figure 10.12. The Fed's purchase of bonds shifts the demand curve for bonds to the right, raising bond prices to P^b_2. As we learned, when the Fed buys bonds, the supply of money increases. Panel (b) of Figure 10.12 shows an economy with a money supply of M, which is in equilibrium at an interest rate of r_1. Now suppose the bond purchases by the Fed as shown in Panel (a) result in an increase in the money supply to M'; that policy change shifts the supply curve for money to the right to S_2. At the original interest rate r_1, people do not wish to hold the newly supplied money; they would prefer to hold non-money assets. To reestablish equilibrium in the money market, the interest rate must fall to increase the quantity of money demanded. In the economy shown, the interest rate must fall to r_2 to increase the quantity of money demanded to M'.

FIGURE 10.12 An Increase in the Money Supply

The Fed increases the money supply by buying bonds, increasing the demand for bonds in Panel (a) from D_1 to D_2 and the price of bonds to P^b_2. This corresponds to an increase in the money supply to M' in Panel (b). The interest rate must fall to r_2 to achieve equilibrium. The lower interest rate leads to an increase in investment and net exports, which shifts the aggregate demand curve from AD_1 to AD_2 in Panel (c). Real GDP and the price level rise.

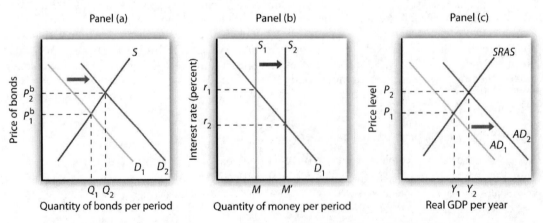

The reduction in interest rates required to restore equilibrium to the market for money after an increase in the money supply is achieved in the bond market. The increase in bond prices lowers interest rates, which will increase the quantity of money people demand. Lower interest rates will stimulate investment and net exports, via changes in the foreign exchange market, and cause the aggregate demand curve to shift to the right, as shown in Panel (c), from AD_1 to AD_2. Given the short-run aggregate supply curve $SRAS$, the economy moves to a higher real GDP and a higher price level.

Open-market operations in which the Fed sells bonds—that is, a contractionary monetary policy—will have the opposite effect. When the Fed sells bonds, the supply curve of bonds shifts to the right and the price of bonds falls. The bond sales lead to a reduction in the money supply, causing the money supply curve to shift to the left and raising the equilibrium interest rate. Higher interest rates lead to a shift in the aggregate demand curve to the left.

As we have seen in looking at both changes in demand for and in supply of money, the process of achieving equilibrium in the money market works in tandem with the achievement of equilibrium in the bond market. The interest rate determined by money market equilibrium is consistent with the interest rate achieved in the bond market.

KEY TAKEAWAYS

- People hold money in order to buy goods and services (transactions demand), to have it available for contingencies (precautionary demand), and in order to avoid possible drops in the value of other assets such as bonds (speculative demand).
- The higher the interest rate, the lower the quantities of money demanded for transactions, for precautionary, and for speculative purposes. The lower the interest rate, the higher the quantities of money demanded for these purposes.
- The demand for money will change as a result of a change in real GDP, the price level, transfer costs, expectations, or preferences.
- We assume that the supply of money is determined by the Fed. The supply curve for money is thus a vertical line. Money market equilibrium occurs at the interest rate at which the quantity of money demanded equals the quantity of money supplied.
- All other things unchanged, a shift in money demand or supply will lead to a change in the equilibrium interest rate and therefore to changes in the level of real GDP and the price level.

TRY IT!

In 2005 the Fed was concerned about the possibility that the United States was moving into an inflationary gap, and it adopted a contractionary monetary policy as a result. Draw a four-panel graph showing this policy and its expected results. In Panel (a), use the model of aggregate demand and aggregate supply to illustrate an economy with an inflationary gap. In Panel (b), show how the Fed's policy will affect the market for bonds. In Panel (c), show how it will affect the demand for and supply of money. In Panel (d), show how it will affect the exchange rate. Finally, return to Panel (a) and incorporate these developments into your analysis of aggregate demand and aggregate supply, and show how the Fed's policy will affect real GDP and the price level in the short run.

Case in Point: Money in Today's World

The models of the money and bond markets presented in this chapter suggest that the Fed can control the interest rate by deciding on a money supply that would lead to the desired equilibrium interest rate in the money market. Yet, Fed policy announcements typically focus on what it wants the federal funds rate to be with scant attention to the money supply. Whereas throughout the 1990s, the Fed would announce a target federal funds rate and also indicate an expected change in the money supply, in 2000, when legislation requiring it to do so expired, it abandoned the practice of setting money supply targets.

Why the shift? The factors that have made focusing on the money supply as a policy target difficult for the past 25 years are first banking deregulation in the 1980s followed by financial innovations associated with technological changes—in particular the maturation of electronic payment and transfer mechanisms—thereafter.

Before the 1980s, M1 was a fairly reliable measure of the money people held, primarily for transactions. To buy things, one used cash, checks written on demand deposits, or traveler's checks. The Fed could thus use reliable estimates of the money demand curve to predict what the money supply would need to be in order to bring about a certain interest rate in the money market.

Legislation in the early 1980s allowed for money market deposit accounts (MMDAs), which are essentially interest-bearing savings accounts on which checks can be written. MMDAs are part of M2. Shortly after, other forms of payments for transactions developed or became more common. For example, credit and debit card use has mushroomed (from $10.8 billion in 1990 to $30 billion in 2000), and people can pay their credit card bills, electronically or with paper checks, from accounts that are part of either M1 or M2. Another innovation of the last 20 years is the automatic transfer service (ATS) that allows consumers to move money between checking and savings accounts at an ATM machine, or online, or through prearranged agreements with their financial institutions. While we take these methods of payment for granted today, they did not exist before 1980 because of restrictive banking legislation and the lack of technological know-how. Indeed, before 1980, being able to pay bills from accounts that earned interest was unheard of.

Further blurring the lines between M1 and M2 has been the development and growing popularity of what are called retail sweep programs. Since 1994, banks have been using retail-sweeping software to dynamically re-classify balances as either checking account balances (part of M1) or MMDAs (part of M2). They do this to avoid reserve requirements on checking accounts. The software not only moves the funds but also ensures that the bank does not exceed the legal limit of six reclassifications in any month. In the last 10 years these retail sweeps rose from zero to nearly the size of M1 itself!

Such changes in the ways people pay for transactions and banks do their business have led economists to think about new definitions of money that would better track what is actually used for the purposes behind the money demand curve. One notion is called MZM, which stands for "money zero maturity." The idea behind MZM is that people can easily use any deposits that do not have specified maturity terms to pay for transactions, as these accounts are quite liquid, regardless of what classification of money they fall into. Some research shows that using MZM allows for a stable picture of the money market. Until more agreement has been reached, though, we should expect the Fed to continue to downplay the role of the money supply in its policy deliberations and to continue to announce its intentions in terms of the federal funds rate.

Source: *Pedre Teles and Ruilin Zhou, "A Stable Money Demand: Looking for the Right Monetary Aggregate," Federal Reserve Bank of Chicago Economic Perspectives 29 (First Quarter, 2005): 50–59.*

In Panel (a), with the aggregate demand curve AD_1, short-run aggregate supply curve $SRAS$, and long-run aggregate supply curve $LRAS$, the economy has an inflationary gap of $Y_1 - Y_P$. The contractionary monetary policy means that the Fed sells bonds—a rightward shift of the bond supply curve in Panel (b), which decreases the money supply—as shown by a leftward shift in the money supply curve in Panel (c). In Panel (b), we see that the price of bonds falls, and in Panel (c) that the interest rate rises. A higher interest rate will reduce the quantity of investment demanded. The higher interest rate also leads to a higher exchange rate, as shown in Panel (d), as the demand for dollars increases and the supply decreases. The higher exchange rate will lead to a decrease in net exports. As a result of these changes in financial markets, the aggregate demand curve shifts to the left to AD_2 in Panel (a). If all goes according to plan (and we will learn in the next chapter that it may not!), the new aggregate demand curve will intersect $SRAS$ and $LRAS$ at Y_P.

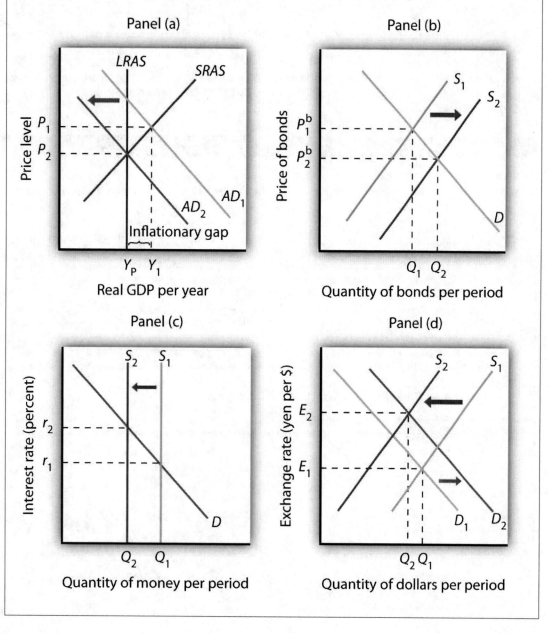

3. REVIEW AND PRACTICE

Summary

We began this chapter by looking at bond and foreign exchange markets and showing how each is related to the level of real GDP and the price level. Bonds represent the obligation of the seller to repay the buyer the face value by the maturity date; their interest rate is determined by the demand and supply for bonds. An increase in bond prices means a drop in interest rates. A reduction in bond prices means interest rates have risen. The price of the dollar is determined in foreign exchange markets by the demand and supply for dollars.

We then saw how the money market works. The quantity of money demanded varies negatively with the interest rate. Factors that cause the demand curve for money to shift include changes in real GDP, the price level, expectations, the cost of transferring funds between money and nonmoney accounts, and preferences, especially preferences concerning risk. Equilibrium in the market for money is achieved at the interest rate at which the quantity of money demanded equals the quantity of money supplied. We assumed that the supply of money is determined by the Fed. An increase in money demand raises the equilibrium interest rate, and a decrease in money demand lowers the equilibrium interest rate. An increase in the money supply lowers the equilibrium interest rate; a reduction in the money supply raises the equilibrium interest rate.

CONCEPT PROBLEMS

1. What factors might increase the demand for bonds? The supply?
2. What would happen to the market for bonds if a law were passed that set a minimum price on bonds that was above the equilibrium price?
3. When the price of bonds decreases, the interest rate rises. Explain.
4. One journalist writing about the complex interactions between various markets in the economy stated: "When the government spends more than it takes in taxes it must sell bonds to finance its excess expenditures. But selling bonds drives interest rates down and thus stimulates the economy by encouraging more investment and decreasing the foreign exchange rate, which helps our export industries." Carefully analyze the statement. Do you agree? Why or why not?
5. What do you predict will happen to the foreign exchange rate if interest rates in the United States increase dramatically over the next year? Explain, using a graph of the foreign exchange market. How would such a change affect real GDP and the price level?
6. Suppose the government were to increase its purchases, issuing bonds to finance these purchases. Use your knowledge of the bond and foreign exchange markets to explain how this would affect investment and net exports.
7. How would each of the following affect the demand for money?
   a. A tax on bonds held by individuals
   b. A forecast by the Fed that interest rates will rise sharply in the next quarter
   c. A wave of muggings
   d. An announcement of an agreement between Congress and the president that, beginning in the next fiscal year, government spending will be reduced by an amount sufficient to eliminate all future borrowing
8. Some low-income countries do not have a bond market. In such countries, what substitutes for money do you think people would hold?
9. Explain what is meant by the statement that people are holding more money than they want to hold.
10. Explain how the Fed's sale of government bonds shifts the supply curve for money.
11. Trace the impact of a sale of government bonds by the Fed on bond prices, interest rates, investment, net exports, aggregate demand, real GDP, and the price level.

NUMERICAL PROBLEMS

1. Compute the rate of interest associated with each of these bonds that matures in one year:

	Face Value		Selling Price
a.	$100		$80
b.	$100		$90
c.	$100		$95
d.	$200		$180
e.	$200		$190
f.	$200		$195

   g. Describe the relationship between the selling price of a bond and the interest rate.

2. Suppose that the demand and supply schedules for bonds that have a face value of $100 and a maturity date one year hence are as follows:

Price	Quantity Demanded	Quantity Supplied
$100	0	600
95	100	500
90	200	400
85	300	300
80	400	200
75	500	100
70	600	0

   a. Draw the demand and supply curves for these bonds, find the equilibrium price, and determine the interest rate.

   b. Now suppose the quantity demanded increases by 200 bonds at each price. Draw the new demand curve and find the new equilibrium price. What has happened to the interest rate?

3. Compute the dollar price of a German car that sells for 40,000 euros at each of the following exchange rates:

   a. $1 = 1 euro

   b. $1 = 0.8 euro

   c. $1 = 0.75 euro

4. Consider the euro-zone of the European Union and Japan. The demand and supply curves for euros are given by the following table (prices for the euro are given in Japanese yen; quantities of euros are in millions):

Price (in euros)	Euros Demanded	Euros Supplied
¥75	0	600
70	100	500
65	200	400
60	300	300
55	400	200
50	500	100
45	600	0

   a. Draw the demand and supply curves for euros and state the equilibrium exchange rate (in yen) for the euro. How many euros are required to purchase one yen?

   b. Suppose an increase in interest rates in the European Union increases the demand for euros by 100 million at each price. At the same time, it reduces the supply by 100 million at each price. Draw the new demand and supply curves and state the new equilibrium exchange rate for the euro. How many euros are now required to purchase one yen?

   c. How will the event in (b) affect net exports in the European Union?

   d. How will the event in (b) affect aggregate demand in the European Union?

e. How will the event in (b) affect net exports in Japan?

f. How will the event in (b) affect aggregate demand in Japan?

5. Suppose you earn $6,000 per month and spend $200 in each of the month's 30 days. Compute your average quantity of money demanded if:

a. You deposit your entire earnings in your checking account at the beginning of the month.

b. You deposit $2,000 into your checking account on the 1st, 11th, and 21st days of the month.

c. You deposit $1,000 into your checking account on the 1st, 6th, 11th, 16th, 21st, and 26th days of the month.

d. How would you expect the interest rate to affect your decision to opt for strategy (a), (b), or (c)?

6. Suppose the quantity demanded of money at an interest rate of 5% is $2 billion per day, at an interest rate of 3% is $3 billion per day, and at an interest rate of 1% is $4 billion per day. Suppose the money supply is $3 billion per day.

a. Draw a graph of the money market and find the equilibrium interest rate.

b. Suppose the quantity of money demanded decreases by $1 billion per day at each interest rate. Graph this situation and find the new equilibrium interest rate. Explain the process of achieving the new equilibrium in the money market.

c. Suppose instead that the money supply decreases by $1 billion per day. Explain the process of achieving the new equilibrium in the money market.

7. We know that the U.S. economy faced a recessionary gap in 2008 and that the Fed responded with an expansionary monetary policy. Present the results of the Fed's action in a four-panel graph. In Panel (a), show the initial situation, using the model of aggregate demand and aggregate supply. In Panel (b), show how the Fed's policy affects the bond market and bond prices. In Panel (c), show how the market for U.S. dollars and the exchange rate will be affected. In Panel (d), incorporate these developments into your analysis of aggregate demand and aggregate supply, and show how the Fed's policy will affect real GDP and the price level in the short run.

ENDNOTES

1. Consumption may also be affected by changes in interest rates. For example, if interest rates fall, consumers can more easily obtain credit and thus are more likely to purchase cars and other durable goods. To simplify, we ignore this effect.

2. In this chapter we are looking only at changes that originate in financial markets to see their impact on aggregate demand and aggregate supply. Changes in the price level and in real GDP also shift the money demand curve, but these changes are the result of changes in aggregate demand or aggregate supply and are considered in more advanced courses in macroeconomics.

CHAPTER 11
Monetary Policy and the Fed

START UP: THE FED'S EXTRAORDINARY CHALLENGES IN 2008

"The Federal Reserve will employ all available tools to promote the resumption of sustainable economic growth and to preserve price stability. In particular, the Committee anticipates that weak economic conditions are likely to warrant exceptionally low levels of the federal funds rate for some time." So went the statement issued by the Federal Open Market Committee on December 16, 2008, that went on to say that the new target range for the federal funds rate would be between 0% and 0.25%. For the first time in its history, the Fed was targeting a rate below 1%. It was also acknowledging the difficulty of hitting a specific rate target when the target is so low. And, finally, it was experimenting with extraordinary measures based on a section of the Federal Reserve Act that allows it to take such measures when conditions in financial markets are deemed "unusual and exigent."

The Fed was responding to the broad-based weakness of the U.S. economy, the strains in financial markets, and the tightness of credit. Unlike some other moments in U.S. economic history, it did not have to worry about inflation, at least not in the short term. On the same day, consumer prices were reported to have fallen by 1.7% for the month of November. Indeed, commentators were beginning to fret over the possibility of deflation and how the Fed could continue to support the economy when it had already used all of its federal funds rate ammunition.

Anticipating this concern, the Fed's statement went on to discuss other ways it was planning to support the economy over the months to come. These included buying mortgage-backed securities to support the mortgage and housing markets, buying long-term Treasury bills, and creating other new credit facilities to make credit more easily available to households and small businesses. These options recalled a speech that Ben Bernanke had made six years earlier, when he was a member of the Federal Reserve Board of Governors but still nearly four years away from being named its chair, titled "Deflation: Making Sure 'It' Doesn't Happen Here." In the 2002 speech he laid out how these tools, along with tax cuts, were the equivalent of what Nobel prize winning economist Milton Friedman meant by a "helicopter drop" of money. The speech earned Bernanke the nickname of Helicopter Ben.

The Fed's decisions of mid-December put it in uncharted territory. Japan had tried a similar strategy, though somewhat less comprehensively and more belatedly, in the 1990s when faced with a situation similar to that of the United States in 2008 with only limited success. In his 2002 speech, Bernanke suggested that Japanese authorities had not gone far enough. Only history will tell us whether the Fed will be more successful and how well these new strategies will work.

This chapter examines in greater detail monetary policy and the roles of central banks in carrying out that policy. Our primary focus will be on the U.S. Federal Reserve System. The basic tools used by central banks in many countries are similar, but their institutional structure and their roles in their respective countries can differ.

1. MONETARY POLICY IN THE UNITED STATES

In many respects, the Fed is the most powerful maker of economic policy in the United States. Congress can pass laws, but the president must execute them; the president can propose laws, but only Congress can pass them. The Fed, however, both sets and carries out monetary policy. Deliberations about fiscal policy can drag on for months, even years, but the Federal Open Market Committee (FOMC) can, behind closed doors, set monetary policy in a day—and see that policy implemented within hours. The Board of Governors can change the discount rate or reserve requirements at any time. The impact of the Fed's policies on the economy can be quite dramatic. The Fed can push interest rates up or down. It can promote a recession or an expansion. It can cause the inflation rate to rise or fall. The Fed wields enormous power.

But to what ends should all this power be directed? With what tools are the Fed's policies carried out? And what problems exist in trying to achieve the Fed's goals? This section reviews the goals of monetary policy, the tools available to the Fed in pursuing those goals, and the way in which monetary policy affects macroeconomic variables.

1.1 Goals of Monetary Policy

When we think of the goals of monetary policy, we naturally think of standards of macroeconomic performance that seem desirable—a low unemployment rate, a stable price level, and economic growth. It thus seems reasonable to conclude that the goals of monetary policy should include the maintenance of full employment, the avoidance of inflation or deflation, and the promotion of economic growth.

But these goals, each of which is desirable in itself, may conflict with one another. A monetary policy that helps to close a recessionary gap and thus promotes full employment may accelerate inflation. A monetary policy that seeks to reduce inflation may increase unemployment and weaken economic growth. You might expect that in such cases, monetary authorities would receive guidance from legislation spelling out goals for the Fed to pursue and specifying what to do when achieving one goal means not achieving another. But as we shall see, that kind of guidance does not exist.

The Federal Reserve Act

When Congress established the Federal Reserve System in 1913, it said little about the policy goals the Fed should seek. The closest it came to spelling out the goals of monetary policy was in the first paragraph of the Federal Reserve Act, the legislation that created the Fed:

> *"An Act to provide for the establishment of Federal reserve banks, to furnish an elastic currency, [to make loans to banks], to establish a more effective supervision of banking in the United States, and for other purposes."*

In short, nothing in the legislation creating the Fed anticipates that the institution will act to close recessionary or inflationary gaps, that it will seek to spur economic growth, or that it will strive to keep the price level steady. There is no guidance as to what the Fed should do when these goals conflict with one another.

The Employment Act of 1946

The first U.S. effort to specify macroeconomic goals came after World War II. The Great Depression of the 1930s had instilled in people a deep desire to prevent similar calamities in the future. That desire, coupled with the 1936 publication of John Maynard Keynes's prescription for avoiding such problems through government policy (*The General Theory of Employment, Interest and Money*), led to the passage of the Employment Act of 1946, which declared that the federal government should "use all practical means . . . to promote maximum employment, production and purchasing power." The act also created the Council of Economic Advisers (CEA) to advise the president on economic matters.

The Fed might be expected to be influenced by this specification of federal goals, but because it is an independent agency, it is not required to follow any particular path. Furthermore, the legislation does not suggest what should be done if the goals of achieving full employment and maximum purchasing power conflict.

The Full Employment and Balanced Growth Act of 1978

The clearest, and most specific, statement of federal economic goals came in the Full Employment and Balanced Growth Act of 1978. This act, generally known as the Humphrey–Hawkins Act, specified that by 1983 the federal government should achieve an unemployment rate among adults of 3% or less, a civilian unemployment rate of 4% or less, and an inflation rate of 3% or less. Although these goals have the virtue of specificity, they offer little in terms of practical policy guidance. The last time the civilian unemployment rate in the United States fell below 4% was 1969, and the inflation rate that year was 6.2%. In 2000, the unemployment rate touched 4%, and the inflation rate that year was 3.4%, so the goals were close to being met. Except for 2007 when inflation hit 4.1%, inflation has hovered between 1.6% and 3.4% in all the other years between 1991 and 2008, so the inflation goal was met or nearly met, but unemployment fluctuated between 4.0% and 7.5% during those years.

The Humphrey-Hawkins Act requires that the chairman of the Fed's Board of Governors report twice each year to Congress about the Fed's monetary policy. These sessions provide an opportunity for members of the House and Senate to express their views on monetary policy.

Federal Reserve Policy and Goals

Perhaps the clearest way to see the Fed's goals is to observe the policy choices it makes. Since 1979, following a bout of double-digit inflation, its actions have suggested that the Fed's primary goal is to keep inflation under control. Provided that the inflation rate falls within acceptable limits, however, the Fed will also use stimulative measures to close recessionary gaps.

In 1979, the Fed, then led by Paul Volcker, launched a deliberate program of reducing the inflation rate. It stuck to that effort through the early 1980s, even in the face of a major recession. That effort achieved its goal: the annual inflation rate fell from 13.3% in 1979 to 3.8% in 1982. The cost, however, was great. Unemployment soared past 9% during the recession. With the inflation rate below 4%, the Fed shifted to a stimulative policy early in 1983.

In 1990, when the economy slipped into a recession, the Fed, with Alan Greenspan at the helm, engaged in aggressive open-market operations to stimulate the economy, despite the fact that the inflation rate had jumped to 6.1%. Much of that increase in the inflation rate, however, resulted from an oil-price boost that came in the wake of Iraq's invasion of Kuwait that year. A jump in prices that occurs at the same time as real GDP is slumping suggests a leftward shift in short-run aggregate supply, a shift that creates a recessionary gap. Fed officials concluded that the upturn in inflation in 1990 was a temporary phenomenon and that an expansionary policy was an appropriate response to a weak economy. Once the recovery was clearly under way, the Fed shifted to a neutral policy, seeking neither to boost nor to reduce aggregate demand. Early in 1994, the Fed shifted to a contractionary policy, selling bonds to reduce the money supply and raise interest rates. Then Fed Chairman Greenspan indicated that the move was intended to head off any possible increase in inflation from its 1993 rate of 2.7%. Although the economy was still in a recessionary gap when the Fed acted, Greenspan indicated that any acceleration of the inflation rate would be unacceptable.

By March 1997 the inflation rate had fallen to 2.4%. The Fed became concerned that inflationary pressures were increasing and tightened monetary policy, raising the goal for the federal funds interest rate to 5.5%. Inflation remained well below 2.0% throughout the rest of 1997 and 1998. In the fall of 1998, with inflation low, the Fed was concerned that the economic recession in much of Asia and slow growth in Europe would reduce growth in the United States. In quarter-point steps it reduced the goal for the federal funds rate to 4.75%. With real GDP growing briskly in the first half of 1999, the Fed became concerned that inflation would increase, even though the inflation rate at the time was about 2%, and in June 1999, it raised its goal for the federal funds rate to 5% and continued raising the rate until it reached 6.5% in May 2000.

With inflation under control, it then began lowering the federal funds rate to stimulate the economy. It continued lowering through the brief recession of 2001 and beyond. There were 11 rate cuts in 2001, with the rate at the end of that year at 1.75%; in late 2002 the rate was cut to 1.25%, and in mid-2003 it was cut to 1.0%.

Then, with growth picking up and inflation again a concern, the Fed began again in the middle of 2004 to increase rates. By the end of 2006, the rate stood at 5.25% as a result of 17 quarter-point rate increases.

Starting in September 2007, the Fed, since 2006 led by Ben Bernanke, shifted gears and began lowering the federal funds rate, mostly in larger steps or 0.5 to 0.75 percentage points. Though initially somewhat concerned with inflation, it sensed that the economy was beginning to slow down. It moved aggressively to lower rates over the course of the next 15 months, and by the end of 2008, the rate was targeted at between 0% and 0.25%. In late 2008 and for at least the following two years, with inflation running quite low and deflation threatening, the Fed seemed quite willing to use all of its options to try to keep financial markets running smoothly and to moderate the recession.

What can we infer from these episodes in the 1980s, 1990s, and the first years of this century? It seems clear that the Fed is determined not to allow the high inflation rates of the 1970s to occur again. When the inflation rate is within acceptable limits, the Fed will undertake stimulative measures in response to a recessionary gap or even in response to the possibility of a growth slowdown. Those limits seem to have tightened over time. In the late 1990s and early 2000s, it appeared that an inflation rate above 3%—or any indication that inflation might rise above 3%—would lead the Fed to adopt a contractionary policy. While on the Federal Reserve Board in the early 2000s, Ben Bernanke had been an advocate of inflation targeting. Under that system, the central bank announces its inflation target and then adjusts the federal funds rate if the inflation rate moves above or below the central bank's target. Mr. Bernanke indicated his preferred target to be an expected increase in the price level, as measured by the price index for consumer goods and services excluding food and energy, of between 1% and 2%. Thus, the inflation goal appears to have tightened even more—to a rate of 2% or less. If inflation were expected to remain below 2%, however, the Fed would undertake stimulative measures to close a recessionary gap. Whether the Fed will hold to that goal will not really be tested until further macroeconomic experiences unfold.

1.2 Monetary Policy and Macroeconomic Variables

We saw in an earlier chapter that the Fed has three tools at its command to try to change aggregate demand and thus to influence the level of economic activity. It can buy or sell federal government bonds through open-market operations, it can change the discount rate, or it can change reserve requirements. It can also use these tools in combination. In the next section of this chapter, where we discuss the notion of a liquidity trap, we will also introduce more extraordinary measures that the Fed has at its disposal.

Most economists agree that these tools of monetary policy affect the economy, but they sometimes disagree on the precise mechanisms through which this occurs, on the strength of those mechanisms, and on the ways in which monetary policy should be used. Before we address some of these issues, we shall review the ways in which monetary policy affects the economy in the context of the model of aggregate demand and aggregate supply. Our focus will be on open-market operations, the purchase or sale by the Fed of federal bonds.

Expansionary Monetary Policy

The Fed might pursue an expansionary monetary policy in response to the initial situation shown in Panel (a) of Figure 11.1. An economy with a potential output of Y_P is operating at Y_1; there is a recessionary gap. One possible policy response is to allow the economy to correct this gap on its own, waiting for reductions in nominal wages and other prices to shift the short-run aggregate supply curve $SRAS_1$ to the right until it intersects the aggregate demand curve AD_1 at Y_P. An alternative is a stabilization policy that seeks to increase aggregate demand to AD_2 to close the gap. An expansionary monetary policy is one way to achieve such a shift.

To carry out an expansionary monetary policy, the Fed will buy bonds, thereby increasing the money supply. That shifts the demand curve for bonds to D_2, as illustrated in Panel (b). Bond prices rise to P^b_2. The higher price for bonds reduces the interest rate. These changes in the bond market are consistent with the changes in the money market, shown in Panel (c), in which the greater money supply leads to a fall in the interest rate to r_2. The lower interest rate stimulates investment. In addition, the lower interest rate reduces the demand for and increases the supply of dollars in the currency market, reducing the exchange rate to E_2 in Panel (d). The lower exchange rate will stimulate net exports. The combined impact of greater investment and net exports will shift the aggregate demand curve to the right. The curve shifts by an amount equal to the multiplier times the sum of the initial changes in investment and net exports. In Panel (a), this is shown as a shift to AD_2, and the recessionary gap is closed.

FIGURE 11.1 Expansionary Monetary Policy to Close a Recessionary Gap

In Panel (a), the economy has a recessionary gap $Y_P - Y_1$. An expansionary monetary policy could seek to close this gap by shifting the aggregate demand curve to AD_2. In Panel (b), the Fed buys bonds, shifting the demand curve for bonds to D_2 and increasing the price of bonds to P^b_2. By buying bonds, the Fed increases the money supply to M' in Panel (c). The Fed's action lowers interest rates to r_2. The lower interest rate also reduces the demand for and increases the supply of dollars, reducing the exchange rate to E_2 in Panel (d). The resulting increases in investment and net exports shift the aggregate demand curve in Panel (a).

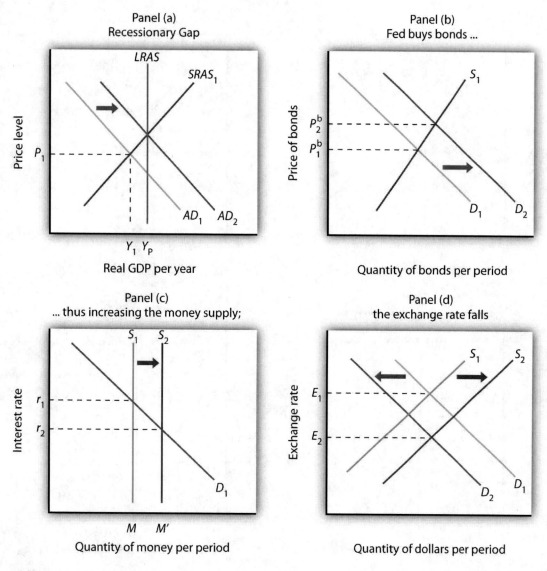

Contractionary Monetary Policy

The Fed will generally pursue a contractionary monetary policy when it considers inflation a threat. Suppose, for example, that the economy faces an inflationary gap; the aggregate demand and short-run aggregate supply curves intersect to the right of the long-run aggregate supply curve, as shown in Panel (a) of Figure 11.2.

FIGURE 11.2 A Contractionary Monetary Policy to Close an Inflationary Gap

In Panel (a), the economy has an inflationary gap $Y_1 - Y_P$. A contractionary monetary policy could seek to close this gap by shifting the aggregate demand curve to AD_2. In Panel (b), the Fed sells bonds, shifting the supply curve for bonds to S_2 and lowering the price of bonds to P^b_2. The lower price of bonds means a higher interest rate, r_2, as shown in Panel (c). The higher interest rate also increases the demand for and decreases the supply of dollars, raising the exchange rate to E_2 in Panel (d), which will increase net exports. The decreases in investment and net exports are responsible for decreasing aggregate demand in Panel (a).

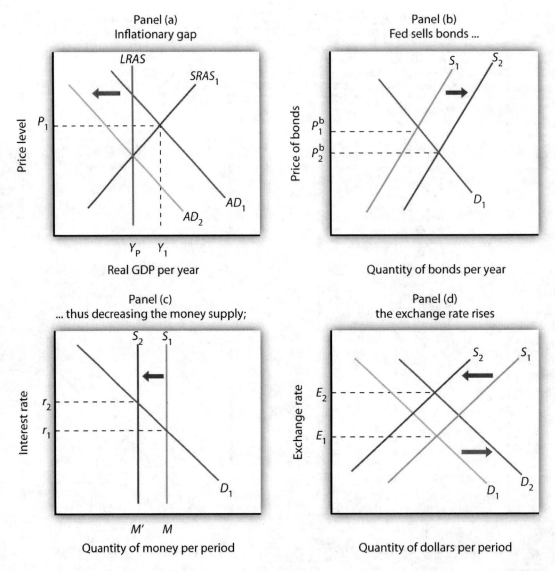

To carry out a contractionary policy, the Fed sells bonds. In the bond market, shown in Panel (b) of Figure 11.2, the supply curve shifts to the right, lowering the price of bonds and increasing the interest rate. In the money market, shown in Panel (c), the Fed's bond sales reduce the money supply and raise the interest rate. The higher interest rate reduces investment. The higher interest rate also induces a greater demand for dollars as foreigners seek to take advantage of higher interest rates in the United States. The supply of dollars falls; people in the United States are less likely to purchase foreign interest-earning assets now that U.S. assets are paying a higher rate. These changes boost the exchange rate, as shown in Panel (d), which reduces exports and increases imports and thus causes net exports to fall. The contractionary monetary policy thus shifts aggregate demand to the left, by an amount equal to the multiplier times the combined initial changes in investment and net exports, as shown in Panel (a).

KEY TAKEAWAYS

- The Federal Reserve Board and the Federal Open Market Committee are among the most powerful institutions in the United States.
- The Fed's primary goal appears to be the control of inflation. Providing that inflation is under control, the Fed will act to close recessionary gaps.
- Expansionary policy, such as a purchase of government securities by the Fed, tends to push bond prices up and interest rates down, increasing investment and aggregate demand. Contractionary policy, such as a sale of government securities by the Fed, pushes bond prices down, interest rates up, investment down, and aggregate demand shifts to the left.

TRY IT!

The figure shows an economy operating at a real GDP of Y_1 and a price level of P_1, at the intersection of AD_1 and $SRAS_1$.

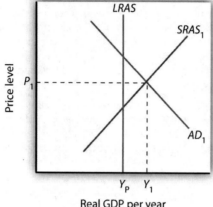

1. What kind of gap is the economy experiencing?
2. What type of monetary policy (expansionary or contractionary) would be appropriate for closing the gap?
3. If the Fed decided to pursue this policy, what type of open-market operations would it conduct?
4. How would bond prices, interest rates, and the exchange rate change?
5. How would investment and net exports change?
6. How would the aggregate demand curve shift?

Case in Point: A Brief History of the Greenspan Fed

With the passage of time and the fact that the fallout on the economy turned out to be relatively minor, it is hard in retrospect to realize how scary a situation Alan Greenspan and the Fed faced just two months after his appointment as Chairman of the Federal Reserve Board. On October 12, 1987, the stock market had its worst day ever. The Dow Jones Industrial Average plunged 508 points, wiping out more than $500 billion in a few hours of feverish trading on Wall Street. That drop represented a loss in value of over 22%. In comparison, the largest daily drop in 2008 of 778 points on September 29, 2008, represented a loss in value of about 7%.

When the Fed faced another huge plunge in stock prices in 1929—also in October—members of the Board of Governors met and decided that no action was necessary. Determined not to repeat the terrible mistake of 1929, one that helped to usher in the Great Depression, Alan Greenspan immediately reassured the country, saying that the Fed would provide adequate liquidity, by buying federal securities, to assure that economic activity would not fall. As it turned out, the damage to the economy was minor and the stock market quickly regained value.

In the fall of 1990, the economy began to slip into recession. The Fed responded with expansionary monetary policy—cutting reserve requirements, lowering the discount rate, and buying Treasury bonds.

Interest rates fell quite quickly in response to the Fed's actions, but, as is often the case, changes to the components of aggregate demand were slower in coming. Consumption and investment began to rise in 1991, but their growth was weak, and unemployment continued to rise because growth in output was too slow to keep up with growth in the labor force. It was not until the fall of 1992 that the economy started to pick up steam. This episode demonstrates an important difficulty with stabilization policy: attempts to manipulate aggregate demand achieve shifts in the curve, but with a lag.

Throughout the rest of the 1990s, with some tightening when the economy seemed to be moving into an inflationary gap and some loosening when the economy seemed to be possibly moving toward a recessionary gap—especially in 1998 and 1999 when parts of Asia experienced financial turmoil and recession and European growth had slowed down—the Fed helped steer what is now referred to as the Goldilocks (not too hot, not too cold, just right) economy.

The U.S. economy again experienced a mild recession in 2001 under Greenspan. At that time, the Fed systematically conducted expansionary policy. Similar to its response to the 1987 stock market crash, the Fed has been credited with maintaining liquidity following the dot-com stock market crash in early 2001 and the attacks on the World Trade Center and the Pentagon in September 2001.

When Greenspan retired in January 2006, many hailed him as the greatest central banker ever. As the economy faltered in 2008 and as the financial crisis unfolded throughout the year, however, the question of how the policies of Greenspan's Fed played into the current difficulties took center stage. Testifying before Congress in October 2008, he said that the country faces a "once-in-a-century credit tsunami," and he admitted, "I made a mistake in presuming that the self-interests of organizations, specifically banks and others, were such as that they were best capable of protecting their own shareholders and their equity in their firms." The criticisms he has faced are twofold: that the very low interest rates used to fight the 2001 recession and maintained for too long fueled the real estate bubble and that he did not promote appropriate regulations to deal with the new financial instruments that were created in the early 2000s. While supporting some additional regulations when he testified before Congress, he also warned that overreacting could be dangerous: "We have to recognize that this is almost surely a once-in-a-century phenomenon, and, in that regard, to realize the types of regulation that would prevent this from happening in the future are so onerous as to basically suppress the growth rate in the economy and . . . the standards of living of the American people."

A N S W E R S   T O   T R Y   I T !   P R O B L E M S

1. Inflationary gap
2. Contractionary
3. Open-market sales of bonds
4. The price of bonds would fall. The interest rate and the exchange rate would rise.
5. Investment and net exports would fall.
6. The aggregate demand curve would shift to the left.

2. PROBLEMS AND CONTROVERSIES OF MONETARY POLICY

L E A R N I N G   O B J E C T I V E S

1. Explain the three kinds of lags that can influence the effectiveness of monetary policy.
2. Identify the macroeconomic targets at which the Fed can aim in managing the economy, and discuss the difficulties inherent in using each of them as a target.
3. Discuss how each of the following influences a central bank's ability to achieve its desired macroeconomic outcomes: political pressures, the degree of impact on the economy (including the situation of a liquidity trap), and the rational expectations hypothesis.

The Fed has some obvious advantages in its conduct of monetary policy. The two policy-making bodies, the Board of Governors and the Federal Open Market Committee (FOMC), are small and largely independent from other political institutions. These bodies can thus reach decisions quickly and implement them immediately. Their relative independence from the political process, together with the fact that they meet in secret, allows them to operate outside the glare of publicity that might otherwise be focused on bodies that wield such enormous power.

Despite the apparent ease with which the Fed can conduct monetary policy, it still faces difficulties in its efforts to stabilize the economy. We examine some of the problems and uncertainties associated with monetary policy in this section.

2.1 Lags

Perhaps the greatest obstacle facing the Fed, or any other central bank, is the problem of lags. It is easy enough to show a recessionary gap on a graph and then to show how monetary policy can shift aggregate demand and close the gap. In the real world, however, it may take several months before anyone even realizes that a particular macroeconomic problem is occurring. When monetary authorities become aware of a problem, they can act quickly to inject reserves into the system or to withdraw reserves from it. Once that is done, however, it may be a year or more before the action affects aggregate demand.

The delay between the time a macroeconomic problem arises and the time at which policy makers become aware of it is called a **recognition lag**. The 1990–1991 recession, for example, began in July 1990. It was not until late October that members of the FOMC noticed a slowing in economic activity, which prompted a stimulative monetary policy. In contrast, the most recent recession began in December 2007, and Fed easing began in September 2007.

Recognition lags stem largely from problems in collecting economic data. First, data are available only after the conclusion of a particular period. Preliminary estimates of real GDP, for example, are released about a month after the end of a quarter. Thus, a change that occurs early in a quarter will not be reflected in the data until several months later. Second, estimates of economic indicators are subject to revision. The first estimates of real GDP in the third quarter of 1990, for example, showed it increasing. Not until several months had passed did revised estimates show that a recession had begun. And finally, different indicators can lead to different interpretations. Data on employment and retail sales might be pointing in one direction while data on housing starts and industrial production might be pointing in another. It is one thing to look back after a few years have elapsed and determine whether the economy was expanding or contracting. It is quite another to decipher changes in real GDP when

recognition lag

The delay between the time a macroeconomic problem arises and the time at which policy makers become aware of it.

one is right in the middle of events. Even in a world brimming with computer-generated data on the economy, recognition lags can be substantial.

Only after policy makers recognize there is a problem can they take action to deal with it. The delay between the time at which a problem is recognized and the time at which a policy to deal with it is enacted is called the **implementation lag**. For monetary policy changes, the implementation lag is quite short. The FOMC meets eight times per year, and its members may confer between meetings through conference calls. Once the FOMC determines that a policy change is in order, the required open-market operations to buy or sell federal bonds can be put into effect immediately.

Policy makers at the Fed still have to contend with the **impact lag**, the delay between the time a policy is enacted and the time that policy has its impact on the economy.

The impact lag for monetary policy occurs for several reasons. First, it takes some time for the deposit multiplier process to work itself out. The Fed can inject new reserves into the economy immediately, but the deposit expansion process of bank lending will need time to have its full effect on the money supply. Interest rates are affected immediately, but the money supply grows more slowly. Second, firms need some time to respond to the monetary policy with new investment spending—if they respond at all. Third, a monetary change is likely to affect the exchange rate, but that translates into a change in net exports only after some delay. Thus, the shift in the aggregate demand curve due to initial changes in investment and in net exports occurs after some delay. Finally, the multiplier process of an expenditure change takes time to unfold. It is only as incomes start to rise that consumption spending picks up.

The problem of lags suggests that monetary policy should respond not to statistical reports of economic conditions in the recent past but to conditions *expected* to exist in the future. In justifying the imposition of a contractionary monetary policy early in 1994, when the economy still had a recessionary gap, Greenspan indicated that the Fed expected a one-year impact lag. The policy initiated in 1994 was a response not to the economic conditions thought to exist at the time but to conditions expected to exist in 1995. When the Fed used contractionary policy in the middle of 1999, it argued that it was doing so to forestall a possible increase in inflation. When the Fed began easing in September 2007, it argued that it was doing so to forestall adverse effects to the economy of falling housing prices. In these examples, the Fed appeared to be looking forward. It must do so with information and forecasts that are far from perfect.

Estimates of the length of time required for the impact lag to work itself out range from six months to two years. Worse, the length of the lag can vary—when they take action, policy makers cannot know whether their choices will affect the economy within a few months or within a few years. Because of the uncertain length of the impact lag, efforts to stabilize the economy through monetary policy could be destabilizing. Suppose, for example, that the Fed responds to a recessionary gap with an expansionary policy but that by the time the policy begins to affect aggregate demand, the economy has already returned to potential GDP. The policy designed to correct a recessionary gap could create an inflationary gap. Similarly, a shift to a contractionary policy in response to an inflationary gap might not affect aggregate demand until after a self-correction process had already closed the gap. In that case, the policy could plunge the economy into a recession.

2.2 Choosing Targets

In attempting to manage the economy, on what macroeconomic variables should the Fed base its policies? It must have some target, or set of targets, that it wants to achieve. The failure of the economy to achieve one of the Fed's targets would then trigger a shift in monetary policy. The choice of a target, or set of targets, is a crucial one for monetary policy. Possible targets include interest rates, money growth rates, and the price level or expected changes in the price level.

Interest Rates

Interest rates, particularly the federal funds rate, played a key role in recent Fed policy. The FOMC does not decide to increase or decrease the money supply. Rather, it engages in operations to nudge the federal funds rate up or down.

Up until August 1997, it had instructed the trading desk at the New York Federal Reserve Bank to conduct open-market operations in a way that would either maintain, increase, or ease the current "degree of pressure" on the reserve positions of banks. That degree of pressure was reflected by the federal funds rate; if existing reserves were less than the amount banks wanted to hold, then the bidding for the available supply would send the federal funds rate up. If reserves were plentiful, then the federal funds rate would tend to decline. When the Fed increased the degree of pressure on reserves, it sold bonds, thus reducing the supply of reserves and increasing the federal funds rate. The Fed decreased the degree of pressure on reserves by buying bonds, thus injecting new reserves into the system and reducing the federal funds rate.

---

implementation lag

The delay between the time at which a problem is recognized and the time at which a policy to deal with it is enacted.

impact lag

The delay between the time a policy is enacted and the time that policy has its impact on the economy.

The current operating procedures of the Fed focus explicitly on interest rates. At each of its eight meetings during the year, the FOMC sets a specific target or target range for the federal funds rate. When the Fed lowers the target for the federal funds rate, it buys bonds. When it raises the target for the federal funds rate, it sells bonds.

Money Growth Rates

Until 2000, the Fed was required to announce to Congress at the beginning of each year its target for money growth that year and each report dutifully did so. At the same time, the Fed report would mention that its money growth targets were benchmarks based on historical relationships rather than guides for policy. As soon as the legal requirement to report targets for money growth ended, the Fed stopped doing so. Since in recent years the Fed has placed more importance on the federal funds rate, it must adjust the money supply in order to move the federal funds rate to the level it desires. As a result, the money growth targets tended to fall by the wayside, even over the last decade in which they were being reported. Instead, as data on economic conditions unfolded, the Fed made, and continues to make, adjustments in order to affect the federal funds interest rate.

Price Level or Expected Changes in the Price Level

Some economists argue that the Fed's primary goal should be price stability. If so, an obvious possible target is the price level itself. The Fed could target a particular price level or a particular rate of change in the price level and adjust its policies accordingly. If, for example, the Fed sought an inflation rate of 2%, then it could shift to a contractionary policy whenever the rate rose above 2%. One difficulty with such a policy, of course, is that the Fed would be responding to past economic conditions with policies that are not likely to affect the economy for a year or more. Another difficulty is that inflation could be rising when the economy is experiencing a recessionary gap. An example of this, mentioned earlier, occurred in 1990 when inflation increased due to the seemingly temporary increase in oil prices following Iraq's invasion of Kuwait. The Fed was faced with a similar situation in the first half of 2008 when oil prices were again rising. If the Fed undertakes contractionary monetary policy at such times, then its efforts to reduce the inflation rate could worsen the recessionary gap.

The solution proposed by Chairman Bernanke, who is an advocate of inflation rate targeting, is to focus not on the past rate of inflation or even the current rate of inflation, but on the expected rate of inflation, as revealed by various indicators, over the next year. This concept is discussed in the Case in Point essay that follows this section.

2.3 Political Pressures

The institutional relationship between the leaders of the Fed and the executive and legislative branches of the federal government is structured to provide for the Fed's independence. Members of the Board of Governors are appointed by the president, with confirmation by the Senate, but the 14-year terms of office provide a considerable degree of insulation from political pressure. A president exercises greater influence in the choice of the chairman of the Board of Governors; that appointment carries a four-year term. Neither the president nor Congress has any direct say over the selection of the presidents of Federal Reserve district banks. They are chosen by their individual boards of directors with the approval of the Board of Governors.

The degree of independence that central banks around the world have varies. A central bank is considered to be more independent if it is insulated from the government by such factors as longer term appointments of its governors and fewer requirements to finance government budget deficits. Studies in the 1980s and early 1990s showed that, in general, greater central bank independence was associated with lower average inflation and that there was no systematic relationship between central bank independence and other indicators of economic performance, such as real GDP growth or unemployment.[1] By the rankings used in those studies, the Fed was considered quite independent, second only to Switzerland and the German *Bundesbank* at the time. Perhaps as a result of such findings, a number of countries have granted greater independence to their central banks in the last decade. The charter for the European Central Bank, which began operations in 1998, was modeled on that of the German *Bundesbank*. Its charter states explicitly that its primary objective is to maintain price stability. Also, since 1998, central bank independence has increased in the United Kingdom, Canada, Japan, and New Zealand.

While the Fed is formally insulated from the political process, the men and women who serve on the Board of Governors and the FOMC are human beings. They are not immune to the pressures that can be placed on them by members of Congress and by the president. The chairman of the Board of Governors meets regularly with the president and the executive staff and also reports to and meets with congressional committees that deal with economic matters.

The Fed was created by the Congress; its charter could be altered—or even revoked—by that same body. The Fed is in the somewhat paradoxical situation of having to cooperate with the legislative and executive branches in order to preserve its independence.

2.4   The Degree of Impact on the Economy

The problem of lags suggests that the Fed does not know with certainty *when* its policies will work their way through the financial system to have an impact on macroeconomic performance. The Fed also does not know with certainty *to what extent* its policy decisions will affect the macroeconomy.

For example, investment can be particularly volatile. An effort by the Fed to reduce aggregate demand in the face of an inflationary gap could be partially offset by rising investment demand. But, generally, contractionary policies do tend to slow down the economy as if the Fed were "pulling on a rope." That may not be the case with expansionary policies. Since investment depends crucially on expectations about the future, business leaders must be optimistic about economic conditions in order to expand production facilities and buy new equipment. That optimism might not exist in a recession. Instead, the pessimism that might prevail during an economic slump could prevent lower interest rates from stimulating investment. An effort to stimulate the economy through monetary policy could be like "pushing on a string." The central bank could push with great force by buying bonds and engaging in quantitative easing, but little might happen to the economy at the other end of the string.

What if the Fed cannot bring about a change in interest rates? A **liquidity trap** is said to exist when a change in monetary policy has no effect on interest rates. This would be the case if the money demand curve were horizontal at some interest rate, as shown in Figure 11.5. If a change in the money supply from M to M' cannot change interest rates, then, unless there is some other change in the economy, there is no reason for investment or any other component of aggregate demand to change. Hence, traditional monetary policy is rendered totally ineffective; its degree of impact on the economy is nil. At an interest rate of zero, since bonds cease to be an attractive alternative to money, which is at least useful for transactions purposes, there would be a liquidity trap.

liquidity trap

Situation that exists when a change in monetary policy has no effect on interest rates.

FIGURE 11.5   A Liquidity Trap

When a change in the money supply has no effect on the interest rate, the economy is said to be in a liquidity trap.

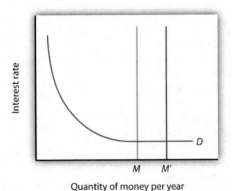

Quantity of money per year

quantitative easing

Policy in which a bank convinces the public that it will keep interest rates very low by providing substantial reserves for as long as is necessary to avoid deflation.

With the federal funds rate in the United States close to zero at the end of 2008, the possibility that the country is in or nearly in a liquidity trap cannot be dismissed. As discussed in the introduction to the chapter, at the same time the Fed lowered the federal funds rate to close to zero, it mentioned that it intended to pursue additional, nontraditional measures. What the Fed seeks to do is to make firms and consumers want to spend now by using a tool not aimed at reducing the interest rate, since it cannot reduce the interest rate below zero. It thus shifts its focus to the price level and to avoiding expected deflation. For example, if the public expects the price level to fall by 2% and the interest rate is zero, by holding money, the money is actually earning a positive *real* interest rate of 2%—the difference between the *nominal* interest rate and the expected deflation rate. Since the nominal rate of interest cannot fall below zero (Who would, for example, want to lend at an interest rate below zero when lending is risky whereas cash is not? In short, it does not make sense to lend $10 and get less than $10 back.), expected deflation makes holding cash very attractive and discourages spending since people will put off purchases because goods and services are expected to get cheaper.

To combat this "wait-and-see" mentality, the Fed or other central bank, using a strategy referred to as **quantitative easing**, must convince the public that it will keep interest rates very low by providing substantial reserves for as long as is necessary to avoid deflation. In other words, it is aimed at creating expected inflation. For example, at the Fed's October 2003 meeting, it announced that it would keep the federal funds rate at 1% for "a considerable period." When the Fed lowered the rate to between 0% and 0.25% in December 2008, it added that "the Committee anticipates that weak economic conditions are likely to warrant exceptionally low levels of the federal funds rate for some time." After working so hard to convince economic players that it will not tolerate inflation above 2%, the Fed must now convince the public that it will, but of course not too much! If it is successful, this extraordinary form of expansionary monetary policy will lead to increased purchases of goods and services, compared to what they would have been with expected deflation. Also, by providing banks with lots of liquidity, it is hoping to encourage them to lend.

The Japanese economy provides an interesting modern example of a country that attempted quantitative easing. With a recessionary gap starting in the early 1990s and deflation in most years from 1995 on, Japan's central bank, the Bank of Japan, began to lower the call money rate (equivalent to the federal funds rate in the United States), reaching near zero by the late 1990s. With growth still languishing, Japan appeared to be in a traditional liquidity trap. In late 1999, the Bank of Japan announced that it would maintain a zero interest rate policy for the foreseeable future, and in March 2001 it officially began a policy of quantitative easing. In 2006, with the price level rising modestly, Japan ended quantitative easing and began increasing the call rate again. It should be noted that the government simultaneously engaged in expansionary fiscal policy.

How well did these policies work? The economy began to grow modestly in 2003, though deflation between 1% and 2% remained. Some researchers feel that the Bank of Japan ended quantitative easing too early. Also, delays in implementing the policy, as well as delays in restructuring the banking sector, exacerbated Japan's problems.[2]

Fed Chairman Bernanke and other Fed officials have argued that the Fed is also engaged in credit easing.[3] **Credit easing** is a strategy that involves the extension of central bank lending to influence more broadly the proper functioning of credit markets and to improve liquidity. The specific new credit facilities that the Fed has created were discussed in the Case in Point in the chapter on the nature and creation of money. In general, the Fed is hoping that these new credit facilities will improve liquidity in a variety of credit markets, ranging from those used by money market mutual funds to those involved in student and car loans.

credit easing

A strategy that involves the extension of central bank lending to influence more broadly the proper functioning of credit markets and to improve liquidity.

2.5 Rational Expectations

One hypothesis suggests that monetary policy may affect the price level but not real GDP. The **rational expectations hypothesis** states that people use all available information to make forecasts about future economic activity and the price level, and they adjust their behavior to these forecasts.

Figure 11.6 uses the model of aggregate demand and aggregate supply to show the implications of the rational expectations argument for monetary policy. Suppose the economy is operating at Y_P, as illustrated by point A. An increase in the money supply boosts aggregate demand to AD_2. In the analysis we have explored thus far, the shift in aggregate demand would move the economy to a higher level of real GDP and create an inflationary gap. That, in turn, would put upward pressure on wages and other prices, shifting the short-run aggregate supply curve to $SRAS_2$ and moving the economy to point B, closing the inflationary gap in the long run. The rational expectations hypothesis, however, suggests a quite different interpretation.

Suppose people observe the initial monetary policy change undertaken when the economy is at point A and calculate that the increase in the money supply will ultimately drive the price level up to point B. Anticipating this change in prices, people adjust their behavior. For example, if the increase in the price level from P_1 to P_2 is a 10% change, workers will anticipate that the prices they pay will rise 10%, and they will demand 10% higher wages. Their employers, anticipating that the prices they will receive will also rise, will agree to pay those higher wages. As nominal wages increase, the short-run aggregate supply curve *immediately* shifts to $SRAS_2$. The result is an upward movement along the long-run aggregate supply curve, $LRAS$. There is no change in real GDP. The monetary policy has no effect, other than its impact on the price level. This rational expectations argument relies on wages and prices being sufficiently flexible—not sticky, as described in an earlier chapter—so that the change in expectations will allow the short-run aggregate supply curve to shift quickly to $SRAS_2$.

One important implication of the rational expectations argument is that a contractionary monetary policy could be painless. Suppose the economy is at point B in Figure 11.6, and the Fed reduces the money supply in order to shift the aggregate demand curve back to AD_1. In the model of aggregate demand and aggregate supply, the result would be a recession. But in a rational expectations world, people's expectations change, the short-run aggregate supply immediately shifts to the right, and the economy moves painlessly down its long-run aggregate supply curve $LRAS$ to point A. Those who support the rational expectations hypothesis, however, also tend to argue that monetary policy should not be used as a tool of stabilization policy.

For some, the events of the early 1980s weakened support for the rational expectations hypothesis; for others, those same events strengthened support for this hypothesis. As we saw in the introduction to an earlier chapter, in 1979 President Jimmy Carter appointed Paul Volcker as Chairman of the Federal Reserve and pledged his full support for whatever the Fed might do to contain inflation. Mr. Volcker made it clear that the Fed was going to slow money growth and boost interest rates. He acknowledged that this policy would have costs but said that the Fed would stick to it as long as necessary to control inflation. Here was a monetary policy that was clearly announced and carried out as advertised. But the policy brought on the most severe recession since the Great Depression—a result that seems inconsistent with the rational expectations argument that changing expectations would prevent such a policy from having a substantial effect on real GDP.

Others, however, argue that people were aware of the Fed's pronouncements but were skeptical about whether the anti-inflation effort would persist, since the Fed had not vigorously fought inflation

rational expectations hypothesis

Individuals form expectations about the future based on the information available to them, and they act on those expectations.

FIGURE 11.6 Monetary Policy and Rational Expectations

Suppose the economy is operating at point A and that individuals have rational expectations. They calculate that an expansionary monetary policy undertaken at price level P_1 will raise prices to P_2. They adjust their expectations—and wage demands—accordingly, quickly shifting the short-run aggregate supply curve to $SRAS_2$. The result is a movement along the long-run aggregate supply curve $LRAS$ to point B, with no change in real GDP.

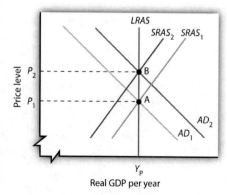

in the late 1960s and the 1970s. Against this history, people adjusted their estimates of inflation downward slowly. In essence, the recession occurred because people were surprised that the Fed was serious about fighting inflation.

Regardless of where one stands on this debate, one message does seem clear: once the Fed has proved it is serious about maintaining price stability, doing so in the future gets easier. To put this in concrete terms, Volcker's fight made Greenspan's work easier, and Greenspan's legacy of low inflation should make Bernanke's easier.

KEY TAKEAWAYS

- Macroeconomic policy makers must contend with recognition, implementation, and impact lags.
- Potential targets for macroeconomic policy include interest rates, money growth rates, and the price level or expected rates of change in the price level.
- Even if a central bank is structured to be independent of political pressure, its officers are likely to be affected by such pressure.
- To counteract liquidity traps, central banks have used quantitative-easing and credit-easing strategies.
- No central bank can know in advance how its policies will affect the economy; the rational expectations hypothesis predicts that central bank actions will affect the money supply and the price level but not the real level of economic activity.

TRY IT!

The scenarios below describe the U.S. recession and recovery in the early 1990s. Identify the lag that may have contributed to the difficulty in using monetary policy as a tool of economic stabilization.

1. The U.S. economy entered into a recession in July 1990. The Fed countered with expansionary monetary policy in October 1990, ultimately lowering the federal funds rate from 8% to 3% in 1992.
2. Investment began to increase, although slowly, in early 1992, and surged in 1993.

Case in Point: Targeting Monetary Policy

Ben Bernanke, the chairman of the Federal Reserve Board, is among a growing group of economists who (at least under normal macroeconomic circumstances!) advocate targeting as an approach to monetary policy. The idea, first proposed in 1993 by Stanford University economist John Taylor, calls for the central bank to set an inflation target and, if the actual rate is above or below it, raise or lower the federal funds rate.

The approach would be a change from the policy carried out under Alan Greenspan, who chaired the board from 1987 to 2006. Mr. Greenspan, who opposed targeting, favors a discretionary approach, one that some critics (and admirers) have called a "seat-of-the-pants" approach to monetary policy.

Targeting would not, according to Mr. Bernanke, be entirely formulaic, replacing the judgment of the Open Market Committee with a rigid rule. Mr. Bernanke has noted, for example, that if the inflation were to increase as a result of a supply side shock (such as an increase in oil prices), then an automatic increase in the federal funds rate would not be appropriate.

One danger of using the current inflation rate as a target is that it might be destabilizing. After all, the current rate is actually the rate for the past month or past several months. Adjusting the federal funds rate to past inflation could, given the inherent recognition and impact lags of monetary policy, easily lead to a worsening of the business cycle. Imagine that past inflation has increased as a result of a much earlier increase in the money supply. That inflation might already be correcting itself by the time a tightening effort takes hold in the economy. It thus could cause a contraction.

Bernanke has said that his preferred target is the expected rate of increase for the next year in the price index for consumer goods and services, excluding food and energy prices. That would avoid the danger of relying on previous inflation rates. He has said that his "comfort zone" for expected inflation is between 1% and 2%.

The central banks of Australia, Brazil, Canada, Great Britain, New Zealand, South Korea, and Sweden adopted targeting. Japan and the United States did not. A study by Goldman Sachs, the investment consulting and management firm, examined the performance of countries that did and did not engage in targeting. It found that countries that used targeting had more stable interest rates and sustained steady growth. Japan and the United States had much more volatile stock and bond markets. In short, the results of the study tended to support the practice of targeting inflation.

Sources: *Peter Coy, "What's the Fuss over Inflation Targeting? Business Week 3958 (November 7, 2005): 34; Justin Fox, "Who Will Replace Greenspan? Who Cares?" Fortune 152, no. 9 (October 31, 2005): 114.*

ANSWERS TO TRY IT! PROBLEMS

1. The recognition lag: the Fed did not seem to "recognize" that the economy was in a recession until several months after the recession began.

2. The impact lag: investment did not pick up quickly after interest rates were reduced. Alternatively, it could be attributed to the expansionary monetary policy's not having its desired effect, at least initially, on investment.

3. MONETARY POLICY AND THE EQUATION OF EXCHANGE

LEARNING OBJECTIVES

1. Explain the meaning of the equation of exchange, $MV = PY$, and tell why it must hold true.
2. Discuss the usefulness of the quantity theory of money in explaining the behavior of nominal GDP and inflation in the long run.
3. Discuss why the quantity theory of money is less useful in analyzing the short run.

So far we have focused on how monetary policy affects real GDP and the price level in the short run. That is, we have examined how it can be used—however imprecisely—to close recessionary or inflationary gaps and to stabilize the price level. In this section, we will explore the relationship between money and the economy in the context of an equation that relates the money supply directly to nominal GDP. As we shall see, it also identifies circumstances in which changes in the price level are directly related to changes in the money supply.

3.1 The Equation of Exchange

We can relate the money supply to the aggregate economy by using the equation of exchange:

EQUATION 11.1

$$MV = \text{nominal GDP}$$

The **equation of exchange** shows that the money supply M times its velocity V equals nominal GDP. **Velocity** is the number of times the money supply is spent to obtain the goods and services that make up GDP during a particular time period.

To see that nominal GDP is the price level multiplied by real GDP, recall from an earlier chapter that the implicit price deflator P equals nominal GDP divided by real GDP:

EQUATION 11.2

$$P = \frac{\text{Nominal GDP}}{\text{Real GDP}}$$

Multiplying both sides by real GDP, we have

EQUATION 11.3

$$\text{Nominal GDP} = P \times \text{real GDP}$$

Letting Y equal real GDP, we can rewrite the equation of exchange as

EQUATION 11.4

$$MV = PY$$

We shall use the equation of exchange to see how it represents spending in a hypothetical economy that consists of 50 people, each of whom has a car. Each person has $10 in cash and no other money. The money supply of this economy is thus $500. Now suppose that the sole economic activity in this economy is car washing. Each person in the economy washes one other person's car once a month, and the price of a car wash is $10. In one month, then, a total of 50 car washes are produced at a price of $10 each. During that month, the money supply is spent once.

Applying the equation of exchange to this economy, we have a money supply M of $500 and a velocity V of 1. Because the only good or service produced is car washing, we can measure real GDP as the number of car washes. Thus Y equals 50 car washes. The price level P is the price of a car wash: $10. The equation of exchange for a period of 1 month is

$$\$500 \times 1 = \$10 \times 50$$

Now suppose that in the second month everyone washes someone else's car again. Over the full two-month period, the money supply has been spent twice—the velocity over a period of two months is 2. The total output in the economy is $1,000—100 car washes have been produced over a two-month period at a price of $10 each. Inserting these values into the equation of exchange, we have

$$\$500 \times 2 = \$10 \times 100$$

Suppose this process continues for one more month. For the three-month period, the money supply of $500 has been spent three times, for a velocity of 3. We have

$$\$500 \times 3 = \$10 \times 150$$

The essential thing to note about the equation of exchange is that it always holds. That should come as no surprise. The left side, MV, gives the money supply times the number of times that money is spent on goods and services during a period. It thus measures total spending. The right side is nominal GDP. But that is a measure of total spending on goods and services as well. Nominal GDP is the value of all final goods and services produced during a particular period. Those goods and services are either sold or added to inventory. If they are sold, then they must be part of total spending. If they are added to inventory, then some firm must have either purchased them or paid for their production; they thus represent a portion of total spending. In effect, the equation of exchange says simply that total spending on goods and services, measured as MV, equals total spending on goods and services, measured as PY (or nominal GDP). The equation of exchange is thus an identity, a mathematical expression that is true by definition.

To apply the equation of exchange to a real economy, we need measures of each of the variables in it. Three of these variables are readily available. The Department of Commerce reports the price level (that is, the implicit price deflator) and real GDP. The Federal Reserve Board reports M2, a measure of the money supply. For the second quarter of 2008, the values of these variables at an annual rate were

$M = \$7,635.4$ billion

$P = 1.22$

$Y = 11,727.4$ billion

To solve for the velocity of money, V, we divide both sides of Equation 11.4 by M:

EQUATION 11.5

$$V = \frac{PY}{M}$$

Using the data for the second quarter of 2008 to compute velocity, we find that V then was equal to 1.87. A velocity of 1.87 means that the money supply was spent 1.87 times in the purchase of goods and services in the second quarter of 2008.

3.2   Money, Nominal GDP, and Price-Level Changes

Assume for the moment that velocity is constant, expressed as $\bar{V}$. Our equation of exchange is now written as

EQUATION 11.6

$$M\bar{V} = PY$$

A constant value for velocity would have two important implications:

1. Nominal GDP could change *only* if there were a change in the money supply. Other kinds of changes, such as a change in government purchases or a change in investment, could have no effect on nominal GDP.

2. A change in the money supply would always change nominal GDP, and by an equal percentage.

In short, if velocity were constant, a course in macroeconomics would be quite simple. The quantity of money would determine nominal GDP; nothing else would matter.

Indeed, when we look at the behavior of economies over long periods of time, the prediction that the quantity of money determines nominal output holds rather well. Figure 11.8 compares long-term averages in the growth rates of M2 and nominal GNP in the United States for more than a century. The lines representing the two variables do seem to move together most of the time, suggesting that velocity is constant when viewed over the long run.

FIGURE 11.8 Inflation, M2 Growth, and GDP Growth

The chart shows the behavior of price-level changes, the growth of M2, and the growth of nominal GDP using 10-year moving averages. Viewed in this light, the relationship between money growth and nominal GDP seems quite strong.

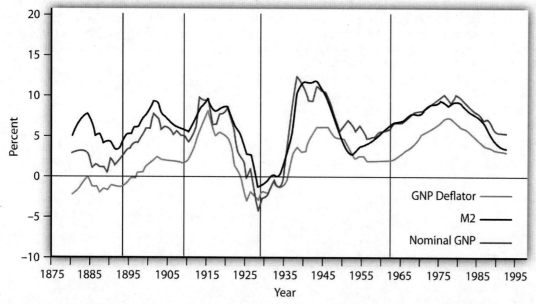

Source: William G. Dewald, "Historical U.S. Money Growth, Inflation, and Inflation Credibility," Federal Reserve Bank of St. Louis Review 80:6 (November/December 1998): 13-23.

Moreover, price-level changes also follow the same pattern that changes in M2 and nominal GNP do. Why is this?

We can rewrite the equation of exchange, $M \bar{V} = PY$, in terms of percentage rates of change. When two products, such as $M \bar{V}$ and PY, are equal, and the variables themselves are changing, then the sums of the percentage rates of change are approximately equal:

EQUATION 11.7

$$\%\Delta M + \%\Delta V \cong \%\Delta P + \%\Delta Y$$

The Greek letter Δ (delta) means "change in." Assume that velocity is constant in the long run, so that $\%\Delta V = 0$. We also assume that real GDP moves to its potential level, Y_P, in the long run. With these assumptions, we can rewrite Equation 11.7 as follows:

EQUATION 11.8

$$\%\Delta M \cong \%\Delta P + \%\Delta Y_P$$

Subtracting $\%\Delta Y_P$ from both sides of Equation 11.8, we have the following:

EQUATION 11.9

$$\%\Delta M - \%\Delta Y_P \cong \%\Delta P$$

Equation 11.9 has enormously important implications for monetary policy. It tells us that, in the long run, the rate of inflation, $\%\Delta P$, equals the difference between the rate of money growth and the rate of increase in potential output, $\%\Delta Y_P$, given our assumption of constant velocity. Because potential output is likely to rise by at most a few percentage points per year, the rate of money growth will be close to the rate of inflation in the long run.

Several recent studies that looked at all the countries on which they could get data on inflation and money growth over long periods found a very high correlation between growth rates of the money supply and of the price level for countries with high inflation rates, but the relationship was much weaker for countries with inflation rates of less than 10%.[4] These findings support the **quantity theory of money**, which holds that in the long run the price level moves in proportion with changes in the money supply, at least for high-inflation countries.

quantity theory of money

In the long run, the price level moves in proportion with changes in the money supply, at least for high-inflation countries.

3.3 Why the Quantity Theory of Money Is Less Useful in Analyzing the Short Run

The stability of velocity in the long run underlies the close relationship we have seen between changes in the money supply and changes in the price level. But velocity is not stable in the short run; it varies significantly from one period to the next. Figure 11.9 shows annual values of the velocity of M2 from 1970 through 2009. Velocity is quite variable, so other factors must affect economic activity. Any change in velocity implies a change in the demand for money. For analyzing the effects of monetary policy from one period to the next, we apply the framework that emphasizes the impact of changes in the money market on aggregate demand.

FIGURE 11.9   The Velocity of M2, 1970–2009

The annual velocity of M2 varied about an average of 1.78 between 1970 and 2009.

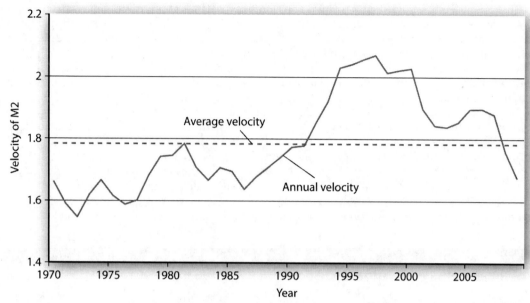

Source: Economic Report of the President, 2010, Tables B-1 and B-69.

The factors that cause velocity to fluctuate are those that influence the demand for money, such as the interest rate and expectations about bond prices and future price levels. We can gain some insight about the demand for money and its significance by rearranging terms in the equation of exchange so that we turn the equation of exchange into an equation for the demand for money. If we multiply both sides of Equation 11.1 by the reciprocal of velocity, $1/V$, we have this equation for money demand:

EQUATION 11.10

$$M = \tfrac{1}{V}PY$$

The equation of exchange can thus be rewritten as an equation that expresses the demand for money as a percentage, given by $1/V$, of nominal GDP. With a velocity of 1.87, for example, people wish to hold a quantity of money equal to 53.4% (1/1.87) of nominal GDP. Other things unchanged, an increase in money demand reduces velocity, and a decrease in money demand increases velocity.

If people wanted to hold a quantity of money equal to a larger percentage of nominal GDP, perhaps because interest rates were low, velocity would be a smaller number. Suppose, for example, that people held a quantity of money equal to 80% of nominal GDP. That would imply a velocity of 1.25. If people held a quantity of money equal to a smaller fraction of nominal GDP, perhaps owing to high interest rates, velocity would be a larger number. If people held a quantity of money equal to 25% of nominal GDP, for example, the velocity would be 4.

As another example, in the chapter on financial markets and the economy, we learned that money demand falls when people expect inflation to increase. In essence, they do not want to hold money that they believe will only lose value, so they turn it over faster, that is, velocity rises. Expectations of deflation lower the velocity of money, as people hold onto money because they expect it will rise in value.

In our first look at the equation of exchange, we noted some remarkable conclusions that would hold if velocity were constant: a given percentage change in the money supply M would produce an equal percentage change in nominal GDP, and no change in nominal GDP could occur without an equal percentage change in M. We have learned, however, that velocity varies in the short run. Thus, the conclusions that would apply if velocity were constant must be changed.

First, we do not expect a given percentage change in the money supply to produce an equal percentage change in nominal GDP. Suppose, for example, that the money supply increases by 10%. Interest rates drop, and the quantity of money demanded goes up. Velocity is likely to decline, though not by as large a percentage as the money supply increases. The result will be a reduction in the degree to which a given percentage increase in the money supply boosts nominal GDP.

Second, nominal GDP could change even when there is no change in the money supply. Suppose government purchases increase. Such an increase shifts the aggregate demand curve to the right, increasing real GDP and the price level. That effect would be impossible if velocity were constant. The fact that velocity varies, and varies positively with the interest rate, suggests that an increase in government purchases could boost aggregate demand and nominal GDP. To finance increased spending, the government borrows money by selling bonds. An increased supply of bonds lowers their price, and that means higher interest rates. The higher interest rates produce the increase in velocity that must occur if increased government purchases are to boost the price level and real GDP.

Just as we cannot assume that velocity is constant when we look at macroeconomic behavior period to period, neither can we assume that output is at potential. With both V and Y in the equation of exchange variable, in the short run, the impact of a change in the money supply on the price level depends on the degree to which velocity and real GDP change.

In the short run, it is not reasonable to assume that velocity and output are constants. Using the model in which interest rates and other factors affect the quantity of money demanded seems more fruitful for understanding the impact of monetary policy on economic activity in that period. However, the empirical evidence on the long-run relationship between changes in money supply and changes in the price level that we presented earlier gives us reason to pause. As Federal Reserve Governor from 1996 to 2002 Laurence H. Meyer put it: "I believe monitoring money growth has value, even for central banks that follow a disciplined strategy of adjusting their policy rate to ongoing economic developments. The value may be particularly important at the extremes: during periods of very high inflation, as in the late 1970s and early 1980s in the United States … and in deflationary episodes."[5]

It would be a mistake to allow short-term fluctuations in velocity and output to lead policy makers to completely ignore the relationship between money and price level changes in the long run.

KEY TAKEAWAYS

- The equation of exchange can be written $MV = PY$.
- When M, V, P, and Y are changing, then $\%\Delta M + \%\Delta V = \%\Delta P + \%\Delta Y$, where Δ means "change in."
- In the long run, V is constant, so $\%\Delta V = 0$. Furthermore, in the long run Y tends toward Y_P, so $\%\Delta M = \%\Delta P$.
- In the short run, V is not constant, so changes in the money supply can affect the level of income.

TRY IT!

The Case in Point on velocity in the Confederacy during the Civil War shows that, assuming real GDP in the South was constant, velocity rose. What happened to money demand? Why did it change?

Case in Point: Velocity and the Confederacy

The Union and the Confederacy financed their respective efforts during the Civil War largely through the issue of paper money. The Union roughly doubled its money supply through this process, and the Confederacy printed enough "Confederates" to increase the money supply in the South 20-fold from 1861 to 1865. That huge increase in the money supply boosted the price level in the Confederacy dramatically. It rose from an index of 100 in 1861 to 9,200 in 1865.

Estimates of real GDP in the South during the Civil War are unavailable, but it could hardly have increased very much. Although production undoubtedly rose early in the period, the South lost considerable capital and an appalling number of men killed in battle. Let us suppose that real GDP over the entire period remained constant. For the price level to rise 92-fold with a 20-fold increase in the money supply, there must have been a 4.6-fold increase in velocity. People in the South must have reduced their demand for Confederates.

An account of an exchange for eggs in 1864 from the diary of Mary Chestnut illustrates how eager people in the South were to part with their Confederate money. It also suggests that other commodities had assumed much greater relative value:

> "She asked me 20 dollars for five dozen eggs and then said she would take it in "Confederate."
> Then I would have given her 100 dollars as easily. But if she had taken my offer of yarn! I
> haggle in yarn for the millionth part of a thread! … When they ask for Confederate money, I
> never stop to chafer [bargain or argue]. I give them 20 or 50 dollars cheerfully for anything."

Sources: C. Vann Woodward, ed., Mary Chestnut's Civil War (New Haven, CT: Yale University Press, 1981), 749. Money and price data from E. M. Lerner, "Money, Prices, and Wages in the Confederacy, 1861–1865," Journal of Political Economy 63 (February 1955): 20–40.

ANSWER TO TRY IT! PROBLEM

People in the South must have reduced their demand for money. The fall in money demand was probably due to the expectation that the price level would continue to rise. In periods of high inflation, people try to get rid of money quickly because it loses value rapidly.

4. REVIEW AND PRACTICE

Summary

Part of the Fed's power stems from the fact that it has no legislative mandate to seek particular goals. That leaves the Fed free to set its own goals. In recent years, its primary goal has seemed to be the maintenance of an inflation rate below 2% to 3%. Given success in meeting that goal, the Fed has used its tools to stimulate the economy to close recessionary gaps. Once the Fed has made a choice to undertake an expansionary or contractionary policy, we can trace the impact of that policy on the economy.

There are a number of problems in the use of monetary policy. These include various types of lags, the issue of the choice of targets in conducting monetary policy, political pressures placed on the process of policy setting, and uncertainty as to how great an impact the Fed's policy decisions have on macroeconomic variables. We highlighted the difficulties for monetary policy if the economy is in or near a liquidity trap and discussed the use of quantitative easing and credit easing in such situations. If people have rational expectations and respond to those expectations in their wage and price choices, then changes in monetary policy may have no effect on real GDP.

We saw in this chapter that the money supply is related to the level of nominal GDP by the equation of exchange. A crucial issue in that relationship is the stability of the velocity of money and of real GDP. If the velocity of money were constant, nominal GDP could change only if the money supply changed, and a change in the money supply would produce an equal percentage change in nominal GDP. If velocity were constant and real GDP were at its potential level, then the price level would change by about the same percentage as the money supply. While these predictions seem to hold up in the long run, there is less support for them when we look at macroeconomic behavior in the short run. Nonetheless, policy makers must be mindful of these long-run relationships as they formulate policies for the short run.

CONCEPT PROBLEMS

1. Suppose the Fed were required to conduct monetary policy so as to hold the unemployment rate below 4%, the goal specified in the Humphrey–Hawkins Act. What implications would this have for the economy?

2. The statutes of the recently established European Central Bank (ECB) state that its primary objective is to maintain price stability. How does this charter differ from that of the Fed? What significance does it have for monetary policy?

3. Do you think the Fed should be given a clearer legislative mandate concerning macroeconomic goals? If so, what should it be?

4. Referring to the Case in Point on targeting, what difference does it make whether the target is the inflation rate of the past year or the expected inflation rate over the next year?

5. In a speech in January 1995,[6] Federal Reserve Chairman Alan Greenspan used a transportation metaphor to describe some of the difficulties of implementing monetary policy. He referred to the criticism levied against the Fed for shifting in 1994 to an anti-inflation, contractionary policy when the inflation rate was still quite low:

    > "To successfully navigate a bend in the river, the barge must begin the turn well before the bend is reached. Even so, currents are always changing and even an experienced crew cannot foresee all the events that might occur as the river is being navigated. A year ago, the Fed began its turn (a shift toward an expansionary monetary policy), and it was successful."

    Mr. Greenspan was referring, of course, to the problem of lags. What kind of lag do you think he had in mind? What do you suppose the reference to changing currents means?

6. In a speech in August 1999,[7] Mr. Greenspan said,

    We no longer have the luxury to look primarily to the flow of goods and services, as conventionally estimated, when evaluating the macroeconomic environment in which monetary policy must function. There are important—but extremely difficult—questions surrounding the behavior of asset prices and the implications of this behavior for the decisions of households and businesses.

    The asset price that Mr. Greenspan was referring to was the U.S. stock market, which had been rising sharply in the weeks and months preceding this speech. Inflation and unemployment were both low at that time. What issues concerning the conduct of monetary policy was Mr. Greenspan raising?

7. Suppose we observed an economy in which changes in the money supply produce no changes whatever in nominal GDP. What could we conclude about velocity?

8. Suppose the price level were falling 10% per day. How would this affect the demand for money? How would it affect velocity? What can you conclude about the role of velocity during periods of rapid price change?

9. Suppose investment increases and the money supply does not change. Use the model of aggregate demand and aggregate supply to predict the impact of such an increase on nominal GDP. Now what happens in terms of the variables in the equation of exchange?

10. The text notes that prior to August 1997 (when it began specifying a target value for the federal funds rate), the FOMC adopted directives calling for the trading desk at the New York Federal Reserve Bank to increase, decrease, or maintain the existing degree of pressure on reserve positions. On the meeting dates given in the first column, the FOMC voted to decrease pressure on reserve positions (that is, adopt a more expansionary policy). On the meeting dates given in the second column, it voted to increase reserve pressure:

July 5–6, 1995	February 3–4, 1994
December 19, 1995	January 31–February 1, 1995
January 30–31, 1996	March 25, 1997

    Recent minutes of the FOMC can be found at the Federal Reserve Board of Governors website. Pick one of these dates on which a decrease in reserve pressure was ordered and one on which an increase was ordered and find out why that particular policy was chosen.

11. Since August 1997, the Fed has simply set a specific target for the federal funds rate. The four dates below show the first four times after August 1997 that the Fed voted to set a new target for the federal funds rate on the following dates:

| September 29, 1998 | November 17, 1998 |
| June 29, 1999 | August 24, 1999 |

Pick one of these dates and find out why it chose to change its target for the federal funds rate on that date.

12. Four recent meetings at which the Fed changed the target for the federal funds rate are shown below.

| January 30, 2008 | March 18, 2008 |
| October 8, 2008 | October 29, 2008 |

Pick one of these dates and find out why it chose to change its target for the federal funds rate on that date.

13. The text notes that a 10% increase in the money supply may not increase the price level by 10% in the short run. Explain why.

14. Trace the impact of an expansionary monetary policy on bond prices, interest rates, investment, the exchange rate, net exports, real GDP, and the price level. Illustrate your analysis graphically.

15. Trace the impact of a contractionary monetary policy on bond prices, interest rates, investment, the exchange rate, net exports, real GDP, and the price level. Illustrate your analysis graphically.

NUMERICAL PROBLEMS

1. Here are annual values for M2 and for nominal GDP (all figures are in billions of dollars) for the mid-1990s.

Year	M2	Nominal GDP
1993	3,482.0	$6,657.4
1994	3,498.1	7,072.2
1995	3,642.1	7,397.7
1996	3,820.5	7,816.9
1997	4,034.1	8,304.3

   a. Compute the velocity for each year.
   b. Compute the fraction of nominal GDP that was being held as money.
   c. What is your conclusion about the stability of velocity in this five-year period?

2. Here are annual values for M2 and for nominal GDP (all figures are in billions of dollars) for the mid-2000s.

Year	M2	Nominal GDP
2003	6,055.5	$10,960.8
2004	6,400.7	11,685.9
2005	6,659.7	12,421.9
2006	7,012.3	13,178.4
2007	7,404.3	13,807.5

   a. Compute the velocity for each year.
   b. Compute the fraction of nominal GDP that was being held as money.
   c. What is your conclusion about the stability of velocity in this five-year period?

3. The following data show M1 for the years 1993 to 1997, respectively (all figures are in billions of dollars):
1,129.6; 1,150.7; 1,127.4; 1,081.3; 1,072.5.

   a. Compute the M1 velocity for these years. (Nominal GDP for these years is shown in problem 1.)
   b. If you were going to use a money target, would M1 or M2 have been preferable during the 1990s? Explain your reasoning.

4. The following data show M1 for the years 2003 to 2007, respectively (all figures are in billions of dollars):
1,306.1; 1,376.3; 1,374.5; 1,366.5; 1,366.5

   a. Compute the M1 velocity for these years. (Nominal GDP for these years is shown in problem 2.)
   b. If you were going to use a money target, would M1 or M2 have been preferable during the 2000s? Explain your reasoning.

5. Assume a hypothetical economy in which the velocity is constant at 2 and real GDP is always at a constant potential of $4,000. Suppose the money supply is $1,000 in the first year, $1,100 in the second year, $1,200 in the third year, and $1,300 in the fourth year.

   a. Using the equation of exchange, compute the price level in each year.
   b. Compute the inflation rate for each year.
   c. Explain why inflation varies, even though the money supply rises by $100 each year.
   d. If the central bank wanted to keep inflation at zero, what should it have done to the money supply each year?
   e. If the central bank wanted to keep inflation at 10% each year, what money supply should it have targeted in each year?

6. Suppose the velocity of money is constant and potential output grows by 3% per year. By what percentage should the money supply grow in order to achieve the following inflation rate targets?

   a. 0%
   b. 1%
   c. 2%

7. Suppose the velocity of money is constant and potential output grows by 5% per year. For each of the following money supply growth rates, what will the inflation rate be?

   a. 4%

b. 5%

c. 6%

8. Suppose that a country whose money supply grew by about 20% a year over the long run had an annual inflation rate of about 20% and that a country whose money supply grew by about 50% a year had an annual inflation rate of about 50%. Explain this finding in terms of the equation of exchange.

ENDNOTES

1. See, for example, Alberto Alesina and Lawrence H. Summers, "Central Bank Independence and Macroeconomic Performance: Some Comparative Evidence," *Journal of Money, Credit, and Banking* 25, no. 2 (May 1993): 151–62.

2. "Bringing an End to Deflation under the New Monetary Policy Framework," *OECD Economic Surveys: Japan 2008* 4 (April 2008): 49–61 and Mark M. Spiegel, "Did Quantitative Easing by the Bank of Japan Work?" *FRBSF Economic Letter* 2006, no. 28 (October 20, 2006): 1–3.

3. Ben S. Bernanke, "The Crisis and the Policy Response" (Stamp Lecture, London School of Economics, London, England, January 13, 2009) and Janet L. Yellen, "U.S. Monetary Policy Objectives in the Short Run and the Long Run" (speech, Allied Social Sciences Association annual meeting, San Francisco, California, January 4, 2009).

4. For example, one study examined data on 81 countries using inflation rates averaged for the period 1980 to 1993 (John R. Moroney, "Money Growth, Output Growth, and Inflation: Estimation of a Modern Quantity Theory," *Southern Economic Journal* 69, no. 2 [2002]: 398–413) while another examined data on 160 countries over the period 1969–1999 (Paul De Grauwe and Magdalena Polan, "Is Inflation Always and Everywhere a Monetary Phenomenon?" *Scandinavian Journal of Economics* 107, no. 2 [2005]: 239–59).

5. Laurence H. Meyer, "Does Money Matter?" *Federal Reserve Bank of St. Louis Review* 83, no. 5 (September/October 2001): 1–15.

6. Speech by Alan Greenspan before the Board of Directors of the National Association of Home Builders, January 28, 1995.

7. Alan Greenspan, "New challenges for monetary policy," speech delivered before a symposium sponsored by the Federal Reserve Bank of Kansas City in Jackson Hole, Wyoming, on August 27, 1999. Mr. Greenspan was famous for his convoluted speech, which listeners often found difficult to understand. CBS correspondent Andrea Mitchell, to whom Mr. Greenspan is married, once joked that he had proposed to her three times and that she had not understood what he was talking about on his first two efforts.

CHAPTER 12

Government and Fiscal Policy

START UP: A MASSIVE STIMULUS

Shaken by the severity of the recession that began in December 2007, Congress passed a huge $787 billion stimulus package in February 2009. President Obama described the measure as only "the beginning" of what the federal government ultimately would do to right the economy.

Roughly a third of the Recovery and Reinvestment Act is for a variety of tax cuts for individuals and firms. For example, each worker making less than $75,000 a year will receive $400 ($800 for a working couple earning up to $150,000) as a kind of rebate for payroll taxes. That works out to $8 a week. Qualifying college students are eligible for $2,500 tax credits for educational expenses. The other two-thirds is for a variety of government spending programs. The president said that the measure would "ignite spending by businesses and consumers … and make the investment necessary for lasting growth and economic prosperity."[1]

The measure illustrates an important difficulty of using fiscal policy in an effort to stabilize economic activity. It was passed over a year after the recession began. According to an estimate by the Congressional Budget Office (CBO), only about 20% of the spending called for by the legislation will take place in 2009, rising to about two-thirds through the middle of 2010. It is a guess what state the economy will be in then.

A fiscal stimulus package of over $150 billion had already been tried earlier in February 2008. It included $100 billion in tax rebates to households—up to $600 for individuals and $1,200 for couples— and over $50 billion in tax breaks for businesses. The boost to aggregate demand seemed slight—consumers saved much of their rebate money. In November 2008, unemployment insurance benefits were extended for seven additional weeks, in recognition of the growing unemployment problem.

President Obama argued that his proposals for dealing with the economy in the short term would, coincidentally, also promote long-term economic health. Some critics argued for a greater focus on tax cuts while others were concerned about whether the spending would focus on getting the greatest employment increase or be driven by political considerations.

How do government tax and expenditure policies affect real GDP and the price level? Why do economists differ so sharply in assessing the likely impact of such policies? Can fiscal policy be used to stabilize the economy in the short run? What are the long-run effects of government spending and taxing?

We begin with a look at the government's budget to see how it spends the tax revenue it collects. Clearly, the government's budget is not always in balance, so we will also look at government deficits and debt. We will then look at how fiscal policy works to stabilize the economy, distinguishing between built-in stabilization methods and discretionary measures. We will end the chapter with a discussion of why fiscal policy is so controversial.

As in the previous chapter on monetary policy, our primary focus will be U.S. policy. However, the tools available to governments around the world are quite similar, as are the issues surrounding the use of fiscal policy.

1.   GOVERNMENT AND THE ECONOMY

We begin our analysis of fiscal policy with an examination of government purchases, transfer payments, and taxes in the U.S. economy.

1.1 Government Purchases

The government-purchases component of aggregate demand includes all purchases by government agencies of goods and services produced by firms, as well as direct production by government agencies themselves. When the federal government buys staples and staplers, the transaction is part of government purchases. The production of educational and research services by public colleges and universities is also counted in the government-purchases component of GDP.

While government spending has grown over time, government purchases as a share of GDP generally declined from over 20% until the early 1990s to under 18% in 2001. Since then, though, the percentage of government purchases in GDP began to increase back toward 20%, first as military spending picked up and then more recently to over 20% during the 2007-2009 recession.

Figure 12.1 shows federal as well as state and local government purchases as a percentage of GDP from 1960 to 2009. Notice the changes that have occurred over this period. In 1960, the federal government accounted for the majority share of total purchases. Since then, however, federal purchases have fallen by almost half relative to GDP, while state and local purchases relative to GDP have risen.

FIGURE 12.1 Federal, State, and Local Purchases Relative to GDP, 1960–2009

Government purchases were generally above 20% of GDP from 1960 until the early 1990s and then below 20% of GDP until the 2007-2009 recession. The share of government purchases in GDP began rising again in the 21st century.

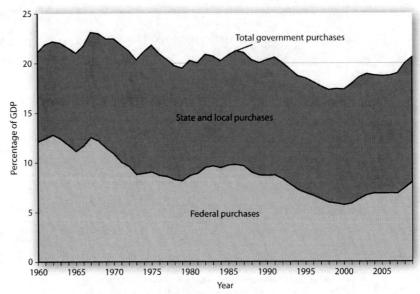

Source: Bureau of Economic Analysis, NIPA Table 1.1 and 3.1 (November 23, 2010 revision).

1.2   Transfer Payments

A **transfer payment** is the provision of aid or money to an individual who is not required to provide anything in exchange. Social Security and welfare benefits are examples of transfer payments. During the 2007-2009 recession, transfers again rose.

A number of changes have influenced transfer payments over the past several decades. First, they increased rapidly during the late 1960s and early 1970s. This was the period in which federal programs such as Medicare (health insurance for the elderly) and Medicaid (health insurance for the poor) were created and other programs were expanded.

Figure 12.2 shows that transfer payment spending by the federal government and by state and local governments has risen as a percentage of GDP. In 1960, such spending totaled about 6% of GDP; by 2009, it had risen to about 18%. The federal government accounts for the bulk of transfer payment spending in the United States.

transfer payment

The provision of aid or money to an individual who is not required to provide anything in exchange.

FIGURE 12.2   Federal, State, and Local Transfer Payments as a Percentage of GDP, 1960–2009

The chart shows transfer payment spending as a percentage of GDP from 1960 through 2009. This spending rose dramatically relative to GDP during the late 1960s and the 1970s as federal programs expanded. More recently, sharp increases in health-care costs have driven upward the spending for transfer payment programs such as Medicare and Medicaid. Transfer payments fluctuate with the business cycle, rising in times of recession and falling during times of expansion. As such, they rose sharply during the deep 2007-2009 recession.

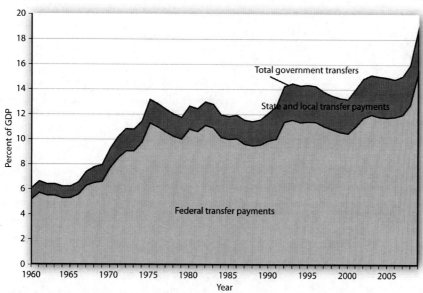

Source: Bureau of Economic Analysis, NIPA Table 1.1, 3.2, and 3.3 (November 23, 2010 revision).

Transfer payment spending relative to GDP tends to fluctuate with the business cycle. Transfer payments fell during the late 1970s, a period of expansion, then rose as the economy slipped into a recessionary gap during the 1979–1982 period. Transfer payments fell during the expansion that began late in 1982, then began rising in 1989 as the expansion began to slow. Transfer payments continued to rise relative to GDP during the recessions of 1990–1991 and 2001–2002 and then fell as the economy entered expansionary phases after each of those recessions. During the 2007—2009 recession, transfers again rose.

When economic activity falls, incomes fall, people lose jobs, and more people qualify for aid. People qualify to receive welfare benefits, such as cash, food stamps, or Medicaid, only if their income falls below a certain level. They qualify for unemployment compensation by losing their jobs. More people qualify for transfer payments during recessions. When the economy expands, incomes and employment rise, and fewer people qualify for welfare or unemployment benefits. Spending for those programs therefore tends to fall during an expansion.

Figure 12.3 summarizes trends in government spending since 1960. It shows three categories of government spending relative to GDP: government purchases, transfer payments, and net interest. Net interest includes payments of interest by governments at all levels on money borrowed, less interest earned on saving.

FIGURE 12.3 Government Spending as a Percentage of GDP, 1960–2009

This chart shows three major categories of government spending as percentages of GDP: government purchases, transfer payments, and net interest.

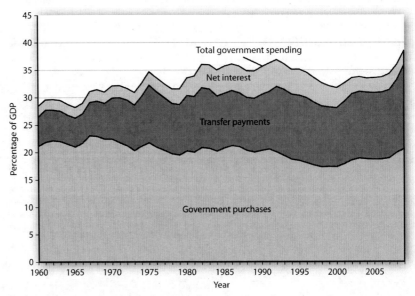

Source: Bureau of Economic Analysis, NIPA Table 1.1 and 3.1 (November 23, 2010 revision).

1.3 Taxes

Taxes affect the relationship between real GDP and personal disposable income; they therefore affect consumption. They also influence investment decisions. Taxes imposed on firms affect the profitability of investment decisions and therefore affect the levels of investment firms will choose. Payroll taxes imposed on firms affect the costs of hiring workers; they therefore have an impact on employment and on the real wages earned by workers.

The bulk of federal receipts come from the personal income tax and from payroll taxes. State and local tax receipts are dominated by property taxes and sales taxes. The federal government, as well as state and local governments, also collects taxes imposed on business firms, such as taxes on corporate profits. Figure 12.4 shows the composition of federal, state, and local receipts in a recent year.

FIGURE 12.4   The Composition of Federal, State, and Local Revenues

Federal receipts come primarily from payroll taxes and from personal taxes such as the personal income tax. State and local tax receipts come from a variety of sources; the most important are property taxes, sales taxes, income taxes, and grants from the federal government. Revenue shares are for 2009.

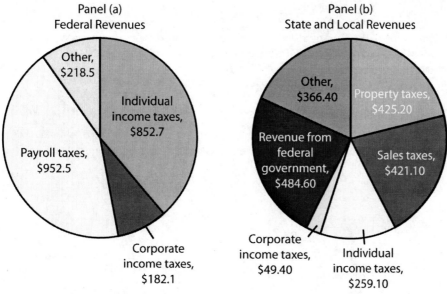

Source: Bureau of Economic Analysis, NIPA Table 3.2 and 3.3 (November 23, 2010 revision).

1.4   The Government Budget Balance

The government's budget balance is the difference between the government's revenues and its expenditures. A **budget surplus** occurs if government revenues exceed expenditures. A **budget deficit** occurs if government expenditures exceed revenues. The minus sign is often omitted when reporting a deficit. If the budget surplus equals zero, we say the government has a **balanced budget**.

Figure 12.5 compares federal, state, and local government revenues to expenditures relative to GDP since 1960. The government's budget was generally in surplus in the 1960s, then mostly in deficit since, except for a brief period between 1998 and 2001. Bear in mind that these data are for all levels of government.

budget surplus

Situation that occurs if government revenues exceed expenditures.

budget deficit

Situation that occurs if government expenditures exceed revenues.

balanced budget

Situation that occurs if the budget surplus equals zero.

FIGURE 12.5   Government Revenue and Expenditure as a Percentage of GDP, 1960–2009

The government's budget was generally in surplus in the 1960s, then mostly in deficit since, except for a brief period between 1998 and 2001.

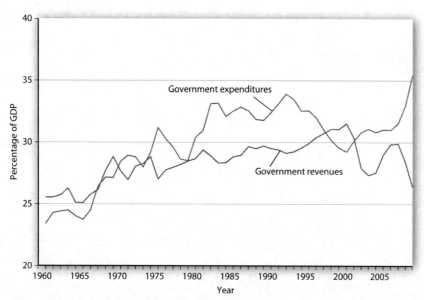

Source: Bureau of Economic Analysis, NIPA Table 1.1 and 3.1 (November 23, 2010 revision).

The administration of George W. Bush saw a large increase in the federal deficit. In part, this is the result of the government's response to the terrorist attacks in 2001. It also results, however, from large increases in federal spending at all levels together with tax cuts in 2001, 2002, and 2003. The federal deficit is projected to be even larger during the administration of Barack Obama.

1.5   The National Debt

national debt

The sum of all past federal deficits, minus any surpluses.

The **national debt** is the sum of all past federal deficits, minus any surpluses. Figure 12.6 shows the national debt as a percentage of GDP. It suggests that, relative to the level of economic activity, the debt is well below the levels reached during World War II. The ratio of debt to GDP rose from 1981 to 1996 and fell in the last years of the 20th century; it began rising again in 2002.

FIGURE 12.6   The National Debt and the Economy, 1929–2009

The national debt relative to GDP is much smaller today than it was during World War II. The ratio of debt to GDP rose from 1981 to 1996 and fell in the last years of the 20th century; it began rising again in 2002.

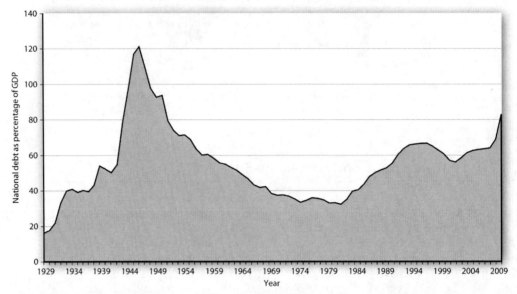

Sources: Data for 1929–1938 from Historical Statistics of the United States, Colonial Times to 1957—not strictly comparable with later data. Data for remaining years from Office of Management and Budget, Budget of the United States Government, Fiscal Year 2011, Historical Tables.

Judged by international standards, the U.S. national debt relative to its GDP is somewhat above average among developed nations. Figure 12.7 shows national debt as a percentage of GDP for 26 countries in 2008. It also shows deficits or surpluses as a percentage of GDP.

FIGURE 12.7 Debts and Deficits for 26 Nations, 2008

The chart shows national debt as a percentage of GDP and deficits or surpluses as a percentage of GDP in 2008. The national debt of the United States relative to its GDP was somewhat above average among these nations.

Country	National Debt as percentage of GDP	Deficit (−) or surplus as percentage of GDP
Japan	172.1	−2.7
Italy	114.4	−2.7
Greece	102.6	−7.8
Iceland	96.3	−13.6
Belgium	93.5	−1.2
Hungary	77.0	−3.7
France	75.7	−3.4
Portugal	75.2	−2.8
United States	70.0	−6.5
Canada	69.7	0.1
Germany	68.8	−0.2
Austria	66.2	−0.5
Netherlands	65.8	0.7
United Kingdom	56.8	−5.3
Norway	56.0	18.8
Poland	54.0	−3.7
Sweden	47.1	2.5
Spain	47.0	−4.1
Switzerland	44.0	1.6
Finland	40.7	4.4
Denmark	39.8	3.4
Slovak Republic	30.8	−2.3
Korea	26.8	3.3
New Zealand	25.3	3.1
Luxembourg	16.3	2.5
Australia	14.3	1.0
Average	63.3	

Source: Organisation for Economic Co-operation and Development (OECD). Factbook 2010. OECD Publishing, May 25, 2010.

KEY TAKEAWAYS

- Over the last 50 years, government purchases fell from about 20% of U.S. GDP to below 20%, but have been rising over the last decade.
- Transfer payment spending has risen sharply, both in absolute terms and as a percentage of real GDP since 1960.
- The bulk of federal revenues comes from income and payroll taxes. State and local revenues consist primarily of sales and property taxes.
- The government budget balance is the difference between government revenues and government expenditures.
- The national debt is the sum of all past federal deficits minus any surpluses.

TRY IT!

What happens to the national debt when there is a budget surplus? What happens to it when there is a budget deficit? What happens to the national debt if there is a decrease in a surplus? What happens to it if the deficit falls?

Case in Point: Generational Accounting

One method of assessing the degree to which current fiscal policies affect future generations is through a device introduced in the early 1990s called generational accounting. It measures the impact of current fiscal policies on different generations in the economy, including future generations. Generational accounting is now practiced by governments in many countries, including the United States and the European Union.

As populations age, the burden of current fiscal policy is increasingly borne by younger people in the population. In most countries, economists computing generational accounts have found that people age 40 or below will pay more in taxes than they receive in transfer payments, while those age 60 or above will receive more in transfers than they pay in taxes. The differences are huge. According to a recent study by Jagadeesh Gokhale, summarized in the table below, in 2004 in the United States, a male age 30 could expect to pay $201,300 more than he receives in government transfers during his lifetime, while another male age 75 could expect to receive $171,100 more in transfers than he paid in taxes during his lifetime. That is a difference of $372,400! For future generations, those born after the year 2004, the difference is even more staggering. A male born after the year 2005 can expect to pay $332,200 more in taxes than he will receive in transfer payments. For a woman, the differences are also large but not as great. A woman age 30 in 2004 could expect to pay $30,200 more in taxes than she will receive in transfers during her lifetime, while a woman age 75 could expect to receive transfers of $184,100 in excess of her lifetime tax burden.

The table below gives generational accounting estimates for the United States for the year 2004 for males and females. Notice that the net burden on females is much lower than for males. That is because women live longer than men and thus receive Social Security and Medicare benefits over a longer period of time. Women also have lower labor force participation rates and earn less than men, and pay lower taxes as a result.

Generational Accounts for the United States (thousands of 2004 dollars)

Year of birth	Age in 2004	Male	Female
2005 (future born)	−1	333.2	26.0
2004 (newborn)	0	104.3	8.1
1989	15	185.7	42.0
1974	30	201.3	30.2
1959	45	67.8	−54.1
1944	60	−162.6	−189.4
1929	75	−171.1	−184.1
1914	90	−65.0	−69.2

Generational accounting has its critics—for example, the table above only measures direct taxes and transfers but omits benefits from government spending on public goods and services. In addition, government spending programs can be modified, which would alter the impact on future generations. Nonetheless, it does help to focus attention on the sustainability of current fiscal policies. Can future generations pay for Social Security, Medicare, and other retirement and health care spending as currently configured? Should they be asked to do so?

Sources: *Jagadeesh Gokhale, "Generational Accounting," The New Palgrave Dictionary of Economics, 2nd ed. (forthcoming).*

2.   THE USE OF FISCAL POLICY TO STABILIZE THE ECONOMY

LEARNING OBJECTIVES

1. Define automatic stabilizers and explain how they work.
2. Explain and illustrate graphically how discretionary fiscal policy works and compare the changes in aggregate demand that result from changes in government purchases, income taxes, and transfer payments.

Fiscal policy—the use of government expenditures and taxes to influence the level of economic activity—is the government counterpart to monetary policy. Like monetary policy, it can be used in an effort to close a recessionary or an inflationary gap.

Some tax and expenditure programs change automatically with the level of economic activity. We will examine these first. Then we will look at how discretionary fiscal policies work. Four examples of discretionary fiscal policy choices were the tax cuts introduced by the Kennedy, Reagan, and George W. Bush administrations and the increase in government purchases proposed by President Clinton in 1993. The 2009 fiscal stimulus bill passed in the first months of the administration of Barack Obama included both tax cuts and spending increases. All were designed to stimulate aggregate demand and close recessionary gaps.

2.1   Automatic Stabilizers

Certain government expenditure and taxation policies tend to insulate individuals from the impact of shocks to the economy. Transfer payments have this effect. Because more people become eligible for income supplements when income is falling, transfer payments reduce the effect of a change in real GDP on disposable personal income and thus help to insulate households from the impact of the change. Income taxes also have this effect. As incomes fall, people pay less in income taxes.

Any government program that tends to reduce fluctuations in GDP automatically is called an **automatic stabilizer**. Automatic stabilizers tend to increase GDP when it is falling and reduce GDP when it is rising.

To see how automatic stabilizers work, consider the decline in real GDP that occurred during the recession of 1990–1991. Real GDP fell 1.6% from the peak to the trough of that recession. The reduction in economic activity automatically reduced tax payments, reducing the impact of the downturn on disposable personal income. Furthermore, the reduction in incomes increased transfer payment spending, boosting disposable personal income further. Real disposable personal income thus fell by only 0.9% during the 1990—1991 recession, a much smaller percentage than the reduction in real GDP. Rising transfer payments and falling tax collections helped cushion households from the impact of the recession and kept real GDP from falling as much as it would have otherwise.

Automatic stabilizers have emerged as key elements of fiscal policy. Increases in income tax rates and unemployment benefits have enhanced their importance as automatic stabilizers. The introduction in the 1960s and 1970s of means-tested federal transfer payments, in which individuals qualify depending on their income, added to the nation's arsenal of automatic stabilizers. The advantage of automatic stabilizers is suggested by their name. As soon as income starts to change, they go to work. Because they affect disposable personal income directly, and because changes in disposable personal income are closely linked to changes in consumption, automatic stabilizers act swiftly to reduce the degree of changes in real GDP.

It is important to note that changes in expenditures and taxes that occur through automatic stabilizers do not shift the aggregate demand curve. Because they are automatic, their operation is already incorporated in the curve itself.

automatic stabilizer

Any government program that tends to reduce fluctuations in GDP automatically.

2.2 Discretionary Fiscal Policy Tools

As we begin to look at deliberate government efforts to stabilize the economy through fiscal policy choices, we note that most of the government's taxing and spending is for purposes other than economic stabilization. For example, the increase in defense spending in the early 1980s under President Ronald Reagan and in the administration of George W. Bush were undertaken primarily to promote national security. That the increased spending affected real GDP and employment was a by-product. The effect of such changes on real GDP and the price level is secondary, but it cannot be ignored. Our focus here, however, is on discretionary fiscal policy that is undertaken with the intention of stabilizing the economy. As we have seen, the tax cuts introduced by the Bush administration were justified as expansionary measures.

Discretionary government spending and tax policies can be used to shift aggregate demand. Expansionary fiscal policy might consist of an increase in government purchases or transfer payments, a reduction in taxes, or a combination of these tools to shift the aggregate demand curve to the right. A contractionary fiscal policy might involve a reduction in government purchases or transfer payments, an increase in taxes, or a mix of all three to shift the aggregate demand curve to the left.

Figure 12.9 illustrates the use of fiscal policy to shift aggregate demand in response to a recessionary gap and an inflationary gap. In Panel (a), the economy produces a real GDP of Y_1, which is below its potential level of Y_p. An expansionary fiscal policy seeks to shift aggregate demand to AD_2 in order to close the gap. In Panel (b), the economy initially has an inflationary gap at Y_1. A contractionary fiscal policy seeks to reduce aggregate demand to AD_2 and close the gap. Now we shall look at how specific fiscal policy options work. In our preliminary analysis of the effects of fiscal policy on the economy, we will assume that at a given price level these policies do not affect interest rates or exchange rates. We will relax that assumption later in the chapter.

FIGURE 12.9 Expansionary and Contractionary Fiscal Policies to Shift Aggregate Demand

In Panel (a), the economy faces a recessionary gap ($Y_P - Y_1$). An expansionary fiscal policy seeks to shift aggregate demand to AD_2 to close the gap. In Panel (b), the economy faces an inflationary gap ($Y_1 - Y_P$). A contractionary fiscal policy seeks to reduce aggregate demand to AD_2 to close the gap.

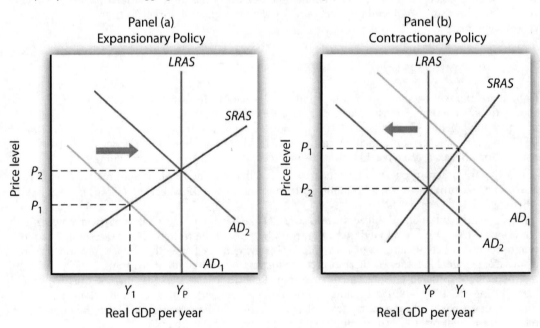

2.3 Changes in Government Purchases

One policy through which the government could seek to shift the aggregate demand curve is a change in government purchases. We learned that the aggregate demand curve shifts to the right by an amount equal to the initial change in government purchases times the multiplier. This multiplied effect of a change in government purchases occurs because the increase in government purchases increases income, which in turn increases consumption. Then, part of the impact of the increase in aggregate demand is absorbed by higher prices, preventing the full increase in real GDP that would have occurred if the price level did not rise.

Figure 12.10 shows the effect of an increase in government purchases of $200 billion. The initial price level is P_1 and the initial equilibrium real GDP is $12,000 billion. Suppose the multiplier is 2. The $200 billion increase in government purchases increases the total quantity of goods and services demanded, at a price level of P_1, by $400 billion (the $200 billion increase in government purchases times the multiplier) to $12,400 billion. The aggregate demand thus shifts to the right by that amount to AD_2. The equilibrium level of real GDP rises to $12,300 billion, and the price level rises to P_2.

A reduction in government purchases would have the opposite effect. The aggregate demand curve would shift to the left by an amount equal to the initial change in government purchases times the multiplier. Real GDP and the price level would fall.

2.4   Changes in Business Taxes

One of the first fiscal policy measures undertaken by the Kennedy administration in the 1960s was an investment tax credit. An investment tax credit allows a firm to reduce its tax liability by a percentage of the investment it undertakes during a particular period. With an investment tax credit of 10%, for example, a firm that engaged in $1 million worth of investment during a year could reduce its tax liability for that year by $100,000. The investment tax credit introduced by the Kennedy administration was later repealed. It was reintroduced during the Reagan administration in 1981, then abolished by the Tax Reform Act of 1986. President Clinton called for a new investment tax credit in 1993 as part of his job stimulus proposal, but that proposal was rejected by Congress. The Bush administration reinstated the investment tax credit as part of its tax cut package.

An investment tax credit is intended, of course, to stimulate additional private sector investment. A reduction in the tax rate on corporate profits would be likely to have a similar effect. Conversely, an increase in the corporate income tax rate or a reduction in an investment tax credit could be expected to reduce investment.

A change in investment affects the aggregate demand curve in precisely the same manner as a change in government purchases. It shifts the aggregate demand curve by an amount equal to the initial change in investment times the multiplier.

An increase in the investment tax credit, or a reduction in corporate income tax rates, will increase investment and shift the aggregate demand curve to the right. Real GDP and the price level will rise. A reduction in the investment tax credit, or an increase in corporate income tax rates, will reduce investment and shift the aggregate demand curve to the left. Real GDP and the price level will fall.[2]

2.5   Changes in Income Taxes

Income taxes affect the consumption component of aggregate demand. An increase in income taxes reduces disposable personal income and thus reduces consumption (but by less than the change in disposable personal income). That shifts the aggregate demand curve leftward by an amount equal to the initial change in consumption that the change in income taxes produces times the multiplier.[3] A reduction in income taxes increases disposable personal income, increases consumption (but by less than the change in disposable personal income), and increases aggregate demand.

Suppose, for example, that income taxes are reduced by $200 billion. Only some of the increase in disposable personal income will be used for consumption and the rest will be saved. Suppose the initial increase in consumption is $180 billion. Then the shift in the aggregate demand curve will be a multiple of $180 billion; if the multiplier is 2, aggregate demand will shift to the right by $360 billion. Thus, as compared to the $200-billion increase in government purchases that we saw in Figure 12.10, the shift in the aggregate demand curve due to an income tax cut is somewhat less, as is the effect on real GDP and the price level.

2.6   Changes in Transfer Payments

Changes in transfer payments, like changes in income taxes, alter the disposable personal income of households and thus affect their consumption, which is a component of aggregate demand. A change in transfer payments will thus shift the aggregate demand curve because it will affect consumption. Because consumption will change by less than the change in disposable personal income, a change in transfer payments of some amount will result in a smaller change in real GDP than would a change in government purchases of the same amount. As with income taxes, a $200-billion increase in transfer

FIGURE 12.10   An Increase in Government Purchases

The economy shown here is initially in equilibrium at a real GDP of $12,000 billion and a price level of P_1. An increase of $200 billion in the level of government purchases (ΔG) shifts the aggregate demand curve to the right by $400 billion to AD_2. The equilibrium level of real GDP rises to $12,300 billion, while the price level rises to P_2.

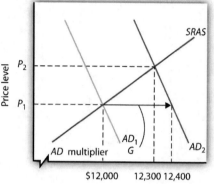

Real GDP (billions of base-year dollars) per year

payments will shift the aggregate demand curve to the right by less than the $200-billion increase in government purchases that we saw in Figure 12.10.

Table 12.2 summarizes U.S. fiscal policies undertaken to shift aggregate demand since the 1964 tax cuts. We see that expansionary policies have been chosen in response to recessionary gaps and that contractionary policies have been chosen in response to inflationary gaps. Changes in government purchases and in taxes have been the primary tools of fiscal policy in the United States.

TABLE 12.2 Fiscal Policy in the United States Since 1964

The table lists the major proposed uses of discretionary policy over the last four decades.

Year	Situation	Policy response
1968	Inflationary gap	A temporary tax increase, first recommended by President Johnson's Council of Economic Advisers in 1965, goes into effect. This one-time surcharge of 10% is added to individual income tax liabilities.
1969	Inflationary gap	President Nixon, facing a continued inflationary gap, orders cuts in government purchases.
1975	Recessionary gap	President Ford, facing a recession induced by an OPEC oil-price increase, proposes a temporary 10% tax cut. It is passed almost immediately and goes into effect within two months.
1981	Recessionary gap	President Reagan had campaigned on a platform of increased defense spending and a sharp cut in income taxes. The tax cuts are approved in 1981 and are implemented over a period of three years. The increased defense spending begins in 1981. While the Reagan administration rejects the use of fiscal policy as a stabilization tool, its policies tend to increase aggregate demand early in the 1980s.
1992	Recessionary gap	President Bush had rejected the use of expansionary fiscal policy during the recession of 1990–1991. Indeed, he agreed late in 1990 to a cut in government purchases and a tax increase. In a campaign year, however, he orders a cut in withholding rates designed to increase disposable personal income in 1992 and to boost consumption.
1993	Recessionary gap	President Clinton calls for a $16-billion jobs package consisting of increased government purchases and tax cuts aimed at stimulating investment. The president says the plan will create 500,000 new jobs. The measure is rejected by Congress.
2001	Recessionary gap	President Bush campaigned to reduce taxes in order to reduce the size of government and encourage long-term growth. When he took office in 2001, the economy was weak and the $1.35-billion tax cut was aimed at both long-term tax relief and at stimulating the economy in the short term. It included, for example, a personal income tax rebate of $300 to $600 per household. With unemployment still high a couple of years into the expansion, another tax cut was passed in 2003.
2008	Recessionary gap	Fiscal stimulus package of $150 billion to spur economy. It included $100 billion in tax rebates and $50 in tax cuts for businesses.
2009	Recessionary gap	Fiscal stimulus package of $787 billion included tax cuts and increased government spending passed in early days of President Obama's administration.

KEY TAKEAWAYS

- Discretionary fiscal policy may be either expansionary or contractionary.
- A change in government purchases shifts the aggregate demand curve at a given price level by an amount equal to the initial change in government purchases times the multiplier. The change in real GDP, however, will be reduced by the fact that the price level will change.
- A change in income taxes or government transfer payments shifts the aggregate demand curve by a multiple of the initial change in consumption (which is less than the change in personal disposable income) that the change in income taxes or transfer payments causes. Then, the change in real GDP will be reduced by the fact that the price level will change.
- A change in government purchases has a larger impact on the aggregate demand curve than does an equal change in income taxes or transfers.
- Changes in business tax rates, including an investment tax credit, can be used to influence the level of investment and thus the level of aggregate demand.

TRY IT!

Suppose the economy has an inflationary gap. What fiscal policies might be used to close the gap? Using the model of aggregate demand and aggregate supply, illustrate the effect of these policies.

Case in Point: Post–World War II Experiences with Fiscal Policy in the United States

Christina Romer, tapped by Barack Obama to head the Council of Economic Advisers, has a long history of writing on economic history. Much of her work focuses on the macroeconomic performance of the United States economy over the past 100-plus years and hence also involves painstaking work to construct historical data series.

One such study titled "Changes in Business Cycles: Evidence and Explanations" draws on a number of her research efforts to compare economic fluctuations before World War I to those after World War II in order to see if the advent of macroeconomic stabilization policy has affected macroeconomic performance. After first showing that macroeconomic performance has not improved as markedly as we might think (excluding the interwar period when "all hell broke loose in the American economy"), she does conclude that monetary and fiscal policies to influence aggregate demand since World War II have "served to dampen many recessions and counteract some shocks entirely."

She notes that before World War I, changes in macroeconomic policy could not have affected economic performance, because the government was simply too small, with, for example, government spending as a percent of GNP averaging between 1.5% and 2.5% between 1901 and 1916. During that period, the government did operate under specified monetary standards and banking regulations, but the Federal Reserve was not created until 1914, so there was no monetary institution to respond to macroeconomic instability. Thus, macroeconomic policy can truly be seen as a post–World War II phenomenon.

Germaine to the focus on fiscal policy in this chapter, Romer found that discretionary fiscal policy after World War II contributed 0.5 percentage points to the rate of growth of real GDP in years following the troughs of recessions, while automatic stabilizers contributed 0.85 percentage points. Adding in the average contribution of monetary policy of 1.5 percentage points, macroeconomic policy in total contributed 2.85 percentage points to the average actual growth of GDP in the years following troughs of 4.6%. She also concluded that macroeconomic policies likely prevented some recessions or near-recessions. For example, automatic stabilizers muted fluctuations in years of extreme changes in GDP, up or down, by 1 to 2 percentage points in absolute value and fluctuations in years of moderate changes in GDP by about 0.5 percentage points in absolute value.

Especially in light of the active use of both monetary and fiscal policies to counter the recession that began in December 2007, she also found that there has been a rise in policy-induced recessions and that this phenomenon explains both why output and other macroeconomic variables have not been more stable in the past half-century and why post–World War II business cycles have been in the moderate range. In particular, she argues that the Fed has generally been too expansionary when the economy was growing, which has led to inflation. Then the Fed has used contractionary policy to reduce inflation. She concludes, "In essence, we have replaced the prewar boom-bust cycle driven by animal spirits and financial panics with the postwar boom-bust cycle driven by policy."

Source: Christina Romer, "Changes in Business Cycles: Evidence and Explanations," Journal of Economic Perspectives 13, no. 2 (Spring 1999): 23–44.

3. ISSUES IN FISCAL POLICY

LEARNING OBJECTIVES

1. Explain how the various kinds of lags influence the effectiveness of discretionary fiscal policy.
2. Explain and illustrate graphically how crowding out (and its reverse) influences the impact of expansionary or contractionary fiscal policy.
3. Discuss the controversy concerning which types of fiscal policies to use, including the arguments from supply-side economics.

The discussion in the previous section about the use of fiscal policy to close gaps suggests that economies can be easily stabilized by government actions to shift the aggregate demand curve. However, as we discovered with monetary policy in the previous chapter, government attempts at stabilization are fraught with difficulties.

3.1 Lags

Discretionary fiscal policy is subject to the same lags that we discussed for monetary policy. It takes some time for policy makers to realize that a recessionary or an inflationary gap exists—the *recognition lag*. Recognition lags stem largely from the difficulty of collecting economic data in a timely and accurate fashion. The current recession was not identified until October 2008, when the Business Cycle Dating Committee of the National Bureau of Economic Research announced that it had begun in December 2007. Then, more time elapses before a fiscal policy, such as a change in government purchases or a change in taxes, is agreed to and put into effect—the *implementation lag*. Finally, still more time goes by before the policy has its full effect on aggregate demand—the *impact lag*.

Changes in fiscal policy are likely to involve a particularly long implementation lag. A tax cut was proposed to presidential candidate John F. Kennedy in 1960 as a means of ending the recession that year. He recommended it to Congress in 1962. It was not passed until 1964, three years after the recession had ended. Some economists have concluded that the long implementation lag for discretionary fiscal policy makes this stabilization tool ineffective. Fortunately, automatic stabilizers respond automatically to changes in the economy. They thus avoid not only the implementation lag but also the recognition lag.

The implementation lag results partly from the nature of bureaucracy itself. The CBO estimate that only a portion of the spending for the stimulus plan passed in 2009 will be spent in the next two years is an example of the implementation lag. Government spending requires bureaucratic approval of that spending. For example, a portion of the stimulus plan must go through the Department of Energy. One division of the department focuses on approving loan guarantees for energy-saving industrial projects. It was created early in 2007 as part of another effort to stimulate economic activity. A Minnesota company, Sage Electrochromics, has developed a process for producing windows that can be darkened or lightened on demand to reduce energy use in buildings. Sage applied two years ago for a guarantee on a loan of $66 million to build a plant that would employ 250 workers. Its application has not been approved. In fact, the loan approval division, which will be crucial for projects in the stimulus plan, has never approved any application made to it in its two years in existence!

Energy Secretary Steven Chu, a Nobel Prize-winning physicist, recognizes the urgency of the problem. In an interview with the *Wall Street Journal*, Dr. Chu said that his agency would have to do better. "Otherwise, it's just going to be a bust," he said.[4]

3.2 Crowding Out

Because an expansionary fiscal policy either increases government spending or reduces revenues, it increases the government budget deficit or reduces the surplus. A contractionary policy is likely to reduce a deficit or increase a surplus. In either case, fiscal policy thus affects the bond market. Our analysis of monetary policy showed that developments in the bond market can affect investment and net exports. We shall find in this section that the same is true for fiscal policy.

Figure 12.12 shows the impact of an expansionary fiscal policy: an increase in government purchases. The increase in government purchases increases the deficit or reduces the surplus. In either case, the Treasury will sell more bonds than it would have otherwise, shifting the supply curve for bonds to the right in Panel (a). That reduces the price of bonds, raising the interest rate. The increase in the interest rate reduces the quantity of private investment demanded. The higher interest rate increases the demand for and reduces the supply of dollars in the foreign exchange market, raising the exchange rate in Panel (b). A higher exchange rate reduces net exports. Panel (c) shows the effects of all these changes on the aggregate demand curve. Before the change in government purchases, the economy is in equilibrium at a real GDP of Y_1, determined by the intersection of AD_1 and the short-run aggregate supply curve. The increase in government expenditures would shift the curve outward to AD_2 if there were no adverse impact on investment and net exports. But the reduction in investment and net exports partially offsets this increase. Taking the reduction in investment and net exports into account means that the aggregate demand curve shifts only to AD_3. The tendency for an expansionary fiscal policy to reduce other components of aggregate demand is called **crowding out**. In the short run, this policy leads to an increase in real GDP to Y_2 and a higher price level, P_2.

crowding out

The tendency for an expansionary fiscal policy to reduce other components of aggregate demand.

FIGURE 12.12   An Expansionary Fiscal Policy and Crowding Out

In Panel (a), increased government purchases are financed through the sale of bonds, lowering their price to P^b_2. In Panel (b), the higher interest rate causes the exchange rate to rise, reducing net exports. Increased government purchases would shift the aggregate demand curve to AD_2 in Panel (c) if there were no crowding out. Crowding out of investment and net exports, however, causes the aggregate demand curve to shift only to AD_3. Then a higher price level means that GDP rises only to Y_2.

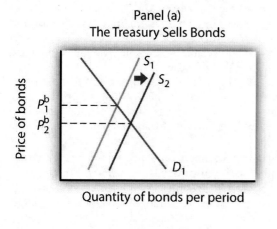

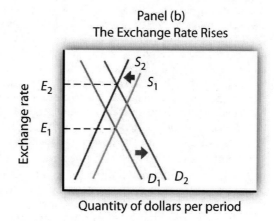

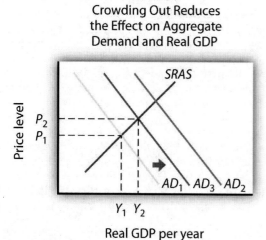

Crowding out reduces the effectiveness of any expansionary fiscal policy, whether it be an increase in government purchases, an increase in transfer payments, or a reduction in income taxes. Each of these policies increases the deficit and thus increases government borrowing. The supply of bonds increases, interest rates rise, investment falls, the exchange rate rises, and net exports fall.

Note, however, that it is private investment that is crowded out. The expansionary fiscal policy could take the form of an increase in the investment component of government purchases. As we have learned, some government purchases are for goods, such as office supplies, and services. But the government can also purchase investment items, such as roads and schools. In that case, government investment may be crowding out private investment.

The reverse of crowding out occurs with a contractionary fiscal policy—a cut in government purchases or transfer payments, or an increase in taxes. Such policies reduce the deficit (or increase the surplus) and thus reduce government borrowing, shifting the supply curve for bonds to the left. Interest rates drop, inducing a greater quantity of investment. Lower interest rates also reduce the demand for and increase the supply of dollars, lowering the exchange rate and boosting net exports. This phenomenon is known as "**crowding in.**"

> **crowding in**
>
> The tendency for a contractionary fiscal policy to increase other components of aggregate demand.

Crowding out and crowding in clearly weaken the impact of fiscal policy. An expansionary fiscal policy has less punch; a contractionary policy puts less of a damper on economic activity. Some economists argue that these forces are so powerful that a change in fiscal policy will have no effect on aggregate demand. Because empirical studies have been inconclusive, the extent of crowding out (and its reverse) remains a very controversial area of study.

Also, the fact that government deficits today may reduce the capital stock that would otherwise be available to future generations does not imply that such deficits are wrong. If, for example, the deficits are used to finance public sector investment, then the reduction in private capital provided to the future is offset by the increased provision of public sector capital. Future generations may have fewer office buildings but more schools.

3.3 Choice of Policy

Suppose Congress and the president agree that something needs to be done to close a recessionary gap. We have learned that fiscal policies that increase government purchases, reduce taxes, or increase transfer payments—or do a combination of these—all have the potential, theoretically, to raise real GDP. The government must decide which kind of fiscal policy to employ. Because the decision makers who determine fiscal policy are all elected politicians, the choice among the policy options available is an intensely political matter, often reflecting the ideology of the politicians.

For example, those who believe that government is too big would argue for tax cuts to close recessionary gaps and for spending cuts to close inflationary gaps. Those who believe that the private sector has failed to provide adequately a host of services that would benefit society, such as better education or public transportation systems, tend to advocate increases in government purchases to close recessionary gaps and tax increases to close inflationary gaps.

> **supply-side economics**
>
> The school of thought that promotes the use of fiscal policy to stimulate long-run aggregate supply.

Another area of contention comes from those who believe that fiscal policy should be constructed primarily so as to promote long-term growth. **Supply-side economics** is the school of thought that promotes the use of fiscal policy to stimulate long-run aggregate supply. Supply-side economists advocate reducing tax rates in order to encourage people to work more or more individuals to work and providing investment tax credits to stimulate capital formation.

While there is considerable debate over how strong the supply-side effects are in relation to the demand-side effects, such considerations may affect the choice of policies. Supply-siders tend to favor tax cuts over increases in government purchases or increases in transfer payments. President Reagan advocated tax cuts in 1981 on the basis of their supply-side effects. Coupled with increased defense spending in the early 1980s, fiscal policy under Mr. Reagan clearly stimulated aggregate demand by increasing both consumption and investment. Falling inflation and accelerated growth are signs that supply-side factors may also have been at work during that period. President George W. Bush's chief economic adviser, N. Gregory Mankiw, argued that the Bush tax cuts would encourage economic growth, a supply-side argument. Mr. Bush's next chief economic adviser, Ben Bernanke, who became the next chairman of the Federal Reserve Board in 2006, made a similar argument and urged that the Bush tax cuts be made permanent.

Finally, even when there is agreement to stimulate the economy, say through increasing government expenditures on highways, the *how* question remains. How should the expenditures be allocated? Specifically, which states should the highways run through? Each member of Congress has a political stake in the outcome. These types of considerations make the implementation lag particularly long for fiscal policy.

KEY TAKEAWAYS

- Discretionary fiscal policy involves the same kind of lags as monetary policy. However, the implementation lag in fiscal policy is likely to be more pronounced, while the impact lag is likely to be less pronounced.
- Expansionary fiscal policy may result in the crowding out of private investment and net exports, reducing the impact of the policy. Similarly, contractionary policy may "crowd in" additional investment and net exports, reducing the contractionary impact of the policy.
- Supply-side economics stresses the use of fiscal policy to stimulate economic growth. Advocates of supply-side economics generally favor tax cuts to stimulate economic growth.

TRY IT!

Do the following hypothetical situations tend to enhance or make more difficult the use of fiscal policy as a stabilization tool?

1. Better and more speedily available data on the state of the economy
2. A finding that private sector investment spending is not much affected by interest rate changes
3. A finding that the supply-side effects of a tax cut are substantial

Case in Point: Crowding Out in Canada

In an intriguing study, economist Baotai Wang examined the degree of crowding out of Canadian private investment as a result of government expenditures from 1961–2000. What made Professor Wang's analysis unusual was that he divided Canadian government expenditures into five categories: expenditures for health and education, expenditures for capital and infrastructure, expenditures for the protection of persons and property (which included defense spending), expenditures for debt services, and expenditures for government and social services.

Mr. Wang found that only government expenditures for capital and infrastructure crowded out private investment. While these expenditures reduced private investment, they represented increased public sector investment for things such as highways and ports.

Expenditures for health and education actually "crowded in" private sector investment. These expenditures, Mr. Wang argued, represented increases in human capital. Such increases complement returns on private sector investment and therefore increase it.

Mr. Wang found that Canadian government expenditures for debt service, the protection of persons and property, and for government and social services had no effect on private sector investment. He argued that expenditures for protection of persons and property may involve some crowding out, but that they also stimulated private investment by firms winning government contracts for defense purchases. The same explanation could be applied to government expenditures for government and social services. These also include an element of investment in human capital.

His results suggest that crowding out depends on the nature of spending done by the government. Some kinds of spending clearly did not crowd out private sector investment in Canada.

Source: Baotai Wang, "Effects of Government Expenditure on Private Investment: Canadian Empirical Evidence," *Empirical Economics* 30, no. 2 (September 2005): 493–504.

1. Data on the economy that are more accurate and more speedily available should enhance the use of fiscal policy by reducing the length of the recognition lag.

2. If private sector investment does not respond much to interest rate changes, then there will be less crowding out when expansionary policies are undertaken. That is, the rising interest rates that accompany expansionary fiscal policy will not reduce investment spending much, making the shift in the aggregate demand curve to the right greater than it would be otherwise. Also, the use of contractionary fiscal policy would be more effective, since the fall in interest rates would "invite in" less investment spending, making the shift in the aggregate demand curve to the left greater than it would otherwise be.

3. Large supply-side effects enhance the impact of tax cuts. For a given expansionary policy, without the supply-side effects, GDP would advance only to the point where the aggregate demand curve intersects the short-run aggregate supply curve. With the supply-side effects, both the short-run and long-run aggregate supply curves shift to the right. The intersection of the *AD* curve with the now increased short-run aggregate supply curve will be farther to the right than it would have been in the absence of the supply-side effects. The potential level of real GDP will also increase.

4. REVIEW AND PRACTICE

Summary

The government sector plays a major role in the economy. The spending, tax, and transfer policies of local, state, and federal agencies affect aggregate demand and aggregate supply and thus affect the level of real GDP and the price level. An expansionary policy tends to increase real GDP. Such a policy could be used to close a recessionary gap. A contractionary fiscal policy tends to reduce real GDP. A contractionary policy could be used to close an inflationary gap.

Government purchases of goods and services have a direct impact on aggregate demand. An increase in government purchases shifts the aggregate demand curve by the amount of the initial change in government purchases times the multiplier. Changes in personal income taxes or in the level of transfer payments affect disposable personal income. They change consumption, though initially by less than the amount of the change in taxes or transfers. They thus cause somewhat smaller shifts in the aggregate demand curve than do equal changes in government purchases.

There are several issues in the use of fiscal policies for stabilization purposes. They include lags associated with fiscal policy, crowding out, the choice of which fiscal policy tool to use, and the possible burdens of accumulating national debt.

CONCEPT PROBLEMS

1. What is the difference between government expenditures and government purchases? How do the two variables differ in terms of their effect on GDP?

2. Federally funded student aid programs generally reduce benefits by $1 for every $1 that recipients earn. Do such programs represent government purchases or transfer payments? Are they automatic stabilizers?

3. Crowding out reduces the degree to which a change in government purchases influences the level of economic activity. Is it a form of automatic stabilizer?

4. The Case in Point on fiscal policy before World War I and after World War II mentions the idea of policy-induced recessions. Explain how this notion relates to the difficulties discussed in the text of using discretionary policy to stabilize the economy.

5. Suppose an economy has an inflationary gap. How does the government's actual budget deficit or surplus compare to the deficit or surplus it would have at potential output?

6. Suppose the president were given the authority to increase or decrease federal spending by as much as $100 billion in order to stabilize economic activity. Do you think this would tend to make the economy more or less stable?

7. Suppose the government increases purchases in an economy with a recessionary gap. How would this policy affect bond prices, interest rates, investment, net exports, real GDP, and the price level? Show your results graphically.

8. Suppose the government cuts transfer payments in an economy with an inflationary gap. How would this policy affect bond prices, interest rates, investment, the exchange rate, net exports, real GDP, and the price level? Show your results graphically.

9. Suppose that at the same time the government undertakes expansionary fiscal policy, such as a cut in taxes, the Fed undertakes contractionary monetary policy. How would this policy affect bond prices, interest rates, investment, net exports, real GDP, and the price level? Show your results graphically.

10. Given the nature of the implementation lag discussed in the text, discuss possible measures that might reduce the lag.

NUMERICAL PROBLEMS

1. Look up the table on Federal Receipts and Outlays, by Major Category, in the most recent *Economic Report of the President* available in your library or on the Internet.

   a. Complete the following table:

Category	Total outlays	Percentage of total outlays
National defense		
International affairs		
Health		
Medicare		
Income security		
Social Security		
Net interest		
Other		

   b. Construct a pie chart showing the percentages of spending for each category in the total.

2. Look up the table on ownership of U.S. Treasury securities in the most recent *Economic Report of the President* available in your library or on the Internet.

   a. Make a pie chart showing the percentage owned by various groups in the earliest year shown in the table.

   b. Make a pie chart showing the percentage owned by various groups in the most recent year shown in the table.

   c. What are some of the major changes in ownership of U.S. government debt over the period?

3. Suppose a country has a national debt of $5,000 billion, a GDP of $10,000 billion, and a budget deficit of $100 billion.

   a. How much will its new national debt be?

   b. Compute its debt-GDP ratio.

   c. Suppose its GDP grows by 1% in the next year and the budget deficit is again $100 billion. Compute its new level of national debt and its new debt-GDP ratio.

4. Suppose a country's debt rises by 10% and its GDP rises by 12%.

   a. What happens to the debt-GDP ratio?

   b. Does the relative level of the initial values affect your answer?

5. The data below show a country's national debt and its prime lending rate.

Year	National debt (billions of $)	Lending rate (%)
1992	4,064	6.0
1993	4,411	6.0
1994	4,692	8.5
1995	4,973	8.7
1996	5,224	8.3
1997	5,413	8.5

   a. Plot the relationship between national debt and the lending rate.

   b. Based on your graph, does crowding out appear to be a problem?

6. Suppose a country increases government purchases by $100 billion. Suppose the multiplier is 1.5 and the economy's real GDP is $5,000 billion.

   a. In which direction will the aggregate demand curve shift and by how much?

   b. Explain using a graph why the change in real GDP is likely to be smaller than the shift in the aggregate demand curve.

7. Suppose a country decreases government purchases by $100 billion. Suppose the multiplier is 1.5 and the economy's real GDP is $5,000 billion.

   a. In which direction will the aggregate demand curve shift and by how much?
   b. Explain using a graph why the change in real GDP is likely to be smaller than the shift in the aggregate demand curve.

8. Suppose a country decreases income taxes by $100 billion, and this leads to an increase in consumption spending of $90 billion. Suppose the multiplier is 1.5 and the economy's real GDP is $5,000 billion.

   a. In which direction will the aggregate demand curve shift and by how much?
   b. Explain using a graph why the change in real GDP is likely to be smaller than the shift in the aggregate demand curve.

9. Suppose a country increases income taxes by $100 billion, and this leads to a decrease in consumption spending of $90 billion. Suppose the multiplier is 1.5 and the economy's real GDP is $5,000 billion.

   a. In which direction will the aggregate demand curve shift and by how much?
   b. Explain using a graph why the change in real GDP is likely to be smaller than the shift in the aggregate demand curve.

10. Suppose a country institutes an investment tax credit, and this leads to an increase in investment spending of $100 billion. Suppose the multiplier is 1.5 and the economy's real GDP is $5,000 billion.

    a. In which direction will the aggregate demand curve shift and by how much?
    b. Explain using a graph why the change in real GDP is likely to be smaller than the shift in the aggregate demand curve.

11. Suppose a country repeals an investment tax credit, and this leads to a decrease in investment spending of $100 billion. Suppose the multiplier is 1.5 and the economy's real GDP is $5,000 billion.

    a. In which direction will the aggregate demand curve shift and by how much?
    b. Explain using a graph why the change in real GDP is likely to be smaller than the shift in the aggregate demand curve.

12. Explain why the shifts in the aggregate demand curves in questions 7 through 11 above are the same or different in absolute value.

ENDNOTES

1. Barack Obama, Weekly Address of the President to the Nation, February 14, 2009, available at http://www.whitehouse.gov/blog/09/02/14/A-major-milestone/.

2. Investment also affects the long-run aggregate supply curve, since a change in the capital stock changes the potential level of real GDP. We examined this earlier in the chapter on economic growth.

3. A change in tax rates will change the value of the multiplier. The reason is explained in another chapter.

4. Stephen Power and Neil King, Jr., "Next Challenge on Stimulus: Spending All That Money," *Wall Street Journal*, February 13, 2009, p. A1.

CHAPTER 13

Consumption and the Aggregate Expenditures Model

START UP: A DISMAL 2008 FOR RETAILERS

2008 turned out to be the worst holiday shopping season in decades. Why? U.S. consumers were battered from many directions. Housing prices had fallen nearly 20% over the year. The stock market had fallen over 40%. Interest rates were falling, but credit was extremely hard to come by. By December, consumer confidence hit an all-time low amid concerns of rising unemployment. Cutting back seemed like the best defense for weathering this tough environment.

Consumption accounts for the bulk of aggregate demand in the United States and in other countries. In this chapter, we will examine the determinants of consumption and introduce a new model, the aggregate expenditures model, which will give insights into the aggregate demand curve. Any change in aggregate demand causes a change in income, and a change in income causes a change in consumption—which changes aggregate demand and thus income and thus consumption. The aggregate expenditures model will help us to unravel the important relationship between consumption and real GDP.

1. DETERMINING THE LEVEL OF CONSUMPTION

LEARNING OBJECTIVES

1. Explain and graph the consumption function and the saving function, explain what the slopes of these curves represent, and explain how the two are related to each other.
2. Compare the current income hypothesis with the permanent income hypothesis, and use each to predict the effect that temporary versus permanent changes in income will have on consumption.
3. Discuss two factors that can cause the consumption function to shift upward or downward.

J. R. McCulloch, an economist of the early nineteenth century, wrote, "Consumption … is, in fact, the object of industry."[1] Goods and services are produced so that people can use them. The factors that determine consumption thus determine how successful an economy is in fulfilling its ultimate purpose: providing goods and services for people. So, consumption is not just important because it is such a large component of economic activity. It is important because, as McCulloch said, consumption is at the heart of the economy's fundamental purpose.

1.1 Consumption and Disposable Personal Income

It seems reasonable to expect that consumption spending by households will be closely related to their disposable personal income, which equals the income households receive less the taxes they pay. Note that disposable personal income and GDP are not the same thing. GDP is a measure of total income; disposable personal income is the income households have available to spend during a specified period.

Real values of disposable personal income and consumption per year from 1960 through 2010 are plotted in Figure 13.1. The data suggest that consumption generally changes in the same direction as does disposable personal income.

The relationship between consumption and disposable personal income is called the **consumption function**. It can be represented algebraically as an equation, as a schedule in a table, or as a curve on a graph.

FIGURE 13.1 The Relationship Between Consumption and Disposable Personal Income, 1960–2010

Plots of consumption and disposable personal income over time suggest that consumption increases as disposable personal income increases.

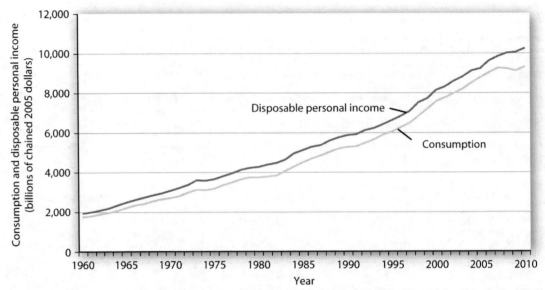

Source: U. S. Department of Commerce, Bureau of Economic Analysis, NIPA Tables 1.16 and 2.1 (November 23, 2010 revision; Data are through 3rd quarter 2010).

Figure 13.2 illustrates the consumption function. The relationship between consumption and disposable personal income that we encountered in Figure 13.1 is evident in the table and in the curve: consumption in any period increases as disposable personal income increases in that period. The slope of the consumption function tells us by how much. Consider points C and D. When disposable personal income (Y_d) rises by $500 billion, consumption rises by $400 billion. More generally, the slope equals the change in consumption divided by the change in disposable personal income. The ratio of the change in consumption (ΔC) to the change in disposable personal income (ΔY_d) is the **marginal propensity to consume** (*MPC*). The Greek letter delta (Δ) is used to denote "change in."

EQUATION 13.1

$$MPC = \frac{\Delta C}{\Delta Y_d}$$

In this case, the marginal propensity to consume equals $400/$500 = 0.8. It can be interpreted as the fraction of an extra $1 of disposable personal income that people spend on consumption. Thus, if a person with an *MPC* of 0.8 received an extra $1,000 of disposable personal income, that person's consumption would rise by $0.80 for each extra $1 of disposable personal income, or $800.

We can also express the consumption function as an equation

EQUATION 13.2

$$C = \$300 \text{ billion} + 0.8 Y_d$$

FIGURE 13.2 Plotting a Consumption Function

The consumption function relates consumption C to disposable personal income Y_d. The equation for the consumption function shown here in tabular and graphical form is $C = \$300$ billion $+ 0.8Y_d$.

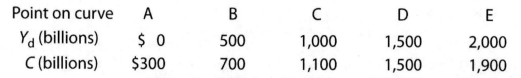

Point on curve	A	B	C	D	E
Y_d (billions)	$ 0	500	1,000	1,500	2,000
C (billions)	$300	700	1,100	1,500	1,900

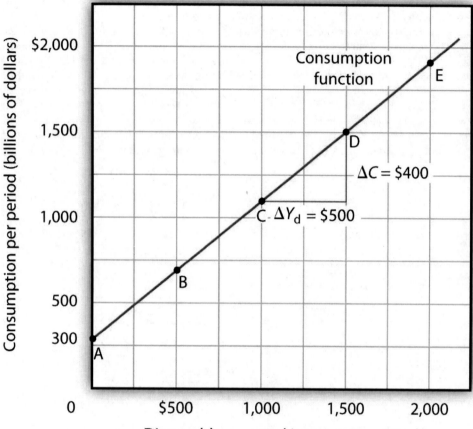

Heads Up!

It is important to note carefully the definition of the marginal propensity to consume. It is the change in consumption divided by the change in disposable personal income. It is not the level of consumption divided by the level of disposable personal income. Using Equation 13.2, at a level of disposable personal income of $500 billion, for example, the level of consumption will be $700 billion so that the ratio of consumption to disposable personal income will be 1.4, while the marginal propensity to consume remains 0.8. The marginal propensity to consume is, as its name implies, a marginal concept. It tells us what will happen to an additional dollar of personal disposable income.

Notice from the curve in Figure 13.2 that when disposable personal income equals 0, consumption is $300 billion. The vertical intercept of the consumption function is thus $300 billion. Then, for every $500 billion increase in disposable personal income, consumption rises by $400 billion. Because the consumption function in our example is linear, its slope is the same between any two points. In this case, the slope of the consumption function, which is the same as the marginal propensity to consume, is 0.8 all along its length.

We can use the consumption function to show the relationship between personal saving and disposable personal income. **Personal saving** is disposable personal income not spent on consumption during a particular period; the value of personal saving for any period is found by subtracting consumption from disposable personal income for that period:

EQUATION 13.3

$$\text{Personal saving} = \text{disposable personal income} - \text{consumption}$$

The **saving function** relates personal saving in any period to disposable personal income in that period. Personal saving is not the only form of saving—firms and government agencies may save as well. In this chapter, however, our focus is on the choice households make between using disposable personal income for consumption or for personal saving.

Figure 13.3 shows how the consumption function and the saving function are related. Personal saving is calculated by subtracting values for consumption from values for disposable personal income, as shown in the table. The values for personal saving are then plotted in the graph. Notice that a 45-degree line has been added to the graph. At every point on the 45-degree line, the value on the vertical axis equals that on the horizontal axis. The consumption function intersects the 45-degree line at an income of $1,500 billion (point D). At this point, consumption equals disposable personal income and personal saving equals 0 (point D' on the graph of personal saving). Using the graph to find personal saving at other levels of disposable personal income, we subtract the value of consumption, given by the consumption function, from disposable personal income, given by the 45-degree line.

FIGURE 13.3   Consumption and Personal Saving

Personal saving equals disposable personal income minus consumption. The table gives hypothetical values for these variables. The consumption function is plotted in the upper part of the graph. At points along the 45-degree line, the values on the two axes are equal; we can measure personal saving as the distance between the 45-degree line and consumption. The curve of the saving function is in the lower portion of the graph.

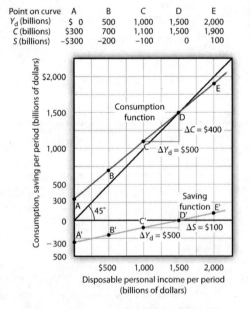

Point on curve	A	B	C	D	E
Y_d (billions)	$ 0	500	1,000	1,500	2,000
C (billions)	$300	700	1,100	1,500	1,900
S (billions)	–$300	–200	–100	0	100

At a disposable personal income of $2,000 billion, for example, consumption is $1,900 billion (point E). Personal saving equals $100 billion (point E')—the vertical distance between the 45-degree line and the consumption function. At an income of $500 billion, consumption totals $700 billion (point B). The consumption function lies above the 45-degree line at this point; personal saving is –$200 billion (point B'). A negative value for saving means that consumption exceeds disposable personal income; it must have come from saving accumulated in the past, from selling assets, or from borrowing.

Notice that for every $500 billion increase in disposable personal income, personal saving rises by $100 billion. Consider points C' and D' in Figure 13.3. When disposable personal income rises by $500 billion, personal saving rises by $100 billion. More generally, the slope of the saving function equals the change in personal saving divided by the change in disposable personal income. The ratio of the change in personal saving (ΔS) to the change in disposable personal income (ΔY_d) is the **marginal propensity to save** (*MPS*).

EQUATION 13.4

$$MPS = \frac{\Delta S}{\Delta Y_d}$$

In this case, the marginal propensity to save equals $100/$500 = 0.2. It can be interpreted as the fraction of an extra $1 of disposable personal income that people save. Thus, if a person with an *MPS* of 0.2 received an extra $1,000 of disposable personal income, that person's saving would rise by $0.20 for each extra $1 of disposable personal income, or $200. Since people have only two choices of what to do with additional disposable personal income—that is, they can use it either for consumption or for personal saving—the fraction of disposable personal income that people consume (*MPC*) plus the fraction of disposable personal income that people save (*MPS*) must add to 1:

EQUATION 13.5

$$MPC + MPS = 1$$

1.2   Current versus Permanent Income

The discussion so far has related consumption in a particular period to income in that same period. The **current income hypothesis** holds that consumption in any one period depends on income during that period, or current income.

Although it seems obvious that consumption should be related to disposable personal income, it is not so obvious that consumers base their consumption in any one period on the income they receive during that period. In buying a new car, for example, consumers might base their decision not only on their current income but on the income they expect to receive during the three or four years they expect to be making payments on the car. Parents who purchase a college education for their children might base their decision on their own expected lifetime income.

Indeed, it seems likely that virtually all consumption choices could be affected by expectations of income over a very long period. One reason people save is to provide funds to live on during their retirement years. Another is to build an estate they can leave to their heirs through bequests. The amount people save for their retirement or for bequests depends on the income they expect to receive for the rest of their lives. For these and other reasons, then, personal saving (and thus consumption) in any one year is influenced by permanent income. **Permanent income** is the average annual income people expect to receive for the rest of their lives.

People who have the same current income but different permanent incomes might reach very different saving decisions. Someone with a relatively low current income but a high permanent income (a college student planning to go to medical school, for example) might save little or nothing now, expecting to save for retirement and for bequests later. A person with the same low income but no expectation of higher income later might try to save some money now to provide for retirement or bequests later. Because a decision to save a certain amount determines how much will be available for consumption, consumption decisions can also be affected by expected lifetime income. Thus, an alternative approach to explaining consumption behavior is the **permanent income hypothesis**, which assumes that consumption in any period depends on permanent income. An important implication of the permanent income hypothesis is that a change in income regarded as temporary will not affect consumption much, since it will have little effect on average lifetime income; a change regarded as permanent will have an effect. The current income hypothesis, though, predicts that it does not matter whether consumers view a change in disposable personal income as permanent or temporary; they will move along the consumption function and change consumption accordingly.

The question of whether permanent or current income is a determinant of consumption arose in 1992 when President George H. W. Bush ordered a change in the withholding rate for personal income taxes. Workers have a fraction of their paychecks withheld for taxes each pay period; Mr. Bush directed that this fraction be reduced in 1992. The change in the withholding rate did not change income tax rates; by withholding less in 1992, taxpayers would either receive smaller refund checks in 1993 or owe more taxes. The change thus left taxpayers' permanent income unaffected.

President Bush's measure was designed to increase aggregate demand and close the recessionary gap created by the 1990–1991 recession. Economists who subscribed to the permanent income hypothesis predicted that the change would not have any effect on consumption. Those who subscribed to the current income hypothesis predicted that the measure would boost consumption substantially in 1992. A survey of households taken during this period suggested that households planned to spend about 43% of the temporary increase in disposable personal income produced by the withholding experiment.[2] That is considerably less than would be predicted by the current income hypothesis, but more than the zero change predicted by the permanent income hypothesis. This result, together with

current income hypothesis

Consumption in any one period depends on income during that period.

permanent income

The average annual income people expect to receive for the rest of their lives.

permanent income hypothesis

Consumption in any period depends on permanent income.

related evidence, suggests that temporary changes in income can affect consumption, but that changes regarded as permanent will have a much stronger impact.

Many of the tax cuts passed during the administration of President George W. Bush are set to expire in 2010. The proposal to make these tax cuts permanent is aimed toward having a stronger impact on consumption, since tax cuts regarded as permanent have larger effects than do changes regarded as temporary.

1.3   Other Determinants of Consumption

The consumption function graphed in Figure 13.2 and Figure 13.3 relates consumption spending to the level of disposable personal income. Changes in disposable personal income cause movements *along* this curve; they do not shift the curve. The curve shifts when other determinants of consumption change. Examples of changes that could shift the consumption function are changes in real wealth and changes in expectations. Figure 13.4 illustrates how these changes can cause shifts in the curve.

FIGURE 13.4 Shifts in the Consumption Function

An increase in the level of consumption at each level of disposable personal income shifts the consumption function upward in Panel (a). Among the events that would shift the curve upward are an increase in real wealth and an increase in consumer confidence. A reduction in the level of consumption at each level of disposable personal income shifts the curve downward in Panel (b). The events that could shift the curve downward include a reduction in real wealth and a decline in consumer confidence.

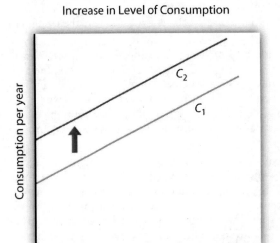

Panel (a)
Increase in Level of Consumption

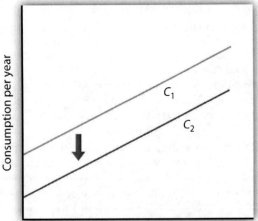

Panel (b)
Decrease in Level of Consumption

Changes in Real Wealth

An increase in stock and bond prices, for example, would make holders of these assets wealthier, and they would be likely to increase their consumption. An increase in real wealth shifts the consumption function upward, as illustrated in Panel (a) of Figure 13.4. A reduction in real wealth shifts it downward, as shown in Panel (b).

A change in the price level changes real wealth. We learned in an earlier chapter that the relationship among the price level, real wealth, and consumption is called the *wealth effect*. A reduction in the price level increases real wealth and shifts the consumption function upward, as shown in Panel (a). An increase in the price level shifts the curve downward, as shown in Panel (b).

Changes in Expectations

Consumers are likely to be more willing to spend money when they are optimistic about the future. Surveyors attempt to gauge this optimism using "consumer confidence" surveys that ask respondents to report whether they are optimistic or pessimistic about their own economic situation and about the prospects for the economy as a whole. An increase in consumer optimism tends to shift the consumption function upward as in Panel (a) of Figure 13.4; an increase in pessimism tends to shift it downward as in Panel (b). The sharp reduction in consumer confidence in 2008 and early in 2009 contributed to a downward shift in the consumption function and thus to the severity of the recession.

The relationship between consumption and consumer expectations concerning future economic conditions tends to be a form of self-fulfilling prophecy. If consumers expect economic conditions to worsen, they will cut their consumption—and economic conditions will worsen! Political leaders often try to persuade people that economic prospects are good. In part, such efforts are an attempt to increase economic activity by boosting consumption.

KEY TAKEAWAYS

- Consumption is closely related to disposable personal income and is represented by the consumption function, which can be presented in a table, in a graph, or in an equation.
- Personal saving is disposable personal income not spent on consumption.
- The marginal propensity to consume is $MPC = \Delta C/\Delta Y_d$ and the marginal propensity to save is $MPS = \Delta S/\Delta Y_d$. The sum of the MPC and MPS is 1.
- The current income hypothesis holds that consumption is a function of current disposable personal income, whereas the permanent income hypothesis holds that consumption is a function of permanent income, which is the income households expect to receive annually during their lifetime. The permanent income hypothesis predicts that a temporary change in income will have a smaller effect on consumption than is predicted by the current income hypothesis.
- Other factors that affect consumption include real wealth and expectations.

TRY IT!

For each of the following events, draw a curve representing the consumption function and show how the event would affect the curve.

1. A sharp increase in stock prices increases the real wealth of most households.
2. Consumers decide that a recession is ahead and that their incomes are likely to fall.
3. The price level falls.

Case in Point: Consumption and the Tax Rebate of 2001

The first round of the Bush tax cuts was passed in 2001. Democrats in Congress insisted on a rebate aimed at stimulating consumption. In the summer of 2001, rebates of $300 per single taxpayer and of $600 for married couples were distributed. The Department of Treasury reported that 92 million people received the rebates. While the rebates were intended to stimulate consumption, the extent to which the tax rebates stimulated consumption, especially during the recession, is an empirical question.

It is difficult to analyze the impact of a tax rebate that is a single event experienced by all households at the same time. If spending does change at that moment, is it because of the tax rebate or because of some other event that occurred at that time?

Fortunately for researchers Sumit Agarwal, Chunlin Liu, and Nicholas Souleles, using data from credit card accounts, the 2001 tax rebate checks were distributed over 10 successive weeks from July to September of 2001. The timing of receipt was random, since it was based on the next-to-last digit of one's Social Security number, and taxpayers were informed well in advance that the checks were coming. The researchers found that consumers initially saved much of their rebates, by paying down their credit card debts, but over a nine-month period, spending increased to about 40% of the rebate. They also found that consumers who were most liquidity constrained (for example, close to their credit card debt limits) spent more than consumers who were less constrained.

The researchers thus conclude that their findings do not support the permanent income hypothesis, since consumers responded to spending based on when they received their checks and because the results indicate that consumers do respond to what they call "lumpy" changes in income, such as those generated by a tax rebate. In other words, current income does seem to matter.

Two other studies of the 2001 tax rebate reached somewhat different conclusions. Using survey data, researchers Matthew D. Shapiro and Joel Slemrod estimated an *MPC* of about one-third. They note that this low increased spending is particularly surprising, since the rebate was part of a general tax cut that was expected to last a long time. At the other end, David S. Johnson, Jonathan A. Parker, and Nicholas S. Souleles, using yet another data set, found that looking over a six-month period, the *MPC* was about two-thirds. So, while there is disagreement on the size of the *MPC*, all conclude that the impact was non-negligible.

Sources: *Sumit Agarwal, Chunlin Liu, and Nicholas S. Souleles, "The Reaction of Consumer Spending and Debt to Tax Rebates—Evidence from Consumer Credit Data," NBER Working Paper No. 13694, December 2007; David S. Johnson, Jonathan A. Parker, and Nicholas S. Souleles, "Household Expenditure and the Income Tax Rebates of 2001," American Economic Review 96, no. 5 (December 2006): 1589–1610; Matthew D. Shapiro and Joel Slemrod, "Consumer Response to Tax Rebates," American Economic Review 93, no. 1 (March 2003): 381–96; and Matthew D. Shapiro and Joel Slemrod, "Did the 2001 Rebate Stimulate Spending? Evidence from Taxpayer Surveys," NBER Tax Policy & the Economy 17, no. 1 (2003): 83–109.*

ANSWERS TO TRY IT! PROBLEMS

1. A sharp increase in stock prices makes people wealthier and shifts the consumption function upward, as in Panel (a) of Figure 13.4.

2. This would be reported as a reduction in consumer confidence. Consumers are likely to respond by reducing their purchases, particularly of durable items such as cars and washing machines. The consumption function will shift downward, as in Panel (b) of Figure 13.4.

3. A reduction in the price level increases real wealth and thus boosts consumption. The consumption function will shift upward, as in Panel (a) of Figure 13.4.

---

2. THE AGGREGATE EXPENDITURES MODEL

LEARNING OBJECTIVES

1. **Explain and illustrate the aggregate expenditures model and the concept of equilibrium real GDP.**

2. **Distinguish between autonomous and induced aggregate expenditures and explain why a change in autonomous expenditures leads to a multiplied change in equilibrium real GDP.**

3. **Discuss how adding taxes, government purchases, and net exports to a simplified aggregate expenditures model affects the multiplier and hence the impact on real GDP that arises from an initial change in autonomous expenditures.**

aggregate expenditures model

Model that relates aggregate expenditures to the level of real GDP.

aggregate expenditures

The sum of planned levels of consumption, investment, government purchases, and net exports at a given price level.

The consumption function relates the level of consumption in a period to the level of disposable personal income in that period. In this section, we incorporate other components of aggregate demand: investment, government purchases, and net exports. In doing so, we shall develop a new model of the determination of equilibrium real GDP, the **aggregate expenditures model**. This model relates **aggregate expenditures**, which equal the sum of planned levels of consumption, investment, government purchases, and net exports at a given price level, to the level of real GDP. We shall see that people, firms, and government agencies may not always spend what they had planned to spend. If so, then actual real GDP will not be the same as aggregate expenditures, and the economy will not be at the equilibrium level of real GDP.

One purpose of examining the aggregate expenditures model is to gain a deeper understanding of the "ripple effects" from a change in one or more components of aggregate demand. As we saw in the chapter that introduced the aggregate demand and aggregate supply model, a change in investment, government purchases, or net exports leads to greater production; this creates additional income for households, which induces additional consumption, leading to more production, more income, more consumption, and so on. The aggregate expenditures model provides a context within which this series of ripple effects can be better understood. A second reason for introducing the model is that we can use it to derive the aggregate demand curve for the model of aggregate demand and aggregate supply.

To see how the aggregate expenditures model works, we begin with a very simplified model in which there is neither a government sector nor a foreign sector. Then we use the findings based on this simplified model to build a more realistic model. The equations for the simplified economy are easier to work with, and we can readily apply the conclusions reached from analyzing a simplified economy to draw conclusions about a more realistic one.

2.1   The Aggregate Expenditures Model: A Simplified View

To develop a simple model, we assume that there are only two components of aggregate expenditures: consumption and investment. In the chapter on measuring total output and income, we learned that real gross domestic product and real gross domestic income are the same thing. With no government or foreign sector, gross domestic income in this economy and disposable personal income would be nearly the same. To simplify further, we will assume that depreciation and undistributed corporate profits (retained earnings) are zero. Thus, for this example, we assume that disposable personal income and real GDP are identical.

Finally, we shall also assume that the only component of aggregate expenditures that may not be at the planned level is investment. Firms determine a level of investment they intend to make in each period. The level of investment firms intend to make in a period is called **planned investment**. Some investment is unplanned. Suppose, for example, that firms produce and expect to sell more goods during a period than they actually sell. The unsold goods will be added to the firms' inventories, and they will thus be counted as part of investment. **Unplanned investment** is investment during a period that firms did not intend to make. It is also possible that firms may sell more than they had expected. In this case, inventories will fall below what firms expected, in which case, unplanned investment would be negative. Investment during a period equals the sum of planned investment (I_P) and unplanned investment (I_U).

> **planned investment**
>
> The level of investment firms intend to make in a period.
>
> **unplanned investment**
>
> Investment during a period that firms did not intend to make.

EQUATION 13.6

$$I = I_P + I_U$$

We shall find that planned and unplanned investment play key roles in the aggregate expenditures model.

Autonomous and Induced Aggregate Expenditures

Economists distinguish two types of expenditures. Expenditures that do not vary with the level of real GDP are called **autonomous aggregate expenditures**. In our example, we assume that planned investment expenditures are autonomous. Expenditures that vary with real GDP are called **induced aggregate expenditures**. Consumption spending that rises with real GDP is an example of an induced aggregate expenditure. Figure 13.6 illustrates the difference between autonomous and induced aggregate expenditures. With real GDP on the horizontal axis and aggregate expenditures on the vertical axis, autonomous aggregate expenditures are shown as a horizontal line in Panel (a). A curve showing induced aggregate expenditures has a slope greater than zero; the value of an induced aggregate expenditure changes with changes in real GDP. Panel (b) shows induced aggregate expenditures that are positively related to real GDP.

> **autonomous aggregate expenditures**
>
> Expenditures that do not vary with the level of real GDP.
>
> **induced aggregate expenditures**
>
> Expenditures that vary with real GDP.

FIGURE 13.6 Autonomous and Induced Aggregate Expenditures

Autonomous aggregate expenditures do not vary with the level of real GDP; induced aggregate expenditures do. Autonomous aggregate expenditures are shown by the horizontal line in Panel (a). Induced aggregate expenditures vary with real GDP, as in Panel (b).

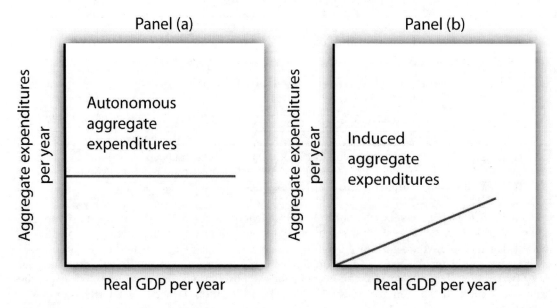

Autonomous and Induced Consumption

The concept of the marginal propensity to consume suggests that consumption contains induced aggregate expenditures; an increase in real GDP raises consumption. But consumption contains an autonomous component as well. The level of consumption at the intersection of the consumption function and the vertical axis is regarded as autonomous consumption; this level of spending would occur regardless of the level of real GDP.

Consider the consumption function we used in deriving the schedule and curve illustrated in Figure 13.2:

$$C = \$300 \text{ billion} + 0.8Y$$

We can omit the subscript on disposable personal income because of the simplifications we have made in this section, and the symbol Y can be thought of as representing both disposable personal income and GDP. Because we assume that the price level in the aggregate expenditures model is constant, GDP equals real GDP. At every level of real GDP, consumption includes $300 billion in autonomous aggregate expenditures. It will also contain expenditures "induced" by the level of real GDP. At a level of real GDP of $2,000 billion, for example, consumption equals $1,900 billion: $300 billion in autonomous aggregate expenditures and $1,600 billion in consumption induced by the $2,000 billion level of real GDP.

Figure 13.7 illustrates these two components of consumption. Autonomous consumption, C_a, which is always $300 billion, is shown in Panel (a); its equation is

EQUATION 13.7

$$C_a = \$300 \text{ billion}$$

Induced consumption C_i is shown in Panel (b); its equation is

EQUATION 13.8

$$C_i = 0.8Y$$

The consumption function is given by the sum of Equation 13.7 and Equation 13.8; it is shown in Panel (c) of Figure 13.7. It is the same as the equation $C = \$300$ billion $+ 0.8Y_d$, since in this simple example, Y and Y_d are the same.

FIGURE 13.7 Autonomous and Induced Consumption

Consumption has an autonomous component and an induced component. In Panel (a), autonomous consumption C_a equals $300 billion at every level of real GDP. Panel (b) shows induced consumption C_i. Total consumption C is shown in Panel (c).

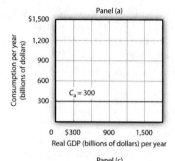
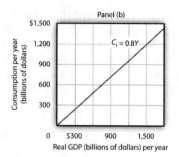
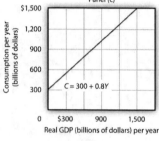

Plotting the Aggregate Expenditures Curve

In this simplified economy, investment is the only other component of aggregate expenditures. We shall assume that investment is autonomous and that firms plan to invest $1,100 billion per year.

EQUATION 13.9

$$I_P = \$1,100 \text{ billion}$$

The level of planned investment is unaffected by the level of real GDP.

Aggregate expenditures equal the sum of consumption C and planned investment I_P. The **aggregate expenditures function** is the relationship of aggregate expenditures to the value of real GDP. It can be represented with an equation, as a table, or as a curve.

We begin with the definition of aggregate expenditures AE when there is no government or foreign sector:

EQUATION 13.10

$$AE = C + I_P$$

Substituting the information from above on consumption and planned investment yields (throughout this discussion all values are in billions of base-year dollars)

$$AE = \$300 + 0.8Y + \$1,100$$

or

EQUATION 13.11

$$AE = \$1,400 + 0.8Y$$

Equation 13.11 is the algebraic representation of the aggregate expenditures function. We shall use this equation to determine the equilibrium level of real GDP in the aggregate expenditures model. It is important to keep in mind that aggregate expenditures measure total planned spending at each level of real GDP (for any given price level). Real GDP is total production. Aggregate expenditures and real GDP need not be equal, and indeed will not be equal except when the economy is operating at its equilibrium level, as we will see in the next section.

In Equation 13.11, the autonomous component of aggregate expenditures is $1,400 billion, and the induced component is $0.8Y$. We shall plot this aggregate expenditures function. To do so, we arbitrarily select various levels of real GDP and then use Equation 13.10 to compute aggregate expenditures at

aggregate expenditures function

The relationship of aggregate expenditures to the value of real GDP.

each level. At a level of real GDP of $6,000 billion, for example, aggregate expenditures equal $6,200 billion:

$$AE = \$1,400 + 0.8(\$6,000) = \$6,200$$

The table in Figure 13.8 shows the values of aggregate expenditures at various levels of real GDP. Based on these values, we plot the aggregate expenditures curve. To obtain each value for aggregate expenditures, we simply insert the corresponding value for real GDP into Equation 13.11. The value at which the aggregate expenditures curve intersects the vertical axis corresponds to the level of autonomous aggregate expenditures. In our example, autonomous aggregate expenditures equal $1,400 billion. That figure includes $1,100 billion in planned investment, which is assumed to be autonomous, and $300 billion in autonomous consumption expenditure.

FIGURE 13.8   Plotting the Aggregate Expenditures Curve

Values for aggregate expenditures *AE* are computed by inserting values for real GDP into Equation 13.10; these are given in the aggregate expenditures schedule. The point at which the aggregate expenditures curve intersects the vertical axis is the value of autonomous aggregate expenditures, here $1,400 billion. The slope of this aggregate expenditures curve is 0.8.

Point on curve	A	B	C	D	E	F
Y (billions)	$0	2,000	4,000	6,000	8,000	10,000
AE (billions)	$1,400	3,000	4,600	6,200	7,800	9,400

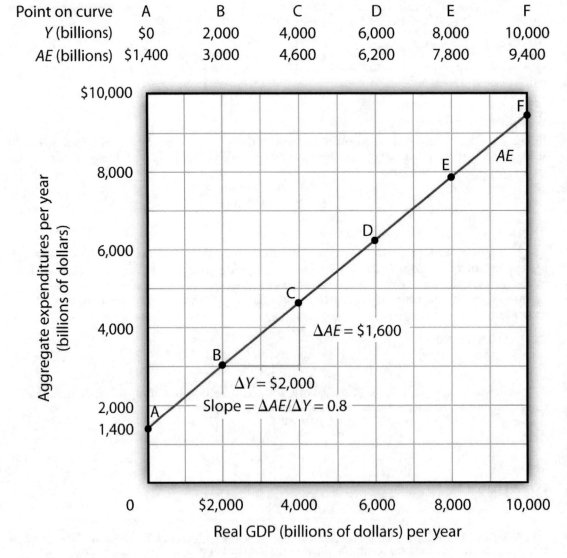

The Slope of the Aggregate Expenditures Curve

The slope of the aggregate expenditures curve, given by the change in aggregate expenditures divided by the change in real GDP between any two points, measures the additional expenditures induced by increases in real GDP. The slope for the aggregate expenditures curve in Figure 13.8 is shown for points B and C: it is 0.8.

In Figure 13.8, the slope of the aggregate expenditures curve equals the marginal propensity to consume. This is because we have assumed that the only other expenditure, planned investment, is autonomous and that real GDP and disposable personal income are identical. Changes in real GDP thus affect only consumption in this simplified economy.

Equilibrium in the Aggregate Expenditures Model

Real GDP is a measure of the total output of firms. Aggregate expenditures equal total planned spending on that output. Equilibrium in the model occurs where aggregate expenditures in some period equal real GDP in that period. One way to think about equilibrium is to recognize that firms, except for some inventory that they plan to hold, produce goods and services with the intention of selling them. Aggregate expenditures consist of what people, firms, and government agencies plan to spend. If the economy is at its equilibrium real GDP, then firms are selling what they plan to sell (that is, there are no unplanned changes in inventories).

Figure 13.9 illustrates the concept of equilibrium in the aggregate expenditures model. A 45-degree line connects all the points at which the values on the two axes, representing aggregate expenditures and real GDP, are equal. Equilibrium must occur at some point along this 45-degree line. The point at which the aggregate expenditures curve crosses the 45-degree line is the equilibrium real GDP, here achieved at a real GDP of $7,000 billion.

FIGURE 13.9 Determining Equilibrium in the Aggregate Expenditures Model

The 45-degree line shows all the points at which aggregate expenditures *AE* equal real GDP, as required for equilibrium. The equilibrium solution occurs where the *AE* curve crosses the 45-degree line, at a real GDP of $7,000 billion.

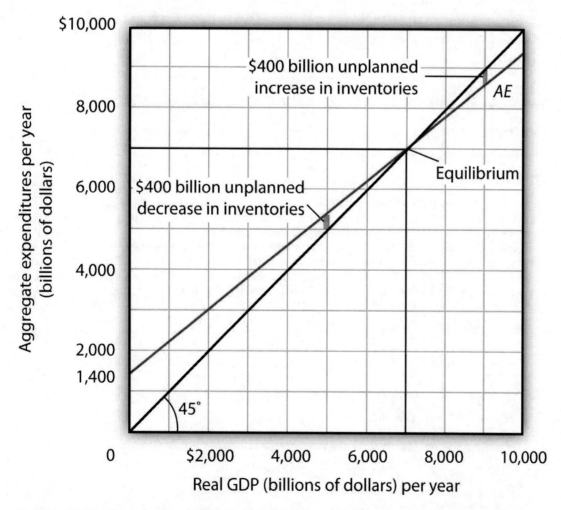

Equation 13.11 tells us that at a real GDP of $7,000 billion, the sum of consumption and planned investment is $7,000 billion—precisely the level of output firms produced. At that level of output, firms sell what they planned to sell and keep inventories that they planned to keep. A real GDP of $7,000 billion represents equilibrium in the sense that it generates an equal level of aggregate expenditures.

If firms were to produce a real GDP greater than $7,000 billion per year, aggregate expenditures would fall short of real GDP. At a level of real GDP of $9,000 billion per year, for example, aggregate expenditures equal $8,600 billion. Firms would be left with $400 billion worth of goods they intended to sell but did not. Their actual level of investment would be $400 billion greater than their planned level of investment. With those unsold goods on hand (that is, with an unplanned increase in inventories), firms would be likely to cut their output, moving the economy toward its equilibrium GDP of $7,000 billion. If firms were to produce $5,000 billion, aggregate expenditures would be $5,400 billion. Consumers and firms would demand more than was produced; firms would respond by reducing their inventories below the planned level (that is, there would be an unplanned decrease in inventories) and increasing their output in subsequent periods, again moving the economy toward its equilibrium real GDP of $7,000 billion. Figure 13.10 shows possible levels of real GDP in the economy for the aggregate expenditures function illustrated in Figure 13.9. It shows the level of aggregate expenditures at various levels of real GDP and the direction in which real GDP will change whenever AE does not equal real GDP. At any level of real GDP other than the equilibrium level, there is unplanned investment.

FIGURE 13.10 Adjusting to Equilibrium Real GDP

Each level of real GDP will result in a particular amount of aggregate expenditures. If aggregate expenditures are less than the level of real GDP, firms will reduce their output and real GDP will fall. If aggregate expenditures exceed real GDP, then firms will increase their output and real GDP will rise. If aggregate expenditures equal real GDP, then firms will leave their output unchanged; we have achieved equilibrium in the aggregate expenditures model. At equilibrium, there is no unplanned investment. Here, that occurs at a real GDP of $7,000 billion.

If real GDP is	Consumption expenditures will be	Planned investment will be	Aggregate expenditures will equal	Unplanned investment will be	Real GDP will
$9,000	$7,500	$1,100	$8,600	$400	Fall ↓
8,000	6,700	1,100	7,800	200	Fall ↓
7,000	5,900	1,100	7,000	0	Remain unchanged
6,000	5,100	1,100	6,200	−200	Rise ↑
5,000	4,300	1,100	5,400	−400	Rise ↑

Changes in Aggregate Expenditures: The Multiplier

In the aggregate expenditures model, equilibrium is found at the level of real GDP at which the aggregate expenditures curve crosses the 45-degree line. It follows that a shift in the curve will change equilibrium real GDP. Here we will examine the magnitude of such changes.

Figure 13.11 begins with the aggregate expenditures curve shown in Figure 13.9. Now suppose that planned investment increases from the original value of $1,100 billion to a new value of $1,400 billion—an increase of $300 billion. This increase in planned investment shifts the aggregate expenditures curve upward by $300 billion, all other things unchanged. Notice, however, that the new aggregate expenditures curve intersects the 45-degree line at a real GDP of $8,500 billion. The $300 billion increase in planned investment has produced an increase in equilibrium real GDP of $1,500 billion.

FIGURE 13.11   A Change in Autonomous Aggregate Expenditures Changes Equilibrium Real GDP

An increase of $300 billion in planned investment raises the aggregate expenditures curve by $300 billion. The $300 billion increase in planned investment results in an increase in equilibrium real GDP of $1,500 billion.

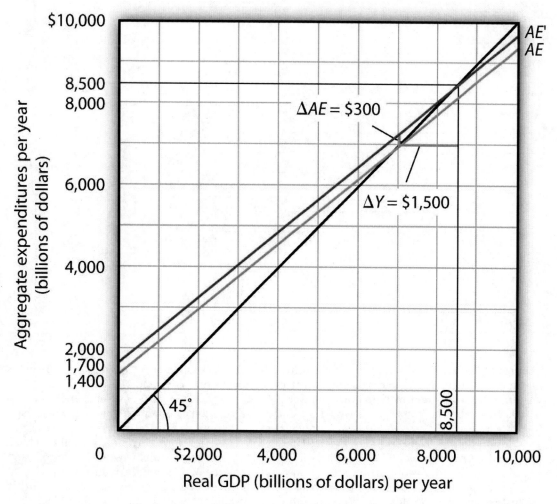

How could an increase in aggregate expenditures of $300 billion produce an increase in equilibrium real GDP of $1,500 billion? The answer lies in the operation of the multiplier. Because firms have increased their demand for investment goods (that is, for capital) by $300 billion, the firms that produce those goods will have $300 billion in additional orders. They will produce $300 billion in additional real GDP and, given our simplifying assumption, $300 billion in additional disposable personal income. But in this economy, each $1 of additional real GDP induces $0.80 in additional consumption. The $300 billion increase in autonomous aggregate expenditures initially induces $240 billion (= 0.8 × $300 billion) in additional consumption.

The $240 billion in additional consumption boosts production, creating another $240 billion in real GDP. But that second round of increase in real GDP induces $192 billion (= 0.8 × $240) in additional consumption, creating still more production, still more income, and still more consumption. Eventually (after many additional rounds of increases in induced consumption), the $300 billion increase in aggregate expenditures will result in a $1,500 billion increase in equilibrium real GDP. Table 13.1 shows the multiplied effect of a $300 billion increase in autonomous aggregate expenditures, assuming each $1 of additional real GDP induces $0.80 in additional consumption.

TABLE 13.1 The Multiplied Effect of an Increase in Autonomous Aggregate Expenditures

A $300 billion increase in autonomous aggregate expenditures initially increases real GDP and income by that amount. This is shown in the first round of spending. The increased income leads to additional consumption. The additional consumption boosts production and thus leads to even higher real GDP and income. Assuming each $1 of additional real GDP induces $0.80 in additional consumption, the multiplied effect of a $300 billion increase in autonomous aggregate expenditures leads to additional rounds of spending such that, in this example, real GDP rises by $1,500 billion.

Round of spending	Increase in real GDP (billions of dollars)
1	$300
2	240
3	192
4	154
5	123
6	98
7	79
8	63
9	50
10	40
11	32
12	26
Subsequent rounds	+103
Total increase in real GDP	$1,500

The size of the additional rounds of expenditure is based on the slope of the aggregate expenditures function, which in this example is simply the marginal propensity to consume. Had the slope been flatter (if the marginal propensity to consume were smaller), the additional rounds of spending would have been smaller. A steeper slope would mean that the additional rounds of spending would have been larger.

This process could also work in reverse. That is, a decrease in planned investment would lead to a multiplied decrease in real GDP. A reduction in planned investment would reduce the incomes of some households. They would reduce their consumption by the *MPC* times the reduction in their income. That, in turn, would reduce incomes for households that would have received the spending by the first group of households. The process continues, thus multiplying the impact of the reduction in aggregate expenditures resulting from the reduction in planned investment.

Computation of the Multiplier

The **multiplier** is the number by which we multiply an initial change in aggregate demand to get the full amount of the shift in the aggregate demand curve. Because the multiplier shows the amount by which the aggregate demand curve shifts at a given price level, and the aggregate expenditures model assumes a given price level, we can use the aggregate expenditures model to derive the multiplier explicitly.

Let Y_{eq} be the equilibrium level of real GDP in the aggregate expenditures model, and let A be autonomous aggregate expenditures. Then the multiplier is

EQUATION 13.12

$$Multiplier = \frac{\Delta Y_{eq}}{\Delta A}$$

In the example we have just discussed, a change in autonomous aggregate expenditures of $300 billion produced a change in equilibrium real GDP of $1,500 billion. The value of the multiplier is therefore $1,500/$300 = 5.

The multiplier effect works because a change in autonomous aggregate expenditures causes a change in real GDP and disposable personal income, inducing a further change in the level of aggregate expenditures, which creates still more GDP and thus an even higher level of aggregate expenditures. The degree to which a given change in real GDP induces a change in aggregate expenditures is given in this simplified economy by the marginal propensity to consume, which, in this case, is the slope of the aggregate expenditures curve. The slope of the aggregate expenditures curve is thus linked to the size of

Multiplier

The number by which we multiply an initial change in aggregate demand to get the full amount of the shift in the aggregate demand curve.

the multiplier. We turn now to an investigation of the relationship between the marginal propensity to consume and the multiplier.

The Marginal Propensity to Consume and the Multiplier

We can compute the multiplier for this simplified economy from the marginal propensity to consume. We know that the amount by which equilibrium real GDP will change as a result of a change in aggregate expenditures consists of two parts: the change in autonomous aggregate expenditures itself, $\Delta \bar{A}$, and the induced change in spending. This induced change equals the marginal propensity to consume times the change in equilibrium real GDP, ΔY_{eq}. Thus

EQUATION 13.13

$$\Delta Y_{eq} = \Delta \bar{A} + MPC\,\Delta Y_{eq}$$

Subtract the $MPC\Delta Y_{eq}$ term from both sides of the equation:

$$\Delta Y_{eq} - MPC\,\Delta Y_{eq} = \Delta \bar{A}$$

Factor out the ΔY_{eq} term on the left:

$$\Delta Y_{eq}(1 - MPC) = \Delta \bar{A}$$

Finally, solve for the multiplier $\Delta Y^{eq} / \Delta \bar{A}$ by dividing both sides of the equation above by ΔA and by dividing both sides by $(1 - MPC)$. We get the following:

EQUATION 13.14

$$\frac{\Delta Y_{eq}}{\Delta \bar{A}} = \frac{1}{1 - MPC}$$

We thus compute the multiplier by taking 1 minus the marginal propensity to consume, then dividing the result into 1. In our example, the marginal propensity to consume is 0.8; the multiplier is 5, as we have already seen [multiplier = $1/(1 - MPC) = 1/(1 - 0.8) = 1/0.2 = 5$]. Since the sum of the marginal propensity to consume and the marginal propensity to save is 1, the denominator on the right-hand side of Equation 13.13 is equivalent to the MPS, and the multiplier could also be expressed as $1/MPS$.

EQUATION 13.15

$$\text{Multiplier} = \frac{1}{MPS}$$

We can rearrange terms in Equation 13.14 to use the multiplier to compute the impact of a change in autonomous aggregate expenditures. We simply multiply both sides of the equation by $\bar{A}$ to obtain the following:

EQUATION 13.16

$$\Delta Y_{eq} = \frac{\Delta \bar{A}}{1 - MPC}$$

The change in the equilibrium level of income in the aggregate expenditures model (remember that the model assumes a constant price level) equals the change in autonomous aggregate expenditures times the multiplier. Thus, the greater the multiplier, the greater will be the impact on income of a change in autonomous aggregate expenditures.

2.2   The Aggregate Expenditures Model in a More Realistic Economy

Four conclusions emerge from our application of the aggregate expenditures model to the simplified economy presented so far. These conclusions can be applied to a more realistic view of the economy.

1. The aggregate expenditures function relates aggregate expenditures to real GDP. The intercept of the aggregate expenditures curve shows the level of autonomous aggregate expenditures. The

slope of the aggregate expenditures curve shows how much increases in real GDP induce additional aggregate expenditures.

2. Equilibrium real GDP occurs where aggregate expenditures equal real GDP.

3. A change in autonomous aggregate expenditures changes equilibrium real GDP by a multiple of the change in autonomous aggregate expenditures.

4. The size of the multiplier depends on the slope of the aggregate expenditures curve. The steeper the aggregate expenditures curve, the larger the multiplier; the flatter the aggregate expenditures curve, the smaller the multiplier.

These four points still hold as we add the two other components of aggregate expenditures—government purchases and net exports—and recognize that government not only spends but also collects taxes. We look first at the effect of adding taxes to the aggregate expenditures model and then at the effect of adding government purchases and net exports.

Taxes and the Aggregate Expenditure Function

Suppose that the only difference between real GDP and disposable personal income is personal income taxes. Let us see what happens to the slope of the aggregate expenditures function.

As before, we assume that the marginal propensity to consume is 0.8, but we now add the assumption that income taxes take ¼ of real GDP. This means that for every additional $1 of real GDP, disposable personal income rises by $0.75 and, in turn, consumption rises by $0.60 (= 0.8 × $0.75). In the simplified model in which disposable personal income and real GDP were the same, an additional $1 of real GDP raised consumption by $0.80. The slope of the aggregate expenditures curve was 0.8, the marginal propensity to consume. Now, as a result of taxes, the aggregate expenditures curve will be flatter than the one shown in Figure 13.8 and Figure 13.10. In this example, the slope will be 0.6; an additional $1 of real GDP will increase consumption by $0.60.

Other things the same, the multiplier will be smaller than it was in the simplified economy in which disposable personal income and real GDP were identical. The wedge between disposable personal income and real GDP created by taxes means that the additional rounds of spending induced by a change in autonomous aggregate expenditures will be smaller than if there were no taxes. Hence, the multiplied effect of any change in autonomous aggregate expenditures is smaller.

The Addition of Government Purchases and Net Exports

Suppose that government purchases and net exports are autonomous. If so, they enter the aggregate expenditures function in the same way that investment did. Compared to the simplified aggregate expenditures model, the aggregate expenditures curve shifts up by the amount of government purchases and net exports.[3]

Figure 13.12 shows the difference between the aggregate expenditures model of the simplified economy in Figure 13.9 and a more realistic view of the economy. Panel (a) shows an *AE* curve for an economy with only consumption and investment expenditures. In Panel (b), the *AE* curve includes all four components of aggregate expenditures.

FIGURE 13.12 The Aggregate Expenditures Function: Comparison of a Simplified Economy and a More Realistic Economy

Panel (a) shows an aggregate expenditures curve for a simplified view of the economy; Panel (b) shows an aggregate expenditures curve for a more realistic model. The *AE* curve in Panel (b) has a higher intercept than the *AE* curve in Panel (a) because of the additional components of autonomous aggregate expenditures in a more realistic view of the economy. The slope of the *AE* curve in Panel (b) is flatter than the slope of the *AE* curve in Panel (a). In a simplified economy, the slope of the *AE* curve is the marginal propensity to consume (*MPC*). In a more realistic view of the economy, it is less than the *MPC* because of the difference between real GDP and disposable personal income.

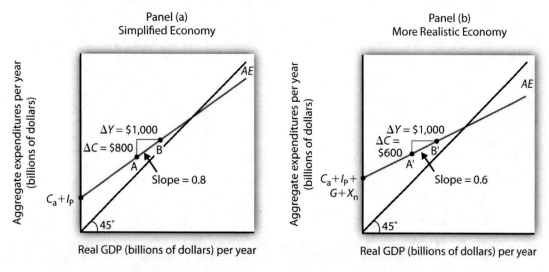

There are two major differences between the aggregate expenditures curves shown in the two panels. Notice first that the intercept of the *AE* curve in Panel (b) is higher than that of the *AE* curve in Panel (a). The reason is that, in addition to the autonomous part of consumption and planned investment, there are two other components of aggregate expenditures—government purchases and net exports—that we have also assumed are autonomous. Thus, the intercept of the aggregate expenditures curve in Panel (b) is the sum of the four autonomous aggregate expenditures components: consumption (C_a), planned investment (I_P), government purchases (G), and net exports (X_n). In Panel (a), the intercept includes only the first two components.

Second, notice that the slope of the aggregate expenditures curve is flatter for the more realistic economy in Panel (b) than it is for the simplified economy in Panel (a). This can be seen by comparing the slope of the aggregate expenditures curve between points A and B in Panel (a) to the slope of the aggregate expenditures curve between points A′ and B′ in Panel (b). Between both sets of points, real GDP changes by the same amount, $1,000 billion. In Panel (a), consumption rises by $800 billion, whereas in Panel (b) consumption rises by only $600 billion. This difference occurs because, in the more realistic view of the economy, households have only a fraction of real GDP available as disposable personal income. Thus, for a given change in real GDP, consumption rises by a smaller amount.

Let us examine what happens to equilibrium real GDP in each case if there is a shift in autonomous aggregate expenditures, such as an increase in planned investment, as shown in Figure 13.13. In both panels, the initial level of equilibrium real GDP is the same, Y_1. Equilibrium real GDP occurs where the given aggregate expenditures curve intersects the 45-degree line. The aggregate expenditures curve shifts up by the same amount—ΔA is the same in both panels. The new level of equilibrium real GDP occurs where the new *AE* curve intersects the 45-degree line. In Panel (a), we see that the new level of equilibrium real GDP rises to Y_2, but in Panel (b) it rises only to Y_3. Since the same change in autonomous aggregate expenditures led to a greater increase in equilibrium real GDP in Panel (a) than in Panel (b), the multiplier for the more realistic model of the economy must be smaller. The multiplier is smaller, of course, because the slope of the aggregate expenditures curve is flatter.

FIGURE 13.13 A Change in Autonomous Aggregate Expenditures: Comparison of a Simplified Economy and a More Realistic Economy

In Panels (a) and (b), equilibrium real GDP is initially Y_1. Then autonomous aggregate expenditures rise by the same amount, ΔI_P. In Panel (a), the upward shift in the AE curve leads to a new level of equilibrium real GDP of Y_2; in Panel (b) equilibrium real GDP rises to Y_3. Because equilibrium real GDP rises by more in Panel (a) than in Panel (b), the multiplier in the simplified economy is greater than in the more realistic one.

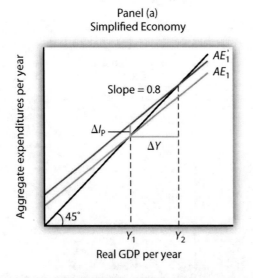
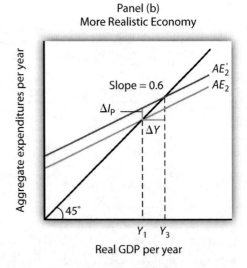

KEY TAKEAWAYS

- The aggregate expenditures model relates aggregate expenditures to real GDP. Equilibrium in the model occurs where aggregate expenditures equal real GDP and is found graphically at the intersection of the aggregate expenditures curve and the 45-degree line.

- Economists distinguish between autonomous and induced aggregate expenditures. The former do not vary with GDP; the latter do.

- Equilibrium in the aggregate expenditures model implies that unintended investment equals zero.

- A change in autonomous aggregate expenditures leads to a change in equilibrium real GDP, which is a multiple of the change in autonomous aggregate expenditures.

- The size of the multiplier depends on the slope of the aggregate expenditures curve. In general, the steeper the aggregate expenditures curve, the greater the multiplier. The flatter the aggregate expenditures curve, the smaller the multiplier.

- Income taxes tend to flatten the aggregate expenditures curve.

TRY IT!

Suppose you are given the following data for an economy. All data are in billions of dollars. Y is actual real GDP, and C, I_P, G, and X_n are the consumption, planned investment, government purchases, and net exports components of aggregate expenditures, respectively.

Y	C	I_P	G	X_n
$0	$800	$1,000	$1,400	−$200
2,500	2,300	1,000	1,400	−200
5,000	3,800	1,000	1,400	−200
7,500	5,300	1,000	1,400	−200
10,000	6,800	1,000	1,400	−200

1. Plot the corresponding aggregate expenditures curve and draw in the 45-degree line.
2. What is the intercept of the AE curve? What is its slope?
3. Determine the equilibrium level of real GDP.
4. Now suppose that net exports fall by $1,000 billion and that this is the only change in autonomous aggregate expenditures. Plot the new aggregate expenditures curve. What is the new equilibrium level of real GDP?
5. What is the value of the multiplier?

Case in Point: Fiscal Policy in the Kennedy Administration

It was the first time expansionary fiscal policy had ever been proposed. The economy had slipped into a recession in 1960. Presidential candidate John Kennedy received proposals from several economists that year for a tax cut aimed at stimulating the economy. As a candidate, he was unconvinced. But, as president he proposed the tax cut in 1962. His chief economic adviser, Walter Heller, defended the tax cut idea before Congress and introduced what was politically a novel concept: the multiplier.

In testimony to the Senate Subcommittee on Employment and Manpower, Mr. Heller predicted that a $10 billion cut in personal income taxes would boost consumption "by over $9 billion."

To assess the ultimate impact of the tax cut, Mr. Heller applied the aggregate expenditures model. He rounded the increased consumption off to $9 billion and explained,

"This is far from the end of the matter. The higher production of consumer goods to meet this extra spending would mean extra employment, higher payrolls, higher profits, and higher farm and professional and service incomes. This added purchasing power would generate still further increases in spending and incomes. … The initial rise of $9 billion, plus this extra consumption spending and extra output of consumer goods, would add over $18 billion to our annual GDP."

We can summarize this continuing process by saying that a "multiplier" of approximately 2 has been applied to the direct increment of consumption spending.

Mr. Heller also predicted that proposed cuts in corporate income tax rates would increase investment by about $6 billion. The total change in autonomous aggregate expenditures would thus be $15 billion: $9 billion in consumption and $6 billion in investment. He predicted that the total increase in equilibrium GDP would be $30 billion, the amount the Council of Economic Advisers had estimated would be necessary to reach full employment.

In the end, the tax cut was not passed until 1964, after President Kennedy's assassination in 1963. While the Council of Economic Advisers concluded that the tax cut had worked as advertised, it came long after the economy had recovered and tended to push the economy into an inflationary gap. As we will see in later chapters, the tax cut helped push the economy into a period of rising inflation.

Source: *Economic Report of the President 1964 (Washington, DC: U.S. Government Printing Office, 1964), 172–73.*

ANSWERS TO TRY IT! PROBLEMS

1. The aggregate expenditures curve is plotted in the accompanying chart as AE_1.

2. The intercept of the AE_1 curve is $3,000. It is the amount of aggregate expenditures ($C + I_P + G + X_n$) when real GDP is zero. The slope of the AE_1 curve is 0.6. It can be found by determining the amount of aggregate expenditures for any two levels of real GDP and then by dividing the change in aggregate expenditures by the change in real GDP over the interval. For example, between real GDP of $2,500 and $5,000, aggregate expenditures go from $4,500 to $6,000. Thus,

$$\frac{\Delta AE_1}{\Delta Y} = \frac{\$6,000 - \$4,500}{\$5,000 - \$2,500} = \frac{\$1,500}{\$2,500} = 0.6$$

3. The equilibrium level of real GDP is $7,500. It can be found by determining the intersection of AE_1 and the 45-degree line. At $Y = \$7,500$, $AE_1 = \$5,300 + 1,000 + 1,400 - 200 = \$7,500$.

4. A reduction of net exports of $1,000 shifts the aggregate expenditures curve down by $1,000 to AE_2. The equilibrium real GDP falls from $7,500 to $5,000. The new aggregate expenditures curve, AE_2, intersects the 45-degree line at real GDP of $5,000.

5. The multiplier is 2.5 [= (−$2,500)/(−$1,000)].

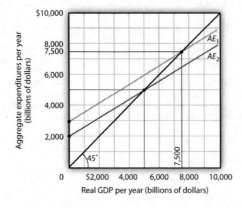

3.   AGGREGATE EXPENDITURES AND AGGREGATE DEMAND

LEARNING OBJECTIVES

1. Explain and illustrate how a change in the price level affects the aggregate expenditures curve.
2. Explain and illustrate how to derive an aggregate demand curve from the aggregate expenditures curve for different price levels.
3. Explain and illustrate how an increase or decrease in autonomous aggregate expenditures affects the aggregate demand curve.

We can use the aggregate expenditures model to gain greater insight into the aggregate demand curve. In this section we shall see how to derive the aggregate demand curve from the aggregate expenditures model. We shall also see how to apply the analysis of multiplier effects in the aggregate expenditures model to the aggregate demand–aggregate supply model.

3.1   Aggregate Expenditures Curves and Price Levels

An aggregate expenditures curve assumes a fixed price level. If the price level were to change, the levels of consumption, investment, and net exports would all change, producing a new aggregate expenditures curve and a new equilibrium solution in the aggregate expenditures model.

A change in the price level changes people's real wealth. Suppose, for example, that your wealth includes $10,000 in a bond account. An increase in the price level would reduce the real value of this money, reduce your real wealth, and thus reduce your consumption. Similarly, a reduction in the price level would increase the real value of money holdings and thus increase real wealth and consumption. The tendency for price level changes to change real wealth and consumption is called the **wealth effect**.

Because changes in the price level also affect the real quantity of money, we can expect a change in the price level to change the interest rate. A reduction in the price level will increase the real quantity of money and thus lower the interest rate. A lower interest rate, all other things unchanged, will increase the level of investment. Similarly, a higher price level reduces the real quantity of money, raises interest rates, and reduces investment. This is called the **interest rate effect**.

Finally, a change in the domestic price level will affect exports and imports. A higher price level makes a country's exports fall and imports rise, reducing net exports. A lower price level will increase exports and reduce imports, increasing net exports. This impact of different price levels on the level of net exports is called the **international trade effect**.

Panel (a) of Figure 13.16 shows three possible aggregate expenditures curves for three different price levels. For example, the aggregate expenditures curve labeled $AE_{P=1.0}$ is the aggregate expenditures curve for an economy with a price level of 1.0. Since that aggregate expenditures curve crosses the 45-degree line at $6,000 billion, equilibrium real GDP is $6,000 billion at that price level. At a lower price level, aggregate expenditures would rise because of the wealth effect, the interest rate effect, and the international trade effect. Assume that at every level of real GDP, a reduction in the price level to 0.5 would boost aggregate expenditures by $2,000 billion to $AE_{P=0.5}$, and an increase in the price level from 1.0 to 1.5 would reduce aggregate expenditures by $2,000 billion. The aggregate expenditures curve for a price level of 1.5 is shown as $AE_{P=1.5}$. There is a different aggregate expenditures curve, and a different level of equilibrium real GDP, for each of these three price levels. A price level of 1.5 produces equilibrium at point A, a price level of 1.0 does so at point B, and a price level of 0.5 does so at point C. More generally, there will be a different level of equilibrium real GDP for every price level; the higher the price level, the lower the equilibrium value of real GDP.

wealth effect

The tendency for price level changes to change real wealth and consumption.

interest rate effect

The tendency for a higher price level to reduce the real quantity of money, raise interest rates, and reduce investment.

international trade effect

The impact of different price levels on the level of net exports.

FIGURE 13.16 From Aggregate Expenditures to Aggregate Demand

Because there is a different aggregate expenditures curve for each price level, there is a different equilibrium real GDP for each price level. Panel (a) shows aggregate expenditures curves for three different price levels. Panel (b) shows that the aggregate demand curve, which shows the quantity of goods and services demanded at each price level, can thus be derived from the aggregate expenditures model. The aggregate expenditures curve for a price level of 1.0, for example, intersects the 45-degree line in Panel (a) at point B, producing an equilibrium real GDP of $6,000 billion. We can thus plot point B' on the aggregate demand curve in Panel (b), which shows that at a price level of 1.0, a real GDP of $6,000 billion is demanded.

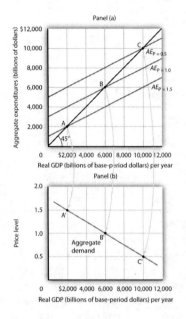

Panel (b) of Figure 13.16 shows how an aggregate demand curve can be derived from the aggregate expenditures curves for different price levels. The equilibrium real GDP associated with each price level in the aggregate expenditures model is plotted as a point showing the price level and the quantity of goods and services demanded (measured as real GDP). At a price level of 1.0, for example, the equilibrium level of real GDP in the aggregate expenditures model in Panel (a) is $6,000 billion at point B. That means $6,000 billion worth of goods and services is demanded; point B' on the aggregate demand curve in Panel (b) corresponds to a real GDP demanded of $6,000 billion and a price level of 1.0. At a price level of 0.5 the equilibrium GDP demanded is $10,000 billion at point C', and at a price level of 1.5 the equilibrium real GDP demanded is $2,000 billion at point A'. The aggregate demand curve thus shows the equilibrium real GDP from the aggregate expenditures model at each price level.

3.2 The Multiplier and Changes in Aggregate Demand

In the aggregate expenditures model, a change in autonomous aggregate expenditures changes equilibrium real GDP by the multiplier times the change in autonomous aggregate expenditures. That model, however, assumes a constant price level. How can we incorporate the concept of the multiplier into the model of aggregate demand and aggregate supply?

Consider the aggregate expenditures curves given in Panel (a) of Figure 13.17, each of which corresponds to a particular price level. Suppose net exports rise by $1,000 billion. Such a change increases aggregate expenditures at each price level by $1,000 billion.

A $1,000-billion increase in net exports shifts each of the aggregate expenditures curves up by $1,000 billion, to $AE'_{P=1.0}$ and $AE'_{P=1.5}$. That changes the equilibrium real GDP associated with each price level; it thus shifts the aggregate demand curve to AD_2 in Panel (b). In the aggregate expenditures model, equilibrium real GDP changes by an amount equal to the initial change in autonomous aggregate expenditures times the multiplier, so the aggregate demand curve shifts by the same amount. In this example, we assume the multiplier is 2. The aggregate demand curve thus shifts to the right by $2,000 billion, two times the $1,000-billion change in autonomous aggregate expenditures.

FIGURE 13.17   Changes in Aggregate Demand

The aggregate expenditures curves for price levels of 1.0 and 1.5 are the same as in Figure 13.16, as is the aggregate demand curve. Now suppose a $1,000-billion increase in net exports shifts each of the aggregate expenditures curves up; $AE_{P=1.0}$, for example, rises to $AE'_{P=1.0}$. The aggregate demand curve thus shifts to the right by $2,000 billion, the change in aggregate expenditures times the multiplier, assumed to be 2 in this example.

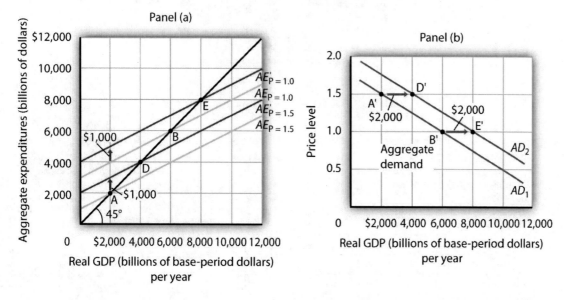

In general, any change in autonomous aggregate expenditures shifts the aggregate demand curve. The amount of the shift is always equal to the change in autonomous aggregate expenditures times the multiplier. An increase in autonomous aggregate expenditures shifts the aggregate demand curve to the right; a reduction shifts it to the left.

KEY TAKEAWAYS

- There will be a different aggregate expenditures curve for each price level.
- Aggregate expenditures will vary with the price level because of the wealth effect, the interest rate effect, and the international trade effect. The higher the price level, the lower the aggregate expenditures curve and the lower the equilibrium level of real GDP. The lower the price level, the higher the aggregate expenditures curve and the higher the equilibrium level of real GDP.
- A change in autonomous aggregate expenditures shifts the aggregate expenditures curve for each price level. That shifts the aggregate demand curve by an amount equal to the change in autonomous aggregate expenditures times the multiplier.

TRY IT!

Sketch three aggregate expenditures curves for price levels of P_1, P_2, and P_3, where P_1 is the lowest price level and P_3 the highest (you do not have numbers for this exercise; simply sketch curves of the appropriate shape). Label the equilibrium levels of real GDP Y_1, Y_2, and Y_3. Now draw the aggregate demand curve implied by your analysis, labeling points that correspond to P_1, P_2, and P_3 and Y_1, Y_2, and Y_3. You can use Figure 13.16 as a model for your work.

Case in Point: Predicting the Impact of Alternative Fiscal Policies in 2008

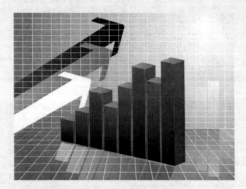

Economists are often asked to simulate the effects of policy changes on the economy. In 2008, as the economy weakened and Congress and the president debated a stimulus package, Mark M. Zandi, an economist at Moody's Economy.com, produced a paper assessing the impact of various possible stimulus packages. His research produced the following table.

Fiscal Economic Bang for the Buck
One year $ change in real GDP for a given $ reduction in federal tax revenue or increase in spending

Tax cuts	
Nonrefundable lump-sum tax rebate	1.02
Refundable lump-sum tax rebate	1.26
Temporary tax cuts	
Payroll tax holiday	1.29
Across-the-board tax cut	1.03
Accelerated depreciation	0.27
Permanent tax cuts	
Extend alternative minimum tax patch	0.48
Make Bush income tax cuts permanent	0.29
Make dividend and capital gains tax cuts permanent	0.37
Spending increases	
Extending UI benefits	1.64
Temporary increase in food stamps	1.73
General aid to state governments	1.36
Increased infrastructure spending	1.59

The $100-billion tax rebate for households that was actually passed was of the nonrefundable lump-sum type. "Nonrefundable" refers to the fact those not earning enough to pay income taxes would not receive a rebate, meaning that many households received zero or partial refunds. As shown, he estimated that a $100-billion tax rebate would shift the aggregate demand curve by $102 billion, assuming a constant price level. As part of the analysis, in the article he mentioned that he assumed an *MPC* of about two-thirds, since many households at the time were living paycheck-to-paycheck. So, consumption would increase by about $67 billion. The implied multiplier is thus 1.54 (= 102/67).

The table shows that other stimuli would have smaller or larger effects. He reasoned that making various tax cuts permanent would have little impact on consumption now, since households in 2008 were cash-strapped. The table shows an estimated bigger bang for the buck from various kinds of government spending increases. That follows, since the change in aggregate expenditure is the full amount of the spending increase instead of the portion of a tax rebate of the same magnitude that consumers decide to spend.

Source: *Mark M. Zandi, "Assessing the Macro Economic Impact of Fiscal Stimulus 2008," Moody's Economy.com, January 2008.*

The lowest price level, P_1, corresponds to the highest AE curve, $AE_{P = P_1}$, as shown. This suggests a downward-sloping aggregate demand curve. Points A, B, and C on the AE curve correspond to points A', B', and C' on the AD curve, respectively.

Panel (a)

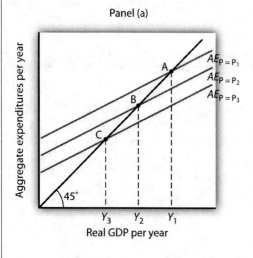

Panel (b)

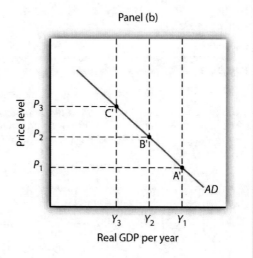

4.   REVIEW AND PRACTICE

Summary

This chapter presented the aggregate expenditures model. Aggregate expenditures are the sum of planned levels of consumption, investment, government purchases, and net exports at a given price level. The aggregate expenditures model relates aggregate expenditures to the level of real GDP.

We began by observing the close relationship between consumption and disposable personal income. A consumption function shows this relationship. The saving function can be derived from the consumption function.

The time period over which income is considered to be a determinant of consumption is important. The current income hypothesis holds that consumption in one period is a function of income in that same period. The permanent income hypothesis holds that consumption in a period is a function of permanent income. An important implication of the permanent income hypothesis is that the marginal propensity to consume will be smaller for temporary than for permanent changes in disposable personal income.

Changes in real wealth and consumer expectations can affect the consumption function. Such changes shift the curve relating consumption to disposable personal income, the graphical representation of the consumption function; changes in disposable personal income do not shift the curve but cause movements along it.

An aggregate expenditures curve shows total planned expenditures at each level of real GDP. This curve is used in the aggregate expenditures model to determine the equilibrium real GDP (at a given price level). A change in autonomous aggregate expenditures produces a multiplier effect that leads to a larger change in equilibrium real GDP. In a simplified economy, with only consumption and investment expenditures, in which the slope of the aggregate expenditures curve is the marginal propensity to consume (MPC), the multiplier is equal to $1/(1 - MPC)$. Because the sum of the marginal propensity to consume and the marginal propensity to save (MPS) is 1, the multiplier in this simplified model is also equal to $1/MPS$.

Finally, we derived the aggregate demand curve from the aggregate expenditures model. Each point on the aggregate demand curve corresponds to the equilibrium level of real GDP as derived in the aggregate expenditures model for each price level. The downward slope of the aggregate demand curve (and the shifting of the aggregate expenditures curve at each price level) reflects the wealth effect, the interest rate effect, and the international trade effect. A change in autonomous aggregate expenditures shifts the aggregate demand curve by an amount equal to the change in autonomous aggregate expenditures times the multiplier.

In a more realistic aggregate expenditures model that includes all four components of aggregate expenditures (consumption, investment, government purchases, and net exports), the slope of the aggregate expenditures curve shows the additional aggregate expenditures induced by increases in real GDP, and the size of the multiplier depends on the slope of the aggregate expenditures curve. The steeper the aggregate expenditures curve, the larger the multiplier; the flatter the aggregate expenditures curve, the smaller the multiplier.

CONCEPT PROBLEMS

1. Explain the difference between autonomous and induced expenditures. Give examples of each.

2. The consumption function we studied in the chapter predicted that consumption would sometimes exceed disposable personal income. How could this be?

3. The consumption function can be represented as a table, as an equation, or as a curve. Distinguish among these three representations.

4. The introduction to this chapter described the behavior of consumer spending at the end of 2008. Explain this phenomenon in terms of the analysis presented in this chapter.

5. Explain the role played by the 45-degree line in the aggregate expenditures model.

6. Your college or university, if it does what many others do, occasionally releases a news story claiming that its impact on the total employment in the local economy is understated by its own employment statistics. If the institution keeps accurate statistics, is that possible?

7. Suppose the level of investment in a certain economy changes when the level of real GDP changes; an increase in real GDP induces an increase in investment, while a reduction in real GDP causes investment to fall. How do you think such behavior would affect the slope of the aggregate expenditures curve? The multiplier?

8. Give an intuitive explanation for how the multiplier works on a reduction in autonomous aggregate expenditures. Why does equilibrium real GDP fall by more than the change in autonomous aggregate expenditures?

9. Explain why the marginal propensity to consume out of a temporary tax rebate would be lower than that for a permanent rebate.

10. Pretend you are a member of the Council of Economic Advisers and are trying to persuade the members of the House Appropriations Committee to purchase $100 billion worth of new materials, in part to stimulate the economy. Explain to the members how the multiplier process will work.

NUMERICAL PROBLEMS

1. Suppose the following information describes a simple economy. Figures are in billion of dollars.

Disposable personal income	Consumption
0	100
100	120
200	140
300	160

    a. What is the marginal propensity to consume?

    b. What is the marginal propensity to save?

    c. Write an equation that describes consumption.

    d. Write an equation that describes saving.

2. The graph below shows a consumption function.

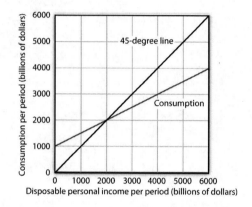

    a. When disposable personal income is equal to zero, how much is consumption?

    b. When disposable personal income is equal to $4,000 billion, how much is consumption?

    c. At what level of personal disposable income are consumption and disposable personal income equal?

    d. How much is personal saving when consumption is $2,500 billion?

    e. How much is personal saving when consumption is $5,000 billion?

    f. What is the marginal propensity to consume?

    g. What is the marginal propensity to save?

    h. Draw the saving function implied by the consumption function above.

3. For the purpose of this exercise, assume that the consumption function is given by $C = \$500$ billion $+ 0.8Y_d$. Construct a consumption and saving table showing how income is divided between consumption and personal saving when disposable personal income (in billions) is $0, $500, $1,000, $1,500, $2,000, $2,500, $3,000, and $3,500.

    a. Graph your results, placing disposable personal income on the horizontal axis and consumption on the vertical axis.

    b. What is the value of the marginal propensity to consume?

    c. What is the value of the marginal propensity to save?

4. The graph below characterizes a simple economy with only two components of aggregate expenditures, consumption and investment.

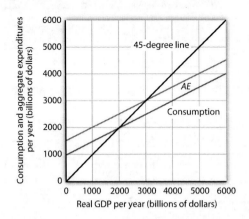

a. How much is planned investment? How do you know?

b. Is planned investment autonomous or induced? How do you know?

c. How much is autonomous aggregate expenditures?

d. What is the value of equilibrium real GDP?

e. If real GDP were $2,000 billion, how much would unplanned investment be? How would you expect firms to respond?

f. If real GDP were $4,000 billion, how much would unplanned investment be? How would you expect firms to respond?

g. Write an equation for aggregate expenditures based on the graph above.

h. What is the value of the multiplier in this example?

5. Explain and illustrate graphically how each of the following events affects aggregate expenditures and equilibrium real GDP. In each case, state the nature of the change in aggregate expenditures, and state the relationship between the change in AE and the change in equilibrium real GDP.

    a. Investment falls.

    b. Government purchases go up.

    c. The government sends $1,000 to every person in the United States.

    d. Real GDP rises by $500 billion.

6. Mary Smith, whose marginal propensity to consume is 0.75, is faced with an unexpected increase in taxes of $1,000. Will she cut back her consumption expenditures by the full $1,000? How will she pay for the higher tax? Explain.

7. The equations below give consumption functions for economies in which planned investment is autonomous and is the only other component of GDP. Compute the marginal propensity to consume and the multiplier for each economy.

    a. $C = \$650 + 0.33Y$

    b. $C = \$180 + 0.9Y$

    c. $C = \$1,500$

    d. $C = \$700 + 0.8Y$

8. Suppose that in Economies A and B the only components of aggregate expenditure are consumption and planned investment. The marginal propensity to consume in Economy A is 0.9, while in Economy B it is 0.7. Both economies experience an increase in planned investment, which is assumed to be autonomous, of $100 billion. Compare the changes in the equilibrium level of real GDP and the shifts in aggregate demand this will produce in the two economies.

9. Assume an economy in which people would spend $200 billion on consumption even if real GDP were zero and, in addition, increase their consumption by $0.50 for each additional $1 of real GDP. Assume further that the sum of planned investment plus government purchases plus net exports is $200 billion regardless of the level of real GDP.

    a. What is the equilibrium level of income in this economy?

    b. If the economy is currently operating at an output level of $1,200 billion, what do you predict will happen to real GDP in the future?

10. Suppose the aggregate expenditures curve in Numerical Problem 9 is drawn for a price level of 1.2. A reduction in the price level to 1 increases aggregate expenditures by $400 billion at each level of real GDP. Draw the implied aggregate demand curve.

ENDNOTES

1. J. R. Mc Culloch, *A Discourse on the Rise, Progress, Peculiar Objects, and Importance, of Political Economy: Containing the Outline of a Course of Lectures on the Principles and Doctrines of That Science* (Edinburgh: Archibald Constable, 1824), 103.

2. Matthew D. Shapiro and Joel Slemrod, "Consumer Response to the Timing of Income: Evidence from a Change in Tax Withholding," *American Economic Review* 85 (March 1995): 274–83.

3. An even more realistic view of the economy might assume that imports are induced, since as a country's real GDP rises it will buy more goods and services, some of which will be imports. In that case, the slope of the aggregate expenditures curve would change.

CHAPTER 14
Investment and Economic Activity

START UP: JITTERY FIRMS SLASH INVESTMENT

In the recession that began in late 2007 in the United States, the first main element of GDP that faltered was the part of investment called residential structures. When housing prices started falling in 2006, new home construction slowed down. In 2008, this sector had shrunk by more than 40% from where it had been just a few years earlier.

In 2008, the part of investment that reflects business spending on equipment ranging from computers to machines to trucks also turned down. The only major part of investment left standing was business spending on structures—factories, hospitals, office buildings, and such. In late 2008, firms around the world seemed to be trying to outdo each other in announcing cutbacks.

Among automakers, it was not just the Detroit 3 cutting back. Toyota announced an indefinite delay in building a Prius hybrid sedan plant in Mississippi.[1] Walgreen's, which had been increasing drugstore locations by about 8% a year, said it would expand by only about 4% in 2009 and by less than 3% in 2010.[2] Package carrier FedEx announced a 20% decline in capital spending, on top of suspending pension contributions and cutting salaries.[3] Even hospitals began scaling back on construction.[4]

Companies around the world were announcing similar cutbacks. Consumer electronics maker Sony announced is was not only closing plants but also not moving forward in constructing an LCD television plant in Slovakia.[5] With the drop in oil prices, oil companies were also cancelling planned projects right and left.[6]

Choices about how much to invest must always be made in the face of uncertainty; firms cannot know what the marketplace has in store. Investment is a gamble; firms that make the gamble hope for a profitable payoff. And, if they are concerned that the payoff may not materialize, they will be quick to take the kinds of actions cited above—to slash investment spending.

Private investment plays an important role, not only in the short run, by influencing aggregate demand, but also in the long run, for it influences the rate at which the economy grows.

In this chapter, we will examine factors that determine investment by firms, and we will study its relationship to output in the short run and in the long run. One determinant of investment is public policy; we will examine the ways in which public policy affects investment.

Private firms are not the only source of investment; government agencies engage in investment as well. We examined the impact of the public sector on macroeconomic performance in the chapter devoted to fiscal policy. When we refer to "investment" in this chapter, we will be referring to investment carried out in the private sector.

1. THE ROLE AND NATURE OF INVESTMENT

LEARNING OBJECTIVES

1. Discuss the components of the investment spending category of GDP and distinguish between gross and net investment.
2. Discuss the relationship between consumption, saving, and investment, and explain the relationship using the production possibilities model.

How important is investment? Consider any job you have ever performed. Your productivity in that job was largely determined by the investment choices that had been made before you began to work. If you worked as a clerk in a store, the equipment used in collecting money from customers affected your productivity. It may have been a simple cash register, or a sophisticated computer terminal that scanned purchases and was linked to the store's computer, which computed the store's inventory and did an analysis of the store's sales as you entered each sale. If you have worked for a lawn maintenance firm, the kind of equipment you had to work with influenced your productivity. You were more productive if you had the latest mulching power lawn mowers than if you struggled with a push mower. Whatever the work you might have done, the kind and quality of capital you had to work with strongly influenced your productivity. And that capital was available because investment choices had provided it.

Investment adds to the nation's capital stock. We saw in the chapter on economic growth that an increase in capital shifts the aggregate production function outward, increases the demand for labor, and shifts the long-run aggregate supply curve to the right. Investment therefore affects the economy's potential output and thus its standard of living in the long run.

Investment is a component of aggregate demand. Changes in investment shift the aggregate demand curve and thus change real GDP and the price level in the short run. An increase in investment shifts the aggregate demand curve to the right; a reduction shifts it to the left.

1.1 Components of Investment

Additions to the stock of private capital are called Gross Private Domestic Investment (GPDI). GPDI includes four categories of investment:

1. Nonresidential Structures. This category of investment includes the construction of business structures such as private office buildings, warehouses, factories, private hospitals and universities, and other structures in which the production of goods and services takes place. A structure is counted as GPDI only during the period in which it is built. It may be sold several times after being built, but such sales are not counted as investment. Recall that investment is part of GDP, and GDP is the value of production in any period, not total sales.

2. Nonresidential Equipment and Software. Producers' equipment includes computers and software, machinery, computers, trucks, cars, and desks, that is, any business equipment that is expected to last more than a year. Equipment and software are counted as investment only in the period in which it is produced.

3. Residential Investment. This category includes all forms of residential construction, whether apartment houses or single-family homes, as well as residential equipment such as computers and software.

4. Change in Private Inventories. Private inventories are considered part of the nation's capital stock, because those inventories are used to produce other goods. All private inventories are capital; additions to private inventories are thus investment. When private inventories fall, that is recorded as negative investment.

Figure 14.1 shows the components of gross private domestic investment from 1995 through 2010. We see that producers' equipment and software constitute the largest component of GPDI in the United States. Residential investment was the second largest component of GPDI for most of the period shown but it shrank considerably during the 2007-2009 recession.

FIGURE 14.1 Components of Gross Private Domestic Investment, 1995–2010

This chart shows the levels of each of the four components of gross private domestic investment from 1990 through the third quarter of 2010. Nonresidential equipment and software is the largest component of GPDI and has shown the most substantial growth over the period.

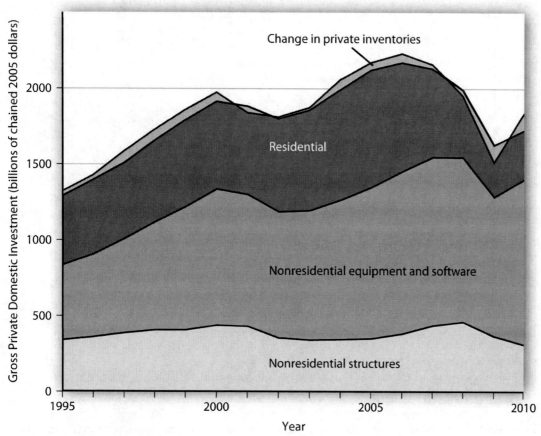

Source: Bureau of Economic Analysis, NIPA Table 1.1.6 (revised November 23, 2010). Data are through the third quarter of 2010.

1.2   Gross and Net Investment

As capital is used, some of it wears out or becomes obsolete; it depreciates (the Commerce Department reports depreciation as "consumption of fixed capital"). Investment adds to the capital stock, and depreciation reduces it. Gross investment minus depreciation is net investment. If gross investment is greater than depreciation in any period, then net investment is positive and the capital stock increases. If gross investment is less than depreciation in any period, then net investment is negative and the capital stock declines.

In the official estimates of total output, gross investment (GPDI) minus depreciation equals net private domestic investment (NPDI). The value for NPDI in any period gives the amount by which the privately held stock of physical capital increased during that period.

Figure 14.2 reports the real values of GPDI, depreciation, and NPDI from 1990 to 2009. We see that the bulk of GPDI replaces capital that has been depreciated. Notice the sharp reductions in NPDI during the recessions of 1990–1991, 2001, and especially 2007 – 2009.

FIGURE 14.2 Gross Private Domestic Investment, Depreciation, and Net Private Domestic Investment, 1990–2009

The bulk of gross private domestic investment goes to the replacement of capital that has depreciated, as shown by the experience of the past two decades.

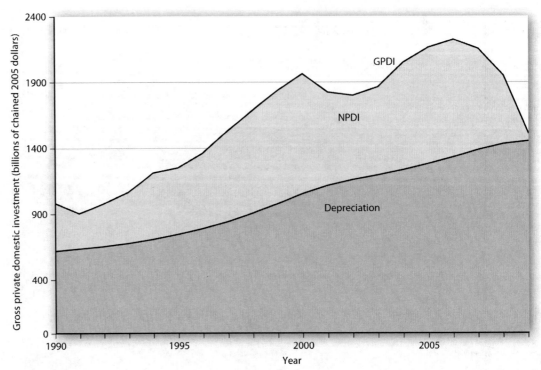

Source: Bureau of Economic Analysis, NIPA Table 5.2.6 (revised August 5, 2010).

1.3 The Volatility of Investment

Investment, measured as GPDI, is among the most volatile components of GDP. In percentage terms, year-to-year changes in GPDI are far greater than the year-to-year changes in consumption or government purchases. Net exports are also quite volatile, but they represent a much smaller share of GDP. Figure 14.3 compares annual percentage changes in GPDI, personal consumption, and government purchases. Of course, a dollar change in investment will be a much larger change in percentage terms than a dollar change in consumption, which is the largest component of GDP. But compare investment and government purchases: their shares in GDP are comparable, but investment is clearly more volatile.

FIGURE 14.3 Changes in Components of Real GDP, 1990–2010

Annual percentage changes in real GPDI have been much greater than annual percentage changes in the real values of personal consumption or government purchases.

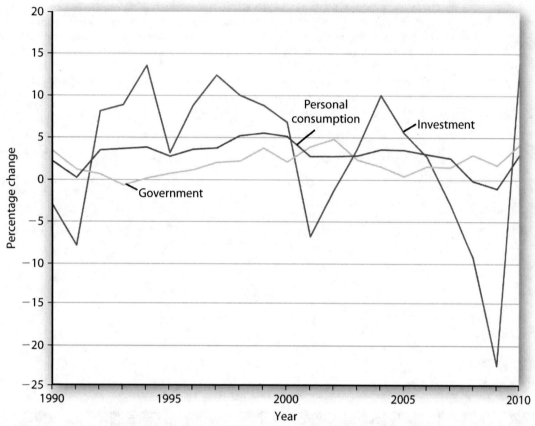

Source: Bureau of Economic Analysis, NIPA Table 1.1.1 (revised November 23, 2010). Data are through the third quarter of 2010.

Given that the aggregate demand curve shifts by an amount equal to the multiplier times an initial change in investment, the volatility of investment can cause real GDP to fluctuate in the short run. Downturns in investment may trigger recessions.

1.4 Investment, Consumption, and Saving

Earlier we used the production possibilities curve to illustrate how choices are made about investment, consumption, and saving. Because such choices are crucial to understanding how investment affects living standards, it will be useful to reexamine them here.

Figure 14.4 shows a production possibilities curve for an economy that can produce two kinds of goods: consumption goods and investment goods. An economy operating at point A on PPC_1 is using its factors of production fully and efficiently. It is producing C_A units of consumption goods and I_A units of investment each period. Suppose that depreciation equals I_A, so that the quantity of investment each period is just sufficient to replace depreciated capital; net investment equals zero. If there is no change in the labor force, in natural resources, or in technology, the production possibilities curve will remain fixed at PPC_1.

FIGURE 14.4 The Choice between Consumption and Investment

A society with production possibilities curve PPC_1 could choose to produce at point A, producing C_A consumption goods and investment of I_A. If depreciation equals I_A, then net investment is zero, and the production possibilities curve will not shift, assuming no other determinants of the curve change. By cutting its production of consumption goods and increasing investment to I_B, however, the society can, over time, shift its production possibilities curve out to PPC_2, making it possible to enjoy greater production of consumption goods in the future.

Now suppose decision makers in this economy decide to sacrifice the production of some consumption goods in favor of greater investment. The economy moves to point B on PPC_1. Production of consumption goods falls to C_B, and investment rises to I_B. Assuming depreciation remains I_A, net investment is now positive. As the nation's capital stock increases, the production possibilities curve shifts outward to PPC_2. Once that shift occurs, it will be possible to select a point such as D on the new production possibilities curve. At this point, consumption equals C_D, and investment equals I_D. By sacrificing consumption early on, the society is able to increase both its consumption and investment in the future. That early reduction in consumption requires an *increase* in saving.

We see that a movement along the production possibilities curve in the direction of the production of more investment goods and fewer consumption goods allows the production of more of both types of goods in the future.

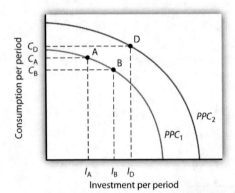

TRY IT!

Which of the following would be counted as gross private domestic investment?

1. Millie hires a contractor to build a new garage for her home.
2. Millie buys a new car for her teenage son.
3. Grandpa buys Tommy a savings bond.
4. General Motors builds a new automobile assembly plant.

Case in Point: The Reduction of Private Capital in the Depression

Net private domestic investment (NPDI) has been negative during only two periods in the last 70 years. During one period, World War II, massive defense spending forced cutbacks in private sector spending. (Recall that government investment is not counted as part of net private domestic investment in the official accounts; production of defense capital thus is not reflected in these figures.) The other period in which NPDI was negative was the Great Depression.

Aggregate demand plunged during the first four years of the Depression. As firms cut their output in response to reductions in demand, their need for capital fell as well. They reduced their capital by holding gross private domestic investment below depreciation beginning in 1931. That produced negative net private domestic investment; it remained negative until 1936 and became negative again in 1938. In all, firms reduced the private capital stock by more than $529.5 billion (in 2007 dollars) during the period.

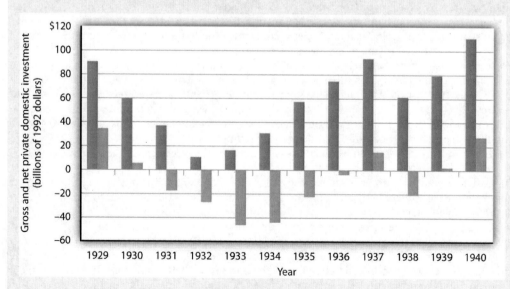

2. DETERMINANTS OF INVESTMENT

LEARNING OBJECTIVES

1. Draw a hypothetical investment demand curve, and explain what it shows about the relationship between investment and the interest rate.
2. Discuss the factors that can cause an investment demand curve to shift.

We will see in this section that interest rates play a key role in the determination of the desired stock of capital and thus of investment. Because investment is a process through which capital is increased in one period for use in future periods, expectations play an important role in investment as well.

Capital is one factor of production, along with labor and natural resources. A decision to invest is a decision to use more capital in producing goods and services. Factors that affect firms' choices in the mix of capital, labor, and natural resources will affect investment as well.

We will also see in this section that public policy affects investment. Some investment is done by government agencies as they add to the public stock of capital. In addition, the tax and regulatory policies chosen by the public sector can affect the investment choices of private firms and individuals.

2.1 Interest Rates and Investment

We often hear reports that low interest rates have stimulated housing construction or that high rates have reduced it. Such reports imply a negative relationship between interest rates and investment in residential structures. This relationship applies to all forms of investment: higher interest rates tend to reduce the quantity of investment, while lower interest rates increase it.

To see the relationship between interest rates and investment, suppose you own a small factory and are considering the installation of a solar energy collection system to heat your building. You have determined that the cost of installing the system would be $10,000 and that the system would lower your energy bills by $1,000 per year. To simplify the example, we shall suppose that these savings will continue forever and that the system will never need repair or maintenance. Thus, we need to consider only the $10,000 purchase price and the $1,000 annual savings.

If the system is installed, it will be an addition to the capital stock and will therefore be counted as investment. Should you purchase the system?

Suppose that your business already has the $10,000 on hand. You are considering whether to use the money for the solar energy system or for the purchase of a bond. Your decision to purchase the system or the bond will depend on the interest rate you could earn on the bond.

Putting $10,000 into the solar energy system generates an effective income of $1,000 per year—the saving the system will produce. That is a return of 10% per year. Suppose the bond yields a 12% annual interest. It thus generates interest income of $1,200 per year, enough to pay the $1,000 in heating bills and have $200 left over. At an interest rate of 12%, the bond is the better purchase. If, however, the interest rate on bonds were 8%, then the solar energy system would yield a higher income than the bond. At interest rates below 10%, you will invest in the solar energy system. At interest rates above 10%, you will buy a bond instead. At an interest rate of precisely 10%, it is a toss-up.

If you do not have the $10,000 on hand and would need to borrow the money to purchase the solar energy system, the interest rate still governs your decision. At interest rates below 10%, it makes sense to borrow the money and invest in the system. At interest rates above 10%, it does not.

In effect, the interest rate represents the opportunity cost of putting funds into the solar energy system rather than into a bond. The cost of putting the $10,000 into the system is the interest you would forgo by not purchasing the bond.

At any one time, millions of investment choices hinge on the interest rate. Each decision to invest will make sense at some interest rates but not at others. The higher the interest rate, the fewer potential investments will be justified; the lower the interest rate, the greater the number that will be justified. There is thus a negative relationship between the interest rate and the level of investment.

Figure 14.7 shows an **investment demand curve** for the economy—a curve that shows the quantity of investment demanded at each interest rate, with all other determinants of investment unchanged. At an interest rate of 8%, the level of investment is $950 billion per year at point A. At a lower interest rate of 6%, the investment demand curve shows that the quantity of investment demanded will rise to $1,000 billion per year at point B. A reduction in the interest rate thus causes a movement along the investment demand curve.

investment demand curve

A curve that shows the quantity of investment demanded at each interest rate, with all other determinants of investment unchanged.

FIGURE 14.7   The Investment Demand Curve

The investment demand curve shows the volume of investment spending per year at each interest rate, assuming all other determinants of investment are unchanged. The curve shows that as the interest rate falls, the level of investment per year rises. A reduction in the interest rate from 8% to 6%, for example, would increase investment from $950 billion to $1,000 billion per year, all other determinants of investment unchanged.

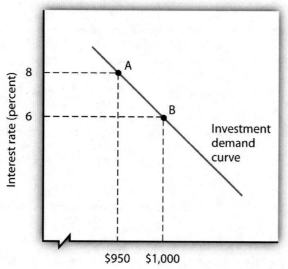

Heads Up!

To make sense of the relationship between interest rates and investment, you must remember that investment is an addition to capital, and that capital is something that has been produced in order to produce other goods and services. A bond is not capital. The purchase of a bond is not an investment. We can thus think of purchasing bonds as a financial investment—that is, as an alternative to investment. The more attractive bonds are (i.e., the higher their interest rate), the less attractive investment becomes. If we forget that investment is an addition to the capital stock and that the purchase of a bond is not investment, we can fall into the following kind of error: "Higher interest rates mean a greater return on bonds, so more people will purchase them. Higher interest rates will therefore lead to greater investment." That is a mistake, of course, because the purchase of a bond is not an investment. Higher interest rates increase the opportunity cost of using funds for investment. They reduce investment.

2.2   Other Determinants of Investment Demand

Perhaps the most important characteristic of the investment demand curve is not its negative slope, but rather the fact that it shifts often. Although investment certainly responds to changes in interest rates, changes in other factors appear to play a more important role in driving investment choices.

This section examines eight additional determinants of investment demand: expectations, the level of economic activity, the stock of capital, capacity utilization, the cost of capital goods, other factor costs, technological change, and public policy. A change in any of these can shift the investment demand curve.

Expectations

A change in the capital stock changes future production capacity. Therefore, plans to change the capital stock depend crucially on expectations. A firm considers likely future sales; a student weighs prospects in different occupations and their required educational and training levels. As expectations change in a way that increases the expected return from investment, the investment demand curve shifts to the right. Similarly, expectations of reduced profitability shift the investment demand curve to the left.

The Level of Economic Activity

Firms need capital to produce goods and services. An increase in the level of production is likely to boost demand for capital and thus lead to greater investment. Therefore, an increase in GDP is likely to shift the investment demand curve to the right.

To the extent that an increase in GDP boosts investment, the multiplier effect of an initial change in one or more components of aggregate demand will be enhanced. We have already seen that the increase in production that occurs with an initial increase in aggregate demand will increase household incomes, which will increase consumption, thus producing a further increase in aggregate demand. If the increase also induces firms to increase their investment, this multiplier effect will be even stronger.

The Stock of Capital

The quantity of capital already in use affects the level of investment in two ways. First, because most investment replaces capital that has depreciated, a greater capital stock is likely to lead to more investment; there will be more capital to replace. But second, a greater capital stock can tend to reduce investment. That is because investment occurs to adjust the stock of capital to its desired level. Given that desired level, the amount of investment needed to reach it will be lower when the current capital stock is higher.

Suppose, for example, that real estate analysts expect that 100,000 homes will be needed in a particular community by 2010. That will create a boom in construction—and thus in investment—if the current number of houses is 50,000. But it will create hardly a ripple if there are now 99,980 homes.

How will these conflicting effects of a larger capital stock sort themselves out? Because most investment occurs to replace existing capital, a larger capital stock is likely to increase investment. But that larger capital stock will certainly act to reduce net investment. The more capital already in place, the less new capital will be required to reach a given level of capital that may be desired.

Capacity Utilization

capacity utilization rate
A measure of the percentage of the capital stock in use.

The **capacity utilization rate** measures the percentage of the capital stock in use. Because capital generally requires downtime for maintenance and repairs, the measured capacity utilization rate typically falls below 100%. For example, the average manufacturing capacity utilization rate was 79.7% for the period from 1972 to 2007. In November 2008 it stood at 72.3.

If a large percentage of the current capital stock is being utilized, firms are more likely to increase investment than they would if a large percentage of the capital stock were sitting idle. During recessions, the capacity utilization rate tends to fall. The fact that firms have more idle capacity then depresses investment even further. During expansions, as the capacity utilization rate rises, firms wanting to produce more often must increase investment to do so.

The Cost of Capital Goods

The demand curve for investment shows the quantity of investment at each interest rate, all other things unchanged. A change in a variable held constant in drawing this curve shifts the curve. One of those variables is the cost of capital goods themselves. If, for example, the construction cost of new buildings rises, then the quantity of investment at any interest rate is likely to fall. The investment demand curve thus shifts to the left.

The $10,000 cost of the solar energy system in the example given earlier certainly affects a decision to purchase it. We saw that buying the system makes sense at interest rates below 10% and does not make sense at interest rates above 10%. If the system costs $5,000, then the interest return on the investment would be 20% (the annual saving of $1,000 divided by the $5,000 initial cost), and the investment would be undertaken at any interest rate below 20%.

Other Factor Costs

Firms have a range of choices concerning how particular goods can be produced. A factory, for example, might use a sophisticated capital facility and relatively few workers, or it might use more workers and relatively less capital. The choice to use capital will be affected by the cost of the capital goods and the interest rate, but it will also be affected by the cost of labor. As labor costs rise, the demand for capital is likely to increase.

Our solar energy collector example suggests that energy costs influence the demand for capital as well. The assumption that the system would save $1,000 per year in energy costs must have been based on the prices of fuel oil, natural gas, and electricity. If these prices were higher, the savings from the solar energy system would be greater, increasing the demand for this form of capital.

Technological Change

The implementation of new technology often requires new capital. Changes in technology can thus increase the demand for capital. Advances in computer technology have encouraged massive investments in computers. The development of fiber-optic technology for transmitting signals has stimulated huge investments by telephone and cable television companies.

Public Policy

Public policy can have significant effects on the demand for capital. Such policies typically seek to affect the cost of capital to firms. The Kennedy administration introduced two such strategies in the early 1960s. One strategy, accelerated depreciation, allowed firms to depreciate capital assets over a very short period of time. They could report artificially high production costs in the first years of an asset's life and thus report lower profits and pay lower taxes. Accelerated depreciation did not change the actual rate at which assets depreciated, of course, but it cut tax payments during the early years of the assets' use and thus reduced the cost of holding capital.

The second strategy was the investment tax credit, which permitted a firm to reduce its tax liability by a percentage of its investment during a period. A firm acquiring new capital could subtract a fraction of its cost—10% under the Kennedy administration's plan—from the taxes it owed the government. In effect, the government "paid" 10% of the cost of any new capital; the investment tax credit thus reduced the cost of capital for firms.

Though less direct, a third strategy for stimulating investment would be a reduction in taxes on corporate profits (called the corporate income tax). Greater after-tax profits mean that firms can retain a greater portion of any return on an investment.

A fourth measure to encourage greater capital accumulation is a capital gains tax rate that allows gains on assets held during a certain period to be taxed at a different rate than other income. When an asset such as a building is sold for more than its purchase price, the seller of the asset is said to have realized a capital gain. Such a gain could be taxed as income under the personal income tax. Alternatively, it could be taxed at a lower rate reserved exclusively for such gains. A lower capital gains tax rate makes assets subject to the tax more attractive. It thus increases the demand for capital. Congress reduced the capital gains tax rate from 28% to 20% in 1996 and reduced the required holding period in 1998. The Jobs and Growth Tax Relief Reconciliation Act of 2003 reduced the capital gains tax further to 15% and also reduced the tax rate on dividends from 38% to 15%. A proposal to eliminate capital gains taxation for smaller firms was considered but dropped before the stimulus bill of 2009 was enacted.

Accelerated depreciation, the investment tax credit, and lower taxes on corporate profits and capital gains all increase the demand for private physical capital. Public policy can also affect the demands for other forms of capital. The federal government subsidizes state and local government production of transportation, education, and many other facilities to encourage greater investment in public sector capital. For example, the federal government pays 90% of the cost of investment by local government in new buses for public transportation.

KEY TAKEAWAYS

- The quantity of investment demanded in any period is negatively related to the interest rate. This relationship is illustrated by the investment demand curve.
- A change in the interest rate causes a movement along the investment demand curve. A change in any other determinant of investment causes a shift of the curve.
- The other determinants of investment include expectations, the level of economic activity, the stock of capital, the capacity utilization rate, the cost of capital goods, other factor costs, technological change, and public policy.

Show how the investment demand curve would be affected by each of the following:

1. A sharp increase in taxes on profits earned by firms
2. An increase in the minimum wage
3. The expectation that there will be a sharp upsurge in the level of economic activity
4. An increase in the cost of new capital goods
5. An increase in interest rates
6. An increase in the level of economic activity
7. A natural disaster that destroys a significant fraction of the capital stock

Case in Point: Assessing the Impact of a One-Year Tax Break on Investment

The U.S. economy was expanding in 2004, but there was a feeling that it still was not functioning as well as it could, as job growth was rather sluggish. To try to spur growth, Congress, supported by President Bush, passed a law in 2004 called the American Jobs Creation Act that gave businesses a one-year special tax break on any profits accumulating overseas that were transferred to the United States. Such profits are called repatriated profits and were estimated at the time to be about $800 billion. For 2005, the tax rate on repatriated profits essentially fell from 25% to 5.25%.

Did the tax break have the desired effect on the economy? To some extent yes, though business also found other uses for the repatriated funds. There were 843 companies that repatriated $312 billion that qualified for the tax break. The Act thus generated about $18 billion in tax revenue, a higher level than had been expected. Some companies announced they were repatriating profits and continuing to downsize. For example, Colgate-Palmolive brought back $800 million and made known it was closing a third of its factories and eliminating 12% of its workforce. However, other companies' plans seemed more in line with the objectives of the special tax break—to create jobs and spur investment.

For example, spokesman Chuck Mulloy of Intel, which repatriated over $6 billion, said the company was building a $3-billion wafer fabrication facility and spending $345 million on expanding existing facilities. "I can't say dollar-for-dollar how much of the funding for those comes from off-shore cash," but he felt that the repatriated funds were contributing to Intel's overall investments. Spokeswoman Margaret Graham of Bausch and Lomb, which makes eye-care products and repatriated $805 million, said, "We plan to use that cash for capital expenditures, investment in research and development, and paying nonofficer compensation."

Analysts are skeptical, though, that the repatriated profits really contributed to investment. The *New York Times* reported on one study that suggested it had not. Rather, the repatriated funds were used for other purposes, such as stock repurchases. The argument is that the companies made investments that they were planning to make and the repatriated funds essentially freed up funding for other purposes.

Sources: Timothy Aeppel, "Tax Break Brings Billion to U.S., But Impact on Hiring Is Unclear," Wall Street Journal, October 5, 2005, p. A1; Lynnley Browning, "A One-Time Tax Break Saved 843 U.S. Corporations $265 Billion," New York Times, June 24, 2008, p. C3.

1. The investment demand curve shifts to the left: Panel (b).
2. A higher minimum wage makes labor more expensive. Firms are likely to shift to greater use of capital, so the investment demand curve shifts to the right: Panel (a).
3. The investment demand curve shifts to the right: Panel (a).
4. The investment demand curve shifts to the left: Panel (b).
5. An increase in interest rates causes a movement along the investment demand curve: Panel (c).
6. The investment demand curve shifts to the right: Panel (a).
7. The need to replace capital shifts the investment demand curve to the right: Panel (a).

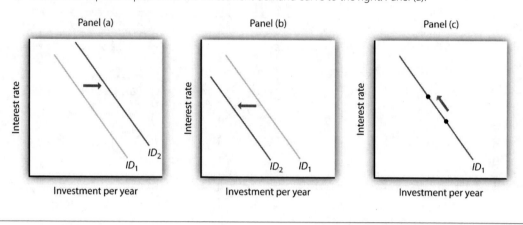

3. INVESTMENT AND THE ECONOMY

L E A R N I N G   O B J E C T I V E S

1. Explain how investment affects aggregate demand.
2. Explain how investment affects economic growth.

We shall examine the impact of investment on the economy in the context of the model of aggregate demand and aggregate supply. Investment is a component of aggregate demand; changes in investment shift the aggregate demand curve by the amount of the initial change times the multiplier. Investment changes the capital stock; changes in the capital stock shift the production possibilities curve and the economy's aggregate production function and thus shift the long- and short-run aggregate supply curves to the right or to the left.

3.1 Investment and Aggregate Demand

In the short run, changes in investment cause aggregate demand to change. Consider, for example, the impact of a reduction in the interest rate, given the investment demand curve (*ID*). In Figure 14.10, Panel (a), which uses the investment demand curve introduced in Figure 14.7, a reduction in the interest rate from 8% to 6% increases investment by $50 billion per year. Assume that the multiplier is 2. With an increase in investment of $50 billion per year and a multiplier of 2, the aggregate demand curve shifts to the right by $100 billion to AD_2 in Panel (b). The quantity of real GDP demanded at each price level thus increases. At a price level of 1.0, for example, the quantity of real GDP demanded rises from $8,000 billion to $8,100 billion per year.

FIGURE 14.10 A Change in Investment and Aggregate Demand

A reduction in the interest rate from 8% to 6% increases the level of investment by $50 billion per year in Panel (a). With a multiplier of 2, the aggregate demand curve shifts to the right by $100 billion in Panel (b). The total quantity of real GDP demanded increases at each price level. Here, for example, the quantity of real GDP demanded at a price level of 1.0 rises from $8,000 billion per year at point C to $8,100 billion per year at point D.

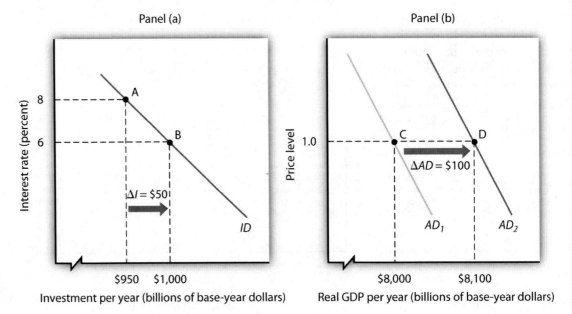

A reduction in investment would shift the aggregate demand curve to the left by an amount equal to the multiplier times the change in investment.

The relationship between investment and interest rates is one key to the effectiveness of monetary policy to the economy. When the Fed seeks to increase aggregate demand, it purchases bonds. That raises bond prices, reduces interest rates, and stimulates investment and aggregate demand as illustrated in Figure 14.10. When the Fed seeks to decrease aggregate demand, it sells bonds. That lowers bond prices, raises interest rates, and reduces investment and aggregate demand. The extent to which investment responds to a change in interest rates is a crucial factor in how effective monetary policy is.

3.2 Investment and Economic Growth

Investment adds to the stock of capital, and the quantity of capital available to an economy is a crucial determinant of its productivity. Investment thus contributes to economic growth. We saw in Figure 14.4 that an increase in an economy's stock of capital shifts its production possibilities curve outward. (Recall from the chapter on economic growth that it also shifts the economy's aggregate production function upward.) That also shifts its long-run aggregate supply curve to the right. At the same time, of course, an increase in investment affects aggregate demand, as we saw in Figure 14.10.

KEY TAKEAWAYS

- Changes in investment shift the aggregate demand curve to the right or left by an amount equal to the initial change in investment times the multiplier.
- Investment adds to the capital stock; it therefore contributes to economic growth

TRY IT!

The text notes that rising investment shifts the aggregate demand curve to the right and at the same time shifts the long-run aggregate supply curve to the right by increasing the nation's stock of physical and human capital. Show this simultaneous shifting in the two curves with three graphs. One graph should show growth in which the price level rises, one graph should show growth in which the price level remains unchanged, and another should show growth with the price level falling.

Case in Point: Investment by Businesses Saves the Australian Expansion

With consumer and export spending faltering in 2005, increased business investment spending seemed to be keeping the Australian economy afloat. "Corporate Australia is solidly behind the steering wheel of the Australian economy," said Craig James, an economist for Commonwealth Securities, an Australian Internet securities brokerage firm. "The clear message from the latest investment survey is that corporate Australia is flush with cash and ready to spend," he continued.

The data supported his conclusions. The level of investment spending in Australia on new buildings, plant, and equipment was 17% higher in 2005 than in 2004. Within the investment category, mining investment, spurred on by high prices for natural resources, was particularly strong.

Source: Scott Murdoch, "Equipment Investment Gives Boost to Economy," *Courier Mail* (Queensland, Australia), September 2, 2005, Finance section, p. 35.

ANSWER TO TRY IT! PROBLEM

Panel (a) shows *AD* shifting by more than *LRAS*; the price level will rise in the long run.

Panel (b) shows *AD* and *LRAS* shifting by equal amounts; the price level will remain unchanged in the long run.

Panel (c) shows *LRAS* shifting by more than *AD*; the price level falls in the long run.

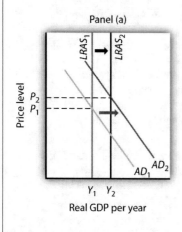
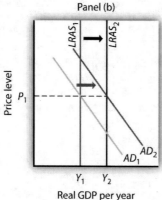
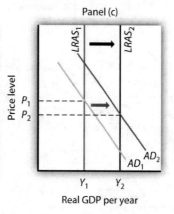

4.   REVIEW AND PRACTICE

Summary

Investment is an addition to the capital stock. Investment may occur as a net addition to capital or as a re-placement of depreciated capital. The bulk of investment spending in the United States falls into the latter category. Investment is a highly volatile component of GDP.

The decision to save is linked directly to the decision to invest. If a nation is to devote a larger share of its production to investment, then it must devote a smaller share to consumption, all other things unchanged. And that requires people to save more.

Investment is affected by the interest rate; the negative relationship between investment and the interest rate is illustrated by the investment demand curve. The position of this curve is affected by expectations, the level of economic activity, the stock of capital, the price of capital, the prices of other factors, technology, and public policy.

Because investment is a component of aggregate demand, a change in investment shifts the aggregate demand curve to the right or left. The amount of the shift will equal the initial change in investment times the multiplier.

In addition to its impact on aggregate demand, investment can also affect economic growth. Investment shifts the production possibilities curve outward, shifts the economy's aggregate production function upward, and shifts the long-run aggregate supply curve to the right.

CONCEPT PROBLEMS

1. Which of the following would be counted as gross private domestic investment?
    a. General Motors issues 1 million shares of stock.
    b. Consolidated Construction purchases 1,000 acres of land for a regional shopping center it plans to build in a few years.
    c. A K-Mart store adds 1,000 T-shirts to its inventory.
    d. Crew buys computers for its office staff.
    e. Your family buys a house.

2. If saving dropped sharply in the economy, what would likely happen to investment? Why?

3. Suppose local governments throughout the United States increase their tax on business inventories. What would you expect to happen to U.S. investment? Why?

4. Suppose the government announces it will pay for half of any new investment undertaken by firms. How will this affect the investment demand curve?

5. White House officials often exude more confidence than they actually feel about future prospects for the economy. Why might this be a good strategy? Are there any dangers inherent in it?

6. Suppose everyone expects investment to rise sharply in three months. How would this expectation be likely to affect bond prices?

7. Suppose that every increase of $1 in real GDP automatically stimulates $0.20 in additional investment spending. How would this affect the multiplier?

8. If environmental resources were counted as part of the capital stock, how would a major forest fire affect net investment?

9. In the Case in Point on reducing private capital in the Great Depression, we saw that net investment was negative during that period. Could gross investment ever be negative? Explain.

10. The Case in Point on lowering the tax rate for one year for companies that repatriated profits suggests that investment did not increase, even though company representatives are quoted as saying that they were using the repatriated profits for investment. Explain this seeming contradiction.

11. Use the model of aggregate demand and aggregate supply to evaluate the argument that an increase in investment would raise the standard of living.

NUMERICAL PROBLEMS

1. Suppose a construction company is trying to decide whether to buy a new nail gun. The table below shows the hypothetical costs for the nail gun and the amount the gun will save the company each year. Assume the gun will last forever. In each case, determine the highest interest rate the company should pay for a loan that makes purchase of the nail gun possible.

	Cost	Savings
a.	$1,000	$100
b.	$1,000	$200
c.	$1,000	$300

2. A car company currently has capital stock of $100 million and desires a capital stock of $110 million.

   a. If it experiences no depreciation, how much will it need to invest to get to its desired level of capital stock?

   b. If its annual depreciation is 5%, how much will it need to invest to get to its desired level?

   c. If its annual depreciation is 10%, how much will it need to invest to get to its desired level?

3. Burger World is contemplating installing an automated ordering system. The ordering system will allow Burger World to permanently replace five employees for an annual (and permanent) cost savings of $100,000.

   a. If the automated system cost $1,000,000, what is the rate of return on the investment?

   b. If the system cost $2,000,000, what would be its rate of return?

   c. If the government were to introduce an investment tax credit that allows firms to deduct 10% of its investment from its tax liability, what would happen to the rate of return if the system costs $1,000,000?

   d. If Burger World has to pay 8% to borrow the funds to purchase the system, what is the most it should pay for the system? Assume that there is no investment tax credit.

4. The table below shows a number of investment projects and their effective earned interest rates or returns. Given the market interest rates shown below, identify which projects will be undertaken and the total amount of investment spending that will ensue.

Project	Return on project	Cost
A	30%	$1,000
B	28	500
C	22	2,500
D	17	1,000
E	8	750
F	4	1,200

   a. 20%

   b. 15%

   c. 10%

   d. 5%

   e. 3%

   f. Sketch out the investment demand curve implied by these data.

5. The table below describes the amounts of investment for different interest rates.

Interest rate	Amount of investment (billions)
25%	$5
20	$10
15	$15
10	$20
5	$25

   a. Draw the investment demand curve for this economy.

b. Show the effect you would expect a decrease in the cost of capital goods to have on this investment demand curve.

c. Show the effect you would expect an investment tax credit to have on this investment demand curve.

d. Show the effect you would expect a recession to have on this investment demand curve.

6. Suppose real GDP in an economy equals its potential output of $2,000 billion, the multiplier is 2.5, investment is raised by $200 billion, and the increased investment does not affect the economy's potential.

a. Show the short- and long-run effects of the change upon real GDP and the price level, using the graphical framework for the model of aggregate demand and aggregate supply.

b. Would real GDP rise by the multiplier times the change in investment in the short run? In the long run? Explain.

7. Use the information below to compute the levels of gross and net private domestic investment. Data are in billions of dollars.

Change in business inventories $ 59.3

Residential construction 369.6

Producers' durable equipment 691.3

Nonresidential structures 246.9

Depreciation 713.9

8. Complete the table, which shows investment in the United States in billions of 2000 chained dollars.

	Year	Gross private domestic investment	Depreciation	Net private domestic investment
a.	2005	1,873.5	1,266.6	
b.	2006		1,216.1	696.4
c.	2007	1,809.7		546.7

ENDNOTES

1. Kate Linebaugh, "Toyota Delays Mississippi Prius Factor Amid Slump," *Wall Street Journal*, December 16, 2008, p. B1.

2. Amy Merrick, "Walgreen to Cut Back on Opening New Stores," *Wall Street Journal*, December 23, 2008, p. B1.

3. Darren Shannon, "FedEx Takes More Measures to Offset Fiscal Uncertainty," *Aviation Daily*, December 19, 2008, p. 6.

4. Reed Abelson, "Hurting for Business," *New York Times*, November 7, 2008, p. B1.

5. Bettina Wassener, "Sony to Cut 8,000 Workers and Shut Plants," *New York Times*, December 10, 2008, p. B8.

6. Steve LeVine, "Pullback in the Oil Patch," *Business Week*, December 8, 2008, p. 60.

CHAPTER 15

Net Exports and International Finance

START UP: CURRENCY CRISES SHAKE THE WORLD

It became known as the "Asian Contagion," and it swept the world as the 20th century came to a close.

Japan, crippled by the threat of collapse of many of its banks, seemed stuck in a recessionary gap for most of the decade. Because Japan was a major market for the exports of economies throughout East Asia, the slump in Japan translated into falling exports in neighboring economies. Slowed growth in a host of economies that had grown accustomed to phenomenal growth set the stage for trouble throughout the world.

The first crack appeared in Thailand, whose central bank had successfully maintained a stable exchange rate between the baht, Thailand's currency, and the U.S. dollar. But weakened demand for Thai exports, along with concerns about the stability of Thai banks, put downward pressure on the baht. Thailand's effort to shore up its currency ultimately failed, and the country's central bank gave up the effort in July of 1997. The baht's value dropped nearly 20% in a single day.

Holders of other currencies became worried about their stability and began selling. Central banks that, like Thailand's, had held their currencies stable relative to the dollar, gave up their efforts as well. Malaysia quit propping up the ringgit less than two weeks after the baht's fall. Indonesia's central bank gave up trying to hold the rupiah's dollar value a month later. South Korea let the won fall in November.

Currency crises continued to spread in 1998, capped by a spectacular plunge in the Russian ruble. As speculators sold other currencies, they bought dollars, driving the U.S. exchange rate steadily upward.

What was behind the currency crises that shook the world? How do changes in a country's exchange rate affect its economy? How can events such as the fall of the baht and the ringgit spread to other countries?

We will explore the answers to these questions by looking again at how changes in a country's exchange rate can affect its economy—and how changes in one economy can spread to others. We will be engaged in a study of **international finance**, the field that examines the macroeconomic consequences of the financial flows associated with international trade.

We will begin by reviewing the reasons nations trade. International trade has the potential to increase the availability of goods and services to everyone. We will look at the effects of trade on the welfare of people and then turn to the macroeconomic implications of financing trade.

international finance

The field that examines the macroeconomic consequences of the financial flows associated with international trade.

1. THE INTERNATIONAL SECTOR: AN INTRODUCTION

LEARNING OBJECTIVES

1. Discuss the main arguments economists make in support of free trade.
2. Explain the determinants of net exports and tell how each affects aggregate demand.

How important is international trade?

Take a look at the labels on some of your clothing. You are likely to find that the clothes in your closet came from all over the globe. Look around any parking lot. You may find cars from Japan, Korea, Sweden, Britain, Germany, France, and Italy—and even the United States! Do you use a computer? Even if it is an American computer, its components are likely to have been assembled in Indonesia or in some other country. Visit the grocery store. Much of the produce may come from Latin America and Asia.

The international market is important not just in terms of the goods and services it provides to a country, but as a market for that country's goods and services. Because foreign demand for U.S. exports is almost as large as investment and government purchases as a component of aggregate demand, it can be very important in terms of growth. The increase in exports from 2000 to 2007, for example, accounted for almost 20% of the gain in U.S. real GDP during that period. For the period 2004 to 2007, the increase in exports accounted for about 30% of the gain.

1.1 The Case for Trade

International trade increases the quantity of goods and services available to the world's consumers. By allocating resources according to the principle of comparative advantage, trade allows nations to consume combinations of goods and services they would be unable to produce on their own, combinations that lie outside each country's production possibilities curve.

A country has a comparative advantage in the production of a good if it can produce that good at a lower opportunity cost than can other countries. If each country specializes in the production of goods in which it has a comparative advantage and trades those goods for things in which other countries have a comparative advantage, global production of all goods and services will be increased. The result can be higher levels of consumption for all.

If international trade allows expanded world production of goods and services, it follows that restrictions on trade will reduce world production. That, in a nutshell, is the economic case for free trade. It suggests that restrictions on trade, such as a **tariff**, a tax imposed on imported goods and services, or a **quota**, a ceiling on the quantity of specific goods and services that can be imported, reduce world living standards.

tariff

A tax imposed on imported goods and services.

quota

A ceiling on the quantity of specific goods and services that can be imported, which reduces world living standards.

The conceptual argument for free trade is a compelling one; virtually all economists support policies that reduce barriers to trade. Economists were among the most outspoken advocates for the 1993 ratification of the North American Free Trade Agreement (NAFTA), which virtually eliminated trade restrictions between Mexico, the United States, and Canada, and the 2004 Central American Free Trade Agreement (CAFTA), which did the same for trade between the United States, Central America, and the Dominican Republic. Most economists have also been strong supporters of worldwide reductions in trade barriers, including the 1994 ratification of the General Agreement on Tariffs and Trade (GATT), a pact slashing tariffs and easing quotas among 117 nations, including the United States, and the Doha round of World Trade Organization negotiations, named after the site of the first meeting in Doha, Qatar, in 2001 and still continuing. In Europe, member nations of the European Union (EU) have virtually eliminated trade barriers among themselves, and 15 EU nations now have a common currency, the euro, and a single central bank, the European Central Bank, established in 1999. Trade barriers have also been slashed among the economies of Latin America and of Southeast Asia. A treaty has been signed that calls for elimination of trade barriers among the developed nations of the Pacific Rim (including the United States and Japan) by 2010 and among all Pacific rim nations by 2020.

The global embrace of the idea of free trade demonstrates the triumph of economic ideas over powerful forces that oppose free trade. One source of opposition to free trade comes from the owners of factors of production used in industries in which a nation lacks a comparative advantage.

A related argument against free trade is that it not only reduces employment in some sectors but also reduces employment in the economy as a whole. In the long run, this argument is clearly wrong. The economy's natural level of employment is determined by forces unrelated to trade policy, and employment moves to its natural level in the long run.

Further, trade has no effect on real wage levels for the economy as a whole. The equilibrium real wage depends on the economy's demand for and supply curve of labor. Trade affects neither.

In the short run, trade does affect aggregate demand. Net exports are one component of aggregate demand; a change in net exports shifts the aggregate demand curve and affects real GDP in the short run. All other things unchanged, a reduction in net exports reduces aggregate demand, and an increase in net exports increases it.

Protectionist sentiment always rises during recessions. The recession that began in the United States in 2007 is no exception. The stimulus bill contained a provision ordering U.S. government agencies and contractors to purchase goods and services produced in the United States in preference to goods and services from other countries. Our trading partners have already begun threatening a trade war as a result of this provision. The stimulus bill does say that the "buy America first" provision should be "consistent with international obligations." As yet, it is not clear how significant this provision would become.

1.2 The Rising Importance of International Trade

International trade is important, and its importance is increasing. From 1965 to 2007, world output rose by about 300%. But the gains in total exports were even more spectacular; they soared by over 1,000%!

While international trade was rising around the world, it was playing a more significant role in the United States as well. In 1960, exports represented just 3.5% of real GDP; by 2010, exports accounted for 12.6% of real GDP. Figure 15.1 shows the growth in exports and imports as a percentage of real GDP in the United States from 1960 to 2010.

Why has world trade risen so spectacularly? Two factors have been important. First, advances in transportation and communication have dramatically reduced the costs of moving goods around the globe. The development of shipping containerization that allows cargo to be moved seamlessly from trucks or trains to ships, which began in 1956, drastically reduced the cost of moving goods around the world, by as much as 90%. As a result, the numbers of container ships and their capacities have markedly increased.[1] Second, we have already seen that trade barriers between countries have fallen and are likely to continue to fall.

FIGURE 15.1 U.S. Exports and Imports Relative to U.S. Real GDP, 1960–2010

The chart shows exports and imports as a percentage of real GDP from 1960 through the third quarter of 2010.

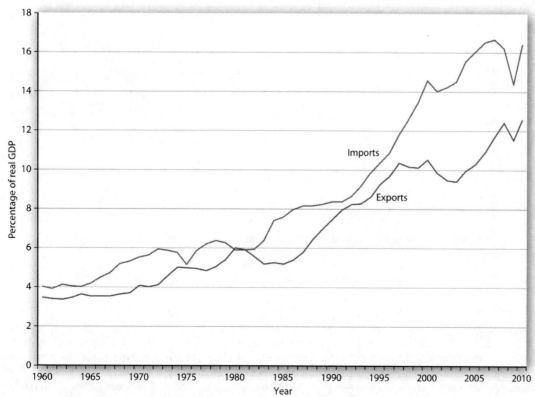

Source: Bureau of Economic Analysis, NIPA Table 1.1.6 (Revised November 23, 2010). Data are through the third quarter of 2010.

1.3 Net Exports and the Economy

As trade has become more important worldwide, exports and imports have assumed increased import-ance in nearly every country on the planet. We have already discussed the increased shares of U.S. real GDP represented by exports and by imports. We will find in this section that the economy both in-fluences, and is influenced by, net exports. First, we will examine the determinants of net exports and then discuss the ways in which net exports affect aggregate demand.

Determinants of Net Exports

Net exports equal exports minus imports. Many of the same forces affect both exports and imports, al-beit in different ways.

Income

As incomes in other nations rise, the people of those nations will be able to buy more goods and ser-vices—including foreign goods and services. Any one country's exports thus will increase as incomes rise in other countries and will fall as incomes drop in other countries.

A nation's own level of income affects its imports the same way it affects consumption. As con-sumers have more income, they will buy more goods and services. Because some of those goods and services are produced in other nations, imports will rise. An increase in real GDP thus boosts imports; a reduction in real GDP reduces imports. Figure 15.2 shows the relationship between real GDP and the real level of import spending in the United States from 1960 through 2010. Notice that the observations lie close to a straight line one could draw through them and resemble a consumption function.

FIGURE 15.2 U.S. Real GDP and Imports, 1960–2010

The chart shows annual values of U.S. real imports and real GDP from 1960 through 2010. The observations lie quite close to a straight line.

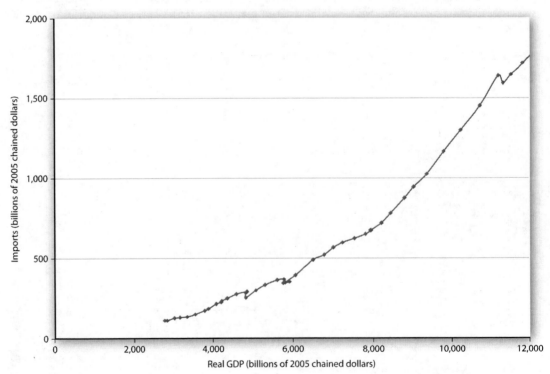

Source: Bureau of Economic Analysis, NIPA Table 1.1.6 (Revised November 23, 2010). Data are through the third quarter of 2010.

Relative Prices

A change in the price level within a nation simultaneously affects exports and imports. A higher price level in the United States, for example, makes U.S. exports more expensive for foreigners and thus tends to reduce exports. At the same time, a higher price level in the United States makes foreign goods and services relatively more attractive to U.S. buyers and thus increases imports. A higher price level therefore reduces net exports. A lower price level encourages exports and reduces imports, increasing net exports. As we saw in the chapter that introduced the aggregate demand and supply model, the negative relationship between net exports and the price level is called the international trade effect and is one reason for the negative slope of the aggregate demand curve.

The Exchange Rate

The purchase of U.S. goods and services by foreign buyers generally requires the purchase of dollars, because U.S. suppliers want to be paid in their own currency. Similarly, purchases of foreign goods and services by U.S. buyers generally require the purchase of foreign currencies, because foreign suppliers want to be paid in their own currencies. An increase in the exchange rate means foreigners must pay more for dollars, and must thus pay more for U.S. goods and services. It therefore reduces U.S. exports. At the same time, a higher exchange rate means that a dollar buys more foreign currency. That makes foreign goods and services cheaper for U.S. buyers, so imports are likely to rise. An increase in the exchange rate should thus tend to reduce net exports. A reduction in the exchange rate should increase net exports.

Trade Policies

A country's exports depend on its own trade policies as well as the trade policies of other countries. A country may be able to increase its exports by providing some form of government assistance (such as special tax considerations for companies that export goods and services, government promotional efforts, assistance with research, or subsidies). A country's exports are also affected by the degree to which other countries restrict or encourage imports. The United States, for example, has sought changes in Japanese policies toward products such as U.S.-grown rice. Japan banned rice imports in the past, arguing it needed to protect its own producers. That has been a costly strategy; consumers in Japan typically pay as much as 10 times the price consumers in the United States pay for rice. Japan has given in to pressure from the United States and other nations to end its ban on foreign rice as part of the GATT accord. That will increase U.S. exports and lower rice prices in Japan.

Similarly, a country's imports are affected by its trade policies and by the policies of its trading partners. A country can limit its imports of some goods and services by imposing tariffs or quotas on them—it may even ban the importation of some items. If foreign governments subsidize the manufacture of a particular good, then domestic imports of the good might increase. For example, if the governments of countries trading with the United States were to subsidize the production of steel, then U.S. companies would find it cheaper to purchase steel from abroad than at home, increasing U.S. imports of steel.

Preferences and Technology

Consumer preferences are one determinant of the consumption of any good or service; a shift in preferences for a foreign-produced good will affect the level of imports of that good. The preference among the French for movies and music produced in the United States has boosted French imports of these services. Indeed, the shift in French preferences has been so strong that the government of France, claiming a threat to its cultural heritage, has restricted the showing of films produced in the United States. French radio stations are fined if more than 40% of the music they play is from "foreign" (in most cases, U.S.) rock groups.

Changes in technology can affect the kinds of capital firms import. Technological changes have changed production worldwide toward the application of computers to manufacturing processes, for example. This has led to increased demand for high-tech capital equipment, a sector in which the United States has a comparative advantage and tends to dominate world production. This has boosted net exports in the United States.

Net Exports and Aggregate Demand

Net exports affect both the slope and the position of the aggregate demand curve. A change in the price level causes a change in net exports that moves the economy along its aggregate demand curve. This is the international trade effect. A change in net exports produced by one of the other determinants of net exports listed above (incomes and price levels in other nations, the exchange rate, trade policies, and preferences and technology) will shift the aggregate demand curve. The magnitude of this shift equals the change in net exports times the multiplier, as shown in Figure 15.3. Panel (a) shows an increase in net exports; Panel (b) shows a reduction. In both cases, the aggregate demand curve shifts by the multiplier times the initial change in net exports, provided there is no other change in the other components of aggregate demand.

FIGURE 15.3 Changes in Net Exports and Aggregate Demand

In Panel (a), an increase in net exports shifts the aggregate demand curve to the right by an amount equal to the multiplier times the initial change in net exports. In Panel (b), an equal reduction in net exports shifts the aggregate demand curve to the left by the same amount.

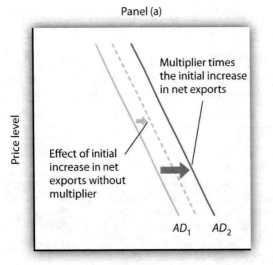
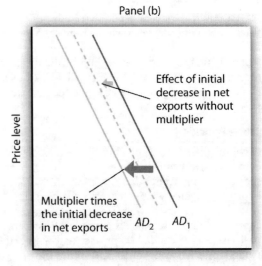

Changes in net exports that shift the aggregate demand curve can have a significant impact on the economy. The United States, for example, experienced a slowdown in the rate of increase in real GDP in the second and third quarters of 1998—virtually all of this slowing was the result of a reduction in net exports caused by recessions that staggered economies throughout Asia. The Asian slide reduced incomes there and thus reduced Asian demand for U.S. goods and services. We will see in the next section another mechanism through which difficulties in other nations can cause changes in a nation's net exports and its level of real GDP in the short run.

KEY TAKEAWAYS

- International trade allows the world's resources to be allocated on the basis of comparative advantage and thus allows the production of a larger quantity of goods and services than would be available without trade.

- Trade affects neither the economy's natural level of employment nor its real wage in the long run; those are determined by the demand for and the supply curve of labor.

- Growth in international trade has outpaced growth in world output over the past five decades.

- The chief determinants of net exports are domestic and foreign incomes, relative price levels, exchange rates, domestic and foreign trade policies, and preferences and technology.

- A change in the price level causes a change in net exports that moves the economy along its aggregate demand curve. This is the international trade effect. A change in net exports produced by one of the other determinants of net exports will shift the aggregate demand curve by an amount equal to the initial change in net exports times the multiplier.

Draw graphs showing the aggregate demand and short-run aggregate supply curves in each of four countries: Mexico, Japan, Germany, and the United States. Assume that each country is initially in equilibrium with a real GDP of Y_1 and a price level of P_1. Now show how each of the following four events would affect aggregate demand, the price level, and real GDP in the country indicated.

1. The United States is the largest foreign purchaser of goods and services from Mexico. How does an expansion in the United States affect real GDP and the price level in Mexico?
2. Japan's exchange rate falls sharply. How does this affect the price level and real GDP in Japan?
3. A wave of pro-German sentiment sweeps France, and the French sharply increase their purchases of German goods and services. How does this affect real GDP and the price level in Germany?
4. Canada, the largest importer of U.S. goods and services, slips into a recession. How does this affect the price level and real GDP in the United States?

Case in Point: Canadian Net Exports Survive the Loonie's Rise

Throughout 2003 and the first half of 2004, the Canadian dollar, nicknamed the loonie after the Canadian bird that is featured on its one-dollar coin, rose sharply in value against the U.S. dollar. Because the United States and Canada are major trading partners, the changing exchange rate suggested that, other things equal, Canadian exports to the United States would fall and imports rise. The resulting fall in net exports, other things equal, could slow the rate of growth in Canadian GDP.

Fortunately for Canada, "all other things" were not equal. In particular, strong income growth in the United States and China increased the demand for Canadian exports. In addition, the loonie's appreciation against other currencies was less dramatic, and so Canadian exports remained competitive in those markets. While imports did increase, as expected due to the exchange rate change, exports grew at a faster rate, and hence net exports increased over the period.

In sum, Canadian net exports grew, although not by as much as they would have had the loonie not appreciated. As Beata Caranci, an economist for Toronto Dominion Bank put it, "We might have some bumpy months ahead but it definitely looks like the worst is over. ... While Canadian exports appear to have survived the loonie's run-up, their fortunes would be much brighter if the exchange rate were still at 65 cents."

Source: *Steven Theobald, "Exports Surviving Loonie's Rise: Study," Toronto Star, July 13, 2004, p. D1.*

1. Mexico's exports increase, shifting its aggregate demand curve to the right. Mexico's real GDP and price level rise, as shown in Panel (a).

2. Japan's net exports rise. This event shifts Japan's aggregate demand curve to the right, increasing its real GDP and price level, as shown in Panel (b).

3. Germany's net exports increase, shifting Germany's aggregate demand curve to the right, increasing its price level and real GDP, as shown in Panel (c).

4. U.S. exports fall, shifting the U.S. aggregate demand curve to the left, which will reduce the price level and real GDP, as shown in Panel (d).

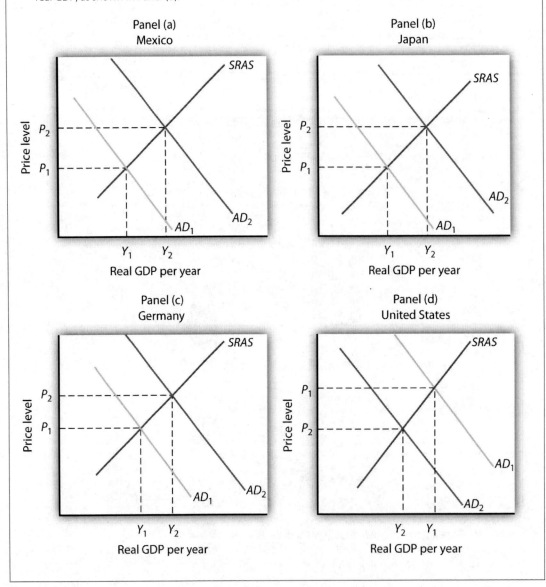

2. INTERNATIONAL FINANCE

LEARNING OBJECTIVES

1. Define a country's balance of payments, and explain what is included on the current and capital accounts.
2. Assuming that the market for a country's currency is in equilibrium, explain why the current account balance will always be the negative of the capital account balance.
3. Summarize the economic arguments per se against public opposition to a current account deficit and a capital account surplus.

There is an important difference between trade that flows, say, from one city to another and trade that flows from one nation to another. Unless they share a common currency, as some of the nations of the European Union do, trade among nations requires that currencies be exchanged as well as goods and services. Suppose, for example, that buyers in Mexico purchase silk produced in China. The Mexican buyers will pay in Mexico's currency, the peso; the manufacturers of the silk must be paid in China's currency, the yuan. The flow of trade between Mexico and China thus requires an exchange of pesos for yuan.

This section examines the relationship between spending that flows into a country and spending that flows out of it. These spending flows include not only spending for a nation's exports and imports, but payments to owners of assets in other countries, international transfer payments, and purchases of foreign assets. The balance between spending flowing into a country and spending flowing out of it is called its **balance of payments**.

We will simplify our analysis by ignoring international transfer payments, which occur when an individual, firm, or government makes a gift to an individual, firm, or government in another country. Foreign aid is an example of an international transfer payment. International transfer payments play a relatively minor role in the international financial transactions of most countries; ignoring them will not change our basic conclusions.

A second simplification will be to treat payments to foreign owners of factors of production used in a country as imports and payments received by owners of factors of production used in other countries as exports. This is the approach when we use GNP rather than GDP as the measure of a country's output.

These two simplifications leave two reasons for demanding a country's currency: for foreigners to purchase a country's goods and services (that is, its exports) and to purchase assets in the country. A country's currency is supplied in order to purchase foreign currencies. A country's currency is thus supplied for two reasons: to purchase goods and services from other countries (that is, its imports) and to purchase assets in other countries.

We studied the determination of exchange rates in the chapter on how financial markets work. We saw that, in general, exchange rates are determined by demand and supply and that the markets for the currencies of most nations can be regarded as being in equilibrium. Exchange rates adjust quickly, so that the quantity of a currency demanded equals the quantity of the currency supplied.

Our analysis will deal with flows of spending between the domestic economy and the rest of the world. Suppose, for example, that we are analyzing Japan's economy and its transactions with the rest of the world. The purchase by a buyer in, say, Germany of bonds issued by a Japanese corporation would be part of the rest-of-world demand for yen to buy Japanese assets. Adding export demand to asset demand by people, firms, and governments outside a country, we get the total demand for a country's currency.

A domestic economy's currency is supplied to purchase currencies in the rest of the world. In an analysis of the market for Japanese yen, for example, yen are supplied when people, firms, and government agencies in Japan purchase goods and services from the rest of the world. This part of the supply of yen equals Japanese imports. Yen are also supplied so that holders of yen can acquire assets from other countries.

Equilibrium in the market for a country's currency implies that the quantity of a particular country's currency demanded equals the quantity supplied. Equilibrium thus implies that

EQUATION 15.1

$$\text{Quantity of currency demanded} = \text{quantity of currency supplied}$$

balance of payments

The balance between spending flowing into a country and spending flowing out.

In turn, the quantity of a currency demanded is from two sources:

1. Exports
2. Rest-of-world purchases of domestic assets

The quantity supplied of a currency is from two sources:

1. Imports
2. Domestic purchases of rest-of-world assets

Therefore, we can rewrite Equation 15.1 as

EQUATION 15.2

Exports+(rest-of-world purchases of domestic assets) = imports+(domestic purchases of rest-of-world assets)

2.1 Accounting for International Payments

In this section, we will build a set of accounts to track international payments. To do this, we will use the equilibrium condition for foreign exchange markets given in Equation 15.2. We will see that the balance between a country's purchases of foreign assets and foreign purchases of the country's assets will have important effects on net exports, and thus on aggregate demand.

We can rearrange the terms in Equation 15.2 to write the following:

EQUATION 15.3

Exports−imports = − [(rest-of-world purchases of domestic assets) − (domestic purchases of rest-of-world asset

Equation 15.3 represents an extremely important relationship. Let us examine it carefully.

The left side of the equation is net exports. It is the balance between spending flowing from foreign countries into a particular country for the purchase of its goods and services and spending flowing out of the country for the purchase of goods and services produced in other countries. The **current account** is an accounting statement that includes all spending flows across a nation's border except those that represent purchases of assets. The **balance on current account** equals spending flowing into an economy from the rest of the world on current account less spending flowing from the nation to the rest of the world on current account. Given our two simplifying assumptions—that there are no international transfer payments and that we can treat rest-of-world purchases of domestic factor services as exports and domestic purchases of rest-of-world factor services as imports—the balance on current account equals net exports. When the balance on current account is positive, spending flowing in for the purchase of goods and services exceeds spending that flows out, and the economy has a **current account surplus** (i.e., net exports are positive in our simplified analysis). When the balance on current account is negative, spending for goods and services that flows out of the country exceeds spending that flows in, and the economy has a **current account deficit** (i.e., net exports are negative in our simplified analysis).

---

current account

An accounting statement that includes all spending flows across a nation's border except those that represent purchases of assets.

balance on current account

Spending flowing into an economy from the rest of the world on current account less spending flowing from the nation to the rest of the world on current account.

current account surplus

Situation that occurs when spending flowing in for the purchase of goods and services exceeds spending that flows out.

current account deficit

Situation that occurs when spending for goods and services that flows out of the country exceeds spending that flows in.

A country's **capital account** is an accounting statement of spending flows into and out of the country during a particular period for purchases of assets. The term within the parentheses on the right side of the equation gives the balance between rest-of-world purchases of domestic assets and domestic purchases of rest-of-world assets; this balance is a country's **balance on capital account**. A positive balance on capital account is a **capital account surplus**. A capital account surplus means that buyers in the rest of the world are purchasing more of a country's assets than buyers in the domestic economy are spending on rest-of-world assets. A negative balance on capital account is a **capital account deficit**. It implies that buyers in the domestic economy are purchasing a greater volume of assets in other countries than buyers in other countries are spending on the domestic economy's assets. Remember that the balance on capital account is the term *inside* the parentheses on the right-hand side of Equation 15.3 and that there is a minus sign *outside* the parentheses.

Equation 15.3 tells us that a country's balance on current account equals the negative of its balance on capital account. Suppose, for example, that buyers in the rest of the world are spending $100 billion per year acquiring assets in a country, while that country's buyers are spending $70 billion per year to acquire assets in the rest of the world. The country thus has a capital account surplus of $30 billion per year. Equation 15.3 tells us the country must have a current account deficit of $30 billion per year.

Alternatively, suppose buyers from the rest of the world acquire $25 billion of a country's assets per year and that buyers in that country buy $40 billion per year in assets in other countries. The economy has a capital account deficit of $15 billion; its capital account balance equals −$15 billion. Equation 15.3 tells us it thus has a current account surplus of $15 billion. In general, we may write the following:

EQUATION 15.4

$$\text{Current account balance} = -(\text{capital account balance})$$

Assuming the market for a nation's currency is in equilibrium, a capital account surplus *necessarily* means a current account deficit. A capital account deficit *necessarily* means a current account surplus. Similarly, a current account surplus implies a capital account deficit; a current account deficit implies a capital account surplus. Whenever the market for a country's currency is in equilibrium, and it virtually always is in the absence of exchange rate controls, Equation 15.3 is an identity—it must be true. Thus, any surplus or deficit in the current account means the capital account has an offsetting deficit or surplus.

The accounting relationships underlying international finance hold as long as a country's currency market is in equilibrium. But what are the economic forces at work that cause these equalities to hold? Consider how global turmoil in 1997 and 1998, discussed in the chapter opening, affected the United States. Holders of assets, including foreign currencies, in the rest of the world were understandably concerned that the values of those assets might fall. To avoid a plunge in the values of their own holdings, many of them purchased U.S. assets, including U.S. dollars. Those purchases of U.S. assets increased the U.S. surplus on capital account. To buy those assets, foreign purchasers had to purchase dollars. Also, U.S. citizens became less willing to hold foreign assets, and their preference for holding U.S. assets increased. United States citizens were thus less willing to supply dollars to the foreign exchange market. The increased demand for dollars and the decreased supply of dollars sent the U.S. exchange rate higher, as shown in Panel (a) of Figure 15.6. Panel (b) shows the actual movement of the U.S. exchange rate in 1997 and 1998. Notice the sharp increases in the exchange rate throughout most of the period. A higher exchange rate in the United States reduces U.S. exports and increases U.S. imports, increasing the current account deficit. Panel (c) shows the movement of the current and capital accounts in the United States in 1997 and 1998. Notice that as the capital account surplus increased, the current account deficit rose. A reduction in the U.S. exchange rate at the end of 1998 coincided with a movement of these balances in the opposite direction.

capital account

An accounting statement of spending flows into and out of the country during a particular period for purchases of assets.

balance on capital account

The balance between rest-of-world purchases of domestic assets and domestic purchases of rest-of-world assets.

capital account surplus

A positive balance on capital account.

capital account deficit

A negative balance on capital account.

FIGURE 15.6 A Change in the Exchange Rate Affected the U.S. Current and Capital Accounts in 1997 and 1998

Turmoil in currency markets all over the world in 1997 and 1998 increased the demand for dollars and decreased the supply of dollars in the foreign exchange market, which caused an increase in the U.S. exchange rate, as shown in Panel (a). Panel (b) shows actual values of the U.S. exchange rate during that period; Panel (c) shows U.S. balances on current and on capital accounts. Notice that the balance on capital account generally rose while the balance on current account generally fell.

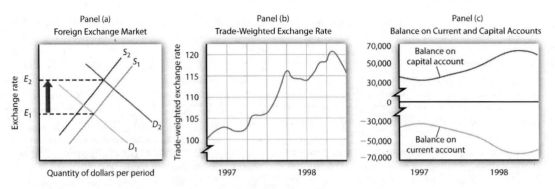

2.2 Deficits and Surpluses: Good or Bad?

For the past quarter century, the United States has had a current account deficit and a capital account surplus. Is this good or bad?

Viewed from the perspective of consumers, neither phenomenon seems to pose a problem. A current account deficit is likely to imply a trade deficit. That means more goods and services are flowing into the country than are flowing out. A capital account surplus means more spending is flowing into the country for the purchase of assets than is flowing out. It is hard to see the harm in any of that.

Public opinion, however, appears to regard a current account deficit and capital account surplus as highly undesirable, perhaps because people associate a trade deficit with a loss of jobs. But that is erroneous; employment in the long run is determined by forces that have nothing to do with a trade deficit. An increase in the trade deficit (that is, a reduction in net exports) reduces aggregate demand in the short run, but net exports are only one component of aggregate demand. Other factors—consumption, investment, and government purchases—affect aggregate demand as well. There is no reason a trade deficit should imply a loss of jobs.

What about foreign purchases of U.S. assets? One objection to such purchases is that if foreigners own U.S. assets, they will receive the income from those assets—spending will flow out of the country. But it is hard to see the harm in paying income to financial investors. When someone buys a bond issued by Microsoft, interest payments will flow from Microsoft to the bond holder. Does Microsoft view the purchase of its bond as a bad thing? Of course not. Despite the fact that Microsoft's payment of interest on the bond and the ultimate repayment of the face value of the bond will exceed what the company originally received from the bond purchaser, Microsoft is surely not unhappy with the arrangement. It expects to put that money to more productive use; that is the reason it issued the bond in the first place.

A second concern about foreign asset purchases is that the United States in some sense loses sovereignty when foreigners buy its assets. But why should this be a problem? Foreign-owned firms competing in U.S. markets are at the mercy of those markets, as are firms owned by U.S. nationals. Foreign owners of U.S. real estate have no special power. What about foreign buyers of bonds issued by the U.S. government? Foreigners owned about 28% of these bonds at the end of September 2008; they are thus the creditors for about 28% of the national debt. But this position hardly puts them in control of the government of the United States. They hold an obligation of the U.S. government to pay them a certain amount of U.S. dollars on a certain date, nothing more. A foreign owner could sell his or her bonds, but more than $100 billion worth of these bonds are sold every day. The resale of U.S. bonds by a foreign owner will not affect the U.S. government.

In short, there is no economic justification for concern about having a current account deficit and a capital account surplus—nor would there be an economic reason to be concerned about the opposite state of affairs. The important feature of international trade is its potential to improve living standards for people. It is not a game in which current account balances are the scorecard.

TRY IT!

Use Equation 15.3 and Equation 15.4 to compute the variables given in each of the following. Assume that the market for a nation's currency is in equilibrium and that the balance on current account equals net exports.

1. Suppose U.S. exports equal $300 billion, imports equal $400 billion, and rest-of-world purchases of U.S. assets equal $150 billion. What is the U.S. balance on current account? The balance on capital account? What is the value of U.S. purchases of rest-of-world assets?

2. Suppose Japanese exports equal ¥200 trillion (¥ is the symbol for the yen, Japan's currency), imports equal ¥120 trillion, and Japan's purchases of rest-of-world assets equal ¥90 trillion. What is the balance on Japan's current account? The balance on Japan's capital account? What is the value of rest-of-world purchases of Japan's assets?

3. Suppose Britain's purchases of rest-of-world assets equal £70 billion (£ is the symbol for the pound, Britain's currency), rest-of-world purchases of British assets equal £90 billion, and Britain's exports equal £40 billion. What is Britain's balance on capital account? Its balance on current account? Its total imports?

4. Suppose Mexico's purchases of rest-of-world assets equal $500 billion ($ is the symbol for the peso, Mexico's currency), rest-of-world purchases of Mexico's assets equal $700 billion, and Mexico's imports equal $550 billion. What is Mexico's balance on capital account? Its balance on current account? Its total exports?

Case in Point: Alan Greenspan on the U.S. Current Account Deficit

The growing U.S. current account deficit has generated considerable alarm. But, is there cause for alarm? In a speech in December 2005, former Federal Reserve Chairman Alan Greenspan analyzed what he feels are the causes of the growing deficit and explains how the U.S. current account deficit may, under certain circumstances, decrease over time without a crisis.

"In November 2003, I noted that we saw little evidence of stress in funding the U.S. current account deficit even though the real exchange rate for the dollar, on net, had declined more than 10% since early 2002. … Two years later, little has changed except that our current account deficit has grown still larger. Most policy makers marvel at the seeming ease with which the United States continues to finance its current account deficit.

"Of course, deficits that cumulate to ever-increasing net external debt, with its attendant rise in servicing costs, cannot persist indefinitely. At some point, foreign investors will balk at a growing concentration of claims against U.S. residents … and will begin to alter their portfolios. … The rise of the U.S. current account deficit over the past decade appears to have coincided with a pronounced new phase of globalization that is characterized by a major acceleration in U.S. productivity growth and the decline in what economists call home bias. In brief, home bias is the parochial tendency of persons, though faced with comparable or superior foreign opportunities, to invest domestic savings in the home country. The decline in home bias is reflected in savers increasingly reaching across national borders to invest in foreign assets. The rise in U.S. productivity attracted much of those savings toward investments in the United States. …

"Accordingly, it is tempting to conclude that the U.S. current account deficit is essentially a byproduct of long-term secular forces, and thus is largely benign. After all, we do seem to have been able to finance our international current account deficit with relative ease in recent years.

"But does the apparent continued rise in the deficits of U.S. individual households and nonfinancial businesses themselves reflect growing economic strain? (We do not think so.) And does it matter how those deficits of individual economic entities are being financed? Specifically, does the recent growing proportion of these deficits being financed, net, by foreigners matter? …

"If the currently disturbing drift toward protectionism is contained and markets remain sufficiently flexible, changing terms of trade, interest rates, asset prices, and exchange rates will cause U.S. saving to rise, reducing the need for foreign finance, and reversing the trend of the past decade toward increasing reliance on it. If, however, the pernicious drift toward fiscal instability in the United States and elsewhere is not arrested and is compounded by a protectionist reversal of globalization, the adjustment process could be quite painful for the world economy."

Source: *Alan Greenspan, "International Imbalances" (speech, Advancing Enterprise Conference, London, England, December 2, 2005), available at http://www.federalreserve.gov/boarddocs/speeches/2005/200512022/default.htm.*

ANSWERS TO TRY IT! PROBLEMS

1. All figures are in billions of U.S. dollars per period. The left-hand side of Equation 15.3 is the current account balance

$$\text{Exports} - \text{imports} = \$300 - \$400 = -\$100$$

Using Equation 15.4, the balance on capital account is

$$-\$100 = -(\text{capital account balance})$$

Solving this equation for the capital account balance, we find that it is $100. The term in parentheses on the right-hand side of Equation 15.3 is also the balance on capital account. We thus have

$$\$100 = \$150 - \text{U.S. purchases of rest-of-world assets}$$

Solving this for U.S. purchase of rest-of-world assets, we find they are $50.

2. All figures are in trillions of yen per period. The left-hand side of Equation 15.3 is the current account balance

$$\text{Exports} - \text{imports} = ¥200 - ¥120 = ¥80$$

Using Equation 15.4, the balance on capital account is

$$¥80 = -(\text{capital account balance})$$

Solving this equation for the capital account balance, we find that it is −¥80. The term in parentheses on the right-hand side of Equation 15.3 is also the balance on capital account. We thus have

$$-¥80 = \text{rest-of-world purchases of Japan's assets} - ¥90$$

Solving this for the rest-of-world purchases of Japan's assets, we find they are ¥10.

3. All figures are in billions of pounds per period. The term in parentheses on the right-hand side of Equation 15.3 is the balance on capital account. We thus have

$$£90 - £70 = £20$$

Using Equation 15.4, the balance on current account is

$$\text{Current account balance} = -(£20)$$

The left-hand side of Equation 15.3 is also the current account balance

$$£40 - \text{imports} = -£20$$

Solving for imports, we find they are £60. Britain's balance on current account is −£20 billion, its balance on capital account is £20 billion, and its total imports equal £60 billion per period.

4. All figures are in billions of pesos per period. The term in parentheses on the right-hand side of Equation 15.3 is the balance on capital account. We thus have

$$\$700 - \$500 = \$200$$

Using Equation 15.4, the balance on current account is

$$\text{Current account balance} = -(\$200)$$

The left-hand side of Equation 15.3 is also the current account balance

$$\text{Exports} - \$550 = -\$200$$

Solving for exports, we find they are $350.

3. EXCHANGE RATE SYSTEMS

Exchange rates are determined by demand and supply. But governments can influence those exchange rates in various ways. The extent and nature of government involvement in currency markets define alternative systems of exchange rates. In this section we will examine some common systems and explore some of their macroeconomic implications.

There are three broad categories of exchange rate systems. In one system, exchange rates are set purely by private market forces with no government involvement. Values change constantly as the demand for and supply of currencies fluctuate. In another system, currency values are allowed to change, but governments participate in currency markets in an effort to influence those values. Finally, governments may seek to fix the values of their currencies, either through participation in the market or through regulatory policy.

3.1 Free-Floating Systems

free-floating exchange rate system

System in which governments and central banks do not participate in the market for foreign exchange.

In a **free-floating exchange rate system**, governments and central banks do not participate in the market for foreign exchange. The relationship between governments and central banks on the one hand and currency markets on the other is much the same as the typical relationship between these institutions and stock markets. Governments may regulate stock markets to prevent fraud, but stock values themselves are left to float in the market. The U.S. government, for example, does not intervene in the stock market to influence stock prices.

The concept of a completely free-floating exchange rate system is a theoretical one. In practice, all governments or central banks intervene in currency markets in an effort to influence exchange rates. Some countries, such as the United States, intervene to only a small degree, so that the notion of a free-floating exchange rate system comes close to what actually exists in the United States.

A free-floating system has the advantage of being self-regulating. There is no need for government intervention if the exchange rate is left to the market. Market forces also restrain large swings in demand or supply. Suppose, for example, that a dramatic shift in world preferences led to a sharply increased demand for goods and services produced in Canada. This would increase the demand for Canadian dollars, raise Canada's exchange rate, and make Canadian goods and services more expensive for foreigners to buy. Some of the impact of the swing in foreign demand would thus be absorbed in a rising exchange rate. In effect, a free-floating exchange rate acts as a buffer to insulate an economy from the impact of international events.

The primary difficulty with free-floating exchange rates lies in their unpredictability. Contracts between buyers and sellers in different countries must not only reckon with possible changes in prices and other factors during the lives of those contracts, they must also consider the possibility of exchange rate changes. An agreement by a U.S. distributor to purchase a certain quantity of Canadian lumber each year, for example, will be affected by the possibility that the exchange rate between the Canadian dollar and the U.S. dollar will change while the contract is in effect. Fluctuating exchange rates make international transactions riskier and thus increase the cost of doing business with other countries.

3.2 Managed Float Systems

managed float

Government or central bank participation in a floating exchange rate system.

Governments and central banks often seek to increase or decrease their exchange rates by buying or selling their own currencies. Exchange rates are still free to float, but governments try to influence their values. Government or central bank participation in a floating exchange rate system is called a **managed float**.

Countries that have a floating exchange rate system intervene from time to time in the currency market in an effort to raise or lower the price of their own currency. Typically, the purpose of such intervention is to prevent sudden large swings in the value of a nation's currency. Such intervention is likely to have only a small impact, if any, on exchange rates. Roughly $1.5 trillion worth of currencies changes hands every day in the world market; it is difficult for any one agency—even an agency the size of the U.S. government or the Fed—to force significant changes in exchange rates.

Still, governments or central banks can sometimes influence their exchange rates. Suppose the price of a country's currency is rising very rapidly. The country's government or central bank might seek to hold off further increases in order to prevent a major reduction in net exports. An announcement that a further increase in its exchange rate is unacceptable, followed by sales of that country's currency by the central bank in order to bring its exchange rate down, can sometimes convince other participants in the currency market that the exchange rate will not rise further. That change in expectations could reduce demand for and increase supply of the currency, thus achieving the goal of holding the exchange rate down.

3.3   Fixed Exchange Rates

In a **fixed exchange rate system**, the exchange rate between two currencies is set by government policy. There are several mechanisms through which fixed exchange rates may be maintained. Whatever the system for maintaining these rates, however, all fixed exchange rate systems share some important features.

A Commodity Standard

In a **commodity standard system**, countries fix the value of their respective currencies relative to a certain commodity or group of commodities. With each currency's value fixed in terms of the commodity, currencies are fixed relative to one another.

For centuries, the values of many currencies were fixed relative to gold. Suppose, for example, that the price of gold were fixed at $20 per ounce in the United States. This would mean that the government of the United States was committed to exchanging 1 ounce of gold to anyone who handed over $20. (That was the case in the United States—and $20 was roughly the price—up to 1933.) Now suppose that the exchange rate between the British pound and gold was £5 per ounce of gold. With £5 and $20 both trading for 1 ounce of gold, £1 would exchange for $4. No one would pay more than $4 for £1, because $4 could always be exchanged for 1/5 ounce of gold, and that gold could be exchanged for £1. And no one would sell £1 for less than $4, because the owner of £1 could always exchange it for 1/5 ounce of gold, which could be exchanged for $4. In practice, actual currency values could vary slightly from the levels implied by their commodity values because of the costs involved in exchanging currencies for gold, but these variations are slight.

Under the gold standard, the quantity of money was regulated by the quantity of gold in a country. If, for example, the United States guaranteed to exchange dollars for gold at the rate of $20 per ounce, it could not issue more money than it could back up with the gold it owned.

The gold standard was a self-regulating system. Suppose that at the fixed exchange rate implied by the gold standard, the supply of a country's currency exceeded the demand. That would imply that spending flowing out of the country exceeded spending flowing in. As residents supplied their currency to make foreign purchases, foreigners acquiring that currency could redeem it for gold, since countries guaranteed to exchange gold for their currencies at a fixed rate. Gold would thus flow out of the country running a deficit. Given an obligation to exchange the country's currency for gold, a reduction in a country's gold holdings would force it to reduce its money supply. That would reduce aggregate demand in the country, lowering income and the price level. But both of those events would increase net exports in the country, eliminating the deficit in the balance of payments. Balance would be achieved, but at the cost of a recession. A country with a surplus in its balance of payments would experience an inflow of gold. That would boost its money supply and increase aggregate demand. That, in turn, would generate higher prices and higher real GDP. Those events would reduce net exports and correct the surplus in the balance of payments, but again at the cost of changes in the domestic economy.

Because of this tendency for imbalances in a country's balance of payments to be corrected only through changes in the entire economy, nations began abandoning the gold standard in the 1930s. That was the period of the Great Depression, during which world trade virtually was ground to a halt. World War II made the shipment of goods an extremely risky proposition, so trade remained minimal during the war. As the war was coming to an end, representatives of the United States and its allies met in 1944 at Bretton Woods, New Hampshire, to fashion a new mechanism through which international trade could be financed after the war. The system was to be one of fixed exchange rates, but with much less emphasis on gold as a backing for the system.

fixed exchange rate system

System in which the exchange rate between two currencies is set by government policy.

commodity standard system

System in which countries fix the value of their respective currencies relative to a certain commodity or group of commodities.

In recent years, a number of countries have set up **currency board arrangements**, which are a kind of commodity standard, fixed exchange rate system in which there is explicit legislative commitment to exchange domestic currency for a specified foreign currency at a fixed rate and a currency board to ensure fulfillment of the legal obligations this arrangement entails. In its simplest form, this type of arrangement implies that domestic currency can be issued only when the currency board has an equivalent amount of the foreign currency to which the domestic currency is pegged. With a currency board arrangement, the country's ability to conduct independent monetary policy is severely limited. It can create reserves only when the currency board has an excess of foreign currency. If the currency board is short of foreign currency, it must cut back on reserves.

Argentina established a currency board in 1991 and fixed its currency to the U.S. dollar. For an economy plagued in the 1980s with falling real GDP and rising inflation, the currency board served to restore confidence in the government's commitment to stabilization policies and to a restoration of economic growth. The currency board seemed to work well for Argentina for most of the 1990s, as inflation subsided and growth of real GDP picked up.

The drawbacks of a currency board are essentially the same as those associated with the gold standard. Faced with a decrease in consumption, investment, and net exports in 1999, Argentina could not use monetary and fiscal policies to try to shift its aggregate demand curve to the right. It abandoned the system in 2002.

Fixed Exchange Rates Through Intervention

The Bretton Woods Agreement called for each currency's value to be fixed relative to other currencies. The mechanism for maintaining these rates, however, was to be intervention by governments and central banks in the currency market.

Again suppose that the exchange rate between the dollar and the British pound is fixed at $4 per £1. Suppose further that this rate is an equilibrium rate, as illustrated in Figure 15.8. As long as the fixed rate coincides with the equilibrium rate, the fixed exchange rate operates in the same fashion as a free-floating rate.

FIGURE 15.8 Maintaining a Fixed Exchange Rate Through Intervention

Initially, the equilibrium price of the British pound equals $4, the fixed rate between the pound and the dollar. Now suppose an increased supply of British pounds lowers the equilibrium price of the pound to $3. The Bank of England could purchase pounds by selling dollars in order to shift the demand curve for pounds to D_2. Alternatively, the Fed could shift the demand curve to D_2 by buying pounds.

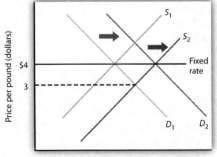

Quantity of British pounds per period

Now suppose that the British choose to purchase more U.S. goods and services. The supply curve for pounds increases, and the equilibrium exchange rate for the pound (in terms of dollars) falls to, say, $3. Under the terms of the Bretton Woods Agreement, Britain and the United States would be required to intervene in the market to bring the exchange rate back to the rate fixed in the agreement, $4. If the adjustment were to be made by the British central bank, the Bank of England, it would have to purchase pounds. It would do so by exchanging dollars it had previously acquired in other transactions for pounds. As it sold dollars, it would take in checks written in pounds. When a central bank sells an asset, the checks that come into the central bank reduce the money supply and bank reserves in that country. We saw in the chapter explaining the money supply, for example, that the sale of bonds by the Fed reduces the U.S. money supply. Similarly, the sale of dollars by the Bank of England would reduce the British money supply. In order to bring its exchange rate back to the agreed-to level, Britain would have to carry out a contractionary monetary policy.

Alternatively, the Fed could intervene. It could purchase pounds, writing checks in dollars. But when a central bank purchases assets, it adds reserves to the system and increases the money supply. The United States would thus be forced to carry out an expansionary monetary policy.

Domestic disturbances created by efforts to maintain fixed exchange rates brought about the demise of the Bretton Woods system. Japan and West Germany gave up the effort to maintain the fixed values of their currencies in the spring of 1971 and announced they were withdrawing from the Bretton Woods system. President Richard Nixon pulled the United States out of the system in August of that year, and the system collapsed. An attempt to revive fixed exchange rates in 1973 collapsed almost immediately, and the world has operated largely on a managed float ever since.

Under the Bretton Woods system, the United States had redeemed dollars held by other governments for gold; President Nixon terminated that policy as he withdrew the United States from the Bretton Woods system. The dollar is no longer backed by gold.

Fixed exchange rate systems offer the advantage of predictable currency values—when they are working. But for fixed exchange rates to work, the countries participating in them must maintain domestic economic conditions that will keep equilibrium currency values close to the fixed rates. Sovereign nations must be willing to coordinate their monetary and fiscal policies. Achieving that kind of coordination among independent countries can be a difficult task.

The fact that coordination of monetary and fiscal policies is difficult does not mean it is impossible. Eleven members of the European Union not only agreed to fix their exchange rates to one another, they agreed to adopt a common currency, the euro. The new currency was introduced in 1998 and became fully adopted in 1999. Since then, four other nations have joined. The nations that have adopted it have agreed to strict limits on their fiscal policies. Each will continue to have its own central bank, but these national central banks will operate similarly to the regional banks of the Federal Reserve System in the United States. The new European Central Bank will conduct monetary policy throughout the area. Details of this revolutionary venture are provided in the accompanying Case in Point.

When exchange rates are fixed but fiscal and monetary policies are not coordinated, equilibrium exchange rates can move away from their fixed levels. Once exchange rates start to diverge, the effort to force currencies up or down through market intervention can be extremely disruptive. And when countries suddenly decide to give that effort up, exchange rates can swing sharply in one direction or another. When that happens, the main virtue of fixed exchange rates, their predictability, is lost.

Thailand's experience with the baht illustrates the potential difficulty with attempts to maintain a fixed exchange rate. Thailand's central bank had held the exchange rate between the dollar and the baht steady, at a price for the baht of $0.04. Several factors, including weakness in the Japanese economy, reduced the demand for Thai exports and thus reduced the demand for the baht, as shown in Panel (a) of Figure 15.9. Thailand's central bank, committed to maintaining the price of the baht at $0.04, bought baht to increase the demand, as shown in Panel (b). Central banks buy their own currency using their reserves of foreign currencies. We have seen that when a central bank sells bonds, the money supply falls. When it sells foreign currency, the result is no different. Sales of foreign currency by Thailand's central bank in order to purchase the baht thus reduced Thailand's money supply and reduced the bank's holdings of foreign currencies. As currency traders began to suspect that the bank might give up its effort to hold the baht's value, they sold baht, shifting the supply curve to the right, as shown in Panel (c). That forced the central bank to buy even more baht—selling even more foreign currency—until it finally gave up the effort and allowed the baht to become a free-floating currency. By the end of 1997, the baht had lost nearly half its value relative to the dollar.

FIGURE 15.9 The Anatomy of a Currency Collapse

Weakness in the Japanese economy, among other factors, led to a reduced demand for the baht (Panel [a]). That put downward pressure on the baht's value relative to other currencies. Committed to keeping the price of the baht at $0.04, Thailand's central bank bought baht to increase the demand, as shown in Panel (b). However, as holders of baht and other Thai assets began to fear that the central bank might give up its effort to prop up the baht, they sold baht, shifting the supply curve for baht to the right (Panel [c]) and putting more downward pressure on the baht's price. Finally, in July of 1997, the central bank gave up its effort to prop up the currency. By the end of the year, the baht's dollar value had fallen to about $0.02.

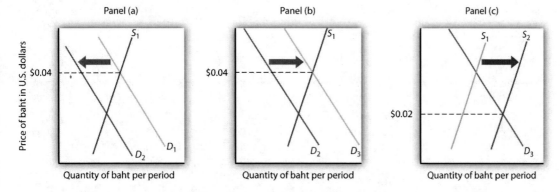

As we saw in the introduction to this chapter, the plunge in the baht was the first in a chain of currency crises that rocked the world in 1997 and 1998. International trade has the great virtue of increasing the availability of goods and services to the world's consumers. But financing trade—and the way nations handle that financing—can create difficulties.

KEY TAKEAWAYS

- In a free-floating exchange rate system, exchange rates are determined by demand and supply.
- Exchange rates are determined by demand and supply in a managed float system, but governments intervene as buyers or sellers of currencies in an effort to influence exchange rates.
- In a fixed exchange rate system, exchange rates among currencies are not allowed to change. The gold standard and the Bretton Woods system are examples of fixed exchange rate systems.

TRY IT!

Suppose a nation's central bank is committed to holding the value of its currency, the mon, at $2 per mon. Suppose further that holders of the mon fear that its value is about to fall and begin selling mon to purchase U.S. dollars. What will happen in the market for mon? Explain your answer carefully, and illustrate it using a demand and supply graph for the market for mon. What action will the nation's central bank take? Use your graph to show the result of the central bank's action. Why might this action fuel concern among holders of the mon about its future prospects? What difficulties will this create for the nation's central bank?

Case in Point: The Euro

It marks the most dramatic development in international finance since the collapse of the Bretton Woods system. A new currency, the euro, began trading among 11 European nations—Austria, Belgium, Finland, France, Germany, Ireland, Italy, Luxembourg, the Netherlands, Portugal, and Spain—in 1999. During a three-year transition, each nation continued to have its own currency, which traded at a fixed rate with the euro. In 2002, the currencies of the participant nations disappeared altogether and were replaced by the euro. In 2007, Slovenia adopted the euro, as did Cyprus and Malta in 2008 and Slovakia in 2009. Several other countries are also hoping to join. Notable exceptions are Britain, Sweden, Switzerland, and Denmark. Still, most of Europe now operates as the ultimate fixed exchange rate regime, a region with a single currency.

To participate in this radical experiment, the nations switching to the euro had to agree to give up considerable autonomy in monetary and fiscal policy. While each nation continues to have its own central bank, those central banks operate more like regional banks of the Federal Reserve System in the United States; they have no authority to conduct monetary policy. That authority is vested in a new central bank, the European Central Bank.

The participants have also agreed in principle to strict limits on their fiscal policies. Their deficits can be no greater than 3% of nominal GDP, and their total national debt cannot exceed 60% of nominal GDP.

Whether sovereign nations will be able—or willing—to operate under economic restrictions as strict as these remains to be seen. Indeed, several of the nations in the eurozone have exceeded the limit on national deficits.

A major test of the euro coincided with its 10th anniversary at about the same time the 2008 world financial crisis occurred. It has been a mixed blessing in getting through this difficult period. For example, guarantees that the Irish government made concerning bank deposits and debt have been better received, because Ireland is part of the euro system. On the other hand, if Ireland had a floating currency, its depreciation might enhance Irish exports, which would help Ireland to get out of its recession.

The 2008 crisis also revealed insights into the value of the euro as an international currency. The dollar accounts for about two-thirds of global currency reserves, while the euro accounts for about 25%. Most of world trade is still conducted in dollars, and even within the eurozone about a third of trade is conducted in dollars. One reason that the euro has not gained more on the dollar in terms of world usage during its first 10 years is that, whereas the U.S. government is the single issuer of its public debt, each of the 16 separate European governments in the eurozone issues its own debt. The smaller market for each country's debt, each with different risk premiums, makes them less liquid, especially in difficult financial times.

When the euro was launched it was hoped that having a single currency would nudge the countries toward greater market flexibility and higher productivity. However, income per capita is about at the same level in the eurozone as it was 10 years ago in comparison to that of the United States—about 70%.

Source: "Demonstrably Durable: The Euro at Ten," Economist, January 3, 2009, p. 50–52.

The value of the mon is initially $2. Fear that the mon might fall will lead to an increase in its supply to S_2, putting downward pressure on the currency. To maintain the value of the mon at $2, the central bank will buy mon, thus shifting the demand curve to D_2. This policy, though, creates two difficulties. First, it requires that the bank sell other currencies, and a sale of any asset by a central bank is a contractionary monetary policy. Second, the sale depletes the bank's holdings of foreign currencies. If holders of the mon fear the central bank will give up its effort, then they might sell mon, shifting the supply curve farther to the right and forcing even more vigorous action by the central bank.

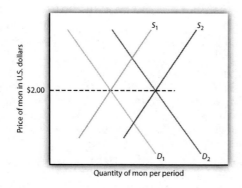

4.   REVIEW AND PRACTICE

Summary

In this chapter we examined the role of net exports in the economy. We found that export and import demand are influenced by many different factors, the most important being domestic and foreign income levels, changes in relative prices, the exchange rate, and preferences and technology. An increase in net exports shifts the aggregate demand curve to the right; a reduction shifts it to the left.

In the foreign exchange market, the equilibrium exchange rate is determined by the intersection of the demand and supply curves for a currency. Given the ease with which most currencies can be traded, we can assume this equilibrium is achieved, so that the quantity of a currency demanded equals the quantity supplied. An economy can experience current account surpluses or deficits. The balance on current account equals the negative of the balance on capital account. We saw that one reason for the current account deficit in the United States is the U.S. capital account surplus; the United States has attracted a great deal of foreign financial investment.

The chapter closed with an examination of floating and fixed exchange rate systems. Fixed exchange rate systems include commodity-based systems and fixed rates that are maintained through intervention. Exchange rate systems have moved from a gold standard, to a system of fixed rates with intervention, to a mixed set of arrangements of floating and fixed exchange rates.

CONCEPT PROBLEMS

1. David Ricardo, a famous English economist of the 19th century, stressed that a nation has a comparative advantage in those products for which its efficiency relative to other nations is the highest. He argued in favor of specialization and trade based on comparative, not absolute, advantage. From a global perspective, what would be the "advantage" of such a system?

2. For several months prior to your vacation trip to Naples, Italy, you note that the exchange rate for the dollar has been increasing relative to the euro (that is, it takes more euro to buy a dollar). Are you pleased or sad? Explain.

3. Who might respond in a way different from your own to the falling value of the euro in Question 2?

4. Suppose a nation has a deficit on capital account. What does this mean? What can you conclude about its balance on current account?

5. Suppose a nation has a surplus on capital account. What does this mean? What can you conclude about its balance on current account?

6. The following analysis appeared in a newspaper editorial:

   "If foreigners own our businesses and land, that's one thing, but when they own billions in U.S. bonds, that's another. We don't care who owns the businesses, but our grandchildren will have to put up with a lower standard of living because of the interest payments sent overseas. Therefore, we must reduce our trade deficit."

   Critically analyze this editorial view. Are the basic premises correct? The conclusion?

7. In the years prior to the abandonment of the gold standard, foreigners cashed in their dollars and the U.S. Treasury "lost gold" at unprecedented rates. Today, the dollar is no longer tied to gold and is free to float. What are the fundamental differences between a currency based on the gold standard and one that is allowed to float? What would the U.S. "lose" if foreigners decided to "cash in" their dollars today?

8. Can there be a deficit on current account and a deficit on capital account at the same time? Explain.

9. Suppose the people of a certain economy increase their spending on foreign-produced goods and services. What will be the effect on real GDP and the price level in the short run? In the long run?

10. Now suppose the people of a certain economy reduce their spending on foreign-produced goods and services. What will be the effect on real GDP and the price level in the short run? In the long run?

11. Canada, Mexico, and the United States have a free trade zone. What would be some of the advantages of having a common currency as well? The disadvantages? Do you think it would be a good idea? Why or why not?

12. The text says that the U.S. capital account surplus necessarily implies a current account deficit. Suppose that the United States were to undertake measures to eliminate its capital account surplus. What sorts of measures might it take? Do you think such measures would be a good idea? Why or why not?

NUMERICAL PROBLEMS

1. For each of the following scenarios, determine whether the aggregate demand curve will shift. If so, in which direction will it shift and by how much?

   a. A change in consumer preferences leads to an initial $25-billion decrease in net exports. The multiplier is 1.5.

   b. A change in trade policies leads to an initial $25-billion increase in net exports. The multiplier is 1.

   c. There is an increase in the domestic price level from 1 to 1.05, while the price level of the country's major trading partner does not change. The multiplier is 2.

   d. Recession in a country's trading partner lowers exports by $20 billion. The multiplier is 2.

2. Fill in the missing items in the table below. All figures are in U.S. billions of dollars.

	U.S. exports	U.S. imports	Domestic purchases of foreign assets	Rest-of-world purchases of U.S. assets
a.	100	100	400	
b.	100	200		200
c.	300		400	600
d.		800	800	1,100

3. Suppose the market for a country's currency is in equilibrium and that its exports equal $700 billion, its purchases of rest-of-world assets equal $1,000 billion, and foreign purchases of its assets equal $1,200 billion. Assuming it has no international transfer payments and that output is measured as GNP:

   a. What are the country's imports?

   b. What is the country's balance on current account?

   c. What is the country's balance on capital account?

4. Suppose that the market for a country's currency is in equilibrium and that its exports equal $400, its imports equal $500 billion, and rest-of-world purchases of the country's assets equal $100. Assuming it has no international transfer payments and that output is measured as GNP:

   a. What is the country's balance on current account?

   b. What is the country's balance on capital account?

   c. What is the value of the country's purchases of rest-of-world assets?

5. The information below describes the trade-weighted exchange rate for the dollar (standardized at a value of 100) and net exports (in billions of dollars) for an eight-month period.

Month	Trade-weighted exchange rate	Net exports
January	100.5	−9.8
February	99.9	−11.6
March	100.5	−13.5
April	100.3	−14.0
May	99.6	−15.6
June	100.9	−14.2
July	101.4	−14.9
August	101.8	−16.7

   a. Plot the data on a graph.

   b. Do the data support the expected relationship between the trade-weighted exchange rate and net exports? Explain.

6. The graph below shows the foreign exchange market between the United States and Japan before and after an increase in the demand for Japanese goods by U.S. consumers.

   a. If the exchange rate was free-floating prior to the change in demand for Japanese goods, what was its likely value?

   b. After the change in demand, the free-floating exchange rate would be how many yen per dollar?

   c. If the Japanese central bank wanted to keep the exchange rate fixed at its initial value, how many dollars would it have to buy?

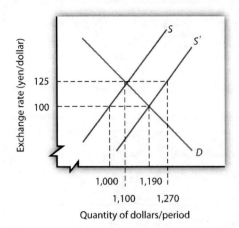

7. Suppose Japan relaxes its restrictions on imports of foreign goods and services and begins importing more from the United States. Illustrate graphically how this will affect the U.S. exchange rate, price level, and level of real GDP in the short run and in the long run. How will it affect these same variables in Japan? (Assume both economies are initially operating at their potential levels of output.)

8. Suppose U.S. investors begin purchasing assets in Mexico. Illustrate graphically how this will affect the U.S. exchange rate, price level, and level of real GDP in the short run and in the long run. How will it affect these same variables in Mexico? (Assume both economies are initially operating at their potential levels of output.)

9. Suppose foreigners begin buying more assets in the United States. Illustrate graphically how this will affect the U.S. exchange rate, price level, and level of real GDP in the short run and in the long run. (Assume the economy is initially operating at its potential output.)

ENDNOTES

1. For an interesting history of this remarkable development, see Marc Levinson, *The Box: How the Shipping Container Made the World Smaller and the World Economy Bigger* (Princeton: Princeton University Press, 2006).

CHAPTER 16

Inflation and Unemployment

START UP: THE INFLATION/UNEMPLOYMENT CONUNDRUM

As the twentieth century drew to a close, the United States could look back on a remarkable achievement. From 1992 through 2000, the unemployment rate *fell* every year. The inflation rate, measured as the annual percentage change in the implicit price deflator, was about 2% or less during this period. The dramatic reduction in the two rates provided welcome relief to a nation that had seen soaring unemployment early in the 1980s, soaring inflation in the late 1970s, and painful increases in both rates early in the 1970s.

Unemployment and inflation rates were also at fairly low levels during the early 2000s. Following a brief recession in 2001, in which unemployment reached nearly 6% (though this actually occurred after the recession officially ended), it fell back to 4.6% in 2006 and 2007. Through 2007, inflation never exceeded 3.3%. With the start of the recession in December 2007, the unemployment rate began to rise. At first, though, it appeared that inflation was becoming a bigger problem, as high gas and food prices until summer 2008 seemed to be driving up other prices and increasing inflationary expectations. Indeed, through much of 2008, a debate over the appropriate direction of monetary policy occurred over just this issue: should the Fed ease in an attempt to reduce unemployment or at least to keep it from rising as much as it would otherwise have, or should it stem rising inflation and inflationary expectations by holding the federal funds rate constant or even increasing it? While the Fed voted during most of its 2008 meetings for easing, the year is notable in that there were often dissenters at the Federal Open Market Committee meetings. For example, the minutes of the March 18, 2008, meeting note that two members, Richard W. Fisher of the Dallas Fed and Charles I. Plosser of the Philadelphia Fed voted against the 0.75% point drop approved at that meeting. Their rationale was that the inflation risks were simply too great. The minutes state,

> *"Incoming data suggested a weaker near-term outlook for economic growth, but the Committee's earlier policy moves had already reduced the target federal funds rate by 225 basis points to address risks to growth, and the full effect of those rate cuts had yet to be felt. ... Both Messrs. Fisher and Plosser were concerned that inflation expectations could potentially become unhinged should the Committee continue to lower the funds rate in the current environment. They pointed to measures of inflation and indicators of inflation expectations that had risen and Mr. Fisher stressed the international influences on U.S. inflation rates. Mr. Plosser noted that the Committee could not afford to wait until there was clear evidence that inflation expectations were no longer anchored, as by then it would be too late to prevent a further increase inflation pressures."[1]*

But as the depth of the recession increased toward the latter part of 2008, with the unemployment rate reaching 7.2% in December and prices of both oil and other commodities falling back substantially, the inflation threat had dissipated. Unanimity had returned to the FOMC: the Fed should use all of its powers to fight the recession.

This chapter examines the relationship between inflation and unemployment. We will find that there have been periods in which a clear trade-off between inflation and unemployment seemed to exist. During such periods, the economy achieved reductions in unemployment at the expense of increased inflation. But there have also been periods in which inflation and unemployment rose together and periods in which both variables fell together. We will examine some explanations for the sometimes perplexing relationship between the two variables.

We will see that the use of stabilization policy, coupled with the lags for monetary and for fiscal policy, have at times led to a cyclical relationship between inflation and unemployment. The explanation for the fact that Americans enjoyed such a long period of falling inflation and unemployment in the 1990s lies partly in improved policy, policy that takes those lags into account. We will see that a bit of macroeconomic luck in aggregate supply has also played a role.

1. RELATING INFLATION AND UNEMPLOYMENT

LEARNING OBJECTIVES

1. Draw a Phillips curve and describe the relationship between inflation and unemployment that it expresses.
2. Describe the other relationships or phases that have been observed between inflation and unemployment.

It has often been the case that progress against inflation comes at the expense of greater unemployment, and that reduced unemployment comes at the expense of greater inflation. This section looks at the record and traces the emergence of the view that a simple trade-off between these macroeconomic "bad guys" exists.

Clearly, it is desirable to reduce unemployment and inflation. Unemployment represents a lost opportunity for workers to engage in productive effort—and to earn income. Inflation erodes the value of money people hold, and more importantly, the threat of inflation adds to uncertainty and makes people less willing to save and firms less willing to invest. If there were a trade-off between the two, we could reduce the rate of inflation or the rate of unemployment, but not both. The fact that the United States did make progress against unemployment and inflation through most of the 1990s and early 2000s represented a macroeconomic triumph, one that appeared impossible just a few years earlier. The next section examines the argument that once dominated macroeconomic thought—that a simple trade-off between inflation and unemployment did, indeed, exist. The argument continues to appear in discussions of macroeconomic policy today; it will be useful to examine it.

1.1 The Phillips Curve

Phillips curve

A curve that suggests a negative relationship between inflation and unemployment.

In 1958, New Zealand-born economist Almarin Phillips reported that his analysis of a century of British wage and unemployment data suggested that an inverse relationship existed between rates of increase in wages and British unemployment.[2] Economists were quick to incorporate this idea into their thinking, extending the relationship to the rate of price-level changes—inflation—and unemployment. The notion that there is a trade-off between the two is expressed by a **Phillips curve**, a curve that suggests a negative relationship between inflation and unemployment. Figure 16.1 shows a Phillips curve.

The Phillips curve seemed to make good theoretical sense. The dominant school of economic thought in the 1960s suggested that the economy was likely to experience either a recessionary or an inflationary gap. An economy with a recessionary gap would have high unemployment and little or no inflation. An economy with an inflationary gap would have very little unemployment and a higher rate of inflation. The Phillips curve suggested a smooth transition between the two. As expansionary policies were undertaken to move the economy out of a recessionary gap, unemployment would fall and inflation would rise. Policies to correct an inflationary gap would bring down the inflation rate, but at a cost of higher unemployment.

The experience of the 1960s suggested that precisely the kind of trade-off the Phillips curve implied did, in fact, exist in the United States. Figure 16.2 shows annual rates of inflation (computed using the implicit price deflator) plotted against annual rates of unemployment from 1961 to 1969. The points appear to follow a path quite similar to a Phillips curve relationship. The civilian unemployment rate fell from 6.7% in 1961 to 3.5% in 1969. The inflation rate rose from 1.1% in 1961 to 4.8% in 1969. While inflation dipped slightly in 1963, it appeared that, for the decade as a whole, a reduction in unemployment had been "traded" for an increase in inflation.

In the mid-1960s, the economy moved into an inflationary gap as unemployment fell below its natural level. The economy had already reached its full employment level of output when the 1964 tax cut was passed. The Fed undertook a more expansionary monetary policy at the same time. The combined effect of the two policies increased aggregate demand and pushed the economy beyond full employment and into an inflationary gap. Aggregate demand continued to rise as U.S. spending for the war in Vietnam expanded and as President Lyndon Johnson launched an ambitious program aimed at putting an end to poverty in the United States.

By the end of the decade, unemployment at 3.5% was substantially below its natural level, estimated by the Congressional Budget Office to be 5.6% that year. When Richard Nixon became president in 1969, it was widely believed that, with an economy operating with an inflationary gap, it was time to move back down the Phillips curve, trading a reduction in inflation for an increase in unemployment. President Nixon moved to do precisely that, serving up a contractionary fiscal policy by ordering cuts in federal government purchases. The Fed pursued a contractionary monetary policy aimed at bringing inflation down.

1.2 The Phillips Curve Goes Awry

The effort to nudge the economy back down the Phillips curve to an unemployment rate closer to the natural level and a lower rate of inflation met with an unhappy surprise in 1970. Unemployment increased as expected. But inflation rose! The inflation rate rose to 5.3% from its 1969 rate of 4.8%.

The tidy relationship between inflation and unemployment that had been suggested by the experience of the 1960s fell apart in the 1970s. Unemployment rose substantially, but inflation remained the same in 1971. In 1972, both rates fell. The economy seemed to fall back into the pattern described by the Phillips curve in 1973, as inflation rose while unemployment fell. But the next two years saw increases in both rates. The Phillips curve relationship between inflation and unemployment that had seemed to hold true in the 1960s no longer prevailed.

Indeed, a look at annual rates of inflation and unemployment since 1961 suggests that the 1960s were quite atypical. Figure 16.3 shows the two variables over the period from 1961 through 2009. It is hard to see a Phillips curve lurking within that seemingly random scatter of points.

FIGURE 16.1 The Phillips Curve

The relationship between inflation and unemployment suggested by the work of Almarin Phillips is shown by a Phillips curve.

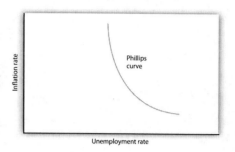

FIGURE 16.2 The Phillips Curve in the 1960s

Values of U.S. inflation and unemployment rates during the 1960s generally conformed to the trade-off implied by the Phillips curve. The points for each year lie close to a curve with the shape that Phillips's analysis predicted.

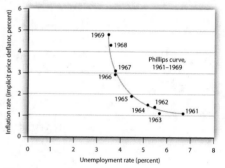

Source: Economic Report of the President, 2009, Tables B-3 and B-42.

FIGURE 16.3 Inflation and Unemployment, 1961–2009

Annual observations of inflation and unemployment in the United States from 1961 to 2009 do not seem consistent with a Phillips curve.

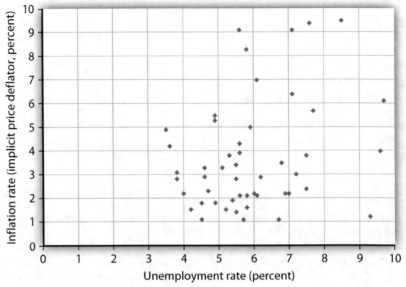

Sources: *Economic Report of the President, 2010, Tables B-3 and B-42.*

1.3 Cycles of Inflation and Unemployment

Although the points plotted in Figure 16.3 are not consistent with a Phillips curve, we can find a relationship. Suppose we draw connecting lines through the sequence of observations, as is done in Figure 16.4. This approach suggests a pattern of clockwise loops, at least until 2002 when we see the beginnings of a counterclockwise loop. We see periods in which inflation rises as unemployment falls, followed by periods in which unemployment rises while inflation remains high or fairly constant. And those periods are followed by periods in which inflation and unemployment both fall.

FIGURE 16.4 Inflation and Unemployment: Loops

Connecting observed values for unemployment and inflation sequentially suggests a cyclical pattern of clockwise loops over the 1961–2002 period, after which we see a counterclockwise loop.

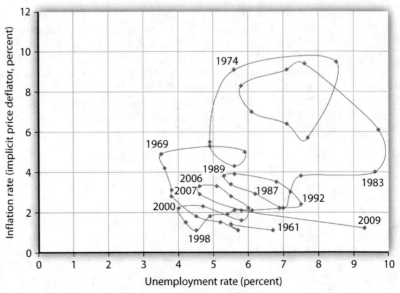

Sources: *Economic Report of the President, 2010, Tables B-3 and B-42.*

Figure 16.5 gives an idealized version of the general cycle suggested by the data in Figure 16.4. There is a **Phillips phase** in which inflation rises as unemployment falls. In this phase, the relationship suggested by the Phillips curve holds. The Phillips phase is followed by a **stagflation phase** in which inflation remains high while unemployment increases. The term, coined by Massachusetts Institute of Technology economist and Nobel laureate Paul Samuelson during the 1970s, suggests a combination of a stagnating economy and continued inflation. And finally, there is a **recovery phase** in which inflation and unemployment both decline. This pattern of a Phillips phase, then stagflation, and then a recovery can be termed the **inflation—unemployment cycle**.

Trace the path of the inflation—unemployment cycle as it unfolds in Figure 16.4. Starting with the Phillips phase in the 1960s, we see that the economy went through three inflation—unemployment cycles through the 1970s. Each took the United States to successively higher rates of inflation and unemployment. As the cycle that began in the late 1970s passed through the stagflation phase, however, something quite significant happened. The economy suffered its highest rate of unemployment since the Great Depression during that period. It also achieved its most dramatic gains against inflation. The recovery phase of the 1990s was the longest since the U.S. government began tracking inflation and unemployment. Good luck explains some of that: oil prices fell in the late 1990s, shifting the short-run aggregate supply curve to the right. That boosted real GDP and put downward pressure on the price level. But one cause of that improved performance seemed to be the better understanding economists gained from some policy mistakes of the 1970s.

In the early 2000s, following the brief recession in 2001, the inflation–unemployment trajectory moves in a counterclockwise direction, as the economy moved back quickly into the Phillips phase of falling unemployment and rising inflation but at higher levels of both compared to what prevailed in the late 1990s. During this recent period, oil and other commodity prices were rising, due primarily to rising demand in developing countries, principally China and India. Thus, the short-run aggregate supply curve was moving to the left while aggregate demand was shifting to the right. During the recession of 2007 to 2009, the unemployment rate spiked while inflation fell. The primary reason was that the aggregate demand curve was shifting to the left.

The next section will explain these experiences in a stylized way in terms of the aggregate demand and supply model.

Phillips phase

Period in which inflation rises as unemployment falls.

stagflation phase

Period in which inflation remains high while unemployment increases.

recovery phase

Period in which inflation and unemployment both decline.

inflation—unemployment cycle

pattern consisting of a Phillips phase, followed by stagflation, and then a recovery.

FIGURE 16.5 Phases of the inflation—unemployment cycle

The figure shows the way an economy may move from a Phillips phase to a stagflation phase and then to a recovery phase.

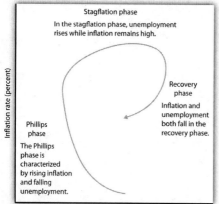

KEY TAKEAWAYS

- The view that there is a trade-off between inflation and unemployment is expressed by a Phillips curve.
- While there are periods in which a trade-off between inflation and unemployment exists, the actual relationship between these variables between 1961 and 2002 followed a cyclical pattern: the inflation—unemployment cycle.
- In a Phillips phase, the inflation rate rises and unemployment falls. A stagflation phase is marked by rising unemployment while inflation remains high. In a recovery phase, inflation and unemployment both fall.

TRY IT!

Suppose an economy has experienced the rates of inflation and of unemployment shown below. Plot these data graphically in a grid with the inflation rate on the vertical axis and the unemployment rate on the horizontal axis. Identify the periods during which the economy experienced each of the three phases of the inflation—unemployment cycle identified in the text.

Period	Unemployment rate (%)	Inflation rate (%)
1	2.5	6.3
2	2.6	5.9
3	2.8	4.8
4	4.7	4.1
5	4.9	5.0
6	5.0	6.1
7	4.5	5.7
8	4.0	5.1

Case in Point: Some Reflections on the 1970s

Looking back, we may find it difficult to appreciate how stunning the experience of 1970 and 1971 was. But those two years changed the face of macroeconomic thought.

Introductory textbooks of that time contained no mention of aggregate supply. The model of choice was the aggregate expenditures model. Students learned that the economy could be in equilibrium below full employment, in which case unemployment would be the primary macroeconomic problem. Alternatively, equilibrium could occur at an income greater than the full employment level, in which case inflation would be the main culprit to worry about.

These ideas could be summarized using a Phillips curve, a new analytical device. It suggested that economists could lay out for policy makers a menu of possibilities. Policy makers could then choose the mix of inflation and unemployment they were willing to accept. Economists would then show them how to attain that mix with the appropriate fiscal and monetary policies.

Then 1970 and 1971 came crashing in on this well-ordered fantasy. President Richard Nixon had come to office with a pledge to bring down inflation. The consumer price index had risen 4.7% during 1968, the highest rate since 1951. Mr. Nixon cut government purchases in 1969, and the Fed produced a sharp slowing in money growth. The president's economic advisers predicted at the beginning of 1970 that inflation and unemployment would both fall. Appraising the 1970 debacle early in 1971, the president's economists said that the experience had not been consistent with what standard models would predict. The economists suggested, however, that this was probably due to a number of transitory factors. Their forecast that inflation and unemployment would improve in 1971 proved wide of the mark—the unemployment rate rose from 4.9% to 5.9% (an increase of 20%), while the rate of inflation measured by the change in the implicit price deflator barely changed from 5.3% to 5.2%.

As we will see, the experience can be readily explained using the model of aggregate demand and aggregate supply. But this tool was not well developed then. The experience of the 1970s forced economists back to their analytical drawing boards and spawned dramatic advances in our understanding of macroeconomic events. We will explore many of those advances in the next chapter.

Source: *Economic Report of the President, 1971, pp. 60–84.*

ANSWER TO TRY IT! PROBLEM

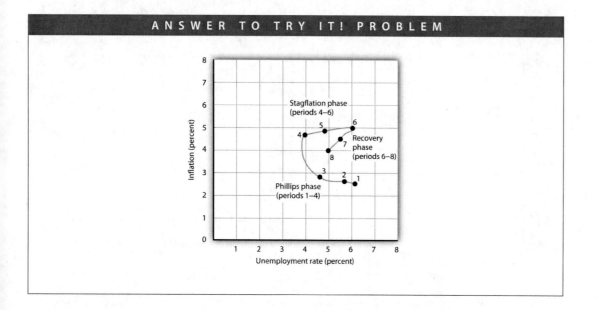

2. EXPLAINING INFLATION–UNEMPLOYMENT RELATIONSHIPS

LEARNING OBJECTIVE

1. Use the model of aggregate demand and aggregate supply to explain a Phillips phase, a stagflation phase, and a recovery phase.

We have examined the cyclical pattern of inflation and unemployment suggested by the experience of the past four decades. Our task now is to explain it. We will apply the model of aggregate demand and aggregate supply, along with our knowledge of monetary and fiscal policy, to explain just why the economy performed as it did. We will find that the relationship between inflation and unemployment depends crucially on macroeconomic policy and on expectations.

The next three sections illustrate the unfolding of the inflation—unemployment cycle. Each phase of the cycle results from a specific pattern of shifts in the aggregate demand and short-run aggregate supply curves.

It is important to be careful in thinking about the meaning of changes in inflation as we examine the cycle of inflation and unemployment. The rise in inflation during the Phillips phase does not simply mean that the price level rises. It means that the price level rises by larger and larger percentages. Rising inflation means that the price level is rising *at an increasing rate*. In the recovery phase, a falling rate of inflation does *not* imply a falling price level. It means the price level is rising, but by smaller and smaller percentages. Falling inflation means that the price level is rising more slowly, not that the price level is falling.

2.1   The Phillips Phase: Increasing Aggregate Demand

As we saw in the last section, the Phillips phase of the inflation—unemployment cycle conforms to the concept of a Phillips curve. It is a period in which inflation tends to rise and unemployment tends to fall.

Figure 16.8 shows how a Phillips phase can unfold. Panel (a) shows the model of aggregate demand and aggregate supply; Panel (b) shows the corresponding path of inflation and unemployment.

FIGURE 16.8   The Phillips Phase

The Phillips phase is marked by increases in aggregate demand pushing real GDP and the price level up along the short-run aggregate supply curve $SRAS_{1,2,3}$. The result is rising inflation and falling unemployment. The points labeled in Panels (a) and (b) correspond to one another; point 1 in Panel (a) corresponds to point 1 in Panel (b), and so on.

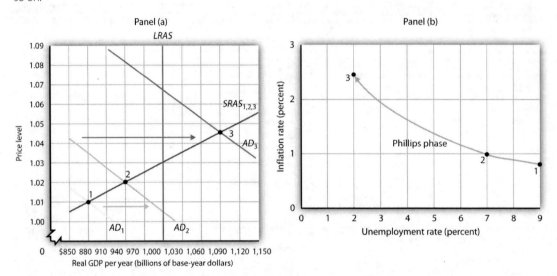

We shall assume in Figure 16.8 and in the next two figures that the following relationship between real GDP and the unemployment rate holds. In our example, the level of potential output will be $1,000 billion, while the natural rate of unemployment is 5.0%. The numbers given in the table correspond to the numbers used in Figure 16.8 through Figure 16.10. Notice that the higher the level of real GDP, the lower the unemployment rate. That is because the production of more goods and services requires more employment. For a given labor force, a higher level of employment implies a lower rate of unemployment.

Real GDP (billions)	Rate of unemployment (%)
$880	9.0
910	8.0
940	7.0
970	6.0
1,000	5.0
1,030	4.0
1,060	3.0
1,090	2.0

Suppose that in Period 1 the price level is 1.01 and real GDP equals $880 billion. The economy is operating below its potential level. The unemployment rate is 9.0%; we shall assume the price level in Period 1 has risen by 0.8% from the previous period. Point 1 in Panel (b) thus shows an initial rate of inflation of 0.8% and an unemployment rate of 9.0%.

Now suppose policy makers respond to the recessionary gap of the first period with an expansionary monetary or fiscal policy. Aggregate demand in Period 2 shifts to AD_2. In Panel (a), we see that the price level rises to 1.02 and real GDP rises to $940 billion. Unemployment falls to 7.0%. The price increase from 1.01 to 1.02 gives us an inflation rate of about 1.0%. Panel (b) shows the new combination of inflation and unemployment rates for Period 2.

Impact lags mean that expansionary policies, even those undertaken in response to the recessionary gap in Periods 1 and 2, continue to expand aggregate demand in Period 3. In the case shown, aggregate demand rises to AD_3, pushing the economy well past its level of potential output into an inflationary gap. Real GDP rises to $1,090 billion, and the price level rises to 1.045 in Panel (a) of Figure 16.8. The increase in real GDP lowers the unemployment rate to 2.0%, and the inflation rate rises to 2.5% at point 3 in Panel (b). Unemployment has fallen at a cost of rising inflation.

The shifts from point 1 to point 2 to point 3 in Panel (b) are characteristic of the Phillips phase. It is crucial to note how these changes occurred. Inflation rose and unemployment fell, because increasing aggregate demand moved along the original short-run aggregate supply curve $SRAS_{1,2,3}$. We saw in the chapter that introduced the model of aggregate demand and aggregate supply that a short-run aggregate supply curve is drawn for a given level of the nominal wage and for a given set of expected prices. The Phillips phase, however, drives prices above what workers and firms expected when they agreed to a given set of nominal wages; real wages are thus driven below their expected level during this phase. Firms that have sticky prices are in the same situation. Firms set their prices based on some expected price level. As rising inflation drives the price level beyond their expectations, their prices will be too low relative to the rest of the economy. Because some firms and workers are committed to their present set of prices and wages for some period of time, they will be stuck with the wrong prices and wages for a while. During that time, their lower-than-expected relative prices will mean greater sales and greater production. The combination of increased production and lower real wages means greater employment and, thus, lower unemployment.

Ultimately, we should expect that workers and firms will begin adjusting nominal wages and other sticky prices to reflect the new, higher level of prices that emerges during the Phillips phase. It is this adjustment that can set the stage for a stagflation phase.

2.2   Changes in Expectations and the Stagflation Phase

As workers and firms become aware that the general price level is rising, they will incorporate this fact into their expectations of future prices. In reaching new agreements on wages, they are likely to settle on higher nominal wages. Firms with sticky prices will adjust their prices upward as they anticipate higher prices throughout the economy.

As we saw in the chapter introducing the model of aggregate demand and aggregate supply, increases in nominal wages and in prices that were sticky will shift the short-run aggregate supply curve to the left. Such a shift is illustrated in Panel (a) of Figure 16.9, where $SRAS_{1,2,3}$ shifts to $SRAS_4$. The result is a shift to point 4; the price level rises to 1.075, and real GDP falls to $970 billion. The increase in the price level to 1.075 from 1.045 implies an inflation rate of 2.9% ([1.075 − 1.045] / 1.045 = 2.9%); unemployment rises to 6.0% with the decrease in real GDP. The new combination of inflation and unemployment is given by point 4 in Panel (b).

FIGURE 16.9   The Stagflation Phase

In the stagflation phase, workers and firms adjust their expectations in a higher price level. As they act on their expectations, the short-run aggregate supply curve shifts leftward in Panel (a). The price level rises to 1.075, and real GDP falls to $970 billion. The inflation rate rises to 2.9% as unemployment rises to 6.0% at point 4 in Panel (b).

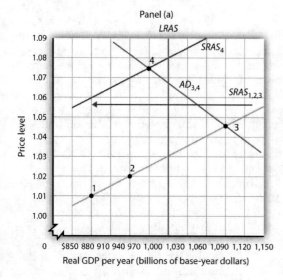

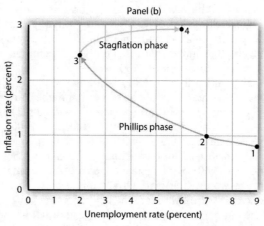

The essential feature of the stagflation phase is a change in expectations. Workers and firms that were blindsided by rising prices during the Phillips phase ended up with lower real wages and lower relative price levels than they intended. In the stagflation phase, they catch up. But the catching up shifts the short-run aggregate supply curve to the left, producing a reduction in real GDP and an increase in the price level.

2.3 The Recovery Phase

The stagflation phase shown in Figure 16.9 leaves the economy with a recessionary gap at point 4 in Panel (a). The economy is bumped into a recession by changing expectations. Policy makers can be expected to respond to the recessionary gap by boosting aggregate demand. That increase in aggregate demand will lead the economy into the recovery phase of the inflation—unemployment cycle.

Figure 16.10 illustrates a recovery phase. In Panel (a), aggregate demand increases to AD_5, boosting the price level to 1.09 and real GDP to $1,060. The new price level represents a 1.4% ([1.09 − 1.075] / 1.075 = 1.4%) increase over the previous price level. The price level is higher, but the inflation rate has fallen sharply. Meanwhile, the increase in real GDP cuts the unemployment rate to 3.0%, shown by point 5 in Panel (b).

FIGURE 16.10 The Recovery Phase

Policy makers act to increase aggregate demand in order to move the economy out of the recessionary gap created during the stagflation phase. Here, aggregate demand shifts to AD_4, boosting the price level to 1.09 and real GDP to $1,060 billion at point 5 in Panel (a). The increase in real GDP reduces unemployment. The price level has risen, but at a slower rate than in the previous period. The result is a reduction in inflation. The new combination of unemployment and inflation is shown by point 5 in Panel (b).

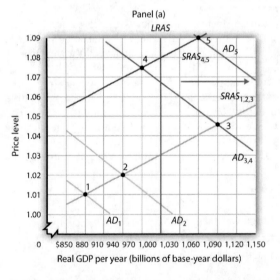

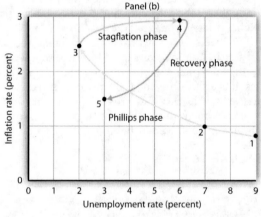

Policies that stimulate aggregate demand and changes in expected price levels are not the only forces that affect the values of inflation and unemployment. Changes in production costs shift the short-run aggregate supply curve. Depending on when these changes occur, they can reinforce or reduce the swings in inflation and unemployment that mark the inflation—unemployment cycle. For example, Figure 16.4 shows that inflation was exceedingly low in the late 1990s. During this period, oil prices were very low—only $12.50 per barrel in 1998, for example. In terms of Figure 16.9, we can represent the low oil prices by a short-run aggregate supply curve that is to the right of $SRAS_{4,5}$. That would mean that output would be somewhat higher, unemployment somewhat lower, and inflation somewhat lower than what is shown as point 5 in Panels (a) and (b) of Figure 16.10.

Comparing the late 1990s to the early 2000s, Figure 16.4 shows that both periods exhibit Phillips phases, but that the early 2000s has both higher inflation and higher unemployment. One way to explain these back-to-back Phillips phases is to look at Figure 16.8. Assume point 1 represents the economy in 2001, with aggregate demand increasing. At the same time, though, oil and other commodity prices were rising markedly—tripling between 2001 and 2007. Thus, the short-run aggregate supply curve was also shifting to the left of $SRAS_{1,2,3}$. This would mean that output would be somewhat lower, unemployment somewhat higher, and inflation somewhat higher than what is shown as points 2 and 3 in Panels (a) and (b) of Figure 16.8. The 2000s Phillips curve would thus be above the late 1990s Phillips curve. While the Phillips phase of the early 2000s is farther from the origin than that of the late 1990s, it is noteworthy that the economy did not go through a severe stagflation phase, suggesting some learning about how to conduct monetary and fiscal policy. It will be interesting to see how the U.S. economy emerges from the 2007-2009 recession. Will the expansionary monetary and fiscal policies generate inflation or will inflation remain low as the unemployment rate drops?

So, while the economy does not move neatly through the phases outlined in the inflation—unemployment cycle, we can conclude that efforts to stimulate aggregate demand, together with changes in expectations, have played an important role in generating the inflation–unemployment patterns we observe in the past half-century.

Lags have played a crucial role in the cycle as well. If policy makers respond to a recessionary gap with an expansionary fiscal or monetary policy, then we know that aggregate demand will increase, but with a lag. Policy makers could thus undertake an expansionary policy and see little or no response at first. They might respond by making further expansionary efforts. When the first efforts finally shift aggregate demand, subsequent expansionary efforts can shift it too far, pushing real GDP beyond potential and creating an inflationary gap. These increases in aggregate demand create a Phillips phase. The economy's correction of the gap creates a stagflation phase. If policy makers respond to the stagflation phase with a new round of expansionary policies, the initial result will be a recovery phase. Sufficiently large increases in aggregate demand can then push the economy into another Phillips phase, and the cycle continues.

KEY TAKEAWAYS

- In a Phillips phase, aggregate demand rises and boosts real GDP, lowering the unemployment rate. The price level rises by larger and larger percentages. Inflation thus rises while unemployment falls.
- A stagflation phase is marked by a leftward shift in short-run aggregate supply as wages and sticky prices are adjusted upwards. Unemployment rises while inflation remains high.
- In a recovery phase, policy makers boost aggregate demand. The price level rises, but at a slower rate than in the stagflation phase, so inflation falls. Unemployment falls as well.

TRY IT!

Using the model of aggregate demand and aggregate supply; sketch the changes in the curve(s) that produced each of the phases you identified in Try It! 16-1. Do not worry about specific numbers; just show the direction of changes in aggregate demand and/or short-run aggregate supply in each phase.

Case in Point: From the Challenging 1970s to the Calm 1990s

The path of U.S. inflation and unemployment followed a fairly consistent pattern of clockwise loops from 1961 to 2002, but the nature of these loops changed with changes in policy.

If we follow the cycle shown in Figure 16.4, we see that the three Phillips phases that began in 1961, 1972, and 1976 started at successively higher rates of inflation. Fiscal and monetary policy became expansionary at the beginnings of each of these phases, despite rising rates of inflation.

As inflation soared into the double-digit range in 1979, President Jimmy Carter appointed a new Fed chairman, Paul Volcker. The president gave the new chairman a clear mandate: bring inflation under control, regardless of the cost. The Fed responded with a sharply contractionary monetary policy and stuck with it even as the economy experienced its worse recession since the Great Depression.

Falling oil prices after 1982 contributed to an unusually long recovery phase: Inflation and unemployment both fell from 1982 to 1986. The inflation rate at which the economy started its next Phillips phase was the lowest since the Phillips phase of the 1960s.

The Fed's policies since then have clearly shown a reduced tolerance for inflation. The Fed shifted to a contractionary monetary policy in 1988, so that inflation during the 1986–1989 Phillips phase never exceeded 4%. When oil prices rose at the outset of the Persian Gulf War in 1990, the resultant swings in inflation and unemployment were much less pronounced than they had been in the 1970s.

The Fed continued its effort to restrain inflation in 1994 and 1995. It shifted to a contractionary policy early in 1994 when the economy was still in a recessionary gap left over from the 1990–1991 recession. The Fed's announced intention was to prevent any future increase in inflation. In effect, the Fed was taking explicit account of the lag in monetary policy. Had it continued an expansionary monetary policy, it might well have put the economy in another Phillips phase. Instead, the Fed has conducted a carefully orchestrated series of slight shifts in policy that succeeded in keeping the economy in the longest recovery phase since World War II.

To be sure, the stellar economic performance of the United States in the late 1990s was due in part to falling oil prices, which shifted the short-run aggregate supply curve to the right and helped push inflation and unemployment down. But it seems clear that a good deal of the credit can be claimed by the Fed, which paid closer attention to the lags inherent in macroeconomic policy. Ignoring those lags helped create the inflation—unemployment cycles that emerged with activist stabilization policies in the 1960s.

ANSWER TO TRY IT! PROBLEM

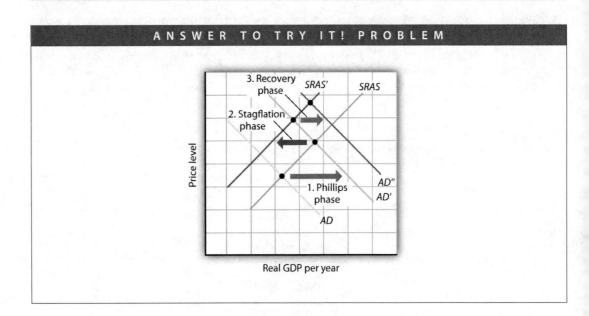

3. INFLATION AND UNEMPLOYMENT IN THE LONG RUN

In the last section, we saw how stabilization policy, together with changes in expectations, can produce the cycles of inflation and unemployment that characterized the past several decades. These cycles, though, are short-run phenomena. They involve swings in economic activity around the economy's potential output.

This section examines forces that affect the values of inflation and the unemployment rate in the long run. We shall see that the rates of money growth and of economic growth determine the inflation rate. Unemployment that persists in the long run includes frictional and structural unemployment. We shall examine some of the forces that affect both types of unemployment, as well as a new theory of unemployment.

3.1 The Inflation Rate in the Long Run

What factors determine the inflation rate? The price level is determined by the intersection of aggregate demand and short-run aggregate supply; anything that shifts either of these two curves changes the price level and thus affects the inflation rate. We have seen how these shifts can generate different inflation–unemployment combinations in the short run. In the long run, the rate of inflation will be determined by two factors: the rate of money growth and the rate of economic growth.

Economists generally agree that the rate of money growth is one determinant of an economy's inflation rate in the long run. The conceptual basis for that conclusion lies in the equation of exchange: $MV = PY$. That is, the money supply times the velocity of money equals the price level times the value of real GDP.

Given the equation of exchange, which holds by definition, we learned in the chapter on monetary policy that the sum of the percentage rates of change in M and V will be roughly equal to the sum of the percentage rates of change in P and Y. That is,

EQUATION 16.1

$$\%\Delta M + \%\Delta V \cong \%\Delta P + \%\Delta Y$$

Suppose that velocity is stable in the long run, so that $\%\Delta V$ equals zero. Then, the inflation rate ($\%\Delta P$) roughly equals the percentage rate of change in the money supply minus the percentage rate of change in real GDP:

EQUATION 16.2

$$\%\Delta P \cong \%\Delta M - \%\Delta Y$$

In the long run, real GDP moves to its potential level, Y_P. Thus, in the long run we can write Equation 16.2 as follows:

EQUATION 16.3

$$\%\Delta P \cong \%\Delta M - \%\Delta Y_P$$

There is a limit to how fast the economy's potential output can grow. Economists generally agree that potential output increases at only about a 2% to 3% annual rate in the United States. Given that the economy stays close to its potential, this puts a rough limit on the speed with which Y can grow. Velocity can vary, but it is not likely to change at a rapid rate over a sustained period. These two facts suggest that very rapid increases in the quantity of money, M, will inevitably produce very rapid increases in the price level, P. If the money supply grows more slowly than potential output, then the right-hand side of Equation 16.3 will be negative. The price level will fall; the economy experiences deflation.

Numerous studies point to the strong relationship between money growth and inflation, especially for high-inflation countries. Figure 16.13 is from a recent study by economists Paul De Grauwe and Magdalena Polan. It is based on a sample of 160 countries over a 30-year period. Panel (a) includes all 160 countries and suggests a positive relationship between money growth and the rate of inflation. The relationship is clearly not precise, and the relationship is strengthened by the presence of countries with very high inflation rates. When the researchers break down the sample into countries with inflation rates of less than 10%, less than 20%, and less than 50%, they find that for countries with single-digit inflation the relationship between inflation and money growth is quite weak. Panel (b) shows that there is still a visible, though of course not perfect, correlation when examining countries with inflation rates of less than 50%.[3]

FIGURE 16.13 Money Growth Rates and Inflation over the Long Run

Data for 160 countries over a 30-year period suggest a positive relationship between the rate of money growth and inflation. The graph shows the inflation rate against a broad definition of the money supply, M2.

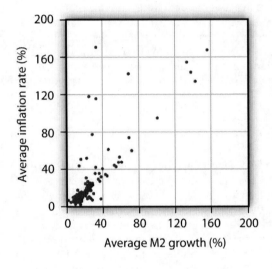

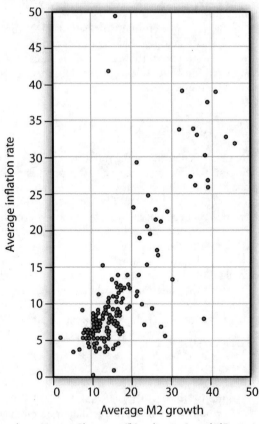

Source: Paul De Grauwe and Magdalena Polan, "Is Inflation Always and Everywhere a Monetary Phenomenon?" Scandinavian Journal of Economics 107, no. 2 (2005): 245–46.

In the model of aggregate demand and aggregate supply, increases in the money supply shift the aggregate demand curve to the right and thus force the price level upward. Money growth thus produces inflation.

Of course, other factors can shift the aggregate demand curve as well. For example, expansionary fiscal policy or an increase in investment will shift aggregate demand. We have already seen that changes in the expected price level or in production costs shift the short-run aggregate supply curve. But such increases are not likely to continue year after year, as money growth can. Factors other than money growth may influence the inflation rate from one year to the next, but they are not likely to cause sustained inflation.

Inflation Rates and Economic Growth

Our conclusion is a simple and an important one. In the long run, the inflation rate is determined by the relative values of the economy's rate of money growth and of its rate of economic growth. If the money supply increases more rapidly than the rate of economic growth, inflation is likely to result. A money growth rate equal to the rate of economic growth will, in the absence of a change in velocity, produce a zero rate of inflation. Finally, a money growth rate that falls short of the rate of economic growth is likely to lead to deflation.

3.2 Unemployment in the Long Run

Economists distinguish three types of unemployment: frictional unemployment, structural unemployment, and cyclical unemployment. The first two exist at all times, even when the economy operates at its potential. These two types of unemployment together determine the natural rate of unemployment. In the long run, the economy will operate at potential, and the unemployment rate will be the natural rate of unemployment. For this reason, in the long run the Phillips curve will be vertical at the natural rate of unemployment. Figure 16.14 explains why. Suppose the economy is operating at Y_P on AD_1 and $SRAS_1$. Suppose the price level is P_0, the same as in the last period. In that case, the inflation rate is 0. Panel (b) shows that the unemployment rate is U_P, the natural rate of unemployment. Now suppose that the aggregate demand curve shifts to AD_2. In the short run, output will increase to Y_1. The price level will rise to P_1, and the unemployment rate will fall to U_1. In Panel (b) we show the new unemployment rate, U_1, to be associated with an inflation rate of π_1, and the beginnings of the negatively sloped short-run Phillips curve emerges. In the long run, as price and nominal wages increase, the short-run aggregate supply curve moves to $SRAS_2$ and output returns to Y_P, as shown in Panel (a). In Panel (b), unemployment returns to U_P, regardless of the rate of inflation. Thus, in the long-run, the Phillips curve is vertical.

FIGURE 16.14 The Phillips Curve in the Long Run

Suppose the economy is operating at Y_P on AD_1 and $SRAS_1$ in Panel (a) with price level of P_0, the same as in the last period. Panel (b) shows that the unemployment rate is U_P, the natural rate of unemployment. If the aggregate demand curve shifts to AD_2, in the short run output will increase to Y_1, and the price level will rise to P_1. In Panel (b), the unemployment rate will fall to U_1, and the inflation rate will be π_1. In the long run, as price and nominal wages increase, the short-run aggregate supply curve moves to $SRAS_2$, and output returns to Y_P, as shown in Panel (a). In Panel (b), unemployment returns to U_P, regardless of the rate of inflation. Thus, in the long-run, the Phillips curve is vertical.

Panel (a)

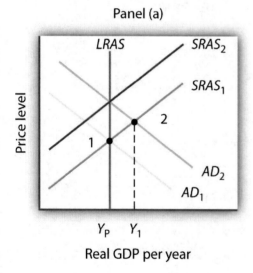

Real GDP per year

Panel (b)

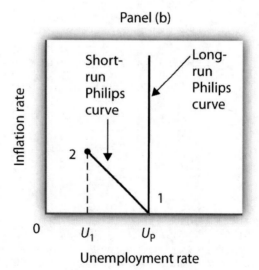

Unemployment rate

An economy operating at its potential would have no cyclical unemployment. Because an economy achieves its potential output in the long run, an analysis of unemployment in the long run is an analysis of frictional and structural unemployment. In this section, we will also look at some new research that challenges the very concept of an economy achieving its potential output.

Frictional Unemployment

Frictional unemployment occurs because it takes time for people seeking jobs and employers seeking workers to find each other. If the amount of time could be reduced, frictional unemployment would fall. The economy's natural rate of unemployment would drop, and its potential output would rise. This section presents a model of frictional unemployment and examines some issues in reducing the frictional unemployment rate.

A period of frictional unemployment ends with the individual getting a job. The process through which the job is obtained suggests some important clues to the nature of frictional unemployment.

By definition, a person who is unemployed is seeking work. At the outset of a job search, we presume that the individual has a particular wage in mind as he or she considers various job possibilities. The lowest wage that an unemployed worker would accept, if it were offered, is called the **reservation wage**. This is the wage an individual would accept; any offer below it would be rejected. Once a firm offers the reservation wage, the individual will take it and the job search will be terminated. Many people may hold out for more than just a wage—they may be seeking a certain set of working conditions, opportunities for advancement, or a job in a particular area. In practice, then, an unemployed worker might be willing to accept a variety of combinations of wages and other job characteristics. We shall simplify our analysis by lumping all these other characteristics into a single reservation wage.

A worker's reservation wage is likely to change as his or her search continues. One might initiate a job search with high expectations and thus have a high reservation wage. As the job search continues, however, this reservation wage might be adjusted downward as the worker obtains better information about what is likely to be available in the market and as the financial difficulties associated with unemployment mount. We can thus draw a reservation wage curve (Figure 16.15), that suggests a negative relationship between the reservation wage and the duration of a person's job search. Similarly, as a job search continues, the worker will accumulate better offers. The "best-offer-received" curve shows what its name implies; it is the best offer the individual has received so far in the job search. The upward slope of the curve suggests that, as a worker's search continues, the best offer received will rise.

FIGURE 16.15 A Model of a Job Search

An individual begins a job search at time t_0 with a reservation wage W_0. As long as the reservation wage exceeds the best offer received, the individual will continue searching. A job is accepted, and the search is terminated, at time t_c, at which the reservation and "best-offer-received" curves intersect at wage W_c.

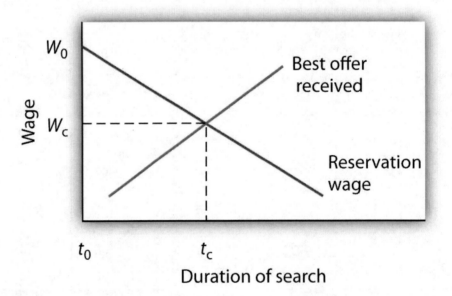

The search begins at time t_0, with the unemployed worker seeking wage W_0. Because the worker's reservation wage exceeds the best offer received, the worker continues the search. The worker reduces his or her reservation wage and accumulates better offers until the two curves intersect at time t_c. The worker accepts wage W_c, and the job search is terminated.

The job search model in Figure 16.15 does not determine an equilibrium duration of job search or an equilibrium initial wage. The reservation wage and best-offer-received curves will be unique to each individual's experience. We can, however, use the model to reach some conclusions about factors that affect frictional unemployment.

First, the duration of search will be shorter when more job market information is available. Suppose, for example, that the only way to determine what jobs and wages are available is to visit each firm separately. Such a situation would require a lengthy period of search before a given offer was received. Alternatively, suppose there are agencies that make such information readily available and that link unemployed workers to firms seeking to hire workers. In that second situation, the time required to obtain a given offer would be reduced, and the best-offer-received curves for individual workers would shift to the left. The lower the cost for obtaining job market information, the lower the average duration of unemployment. Government and private agencies that provide job information and placement services help to reduce information costs to unemployed workers and firms. They tend to lower frictional unemployment by shifting the best-offer-received curves for individual workers to the left, as shown in Panel (a) of Figure 16.16. Workers obtain higher-paying jobs when they do find work; the wage at which searches are terminated rises to W_2.

FIGURE 16.16   Public Policy and Frictional Unemployment

Public policy can influence the time required for job-seeking workers and worker-seeking firms to find each other. Programs that provide labor-market information tend to shift the best-offer-received (*BOR*) curves of individual workers to the left, reducing the duration of job search and reducing unemployment, as in Panel (a). Note that the wage these workers obtain also rises to W_2. Unemployment compensation tends to increase the period over which a worker will hold out for a particular wage, shifting the reservation wage (*RW*) curve to the right, as in Panel (b). Unemployment compensation thus boosts the unemployment rate and increases the wage workers obtain when they find employment.

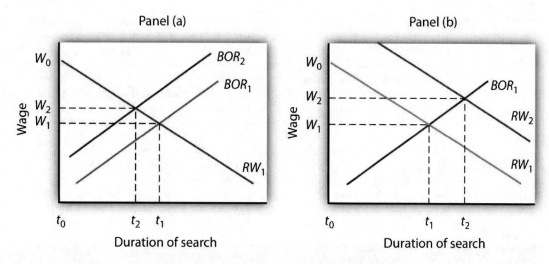

Unemployment compensation, which was introduced in the United States during the Great Depression to help workers who had lost jobs through unemployment, also affects frictional unemployment. Because unemployment compensation reduces the financial burden of being unemployed, it is likely to increase the amount of time people will wait for a given wage. It thus shifts the reservation wage curve to the right, raises the average duration of unemployment, and increases the wage at which searches end, as shown in Panel (b). An increase in the average duration of unemployment implies a higher unemployment rate. Unemployment compensation thus has a paradoxical effect—it tends to increase the problem against which it protects.

Structural Unemployment

Structural unemployment occurs when a firm is looking for a worker and an unemployed worker is looking for a job, but the particular characteristics the firm seeks do not match up with the characteristics the worker offers. Technological change is one source of structural unemployment. New technologies are likely to require different skills than old technologies. Workers with training to equip them for the old technology may find themselves caught up in a structural mismatch.

Technological and managerial changes have, for example, changed the characteristics firms seek in workers they hire. Firms looking for assembly-line workers once sought men and women with qualities such as reliability, integrity, strength, and manual dexterity. Reliability and integrity remain important, but many assembly-line jobs now require greater analytical and communications skills. Automobile manufacturers, for example, now test applicants for entry-level factory jobs on their abilities in algebra, in trigonometry, and in written and oral communications. Strong, agile workers with weak analytical and language skills may find many job openings for which they do not qualify. They would be examples of the structurally unemployed.

Changes in demand can also produce structural unemployment. As consumers shift their demands to different products, firms that are expanding and seeking more workers may need different skills than firms for which demand has shrunk. Similarly, firms may shift their use of different types of jobs in response to changing market conditions, leaving some workers with the "wrong" set of skills. Regional shifts in demand can produce structural unemployment as well. The economy of one region may be expanding rapidly, creating job vacancies, while another region is in a slump, with many workers seeking jobs but not finding them.

Public and private job training firms seek to reduce structural unemployment by providing workers with skills now in demand. Employment services that provide workers with information about jobs in other regions also reduce the extent of structural unemployment.

Cyclical Unemployment and Efficiency Wages

In our model, unemployment above the natural level occurs if, at a given real wage, the quantity of labor supplied exceeds the quantity of labor demanded. In the analysis we've done so far, the failure to achieve equilibrium is a short-run phenomenon. In the long run, wages and prices will adjust so that the real wage reaches its equilibrium level. Employment reaches its natural level.

Some economists, however, argue that a real wage that achieves equilibrium in the labor market may *never* be reached. They suggest that firms may intentionally pay a wage greater than the market equilibrium. Such firms could hire additional workers at a lower wage, but they choose not to do so. The idea that firms may hold to a real wage greater than the equilibrium wage is called **efficiency-wage theory**.

Why would a firm pay higher wages than the market requires? Suppose that by paying higher wages, the firm is able to boost the productivity of its workers. Workers become more contented and more eager to perform in ways that boost the firm's profits. Workers who receive real wages above the equilibrium level may also be less likely to leave their jobs. That would reduce job turnover. A firm that pays its workers wages in excess of the equilibrium wage expects to gain by retaining its employees and by inducing those employees to be more productive. Efficiency-wage theory thus suggests that the labor market may divide into two segments. Workers with jobs will receive high wages. Workers without jobs, who would be willing to work at an even lower wage than the workers with jobs, find themselves closed out of the market.

Whether efficiency wages really exist remains a controversial issue, but the argument is an important one. If it is correct, then the wage rigidity that perpetuates a recessionary gap is transformed from a temporary phenomenon that will be overcome in the long run to a permanent feature of the market. The argument implies that the ordinary processes of self-correction will not eliminate a recessionary gap.[4]

efficiency-wage theory

The idea that firms may hold to a real wage greater than the equilibrium wage.

KEY TAKEAWAYS

- Two factors that can influence the rate of inflation in the long run are the rate of money growth and the rate of economic growth.
- In the long run, the Phillips curve will be vertical since when output is at potential, the unemployment rate will be the natural rate of unemployment, regardless of the rate of inflation.
- The rate of frictional unemployment is affected by information costs and by the existence of unemployment compensation.
- Policies to reduce structural unemployment include the provision of job training and information about labor-market conditions in other regions.
- Efficiency-wage theory predicts that profit-maximizing firms will maintain the wage level at a rate too high to achieve full employment in the labor market.

TRY IT!

Using the model of a job search (see Figure 16.15), show graphically how each of the following would be likely to affect the duration of an unemployed worker's job search and thus the unemployment rate:

1. A new program provides that workers who have lost their jobs will receive unemployment compensation from the government equal to the pay they were earning when they lost their jobs, and that this compensation will continue for at least five years.
2. Unemployment compensation is provided, but it falls by 20% each month a person is out of work.
3. Access to the Internet becomes much more widely available and is used by firms looking for workers and by workers seeking jobs.

Case in Point: Altering the Incentives for Unemployment Insurance Claimants

While the rationale for unemployment insurance is clear—to help people weather bouts of unemployment—especially during economic downturns, designing programs that reduce adverse incentives is challenging. A review article by economists Peter Fredriksson and Bertil Holmlund examined decades of research that looks at how unemployment insurance programs could be improved. In particular, they consider the value of changing the duration and profile of benefit payments, increasing monitoring and sanctions imposed on unemployment insurance recipients, and changing work requirements. Some of the research is theoretical, while some comes out of actual experiments.

Concerning benefit payments, they suggest that reducing payments over time provides better incentives than either keeping payments constant or increasing them over time. Research also suggests that a waiting period might also be useful. Concerning monitoring and sanctions, most unemployment insurance systems require claimants to demonstrate in some way that they have looked for work. For example, they must report regularly to employment agencies or provide evidence they have applied for jobs. If they do not, the benefit may be temporarily cut. A number of experiments support the notion that greater search requirements reduce the length of unemployment. One experiment conducted in Maryland assigned recipients to different processes ranging from the standard requirement at the time of two employer contacts per week to requiring at least four contacts per week, attending a four-day job search workshop, and telling claimants that their employer contacts would be verified. The results showed that increasing the number of employer contacts reduced the duration by 6%, attending the workshop reduced duration by 5%, and the possibility of verification reduced it by 7.5%. Indeed, just telling claimants that they were going to have to attend the workshop led to a reduction in claimants. Evidence on instituting some kind of work requirement is similar to that of instituting workshop attendance.

The authors conclude that the effectiveness of all these instruments results from the fact that they encourage more active job search.

Source: *Peter Fredriksson and Bertil Holmlund, "Improving Incentives in Unemployment Insurance: A Review of Recent Research," Journal of Economic Surveys 20, no. 3 (July 2006): 357–86.*

The duration of an unemployed worker's job search increases in situation (1), as illustrated in panel (a) and decreases in situations (2) and (3), as illustrated in panels (b) and (c) respectively. Thus, the unemployment rate increases in situation (1) and decreases in situations (2) and (3)

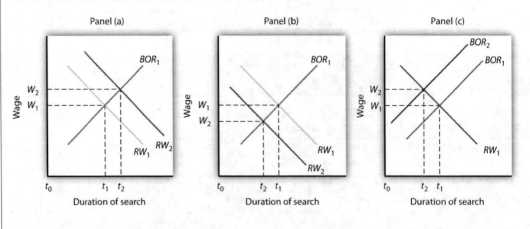

4. REVIEW AND PRACTICE

Summary

During the 1960s, it appeared that there was a stable trade-off between the rate of unemployment and the rate of inflation. The Phillips curve, which describes such a trade-off, suggests that lower rates of unemployment come with higher rates of inflation, and that lower rates of inflation come with higher rates of unemployment. But during subsequent decades, the actual values for unemployment and inflation have not always followed the Phillips curve script.

There has, however, been a relationship between unemployment and inflation over the four decades from 1961. Periods of rising inflation and falling unemployment have been followed by periods of rising unemployment and continued inflation; those periods have, in turn, been followed by periods in which both the inflation rate and the unemployment rate fall. These periods are defined as the Phillips phase, the stagflation phase, and the recovery phase of the inflation—unemployment cycle, respectively. Following the recession of 2001, the economy returned quickly to a Phillips phase.

The Phillips phase is a period in which aggregate demand increases, boosting output and the price level. Unemployment drops and inflation rises. An essential feature of the Phillips phase is that the price increases that occur are unexpected. Workers thus experience lower real wages than they anticipated. Firms with sticky prices find that their prices are low relative to other prices. As workers and firms adjust to the higher inflation of the Phillips phase, they demand higher wages and post higher prices, so the short-run aggregate supply curve shifts leftward. Inflation continues, but real GDP falls. This is the stagflation phase. Finally, aggregate demand begins to increase again, boosting both real GDP and the price level. The higher price level, however, is likely to represent a much smaller percentage increase than had occurred during the stagflation phase. This is the recovery phase: inflation and unemployment fall together.

There is nothing inherent in a market economy that would produce the inflation—unemployment cycle we have observed since 1961. The cycle can begin if expansionary policies are launched to correct a recessionary gap, producing the Phillips phase. If those policies push the economy into an inflationary gap, then the adjustment of short-run aggregate supply will produce the stagflation phase. And, in the economy's first response to an expansionary policy launched to deal with the recession of the stagflation phase, the price level rises, but at a slower rate than before. The economy experiences falling inflation and falling unemployment at the same time: the recovery phase.

In the long run, the Phillips curve is vertical, and inflation is essentially a monetary phenomenon. Assuming stable velocity of money over the long run, the inflation rate roughly equals the money growth rate minus the rate of growth of real GDP. For a given money growth rate, inflation is thus reduced by faster economic growth.

Frictional unemployment is affected by information costs in the labor market. A reduction in those costs would reduce frictional unemployment. Hastening the retraining of workers would reduce structural unemployment. Reductions in frictional or structural unemployment would lower the natural rate of unemployment and thus raise potential output. Unemployment compensation is likely to increase frictional unemployment.

Some economists believe that cyclical unemployment may persist because firms have an incentive to maintain real wages above the equilibrium level. Whether this efficiency-wage argument holds is controversial.

CONCEPT PROBLEMS

1. The Case in Point titled "Some Reflections on the 1970s" describes the changes in inflation and in unemployment in 1970 and 1971 as a watershed development for macroeconomic thought. Why was an increase in unemployment such a significant event?

2. As the economy slipped into recession in 1980 and 1981, the Fed was under enormous pressure to adopt an expansionary monetary policy. Suppose it had begun an expansionary policy early in 1981. What does the text's analysis of the inflation—unemployment cycle suggest about how the macroeconomic history of the 1980s might have been changed?

3. Here are some news reports covering events of the past 35 years. In each case, identify the stage of the inflation—unemployment cycle, and suggest what change in aggregate demand or aggregate supply might have caused it.

   a. "President Nixon expressed satisfaction with last year's economic performance. He said that with inflation and unemployment heading down, the nation 'is on the right course.'"

   b. "The nation's inflation rate rose to a record high last month, the government reported yesterday. The consumer price index jumped 0.3% in January. Coupled with the announcement earlier this month that unemployment had risen by 0.5 percentage points, the reports suggested that the first month of President Nixon's second term had gotten off to a rocky start."

   c. "President Carter expressed concern about reports of rising inflation but insisted the economy is on the right course. He pointed to recent reductions in unemployment as evidence that his economic policies are working."

4. The text notes that changes in oil prices can affect the inflation—unemployment cycle. Should they be incorporated as part of the theory of the cycle?

5. The introduction to this chapter suggests that unemployment fell, and inflation generally fell, through most of the 1990s. What phase of the inflation—unemployment cycle does this represent? Relative to U.S. experience since the 1960s, what was unusual about this?

6. Suppose that declining resource supplies reduce potential output in each period by 4%. What kind of monetary policy would be needed to maintain a zero rate of inflation at full employment?

7. The Humphrey–Hawkins Act of 1978 required that the federal government maintain an unemployment rate of 4% and hold the inflation rate to less than 3%. What does the inflation–unemployment relationship tell you about achieving such goals?

8. The American Economic Association publishes a newsletter (which is available on the AEA's Internet site at http://www.aeaweb.org/joe/) called *Job Openings for Economists* (JOE). Virtually all academic and many nonacademic positions for which applicants are being sought for economics positions are listed in the newsletter, which is quite inexpensive. How do you think that the publication of this journal affects the unemployment rate among economists? What type of unemployment does it affect?

9. Many economists think that we are in the very early stages of putting computer technology to work and that full incorporation of computers will cause a massive restructuring of virtually every institution of modern life. If they are right, what are the implications for unemployment? What kind of unemployment would be affected?

10. The natural unemployment rate in the United States has varied over the last 50 years. According to the Congressional Budget Office, the natural rate was 5.5% in 1960, rose to about 6.5% in the 1970s, and had declined to about 4.8% by 2000. What do you think might have caused this variation?

11. Suppose the Fed begins carrying out an expansionary monetary policy in order to close a recessionary gap. Relate what happens during the next two phases of the inflation—unemployment cycle to the maxim "You can fool some of the people some of the time, but you can't fool all of the people all of the time."

NUMERICAL PROBLEMS

1. Here are annual data for the inflation and unemployment rates for the United States for the 1948–1961 period.

Year	Unemployment rate (%)	Inflation rate (%)
1948	3.8	3.0
1949	5.9	−2.1
1950	5.3	5.9
1951	3.3	6.0
1952	3.0	0.8
1953	2.9	0.7
1954	5.5	−0.7
1955	4.4	0.4
1956	4.1	3.0
1957	4.3	2.9
1958	6.8	1.8
1959	5.5	1.7
1960	5.5	1.4
1961	6.7	0.7

   a. Plot these observations and connect the points as in Figure 16.5.

   b. How does this period compare to the decades that followed?

   c. What do you think accounts for the difference?

2. Here are hypothetical inflation and unemployment data for Econoland.

Time period	Inflation rate (%)	Unemployment rate (%)
1	0	6
2	3	4
3	7	3
4	8	5
5	7	7
6	3	6

   a. Plot these points.

   b. Identify which points correspond to a Phillips phase, which correspond to a stagflation phase, and which correspond to a recovery phase.

3. Relate the observations in Numerical Problem 2 to what must have been happening in the aggregate demand–aggregate supply model.

4. Suppose the full-employment level of real GDP is increasing at a rate of 3% per period and the money supply is growing at a 4% rate. What will happen to the long-run inflation rate, assuming constant velocity?

ENDNOTES

1. Minutes of the Federal Open Market Committee March 18, 2008.

2. Almarin W. Phillips, "The Relation between Unemployment and the Rate of Change of Money Wage Rates in the United Kingdom, 1861–1957," *Economica* 25 (November 1958): 283–99.

3. Paul De Grauwe and Magdalena Polan, "Is Inflation Always and Everywhere a Monetary Phenomenon?" *Scandinavian Journal of Economics* 107, no. 2 (2005): 239–59.

4. For a discussion of the argument, see Janet Yellen, "Efficiency Wage Models of Unemployment," *American Economic Review, Papers and Proceedings* (May 1984): 200–205.

CHAPTER 17

A Brief History of Macroeconomic Thought and Policy

START UP: THREE REVOLUTIONS IN MACROECONOMIC THOUGHT

It is the 1930s. Many people have begun to wonder if the United States will ever escape the Great Depression's cruel grip. Forecasts that prosperity lies just around the corner take on a hollow ring.

The collapse seems to defy the logic of the dominant economic view—that economies should be able to reach full employment through a process of self-correction. The old ideas of macroeconomics do not seem to work, and it is not clear what new ideas should replace them.

In Britain, Cambridge University economist John Maynard Keynes is struggling with ideas that he thinks will stand the conventional wisdom on its head. He is confident that he has found the key not only to understanding the Great Depression but also to correcting it.

It is the 1960s. Most economists believe that Keynes's ideas best explain fluctuations in economic activity. The tools Keynes suggested have won widespread acceptance among governments all over the world; the application of expansionary fiscal policy in the United States appears to have been a spectacular success. But economist Milton Friedman of the University of Chicago continues to fight a lonely battle against what has become the Keynesian orthodoxy. He argues that money, not fiscal policy, is what affects aggregate demand. He insists not only that fiscal policy cannot work, but that monetary policy should not be used to move the economy back to its potential output. He counsels a policy of steady money growth, leaving the economy to adjust to long-run equilibrium on its own.

It is 1970. The economy has just taken a startling turn: Real GDP has fallen, but inflation has remained high. A young economist at Carnegie–Mellon University, Robert E. Lucas, Jr., finds this a paradox, one that he thinks cannot be explained by Keynes's theory. Along with several other economists, he begins work on a radically new approach to macroeconomic thought, one that will challenge Keynes's view head-on. Lucas and his colleagues suggest a world in which self-correction is swift, rational choices by individuals generally cancel the impact of fiscal and monetary policies, and stabilization efforts are likely to slow economic growth.

John Maynard Keynes, Milton Friedman, and Robert E. Lucas, Jr., each helped to establish a major school of macroeconomic thought. Although their ideas clashed sharply, and although there remains considerable disagreement among economists about a variety of issues, a broad consensus among economists concerning macroeconomic policy began to emerge in the 1980s and 1990s. That consensus has sharply affected macroeconomic policy.

And the improved understanding that has grown out of the macroeconomic debate has had dramatic effects on fiscal and on monetary policy.

In this chapter we will examine the macroeconomic developments of five decades: the 1930s, 1960s, 1970s, 1980s, and 1990s. We will use the aggregate demand–aggregate supply model to explain macroeconomic changes during these periods, and we will see how the three major economic schools were affected by these events. We will also see how these schools of thought affected macroeconomic policy. Finally, we will see how the evolution of macroeconomic thought and policy is influencing how economists design policy prescriptions for dealing with the current recession, which many feel has the potential to be the largest since the Great Depression.

In examining the ideas of these schools, we will incorporate concepts such as the potential output and the natural level of employment. While such terms had not been introduced when some of the major schools of thought first emerged, we will use them when they capture the ideas economists were presenting.

1. THE GREAT DEPRESSION AND KEYNESIAN ECONOMICS

LEARNING OBJECTIVES

1. Explain the basic assumptions of the classical school of thought that dominated macroeconomic thinking before the Great Depression, and tell why the severity of the Depression struck a major blow to this view.
2. Compare Keynesian and classical macroeconomic thought, discussing the Keynesian explanation of prolonged recessionary and inflationary gaps as well as the Keynesian approach to correcting these problems.

It is hard to imagine that anyone who lived during the Great Depression was not profoundly affected by it. From the beginning of the Depression in 1929 to the time the economy hit bottom in 1933, real GDP plunged nearly 30%. Real per capita disposable income sank nearly 40%. More than 12 million people were thrown out of work; the unemployment rate soared from 3% in 1929 to 25% in 1933. Some 85,000 businesses failed. Hundreds of thousands of families lost their homes. By 1933, about half of all mortgages on all urban, owner-occupied houses were delinquent.[1]

The economy began to recover after 1933, but a huge recessionary gap persisted. Another downturn began in 1937, pushing the unemployment rate back up to 19% the following year.

The contraction in output that began in 1929 was not, of course, the first time the economy had slumped. But never had the U.S. economy fallen so far and for so long a period. Economic historians estimate that in the 75 years before the Depression there had been 19 recessions. But those contractions had lasted an average of less than two years. The Great Depression lasted for more than a decade. The severity and duration of the Great Depression distinguish it from other contractions; it is for that reason that we give it a much stronger name than "recession."

Figure 17.1 shows the course of real GDP compared to potential output during the Great Depression. The economy did not approach potential output until 1941, when the pressures of world war forced sharp increases in aggregate demand.

FIGURE 17.1 The Depression and the Recessionary Gap

The dark-shaded area shows real GDP from 1929 to 1942, the upper line shows potential output, and the light-shaded area shows the difference between the two—the recessionary gap. The gap nearly closed in 1941; an inflationary gap had opened by 1942. The chart suggests that the recessionary gap remained very large throughout the 1930s.

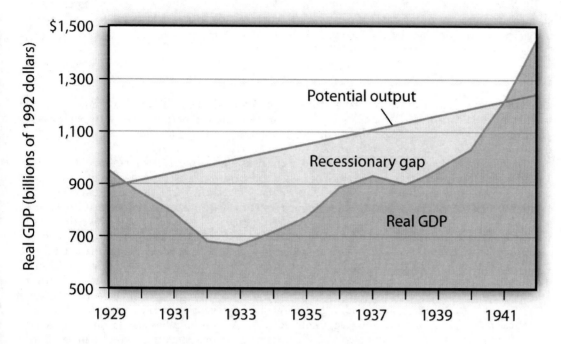

1.1   The Classical School and the Great Depression

The Great Depression came as a shock to what was then the conventional wisdom of economics. To see why, we must go back to the classical tradition of macroeconomics that dominated the economics profession when the Depression began.

Classical economics is the body of macroeconomic thought associated primarily with 19th-century British economist David Ricardo. His *Principles of Political Economy and Taxation*, published in 1817, established a tradition that dominated macroeconomic thought for over a century. Ricardo focused on the long run and on the forces that determine and produce growth in an economy's potential output. He emphasized the ability of flexible wages and prices to keep the economy at or near its natural level of employment.

According to the classical school, achieving what we now call the natural level of employment and potential output is not a problem; the economy can do that on its own. Classical economists recognized, however, that the process would take time. Ricardo admitted that there could be *temporary* periods in which employment would fall below the natural level. But his emphasis was on the long run, and in the long run all would be set right by the smooth functioning of the price system.

Economists of the classical school saw the massive slump that occurred in much of the world in the late 1920s and early 1930s as a short-run aberration. The economy would right itself in the long run, returning to its potential output and to the natural level of employment.

classical economics

The body of macroeconomic thought, associated primarily with nineteenth-century British economist David Ricardo, that focused on the long run and on the forces that determine and produce growth in an economy's potential output.

1.2   Keynesian Economics

In Britain, which had been plunged into a depression of its own, John Maynard Keynes had begun to develop a new framework of macroeconomic analysis, one that suggested that what for Ricardo were "temporary effects" could persist for a long time, and at terrible cost. Keynes's 1936 book, *The General Theory of Employment, Interest and Money*, was to transform the way many economists thought about macroeconomic problems.

Keynes versus the Classical Tradition

In a nutshell, we can say that Keynes's book shifted the thrust of macroeconomic thought from the concept of aggregate supply to the concept of aggregate demand. Ricardo's focus on the tendency of an economy to reach potential output inevitably stressed the supply side—an economy tends to operate at a level of output given by the long-run aggregate supply curve. Keynes, in arguing that what we now call recessionary or inflationary gaps could be created by shifts in aggregate demand, moved the focus of macroeconomic analysis to the demand side. He argued that prices in the short run are quite sticky and suggested that this stickiness would block adjustments to full employment.

Keynes dismissed the notion that the economy would achieve full employment in the long run as irrelevant. "In the long run," he wrote acidly, "we are all dead."

Keynes's work spawned a new school of macroeconomic thought, the Keynesian school. **Keynesian economics** asserts that changes in aggregate demand can create gaps between the actual and potential levels of output, and that such gaps can be prolonged. Keynesian economists stress the use of fiscal and of monetary policy to close such gaps.

Keynesian Economics and the Great Depression

The experience of the Great Depression certainly seemed consistent with Keynes's argument. A reduction in aggregate demand took the economy from above its potential output to below its potential output, and, as we saw in Figure 17.1, the resulting recessionary gap lasted for more than a decade. While the Great Depression affected many countries, we shall focus on the U.S. experience.

The plunge in aggregate demand began with a collapse in investment. The investment boom of the 1920s had left firms with an expanded stock of capital. As the capital stock approached its desired level, firms did not need as much new capital, and they cut back investment. The stock market crash of 1929 shook business confidence, further reducing investment. Real gross private domestic investment plunged nearly 80% between 1929 and 1932. We have learned of the volatility of the investment component of aggregate demand; it was very much in evidence in the first years of the Great Depression.

Other factors contributed to the sharp reduction in aggregate demand. The stock market crash reduced the wealth of a small fraction of the population (just 5% of Americans owned stock at that time), but it certainly reduced the consumption of the general population. The stock market crash also reduced consumer confidence throughout the economy. The reduction in wealth and the reduction in confidence reduced consumption spending and shifted the aggregate demand curve to the left.

Fiscal policy also acted to reduce aggregate demand. As consumption and income fell, governments at all levels found their tax revenues falling. They responded by raising tax rates in an effort to balance their budgets. The federal government, for example, doubled income tax rates in 1932. Total government tax revenues as a percentage of GDP shot up from 10.8% in 1929 to 16.6% in 1933. Higher tax rates tended to reduce consumption and aggregate demand.

Other countries were suffering declining incomes as well. Their demand for U.S. goods and services fell, reducing the real level of exports by 46% between 1929 and 1933. The Smoot–Hawley Tariff Act of 1930 dramatically raised tariffs on products imported into the United States and led to retaliatory trade-restricting legislation around the world. This act, which more than 1,000 economists opposed in a formal petition, contributed to the collapse of world trade and to the recession.

As if all this were not enough, the Fed, in effect, conducted a sharply contractionary monetary policy in the early years of the Depression. The Fed took no action to prevent a wave of bank failures that swept the country at the outset of the Depression. Between 1929 and 1933, one-third of all banks in the United States failed. As a result, the money supply plunged 31% during the period.

The Fed could have prevented many of the failures by engaging in open-market operations to inject new reserves into the system and by lending reserves to troubled banks through the discount window. But it generally refused to do so; Fed officials sometimes even applauded bank failures as a desirable way to weed out bad management!

Keynesian economics

The body of macroeconomic thought that asserts that changes in aggregate demand can create gaps between the actual and potential levels of output, and that such gaps can be prolonged. It stresses the use of fiscal and monetary policy to close such gaps.

Figure 17.2 shows the shift in aggregate demand between 1929, when the economy was operating just above its potential output, and 1933. The plunge in aggregate demand produced a recessionary gap. Our model tells us that such a gap should produce falling wages, shifting the short-run aggregate supply curve to the right. That happened; nominal wages plunged roughly 20% between 1929 and 1933. But we see that the shift in short-run aggregate supply was insufficient to bring the economy back to its potential output.

The failure of shifts in short-run aggregate supply to bring the economy back to its potential output in the early 1930s was partly the result of the magnitude of the reductions in aggregate demand, which plunged the economy into the deepest recessionary gap ever recorded in the United States. We know that the short-run aggregate supply curve began shifting to the right in 1930 as nominal wages fell, but these shifts, which would ordinarily increase real GDP, were overwhelmed by continued reductions in aggregate demand.

A further factor blocking the economy's return to its potential output was federal policy. President Franklin Roosevelt thought that falling wages and prices were in large part to blame for the Depression; programs initiated by his administration in 1933 sought to block further reductions in wages and prices. That stopped further reductions in nominal wages in 1933, thus stopping further shifts in aggregate supply. With recovery blocked from the supply side, and with no policy in place to boost aggregate demand, it is easy to see now why the economy remained locked in a recessionary gap so long.

Keynes argued that expansionary fiscal policy represented the surest tool for bringing the economy back to full employment. The United States did not carry out such a policy until world war prompted increased federal spending for defense. New Deal policies did seek to stimulate employment through a variety of federal programs. But, with state and local governments continuing to cut purchases and raise taxes, the net effect of government at all levels on the economy did not increase aggregate demand during the Roosevelt administration until the onset of world war.[2] As Figure 17.3 shows, expansionary fiscal policies forced by the war had brought output back to potential by 1941. The U.S. entry into World War II after Japan's attack on American forces in Pearl Harbor in December of 1941 led to much sharper increases in government purchases, and the economy pushed quickly into an inflationary gap.

FIGURE 17.2 Aggregate Demand and Short-Run Aggregate Supply: 1929–1933

Slumping aggregate demand brought the economy well below the full-employment level of output by 1933. The short-run aggregate supply curve increased as nominal wages fell. In this analysis, and in subsequent applications in this chapter of the model of aggregate demand and aggregate supply to macroeconomic events, we are ignoring shifts in the long-run aggregate supply curve in order to simplify the diagram.

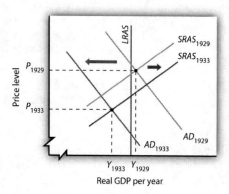

FIGURE 17.3 World War II Ends the Great Depression

Increased U.S. government purchases, prompted by the beginning of World War II, ended the Great Depression. By 1942, increasing aggregate demand had pushed real GDP beyond potential output.

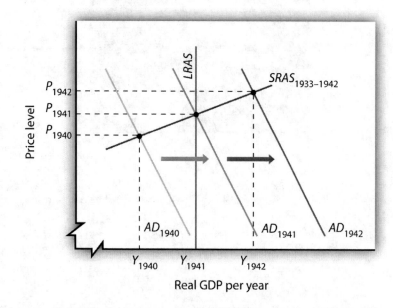

For Keynesian economists, the Great Depression provided impressive confirmation of Keynes's ideas. A sharp reduction in aggregate demand had gotten the trouble started. The recessionary gap created by the change in aggregate demand had persisted for more than a decade. And expansionary fiscal policy had put a swift end to the worst macroeconomic nightmare in U.S. history—even if that policy had been forced on the country by a war that would prove to be one of the worst episodes of world history.

KEY TAKEAWAYS

- Classical economic thought stressed the ability of the economy to achieve what we now call its potential output in the long run. It thus stressed the forces that determine the position of the long-run aggregate supply curve as the determinants of income.

- Keynesian economics focuses on changes in aggregate demand and their ability to create recessionary or inflationary gaps. Keynesian economists argue that sticky prices and wages would make it difficult for the economy to adjust to its potential output.

- Because Keynesian economists believe that recessionary and inflationary gaps can persist for long periods, they urge the use of fiscal and monetary policy to shift the aggregate demand curve and to close these gaps.

- Aggregate demand fell sharply in the first four years of the Great Depression. As the recessionary gap widened, nominal wages began to fall, and the short-run aggregate supply curve began shifting to the right. These shifts, however, were not sufficient to close the recessionary gap. World War II forced the U.S. government to shift to a sharply expansionary fiscal policy, and the Depression ended.

TRY IT!

Imagine that it is 1933. President Franklin Roosevelt has just been inaugurated and has named you as his senior economic adviser. Devise a program to bring the economy back to its potential output. Using the model of aggregate demand and aggregate supply, demonstrate graphically how your proposal could work.

Case in Point: Early Views on Stickiness

Although David Ricardo's focus on the long run emerged as the dominant approach to macroeconomic thought, not all of his contemporaries agreed with his perspective. Many eighteenth- and nineteenth-century economists developed theoretical arguments suggesting that changes in aggregate demand could affect the real level of economic activity in the short run. Like the new Keynesians, they based their arguments on the concept of price stickiness.

Henry Thornton's 1802 book, *An Enquiry into the Nature and Effects of the Paper Credit of Great Britain*, argued that a reduction in the money supply could, because of wage stickiness, produce a short-run slump in output:

"The tendency, however, of a very great and sudden reduction of the accustomed number of bank notes, is to create an unusual and temporary distress, and a fall of price arising from that distress. But a fall arising from temporary distress, will be attended probably with no correspondent fall in the rate of wages; for the fall of price, and the distress, will be understood to be temporary, and the rate of wages, we know, is not so variable as the price of goods. There is reason, therefore, to fear that the unnatural and extraordinary low price arising from the sort of distress of which we now speak, would occasion much discouragement of the fabrication of manufactures."

A half-century earlier, David Hume had noted that an increase in the quantity of money would boost output in the short run, again because of the stickiness of prices. In an essay titled "Of Money," published in 1752, Hume described the process through which an increased money supply could boost output:

"At first, no alteration is perceived; by degrees the price rises, first of one commodity, then of another, till the whole at least reaches a just proportion with the new quantity of (money) which is in the kingdom. In my opinion, it is only in this interval or intermediate situation … that the encreasing quantity of gold and silver is favourable to industry."

Hume's argument implies sticky prices; some prices are slower to respond to the increase in the money supply than others.

Eighteenth- and nineteenth-century economists are generally lumped together as adherents to the classical school, but their views were anything but uniform. Many developed an analytical framework that was quite similar to the essential elements of new Keynesian economists today. Economist Thomas Humphrey, at the Federal Reserve Bank of Richmond, marvels at the insights shown by early economists: "When you read these old guys, you find out first that they didn't speak with one voice. There was no single body of thought to which everyone subscribed. And second, you find out how much they *knew*. You could take Henry Thornton's 1802 book as a textbook in any money course today."

Source: *Thomas M. Humphrey, "Nonneutrality of Money in Classical Monetary Thought," Federal Reserve Bank of Richmond Economic Review 77, no. 2 (March/April 1991): 3–15, and personal interview.*

An expansionary fiscal or monetary policy, or a combination of the two, would shift aggregate demand to the right as shown in Panel (a), ideally returning the economy to potential output. One piece of evidence suggesting that fiscal policy would work is the swiftness with which the economy recovered from the Great Depression once World War II forced the government to carry out such a policy. An alternative approach would be to do nothing. Ultimately, that should force nominal wages down further, producing increases in short-run aggregate supply, as in Panel (b). We do not know if such an approach might have worked; federal policies enacted in 1933 prevented wages and prices from falling further than they already had.

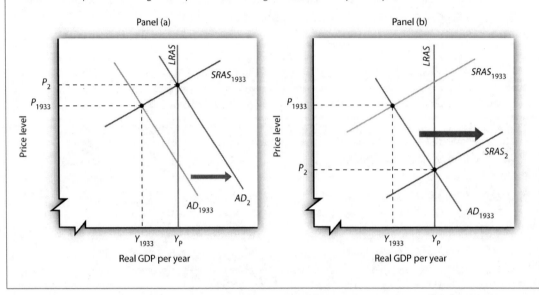

2. KEYNESIAN ECONOMICS IN THE 1960S AND 1970S

LEARNING OBJECTIVES

1. Briefly summarize the monetarist school of thought that emerged in the 1960s, and discuss how the experiences of the 1960s and 1970s seemed to be broadly consistent with it.
2. Briefly summarize the new classical school of thought that emerged in the 1970s, and discuss how the experiences of the 1970s seemed to be broadly consistent with it.
3. Summarize the lessons that economists learned from the decade of the 1970s.

The experience of the Great Depression led to the widespread acceptance of Keynesian ideas among economists, but its acceptance as a basis for economic policy was slower. The administrations of Presidents Roosevelt, Truman, and Eisenhower rejected the notion that fiscal policy could or should be used to manipulate real GDP. Truman vetoed a 1948 Republican-sponsored tax cut aimed at stimulating the economy after World War II (Congress, however, overrode the veto), and Eisenhower resisted stimulative measures to deal with the recessions of 1953, 1957, and 1960.

It was the administration of President John F. Kennedy that first used fiscal policy with the intent of manipulating aggregate demand to move the economy toward its potential output. Kennedy's willingness to embrace Keynes's ideas changed the nation's approach to fiscal policy for the next two decades.

2.1 Expansionary Policy in the 1960s

We can think of the macroeconomic history of the 1960s as encompassing two distinct phases. The first showed the power of Keynesian policies to correct economic difficulties. The second showed the power of these same policies to create them.

Correcting a Recessionary Gap

President Kennedy took office in 1961 with the economy in a recessionary gap. He had appointed a team of economic advisers who believed in Keynesian economics, and they advocated an activist approach to fiscal policy. The new president was quick to act on their advice.

Expansionary policy served the administration's foreign-policy purposes. Kennedy argued that the United States had fallen behind the Soviet Union, its avowed enemy, in military preparedness. He won approval from Congress for sharp increases in defense spending in 1961.

The Kennedy administration also added accelerated depreciation to the tax code. Under the measure, firms could deduct depreciation expenses more quickly, reducing their taxable profits—and thus their taxes—early in the life of a capital asset. The measure encouraged investment. The administration also introduced an investment tax credit, which allowed corporations to reduce their income taxes by 10% of their investment in any one year. The combination of increased defense spending and tax measures to stimulate investment provided a quick boost to aggregate demand.

The Fed followed the administration's lead. It, too, shifted to an expansionary policy in 1961. The Fed purchased government bonds to increase the money supply and reduce interest rates.

As shown in Panel (a) of Figure 17.6, the expansionary fiscal and monetary policies of the early 1960s had pushed real GDP to its potential by 1963. But the concept of potential output had not been developed in 1963; Kennedy administration economists had defined full employment to be an unemployment rate of 4%. The actual unemployment rate in 1963 was 5.7%; the perception of the time was that the economy needed further stimulus.

FIGURE 17.6 The Two Faces of Expansionary Policy in the 1960s

Expansionary fiscal and monetary policy early in the 1960s (Panel [a]) closed a recessionary gap, but continued expansionary policy created an inflationary gap by the end of the decade (Panel [b]). The short-run aggregate supply curve began shifting to the left, but expansionary policy continued to shift aggregate demand to the right and kept the economy in an inflationary gap.

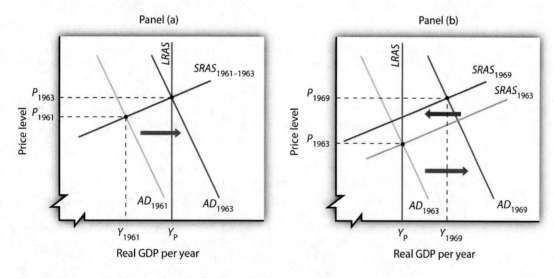

Expansionary Policy and an Inflationary Gap

Kennedy proposed a tax cut in 1963, which Congress would approve the following year, after the president had been assassinated. In retrospect, we may regard the tax cut as representing a kind of a recognition lag— policy makers did not realize the economy had already reached what we now recognize was its potential output. Instead of closing a recessionary gap, the tax cut helped push the economy into an inflationary gap, as illustrated in Panel (b) of Figure 17.6.

The expansionary policies, however, did not stop with the tax cut. Continued increases in federal spending for the newly expanded war in Vietnam and for President Lyndon Johnson's agenda of domestic programs, together with continued high rates of money growth, sent the aggregate demand curve further to the right. While President Johnson's Council of Economic Advisers recommended contractionary policy as early as 1965, macroeconomic policy remained generally expansionary through 1969. Wage increases began shifting the short-run aggregate supply curve to the left, but expansionary policy continued to increase aggregate demand and kept the economy in an inflationary gap for the last six years of the 1960s. Panel (b) of Figure 17.6 shows expansionary policies pushing the economy beyond its potential output after 1963.

The 1960s had demonstrated two important lessons about Keynesian macroeconomic policy. First, stimulative fiscal and monetary policy could be used to close a recessionary gap. Second, fiscal policies could have a long implementation lag. The tax cut recommended by President Kennedy's economic advisers in 1961 was not enacted until 1964—after the recessionary gap it was designed to fight had been closed. The tax increase recommended by President Johnson's economic advisers in 1965 was not passed until 1968—after the inflationary gap it was designed to close had widened.

Macroeconomic policy after 1963 pushed the economy into an inflationary gap. The push into an inflationary gap did produce rising employment and a rising real GDP. But the inflation that came with it, together with other problems, would create real difficulties for the economy and for macroeconomic policy in the 1970s.

2.2 The 1970s: Troubles from the Supply Side

For many observers, the use of Keynesian fiscal and monetary policies in the 1960s had been a triumph. That triumph turned into a series of macroeconomic disasters in the 1970s as inflation and unemployment spiraled to ever-higher levels. The fiscal and monetary medicine that had seemed to work so well in the 1960s seemed capable of producing only instability in the 1970s. The experience of the period shook the faith of many economists in Keynesian remedies and made them receptive to alternative approaches.

This section describes the major macroeconomic events of the 1970s. It then examines the emergence of two schools of economic thought as major challengers to the Keynesian orthodoxy that had seemed so dominant a decade earlier.

Macroeconomic Policy: Coping with the Supply Side

When Richard Nixon became president in 1969, he faced a very different economic situation than the one that had confronted John Kennedy eight years earlier. The economy had clearly pushed beyond full employment; the unemployment rate had plunged to 3.6% in 1968. Inflation, measured using the implicit price deflator, had soared to 4.3%, the highest rate that had been recorded since 1951. The economy needed a cooling off. Nixon, the Fed, and the economy's own process of self-correction delivered it.

Figure 17.7 tells the story—it is a simple one. The economy in 1969 was in an inflationary gap. It had been in such a gap for years, but this time policy makers were no longer forcing increases in aggregate demand to keep it there. The adjustment in short-run aggregate supply brought the economy back to its potential output.

FIGURE 17.7 The Economy Closes an Inflationary Gap

The Nixon administration and the Fed joined to end the expansionary policies that had prevailed in the 1960s, so that aggregate demand did not rise in 1970, but the short-run aggregate supply curve shifted to the left as the economy responded to an inflationary gap.

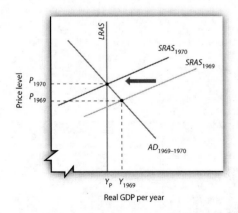

But what we can see now as a simple adjustment seemed anything but simple in 1970. Economists did not think in terms of shifts in short-run aggregate supply. Keynesian economics focused on shifts in aggregate demand, not supply.

For the Nixon administration, the slump in real GDP in 1970 was a recession, albeit an odd one. The price level had risen sharply. That was not, according to the Keynesian story, supposed to happen; there was simply no reason to expect the price level to soar when real GDP and employment were falling.

The administration dealt with the recession by shifting to an expansionary fiscal policy. By 1973, the economy was again in an inflationary gap. The economy's 1974 adjustment to the gap came with another jolt. The Organization of Petroleum Exporting Countries (OPEC) tripled the price of oil. The resulting shift to the left in short-run aggregate supply gave the economy another recession and another jump in the price level.

The second half of the decade was, in some respects, a repeat of the first. The administrations of Gerald Ford and then Jimmy Carter, along with the Fed, pursued expansionary policies to stimulate the economy. Those helped boost output, but they also pushed up prices. As we saw in the chapter on inflation and unemployment, inflation and unemployment followed a cycle to higher and higher levels.

The 1970s presented a challenge not just to policy makers, but to economists as well. The sharp changes in real GDP and in the price level could not be explained by a Keynesian analysis that focused on aggregate demand. Something else was happening. As economists grappled to explain it, their efforts would produce the model with which we have been dealing and around which a broad consensus of economists has emerged. But, before that consensus was to come, two additional elements of the puzzle had to be added. The first was the recognition of the importance of monetary policy. The second was the recognition of the role of aggregate supply, both in the long and in the short run.

The Monetarist Challenge

The idea that changes in the money supply are the principal determinant of the nominal value of total output is one of the oldest in economic thought; it is implied by the equation of exchange, assuming the stability of velocity. Classical economists stressed the long run and thus the determination of the economy's potential output. This meant that changes in the price level were, in the long run, the result of changes in the money supply.

At roughly the same time Keynesian economics was emerging as the dominant school of macroeconomic thought, some economists focused on changes in the money supply as the primary determinant of changes in the nominal value of output. Led by Milton Friedman, they stressed the role of changes in the money supply as the principal determinant of changes in nominal output in the short run as well as in the long run. They argued that fiscal policy had no effect on the economy. Their "money rules" doctrine led to the name *monetarists*. The **monetarist school** holds that changes in the money supply are the primary cause of changes in nominal GDP.

monetarist school

The body of macroeconomic thought that holds that changes in the money supply are the primary cause of changes in nominal GDP.

Monetarists generally argue that the impact lags of monetary policy—the lags from the time monetary policy is undertaken to the time the policy affects nominal GDP—are so long and variable that trying to stabilize the economy using monetary policy can be destabilizing. Monetarists thus are critical of activist stabilization policies. They argue that, because of crowding-out effects, fiscal policy has no effect on GDP. Monetary policy does, but it should not be used. Instead, most monetarists urge the Fed to increase the money supply at a fixed annual rate, preferably the rate at which potential output rises. With stable velocity, that would eliminate inflation in the long run. Recessionary or inflationary gaps could occur in the short run, but monetarists generally argue that self-correction will take care of them more effectively than would activist monetary policy.

While monetarists differ from Keynesians in their assessment of the impact of fiscal policy, the primary difference in the two schools lies in their degree of optimism about whether stabilization policy can, in fact, be counted on to bring the economy back to its potential output. For monetarists, the complexity of economic life and the uncertain nature of lags mean that efforts to use monetary policy to stabilize the economy can be destabilizing. Monetarists argued that the difficulties encountered by policy makers as they tried to respond to the dramatic events of the 1970s demonstrated the superiority of a policy that simply increased the money supply at a slow, steady rate.

Monetarists could also cite the apparent validity of an adjustment mechanism proposed by Milton Friedman in 1968. As the economy continued to expand in the 1960s, and as unemployment continued to fall, Friedman said that unemployment had fallen below its natural rate, the rate consistent with equilibrium in the labor market. Any divergence of unemployment from its natural rate, he insisted, would necessarily be temporary. He suggested that the low unemployment of 1968 (the rate was 3.6% that year) meant that workers had been surprised by rising prices. Higher prices had produced a real wage below what workers and firms had expected. Friedman predicted that as workers demanded and got higher nominal wages, the price level would shoot up and unemployment would rise. That, of course, is precisely what happened in 1970 and 1971. Friedman's notion of the natural rate of unemployment buttressed the monetarist argument that the economy moves to its potential output on its own.

Perhaps the most potent argument from the monetarist camp was the behavior of the economy itself. During the 1960s, monetarist and Keynesian economists alike could argue that economic performance was consistent with their respective views of the world. Keynesians could point to expansions in economic activity that they could ascribe to expansionary fiscal policy, but economic activity also moved closely with changes in the money supply, just as monetarists predicted. During the 1970s, however, it was difficult for Keynesians to argue that policies that affected aggregate demand were having the predicted impact on the economy. Changes in aggregate supply had repeatedly pushed the economy off a Keynesian course. But monetarists, once again, could point to a consistent relationship between changes in the money supply and changes in economic activity.

Figure 17.8 shows the movement of nominal GDP and M2 during the 1960s and 1970s. In the figure, annual percentage changes in M2 are plotted against percentage changes in nominal GDP a year later to account for the lagged effects of changes in the money supply. We see that there was a close relationship between changes in the quantity of money and subsequent changes in nominal GDP.

FIGURE 17.8 M2 and Nominal GDP, 1960–1980

The chart shows annual rates of change in M2 and in nominal GDP, lagged one year. The observation for 1961, for example, shows that nominal GDP increased 3.5% and that M2 increased 4.9% in the previous year, 1960. The two variables showed a close relationship in the 1960s and 1970s.

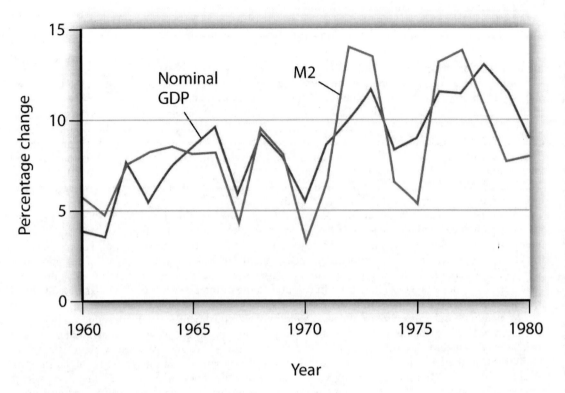

Monetarist doctrine emerged as a potent challenge to Keynesian economics in the 1970s largely because of the close correspondence between nominal GDP and the money supply. The next section examines another school of thought that came to prominence in the 1970s.

New Classical Economics: A Focus on Aggregate Supply

Much of the difficulty policy makers encountered during the decade of the 1970s resulted from shifts in aggregate supply. Keynesian economics and, to a lesser degree, monetarism had focused on aggregate demand. As it became clear that an analysis incorporating the supply side was an essential part of the macroeconomic puzzle, some economists turned to an entirely new way of looking at macroeconomic issues.

These economists started with what we identified at the beginning of this text as a distinguishing characteristic of economic thought: a focus on individuals and their decisions. Keynesian economics employed aggregate analysis and paid little attention to individual choices. Monetarist doctrine was based on the analysis of individuals' maximizing behavior with respect to money demand, but it did not extend that analysis to decisions that affect aggregate supply. The new approach aimed at an analysis of how individual choices would affect the entire spectrum of economic activity.

These economists rejected the entire framework of conventional macroeconomic analysis. Indeed, they rejected the very term. For them there is no macroeconomics, nor is there something called microeconomics. For them, there is only economics, which they regard as the analysis of behavior based on individual maximization. The analysis of the determination of the price level and real GDP becomes an application of basic economic theory, not a separate body of thought. The approach to macroeconomic analysis built from an analysis of individual maximizing choices is called **new classical economics**.

new classical economics

The approach to macroeconomic analysis built from an analysis of individual maximizing choices and emphasizing wage and price flexibility.

Like classical economic thought, new classical economics focuses on the determination of long-run aggregate supply and the economy's ability to reach this level of output quickly. But the similarity ends there. Classical economics emerged in large part before economists had developed sophisticated mathematical models of maximizing behavior. The new classical economics puts mathematics to work in an extremely complex way to generalize from individual behavior to aggregate results.

Because the new classical approach suggests that the economy will remain at or near its potential output, it follows that the changes we observe in economic activity result not from changes in aggregate demand but from changes in long-run aggregate supply. New classical economics suggests that economic changes don't necessarily imply economic problems.

New classical economists pointed to the supply-side shocks of the 1970s, both from changes in oil prices and changes in expectations, as evidence that their emphasis on aggregate supply was on the mark. They argued that the large observed swings in real GDP reflected underlying changes in the economy's potential output. The recessionary and inflationary gaps that so perplexed policy makers during the 1970s were not gaps at all, the new classical economists insisted. Instead, they reflected changes in the economy's own potential output.

Two particularly controversial propositions of new classical theory relate to the impacts of monetary and of fiscal policy. Both are implications of the **rational expectations hypothesis**, which assumes that individuals form expectations about the future based on the information available to them, and that they act on those expectations.

The rational expectations hypothesis suggests that monetary policy, even though it will affect the aggregate demand curve, might have no effect on real GDP. This possibility, which was suggested by Robert Lucas, is illustrated in Figure 17.9. Suppose the economy is initially in equilibrium at point 1 in Panel (a). Real GDP equals its potential output, Y_P. Now suppose a reduction in the money supply causes aggregate demand to fall to AD_2. In our model, the solution moves to point 2; the price level falls to P_2, and real GDP falls to Y_2. There is a recessionary gap. In the long run, the short-run aggregate supply curve shifts to $SRAS_2$, the price level falls to P_3, and the economy returns to its potential output at point 3.

rational expectations hypothesis

Individuals form expectations about the future based on the information available to them, and they act on those expectations.

FIGURE 17.9 Contractionary Monetary Policy: With and Without Rational Expectations

Panels (a) and (b) show an economy operating at potential output (1); a contractionary monetary policy shifts aggregate demand to AD_2. Panel (a) shows the kind of response we have studied up to this point; real GDP falls to Y_2 in period (2); the recessionary gap is closed in the long run by falling nominal wages that cause an increase in short-run aggregate supply in period (3). Panel (b) shows the rational expectations argument. People anticipate the impact of the contractionary policy when it is undertaken, so that the short-run aggregate supply curve shifts to the right at the same time the aggregate demand curve shifts to the left. The result is a reduction in the price level but no change in real GDP; the solution moves from (1) to (2).

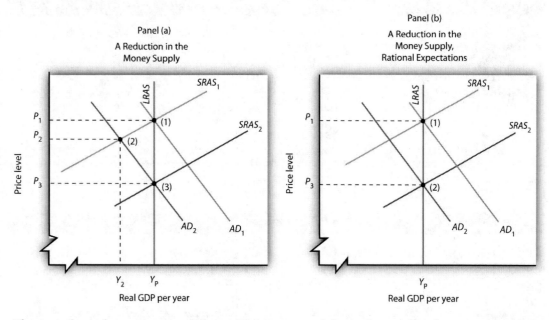

The new classical story is quite different. Consumers and firms observe that the money supply has fallen and anticipate the eventual reduction in the price level to P_3. They adjust their expectations accordingly. Workers agree to lower nominal wages, and the short-run aggregate supply curve shifts to $SRAS_2$. This occurs as aggregate demand falls. As suggested in Panel (b), the price level falls to P_3, and output remains at potential. The solution moves from (1) to (2) with no loss in real GDP.

In this new classical world, there is only one way for a change in the money supply to affect output, and that is for the change to take people by surprise. An unexpected change cannot affect expectations, so the short-run aggregate supply curve does not shift in the short run, and events play out as in Panel (a). Monetary policy can affect output, but only if it takes people by surprise.

The new classical school offers an even stronger case against the operation of fiscal policy. It argues that fiscal policy does not shift the aggregate demand curve at all! Consider, for example, an expansionary fiscal policy. Such a policy involves an increase in government purchases or transfer payments or a cut in taxes. Any of these policies will increase the deficit or reduce the surplus. New classical economists argue that households, when they observe the government carrying out a policy that increases the debt, will anticipate that they, or their children, or their children's children, will end up paying more in taxes. And, according to the new classical story, these households will reduce their consumption as a result. This will, the new classical economists argue, cancel any tendency for the expansionary policy to affect aggregate demand.

Lessons from the 1970s

The 1970s put Keynesian economics and its prescription for activist policies on the defensive. The period lent considerable support to the monetarist argument that changes in the money supply were the primary determinant of changes in the nominal level of GDP. A series of dramatic shifts in aggregate supply gave credence to the new classical emphasis on long-run aggregate supply as the primary determinant of real GDP. Events did not create the new ideas, but they produced an environment in which those ideas could win greater support.

For economists, the period offered some important lessons. These lessons, as we will see in the next section, forced a rethinking of some of the ideas that had dominated Keynesian thought. The experience of the 1970s suggested the following:

1. The short-run aggregate supply curve could not be viewed as something that provided a passive path over which aggregate demand could roam. The short-run aggregate supply curve could shift in ways that clearly affected real GDP, unemployment, and the price level.

2. Money mattered more than Keynesians had previously suspected. Keynes had expressed doubts about the effectiveness of monetary policy, particularly in the face of a recessionary gap. Work by monetarists suggested a close correspondence between changes in M2 and subsequent changes in nominal GDP, convincing many Keynesian economists that money was more important than they had thought.

3. Stabilization was a more difficult task than many economists had anticipated. Shifts in aggregate supply could frustrate the efforts of policy makers to achieve certain macroeconomic goals.

KEY TAKEAWAYS

- Beginning in 1961, expansionary fiscal and monetary policies were used to close a recessionary gap; this was the first major U.S. application of Keynesian macroeconomic policy.
- The experience of the 1960s and 1970s appeared to be broadly consistent with the monetarist argument that changes in the money supply are the primary determinant of changes in nominal GDP.
- The new classical school's argument that the economy operates at its potential output implies that real GDP is determined by long-run aggregate supply. The experience of the 1970s, in which changes in aggregate supply forced changes in real GDP and in the price level, seemed consistent with the new classical economists' arguments that focused on aggregate supply.
- The experience of the 1970s suggested that changes in the money supply and in aggregate supply were more important determinants of economic activity than many Keynesians had previously thought.

TRY IT!

Draw the aggregate demand and the short-run and long-run aggregate supply curves for an economy operating with an inflationary gap. Show how expansionary fiscal and/or monetary policies would affect such an economy. Now show how this economy could experience a recession and an increase in the price level at the same time.

Case in Point: Tough Medicine

The Keynesian prescription for an inflationary gap seems simple enough. The federal government applies contractionary fiscal policy, or the Fed applies contractionary monetary policy, or both. But what seems simple in a graph can be maddeningly difficult in the real world. The medicine for an inflationary gap is tough, and it is tough to take.

President Johnson's new chairman of the Council of Economic Advisers, Gardner Ackley, urged the president in 1965 to adopt fiscal policies aimed at nudging the aggregate demand curve back to the left. The president reluctantly agreed and called in the chairman of the House Ways and Means Committee, the committee that must initiate all revenue measures, to see what he thought of the idea. Wilbur Mills flatly told Johnson that he wouldn't even hold hearings to consider a tax increase. For the time being, the tax boost was dead.

The Federal Reserve System did slow the rate of money growth in 1966. But fiscal policy remained sharply expansionary. Mr. Ackley continued to press his case, and in 1967 President Johnson proposed a temporary 10% increase in personal income taxes. Mr. Mills now endorsed the measure. The temporary tax boost went into effect the following year. The Fed, concerned that the tax hike would be *too* contractionary, countered the administration's shift in fiscal policy with a policy of vigorous money growth in 1967 and 1968.

The late 1960s suggested a sobering reality about the new Keynesian orthodoxy. Stimulating the economy was politically more palatable than contracting it. President Kennedy, while he was not able to win approval of his tax cut during his lifetime, did manage to put the other expansionary aspects of his program into place early in his administration. The Fed reinforced his policies. Dealing with an inflationary gap proved to be quite another matter. President Johnson, a master of the legislative process, took three years to get even a mildly contractionary tax increase put into place, and the Fed acted to counter the impact of this measure by shifting to an expansionary policy.

The second half of the 1960s was marked, in short, by persistent efforts to boost aggregate demand, efforts that kept the economy in an inflationary gap through most of the decade. It was a gap that would usher in a series of supply-side troubles in the next decade.

Even with an inflationary gap, it is possible to pursue expansionary fiscal and monetary policies, shifting the aggregate demand curve to the right, as shown. The inflationary gap will, however, produce an increase in nominal wages, reducing short-run aggregate supply over time. In the case shown here, real GDP rises at first, then falls back to potential output with the reduction in short-run aggregate supply.

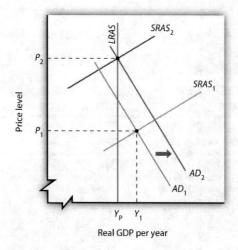

3.   AN EMERGING CONSENSUS: MACROECONOMICS FOR THE TWENTY-FIRST CENTURY

LEARNING OBJECTIVES

1. Discuss how the Fed incorporated a strong inflation constraint and lags into its policies from the 1980s onwards.
2. Describe the fiscal policies that were undertaken from the 1980s onwards and their rationales.
3. Discuss the challenges that events from the 1980s onwards raised for the monetarist and new classical schools of thought.
4. Summarize the views and policy approaches of the new Keynesian school of economic thought.

The last two decades of the twentieth century brought progress in macroeconomic policy and in macroeconomic theory. The outlines of a broad consensus in macroeconomic theory began to take shape in the 1980s. This consensus has grown out of the three bodies of macroeconomic thought that, in turn, grew out of the experiences of the twentieth century. Keynesian economics, monetarism, and new classical economics all developed from economists' attempts to understand macroeconomic change. We shall see how all three schools of macroeconomic thought have contributed to the development of a new school of macroeconomic thought: the new Keynesian school.

New Keynesian economics is a body of macroeconomic thought that stresses the stickiness of prices and the need for activist stabilization policies through the manipulation of aggregate demand to keep the economy operating close to its potential output. It incorporates monetarist ideas about the importance of monetary policy and new classical ideas about the importance of aggregate supply, both in the long and in the short run.

Another "new" element in new Keynesian economic thought is the greater use of microeconomic analysis to explain macroeconomic phenomena, particularly the analysis of price and wage stickiness. We saw in the chapter that introduced the model of aggregate demand and aggregate supply, for example, that sticky prices and wages may be a response to the preferences of consumers and of firms. That idea emerged from research by economists of the new Keynesian school.

New Keynesian ideas guide macroeconomic policy; they are the basis for the model of aggregate demand and aggregate supply with which we have been working. To see how the new Keynesian school has come to dominate macroeconomic policy, we shall review the major macroeconomic events and policies of the 1980s, 1990s, and early 2000s.

3.1   The 1980s and Beyond: Advances in Macroeconomic Policy

The exercise of monetary and of fiscal policy has changed dramatically in the last few decades.

The Revolution in Monetary Policy

It is fair to say that the monetary policy revolution of the last two decades began on July 25, 1979. On that day, President Jimmy Carter appointed Paul Volcker to be chairman of the Fed's Board of Governors. Mr. Volcker, with President Carter's support, charted a new direction for the Fed. The new direction damaged Mr. Carter politically but ultimately produced dramatic gains for the economy.

Oil prices rose sharply in 1979 as war broke out between Iran and Iraq. Such an increase would, by itself, shift the short-run aggregate supply curve to the left, causing the price level to rise and real GDP to fall. But expansionary fiscal and monetary policies had pushed aggregate demand up at the same time. As a result, real GDP stayed at potential output, while the price level soared. The implicit price deflator jumped 8.1%; the CPI rose 13.5%, the highest inflation rate recorded in the twentieth century. Public opinion polls in 1979 consistently showed that most people regarded inflation as the leading problem facing the nation.

Chairman Volcker charted a monetarist course of fixing the growth rate of the money supply at a rate that would bring inflation down. After the high rates of money growth of the past, the policy was sharply contractionary. Its first effects were to shift the aggregate demand curve to the left. Continued oil price increases produced more leftward shifts in the short-run aggregate supply curve, and the economy suffered a recession in 1980. Inflation remained high. Figure 17.12 shows how the combined shifts in aggregate demand and short-run aggregate supply produced a reduction in real GDP and an increase in the price level.

The Fed stuck to its contractionary guns, and the inflation rate finally began to fall in 1981. But the recession worsened. Unemployment soared, shooting above 10% late in the year. It was the worst recession since the Great Depression. The inflation rate, though, fell sharply in 1982, and the Fed began to shift to a modestly expansionary policy in 1983. But inflation had been licked. Inflation, measured by the implicit price deflator, dropped to a 4.1% rate that year, the lowest since 1967.

The Fed's actions represented a sharp departure from those of the previous two decades. Faced with soaring unemployment, the Fed did not shift to an expansionary policy until inflation was well under control. Inflation continued to edge downward through most of the remaining years of the 20th century and into the new century. The Fed has clearly shifted to a stabilization policy with a strong inflation constraint. It shifts to expansionary policy when the economy has a recessionary gap, but only if it regards inflation as being under control.

This concern about inflation was evident again when the U.S. economy began to weaken in 2008, and there was initially discussion among the members of the Federal Open Market Committee about whether or not easing would contribute to inflation. At that time, it looked like inflation was becoming a more serious problem, largely due to increases in oil and other commodity prices. Some members of the Fed, including Chairman Bernanke, argued that these price increases were likely to be temporary and the Fed began using expansionary monetary policy early on. By late summer and early fall, inflationary pressures had subsided, and all the members of the FOMC were behind continued expansionary policy. Indeed, at that point, the Fed let it be known that it was willing to do anything in its power to fight the current recession.

new Keynesian economics

A body of macroeconomic thought that stresses the stickiness of prices and the need for activist stabilization policies through the manipulation of aggregate demand to keep the economy operating close to its potential output. It incorporates monetarist ideas about the importance of monetary policy and new classical ideas about the importance of aggregate supply, both in the long run and in the short run.

FIGURE 17.12 The Fed's Fight Against Inflation

By 1979, expansionary fiscal and monetary policies had brought the economy to its potential output. Then war between Iran and Iraq caused oil prices to increase, shifting the short-run aggregate supply curve to the left. In the second half of 1979, the Fed launched an aggressive contractionary policy aimed at reducing inflation. The Fed's action shifted the aggregate demand curve to the left. The result in 1980 was a recession with continued inflation.

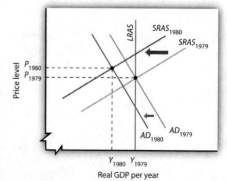

Real GDP per year

The next major advance in monetary policy came in the 1990s, under Federal Reserve Chairman Alan Greenspan. The Fed had shifted to an expansionary policy as the economy slipped into a recession when Iraq's invasion of Kuwait in 1990 began the Persian Gulf War and sent oil prices soaring. By early 1994, real GDP was rising, but the economy remained in a recessionary gap. Nevertheless, the Fed announced on February 4, 1994, that it had shifted to a contractionary policy, selling bonds to boost interest rates and to reduce the money supply. While the economy had not reached its potential output, Chairman Greenspan explained that the Fed was concerned that it might push past its potential output within a year. The Fed, for the first time, had explicitly taken the impact lag of monetary policy into account. The issue of lags was also a part of Fed discussions in the 2000s.

Fiscal Policy: A Resurgence of Interest

President Ronald Reagan, whose 1980 election victory was aided by a recession that year, introduced a tax cut, combined with increased defense spending, in 1981. While this expansionary fiscal policy was virtually identical to the policy President Kennedy had introduced 20 years earlier, President Reagan rejected Keynesian economics, embracing supply-side arguments instead. He argued that the cut in tax rates, particularly in high marginal rates, would encourage work effort. He reintroduced an investment tax credit, which stimulated investment. With people working harder and firms investing more, he expected long-run aggregate supply to increase more rapidly. His policy, he said, would stimulate economic growth.

The tax cut and increased defense spending increased the federal deficit. Increased spending for welfare programs and unemployment compensation, both of which were induced by the plunge in real GDP in the early 1980s, contributed to the deficit as well. As deficits continued to rise, they began to dominate discussions of fiscal policy. In 1990, with the economy slipping into a recession, President George H. W. Bush agreed to a tax increase despite an earlier promise not to do so. President Bill Clinton, whose 1992 election resulted largely from the recession of 1990–1991, introduced another tax increase in 1994, with the economy still in a recessionary gap. Both tax increases were designed to curb the rising deficit.

Congress in the first years of the 1990s rejected the idea of using an expansionary fiscal policy to close a recessionary gap on grounds it would increase the deficit. President Clinton, for example, introduced a stimulus package of increased government investment and tax cuts designed to stimulate private investment in 1993; a Democratic Congress rejected the proposal. The deficit acted like a straitjacket for fiscal policy. The Bush and Clinton tax increases, coupled with spending restraint and increased revenues from economic growth, brought an end to the deficit in 1998.

Initially, it was expected that the budget surplus would continue well into the new century. But, this picture changed rapidly. President George W. Bush campaigned on a platform of large tax cuts, arguing that less government intervention in the economy would be good for long-term economic growth. His administration saw the enactment of two major pieces of tax-cutting legislation in 2001 and 2003. Coupled with increases in government spending, in part for defense but also for domestic purposes including a Medicare prescription drug benefit, the government budget surpluses gave way to budget deficits. To deal with times of economic weakness during President Bush's administration, temporary tax cuts were enacted, both in 2001 and again in 2008.

As the economy continued to weaken in 2008, there seemed to be a resurgence of interest in using discretionary increases in government spending, as discussed in the Case in Point, to respond to the recession. Three factors were paramount: (1) the temporary tax cuts had provided only a minor amount of stimulus to the economy, as sizable portions had been used for saving rather than spending, (2) expansionary monetary policy, while useful, had not seemed adequate, and (3) the recession threatening the global economy seemed to be larger than those in recent economic history.

3.2 The Rise of New Keynesian Economics

New Keynesian economics emerged in the last three decades as the dominant school of macroeconomic thought for two reasons. First, it successfully incorporated important monetarist and new classical ideas into Keynesian economics. Second, developments in the 1980s and 1990s shook economists' confidence in the ability of the monetarist or the new classical school alone to explain macroeconomic change.

Monetary Change and Monetarism

Look again at Figure 17.8. The close relationship between M2 and nominal GDP in the 1960s and 1970s helped win over many economists to the monetarist camp. Now look at Figure 17.13. It shows the same two variables, M2 and nominal GDP, from the 1980s through 2009. The tidy relationship between the two seems to have vanished. What happened?

FIGURE 17.13 M2 and Nominal GDP, 1980–2009

The close relationship between M2 and nominal GDP a year later that had prevailed in the 1960s and 1970s seemed to vanish from the 1980s onward.

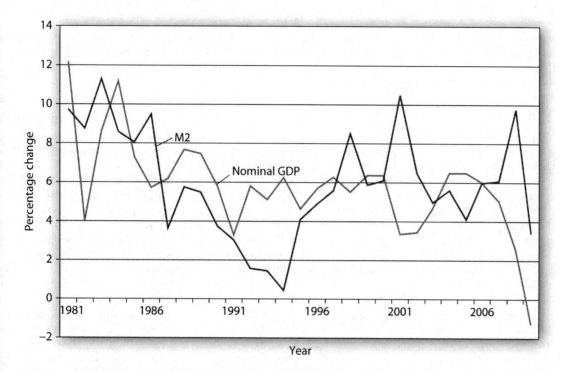

The close relationship between M2 and nominal GDP a year later that had prevailed in the 1960s and 1970s seemed to vanish from the 1980s onward.

The sudden change in the relationship between the money stock and nominal GDP has resulted partly from public policy. Deregulation of the banking industry in the early 1980s produced sharp changes in the ways individuals dealt with money, thus changing the relationship of money to economic activity. Banks have been freed to offer a wide range of financial alternatives to their customers. One of the most important developments has been the introduction of bond funds offered by banks. These funds allowed customers to earn the higher interest rates paid by long-term bonds while at the same time being able to transfer funds easily into checking accounts as needed. Balances in these bond funds are not counted as part of M2. As people shifted assets out of M2 accounts and into bond funds, velocity rose. That changed the once-close relationship between changes in the quantity of money and changes in nominal GDP.

Many monetarists have argued that the experience of the 1980s, 1990s, and 2000s reinforces their view that the instability of velocity in the short run makes monetary policy an inappropriate tool for short-run stabilization. They continue to insist, however, that the velocity of M2 remains stable in the long run. But the velocity of M2 appears to have diverged in recent years from its long-run path. Although it may return to its long-run level, the stability of velocity remains very much in doubt. Because of this instability, in 2000, when the Fed was no longer required by law to report money target ranges, it discontinued the practice.

The New Classical School and Responses to Policy

New classical economics suggests that people should have responded to the fiscal and monetary policies of the 1980s in predictable ways. They did not, and that has created new doubts among economists about the validity of the new classical argument.

The rational expectations hypothesis predicts that if a shift in monetary policy by the Fed is anticipated, it will have no effect on real GDP. The slowing in the rate of growth of the money supply over the period from 1979 to 1982 was surely well known. The Fed announced at the outset what it was going to do, and then did it. It had the full support first of President Carter and then of President Reagan. But the policy plunged the economy into what was then its worst recession since the Great Depression. The experience hardly seemed consistent with new classical logic. New classical economists argued that people may have doubted the Fed would keep its word, but the episode still cast doubt on the rational expectations argument.

The public's response to the huge deficits of the Reagan era also seemed to belie new classical ideas. One new classical argument predicts that people will increase their saving rate in response to an increase in public sector borrowing. The resultant reduction in consumption will cancel the impact of the increase in deficit-financed government expenditures. But the private saving rate in the United States *fell* during the 1980s. New classical economists contend that standard measures of saving do not fully represent the actual saving rate, but the experience of the 1980s did not seem to support the new classical argument.

The events of the 1980s do not suggest that either monetarist or new classical ideas should be abandoned, but those events certainly raised doubts about relying solely on these approaches. Doubts about Keynesian economics raised by the events of the 1970s led Keynesians to modify and strengthen their approach. Perhaps the events of the 1980s and 1990s will produce similar progress within the monetarist and new classical camps.

A Macroeconomic Consensus?

While there is less consensus on macroeconomic policy issues than on some other economic issues (particularly those in the microeconomic and international areas), surveys of economists generally show that the new Keynesian approach has emerged as the preferred approach to macroeconomic analysis. The finding that about 80% of economists agree that expansionary fiscal measures can deal with recessionary gaps certainly suggests that most economists can be counted in the new Keynesian camp. Neither monetarist nor new classical analysis would support such measures. At the same time, there is considerable discomfort about actually using discretionary fiscal policy, as the same survey shows that about 70% of economists feel that discretionary fiscal policy should be avoided and that the business cycle should be managed by the Fed.[3] Just as the new Keynesian approach appears to have won support among most economists, it has become dominant in terms of macroeconomic policy.

Did the experience of the 2007-2009 recession affect the views of economists concerning macroeconomic policy? One source for gauging possible changes in opinions of economists is the National Association For Business Economics twice yearly survey of economic policy.[4] According to the August 2010 survey of 242 members of NABE, almost 60% were supportive of monetary policy at that time, which was expansionary and continued to be so at least through 2010. Concerning fiscal policy, there was less agreement. Still, according to the survey taken at the time the 2009 fiscal stimulus was being debated, 22% characterized it as "about right," another third found it too restrictive, and only one third found it too simulative. In the August 2010 survey, 39% thought fiscal policy "about right," 24% found it too restrictive, and 37% found it too simulative. Also, nearly 75% ranked promotion of economic growth more important than deficit reduction, roughly two thirds supported the extension of unemployment benefits, and 60% agreed that federal assistance funds to states from the 2009 stimulus package was appropriate. Taken together, the new Keynesian approach still seems to reflect the dominant opinion.

KEY TAKEAWAYS

- The actions of the Fed starting in late 1979 reflected a strong inflation constraint and a growing recognition of the impact lag for monetary policy.
- Reducing the deficit dominated much of fiscal policy discussion during the 1980s and 1990s.
- The events of the 1980s and early 1990s do not appear to have been consistent with the hypotheses of either the monetarist or new classical schools.
- New Keynesian economists have incorporated major elements of the ideas of the monetarist and new classical schools into their formulation of macroeconomic theory.

TRY IT!

Show the effect of an expansionary monetary policy on real GDP

1. according to new Keynesian economics
2. according to the rational expectations hypothesis

In both cases, consider both the short-run and the long-run effects.

Case in Point: Steering on a Difficult Course

Imagine that you are driving a test car on a special course. You get to steer, accelerate, and brake, but you cannot be sure whether the car will respond to your commands within a few feet or within a few miles. The windshield and side windows are blackened, so you cannot see where you are going or even where you are. You can only see where you have been with the rear-view mirror. The course is designed so that you will face difficulties you have never experienced. Your job is to get through the course unscathed. Oh, and by the way, you have to observe the speed limit, but you do not know what it is. Have a nice trip.

Now imagine that the welfare of people all over the world will be affected by how well you drive the course. They are watching you. They are giving you a great deal of often-conflicting advice about what you should do. Thinking about the problems you would face driving such a car will give you some idea of the obstacle course fiscal and monetary authorities must negotiate. They cannot know where the economy is going or where it is—economic indicators such as GDP and the CPI only suggest where the economy has been. And the perils through which it must steer can be awesome indeed.

One policy response that most acknowledge as having been successful was how the Fed dealt with the financial crises in Southeast Asia and elsewhere that shook the world economy in 1997 and 1998. There were serious concerns at the time that economic difficulties around the world would bring the high-flying U.S. economy to its knees and worsen an already difficult economic situation in other countries. The Fed had to steer through the pitfalls that global economic crises threw in front of it.

In the fall of 1998, the Fed chose to accelerate to avoid a possible downturn. The Federal Open Market Committee (FOMC) engaged in expansionary monetary policy by lowering its target for the federal funds rate. Some critics argued at the time that the Fed's action was too weak to counter the impact of world economic crisis. Others, though, criticized the Fed for undertaking an expansionary policy when the U.S. economy seemed already to be in an inflationary gap.

In the summer of 1999, the Fed put on the brakes, shifting back to a slightly contractionary policy. It raised the target for the federal funds rate, first to 5.0% and then to 5.25%. These actions reflected concern about speeding when in an inflationary gap.

But was the economy speeding? Was it in an inflationary gap? Certainly, the U.S. unemployment rate of 4.2% in the fall of 1999 stood well below standard estimates of the natural rate of unemployment. There were few, if any, indications that inflation was a problem, but the Fed had to recognize that inflation might not appear for a very long time after the Fed had taken a particular course. As noted in the text, this was also during a time when the once-close relationship between money growth and nominal GDP seemed to break down. The shifts in demand for money created unexplained and unexpected changes in velocity.

The outcome of the Fed's actions has been judged a success. While with 20/20 hindsight the Fed's decisions might seem obvious, in fact it was steering a car whose performance seemed less and less predictable over a course that was becoming more and more treacherous.

Since 2008, both the Fed and the government have been again trying to get the economy back on track. In this case, the car is already in the ditch. The Fed has decided on a "no holds barred" approach. It has moved aggressively to lower the federal funds rate target and engaged in a variety of other measures to improve liquidity to the banking system, to lower other interest rates by purchasing longer-term securities (such as 10-year treasuries and those of Fannie Mae and Freddie Mac), and, working with the Treasury Department, to provide loans related to consumer and business debt.

The Obama administration for its part advocated and Congress passed a massive spending and tax relief package of about $800 billion. Besides the members of his economic team, many economists seem to be on board in using discretionary fiscal policy in this instance. Federal Reserve Bank of San Francisco President Janet Yellen put it this way: "The new enthusiasm for fiscal stimulus, and particularly government spending, represents a huge evolution in mainstream thinking." A notable convert to using fiscal policy to deal with this recession was Harvard economist and former adviser to President Ronald Reagan, Martin Feldstein. His spending proposal encouraged increased military spending and he stated, "While good tax policy can contribute to ending the recession, the heavy lifting will have to be done by increased government spending."

Predictably, not all economists have jumped onto the fiscal policy bandwagon. Concerns included whether so-called shovel-ready projects could really be implemented in time, whether government spending would crowd out private spending, whether monetary policy alone was providing enough stimulus, and whether the spending would flow efficiently to truly worthwhile projects. According to University of California-Berkeley economist Alan J. Auerbach, "We have spent so many years thinking that discretionary fiscal policy was a bad idea, that we have not figured out the right things to do to cure a recession that is scaring all of us."

Sources: *Ben S. Bernanke, "The Crisis and the Policy Response" (speech, London School of Economics, January 13, 2009); Louis Uchitelle, "Economists Warm to Government Spending but Debate Its Form," New York Times, January 7, 2009, p. B1.*

ANSWER TO TRY IT! PROBLEM

Panel (a) shows an expansionary monetary policy according to new Keynesian economics. Aggregate demand increases, with no immediate reduction in short-run aggregate supply. Real GDP rises to Y_2. In the long run, nominal wages rise, reducing short-run aggregate supply and returning real GDP to potential. Panel (b) shows what happens with rational expectations. When the Fed increases the money supply, people anticipate the rise in prices. Workers and firms agree to an increase in nominal wages, so that there is a reduction in short-run aggregate supply at the same time there is an increase in aggregate demand. The result is no change in real GDP; it remains at potential. There is, however, an increase in the price level.

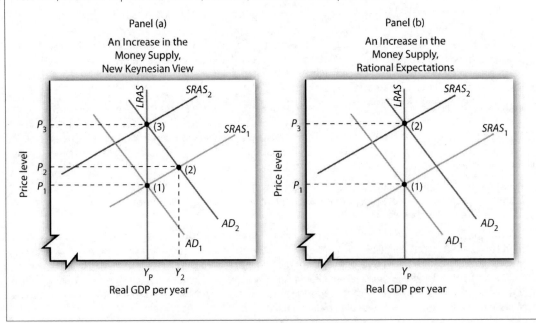

---

4.   REVIEW AND PRACTICE

Summary

We have surveyed the experience of the United States in light of the economic theories that prevailed or emerged during five decades. We have seen that events in the past century have had significant effects on the ways in which economists look at and interpret macroeconomic ideas.

Before the Great Depression, macroeconomic thought was dominated by the classical school. That body of theory stressed the economy's ability to reach full employment equilibrium on its own. The severity and duration of the Depression caused many economists to rethink their acceptance of natural equilibrating forces in the economy.

John Maynard Keynes issued the most telling challenge. He argued that wage rigidities and other factors could prevent the economy from closing a recessionary gap on its own. Further, he showed that expansionary fiscal and monetary policies could be used to increase aggregate demand and move the economy to its potential output. Although these ideas did not immediately affect U.S. policy, the increases in aggregate demand brought by the onset of World War II did bring the economy to full employment. Many economists became convinced of the validity of Keynes's analysis and his prescriptions for macroeconomic policy.

Keynesian economics dominated economic policy in the United States in the 1960s. Fiscal and monetary policies increased aggregate demand and produced what was then the longest expansion in U.S. history. But the economy pushed well beyond full employment in the latter part of the decade, and inflation increased. While Keynesians were dominant, monetarist economists argued that it was monetary policy that accounted for the expansion of the 1960s and that fiscal policy could not affect aggregate demand.

Efforts by the Nixon administration in 1969 and 1970 to cool the economy ran afoul of shifts in the short-run aggregate supply curve. The ensuing decade saw a series of shifts in aggregate supply that contributed to three more recessions by 1982. As economists studied these shifts, they developed further the basic notions we now express in the aggregate demand–aggregate supply model: that changes in aggregate demand and aggregate supply affect income and the price level; that changes in fiscal and monetary policy can affect aggregate demand; and that in the long run, the economy moves to its potential level of output.

The events of the 1980s and beyond raised serious challenges for the monetarist and new classical schools. New Keynesian economists formulated revisions in their theories, incorporating many of the ideas suggested by monetarist and new classical economists. The new, more powerful theory of macroeconomic events has won considerable support among economists today.

PROBLEMS

1. "For many years, the hands-off fiscal policies advocated by the classical economists held sway with American government. When times were hard, the prevailing response was to tough it out, awaiting the 'inevitable' turnaround. The lessons of the Great Depression and a booming wartime economy have since taught us, however, that government intervention is sometimes necessary and desirable—and that to an extent, we can take charge of our own economic lives." Evaluate the foregoing quotation based upon the discussion in this chapter. How would you classify the speaker in terms of a school of economic thought?

2. In his 1982 *Economic Report of the President*, Ronald Reagan said, "We simply cannot blame crop failures and oil price increases for our basic inflation problem. The continuous, underlying cause was poor government policy." What policies might he have been referring to?

3. Many journalists blamed economic policies of the Reagan administration for the extremely high levels of unemployment in 1982 and 1983. Given the record of the rest of the decade, do you agree that President Reagan's economic policies were a failure? Why or why not?

4. The day after the U.S. stock market crash of October 19, 1987, Federal Reserve Board Chairman Alan Greenspan issued the following statement: "The Federal Reserve, consistent with its responsibilities as the nation's central bank, affirmed today its readiness to serve as a source of liquidity to support the economic and financial system." Evaluate why the Fed chairman might have been prompted to make such a statement.

5. Compare the rationale of the Reagan administration for the 1981 tax reductions with the rationale behind the Kennedy–Johnson tax cut of 1964, the Bush tax cut of 2001, and the Bush tax cut of 2003.

6. If the economy is operating below its potential output, what kind of gap exists? What kinds of fiscal or monetary policies might you use to close this gap? Can you think of any objection to the use of such policies?

7. If the economy is operating above its potential output, what kind of gap exists? What kinds of fiscal or monetary policies might you use to close this gap? Can you think of any objection to the use of such policies?

8. In *General Theory*, Keynes wrote of the importance of ideas. The world, he said, is ruled by little else. How important do you think his ideas have been for economic policy today?

9. State whether each of the following events appears to be the result of a shift in short-run aggregate supply or aggregate demand, and state the direction of the shift involved.

    a. The price level rises sharply while real GDP falls.

    b. The price level and real GDP rise.

    c. The price level falls while real GDP rises.

    d. The price level and real GDP fall.

10. Explain whether each of the following events and policies will affect the aggregate demand curve or the short-run aggregate supply curve, and state what will happen to the price level and real GDP.

    a. Oil prices rise

    b. The Fed sells bonds

    c. Government purchases increase

    d. Federal taxes increase

    e. The government slashes transfer payment spending

    f. Oil prices fall

11. Using the model of aggregate demand and aggregate supply, illustrate an economy with a recessionary gap. Show how a policy of nonintervention would ultimately close the gap. Show the alternative of closing the gap through stabilization policy.

12. Using the model of aggregate demand and aggregate supply, illustrate an economy with an inflationary gap. Show how a policy of nonintervention would ultimately close the gap. Show the alternative of closing the gap through stabilization policy.

ENDNOTES

1. David C. Wheelock, "The Federal Response to Home Mortgage Distress: Lessons from the Great Depression," *Federal Reserve Bank of St. Louis Review* 90, no. 3 (Part 1) (May/June 2008): 133–48.

2. For a discussion of fiscal policy during the Great Depression, see E. Cary Brown, "Fiscal Policy in the 'Thirties: A Reappraisal," *American Economic Review* 46, no. 5 (December 1956): 857–79.

3. Dan Fuller and Doris Geide-Stevenson, "Consensus among Economists: Revisited," *Journal of Economic Education* 34, no. 4 (Fall 2003): 369–87.

4. National Association for Business Economics, Economic Policy Surveys, March 2009 and August 2010. Available at www.nabe.com

CHAPTER 18

Inequality, Poverty, and Discrimination

START UP: POVERTY IN THE UNITED STATES

The United States is the richest large country on the planet. Yet, in 2006, 36.5 million people in the United States were, by the official definition, poor. The United States has a greater percentage of its people in poverty than does any other industrialized country. How can a nation that is so rich have so many people that are poor?

It was January 8, 1964 when President Lyndon B. Johnson stood before the Congress of the United States to make his first State of the Union address and to declare a new kind of war, a War on Poverty. "This administration today here and now declares unconditional war on poverty in America," the President said. "Our aim is not only to relieve the symptoms of poverty but to cure it; and, above, all, to prevent it." In the United States that year, 35.1 million people, about 22% of the population, were, by the official definition, poor.

The President's plan included stepped-up federal aid to low-income people, an expanded health-care program for the poor, new housing subsidies, expanded federal aid to education, and job training programs. The proposal became law later that same year.

More than four decades and trillions of dollars in federal antipoverty spending later, the nation seems to have made little progress toward the President's goal. While the percentage of people living in poverty has fallen since Johnson was president, the number of people living in poverty is actually slightly higher than it was then.

Moreover, over the past four decades, the distribution of income has also become more skewed. The share of income going to the rich has risen, while the share going to the poor has fallen.

Income inequality took center stage during the 2008 U.S. presidential election. Both Democratic candidate Barack Obama and Republican candidate John McCain campaigned on platforms to address this issue. McCain advocated making permanent tax cuts voted in under President George W. Bush that are set to expire. Obama advocated an increase in taxes on wealthy Americans and a reduction in taxes for most others. The issue came to the fore in the last presidential debate as the two candidates sparred around the image of "Joe the Plumber." The conversation went like this:

McCain: You know, when Senator Obama ended up his conversation with Joe the plumber—we need to spread the wealth around. In other words, we're going to take Joe's money, give it to Senator Obama, and let him spread the wealth around. I want Joe the plumber to spread that wealth around. You told him you wanted to spread the wealth around. The whole premise behind Senator Obama's plans are class warfare, let's spread the wealth around. I want small businesses—and by the way, the small businesses that we're talking about would receive an increase in their taxes right now. Who—why would you want to increase anybody's taxes right now? Why would you want to do that, anyone, anyone in America, when we have such a tough time, when these small business people, like Joe the plumber, are going to create jobs, unless you take that money from him and spread the wealth around. I'm not going to…

Obama: OK. Can I…

McCain: We're not going to do that in my administration.

Obama: If I can answer the question. Number one, I want to cut taxes for 95% of Americans. Now, it is true that my friend and supporter, Warren Buffett, for example, could afford to pay a little more in taxes in order…

McCain: We're talking about Joe the plumber.

Obama:… in order to give—in order to give additional tax cuts to Joe the plumber before he was at the point where he could make $250,000. Then Exxon Mobil, which made $12 billion, record profits, over the last several quarters, they can afford to pay a little more so that ordinary families who are hurting out there—they're trying to figure out how they're going to afford food, how they're going to save for their kids' college education, they need a break. So, look, nobody likes taxes. I would prefer that none of us had to pay taxes, including myself. But ultimately, we've got to pay for the core investments that make this economy strong and somebody's got to do it.

McCain: Nobody likes taxes. Let's not raise anybody's taxes. OK?

Obama: Well, I don't mind paying a little more.

McCain: The fact is that businesses in America today are paying the second highest tax rate of anywhere in the world. Our tax rate for business in America is 35%. Ireland, it's 11%. Where are companies going to go where they can create jobs and where they can do best in business? We need to cut the business tax rate in America. We need to encourage business. Now, of all times in America, we need to cut people's taxes. We need to encourage business, create jobs, not spread the wealth around.

The candidates thus presented strikingly different views of how to promote prosperity and fairness. In this chapter we shall analyze three issues related to the question of fairness. We begin by looking at income inequality and explanations of why the distribution of income in the United States has grown more unequal in recent years. We shall then analyze poverty. We shall examine government programs designed to alleviate poverty and explore why so little progress appears to have been made toward eliminating it after all these years.

We shall also explore the problem of discrimination. Being at the lower end of the income distribution and being poor are more prevalent among racial minorities and among women than among white males. To a degree, this situation may reflect discrimination. We shall investigate the economics of discrimination and its consequences for the victims and for the economy. We shall also assess efforts by the public sector to eliminate discrimination.

Questions of fairness often accompany discussions of income inequality, poverty, and discrimination. Answering them ultimately involves value judgments; they are normative questions, not positive ones. You must decide for yourself if a particular distribution of income is fair or if society has made adequate progress toward reducing poverty or discrimination. The material in this chapter will not answer those questions for you; rather, in order for you to have a more informed basis for making your own value judgments, it will shed light on what economists have learned about these issues through study and testing of hypotheses.

1.   INCOME INEQUALITY

LEARNING OBJECTIVES

1. Explain how the Lorenz curve and the Gini coefficient provide information on a country's distribution of income.
2. Discuss and evaluate the factors that have been looked at to explain changes in the distribution of income in the United States.

Income inequality in the United States has soared in the last half century. Since 1967, real median household income has risen 30%. For the top 1%, incomes shot up by over 200%. Consider recent experience. Median household-size-adjusted disposable income rose 13% between 1988 and 2004. At the 75th percentile it rose 16%, at the 90th percentile 21%, and at the 95th percentile 27%.[1]

Increasingly, education is the key to a better material life. The gap between the average annual incomes of high school graduates and those with a bachelor's degree increased by nearly a factor of five between 1975 and 2006. Read that sentence again. The gap went from under $5,000 to over $23,000 *per year*. That is a phenomenal change in such a short period of time. A special study by the U.S. Census Bureau estimated that compared to the full-time year-around work-life earnings of a high school graduate, a person with a bachelors degree would earn 75% more, while a person with a professional degree would earn almost four times more over their working lifetime.[2] Moreover, education is not an equal opportunity employer. A student from a family in the top quarter of the income distribution is six times more likely to get a college degree than a student whose family is in the bottom quarter of the income distribution.

That inequality perpetuates itself. College graduates marry other college graduates and earn higher incomes. Those who do not go to college earn lower incomes. Some may have children out of wedlock—an almost sure route to poverty. That does not, of course, mean that young people who go to college are assured high incomes while those who do not are certain to experience poverty, but the odds certainly push in that direction.

We shall learn in this section how the degree of inequality can be measured. We shall examine the sources of rising inequality and consider what policy measures, if any, are suggested. In this section on inequality we are essentially focusing the way the economic pie is shared, while setting aside the important fact that the size of the economic pie has certainly grown over time.

1.1   A Changing Distribution of Income

We have seen that the income distribution has become more unequal. This section describes a graphical approach to measuring the equality, or inequality, of the distribution of income.

Measuring Inequality

The primary evidence of growing inequality is provided by census data. Households are asked to report their income, and they are ranked from the household with the lowest income to the household with the highest income. The Census Bureau then reports the percentage of total income earned by those households ranked among the bottom 20%, the next 20%, and so on, up to the top 20%. Each 20% of households is called a quintile. The bureau also reports the share of income going to the top 5% of households.

Income distribution data can be presented graphically using a **Lorenz curve**, a curve that shows cumulative shares of income received by individuals or groups. It was developed by economist Max O. Lorenz in 1905. To plot the curve, we begin with the lowest quintile and mark a point to show the percentage of total income those households received. We then add the next quintile and its share and mark a point to show the share of the lowest 40% of households. Then, we add the third quintile, and then the fourth. Since the share of income received by all the quintiles will be 100%, the last point on the curve always shows that 100% of households receive 100% of the income.

If every household in the United States received the same income, the Lorenz curve would coincide with the 45-degree line drawn in Figure 18.1. The bottom 20% of households would receive 20% of

Lorenz curve

A curve that shows cumulative shares of income received by individuals or groups.

income; the bottom 40% would receive 40%, and so on. If the distribution of income were completely unequal, with one household receiving all the income and the rest zero, then the Lorenz curve would be shaped like a backward L, with a horizontal line across the bottom of the graph at 0% of income and a vertical line up the right-hand side. The vertical line would show, as always, that 100% of families still receive 100% of income. Actual Lorenz curves lie between these extremes. The closer a Lorenz curve lies to the 45-degree line, the more equal the distribution. The more bowed out the curve, the less equal the distribution. We see in Figure 18.1 that the Lorenz curve for the United States became more bowed out between 1968 and 2006.

FIGURE 18.1   The Distribution of U.S. Income, 1968 and 2006

The distribution of income among households in the United States became more unequal from 1968 to 2006. The shares of income received by each of the first four quintiles fell, while the share received by the top 20% rose sharply. The Lorenz curve for 2006 was more bowed out than was the curve for 1968. (Mean income adjusted for inflation and reported in 2006 dollars; percentages do not sum to 100% due to rounding.)

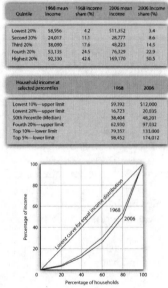

Quintile	1968 mean income	1968 income share (%)	2006 mean income	2006 income share (%)
Lowest 20%	$8,956	4.2	$11,352	3.4
Second 20%	24,017	11.1	28,777	8.6
Third 20%	38,090	17.6	48,223	14.5
Fourth 20%	53,135	24.5	76,329	22.9
Highest 20%	92,330	42.6	169,170	50.5

Household income at selected percentiles	1968	2006
Lowest 10%—upper limit	$9,392	$12,000
Lowest 20%—upper limit	16,723	20,035
50th Percentile (Median)	38,404	48,201
Fourth 20%—upper limit	62,930	97,032
Top 10%—lower limit	79,357	133,000
Top 5%—lower limit	98,452	174,012

Sources: Carmen DeNavas-Walt, Bernadette D. Proctor, and Cheryl Hill Lee, U.S. Census Bureau, Current Population Reports, P60-229, Income, Poverty, and Health Insurance Coverage in the United States: 2004, U.S. Government Printing Office, Washington, DC, 2005, Table A-3; U.S. Census Bureau, Current Population Survey, 2005 Annual Social and Economic Supplement, Table HINC-05.

Gini coefficient

A measure of inequality expressed as the ratio of the area between the Lorenz curve and a 45° line and the total area under the 45° line.

The degree of inequality is often measured with a **Gini coefficient**, the ratio between the Lorenz curve and the 45° line and the total area under the 45° line. The smaller the Gini coefficient, the more equal the income distribution. Larger Gini coefficients mean more unequal distributions. The Census Bureau reported that the Gini coefficient was 0.397 in 1968 and 0.470 in 2006—the highest ever recorded for the United States.[3]

Mobility and Income Distribution

When we speak of the bottom 20% or the middle 20% of families, we are not speaking of a static group. Some families who are in the bottom quintile one year move up to higher quintiles in subsequent years; some families move down. Because people move up and down the distribution, we get a quite different picture of income change when we look at the incomes of a fixed set of persons over time rather than comparing average incomes for a particular quintile at a particular point in time, as was done in Figure 18.1.

Addressing the question of mobility requires that researchers follow a specific group of families over a long period of time. Since 1968, the Panel Survey of Income Dynamics (PSID) at the University of Michigan has followed more than 5,000 families and their descendents. The effort has produced a much deeper understanding of changes in income inequality than it is possible to obtain from census data, which simply take a snapshot of incomes at a particular time.

Based on the University of Michigan's data, Federal Reserve Bank of Boston economists Katharine Bradbury and Jane Katz compared mobility in the 1970s, 1980s, and 1990s. In the 1970s, just under half the families in the poorest quintile at the start of that decade were still in that quintile at the end of that decade and overall about 32% of families moved up one quintile or more. The mobility figures for the 1980s were about the same as for the 1970s. In the 1990s, however, mobility declined. About 30% of families moved up one quintile or more and 53% of families that started the 1990s in the poorest quintile were still in that quintile at the end of the 1990s. In every decade, some of the movement to higher quintiles results simply from gaining age and experience. The researchers further comment that, for the 1990s, moving across quintiles has become harder to achieve precisely because of the increased income inequality.[4]

1.2 Explaining Inequality

Everyone agrees that the distribution of income in the United States generally became more equal during the first two decades after World War II and that it has become more unequal since 1968. While some people conclude that this increase in inequality suggests the latter period was unfair, others want to know why the distribution changed. We shall examine some of the explanations.

Family Structure

Clearly an important source of rising inequality since 1968 has been the sharp increase in the number of families headed by women. In 2006, the median income of families headed by married couples was 2.4 times that of families headed by women with no spouse present. The percentage of families headed by women with no spouse present has more than doubled since 1968 and is thus contributing to increased inequality across households.

Technological and Managerial Change

Technological change has affected the demand for labor. One of the most dramatic changes since the late 1970s has been an increase in the demand for skilled labor and a reduction in the demand for unskilled labor.

The result has been an increase in the gap between the wages of skilled and unskilled workers. That has produced a widening gap between college- and high-school-trained workers. As we saw earlier, that gap has quintupled in the last few decades.

Technological change has meant the integration of computers into virtually every aspect of production. And that has increased the demand for workers with the knowledge to put new methods to work—and to adapt to the even more dramatic changes in production likely to come. At the same time, the demand for workers who do not have that knowledge has fallen.

Along with new technologies that require greater technical expertise, firms are adopting new management styles that require stronger communication skills. The use of production teams, for example, shifts decision-making authority to small groups of assembly-line workers. That means those workers need more than the manual dexterity that was required of them in the past. They need strong communication skills. They must write effectively, speak effectively, and interact effectively with other workers. Workers who cannot do so simply are not in demand to the degree they once were.

The "intellectual wage gap" seems likely to widen as we move even further into the twenty-first century. That is likely to lead to an even higher degree of inequality and to pose a challenge to public policy for decades to come. Increasing education and training could lead to reductions in inequality. Indeed, individuals seem to have already begun to respond to this changing market situation, since the percentage who graduate from high school and college is rising.

Tax Policy

Did tax policy contribute to rising inequality over the past four decades? The tax changes most often cited in the fairness debate are the Bush tax cuts introduced in 2001, 2002, and 2003 and the Reagan tax cuts introduced in 1981.

An analysis of the Bush tax cuts by the Tax Foundation combines the three Bush tax cuts and assumes they occurred in 2003. Table 18.1 gives the share of total income tax liability for each quintile before and after the Bush tax cuts. It also gives the share of the Bush tax cuts received by each quintile.

TABLE 18.1 Income Tax Liability Before and After the Bush Tax Cuts

The share of total tax relief received by the first four quintiles was modest, while those in the top quintile received more than two-thirds of the total benefits of the three tax cuts. However, the share of income taxes paid by each of the first four quintiles fell as a result of the tax cuts, while the share paid by the top quintile rose.

Quintile	Share of income tax liability before tax cuts	Share of income tax liability after tax cuts	Share of total tax relief
First quintile	0.5%	0.3%	1.2%
Second quintile	2.3%	1.9%	4.2%
Third quintile	5.9%	5.2%	9.4%
Fourth quintile	12.6%	11.6%	17.5%
Top quintile	78.7%	81.0%	67.7%

Source: William Ahean, "Comparing the Kennedy, Reagan, and Bush Tax Cuts," Tax Foundation Fiscal Facts, August 24, 2004.

Tax cuts under George W. Bush were widely criticized as being tilted unfairly toward the rich. And certainly, Table 18.1 shows that the share of total tax relief received by the first four quintiles was modest, while those in the top quintile garnered more than two-thirds of the total benefits of the three tax cuts. Looking at the second and third columns of the table, however, gives a different perspective. The share of income taxes paid by each of the first four quintiles fell as a result of the tax cuts, while the share paid by the top quintile rose. Further, we see that each of the first four quintiles paid a very small share of income taxes before and after the tax cuts, while those in the top quintile ended up shouldering more than 80% of the total income tax burden. We saw in Figure 18.1 that those in the top quintile received just over half of total income. After the Bush tax cuts, they paid 81% of income taxes. On that basis, one might conclude that the Bush tax cuts contributed to equalizing income. Others are quick to point out that those same tax cuts were accompanied by reductions in expenditures for some social service programs designed to help lower income families. Still others point out that the tax cuts contributed to an increase in the federal deficit and, therefore, are likely to have distributional effects over many years and across several generations. Whether these changes increased or decreased fairness in the society is ultimately a normative question.

Methodology

The method by which the Census Bureau computes income shares has been challenged by some observers. Robert Rector, of the Heritage Foundation, a conservative think tank, notes three flaws in the Census Bureau approach. First, it ignores taxes. Second, it ignores the $750 billion in spending for the poor and elderly. Third, each quintile does not contain the same number of people. The top quintile, for example, contains 70% more people than the bottom quintile because households in the lowest quintile tend to have fewer people than those in the highest quintile. Taking the Census Bureau finding that the top quintile receives 50.1% of total income while the bottom quintile receives 3.4% of income implies that people in the top quintile receive $14.74 for every $1.00 received by people in the bottom quintile. But, Mr. Rector points out that once one adjusts for taxes, transfers, and the unequal number of people in each quintile, that 14.74:1 gap falls to $4.21 in the top quintile for every $1.00 in the bottom. By this accounting, incomes in the United States are not nearly as unequal as reported by the Census Bureau.[5] This suggests that more precise measurements may provide more insight into explaining inequality.

KEY TAKEAWAYS

- The distribution of income can be illustrated with a Lorenz curve. If all households had the same income, the Lorenz curve would be a 45° line. In general, the more equal the distribution of income, the closer the Lorenz curve will be to the 45° line. A more bowed out curves shows a less equal distribution. The Gini coefficient is another method for describing the distribution of income.
- The distribution of income has, according to the Census Bureau, become somewhat more unequal in the United States during the past 36 years.
- The degree of mobility up and down the distribution of income appears to have declined in recent years.
- Among the factors explaining increased inequality have been changes in family structure and changes in the demand for labor that have rewarded those with college degrees and have penalized unskilled workers.

TRY IT!

The accompanying Lorenz curves show the distribution of income in a country before taxes and welfare benefits are taken into account (curve *A*) and after taxes and welfare benefits are taken into account (curve *B*). Do taxes and benefits serve to make the distribution of income in the country more equal or more unequal?

Case in Point: Attitudes and Inequality

© 2010 Jupiterimages Corporation

In a fascinating examination of attitudes in the United States and in continental Western Europe, economists Alberto Alesina of Harvard University and George-Marios Angeletos of the Massachusetts Institute of Technology suggest that attitudes about the nature of income earning can lead to quite different economic systems and outcomes concerning the distribution of income.

The economists cite survey evidence from the World Values Survey, which concludes that 71% of Americans, and only 40% of Europeans, agree with the proposition: "*The poor could become rich if they worked hard enough.*" Further, Americans are much more likely to attribute material success to hard work, while Europeans tend to attribute success to factors such as luck, connections, and even corruption. The result, according to Professors Alesina and Angeletos, is that Americans select a government that is smaller and engages in less redistributive activity than is selected by Europeans. Government in continental Western Europe is 50% larger than in the United States, the tax system in Europe is much more progressive than in the United States, regulation of labor and product markets is more extensive in Europe, and redistributive programs are more extensive in Europe than in the United States. As a result, the income distribution in Europe is much more equal than in the United States.

People get what they expect. The economists derive two sets of equilibria. Equilibrium in a society in which people think incomes are a result of luck, connections, and corruption turns out to be precisely that. And, in a society in which people believe incomes are chiefly the result of effort and skill, they are. In the latter society, people work harder and invest more. In the United States, the average worker works 1,600 hours per year. In Europe, the average worker works 1,200 hours per year.

So, who is right—Americans with their "you get what you deserve" or Europeans with their "you get what luck, connections, and corruption bring you" attitude? The two economists show that people get, in effect, what they expect. European values and beliefs produce societies that are more egalitarian. American values and beliefs produce the American result: a society in which the distribution of income is more unequal, the government smaller, and redistribution relatively minor. Professors Alesina and Angeletos conclude that Europeans tend to underestimate the degree to which people can improve their material well-being through hard work, while Americans tend to overestimate that same phenomenon.

Source: Alberto Alesina and George-Marios Angeletos, "Fairness and Redistribution," American Economic Review 95:4 (September, 2005) 960–80.

The Lorenz curve showing the distribution of income after taxes and benefits are taken into account is less bowed out than the Lorenz curve showing the distribution of income before taxes and benefits are taken into account. Thus, income is more equally distributed after taking them into account.

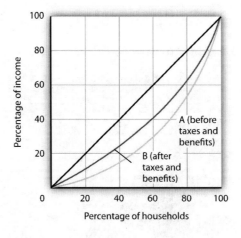

2. THE ECONOMICS OF POVERTY

LEARNING OBJECTIVES

1. Distinguish between relative and absolute measures of poverty and discuss the uses and merits of each.
2. Describe the demographics of poverty in the United States.
3. Describe the forms of welfare programs in the United States and the reform of welfare in the mid-1990s.
4. Discuss the factors that have been looked at to explain the persistence of poverty in the United States.

Poverty in the United States is something of a paradox. Per capita incomes in this country are among the highest on earth. Yet, the United States has a greater percentage of its population below the official poverty line than in the other industrialized nations. How can a nation that is so rich have so many people who are poor?

There is no single answer to the question of why so many people are poor. But we shall see that there are economic factors at work that help to explain poverty. We shall also examine the nature of the government's response to poverty and the impact that response has. First, however, we shall examine the definition of poverty and look at some characteristics of the poor in the United States.

2.1 Defining Poverty

Suppose you were asked to determine whether a particular family was poor or not poor. How would you do it?

You might begin by listing the goods and services that would be needed to provide a minimum standard of living and then finding out if the family's income was enough to purchase those items. If it were not, you might conclude that the family was poor. Alternatively, you might examine the family's income relative to the incomes of other families in the community or in the nation. If the family was on the low end of the income scale, you might classify it as poor.

These two approaches represent two bases on which poverty is defined. The first is an **absolute income test**, which sets a specific income level and defines a person as poor if his or her income falls below that level. The second is a **relative income test**, in which people whose incomes fall at the bottom of the income distribution are considered poor. For example, we could rank households according to income as we did in the previous section on income inequality and define the lowest one-fifth of households as poor. In 2006, any U.S. household with an annual income below $20,035 fell in this category.

In contrast, to determine who is poor according to the absolute income test, we define a specific level of income, independent of how many households fall above or below it. The federal government defines a household as poor if the household's annual income falls below a dollar figure called the **poverty line**. In 2006 the poverty line for a family of four was an income of $20,614. Figure 18.4 shows the poverty line for various family sizes.

FIGURE 18.4 Weighted Average Poverty Thresholds in 2006, by Size of Family

The Census Bureau uses a set of 48 money income thresholds that vary by family size and composition to determine who is in poverty. The "Weighted Average Poverty Thresholds" in the accompanying table is a summary of the 48 thresholds used by the census bureau. It provides a general sense of the "poverty line" based on the relative number of families by size and composition.

Number of people in household	Poverty Line
One person	$10,294
Two people	13,167
Three people	16,079
Four people	20,614
Five people	24,382
Six people	27,560
Seven people	31,205
Eight people	34,774
Nine people or more	41,499

Source: DeNavas-Walt, Carmen, Bernadette D. Proctor, and Jessica Smith, U.S. Census Bureau, Current Population Reports, P60-233, Income, Poverty, and Health Insurance Coverage in the United States: 2006, U.S. Government Printing Office, Washington, D.C., 2007; p. 45.

The concept of a poverty line grew out of a Department of Agriculture study in 1955 that found families spending one-third of their incomes on food. With the one-third figure as a guide, the Department then selected four food plans that met the minimum daily nutritional requirements established by the federal government. The cost of the least expensive plan for each household size was multiplied by three to determine the income below which a household would be considered poor. The government used this method to count the number of poor people from 1959 to 1969. The poverty line was adjusted each year as food prices changed. Beginning in 1969, the poverty line was adjusted annually by the average percentage price change for all consumer goods, not just changes in the price of food.

There is little to be said for this methodology for defining poverty. No attempt is made to establish an income at which a household could purchase basic necessities. Indeed, no attempt is made in the definition to establish what such necessities might be. The day has long passed when the average household devoted one-third of its income to food purchases; today such purchases account for less than one-fifth of household income. Still, it is useful to have some threshold that is consistent from one year to the next so that progress—or the lack thereof—in the fight against poverty can be assessed.

The percentage of the population that falls below the poverty line is called the **poverty rate**. Figure 18.5 shows both the number of people and the percentage of the population that fell below the poverty line each year since 1959.

absolute income test

Income test that sets a specific income level and defines a person as poor if his or her income falls below that level.

relative income test

Income test in which people whose incomes fall at the bottom of the income distribution are considered poor.

poverty line

Amount of annual income below which the federal government defines a household as poor.

poverty rate

The percentage of the population that falls below the poverty line.

FIGURE 18.5 The Poverty Rate in the United States, 1959–2006

The curve shows the percentage of people who lived in households that fell below the poverty line in each year from 1959 to 2006. The poverty rate has generally fallen since 1959. Still, the poverty rate in the United States is greater than that of any other industrialized nation.

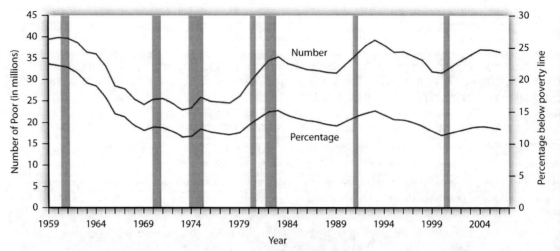

Source: DeNavas-Walt, Carmen, Bernadette D. Proctor, and Jessica Smith, U.S. Census Bureau, Current Population Reports P60-233, Income, Poverty, and Health Insurance Coverage in the United States: 2006, U.S. Government Printing Office, Washington DC, 2007; Table B-1, p. 44.

Despite its shortcomings, measuring poverty using an absolute measure allows for the possibility of progress in reducing it; using a relative measure of poverty does not, since there will always be a lowest 1/5, or 1/10 of the population. But relative measures do make an important point: Poverty is in large measure a relative concept. In the United States, poor people have much higher incomes than most of the world's people or even than average Americans did as recently as the early 1970s. By international and historical standards, the average poor person in the United States is rich! The material possessions of America's poor would be considered lavish in another time and in another place. For example, in 2005, 43% of poor households in the United States owned their own homes, nearly 75% owned a car, and 78% owned a VCR. About 80% of poor households had air conditioning. Forty years ago, only 36% of the entire population in the United States had air conditioning. The average poor person in the United States has more living space than the average *person* in London, Paris, Vienna, or Athens.[6]

We often think of poverty as meaning that poor people are unable to purchase adequate food. Yet, according to Department of Agriculture surveys, 89% of poor people report that they have adequate food. Only 2% reported that they are hungry most of the time. In short, poor people in the United States enjoy a standard of living that would be considered quite comfortable in many parts of the developed world—and lavish in the less developed world.[7]

But people judge their incomes relative to incomes of people around them, not relative to people everywhere on the planet or to people in years past. You may feel poor when you compare yourself to some of your classmates who may have fancier cars or better clothes. And a family of four in a Los Angeles slum with an annual income of $13,000 surely does not feel rich because its income is many times higher than the average family income in Ethiopia or of Americans of several decades ago. While the material possessions of poor Americans are vast by Ethiopian standards, they are low in comparison to how the average American lives. What we think of as poverty clearly depends more on what people around us are earning than on some absolute measure of income.

Both the absolute and relative income approaches are used in discussions of the poverty problem. When we speak of the number of poor people, we are typically using an absolute income test of poverty. When we speak of the problems of those at the bottom of the income distribution, we are speaking in terms of a relative income test. In the European Union, for example, the poverty line is set at 60% of the median income of each member nation in a particular year. That is an example of a relative measure of poverty. In the rest of this section, we focus on the absolute income test of poverty used in the United States.

2.2 The Demographics of Poverty

There is no iron law of poverty that dictates that a household with certain characteristics will be poor. Nonetheless, poverty is much more highly concentrated among some groups than among others. The six characteristics of families that are important for describing who in the United States constitute the poor are whether or not the family is headed by a female, age, the level of education, whether or not the head of the family is working, the race of the household, and geography.

Figure 18.6 shows poverty rates for various groups and for the population as a whole in 2004. What does it tell us?

1. A family headed by a female is more than five times as likely to live in poverty as compared to a family with a husband present. This fact contributes to child poverty.

2. Children under 18 are about two times more likely to be poor than "middle-aged" (45–64) persons.

3. The less education the adults in the family have, the more likely the family is to be poor. A college education is an almost sure ticket out of poverty; the poverty rate for college graduates is just 3.9%.

4. The poverty rate is higher among those who do not work than among those who do. The poverty rate for people who did not work was almost six times the poverty rate of those who worked full time.

5. The prevalence of poverty varies by race and ethnicity. Specifically, the poverty rate in 2006 for whites (non-Hispanic origin) was less than half that for Hispanics or of blacks.

6. The poverty rate in central cities is higher than in other areas of residence.

The incidence of poverty soars when several of these demographic factors associated with poverty are combined. For example, the poverty rate for families with children that are headed by women who lack a high school education is higher than 50%.

FIGURE 18.6 The Demographics of Poverty in the United States, 2006

Poverty rates in the United States vary significantly according to a variety of demographic factors. The data are for 2006.

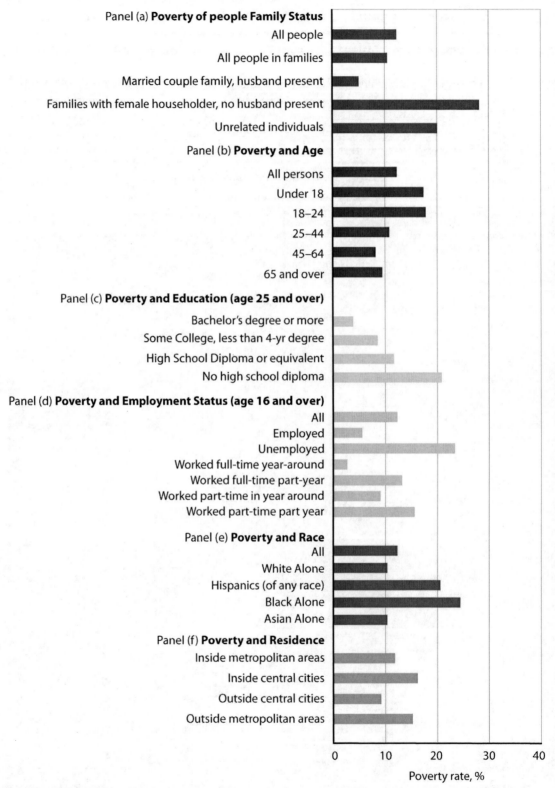

Source: DeNavas-Walt, Carmen, Bernadette D. Proctor, and Jessica Smith, U.S. Census Bureau, Current Population Reports, P60-233, Income, Poverty, and Health Insurance Coverage: 2006, U.S. Government Printing Office, Washington DC, 2007. Data for age, educational attainment, employment status, and residence generated by authors using Current Population Survey (CPS) Table Creator for the Annual Social and Economic Supplement 2007. (http://www.census.gov/hhes/www/cpstc/cps_table_creator.html)

2.3   Government Policy and Poverty

Consider a young single parent with three small children. The parent is not employed and has no support from other relatives. What does the government provide for the family?

The primary form of cash assistance is likely to come from a program called Temporary Assistance for Needy Families (TANF). This program began with the passage of the Personal Responsibility and Work Opportunity Reconciliation Act of 1996. It replaced Aid to Families with Dependent Children (AFDC). TANF is funded by the federal government but administered through the states. Eligibility is limited to two years of continuous payments and to five years in a person's lifetime, although 20% of a state's caseload may be exempted from this requirement.

In addition to this assistance, the family is likely to qualify for food stamps, which are vouchers that can be exchanged for food at the grocery store. The family may also receive rent vouchers, which can be used as payment for private housing. The family may qualify for Medicaid, a program that pays for physician and hospital care as well as for prescription drugs.

A host of other programs provide help ranging from counseling in nutrition to job placement services. The parent may qualify for federal assistance in attending college. The children may participate in the Head Start program, a program of preschool education designed primarily for low-income children. If the poverty rate in the area is unusually high, local public schools the children attend may receive extra federal aid. **Welfare programs** are the array of programs that government provides to alleviate poverty.

In addition to public sector support, a wide range of help is available from private sector charities. These may provide scholarships for education, employment assistance, and other aid.

Figure 18.7 shows participation rates in the major federal programs to help the poor.

welfare programs

The array of programs that government provides to alleviate poverty.

FIGURE 18.7   Welfare Programs and the Poor

Many people who fall below the poverty line have not received aid from particular programs.

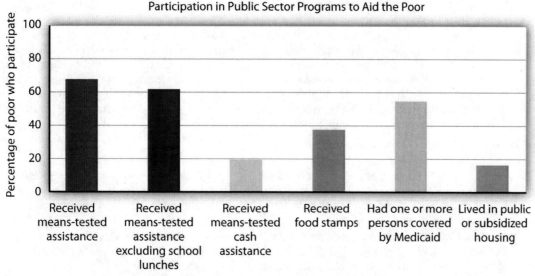

Source: U.S. Census Bureau, Current Population Survey, 2006 Annual Social and Economic Supplement.

Not all people whose incomes fall below the poverty line received aid. In 2006, a substantial majority of those counted as poor received some form of aid. But as shown by Figure 18.7, the percentages who were helped by individual programs were much lower. Less than 20% of people below the poverty line received some form of cash assistance in 2006. Less than 40% received food stamps and slightly more than half lived in a household in which one or more people received medical services through Medicaid. Only about one-sixth of the people living in poverty received some form of housing aid.

Although for the most part poverty programs are federally funded, individual states set eligibility standards and administer the programs. Allowing states to establish their own programs was a hallmark feature of the 1996 welfare reform. As state budgets have come under greater pressure, many states have tightened standards.

Cash Versus Noncash Assistance

cash assistance

A money payment that an aid recipient can spend as he or she wishes.

noncash assistance

The provision of specific goods and services, such as food or medical services, job training, or subsidized child care rather than cash.

Aid provided to people falls into two broad categories: cash and noncash assistance. **Cash assistance** is a money payment that a recipient can spend as he or she wishes. **Noncash assistance** is the provision of specific goods and services, such as food or medical services, job training, or subsidized child care rather than cash.

Noncash assistance is the most important form of aid to the poor. The large share of noncash relative to cash assistance raises two issues. First, since the poor would be better off (that is, reach a higher level of satisfaction) with cash rather than noncash assistance, why is noncash aid such a large percentage of total aid to the poor? Second, the importance of noncash assistance raises an important issue concerning the methodology by which the poverty rate is measured in the United States. We examine these issues in turn.

1. Why Noncash Aid?

   Suppose you had a choice between receiving $515 or a television set worth $515. Neither gift is taxable. Which would you take?

   Given a choice between cash and an equivalent value in merchandise, you would probably take the cash. Unless the television set happened to be exactly what you would purchase with the $515, you could find some other set of goods and services that you would prefer to the TV set. The same is true of funds that you can spend on anything versus funds whose spending is restricted. Given a choice of $515 that you could spend on anything and $515 that you could spend only on food, which would you choose? A given pool of funds allows consumers a greater degree of satisfaction than does a specific set of goods and services.

   We can conclude that poor people who receive government aid would be better off from their own perspectives with cash grants than with noncash aid. Why, then, is most government aid given as noncash benefits?

   Economists have suggested two explanations. The first is based on the preferences of donors. Recipients might prefer cash, but the preferences of donors matter also. The donors, in this case, are taxpayers. Suppose they want poor people to have specific things—perhaps food, housing, and medical care.

   Given such donor preferences, it is not surprising to find aid targeted at providing these basic goods and services. A second explanation has to do with the political clout of the poor. The poor are not likely to be successful competitors in the contest to be at the receiving end of public sector income redistribution efforts; most redistribution goes to people who are not poor. But firms that provide services such as housing or medical care might be highly effective lobbyists for programs that increase the demand for their products. They could be expected to seek more help for the poor in the form of noncash aid that increases their own demand and profits.[8]

2. Poverty Management and Noncash Aid

   Only cash income is counted in determining the official poverty rate. The value of food, medical care, or housing provided through various noncash assistance programs is not included in household income. That is an important omission, because most government aid is noncash aid. Data for the official poverty rate thus do not reflect the full extent to which government programs act to reduce poverty.

   The Census Bureau estimates the impact of noncash assistance on poverty. If a typical household would prefer, say, $515 in cash to $515 in food stamps, then $515 worth of food stamps is not valued at $515 in cash. Economists at the Census Bureau adjust the value of noncash aid downward to reflect an estimate of its lesser value to households. Suppose, for example, that given the choice between $515 in food stamps and $475 in cash, a household reports that it is indifferent between the two—either would be equally satisfactory. That implies that $515 in food stamps generates satisfaction equal to $475 in cash; the food stamps are thus "worth" $475 to the household.

2.4 Welfare Reform

The welfare system in the United States came under increasing attack in the 1980s and early 1990s. It was perceived to be expensive, and it had clearly failed to eliminate poverty. Many observers worried that welfare was becoming a way of life for people who had withdrawn from the labor force, and that existing welfare programs did not provide an incentive for people to work. President Clinton made welfare reform one of the key issues in the 1992 presidential campaign.

The Personal Responsibility and Work Opportunity Reconciliation Act of 1996 was designed to move people from welfare to work. It eliminated the entitlement aspect of welfare by defining a maximum period of eligibility. It gave states considerable scope in designing their own programs. In the first two years following welfare reform, the number of people on welfare dropped by several million.

Advocates of welfare reform proclaimed victory, while critics pointed to the booming economy, the tight labor market, and the general increase in the number of jobs over the same period. The critics also pointed out that the most employable welfare recipients (those with a high school education, no school-aged children living at home, and/or fewer personal problems) were the first to find jobs. The remaining welfare recipients, the critics argue, will have a harder time doing so. Moreover, having a job is not synonymous with getting out of poverty. Though some cities and states have reported notable successes, more experience is required before a final verdict on welfare reform can be reached. The downturn which started in 2008 and which could be prolonged may provide a real–time test.

2.5   Explaining Poverty

Just as the increase in income inequality begs for explanation, so does the question of why poverty seems so persistent. Should not the long periods of economic growth in the 1980s and 1990s and since 2003 have substantially reduced poverty? Have the various government programs been ineffective?

Clearly, some of the same factors that have contributed to rising income inequality have also contributed to the persistence of poverty. In particular, the increases in households headed by females and the growing gaps in wages between skilled and unskilled workers have been major contributors.

Tax policy changes have reduced the extent of poverty. In addition to general reductions in tax rates, the Earned Income Tax Credit, which began in 1975 and was expanded in the 1990s, provides people below a certain income level with a supplement for each dollar of income earned. This supplement, roughly 30 cents for every dollar earned, is received as a tax refund at the end of the year.

FIGURE 18.8 Percentages of Population in Eight Countries with Disposable Incomes Less Than 1/2 the National Median

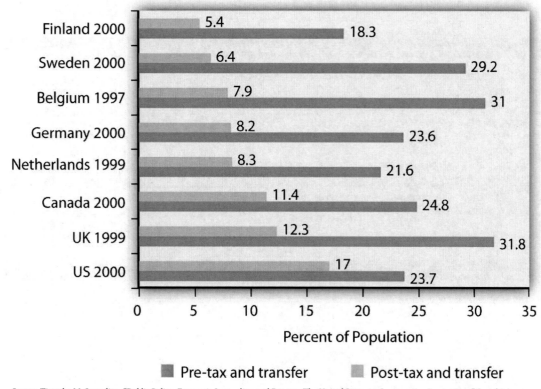

Source: Timothy M. Smeeding, "Public Policy, Economic Inequality, and Poverty: The United States in Comparative Perspectives," Social Science Quarterly, 86 (December 2005): 955–983.

Taken together, though, transfer payment and tax programs in the United States are less effective in reducing poverty that are the programs of other developed countries. Figure 18.8 shows the percentage of the population in eight developed countries with a disposable income (income after taxes) less than one-half the national median. The exhibit shows this percentage both before and after tax and transfer payment programs are considered. Clearly, the United States is the least aggressive in seeking to eliminate poverty among the eight countries shown.

Poverty and Work

How does poverty relate to work? Look back at Figure 18.6. Many of the poor are children or adults who do not work. That suggests one explanation for the weak relationship between poverty and economic growth in recent years. A growing economy reduces poverty by creating more jobs and higher incomes. Neither of those will reach those who, for various reasons, are not in the labor force.

Look at Figure 18.9. Of the nation's 36.5 million poor people in 2006, only about 13.6 million—roughly a third–could be considered available to participate in the labor market. The rest were too young, retired, sick or disabled. Even of the 13.6 million, many were already working part-time or seasonally (3.8 million) and others were college students or people who were unavailable for work because of their family situations, such as responsibility for caring for disabled family members. In sum, most of the nation's poor people are unlikely to be available for additional work.

FIGURE 18.9 Poor People and the Labor Force

Only a small fraction of the nation's poor in 2006 could be considered available to the labor force.

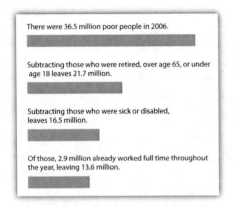

Source: 2006 Annual Social and Economic Supplement;
http://www.census.gov/hhes/www/cpstc/
cps_table_creator.html.

Poverty and Welfare Programs

How effective have government programs been in alleviating poverty? Here, it is important to distinguish between the poverty rate and the degree of poverty. Cash programs might reduce the degree of poverty, but might not affect a family's income enough to actually move that family above the poverty line. Thus, even though the gap between the family's income and the poverty line is lessened, the family is still classified as poor and would thus still be included in the poverty-rate figures. The data in Figure 18.9 show that significant gains in work participation will be difficult to achieve.

Economist Rebecca M. Blank of the University of Michigan argued that empirical studies prior to federal welfare reform generally showed that welfare payments discouraged work effort, but the effect was fairly small.[9] On the other hand, she also concluded that, following welfare reform, welfare caseloads fell more and labor force participation increased more than analysts had expected.[10] Evaluation of the effect of the federal welfare reform program on work participation, particularly over the long term, and on poverty continues.

KEY TAKEAWAYS

- Poverty may be defined according to a relative or an absolute definition.
- Official estimates of the number of people who are "poor" are typically based on an absolute definition of poverty, one that makes very little economic sense.
- Several demographic factors appear to be associated with poverty. Families headed by single women are three times as likely to be poor as are other families. Poverty is also associated with low levels of education and with minority status.
- There is a wide range of welfare programs; the majority of welfare spending is for noncash assistance. Those receiving this aid do not have it counted as income in the official calculations of poverty.
- Welfare reform has focused on requiring recipients to enter the labor force. Many poor people, however, are not candidates for the labor force.

TRY IT!

The Smiths, a family of four, have an income of $20,500 in 2006. Using the absolute income test approach and the data given in the chapter, determine if this family is poor. Use the relative income test to determine if this family is poor.

Case in Point: Welfare Reform in Britain and in the United States

© 2010 Jupiterimages Corporation

The governments of the United States and of Great Britain have taken sharply different courses in their welfare reform efforts. In the United States, the primary reform effort was undertaken in 1996, with the declaration to eliminate welfare as an entitlement and the beginning of programs that required recipients to enter the labor force within two years. President Clinton promised to "end welfare as we know it."

In Britain, the government of Tony Blair took a radically different approach. Prime Minister Blair promised to "make welfare popular again." His government undertook to establish what he called a "third way" to welfare reform, one that emphasized returning recipients to the workforce but that also sought explicitly to end child poverty.

The British program required recipients to get counseling aimed at encouraging them to return to the labor force. It did not, however, require that they obtain jobs. It also included a program of "making work pay," the primary feature of which was the creation of a National Minimum Wage, one that was set higher than the minimum wage in the United States. In the United States, the minimum wage equaled 34% of median private sector wages in 2002; the British minimum wage was set at 45% of the median private sector wage in 2002.

The British program, which was called the New Deal, featured tax benefits for poor families with children, whether they worked or not. It also included a Sure Start program of child care for poor people with children under three years old. In short, the Blair program was a more extensive social welfare program than the 1996 act in the United States.

The table below compares results of the two programs in terms of their impact on child poverty, using an "absolute" poverty line and also using a relative poverty line.

Child Poverty Rates, Pre- and Post- Reform		
United Kingdom	**Absolute (percent)**	**Relative (percent)**
1997–1998	24	25
2002–2003	12	21
Change	−12	−4
United States	**Absolute (percent)**	**Relative (percent)**
1992	19	38
2001	13	35
Change	−6	−3

Child Poverty Rates in Single-Mother Families, Pre- and Post- Reform		
United Kingdom	**Absolute (percent)**	**Relative (percent)**
1997–1998	40	41
2002–2003	15	33
Change	−25	−8
United States	**Absolute (percent)**	**Relative (percent)**
1992	44	67
2001	28	59
Change	−16	−8

The relative measure of child poverty is the method of measuring poverty adopted by the European Union. It draws the poverty line at 60% of median income. The poverty line is thus a moving target against which it is more difficult to make progress.

Hills and Waldfogel compared the British results to those in the United States in terms of the relative impact on welfare caseloads, employment of women having families, and reduction in child poverty. They note that reduction in welfare caseloads was much greater in the United States, with caseloads falling from 5.5 million to 2.3 million. In Britain, the reduction in caseloads was much smaller. In terms of impact on employment among women, the United States again experienced a much more significant increase. In terms of reduction of child poverty, however, the British approach clearly achieved a greater reduction. The British approach also increased incomes of families in the bottom 10% of the income distribution (i.e., the bottom decile) by more than that achieved in the United States. In Britain, incomes of families in the bottom decile rose 22%, and for families with children they rose 24%. In the United States, those in the bottom decile had more modest gains.

Would the United States ever adopt a New Deal program such as the Blair program in Great Britain? That, according to Hills and Waldfogel, would require a change in attitudes in the United States that they regard as unlikely.

Source: John Hills and Jane Waldfogel, "A 'Third Way' in Welfare Reform? Evidence from the United Kingdom," Journal of Policy Analysis and Management, 23(4) (2004): 765–88.

ANSWER TO TRY IT! PROBLEM

According to the absolute income test, the Smiths are poor because their income of $20,500 falls below the 2006 poverty threshold of $20,614. According to the relative income test, they are not poor because their $20,500 income is above the upper limit of the lowest quintile, $20,035.

---

3. THE ECONOMICS OF DISCRIMINATION

LEARNING OBJECTIVES

1. Define discrimination, identify some sources of it, and illustrate Becker's model of discrimination using demand and supply in a hypothetical labor market.
2. Assess the effectiveness of government efforts to reduce discrimination in the United States.

We have seen that being a female head of household or being a member of a racial minority increases the likelihood of being at the low end of the income distribution and of being poor. In the real world, we know that on average women and members of racial minorities receive different wages from white male workers, even though they may have similar qualifications and backgrounds. They might be charged different prices or denied employment opportunities. This section examines the economic forces that create such discrimination, as well as the measures that can be used to address it.

3.1 Discrimination in the Marketplace: A Model

Discrimination occurs when people with similar economic characteristics experience different economic outcomes because of their race, sex, or other noneconomic characteristics. A black worker whose skills and experience are identical to those of a white worker but who receives a lower wage is a victim of discrimination. A woman denied a job opportunity solely on the basis of her gender is the victim of discrimination. To the extent that discrimination exists, a country will not be allocating resources efficiently; the economy will be operating inside its production possibilities curve.

Pioneering work on the economics of discrimination was done by Gary S. Becker, an economist at the University of Chicago, who won the Nobel Prize in economics in 1992. He suggested that discrimination occurs because of people's preferences or attitudes. If enough people have prejudices against certain racial groups, or against women, or against people with any particular characteristic, the market will respond to those preferences.

In Becker's model, discriminatory preferences drive a wedge between the outcomes experienced by different groups. Discriminatory preferences can make salespeople less willing to sell to one group than to another or make consumers less willing to buy from the members of one group than from another or to make workers of one race or sex or ethnic group less willing to work with those of another race, sex, or ethnic group.

Let us explore Becker's model by examining labor-market discrimination against black workers. We begin by assuming that no discriminatory preferences or attitudes exist. For simplicity, suppose that the supply curves of black and white workers are identical; they are shown as a single curve in Figure 18.11. Suppose further that all workers have identical marginal products; they are equally productive. In the absence of racial preferences, the demand for workers of both races would be D. Black and white workers would each receive a wage W per unit of labor. A total of L black workers and L white workers would be employed.

Now suppose that employers have discriminatory attitudes that cause them to assume that a black worker is less productive than an otherwise similar white worker. Now employers have a lower demand, D_B, for black than for white workers. Employers pay black workers a lower wage, W_B, and employ fewer of them, L_B instead of L, than they would in the absence of discrimination.

3.2 Sources of Discrimination

As illustrated in Figure 18.11, racial prejudices on the part of employers produce discrimination against black workers, who receive lower wages and have fewer employment opportunities than white workers. Discrimination can result from prejudices among other groups in the economy as well.

One source of discriminatory prejudices is other workers. Suppose, for example, that white workers prefer not to work with black workers and require a wage premium for doing so. Such preferences would, in effect, raise the cost to the firm of hiring black workers. Firms would respond by demanding fewer of them, and wages for black workers would fall.

Another source of discrimination against black workers could come from customers. If the buyers of a firm's product prefer not to deal with black employees, the firm might respond by demanding fewer of them. In effect, prejudice on the part of consumers would lower the revenue that firms can generate from the output of black workers.

Whether discriminatory preferences exist among employers, employees, or consumers, the impact on the group discriminated against will be the same. Fewer members of that group will be employed, and their wages will be lower than the wages of other workers whose skills and experience are otherwise similar.

Race and sex are not the only characteristics that affect hiring and wages. Some studies have found that people who are short, overweight, or physically unattractive also suffer from discrimination, and charges of discrimination have been voiced by disabled people and by homosexuals. Whenever discrimination occurs, it implies that employers, workers, or customers have discriminatory preferences. For the effects of such preferences to be felt in the marketplace, they must be widely shared.

There are, however, market pressures that can serve to lessen discrimination. For example, if some employers hold discriminatory preferences but others do not, it will be profit enhancing for those who do not to hire workers from the group being discriminated against. Because workers from this group are less expensive to hire, costs for non-discriminating firms will be lower. If the market is at least somewhat competitive, firms who continue to discriminate may be driven out of business.

discrimination

When people with similar economic characteristics experience different economic outcomes because of their race, sex, or other noneconomic characteristics.

FIGURE 18.11 Prejudice and Discrimination

If employers, customers, or employees have discriminatory preferences, and those preferences are widespread, then the marketplace will result in discrimination. Here, black workers receive a lower wage and fewer of them are employed than would be the case in the absence of discriminatory preferences.

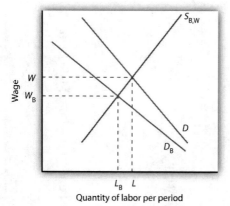

Quantity of labor per period

3.3 Discrimination in the United States Today

Reacting to demands for social change brought on most notably by the civil rights and women's movements, the federal government took action against discrimination. In 1954, the U.S. Supreme Court rendered its decision that so-called separate but equal schools for black and white children were inherently unequal, and the Court ordered that racially segregated schools be integrated. The Equal Pay Act of 1963 requires employers to pay the same wages to men and women who do substantially the same work. Federal legislation was passed in 1965 to ensure that minorities were not denied the right to vote.

Congress passed the most important federal legislation against discrimination in 1964. The Civil Rights Act barred discrimination on the basis of race, sex, or ethnicity in pay, promotion, hiring, firing, and training. An Executive Order issued by President Lyndon Johnson in 1967 required federal contractors to implement affirmative action programs to ensure that members of minority groups and women were given equal opportunities in employment. The practical effect of the order was to require that these employers increase the percentage of women and minorities in their work forces. Affirmative action programs for minorities followed at most colleges and universities.

What has been the outcome of these efforts to reduce discrimination? A starting point is to look at wage differences among different groups. Gaps in wages between males and females and between blacks and whites have fallen over time. In 1955, the wages of black men were about 60% of those of white men; in 2005, they were 75% of those of white men. For black men, the reduction in the wage gap occurred primarily between 1965 and 1973. In contrast, the gap between the wages of black women and white men closed more substantially, and progress in closing the gap continued after 1973, albeit at a slower rate. Specifically, the wages of black women were about 35% of those of white men in 1955, 58% in 1975, and 67% in the 2005. For white women, the pattern of gain is still different. The wages of white women were about 65% of those of white men in 1955, and fell to about 60% from the mid-1960s to the late 1970s. The wages of white females relative to white males did improve, however, over the last 40 years. In 2005, white female wages were 80% of white male wages. While there has been improvement in wage gaps between black men, black women, and white women vis-à-vis white men, a substantial gap still remains. Figure 18.12 shows the wage differences for the period 1969–2006.

FIGURE 18.12 The Wage Gap

The exhibit shows the wages of white women, black women, and black men as a percentage of the wages of white men from 1969–2005. As you can see, the gap has closed considerably, but there remains a substantial gap between the wages of white men and those of other groups in the economy. Part of the difference is a result of discrimination.

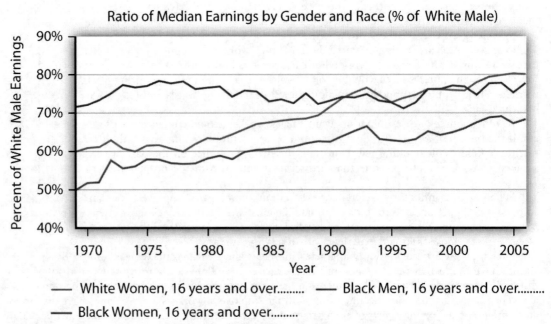

Source: Table 16. Median usual weekly earnings of full-time wage and salary workers, by sex, age, race and Hispanic origin, quarterly average (not seasonally adjusted) and annual averages, 1970–2006. For years after 1979, http://www.bls.gov/cps/wlf-table_16-2007.pdf

One question that economists try to answer is the extent to which the gaps are due to discrimination per se and the extent to which they reflect other factors, such as differences in education, job experience, or choices that individuals in particular groups make about labor-force participation. Once these factors are accounted for, the amount of the remaining wage differential due to discrimination is less than the raw differentials presented in Figure 18.12 would seem to indicate.

There is evidence as well that the wage differential due to discrimination against women and blacks, as measured by empirical studies, has declined over time. For example, a number of studies have concluded that black men in the 1980s and 1990s experienced a 12 to 15% loss in earnings due to labor-market discrimination.[11] University of Chicago economist James Heckman denies that the entire 12% to 15% differential is due to racial discrimination, pointing to problems inherent in measuring and comparing human capital among individuals. Nevertheless, he reports that the earnings loss due to discrimination similarly measured would have been between 30 and 40% in 1940 and still over 20% in 1970.[12]

Can civil rights legislation take credit for the reductions in labor-market discrimination over time? To some extent, yes. A study by Heckman and John J. Donohue III, a law professor at Northwestern University, concluded that the landmark 1964 Civil Rights Act, as well as other civil rights activity leading up to the act, had the greatest positive impact on blacks in the South during the decade following its passage. Evidence of wage gains by black men in other regions of the country was, however, minimal. Most federal activity was directed toward the South, and the civil rights effort shattered an entire way of life that had subjugated black Americans and had separated them from mainstream life.[13]

In recent years, affirmative action programs have been under attack. Proposition 209, passed in California in 1996, and Initiative 200, passed in Washington State in 1998, bar preferential treatment due to race in admission to public colleges and universities in those states. The 1996 Hopwood case against the University of Texas, decided by the United States Court of Appeals for the Fifth Circuit, eliminated the use of race in university admissions, both public and private, in Texas, Louisiana, and Mississippi. Then Supreme Court decisions in 2003 concerning the use of affirmative action at the University of Michigan upheld race conscious admissions, so long as applicants are still considered individually and decisions are based of multiple criteria.

Controversial research by two former Ivy League university presidents, political scientist Derek Bok of Harvard University and economist William G. Bowen of Princeton University, concluded that affirmative action policies have created the backbone of the black middle class and taught white students the value of integration. The study focused on affirmative action at 28 elite colleges and universities. It found that while blacks enter those institutions with lower test scores and grades than those of whites, receive lower grades, and graduate at a lower rate, after graduation blacks earn advanced degrees at rates identical to those of their former white classmates and are more active in civic affairs.[14]

While stricter enforcement of civil rights laws or new programs designed to reduce labor-market discrimination may serve to further improve earnings of groups that have been historically discriminated against, wage gaps between groups also reflect differences in choices and in "premarket" conditions, such as family environment and early education. Some of these premarket conditions may themselves be the result of discrimination.

The narrowing in wage differentials may reflect the dynamics of the Becker model at work. As people's preferences change, or are forced to change due to competitive forces and changes in the legal environment, discrimination against various groups will decrease. However, it may be a long time before discrimination disappears from the labor market, not only due to remaining discriminatory preferences but also because the human capital and work characteristics that people bring to the labor market are decades in the making. The election of Barack Obama as president of the United States in 2008 is certainly a hallmark in the long and continued struggle against discrimination.

KEY TAKEAWAYS

- Discrimination means that people of similar economic characteristics experience unequal economic outcomes as a result of noneconomic factors such as race or sex.
- Discrimination occurs in the marketplace only if employers, employees, or customers have discriminatory preferences and if such preferences are widely shared.
- Competitive markets will tend to reduce discrimination if enough individuals lack such prejudices and take advantage of discrimination practiced by others.
- Government intervention in the form of antidiscrimination laws may have reduced the degree of discrimination in the economy. There is considerable disagreement on this question but wage gaps have declined over time in the United States.

Use a production possibilities curve to illustrate the impact of discrimination on the production of goods and services in the economy. Label the horizontal axis as consumer goods per year. Label the vertical axis as capital goods per year. Label a point A that shows an illustrative bundle of the two which can be produced given the existence of discrimination. Label another point B that lies on the production possibilities curve above and to the right of point A. Use these two points to describe the outcome that might be expected if discrimination were eliminated.

Case in Point: Early Intervention Programs

© 2010 Jupiterimages Corporation

Many authors have pointed out that differences in "pre-market" conditions may drive observed differences in market outcomes for people in different groups. Significant inroads to the reduction of poverty may lie in improving the educational opportunities available to minority children and others living in poverty-level households, but at what point in their lives is the pay-off to intervention the largest? Professor James Heckman, in an op-ed essay in *The Wall Street Journal*, argues that the key to improving student performance and adult competency lies in early intervention in education.

Professor Heckman notes that spending on children after they are already in school has little impact on their later success. Reducing class sizes, for example, does not appear to promote gains in factors such as attending college or earning higher incomes. What does seem to matter is earlier intervention. By the age of eight , differences in learning abilities are essentially fixed. But, early intervention to improve cognitive and especially non-cognitive abilities (the latter include qualities such as perseverance, motivation, and self-restraint) has been shown to produce significant benefits. In an experiment begun several decades ago known as the Perry intervention, four-year-old children from disadvantaged homes were given programs designed to improve their chances for success in school. Evaluations of the program 40 years later found that it had a 15 to 17% rate of return in terms of the higher wages earned by men and women who had participated in the program compared to those from similar backgrounds who did not—the program's benefit-cost ratio was 8 to 1. Professor Heckman argues that even earlier intervention among disadvantaged groups would be desirable—perhaps as early as six months of age.

Economists Rob Grunewald and Art Rolnick of the Federal Reserve Bank of Minneapolis have gone so far as to argue that, because of the high returns to early childhood development programs, which they estimate at 12% per year to the public, state and local governments, can promote more economic development in their areas by supporting early childhood programs than they currently do by offering public subsidies to attract new businesses to their locales or to build new sports stadiums, none of which offers the prospects of such a high rate of return.

Sources: James Heckman, "Catch 'em Young," The Wall Street Journal, January 10, 2006, p. A-14; Rob Grunewald and Art Rolnick, "Early Childhood Development on a Large Scale," Federal Reserve Bank of Minneapolis The Region, June 2005.

ANSWER TO TRY IT! PROBLEM

Discrimination leads to an inefficient allocation of resources and results in production levels that lie inside the production possibilities curve (*PPC*) (point A). If discrimination were eliminated, the economy could increase production to a point on the *PPC*, such as B.

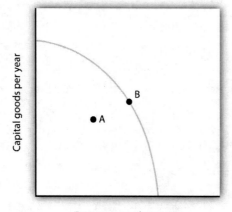

4. REVIEW AND PRACTICE

Summary

In this chapter, we looked at three issues related to the question of fairness: income inequality, poverty, and discrimination.

The distribution of income in the United States has become more unequal in the last four decades. Among the factors contributing to increased inequality have been changes in family structure, technological change, and tax policy. While rising inequality can be a concern, there is a good deal of movement of families up and down the distribution of income, though recently mobility may have decreased somewhat.

Poverty can be measured using an absolute or a relative income standard. The official measure of poverty in the United States relies on an absolute standard. This measure tends to overstate the poverty rate because it does not count noncash welfare aid as income. Poverty is concentrated among female-headed households, minorities, people with relatively little education, and people who are not in the labor force. Children have a particularly high poverty rate.

Welfare reform in 1996 focused on moving people off welfare and into work. It limits the number of years that individuals can receive welfare payments and allows states to design the specific parameters of their own welfare programs. Following the reform, the number of people on welfare fell dramatically. The long-term impact on poverty is still under investigation.

Federal legislation bans discrimination. Affirmative action programs, though controversial, are designed to enhance opportunities for minorities and women. Wage gaps between women and white males and between blacks and white males have declined since the 1950s. For black males, however, most of the reduction occurred between 1965 and 1973. Much of the decrease in wage gaps is due to acquisition of human capital by women and blacks, but some of the decrease also reflects a reduction in discrimination.

CONCEPT PROBLEMS

1. Explain how rising demand for college-educated workers and falling demand for high-school-educated workers contributes to increased inequality of the distribution of income.

2. Discuss the advantages and disadvantages of the following three alternatives for dealing with the rising inequality of wages.

   a. Increase the minimum wage each year so that wages for unskilled workers rise as fast as wages for skilled workers.

   b. Subsidize the wages of unskilled workers.

   c. Do nothing.

3. How would you define poverty? How would you determine whether a particular family is poor? Is the test you have proposed an absolute or a relative test?

4. Why does the failure to adjust the poverty line for regional differences in living costs lead to an understatement of poverty in some states and an overstatement of poverty in others?

5. The text argues that welfare recipients could achieve higher levels of satisfaction if they received cash rather than in-kind aid. Use the same argument to make a case that gifts given at Christmas should be in cash rather than specific items. Why do you suppose they usually are not?

6. Suppose a welfare program provides a basic grant of $10,000 per year to poor families but reduces the grant by $1 for every $1 of income earned. How would such a program affect a household's incentive to work?

7. Welfare reform calls for a two-year limit on welfare payments, after which recipients must go to work. Suppose a recipient with children declines work offers. Should aid be cut? What about the children?

8. How would you tackle the welfare problem? State the goals you would seek, and explain how the measures you propose would work to meet those goals.

9. Suppose a common but unfounded belief held that people with blue eyes were not as smart as people with brown eyes. What would we expect to happen to the relative wages of the two groups? Suppose you were an entrepreneur who knew that the common belief was wrong. What could you do to enhance your profits? Suppose other entrepreneurs acted in the same way. How would the wages of people with blue eyes be affected?

10. The Case in Point on Income Inequality in the United States versus continental Western Europe argues that people get, in effect, what they expect. People in the United States attribute success to hard work and skill, while people in Continental Western Europe attribute success to connections, luck, and corruption. With what set of views do you agree? Explain.

11. The Case in Point on welfare reform in Britain versus that in the United States argues that the British system, before it could be adopted in the United States, would require a change in attitudes in the United States. What sort of change would it require? Do you prefer the British approach? Why or why not?

12. James Heckman of the University of Chicago advocates a program of early intervention targeted at low income families. What are the advantages of such an approach? The disadvantages?

13. Give five reasons that the income distribution in the United States has become more unequal in the last several decades. Do you regard this as a problem for society? Why or why not?

14. Suppose that all welfare aid were converted to programs of cash assistance. Total spending on welfare would remain unchanged. How would this affect the poverty rate? Why?

NUMERICAL PROBLEMS

1. Here are income distribution data for three countries, from the *Human Development Report 2005*, table 15. Note that here we report only four data points rather than the five associated with each quintile. These emphasize the distribution at the extremes of the distribution.

	Poorest 10%	Poorest 20%	Richest 20%	Richest 10%
Panama	0.7	2.4	60.3	43.3
Sweden	3.6	9.1	36.6	22.2
Singapore	1.9	5.0	49.0	32.8

   a. Plot the Lorenz curves for each in a single graph.

   b. Compare the degree of inequality for the three countries. (Do not forget to convert the data to cumulative shares; e.g., the lowest 80% of the population in Panama receives 39.7% of total income.)

   c. Compare your results to the Lorenz curve given in the text for the United States. Which country in your chart appears closest to the United States in terms of its income distribution?

2. Looking at Figure 18.11 suppose the wage that black workers are receiving in a discriminatory environment, W_B, is $25 per hour, while the wage that white workers receive, W, is $30 per hour. Now suppose a regulation is imposed that requires that black workers be paid $30 per hour also.

   a. How does this affect the employment of black workers?

   b. How does this the wages of black workers?

   c. How does this affect their total income? Explain.

3. Suppose the poverty line in the United States was set according to the test required in the European Union: a household is poor if its income is less than 60% of the median household income. Here are annual data for median household income in the United States for the period 1994–2004. The data also give the percentage of the households that fall below 60% of the median household income.

	Median Household Income in the U.S.	Percent of households with income below 60% of median
1994	40,677	30.1
1995	41,943	30.4
1996	42,544	29.9
1997	43,430	29.1
1998	45,003	27.8
1999	46,129	27.1
2000	46,058	26.4
2001	45,062	27.4
2002	44,546	27.8
2003	44,482	28.3
2004	44,389	28.3

Source: U.S Census Bureau, Current Population Reports, P60-229; Income in 2004 CPI-U-RS adjusted dollars; column 3 estimated by authors using Table A-1, p. 31.

a. Plot the data on a graph.

b. Is this a relative or an absolute definition of poverty?

c. Why do you think the percent of households with incomes below 60% of the median fell from 1994 to 2000 and has risen since?

d. Discuss the measurement issues involved in the data you have presented.

e. Discuss the elements of the system of counting the incomes of low income people in the United States and explain how it relates to your answer in (d).

4. Consider the following model of the labor market in the United States. Suppose that the labor market consists of two parts, a market for skilled workers and the market for unskilled workers, with different demand and supply curves for each as given below. The initial wage for skilled workers is $20 per hour; the initial wage for unskilled workers is $7 per hour.

a. Draw the demand and supply curves for the two markets so that they intersect at the wages given above.

b. How does increased demand for skilled workers and a reduced demand for unskilled workers affect the initial solution?

c. How is the Lorenz curve for the United States economy affected by this development? Illustrate the old and the new Lorenz curves.

d. Suppose there is an increase in immigration from Mexico. How will this affect the two markets for labor?

e. Suppose Professor Heckman's recommendation for early intervention for low income children is followed and that it has the impact he predicts. How will this affect the two markets today? In 20 years? Illustrate and explain how the demand and/or supply curves in each market will be affected.

f. What would the impact of the change in (d) be on the Lorenz curve for the United States 20 years from now?

ENDNOTES

1. Gary Burtless, "Inequality Trends: The Facts and Why They Matter," *Cato Unbound Block Archive*, February 20, 2007.

2. The 40 year synthetic earnings estimates (in $millions of 1999 dollars) are: high school dropout, $1.0; high school graduate, $1.2; Bachelors degree, $2.2; Masters degree, $2.5; Doctoral degree, $3.4; Professional degree, $4.4. Jennifer Cheeseman Day and Eric C. Newburger, "The Big Payoff: Education Attainment and Synthetic Estimates of Work-life Earnings," U.S. Census Bureau, *Current Population Reports* (P23-210, July, 2002). Synthetic earnings estimates represent what a typical person with a certain education level could expect to earn over a 40-year worklife.

3. U.S. Census Bureau, Current Population Reports, P60-233, Income, Poverty, and Health Insurance Coverage in the United States: 2006, U.S. Government Printing Office, Washington, D.C.

4. Katharine Bradbury and Jane Katz, "Issues in Economics: Are Lifetime Incomes Growing More Unequal? Looking at New Evidence on Family Income Mobility," *Regional Review* 12:4 (4th Quarter, 2002): 2–5.

5. Robert Rector, "Understanding Poverty and Economic Inequality in the United States," The Heritage Foundation, Policy Research & Analysis, September 15, 2004.

6. Robert Rector, "How Poor Are America's Poor? Examining the "Plague" of Poverty in America," The Heritage Foundation, Policy Research & Analysis, August 27, 2007.

7. Ibid.

8. Students who have studied rent seeking behavior will recognize this argument. It falls within the public choice perspective of public finance theory.

9. For a review of the literature, see Rebecca M. Blank, *It Takes a Nation* (New York: Russell Sage Foundation: 1997).

10. Rebecca M. Blank, "Evaluating Welfare Reform in the United States," *Journal of Economic Literature* 40:4 (December 2002): 1105–66.

11. William A. Darity and Patrick L. Mason, "Evidence on Discrimination in Employment," *Journal of Economic Perspectives* 12:2 (Spring 1998): 63–90.

12. James J. Heckman, "Detecting Discrimination," *Journal of Economic Perspectives* 12:2 (Spring 1998): 101–16.

13. John J. Donohue III and James Heckman, "Continuous Versus Episodic Change: The Impact of Civil Rights Policy on the Economic Status of Blacks," *Journal of Economic Literature* 29 (December 1991): 1603–43.

14. Derek Bok and William G. Bowen, *The Shape of the River: Long-Term Consequences of Considering Race in College and University Admissions* (Princeton, N. J.: Princeton University Press, 1998).

C H A P T E R   1 9
Economic Development

START UP: BEING POOR IN A POOR COUNTRY

You are four years old. You live with your family in the vicinity of Lagos, the capital of Nigeria. You are poor. Very poor.

You and your father, mother, four brothers and sisters, and grandmother live in a shack with a dirt floor. It commands a rather nice view of the Gulf of Guinea to the south, but the amenities end there. Drinking water, which you are learning to help fetch, is badly polluted—so you are sick much of the time. As for sanitation, there is not any in your neighborhood. You are also hungry. You think of the gnawing feeling in your stomach, the slight dizziness you always feel, as normal.

Your newest brother, who was born last month, just died of cholera. Your mother tried to get him to the clinic, but it was closed when your brother needed it. Your father's usual optimism has vanished—he talks of going east to Abuja to find work. He has given up finding a job here.

Your father worked in the peanut fields in the eastern part of the country for several years, but he lost his job. After some very tough years marked by ethnic violence, your family came to the city. You were born shortly after that—you have never known your father to have a regular job. Your mother has had better luck finding work as a maid for some of the wealthy people, with real homes, across town.

You will be old enough to start school next year and are looking forward to that. Your parents say you will be fed there. But if you are like your older brothers and sisters, you will not go to school for more than a couple of years. Your family will need you to earn some money in the streets—begging, running errands, hustling.

You have no reason to think your life will ever get any better. Your own family's fortunes seem to have declined, not risen, all your life.

You cannot know it, but you are not alone. The World Bank estimated that in 2005 about 1.4 billion people, about a quarter of the population of developing countries, were poor, defined as living on less than $1.25 a day, the international poverty line. You are on the poor end even of that group, but there are plenty of others who live pretty much the way you do.

In this chapter, we will take a look at the economies of poor countries. We will see that malnutrition, inadequate health care, high infant mortality, high unemployment, and low levels of education prevail in much of the world. But, we will also see that overall, and especially in some countries, great strides in improving living standards have been made. In 1980, about half of the population of developing countries, or 1.9 billion people, were poor. Poverty reduction in East Asia has been phenomenal, with the poverty rate falling from around 80% to less than 20% over the last 25 years. Declines in the poverty rate, at about 50%, have been minimal in Sub-Saharan Africa over that period.[1]

In 2000, eight Millennium Development Goals were adopted by the international community. They are (1) to eradicate extreme poverty and hunger, (2) to achieve universal primary education, (3) to promote gender equality,

(4) to reduce child mortality, (5) to improve maternal health, (6) to combat HIV/AIDS, malaria, and other diseases, (7) to ensure environmental sustainability, and (8) to develop a global partnership for development.

The United Nations monitors progress on these goals, which have been concretely specified (e.g., between 1990 and 2015, halve the proportion of people whose income is less than $1 a day, reduce the under-five mortality rate by two-thirds, halt and begin to reverse the spread of HIV/AIDS). The United Nations' most recent annual goals report notes that not only have governments been supportive of the goals, but so have many private foundations. As might be expected, it appears that some of the goals will be reached by their target dates, mostly 2015, while other goals are less likely to be achieved. Some that are likely to be achieved are the halving of the absolute poverty rate, the increase in primary school enrollment, reductions in deaths from measles and AIDS, the increase in access to safe drinking water, and the reduction in the use of ozone-depleting substances. Goals that are likely to be missed are reaching the absolute poverty reduction goal in Sub-Saharan Africa, improvements in gender parity and job security, and improvements in conditions in slums.[2]

The challenge of economic development is to find ways to achieve sustained economic growth in poor countries and to improve the living conditions of most of the world's people. It is an enormous task, one often marked by failure. But there have been successes. With those successes have come lessons that can guide us as we face what surely must be the most urgent of global tasks: economic development.

1. THE NATURE AND CHALLENGE OF ECONOMIC DEVELOPMENT

LEARNING OBJECTIVES

1. Define a developing country and discuss how incomes are compared across countries.
2. State and explain the general characteristics of low-income countries.
3. Discuss what is meant by economic development.

Throughout most of history, poverty has been the human condition. For most people life was, in the words of 17th-century English philosopher Thomas Hobbes, "solitary, poor, nasty, brutish, and short." Only within the past 200 years have a handful or so of countries been able to break the chains of economic deprivation and poverty.

Consider these facts:[3]

- Over a third of the world's people live in countries in which total per capita income in 2005 was less than $610 per year; 85% live in countries in which total per capita income in 2005 was $2,808 or less. Adjusting for purchasing power, the per capita income levels would be $2,531 and $7,416, respectively. The latter numbers compare to per capita income in high-income countries of over $30,000.
- Babies born in poor countries are 16 times more likely to die in their first five years than are babies born in rich countries.
- About a quarter of the populations of low-income countries is undernourished.
- About 40% (over 50% for women) of the people 15 years old and older in low-income countries are illiterate.
- Roughly one-fourth of the people in low-income countries do not have access to safe drinking water.

Clearly, the high standards of living enjoyed by people in the world's developed economies are the global exception, not the rule. This chapter looks at the problem of improving the standard of living in poor countries.

1.1 Rich and Poor Nations

The World Bank, an international organization designed to support economic development by providing financial assistance, advice, and other resources to poor countries, classifies over 200 countries according to their levels of per capita gross national income. The categories in its 2008 report, as shown in Table 19.1, were as follows:

- Low-income countries: These countries had per capita incomes of $935 or less in 2007. There were 49 countries in this category. About 20% of the world's total population of about 6.5 billion people lived in low-income nations in 2007.

- Middle-income countries: There were 95 countries with per capita incomes of more than $936 but less than $11,455. Middle-income countries are further subdivided into lower middle-income and upper middle-income countries. Roughly two-thirds of the world's population lived in middle-income countries in 2007. We should note that the percentage of the world's population living in middle-income countries increased dramatically (and the percentage living in low-income countries decreased dramatically) when China and India moved from being low-income to middle-income countries.

- High-income countries: There were 65 nations with per capita incomes of $11,456 or more. Just 16% of the world's total population lived in high-income countries in 2007.

Countries in the low- and middle-income categories are often called developing countries. A **developing country** is thus a country that is not among the high-income nations of the world.[4] Developing countries are sometimes referred to as third-world countries.

How does the World Bank compare incomes across countries? The World Bank converts gross national income (GNI) figures to dollars in two ways. One is to take GNI in a local currency and convert using the exchange rate, averaged over a three-year period in order to smooth out the effects of currency fluctuations. This type of comparison can, however, be misleading. A country could have a relatively high standard of living but, for a variety of reasons, a low exchange rate. The per capita GNI figure would be quite low; the country would appear to be poorer than it is.

A better approach to comparing incomes converts currencies to dollars on the basis of purchasing power. This measure is reported in what are called international dollars. An international dollar has the same purchasing power as does a U.S. dollar in the United States. This is reported in the column labeled "2007 International $" in Table 19.1.

developing country

A country that is not among the high-income nations of the world.

TABLE 19.1 World Incomes, Selected Countries

The table shows the World Bank's 2007 classifications for 30 representative nations selected from among the more than 200 nations in the World Development Report. Nations whose per capita GNI in 2007 was $935 or less were classified as low income, those whose per capita GNI was from $935 to $11,455 were classified as middle income, and nations with higher levels of per capita GNI were classified as high income.

Gross National Income per Capita, 2007								
Low-income countries			Middle-income countries			High-income countries		
Countries	2007 $	2007 International $	Countries	2007 $	2007 International $	Countries	2007 $	2007 International $
Burundi	110	330	India	950	2,740	Czech Republic	14,450	22,020
Sierra Leone	260	660	China	2,360	5,370	Saudi Arabia	15,440	22,910
Mozambique	320	690	Thailand	3,400	7,880	Israel	21,900	25,930
Bangladesh	470	1,340	Iran	3,470	10,800	Greece	29,630	32,330
Haiti	560	1,150	Jamaica	3,710	6,210	Japan	37,670	34,600
Uzbekistan	730	2,430	Costa Rica	5,560	10,700	France	38,500	33,600
Vietnam	790	2,550	Brazil	5,910	9,370	Canada	39,420	35,310
Zambia	800	1,220	Argentina	6,050	12,990	United States	46,040	45,850
Pakistan	870	2,570	Russian Federation	7,560	14,400	Ireland	48,140	37,090
Nigeria	930	1,770	Turkey	8,020	12,350	Norway	76,450	53,320
Average	578	1,494	Average	2,872	5,952	Average	37,566	36,100
			Ave., lower middle	1,887	4,543			
			Ave., upper middle	6,987	11,868			

Source: World Development Indicators database, World Bank, revised October 17, 2008.

The international dollar estimates typically show higher incomes than estimates based on an exchange rate conversion. For example, in 2007 Mozambique's per capita GNI, based on exchange rates, was $320. Its per capita GNI based the international dollars was $690.

Ranking of countries, both rich and poor, by per capita GNI differs depending on the measure used. According to the per capita GNI figures in Table 19.1, which convert data in domestic currencies to dollars using exchange rates, the United States ranked fifteenth of all countries in 2007. Using the international dollars method, its rank is tenth. China is ranked at 132 when per capita GNI is based on the exchange rate conversion method but rises to 122 based on the international dollar method.

1.2 Characteristics of Low-Income Countries

Low incomes are often associated with other characteristics: severe inequality, poor health care and education, high unemployment, heavy reliance on agriculture, and rapid population growth. We will examine most of these problems in this section. Population growth in low-income nations is examined later in the chapter.

Inequality

Not only are incomes in low-income countries quite low; income distribution is often highly unequal. Poverty is far more prevalent than per capita numbers suggest, as illustrated by Lorenz curves, introduced in the chapter on inequality, that show the cumulative shares of income received by individuals or groups.

Consider Costa Rica and Panama, two Latin American countries with roughly equivalent levels of per capita GNI (Costa Rica's was $5,560 and Panama's $5,510 in 2007). Panama's income distribution is comparatively less equal, while Costa Rica's is far more equal. Figure 19.1 compares the 2003 Lorenz curves for Costa Rica and Panama, the most recent year for which the information was available. The 20% of the households with the lowest incomes in Costa Rica had twice as large a share of their country's total income as did the bottom 20% of households in Panama. That means Costa Rica's poor were about twice as well off, in material terms, as Panama's poor.

FIGURE 19.1   Poverty and the Distribution of Income: Costa Rica versus Panama

Costa Rica had about the same per capita GNI as Panama in 2003, but Panama's income distribution was far more unequal. Panama's poor had much lower living standards than Costa Rica's poor, as suggested by the Lorenz curves for the two nations.

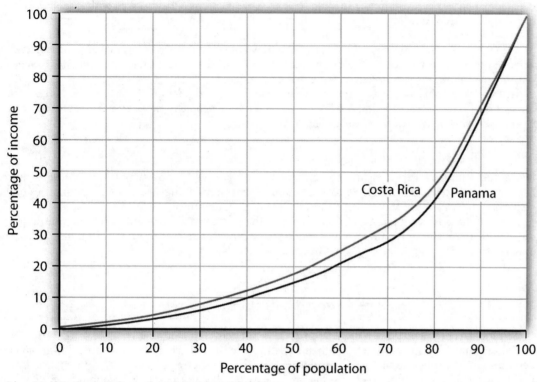

Source: World Development Indicators Online (revised October 17, 2008).

In general, the greater the degree of inequality, the more desperate is the condition of people at the bottom of an income distribution. Given the high degree of inequality in many low-income countries, it is very important to look at income distributions when we compare living standards in different countries.

Health and Education

Poor nations are typically characterized by low levels of human capital. Where health-care facilities are inadequate, that human capital can be reduced further by disease. Where educational resources are poor, there will be little progress in improving human capital.

One indicator of poor health care appears on the supply side. Low-income countries have fewer doctors, relative to their populations, than high-income countries. For example, the UN estimates that in 2006 about 60% of mothers giving birth in developing countries had access to a skilled health-care provider (doctor, nurse, or midwife). While that is up from 47% in 1990, the lack of access to a health-care provider may explain much of the difference in maternal death rates between developed and developing countries: about nine maternal deaths per 100,000 live births in developed countries compared to about 450 per 100,000 in developing countries.[5]

We can also see the results of poor health care in statistics on health. Among the world's developing countries, the infant mortality rate, which reports deaths in the first year of life, was 57 per 1,000 live births in 2005. There were six infant deaths per 1,000 live births among the high-income countries that year.[6]

Another health issue facing the world's low-income countries is malnutrition. Malnutrition rates in all developing countries in the 2002 to 2004 period averaged 17%, 35% in the least developed countries.

Still another issue is the spread of HIV/AIDS. Here there is some progress. The number of people newly infected declined from 3 million in 2001 to 2.7 million in 2005. Antiretroviral treatments are also leading to a reduction in deaths from 2.2 million in 2005 to 2 million in 2007. Longer survival means that the number of people living with HIV (from just under 30 million in 2001 to about 33 million in 2007) is rising and most of the people living with HIV are in Sub-Saharan Africa.[7]

Education in poor and middle-income nations is improving. In 1991, about 80% of children in developing countries were enrolled in primary schools. In 2005, about 85% were. The comparable numbers in developed countries are about 95%. Enrollment rates taper off for high school (about 53% in 2005 in developing countries compared to 91% in developed countries).[8]

Unemployment

Unemployment is pervasive in low-income nations. These nations, already faced with low levels of potential output, are producing well below their potential. Unemployment rates in low-income countries vary widely, reaching as high as 15% or more in some countries. If we count discouraged workers, people who have given up looking for work but who would take it if it were available, and people who work less than full time, not by choice but because more work is unavailable, then unemployment in low-income countries soars—often to more than 30%.

Migration within low-income countries often contributes to unemployment in urban areas. Factors such as ethnic violence, poverty, and drought often force people to move from rural areas to cities, where unemployment rates are already high.

Reliance on Agriculture

One of the dominant characteristics of poor nations is the concentration of employment in agriculture. Another is the very low productivity of that employment. Agriculture in low-income countries often employs a majority of the population but produces less than one-third of GDP.

One of the primary forces behind income growth in wealthy countries has been the shift of labor out of agriculture and into more productive sectors such as manufacturing. This shift is also occurring in low-income nations but has lagged far behind.

The solution to these problems lies in economic development, to which we turn next.

1.3 Economic Development: A Definition

If the problems of low-income nations are pervasive, the development that helps to solve those problems must transform the very nature of their societies. The late Austrian economist Joseph Schumpeter described economic development as a revolutionary process. Whereas economic growth implies quantitative change in production processes that are already familiar to the society, economic development requires qualitative change in virtually every aspect of life.

Robert Heilbroner, an economist at the New School for Social Research in New York, has argued,

> "Economic development is political and social change on a wrenching and tearing scale. … It is a process of institutional birth and institutional death. It is a time when power shifts, often violently and abruptly, a time when old regimes go under and new ones rise in their places. And these are not just the unpleasant side effects of development. They are part and parcel of the process, the very driving force of change itself."[9]

economic development

A process that produces sustained and widely shared gains in per capita real GDP.

Economic development transforms a nation at its core. But what, precisely, is development? Many definitions follow Heilbroner in noting the massive institutional and cultural changes economic development involves. But whatever the requirements of development, its primary characteristics are rising incomes and improving standards of living. That means output must increase—and it must increase relative to population growth. And because inequality is so serious a problem in low-income nations, development must deliver widespread improvement in living conditions. It therefore seems useful to define **economic development** as a process that produces sustained and widely shared gains in per capita real GDP.

In recent years, the United Nations has constructed measures incorporating dimensions of economic development that go beyond the level of per capita GDP. The Human Development Index (HDI) includes three dimensions—life expectancy, educational attainment (adult literacy and combined primary, secondary, and post-secondary enrollment), as well as purchasing-power-adjusted per capita real GDP. The Gender Development Index (GDI) uses the same variables as the HDI but adjusts them downward to take into account the extent of gender inequality. A third index, the Human Poverty Index (HPI), measures human deprivation and includes such indicators as the percentage of people expected to die before age 40, the percentage of underweight children under age 5, the percentage of adults who are illiterate, and the percentage of people who live in poverty. The number reported for the HPI shows the percentage of people in the country who suffer these deprivations.

Table 19.2 shows the HDI, the GDI rank, and the HPI for selected countries, by HDI rank. The HDI is constructed to have an upper limit of 1. Canada's HDI is 0.96; the United States' is 0.95. As the table shows, the HDIs for developing countries range from 0.87 in Argentina to 0.34 in Sierra Leone. The greater the difference between the HDI and the GDI of a country, the greater the disparity in achievement between males and females in the country. Countries can have similar HDIs but different GDIs or HPIs. By looking at a variety of measures, we come closer to examining the extent to which the gains in income growth have been shared or not.

TABLE 19.2 Human Development Index, Gender Development Index, and Human Poverty Index
The Human Development Index and the Gender Development Index are constructed to have an upper limit. The greater the difference between them, the greater the disparity in achievement between males and females in the country. The Human Poverty Index measures the percent of people who suffer various deprivations, such as low life expectancy, illiteracy, and poverty.

HDI rank	Country	Human Development Index (HDI), 2005	Gender-Related Development Index (GDI) 2005, Rank	Human Poverty Index (HPI), % 2005[10]
1	Iceland	0.968	1	NA
2	Norway	0.968	3	6.8
4	Canada	0.961	4	10.9
10	France	0.952	7	11.2
12	United States	0.951	16	15.4
24	Greece	0.926	24	NA
32	Czech Republic	0.891	29	NA
38	Argentina	0.869	36	4.1
48	Costa Rica	0.846	47	4.4
61	Saudi Arabia	0.812	70	NA
67	Russian Federation	0.802	59	NA
70	Brazil	0.8	60	9.7
78	Thailand	0.781	71	10.0
81	China	0.777	73	11.7
84	Turkey	0.775	79	9.2
90	Philippines	0.771	77	15.3
94	Iran	0.759	84	12.9
101	Jamaica	0.736	90	14.3
105	Viet Nam	0.733	91	15.2
114	Mongolia	0.7	100	NA
117	Bolivia	0.695	103	13.6
126	Morocco	0.646	112	33.4
128	India	0.619	113	31.3
135	Ghana	0.553	117	32.3
136	Pakistan	0.551	125	36.2
148	Kenya	0.521	127	30.8
154	Uganda	0.505	132	34.7
156	Senegal	0.499	135	42.9
173	Mali	0.38	151	56.4
177	Sierra Leone	0.336	157	51.7

Source: United Nations Development Program, Human Development Report 2007/2008 (New York: Palgrave Macmillan, 2007).

KEY TAKEAWAYS

- The World Bank classifies countries as being low-income, middle-income, or high-income. More than 80% of the world's people live in low- and middle-income countries.
- Among the problems facing low-income nations are low living standards, inequality, inadequate health care and education, high unemployment, and the concentration of the labor force in low-productivity agricultural work.
- Economic development is a process that generates sustained and widely shared gains in per capita real GDP.

TRY IT!

Provided below is information about two low-income developing countries in Western Africa, Côte d'Ivoire, and Guinea. Use the information to plot their Lorenz curves for consumption, which are similar to Lorenz curves for income distribution, discussed in the chapter on inequality, poverty, and discrimination. Then, based on the material in this section, contrast the concept of economic growth, as discussed in the chapter on that topic, with the concept of economic development, the subject of this chapter. Which of the two countries do you believe fits better the definition of development? Explain.

	Average annual growth rate of GNP (%)	Average annual growth rate of GNP per capita	Percentage Share of Consumption				
			Lowest 20%	Second 20%	Third 20%	Fourth 20%	Highest 20%
Cote d'Ivoire	6.9	4.2	6.8	11.2	15.8	22.2	44.1
Guinea	7.2	4.6	3.0	8.3	14.6	23.9	50.2

Case in Point: (Growth and Development) *or* (Growth or Development)?

The 1971 Nobel laureate in economics, Simon Kuznets, hypothesized that, at low levels of per capita income, increases in income would lead to increases in income inequality. The Kuznets hypothesis was later extended to include concern that early growth might not be associated with improvements in other aspects of development, such as those measured by the HDI or HPI. The rationale for growth pessimism was that the structural changes that often accompany early growth—such as rural–urban migration, occupational changes, and environmental degradation—disproportionately hurt poorer people.

The passage of time and the availability of more information on developing countries' experiences allow us to test whether such pessimism is warranted. The results of a recent study of 95 decade-long episodes of economic growth and decline around the world show that the distribution of income can go either way. Clearly, as the table below shows, with the direction of change in the distribution of income split almost 50-50 during periods of growth, there is no longer any reason to think that growth necessarily increases income inequality. As the table also shows, by a ratio of 7 to 1, the income of the poor usually improves during periods of growth. This means that even when inequality increases, the poor usually gain in absolute terms as income grows.

There were only seven periods of income decline included in the study, but, in general, during those periods the distribution of income grew more unequal and the incomes of the poor fell.

Broad-based measures of development, such as the HDI and the HPI, have not been calculated for a long enough period to allow us to see the trend in these social indicators of development, but we can look at various aspects of human development and poverty over time. As shown in the graphs accompanying this case, there have generally been improvements in the percentage of people with access to safe water, in the adult literacy rate, and in the percentage of underweight children under age 5. On this last indicator, the improvement in Sub-Saharan Africa is very small, but keep in mind that the rate of growth of real GNP per capita in this region has been just over 1% per year.

There is no guarantee that economic growth will improve the plight of the world's poor—there is indeed wide variation in individual countries' experiences. In general, though, economic growth makes most people, including most poor people, better off. As former World Bank Senior Vice President and Chief Economist Joseph Stiglitz put it, "Aggregate economic growth benefits most of the people most of the time; and it is usually associated with progress in other, social dimensions of development."

	Periods of growth (88)		Periods of decline (7)	
Indicator	Improved	Worsened	Improved	Worsened
Inequality	45	43	2	5
Income of the poor	77	11	2	5

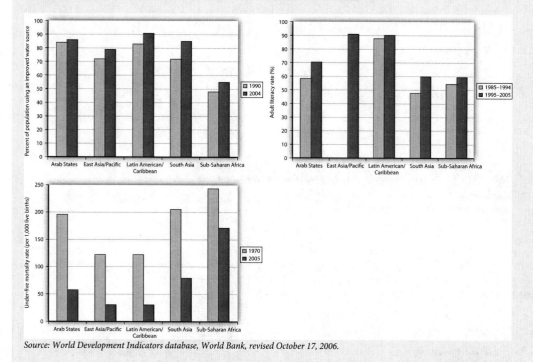

Source: World Development Indicators database, World Bank, revised October 17, 2006.

Sources: *United Nations, Human Development Report, 1997 (New York: Oxford University Press, 1997), 72, 224; Human Development Report, 1998 (New York: Oxford University Press, 1998), 206; Joseph Stiglitz, "International Development: Is It Possible?" Foreign Policy 110 (Spring 1998): 138–51.*

Economic growth refers to the process of increasing a country's potential output. Graphically, this can be represented by rightward shifts in the long-run aggregate supply curve or by the shifting outward of the production possibilities curve. The challenge of economic development, however, is for countries to move toward their level of potential output and to achieve widely shared gains in GDP per capita. This process usually involves widespread structural changes in the way people live—their standards of living, the kinds of jobs they have, their health, and so forth. When comparing Côte d'Ivoire and Guinea, for example, it is clear that the distribution of consumption is much more equal in the former. This implies that Côte d'Ivoire is coming closer to generating widely shared gains in per capita real GDP.

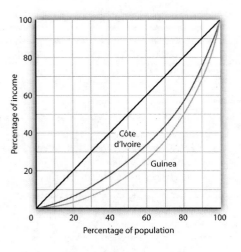

2. POPULATION GROWTH AND ECONOMIC DEVELOPMENT

L E A R N I N G   O B J E C T I V E S

1. **Explain the relationship between population growth and the rate of increase in per capita income.**
2. **Summarize Thomas Malthus's reasoning that led to the concept of a Malthusian trap, and explain why his dire predictions have not occurred in many countries in modern times.**
3. **Explain what is meant by a demographic transition, and describe how it has proceeded in very different ways in developed versus developing countries.**

It is easy to see why some people have become alarmists when it comes to population growth rates in developing nations. Looking at the world's low-income countries, they see a population of more than 2 billion growing at a rate that suggests a doubling every 31 years. How will we cope with so many more people? The following statement captures the essence of widely expressed concerns:

> *"At the end of each day, the world now has over two hundred thousand more mouths to feed than it had the day before; at the end of each week, one and one-half million more; at the close of each year, an additional eighty million. … Humankind, now doubling its numbers every thirty-five years, has fallen into an ambush of its own making; economists call it the "Malthusian trap," after the man who most forcefully stated our biological predicament: population growth tends to outstrip the supply of food."[11]*

But what are we to make of such a statement? Certainly, if the world's population continues to increase at the rate that it grew in the past 50 years, economic growth is less likely to be translated into an improvement in the average standard of living. But the rate of population growth is not a constant; it is affected by other economic forces. This section begins with a discussion of the relationship between population growth and income growth, then turns to an explanation of the sources of population growth in low-income countries, and closes with a discussion of the Malthusian warning suggested in the quote above.

2.1 Population Growth and Income Growth

On a simplistic level, the relationship between growth in population and growth in per capita income is clear. After all, per capita income equals total income divided by population. The growth rate of per capita income roughly equals the difference between the growth rate of income and the growth rate of population. Kenya's annual growth rate in real GDP from 1975 to 2005, for example, was 3.3%. Its population growth rate during that period was 3.2%, leaving it a growth rate of per capita GDP of just 0.1%. A slower rate of population growth, together with the same rate of GDP increase, would have left Kenya with more impressive gains in per capita income. The implication is that if the developing countries want to increase their rate of growth of per capita GDP relative to the developed nations, they must limit their population growth.

Figure 19.5 plots growth rates in population versus growth rates in per capita GDP from 1975 to 2005 for more than 100 developing countries. We do not see a simple relationship. Many countries experienced both rapid population growth and negative changes in real per capita GDP. But still others had relatively rapid population growth, yet they had a rapid increase in per capita GDP. Clearly, there is more to achieving gains in per capita income than a simple slowing in population growth. But the challenge raised at the beginning of this section remains: Can the world continue to feed a population that is growing exponentially—that is, doubling over fixed intervals?

FIGURE 19.5 Population and Income Growth, 1975–2005

A scatter chart of population growth rates versus GNP per capita growth rates for various developing countries for the period 1975–2005 suggests no systematic relationship between the rates of population and of income growth.

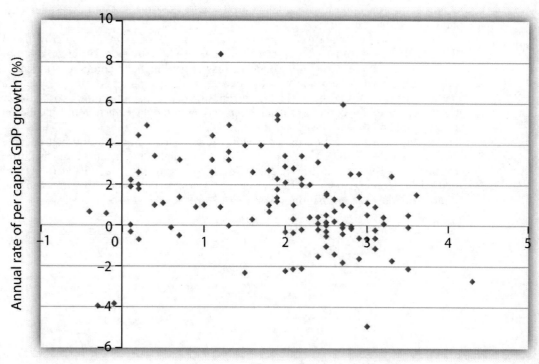

Annual rate of population growth (%)

Source: *United Nations Development Program, Human Development Report 2007/2008 (New York: Palgrave Macmillan, 2007).*

2.2 The Malthusian Trap and the Demographic Transition

In 1798, Thomas Robert Malthus published his *Essay on the Principle of Population*. It proved to be one of the most enduring works of the time. Malthus's fundamental argument was that population growth will inevitably collide with diminishing returns.

Malthusian trap

A point at which the world is no longer able to meet the food requirements of the population, and starvation becomes the primary check to population growth.

Diminishing returns imply that adding more labor to a fixed quantity of land increases output, but by ever smaller amounts. Eventually, Malthus concluded, increases in food production would be too small to sustain the increased number of human beings who consume that output. As the population continued to grow unchecked, the number of people would eventually outstrip the ability of the land to generate enough food. There would be an inevitable **Malthusian trap**, a point at which the world is no longer able to meet the food requirements of the population, and starvation becomes the primary check to population growth.

A Malthusian trap is illustrated in Figure 19.6. We can determine the total amount of food needed by multiplying the population in any period by the amount of food required to keep one person alive. Because population grows exponentially, food requirements rise at an increasing rate, as shown by the curve labeled "Food required." Food produced, according to Malthus, rises by a constant amount each period; its increase is shown by an upward-sloping straight line labeled "Food produced." Food required eventually exceeds food produced, and the Malthusian trap is reached at time t_1. The faster the rate of population growth, the sooner t_1 is reached.

What happens at the Malthusian trap? Clearly, there is not enough food to support the population growth implied by the "Food required" curve. Instead, people starve, and population begins rising arithmetically, held in check by the "Food produced" curve. Starvation becomes the limiting force for population; the population lives at the margin of subsistence. For Malthus, the long-run fate of human beings was a standard of living barely sufficient to keep them alive. As he put it, "the view has a melancholy hue."

Happily, Malthus's predictions do not match the experience of Western societies in the 19th and 20th centuries. One weakness of his argument is that he failed to take into account the gains in output that could be achieved through increased use of physical capital and new technologies in agriculture. Increases in the amount of capital per worker in the form of machines, improved seed, irrigation, and fertilization have made possible huge increases in agricultural output at the same time as the supply of labor was rising. Agricultural productivity rose rapidly in the United States over the last two centuries, just the opposite of the fall in productivity expected by Malthus. Productivity has continued to expand.

Malthus was wrong as well about the relationship between population growth and income. He believed that any increase in income would boost population growth. But the law of demand tells us that the opposite may be true: higher incomes tend to reduce population growth. The primary cost of having children is the opportunity cost of the parents' time in raising them—higher incomes increase this opportunity cost. Higher incomes increase the cost of having children and tend to reduce the number of children people want and thus to slow population growth.

Panel (a) of Figure 19.7 shows the birth rates of low-, middle-, and high-income countries for the period 2000–2005. We see that the higher the income level, the lower the birth rate. Fewer births translate into slower population growth. In Panel (b), we see that high-income nations had much slower rates of population growth than did middle- and low-income nations over the last 30 years.

FIGURE 19.6 The Malthusian Trap

If population grows at a fixed exponential rate, the amount of food required will increase exponentially. But Malthus held that the output of food could increase only by a constant amount each period. Given these two different growth processes, food requirements would eventually catch up with food production. The population hits the subsistence level of food production at the Malthusian trap, shown here at point T.

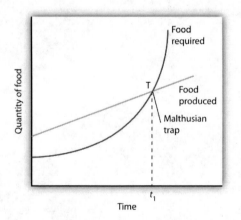

FIGURE 19.7   Income Levels and Population Growth

Panel (a) shows that low-income nations had much higher total fertility rates (births per woman) during the 2000–2005 period than did high-income nations. In Panel (b), we see that low-income nations had a much higher rate of population growth during the 1975–2005 period.

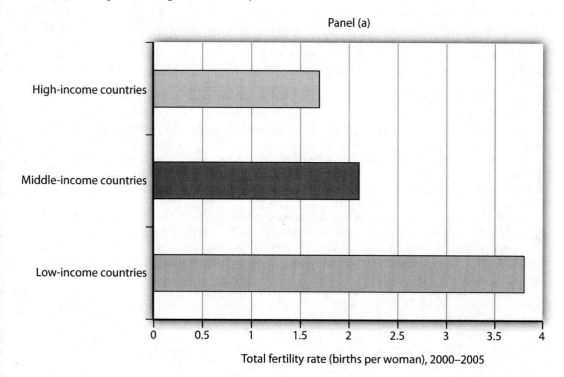

Total fertility rate (births per woman), 2000–2005

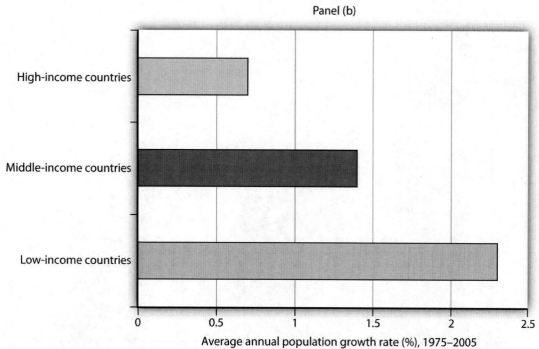

Average annual population growth rate (%), 1975–2005

Source: *World Development Indicators database, World Bank, revised October 17, 2008.*

An increase in a nation's income can be expected to slow its rate of population growth. Hong Kong, for example, has enjoyed dramatic gains in income since the 1960s. Its birth rate and rate of population growth have fallen by over half during that time.

demographic transition

Situation in which population growth rises with a fall in death rates and then falls with a reduction in birth rates.

But if economic development can slow population growth, it can also increase it. One of the first gains a developing nation can achieve is improvements in such basics as the provision of clean drinking water, improved sanitation, and public health measures such as vaccination against childhood diseases. Such gains can dramatically reduce disease and death rates. As desirable as such gains are, they also boost the rate of population growth. Nations are likely to enjoy sharp reductions in death rates before they achieve gains in per capita income. That can accelerate population growth early in the development process. Demographers have identified a process of **demographic transition** in which population growth rises with a fall in death rates and then falls with a reduction in birth rates.

The process of demographic transition has unfolded in a strikingly different manner in developed versus less developed nations over the past two centuries. In 1800, birth rates barely exceeded death rates in both developed and less developed countries. The result was a rate of population growth of only about 0.5% per year worldwide. By 1900, the death rate in developed nations had fallen by about 25%, with little change in the birth rate. Among developing nations, the birth rate was unchanged, while the death rate was down only slightly. The combined result was a modest increase in the rate of world population growth.

Changes were much more rapid in the 20th century. By 1965, the death rate among developed nations had plunged to about one-quarter of its 1800 level, while the birth rate had fallen by half. In developing nations, death rates took a similarly dramatic drop, while birth rates showed little change. The result was dramatic world population growth.

The world's high-income economies have completed the demographic transition. Less developed nations have begun to make progress, with birth rates falling by a slightly greater percentage than death rates. The results have been a sharp slowing in the rate of population growth among high-income nations and a more modest slowing among low-income nations. Continued slowing in population growth at all income levels is suggested in Figure 19.8.

Between 1965 and 1980, the world population grew at an annual rate of 2%, suggesting a doubling time of 36 years. For the world as a whole, it is predicted that population growth will slow to a 1.1% rate during the 2005–2015 period, a rate that would imply a doubling time of 65 years.

FIGURE 19.8 The Demographic Transition at Work: Actual and Projected Population Growth

Population growth has slowed considerably in the past several decades.

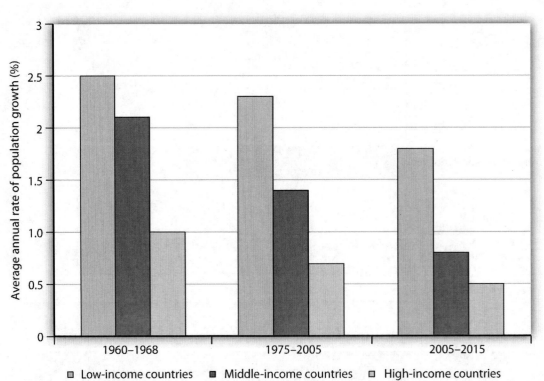

Source: United Nations Development Program, Human Development Report 2007/2008 (New York: Palgrave Macmillan, 2007) for periods 1975–2000 and 2005–2015, United Nations Development Program, Human Development Report 1990 (New York, Oxford: Oxford University Press, 1990) for the 1960–1988 period, in which categories refer to low, middle, and high human development rankings.

KEY TAKEAWAYS

- The rate of increase in per capita income roughly equals the rate of increase in income minus the rate of increase in population. High rates of population growth do not necessarily imply low rates of growth in per capita income.
- Malthus's prediction of a world in which production would be barely sufficient to keep people alive has proven incorrect because of gains generated by increased physical and human capital, advances in technology, and the tendency of higher incomes to slow population growth.
- A demographic transition is achieved when rising incomes begin to reduce birth rates and bring population growth in check.

TRY IT!

The text gives two main reasons why the Malthusian trap did not occur: (1) increased use of physical capital and human capital and technological improvements in agriculture and (2) higher income leading to fewer children. How do these two reasons alter Figure 19.6?

Case in Point: China Curtails Population Growth

China is an example of a country that has achieved a very low rate of population growth and a very high rate of growth in per capita GNP.

China's low rate of population growth represents a dramatic shift. As recently as the early 1970s, China had a relatively high rate of population growth; its population expanded at an annual rate of 2.7% from 1965 to 1973. By the 1980s, that rate had plunged to 1.5%. The World Bank reports a growth rate in China's population of about 1% in the early part of the 21st century.

This dramatic drop in the population growth rate was brought about by a strict government policy by which couples are allowed to have only one child. Disincentives have been known to include fines, loss of employment, confiscation of property, demolition of homes, forced abortions, and sterilization. While the Chinese government has denied that forced abortions and sterilizations are part of its strategy, policies are administered locally, and all of the above means of coercion seem to have been employed at one time or another. If a woman who already has one child becomes pregnant, she will most likely be forced to have an abortion.

Although the policy has achieved its desired result—reduced population growth—it has had some horrible side effects. Given a strong cultural tradition favoring having a son, some couples resort to infanticide as a means of eliminating newborn daughters. When the sex of an unborn baby is determined to be female, abortion is common.

The coercive aspects of China's policies and their undesirable side effects have been condemned by many governments around the world, as well as by nongovernmental organizations. Declarations from United Nations' conferences—the UN Conference on Population in Cairo in 1994 and the UN Conference on Women in Beijing in 1995—have emphasized that birth rates are linked to the economic conditions of women and that improving health, education, and employment opportunities for women constitutes a better and more humane way of reducing birth rates. Fearful that pro-democracy and human rights activists from other countries might stir up those movements locally, the Chinese government actually designed the 1995 Beijing Conference so as to minimize contact between Chinese and foreigners.

There are signs, though, that Chinese officials may have heard the message. In a number of counties in China, experimental programs with slogans such as "Carry out Contraception and Family Planning Measures Voluntarily" are underway. The new approach to family planning emphasizes health care, education, and reduction in poverty to encourage women to have fewer children.

International pressures may only be part of the reason for the emerging Chinese change of heart. In the late 1980s, Chinese officials discovered that the number of births in China was being underreported by about 30%. The aggressive policies may not have been as successful as they were cracked up to be.

ANSWER TO TRY IT! PROBLEM

The first reason raises the curve labeled "Food produced" and suggests that it is exponential rather than linear. The second reason lowers the curve labeled "Food required." The result is that the time t_1, when the amount of food required exceeds the amount produced, is pushed further into the future, perhaps indefinitely if the "Food produced" stays above the "Food required" curve. The latter seems to have been the experience of today's rich countries.

3. KEYS TO ECONOMIC DEVELOPMENT

LEARNING OBJECTIVES

1. List and discuss domestic policies that contribute to economic growth.
2. State the dependency theory view of trade and developing nations, relate this theory to the strategy of import substitution, and evaluate that strategy.
3. Outline some of the factors underlying the successes of newly industrialized countries.

What are the keys to economic development? Clearly, each nation's experience is unique; we cannot isolate the sources of development success in the laboratory. We can, however, identify some factors that appear to have played an important role in successful economic development. We will look separately at policies that relate to the domestic economy and at policies in international trade.

3.1 Domestic Policy and Economic Development

What domestic policies contribute to development? Looking at successful economies, those that have achieved high and sustained increases in per capita output, we can see some clear tendencies. They include a market economy, a high saving rate, and investment in infrastructure and in human capital.

Market Economies and Development

There can be no clearer lesson than that a market-oriented economy is a necessary condition for economic development. We saw in the chapter that introduced the production possibilities model that economic systems can be categorized as market capitalist, command socialist, or as mixed economic systems. There are no examples of development success among command socialist systems, although some people still believe that the former Soviet Union experienced some development advances in its early years.

One of the most dramatic examples is provided by China. Its shift in the late 1970s to a more market-based economy has ushered in a period of phenomenal growth. China, which has shifted from a command socialist to what could most nearly be categorized as a mixed economy, has been among the fastest-growing economies in the world for the past 20 years. Its growth has catapulted China from being one of the world's poorest countries a few decades ago to being a middle-income country today.

The experience of other economies reinforces the general observation that markets matter. South Korea, Hong Kong, Taiwan, Singapore, and Chile—all have achieved gigantic gains with a market-based approach to economic growth.

We should not conclude, however, that growth has been independent of any public sector activity. China, for example, remains a nominally socialist state; its government continues to play a major role. The governments of South Korea, Taiwan, and Singapore all targeted specific sectors for growth and provided government help to those sectors. Even Hong Kong, which became part of China in 1997, has a high degree of government involvement in the provision of housing, health care, and education. A market economy is not a nongovernment economy. But those countries that have left the task of resource allocation primarily to the market have achieved dramatic gains. Hong Kong and Singapore, in fact, are now included in the World Bank's list of high-income economies.

The Rule of Law and Development

If a market is to thrive, individuals must be secure in their property. If crime or government corruption makes it likely that individuals will regularly be subjected to a loss of property, then exchange will be difficult and little investment will occur. Also, the rule of law is necessary for contracts; that is, the rule of law is necessary to provide an institutional framework within which an economy can operate.

We will see in the chapter on socialist economies in transition, for example, that Russia's effort to achieve economic development through the adoption of a market economy has been hampered by widespread lawlessness. An important difficulty of economies with extensive regulation is that the power they grant to government officials inevitably results in widespread corruption that saps entrepreneurial effort and economic growth.

Investment and Saving

Saving is a key to growth and the achievement of high incomes. All other things equal, higher saving allows more resources to be devoted to increases in physical and human capital and to technological improvement. In other words, saving, which is income not spent on consumption, promotes economic growth by making available resources that can be channeled into growth-enhancing uses.

High saving rates generally accompany high levels of investment. The productivity of this investment, however, can be quite variable. Government efforts to invest in human capital by promoting education, for example, may or may not be successful in actually achieving education. Development projects sponsored by international relief agencies may or may not foster development.

However, investment in infrastructure, such as transportation and communication, clearly plays an important role in economic development. Investment in improved infrastructure facilitates the exchange of goods and services and thus fosters development.

3.2 International Economic Issues in Development

In 1974, the poorest nations among the developing nations introduced into the United Nations a Declaration on the Establishment of a New International Economic Order. The program called upon the rich nations to help them reduce the growing gap in real per capita income levels between the developed and developing nations. The declaration has come to be known as the New International Economic Order or NIEO for short.

NIEO called for different and special treatment of the developing nations in the international arena in areas such as trade policy and control over multinational corporations. NIEO reflected a widely held view of international relations known as dependency theory.

Dependency Theory and Trade Policy

Conventional economic theory concerning international trade is based on the idea of comparative advantage. As we have seen in other chapters, the principle of comparative advantage suggests that free trade between two countries will benefit both and, in general, the freer the trade the better. But some economists have proposed a doctrine that challenges this idea. **Dependency theory** concludes that poverty in developing nations is the result of their dependence on high-income nations.

dependency theory

The idea that poverty in developing nations is the result of their dependence on high-income nations.

Dependency theory holds that the industrialized nations control the destiny of the developing nations, particularly in terms of being the ultimate markets for their exports, serving as the source of capital required for development, and controlling the relative prices and exchange rates at which market transactions occur. In addition, export industries in a developing nation are assumed to have small multiplier effects throughout the rest of the economy, severely limiting any positive role than an expanded export sector might play. Specifically, limited transportation, a poorly developed financial sector, and an uneducated work force stand in the way of "multiplying" any positive effects of export expansion. A poor country thus may not experience the kind of development and growth enjoyed by the rich country pursuing free trade. Also, increased trade makes the poor country more dependent on the rich country and its export service firms. In short, the benefits of trade between a rich country and a poor country will go almost entirely to the rich country.

The development strategy that this line of argument suggests is that developing countries would need to become independent of the already developed nations in order to achieve economic development. In relative terms, free trade would leave the poor country poorer and the rich country richer.

Some dependency theorists even argued that trade is likely to make poor countries poorer in absolute terms.

Tanzania's president, Julius Nyerere, speaking before the United Nations in 1975, put it bluntly, "I am poor because you are rich."

Import Substitution Strategies and Export-Led Development

If free trade widens the gap between rich and poor nations and makes poor nations poorer, it follows that a poor country should avoid free trade. Many developing countries, particularly in Latin America, attempted to overcome the implications of dependency theory by adopting a strategy of **import substitution**, a strategy of blocking most imports and substituting domestic production of those goods.

The import substitution strategy calls for rapidly increasing industrialization by mimicking the already industrialized nations. The intent is to reduce the dependence of the developing country on imports of consumer and capital goods from the industrialized countries by manufacturing these goods at home. But in order to protect these relatively high-cost industries at home, the developing country must establish very high protective tariffs. Moreover, the types of industries that produce the previously imported consumer goods and capital goods are unlikely to increase the demand for unskilled labor. Yet unskilled labor is the most abundant resource in the poor countries. Adopting the import substitution strategy raises the demand for expensive capital, managerial talent, and skilled labor—resources in short supply.

High tariffs insulate domestic firms from competition, but that tends to increase their monopoly power. Recognizing that some imported goods, particularly spare parts for industrial equipment, will be needed, countries can establish complex permit systems through which firms can import vital parts and other equipment. But that leaves a company's fortunes in the hands of the government bureaucrats issuing the permits. A highly corrupt system quickly evolves in which a few firms bribe their way to easy access to foreign markets, reducing competition still further. Instead of the jobs expected to result from import substitution, countries implementing the import substitution strategy get the high prices, reduced production, and poor quality that come from reduced competition.

No country that has relied on a general strategy of import substitution has been successful in its development efforts. It is an idea whose time has not come. In contrast, more successful economies in Asia and elsewhere have kept their economies fairly open to both imports and exports. They have shown the greatest ability to move the development process along.

Development and International Financial Markets

Successful development in the developing nations requires more than just redirecting labor and capital resources into newly emerging sectors of the economy. That could be accomplished by both domestic firms and international firms located within the economy. But to complement the reorientation of traditional production processes, economic infrastructure such as roads, schools, communication facilities, ports, warehouses, and many other prerequisites to growth must be put into place. Paying for the projects requires a high level of saving.

The sources of saving are private saving, government saving, and foreign saving. Grants in the form of foreign aid from the developed nations supplement these sources, but they form a relatively small part of the total.

Private domestic saving is an important source of funds. But even high rates of private saving cannot guarantee sufficient funds in a poor economy, where the bulk of the population lives close to the subsistence level. Government saving in the form of tax revenues in excess of government expenditures is almost universally negative. If the required investments are to take place, the developing nations have to borrow the money from foreign savers.

The problem for developing nations borrowing funds from foreigners is the same potential difficulty any borrower faces: the debt can be difficult to repay. Unlike, say, the national debt of the United States government, whose obligations are in its own currency, developing nations typically commit to make loan payments in the currency of the lending institution. Money borrowed by Brazil from a U.S. bank, for example, must generally be paid back in U.S. dollars.

Many developing nations borrowed heavily during the 1970s, only to find themselves in trouble in the 1980s. Countries such as Brazil suspended payments on their debt when required payments exceeded net exports. Much foreign debt was simply written off as bad debt by lending institutions. While foreign debts created a major crisis in the 1980s, subsequent growth appeared to make these payments more manageable.

A somewhat different international financial crisis emerged in the late 1990s. It started in Thailand in the summer of 1997. Thailand had experienced 20 years of impressive economic growth and rising living standards. One element of its development strategy was to maintain a fixed exchange rate between its currency, the baht, and the dollar. The slowing of Japanese growth, which reduced demand for Thai exports, and weaknesses in the Thai banking sector were putting downward pressure on the baht, which Thailand's central bank initially tried to counteract. As discussed there, this effort was abandoned, and the value of the currency declined.

The Thai government, in an effort to keep its exchange rate somewhat stable, appealed to the International Monetary Fund (IMF) for support. The IMF is an international agency that makes financial assistance available to member countries experiencing problems in their international balance of payments in order to support adjustment and reform in those countries. In an agreement between Thailand and the IMF, Thailand's central bank tightened monetary policy, thereby raising interest rates there. The logic behind this move was that higher interest rates in Thailand would make the baht more attractive to both Thai and foreign financial investors, who could thus earn more on Thai bonds and on other Thai financial assets. This would increase the demand for baht and help to keep the currency from falling further. Thailand also agreed to tighten fiscal policy, the rationale for which was to prepare for the anticipated future costs of restructuring its banking system. As we have learned throughout macroeconomics, however, contractionary monetary and fiscal policies will reduce real GDP in the short run. The hope was that growth would resume once the immediate currency crisis was over and plans had been put into place for correcting other imbalances in the Thai economy.

Other countries, such as South Korea and Brazil, soon experienced similar currency disturbances and entered into similar IMF programs to put their domestic houses in order in exchange for financial assistance from the IMF. For some of the other countries that went through similar experiences, notably Indonesia and Malaysia, the situation in 1999 was very unstable. Malaysia decided to forgo IMF assistance and to impose massive currency controls. In Indonesia, the financial crisis and the ensuing economic crisis led to political unrest. It held its first free elections in June 1999, but violence erupted in late 1999, when the overwhelming majority of people in East Timor voted against an Indonesian proposal that the province have limited autonomy within Indonesia and voted for independence from Indonesia.

Remarkably, in the early 2000s, the economies of most of these countries rebounded, though they are now caught up in the global economic downturn.

3.3 Development Successes

As we have seen throughout this chapter, the greatest success stories are found among the newly industrializing economies (NIEs) in East Asia. These economies, including Hong Kong, South Korea, Singapore, and Taiwan, share two common traits. First, they have allowed their economies to develop through an emphasis on export-based, market capitalist strategies. The NIEs achieved higher per capita income and output by entering and competing in the global market for products such as computers, automobiles, plastics, chemicals, steel, shipbuilding, and sporting goods. These countries have succeeded largely by linking standardized production technologies with low-cost labor.

Second, the role of government was relatively limited in the NIEs, which made less use of regulation and bureaucratic controls. Governments were clearly involved in some strategic industries, and, in the wake of recent financial crises, in some cases it appears that this involvement led to some decisions in those industries being made on political rather than on economic grounds. But the principal contribution of governments in the Far Eastern NIEs has been to create a modern infrastructure (especially up-to-date communications facilities essential for the development of a strong financial sector), to provide a stable incentive system (including stable exchange rates), and to ensure that government bureaucracy will help rather than hinder exports (especially by not regulating export trade, labor markets, and capital markets).[12]

Chile adopted sweeping market reforms in the late 1970s, creating the freest economy in Latin America. Chile's growth has accelerated sharply, and the country has moved to the upper-middle-income group of nations. Perhaps more dramatic, the dictator who instituted market reforms, General Augusto Pinochet, agreed to democratic elections that removed him from power in 1989. Chile now has a greatly increased degree of political as well as economic freedom—and has emerged as the most prosperous country in Latin America.

Over the last decade, Mexico also shifted from a strategy of import substitution and began to follow more free-trade-oriented policies. The North American Free Trade Agreement (NAFTA) turned all of North America into a free trade zone. This could not have occurred had Mexico not undergone such a dramatic shift in its development strategy. Mexico's commitment to the new strategy was tested in 1994, when the country underwent a currency crisis, similar to that experienced in many Asian countries in 1997 and 1998. At that time, Mexico, too, entered into an agreement with the IMF to address economic imbalances in return for financial assistance. The U.S. government also provided support to help Mexico at that time. By 1996, the Mexican economy was growing again, and Mexican commitment to more open policies has endured. Only with the passage of time will we know for sure whether the changed strategy worked in Mexico as well, but the early signs are that it is working.

Although the trend in developing countries toward market reforms has been less heralded than the collapse of communism, it is surely significant. Will market reforms translate into development success? The jury is still out. Market reform requires that many wealthy—and powerful—interests be swept aside. Whether that can be achieved, and whether poor people who lack human capital can be included in the development effort, remain open questions. But some dramatic success stories have shown that economic development can be achieved. The fate of billions of desperately poor people rests in the ability of their countries to match that success.

KEY TAKEAWAYS

- A market economy, perhaps with a substantial role for government, appears to be one key to economic growth. A system in which laws and property rights are well established and enforced also promotes growth.
- High rates of saving and investment can boost economic growth.
- Dependency theory suggests that poor countries should seek to insulate themselves from international trade. The import substitution strategies suggested by dependency theory have not been successful in generating economic growth, and a number of countries have moved away from this strategy.

Case in Point: Democracy and Economic Development

Democracy as an economic institution has typically received mixed notices from economists. While virtually all the world's rich nations have democratic systems of government, it isn't clear that democracy is necessary for development.

India long provided the strongest counterexample to the idea that democracy promotes development. It has long been a democracy, yet its per capita income has kept it among the world's poor countries. India's government has traditionally opted for extensive regulation that has curtailed development. Countries such as China, with no democracy and a repressive government, have managed to generate very high rates of economic growth. China's per capita income now exceeds that of India by about 50%. Lee Kuan Yew, Singapore's former prime minister, put it this way: "I believe what a country needs to develop is discipline more than democracy. The exuberance of democracy leads to indiscipline and disorderly conduct which are inimical to development."

Many economists have reached the conclusion that countries are likely to become democratic once they achieve a high degree of economic development. Political freedom, they argue, is a normal good. The demand for freedom thus increases as incomes rise, making the creation of democratic institutions a product of economic growth, not a cause of it.

Two recent studies—one by economists John Mukum Mbaku and Mwangi S. Kimenyi and the other by economists Michael A. Nelson and Ram D. Singh—challenge the conventional view, arguing instead that democracy and economic growth are compatible. Using statistical models that control for a variety of factors that affect economic growth, such as investment and population growth, both studies concluded that there is a positive relationship between political freedom and economic growth. In the latter study, the authors separately tested the direction of causality: does growth cause democracy or does democracy cause growth? They conclude that the direction of causality goes from democracy to economic growth. They also controlled for the level of economic freedom (an index of price stability, government size, discriminatory taxation, and trade restrictions), which many studies have concluded is critical for development. As argued in this chapter, more economic freedom does lead to higher economic growth, but so does more political freedom.

Just as pessimism that economic growth has a negative impact on the poor is dissipating, likewise the notion that developing countries must wait until they are developed in order for their citizens to experience political freedom is also falling by the wayside.

Sources: Jagdish Bhagwati, "Democracy and Development," American Enterprise 6, no. 2 (March/April 1995): 69; John Mukum Mbaku and Mwangi S. Kimenyi, "Macroeconomic Determinants of Growth: Further Evidence on the Role of Political Freedom," Journal of Economic Development 22, no. 2 (December 1997): 119–32; Michael A. Nelson and Ram D. Singh, "Democracy, Economic Freedom, Fiscal Policy, and Growth in LDC: A Fresh Look," Economic Development and Cultural Change 64, no. 4 (July 1998): 677–96.

4. REVIEW AND PRACTICE

Summary

Developing nations face a host of problems: low incomes; unequal distributions of income; inadequate health care and education; high unemployment; and a concentration of workers in agriculture, where productivity is low. Economic development, the process that generates widely shared gains in income, can alleviate these problems.

The sources of economic growth in developing countries are not substantially different from those that apply to the developed countries. Market economies with legal systems that provide for the reliable protection of property rights and enforcement of contracts tend to promote economic growth. Saving and investment, particularly investment in appropriate technologies and human capital, appear to be critical. So, too, does the ability of developing nations to match their population growth rate with the ability of the economy to increase real output.

Dependency theory, the notion that developing countries are in the grip of the industrialized countries, led to import substitution schemes that proved detrimental to the long-run growth prospects of developing nations. The movement of Latin American countries such as Mexico and Chile to market systems is a rejection of dependency theory. There is a general movement toward market-based strategies to support economic development in the future. But even market-based strategies will work only if efforts are made to ensure an adequate infrastructure, including the development of financial institutions capable of providing the required signals to guide individual decision making.

CONCEPT PROBLEMS

1. What is the difference between economic development and economic growth?
2. Look at the Case in Point on the relationship between growth and development. Why do you think that the distribution of income is more likely to become more unequal during economic downturns?
3. What are the implications for the long-run development of a society that is unable to reduce its population growth rate below, say, 4% per year?
4. Explain how technological progress averts the Malthusian trap.
5. China reduced its rate of population growth by force (see the Case in Point). Given the likely effects of population growth on living standards, do you think such a policy is reasonable? Are there other ways a government might seek to limit population growth?
6. On what basis might a poor country argue that its poverty is a result of high incomes in another country? Do you think Mexico's poverty contributed to U.S. wealth?
7. Given the arguments presented in the text, what do you think the United States should do to assist Mexico in its development efforts?

NUMERICAL PROBLEMS

1. Consider two economies, one with an initial per capita income of $16,000 (about the income of Israel) growing at a rate of 1.8% per year, the other with an initial per capita income of $600 (about the income of Guinea) growing twice as fast (that is, at a rate of 3.6% per year). Using the rule of 72 from the chapter on economic growth, calculate how long it will take for the lower-income country to achieve the per capita income enjoyed by the richer one. How long will it take to literally "catch up" to the richer nation, assuming that the growth rates continue unchanged in the future?

2. Use the most recent copy of the *World Development Report* available in your library (or at www.worldbank.org) to determine the five poorest countries in the world. Look up data on the distribution of income, education, health and nutrition, and demography for each country (information on some of these variables will not be available for every country). Do you think that low incomes cause the observations you have made, or do you think that low levels of education, health, and nutrition and high rates of population growth tend to cause poverty?

3. A country's rate of GDP growth is 3% per year. Its population is growing 4% per year. At what rate is its GDP per capita changing?

ENDNOTES

1. Shaohua Chen and Martin Ravallion, "The Developing World Is Poorer than We Thought, but No Less Successful in the Fight against Poverty," World Bank Policy Research Working Paper 4703, August 1, 2008.

2. United Nations, *The Millennium Development Goals Report 2008* (New York: United Nations, 2008).

3. United Nations Development Program, *Human Development Report 2007/2008* (New York: Palgrave Macmillan, 2007).

4. *The World Development Report 2006* (New York: Oxford University Press, 2006), xiv, comments on this usage: "The term *developing countries* includes low- and middle-income economies and thus may include economies in transition from central planning, as a matter of convenience. The term *advanced countries* may be used as a matter of convenience to denote high-income economics."

5. United Nations, *The Millennium Development Goals Report 2008*, 27.

6. United Nations Development Program, *Human Development Report 2007/2008* (New York: Palgrave Macmillan, 2007), 264.

7. United Nations, *The Millennium Development Goals Report 2008*, 30.

8. United Nations Development Program, *Human Development Report 2007/2008* (New York: Palgrave Macmillan, 2007), 272.

9. Robert Heilbroner, *Between Capitalism and Socialism* (New York: Vintage Books, 1970), 53–54.

10. The definition of deprivation for developed countries applies a higher standard than it does for developing countries.

11. Phillip Appleman, ed., *Thomas Robert Malthus: An Essay on the Principle of Population—Text, Sources and Background, Criticism* (New York: Norton, 1976), xi.

12. Bela Balassa, "The Lessons of East Asian Development," *Economic Development and Cultural Change* 36, no. 3 (April 1988): S247–S290.

CHAPTER 20
Socialist Economies in Transition

START UP: THE COLLAPSE OF SOCIALISM

It is hard, even in retrospect, to appreciate how swiftly the collapse came. Command socialism, which had reigned supreme in Russia for more than 70 years and in much of the rest of the world for more than 40 years, appeared to be a permanent institution. Indeed, many observers had expected its influence to increase by the end of the twentieth century. But in the span of five months in 1989, command socialist systems fell in six Eastern European nations. The Soviet Union, which had been the main enemy of the United States in the post-World War II period, and which possesses enough nuclear arms to destroy the world (as does the United States), broke up in 1991.

The start of the collapse can be dated to 1980. The government of Poland, a command socialist state that was part of the Soviet bloc, raised meat prices. The price boosts led to widespread protests and to the organization of Solidarity, the first independent labor union permitted in a Soviet bloc state. After nine years of political clashes, Solidarity won an agreement from the Polish government for wide-ranging economic reforms and for free elections. Solidarity-backed candidates swept the elections in June 1989, and a new government, pledged to democracy and to market capitalism, came to power in August.

Command socialist governments in the rest of the Soviet bloc disappeared quickly in the wake of Poland's transformation. Hungary's government fell in October. East Germany opened the Berlin Wall in November, and the old regime, for which that wall had been a symbol, collapsed. Bulgaria and Czechoslovakia kicked out their command socialist leaders the same month. Romania's dictator, Nicolae Ceausescu, was executed after a bloody uprising in December. Ultimately, every nation in the Warsaw Pact, the bloc making up the Soviet Union and its Eastern European satellite nations, announced its intention to discard the old system of command socialism. The collapse of the command socialist regimes of the former Soviet bloc precipitated an often painful process of transition as countries tried to put in place the institutions of a market capitalist economy. But, by the beginning of the 21st century, many of them were already admitted as members of the European Union.

Meanwhile, a very different process of transition has been under way in China. The Chinese began a gradual process of transition toward a market economy in 1979. It has been a process marked by spectacular economic gain ever since.

In this chapter we will examine the rise of command socialist systems and explore their ideological roots. Then we will see how these economic systems operated and trace the sources of their collapse. Finally, we will investigate the problems and prospects for the transition from command socialism to market capitalism.

1. THE THEORY AND PRACTICE OF SOCIALISM

L E A R N I N G   O B J E C T I V E

1. Discuss and assess Karl Marx's theory of capitalism, including mention of the labor theory of value, the concept of surplus value, periodic capitalist crises, and worker solidarity.

Socialism has a very long history. The earliest recorded socialist society is described in the Book of Acts in the Bible. Following the crucifixion of Jesus, Christians in Jerusalem established a system in which all property was owned in common.

There have been other socialist experiments in which all property was held in common, effectively creating socialist societies. Early in the nineteenth century, such reformers as Robert Owen, Count Claude-Henri de Rouvroy de Saint-Simon, and Charles Fourier established almost 200 communities in which workers shared in the proceeds of their labor. These men, while operating independently, shared a common ideal—that in the appropriate economic environment, people will strive for the good of the community rather than for their own self-interest. Although some of these communities enjoyed a degree of early success, none survived.

Socialism as the organizing principle for a national economy is in large part the product of the revolutionary ideas of one man, Karl Marx. His analysis of what he saw as the inevitable collapse of market capitalist economies provided a rallying spark for the national socialist movements of the twentieth century. Another important contributor to socialist thought was Vladimir Ilyich Lenin, who modified many of Marx's theories for application to the Soviet Union. Lenin put his ideas into practice as dictator of that country from 1917 until his death in 1924. It fell to Joseph Stalin to actually implement the Soviet system. We shall examine the ideas of Marx, Lenin, and Stalin and investigate the operation of the economic systems based upon them.

1.1 The Economics of Karl Marx

Marx is perhaps best known for the revolutionary ideas expressed in the ringing phrases of the *Communist Manifesto*, such as those shown in the Case in Point. Written with Friedrich Engels in 1848, the *Manifesto* was a call to arms. But it was Marx's exhaustive, detailed theoretical analysis of market capitalism, *Das Kapital (Capital)*, that was his most important effort. This four-volume work, most of which was published after Marx's death, examines a theoretical economy that we would now describe as perfect competition. In this context, Marx outlined a dynamic process that would, he argued, inevitably result in the collapse of capitalism.

Marx stressed a historical approach to the analysis of economics. Indeed, he was sharply critical of his contemporaries, complaining that their work was wholly lacking in historical perspective. To Marx, capitalism was merely a stage in the development of economic systems. He explained how feudalism would tend to give way to capitalism and how capitalism would give way to socialism. Marx's conclusions stemmed from his labor theory of value and from his perception of the role of profit in a capitalist economy.

The Labor Theory of Value and Surplus Value

labor theory of value

Theory that states that the relative values of different goods are ultimately determined by the relative amounts of labor used in their production.

surplus value

The difference between the price of a good or service and the labor cost of producing it.

In *The Wealth of Nations*, Adam Smith proposed the idea of the **labor theory of value**, which states that the relative values of different goods are ultimately determined by the relative amounts of labor used in their production. This idea was widely accepted at the time Marx was writing. Economists recognized the roles of demand and supply but argued that these would affect prices only in the short run. In the long run, it was labor that determined value.

Marx attached normative implications to the ideas of the labor theory of value. Not only was labor the ultimate determinant of value, it was the only *legitimate* determinant of value. The price of a good in Marx's system equaled the sum of the labor and capital costs of its production, plus profit to the capitalist. Marx argued that capital costs were determined by the amount of labor used to produce the capital, so the price of a good equaled a return to labor plus profit. Marx defined profit as **surplus value**, the difference between the price of a good or service and the labor cost of producing it. Marx insisted that surplus value was unjustified and represented exploitation of workers.

Marx accepted another piece of conventional economic wisdom of the nineteenth century, the concept of subsistence wages. This idea held that wages would, in the long run, tend toward their subsistence level, a level just sufficient to keep workers alive. Any increase in wages above their subsistence level would simply attract more workers—or induce an increase in population, forcing wages back down. Marx suggested that unemployed workers were important in this process; they represented a surplus of labor that acted to push wages down.

Capital Accumulation and Capitalist Crises

The concepts of surplus value and subsistence wages provide the essential dynamics of Marx's system. He said that capitalists, in an effort to increase surplus value, would seek to acquire more capital. But as they expanded capital, their profit rates, expressed as a percentage of the capital they held, would fall. In a desperate effort to push profit rates up, capitalists would acquire still more capital, which would only push their rate of return down further.

A further implication of Marx's scheme was that as capitalists increased their use of capital, the wages received by workers would become a smaller share of the total value of goods. Marx assumed that capitalists used all their funds to acquire more capital. Only workers, then, could be counted on for consumption. But their wages equaled only a fraction of the value of the output they produced—they could not possibly buy all of it. The result, Marx said, would be a series of crises in which capitalists throughout the economy, unable to sell their output, would cut back production. This would cause still more reductions in demand, exacerbating the downturn in economic activity. Crises would drive the weakest capitalists out of business; they would become unemployed and thus push wages down further. The economy could recover from such crises, but each one would weaken the capitalist system.

Faced with declining surplus values and reeling from occasional crises, capitalists would seek out markets in other countries. As they extended their reach throughout the world, Marx said, the scope of their exploitation of workers would expand. Although capitalists could make temporary gains by opening up international markets, their continuing acquisition of capital meant that profit rates would resume their downward trend. Capitalist crises would now become global affairs.

According to Marx, another result of capitalists' doomed efforts to boost surplus value would be increased solidarity among the working class. At home, capitalist acquisition of capital meant workers would be crowded into factories, building their sense of class identity. As capitalists extended their exploitation worldwide, workers would gain a sense of solidarity with fellow workers all over the planet. Marx argued that workers would recognize that they were the victims of exploitation by capitalists.

Marx was not clear about precisely what forces would combine to bring about the downfall of capitalism. He suggested other theories of crisis in addition to the one based on insufficient demand for the goods and services produced by capitalists. Indeed, modern theories of the business cycle owe much to Marx's discussion of the possible sources of economic downturns. Although Marx spoke sometimes of bloody revolution, it is not clear that this was the mechanism he thought would bring on the demise of capitalism. Whatever the precise mechanism, Marx was confident that capitalism would fall, that its collapse would be worldwide, and that socialism would replace it.

Marx's Theory: An Assessment

To a large degree, Marx's analysis of a capitalist economy was a logical outgrowth of widely accepted economic doctrines of his time. As we have seen, the labor theory of value was conventional wisdom, as was the notion that workers would receive only a subsistence wage. The notion that profit rates would fall over time was widely accepted. Doctrines similar to Marx's notion of recurring crises had been developed by several economists of the period.

What was different about Marx was his tracing of the dynamics of a system in which values would be determined by the quantity of labor, wages would tend toward the subsistence level, profit rates would fall, and crises would occur from time to time. Marx saw these forces as leading inevitably to the fall of capitalism and its replacement with a socialist economic system. Other economists of the period generally argued that economies would stagnate; they did not anticipate the collapse predicted by Marx.

Marx's predictions have turned out to be wildly off the mark. Profit rates have not declined; they have remained relatively stable over the long run. Wages have not tended downward toward their subsistence level; they have risen. Labor's share of total income in market economies has not fallen; it has increased. Most important, the predicted collapse of capitalist economies has not occurred.

Revolutions aimed at establishing socialism have been rare. Perhaps most important, none has occurred in a market capitalist economy. The Cuban economy, for example, had some elements of market capitalism before Castro but also had features of command systems as well.[1] In other cases where socialism has been established through revolution it has replaced systems that could best be described as feudal. The Russian Revolution of 1917 that established the Soviet Union and the revolution that established the People's Republic of China in 1949 are the most important examples of this form of revolution. In the countries of Eastern Europe, socialism was imposed by the former Soviet Union in the wake of World War II. In the early 2000s, a number of Latin American countries, such as Venezuela and Bolivia, seemed to be moving towards nationalizing, rather than privatizing, assets, but it is too early to know the long-term direction of these economies.

Whatever the shortcomings of Marx's economic prognostications, his ideas have had enormous influence. Politically, his concept of the inevitable emergence of socialism promoted the proliferation of socialist-leaning governments during the middle third of the twentieth century. Before socialist systems began collapsing in 1989, fully one-third of the earth's population lived in countries that had adopted Marx's ideas. Ideologically, his vision of a market capitalist system in which one class exploits another has had enormous influence.

KEY TAKEAWAYS

- Marx's theory, based on the labor theory of value and the presumption that wages would approach the subsistence level, predicted the inevitable collapse of capitalism and its replacement by socialist regimes.
- Lenin modified many of Marx's theories for application to the Soviet Union and put his ideas into practice as dictator of that country from 1917 until his death in 1924.
- Before socialist systems began collapsing in 1989, fully one-third of the earth's population lived in countries that had adopted Marx's ideas.

TRY IT!

Briefly explain how each of the following would contribute to the downfall of capitalism: 1) capital accumulation, 2) subsistence wages, and 3) the factory system.

Case in Point: The Powerful Images in the *Communist Manifesto*

© 2010 Jupiterimages Corporation

The *Communist Manifesto* by Karl Marx and Friedrich Engels was originally published in London in 1848, a year in which there were a number of uprisings across Europe that at the time could have been interpreted as the beginning of the end of capitalism. This relatively short (12,000 words) document was thus more than an analysis of the process of historical change, in which class struggles propel societies from one type of economic system to the next, and a prediction about how capitalism would evolve and why it would end. It was also a call to action. It contains powerful images that cannot be easily forgotten. It begins,

> *"A specter is haunting Europe—the specter of communism. All the Powers of old Europe have entered into a holy alliance to exorcise this specter: Pope and Czar, Metternich and Guizot, French Radicals and German police-spies."*

Its description of history begins,

"The history of all hitherto existing society is the history of class struggles. Freeman and slave, patrician and plebeian, lord and serf, guild-master and journeyman, in a word, oppressor and oppressed, stood in constant opposition to one another ..."

In capitalism, the divisions are yet more stark:

"Society as a whole is more and more splitting up into two great hostile camps, into two great classes directly facing each other: Bourgeoisie and Proletariat."

Foreshadowing the globalization of capitalism, Marx and Engels wrote,

"The bourgeoisie, by the rapid improvement of all instruments of production, by the immensely facilitated means of communication, draws all, even the most barbarian, nations into civilization. The cheap prices of its commodities are the heavy artillery with which it batters down all Chinese walls, with which it forces the barbarians' intensely obstinate hatred of foreigners to capitulate. It compels all nations, on pain of extinction, to adopt the bourgeois mode of production: it compels them to introduce what it calls civilization into their midst. ... In one word, it creates a world after its own image."

But the system, like all other class-based systems before it, brings about its own demise:

"The weapons with which the bourgeoisie felled feudalism to the ground are now turned against the bourgeoisie itself. ... Masses of laborers, crowded into the factory, are organized like soldiers. ... It was just this contact that was needed to centralize the numerous local struggles, all of the same character, into one national struggle between classes."

The national struggles eventually become an international struggle in which:

"What the bourgeoisie, therefore, produces, above all, is its own gravediggers."

The *Manifesto* ends,

"Let the ruling classes tremble at a Communistic revolution. The proletarians have nothing to lose but their chains. They have a world to win. WORKING MEN OF ALL COUNTRIES, UNITE!"

ANSWER TO TRY IT!

Marx predicted that capital accumulation would lead to falling profit rates over the long term. Subsistence wages meant that workers would not be able to consume enough of what was produced and this would lead to ever larger economic downturns. Because of the factory system, worker solidarity would grow and workers would come to understand that they were being exploited by capitalists.

2. SOCIALIST SYSTEMS IN ACTION

LEARNING OBJECTIVES

1. Describe the operation of the command socialist system in the Soviet Union, including its major problems.
2. Explain how Yugoslavian-style socialism differed from that of the Soviet Union.
3. Discuss the factors that brought an end to command socialist systems in much of the world.

The most important example of socialism was the economy of the Union of Soviet Socialist Republics, the Soviet Union. The Russian Revolution succeeded in 1917 in overthrowing the czarist regime that had ruled the Russian Empire for centuries. Leaders of the revolution created the Soviet Union in its place and sought to establish a socialist state based on the ideas of Karl Marx.

The leaders of the Soviet Union faced a difficulty in using Marx's writings as a foundation for a socialist system. He had sought to explain why capitalism would collapse; he had little to say about how the socialist system that would replace it would function. He did suggest the utopian notion that, over time, there would be less and less need for a government and the state would wither away. But his writings did not provide much of a blueprint for running a socialist economic system.

Lacking a guide for establishing a socialist economy, the leaders of the new regime in Russia struggled to invent one. In 1917, Lenin attempted to establish what he called "war communism." The national government declared its ownership of most firms and forced peasants to turn over a share of their output to the government. The program sought to eliminate the market as an allocative mechanism; government would control production and distribution. The program of war communism devastated the economy. In 1921, Lenin declared a New Economic Policy. It returned private ownership to some sectors of the economy and reinstituted the market as an allocative mechanism.

Lenin's death in 1924 precipitated a power struggle from which Joseph Stalin emerged victorious. It was under Stalin that the Soviet economic system was created. Because that system served as a model for most of the other command socialist systems that emerged, we shall examine it in some detail. We shall also examine an intriguing alternative version of socialism that was created in Yugoslavia after World War II.

2.1 Command Socialism in the Soviet Union

Stalin began by seizing virtually all remaining privately-owned capital and natural resources in the country. The seizure was a brutal affair; he eliminated opposition to his measures through mass executions, forced starvation of whole regions, and deportation of political opponents to prison camps. Estimates of the number of people killed during Stalin's centralization of power range in the tens of millions. With the state in control of the means of production, Stalin established a rigid system in which a central administration in Moscow determined what would be produced.

The justification for the brutality of Soviet rule lay in the quest to develop "socialist man." Leaders of the Soviet Union argued that the tendency of people to behave in their own self-interest was a by-product of capitalism, not an inherent characteristic of human beings. A successful socialist state required that the preferences of people be transformed so that they would be motivated by the collective interests of society, not their own self-interest. Propaganda was widely used to reinforce a collective identity. Those individuals who were deemed beyond reform were likely to be locked up or executed.

The political arm of command socialism was the Communist party. Party officials participated in every aspect of Soviet life in an effort to promote the concept of socialist man and to control individual behavior. Party leaders were represented in every firm and in every government agency. Party officials charted the general course for the economy as well.

A planning agency, Gosplan, determined the quantities of output that key firms would produce each year and the prices that would be charged. Other government agencies set output levels for smaller firms. These determinations were made in a series of plans. A 1-year plan specified production targets for that year. Soviet planners also developed 5-year and 20-year plans.

Managers of state-owned firms were rewarded on the basis of their ability to meet the annual quotas set by the Gosplan. The system of quotas and rewards created inefficiency in several ways. First, no central planning agency could incorporate preferences of consumers and costs of factors of production in its decisions concerning the quantity of each good to produce. Decisions about what to produce were made by political leaders; they were not a response to market forces. Further, planners could not select prices at which quantities produced would clear their respective markets. In a market economy, prices adjust to changes in demand and supply. Given that demand and supply are always changing, it is inconceivable that central planners could ever select market-clearing prices. Soviet central planners typically selected prices for consumer goods that were below market-clearing levels, causing shortages throughout the economy. Changes in prices were rare.

Plant managers had a powerful incentive for meeting their quotas; they could expect bonuses equal to about 35% of their base salary for producing the quantities required of their firms. Those who exceeded their quotas could boost this to 50%. In addition, successful managers were given vacations, better apartments, better medical care, and a host of other perquisites. Managers thus had a direct interest in meeting their quotas; they had no incentive to select efficient production techniques or to reduce costs.

Perhaps most important, there was no incentive for plant managers to adopt new technologies. A plant implementing a new technology risked start-up delays that could cause it to fall short of its quota. If a plant did succeed in boosting output, it was likely to be forced to accept even larger quotas in the future. A plant manager who introduced a successful technology would only be slapped with tougher quotas; if the technology failed, he or she would lose a bonus. With little to gain and a great deal to lose, Soviet plant managers were extremely reluctant to adopt new technologies. Soviet production was, as a result, characterized by outdated technologies. When the system fell in 1991, Soviet manufacturers were using production methods that had been obsolete for decades in other countries.

Centrally controlled systems often generated impressive numbers for total output but failed in satisfying consumer demands. Gosplan officials, recognizing that Soviet capital was not very productive, ordered up a lot of it. The result was a heavy emphasis on unproductive capital goods and relatively little production of consumer goods. On the eve of the collapse of the Soviet Union, Soviet economists estimated that per capita consumption was less than one-sixth of the U.S. level.

The Soviet system also generated severe environmental problems. In principle, a socialist system should have an advantage over a capitalist system in allocating environmental resources for which private property rights are difficult to define. Because a socialist government owns all capital and natural resources, the ownership problem is solved. The problem in the Soviet system, however, came from the labor theory of value. Since natural resources are not produced by labor, the value assigned to them was zero. Soviet plant managers thus had no incentive to limit their exploitation of environmental resources, and terrible environmental tragedies were common.

Systems similar to that created in the Soviet Union were established in other Soviet bloc countries as well. The most important exceptions were Yugoslavia, which is discussed in the next section, and China, which started with a Soviet-style system and then moved away from it. The Chinese case is examined later in this chapter.

2.2 Yugoslavia: Another Socialist Experiment

Although the Soviet Union was able to impose a system of command socialism on nearly all the Eastern European countries it controlled after World War II, Yugoslavia managed to forge its own path. Yugoslavia's communist leader, Marshal Tito, charted an independent course, accepting aid from Western nations such as the United States and establishing a unique form of socialism that made greater use of markets than the Soviet-style systems did. Most important, however, Tito quickly moved away from the centralized management style of the Soviet Union to a decentralized system in which workers exercised considerable autonomy.

In the Yugoslav system, firms with five or more employees were owned by the state but made their own decisions concerning what to produce and what prices to charge. Workers in these firms elected their managers and established their own systems for sharing revenues. Each firm paid a fee for the use of its state-owned capital. In effect, firms operated as labor cooperatives. Firms with fewer than five employees could be privately owned and operated.

Economic performance in Yugoslavia was impressive. Living standards there were generally higher than those in other Soviet bloc countries. The distribution of income was similar to that of command socialist economies; it was generally more equal than distributions achieved in market capitalist economies. The Yugoslav economy was plagued, however, by persistent unemployment, high inflation, and increasing disparities in regional income levels.

Yugoslavia began breaking up shortly after command socialist systems began falling in Eastern Europe. It had been a country of republics and provinces with uneasy relationships among them. Tito had been the glue that held them together. After his death, the groups began to move apart and a number of countries have formed out of what was once Yugoslavia, in several cases accompanied by war. They all seem to be moving in the market capitalist direction, with Slovenia and Macedonia leading the way. Over time, the others—Croatia, Bosnia, and Herzegovina, and even Serbia and Montenegra–have been following suit.

2.3   Evaluating Economic Performance Under Socialism

Soviet leaders placed great emphasis on Marx's concept of the inevitable collapse of capitalism. While they downplayed the likelihood of a global revolution, they argued that the inherent superiority of socialism would gradually become apparent. Countries would adopt the socialist model in order to improve their living standards, and socialism would gradually assert itself as the dominant world system.

One key to achieving the goal of a socialist world was to outperform the United States economically. Stalin promised in the 1930s that the Soviet economy would surpass that of the United States within a few decades. The goal was clearly not achieved. Indeed, it was the gradual realization that the command socialist system could not deliver high living standards that led to the collapse of the old system.

Figure 20.2 shows the World Bank's estimates of per capita output, measured in dollars of 1995 purchasing power, for the republics that made up the Soviet Union, for the Warsaw Pact nations of Eastern Europe for which data are available, and for the United States in 1995. Nations that had operated within the old Soviet system had quite low levels of per capita output. Living standards were lower still, given that these nations devoted much higher shares of total output to investment and to defense than did the United States.

FIGURE 20.2 Per Capita Output in Former Soviet Bloc States and in the United States, 1995

Per capita output was far lower in the former republics of the Soviet Union and in Warsaw Pact countries in 1995 than in the United States. All values are measured in units of equivalent purchasing power.

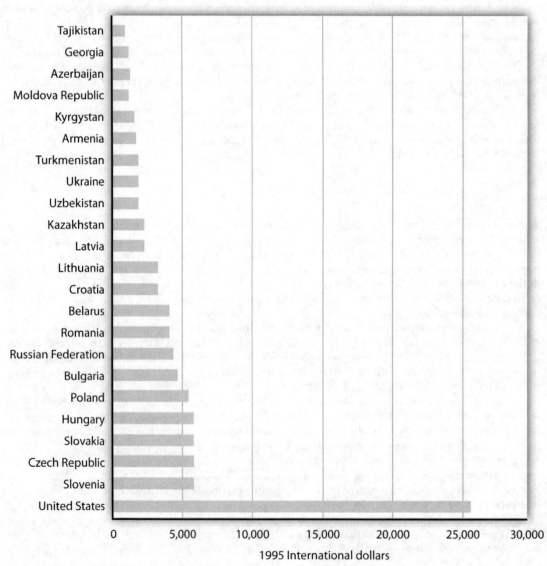

Source: United Nations, Human Development Report, 1998.

Ultimately, it was the failure of the Soviet system to deliver living standards on a par with those achieved by market capitalist economies that brought the system down. Market capitalist economic systems create incentives to allocate resources efficiently; socialist systems do not. Of course, a society may decide that other attributes of a socialist system make it worth retaining. But the lesson of the 1980s was that few that had lived under command socialist systems wanted to continue to do so.

KEY TAKEAWAYS

- In the Soviet Union a central planning agency, Gosplan, set output quotas for enterprises and determined prices.
- The Soviet central planning system was highly inefficient. Sources of this inefficiency included failure to incorporate consumer preferences into decisions about what to produce, failure to take into account costs of factors of production, setting of prices without regard to market equilibrium, lack of incentives for incorporating new technologies, overemphasis on capital goods production, and inattention to environmental problems.
- Yugoslavia developed an alternative system of socialism in which firms were run by their workers as labor cooperatives.
- It was the realization that command socialist systems could not deliver high living standards that contributed to their collapse.

TRY IT!

What specific problem of a command socialist system does each of the cartoons in the Case in Point parodying that system highlight?

Case in Point: Socialist Cartoons

These cartoons came from the Soviet press. Soviet citizens were clearly aware of many of the problems of their planned system.

"But where is the equipment that was sent to us?" "Which year are you talking about?"

"But Santa, it's winter, so we asked for boots for our son!" "I know, but the only thing available in the state store was a pair of sandals."

"Why are they sending us new technology when the old still works?"

3. ECONOMIES IN TRANSITION: CHINA AND RUSSIA

LEARNING OBJECTIVES

1. Discuss the major problems in transitioning from a command socialist economy to a market capitalist one.
2. Compare the approaches to economic transition taken in China and Russia.

Just as leaders of the Soviet Union had to create their own command socialist systems, leaders of the economies making the transition to market capitalist economies must find their own paths to new economic systems. It is a task without historical precedent.

In this section we will examine two countries and the strategies they have chosen for the transition. China was the first socialist nation to begin the process, and in many ways it has been the most successful. Russia was the dominant republic in the old Soviet Union; whether its transition is successful will be crucially important. Before turning to the transition process in these two countries, we will consider some general problems common to all countries seeking to establish market capitalism in the wake of command socialism.

3.1 Problems in Transition

Establishing a system of market capitalism in a command socialist economy is a daunting task. The nations making the attempt must invent the process as they go along. Each of them, though, faces similar problems. Former command socialist economies must establish systems of property rights, establish banking systems, deal with the problem of inflation, and work through a long tradition of ideological antipathy toward the basic nature of a capitalist system.

Property Rights

A market system requires property rights before it can function. A property right details what one can and cannot do with a particular asset. A market system requires laws that specify the actions that are permitted and those that are proscribed, and it also requires institutions for the enforcement of agreements dealing with property rights. These include a court system and lawyers trained in property law and contract law. For the system to work effectively, there must be widespread understanding of the basic nature of private property and of the transactions through which it is allocated.

Command socialist economies possess virtually none of these prerequisites for market capitalism. When the state owned virtually all capital and natural resources, there was little need to develop a legal system that would spell out individual property rights. Governments were largely free to do as they wished.

Countries seeking a transition from command socialism to market capitalism must develop a legal system comparable to those that have evolved in market capitalist countries over centuries. The problem of creating a system of property rights and the institutions necessary to support it is a large hurdle for economies making the transition to a market economy.

One manifestation of the difficulties inherent in establishing clear and widely recognized property rights in formerly socialist countries is widespread criminal activity. Newly established private firms must contend with racketeers who offer protection at a price. Firms that refuse to pay the price may find their property destroyed or some of their managers killed. Criminal activity has been rampant in economies struggling toward a market capitalist system.

Banking

Banks in command socialist countries were operated by the state. There was no tradition of banking practices as they are understood in market capitalist countries.

In a market capitalist economy, a privately owned bank accepts deposits from customers and lends these deposits to borrowers. These borrowers are typically firms or consumers. Banks in command socialist economies generally accepted saving deposits, but checking accounts for private individuals were virtually unknown. Decisions to advance money to firms were made through the economic planning process, not by individual banks. Banks did not have an opportunity to assess the profitability of individual enterprises; such considerations were irrelevant in the old command socialist systems. Bankers in these economies were thus unaccustomed to the roles that would be required of them in a market capitalist system.

Inflation

One particularly vexing problem facing transitional economies is inflation. Under command socialist systems, the government set prices; it could abolish inflation by decree. But such systems were characterized by chronic shortages of consumer goods. Consumers, unable to find the goods they wanted to buy, simply accumulated money. As command socialist economies began their transitions, there was typically a very large quantity of money available for consumers to spend. A first step in transitions was the freeing of prices. Because the old state-determined prices were generally below equilibrium levels, prices typically surged in the early stages of transition. Prices in Poland, for example, shot up 400% within a few months of price decontrol. Prices in Russia went up tenfold within six months.

One dilemma facing transitional economies has been the plight of bankrupt state enterprises. In a market capitalist economy, firms unable to generate revenues that exceed their costs go out of business. In command socialist economies, the central bank simply wrote checks to cover their deficits. As these economies have begun the transition toward market capitalism, they have generally declared their intention to end these bailouts and to let failing firms fail. But the phenomenon of state firms earning negative profits is so pervasive that allowing all of them to fail at once could cause massive disruption.

The practical alternative to allowing firms to fail has been continued bailouts. But in transitional economies, that has meant issuing money to failed firms. This practice increases the money supply and contributes to continuing inflation. Most transition economies experienced high inflation in the initial transition years, but were subsequently able to reduce it.

Ideology

Soviet citizens, and their counterparts in other command socialist economies, were told for decades that market capitalism is an evil institution, that it fosters greed and human misery. They were told that some people become rich in the system, but that they do so only at the expense of others who become poorer.

In the context of a competitive market, this view of market processes as a zero-sum game—one in which the gains for one person come only as a result of losses for another—is wrong. In market transactions, one person gains only by making others better off. But the zero-sum view runs deep, and it is a source of lingering hostility toward market forces.

Countries seeking to transform their economies from command socialist to more market-oriented systems face daunting challenges. Given these challenges, it is remarkable that they have persisted in the effort. There are a thousand reasons for economic reform to fail, but the reform effort has, in general, continued to move forward.

3.2   China: A Gradual Transition

China is a giant by virtually any standard. Larger than the continental United States, it is home to more than 1.3 billion people—more than one-fifth of the earth's population. Although China is poor, its economy has been among the fastest growing in the world since 1980. That rapid growth is the result of a gradual shift toward a market capitalist economy. The Chinese have pursued their transition in a manner quite different from the paths taken by former Soviet bloc nations.

Recent History

China was invaded by Japan during World War II. After Japan's defeat, civil war broke out between Chinese communists, led by Mao Zedong, and nationalists. The communists prevailed, and the People's Republic of China was proclaimed in 1949.

Mao set about immediately to create a socialist state in China. He nationalized many firms and redistributed land to peasants. Many of those who had owned land under the old regime were executed. China's entry into the Korean War in 1950 led to much closer ties to the Soviet Union, which helped China to establish a command socialist economy.

China's first five-year plan, launched in 1953, followed the tradition of Soviet economic development. It stressed capital-intensive production and the development of heavy industry. But China had far less capital and a great many more people than did the Soviet Union. Capital-intensive development made little sense. In 1958, Mao declared a uniquely Chinese approach to development, which he dubbed the Great Leap Forward. It focused on labor-intensive development and the organization of small productive units to quickly turn China into an industrialized country. Indeed, households were encouraged to form their own productive units under the slogan "An iron and steel foundry in every backyard." The Great Leap repudiated the bonuses and other material incentives stressed by the Soviets; motivation was to come from revolutionary zeal, not self-interest.

In agriculture, the new plan placed greater emphasis on collectivization. Farmers were organized into communes containing several thousand households each. Small private plots of land, which had been permitted earlier, were abolished. China's adoption of the plan was a victory for radical leaders in the government.

The Great Leap was an economic disaster. Output plunged and a large-scale famine ensued. Moderate leaders then took over, and the economy got back to its 1957 level of output by the mid-1960s.

Then, again in the mid-1960s, power shifted back towards the radicals with the launching of the Great Proletarian Cultural Revolution. During that time, students formed groups called "red guards" and were encouraged to expose "capitalist roaders." A group dubbed the "Gang of Four," led by Mao's wife Jiang Qing, tried to steer Chinese society towards an ever more revolutionary course until Mao's death in 1976.

China's Reforms

Following Mao's death, pragmatists within the Communist Party, led by Deng Xiaoping, embarked on a course of reform that promoted a more market-oriented economy coupled with retention of political power by the Communists. This policy combination was challenged in 1989 by a large demonstration in Beijing's Tiananmen Square. The authorities ordered the military to remove the demonstrators, resulting in the deaths of several hundred civilians. A period of retrenchment in the reform process followed and lasted for several years. Then, in 1992, Deng ushered in a period of reinvigorated economic reform in a highly publicized trip to southern China, where reforms had progressed farther. Through several leadership changes since then, the path of economic reform, managed by the Communist Party, has continued. The result has been a decades-long period of phenomenal economic growth.

What were some of the major elements of the economic reform? Beginning in 1979, many Chinese provincial leaders instituted a system called *bao gan dao hu*—"contracting all decisions to the household." Under the system, provincial officials contracted the responsibility for operating collectively owned farmland to individual households. Government officials gave households production quotas they were required to meet and purchased that output at prices set by central planners. But farmers were free to sell any additional output they could produce at whatever prices they could get in the marketplace and to keep the profits for themselves.

By 1984, 93% of China's agricultural land had been contracted to individual households and the rate of growth in agricultural output had soared.

At the industrial level, state-owned enterprises (SOEs) were told to meet their quotas and then were free to engage in additional production for sale in free markets. Over time, even those production directives were discontinued. More importantly, manufacturing boomed with the development of township and village enterprises, as well as various types of private endeavors, with much participation from foreign firms. Most price controls were abolished. The entry of China into the World Trade Organization in 2001 symbolized a commitment towards moving even further down the road of economic reform.

In effect, China's economy is increasingly directed by market forces. Even though five-year plans are still announced, they are largely advisory rather than commanding in nature. Recognizing the incomplete nature of the reforms, Chinese authorities continue to work on making the SOEs more competitive, as well as privatizing them, creating a social security system in which social benefits are not tied to a worker's place of employment, and reforming the banking sector.

How well has the gradual approach to transition worked? Between 1980 and 2006, China had one of the fastest-growing economies in the world. Its per capita output, measured in dollars of constant purchasing power, more than quadrupled. The country, which as late as 1997 was one of the poorest of the 59 low-income-countries in the world, is now situated comfortably among the more prosperous lower-middle-income countries, according to the World Bank. Figure 20.6 compares growth rates in China to those achieved by Japan and the United States and to the average annual growth rate of all world economies between 1985 and 2006.

FIGURE 20.6 Soaring Output in China

China's growth in per capita output from 1985 to 2006 greatly exceeded rates recorded for Japan, the United States, or the average of all nations.

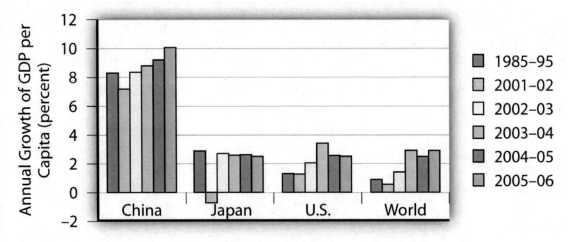

Source: World Bank, World Development Reports, 1997, 1998, 2004, 2005, 2006 Table 1.

Where will China's reforms lead? While the Chinese leadership has continued to be repressive politically, it has generally supported the reform process. The result has been continued expansion of the free economy and a relative shrinking of the state-run sector. Given the rapid progress China has achieved with its gradual approach to reform, it is hard to imagine that the country would reverse course. Given the course it is on, China seems likely to become a market capitalist economy—and a prosperous one—within a few decades.

3.3   Russia: An Uncertain Path to Reform

Russia dominated the former Soviet Union. It contained more than half the Soviet people and more than three-fourths of the nation's land area. Russia's capital, Moscow, was the capital and center of power for the entire country.

Today, Russia retains control over the bulk of the military power that had been accumulated by the former Soviet Union. While it is now an ally of the United States, Russia still possesses the nuclear capability to destroy life on earth. Its success in making the transition to market capitalism and joining as a full partner in the world community thus has special significance for peace.

Recent History

Russia's shift toward market capitalism has its roots in a reform process initiated during the final years of the existence of the Soviet Union. That effort presaged many of the difficulties that have continued to plague Russia.

The Soviet Union, as we have already seen, had a well-established system of command socialism. Leading Soviet economists, however, began arguing as early as the 1970s that the old system could never deliver living standards comparable to those achieved in market capitalist economies. The first political leader to embrace the idea of radical reform was Mikhail Gorbachev, who became General Secretary of the Communist party—the highest leadership post in the Soviet Union—in 1985.

Mr. Gorbachev instituted political reforms that allowed Soviet citizens to speak out, and even to demonstrate, against their government. This policy was dubbed *glasnost*, or "openness." Economically, he called for much greater autonomy for state enterprises and a system in which workers' wages would be tied to productivity. The new policy, dubbed *perestroika*, or "restructuring," appeared to be an effort to move the system toward a mixed economy.

But Mr. Gorbachev's economic advisers wanted to go much further. A small group of economists, which included his top economic adviser, met in August 1990 to draft a radical plan to transform the economy to a market capitalist system—and to do it in 500 days. Stanislav Shatalin, a Soviet economist, led the group. Mr. Gorbachev endorsed the Shatalin plan the following month, and it appeared that the Soviet Union was on its way to a new system. The new plan, however, threatened the Soviet power elite. It called for sharply reduced funding for the military and for the Soviet Union's secret police force, the KGB. It would have stripped central planners, who were very powerful, of their authority. The new plan called for nothing less than the destruction of the old system—and the elimination of the power base of most government officials.

Top Soviet bureaucrats and military leaders reacted to the Shatalin plan with predictable rage. They delivered an ultimatum to Mr. Gorbachev: dump the Shatalin plan or be kicked out.

Caught between advisers who had persuaded him of the necessity for radical reform and Communist party leaders who would have none of it, Mr. Gorbachev chose to leave the command system in place and to seek modest reforms. He announced a new plan that retained control over most prices and he left in place the state's ownership of enterprises. In an effort to deal with shortages of other goods, he ordered sharp price increases early in 1991.

These measures, however, accomplished little. Black market prices for basic consumer goods were typically 10 to 20 times the level of state prices. Those prices, which respond to demand and supply, may be taken as a rough gauge of equilibrium prices. People were willing to pay the higher black market prices because they simply could not find goods at the state-decreed prices. Mr. Gorbachev's order to double and even triple some state prices narrowed the gap between official and equilibrium prices, but did not close it. Table 20.1 shows some of the price changes imposed and compares them to black market prices.

TABLE 20.1 Official Versus Black Market Prices in the Soviet Union, 1991

Mikhail Gorbachev ordered sharp increases in the prices of most consumer goods early in 1991 in an effort to eliminate shortages. As the table shows, however, a large gap remained between official and black market prices.

Item	Old price	New price	Black market price
Children's shoes	2–10 rubles	10–50 rubles	50–300 rubles
Toilet paper	32–40 kopeks	60–75 kopeks	2–3 rubles
Compact car	7,000 rubles	35,000 rubles	70,000–100,000 rubles
Bottle of vodka	10.5 rubles	10.5 rubles	30–35 rubles

Source: Komsomolskaya pravda

Perhaps the most important problem for Mr. Gorbachev's price hikes was that there was no reason for state-owned firms to respond to them by increasing their output. The managers and workers in these firms, after all, were government employees receiving government-determined salaries. There was no mechanism through which they would gain from higher prices. A private firm could be expected to increase its quantity supplied in response to a higher price. State-owned firms did not.

The Soviet people faced the worst of economic worlds in 1991. Soviet output plunged sharply, prices were up dramatically, and there was no relief from severe shortages. A small group of government officials opposed to economic reform staged a coup in the fall of 1991, putting Mr. Gorbachev under house arrest. The coup produced massive protests throughout the country and failed within a few days. Chaos within the central government created an opportunity for the republics of the Soviet Union to declare their independence, and they did. These defections resulted in the collapse of the Soviet Union late in 1991, with Russia as one of 15 countries that emerged.

The Reform Effort

Boris Yeltsin, the first elected president of Russia, had been a leading proponent of market capitalism even before the Soviet Union collapsed. He had supported the Shatalin plan and had been sharply critical of Mr. Gorbachev's failure to implement it. Once Russia became an independent republic, Mr. Yeltsin sought a rapid transition to market capitalism.

Mr. Yeltsin's reform efforts, however, were slowed by Russian legislators, most of them former Communist officials who were appointed to their posts under the old regime. They fought reform and repeatedly sought to impeach Mr. Yeltsin. Citing health reasons, he abruptly resigned from the presidency in 1999, and appointed Vladimir Putin, who had only recently been appointed as Yeltsin's prime minister, as acting president. Mr. Putin has since been elected and re-elected, though many observers have questioned the fairness of those elections as well as Mr. Putin's commitment to democracy. Barred constitutionally from re-election in 2008, Putin became prime minister. Dimitry Medvedev, Putin's close ally, became president.

Despite the hurdles, Russian reformers have accomplished a great deal. Prices of most goods have been freed from state controls. Most state-owned firms have been privatized, and most of Russia's output of goods and services is now produced by the private sector.

To privatize state firms, Russian citizens were issued vouchers that could be used to purchase state enterprises. Under this plan, state enterprises were auctioned off. Individuals, or groups of individuals, could use their vouchers to bid on them. By 1995 most state enterprises in Russia had been privatized.

While Russia has taken major steps toward transforming itself into a market economy, it has not been able to institute its reforms in a coherent manner. For example, despite privatization, restructuring of Russian firms to increase efficiency has been slow. Establishment and enforcement of rules and laws that undergird modern, market-based systems have been lacking in Russia. Corruption has become endemic.

While the quality of the data is suspect, there is no doubt that output and the standard of living fell through the first half of the 1990s. Despite a financial crisis in 1998, when the Russian government defaulted on its debt, output recovered through the last half of the 1990s and Russia has seen substantial growth in the early years of the twenty-first century. In addition, government finances have improved following a major tax reform and inflation has come down from near hyperinflation levels. Despite these gains, there is uneasiness about the long-term sustainability of this progress because of the over-importance of oil and high oil prices in the recovery. Mr. Putin's fight, whether justified or not, with several of Russia's so-called oligarchs, a small group of people who were able to amass large fortunes during the early years of privatization, creates unease for domestic and foreign investors.

To be fair, overcoming the legacy of the Soviet Union would have been difficult at best. Overall, though, most would argue that Russian transition policies have made a difficult situation worse. Why has the transition in Russia been so difficult? One reason may be that Russians lived with command socialism longer than did any other country. In addition, Russia had no historical experience with market capitalism. In countries that did have it, such as the Czech Republic, the switch back to capitalism has gone far more smoothly and has met with far more success.

TRY IT!

Table 20.1 shows three prices for various goods in the Soviet Union in 1991. Illustrate the market for compact cars using a demand and supply diagram. On your diagram, show the old price, the new price, and the black market price.

Case in Point: Eastern Germany's Surprisingly Difficult Transition Experience

© 2010 Jupiterimages Corporation

The transition of eastern Germany was supposed to be the easiest of them all. Quickly merged with western Germany, given its new "Big Brother's" deep pockets, the ease with which it could simply adopt the rules and laws and policies of western Germany, and its automatic entry into the European Union, how could it not do well? And yet, eastern Germany seems to be languishing while some other central European countries that had also been part of the Soviet bloc are doing much better. Specifically, growth in real GDP in eastern Germany was 6% to 8% in the early 1990s, but since then has mostly been around 1%, with three years of negative growth in the early 2000s. In the early 1990s, the Polish economy grew at less than half east Germany's rate, but since then has averaged more than 4% per year. Why the reversal of fortunes?

Most observers point to the quick rise of wages to western German levels, despite the low productivity in the east. Initially, Germans from both east and west supported the move. East Germans obviously liked the idea of huge wage increases while west German workers thought that prolonged low wages in the eastern part of the country would cause companies to relocate there and saw the higher east German wages as protecting their own jobs. While the German government offered subsidies and tax breaks to firms that would move to the east despite the high wages, companies were by and large still reluctant to move their factories there. Instead they chose to relocate in other central European countries, such as the Czech Republic, Slovakia, and Poland. As a result, unemployment in eastern Germany has remained stubbornly high at about 15% and transfer payments to east Germans have totaled $1.65 trillion with no end in sight. "East Germany had the wrong prices: Labor was too expensive, and capital was too cheap," commented Klaus Deutsch, an economist at Deutsche Bank.

While the flow of labor has primarily been from Poland to Germany since the break-up of the Soviet bloc, with mostly senior managers moving from Germany to Poland, there are some less-skilled, unemployed east Germans who are starting to look for jobs in Poland. Tassilo Schlicht is an east German who repaired bicycles and washing machines at a Soviet-era factory and lost his job in 1990. He then worked for a short time at a gas station in his town for no pay with the hope that the experience would be helpful, but he was never hired. He undertook some government-sponsored retraining but still could not find a job. Finally, he was hired at a gas station across the border in Poland. The pay is far less than what employed Germans make for doing similar jobs but it is twice what he had been receiving in unemployment benefits. "These days, a job is a job, wherever it is."

Sources: Marcus Walker and Matthew Karnitschnig, "Eastern Europe Eclipses Eastern Germany," Wall Street Journal, November 9, 2004, p. A16; Keven J. O'Brien, "For Jobs, Some Germans Look to Poland," New York Times, January 8, 2004, p. W1; Doug Saunders, "What's the Matter with Eastern Germany?" The Globe and Mail (Canada), November 27, 2007, p. F3.

TRY IT!

There is a shortage of cars at both the old price of 7,000 rubles and at the new price of 35,000, although the shortage is less at the new price. Equilibrium price is assumed to be 70,000 rubles.

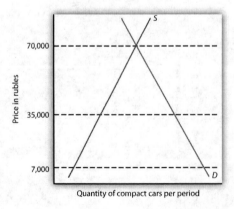

4. REVIEW AND PRACTICE

Summary

Socialism, a system in which factors of production are owned in common or by the public sector, is a very old idea. The impetus for installing it as a national economic system came from the writings of Karl Marx.

Marx argued that capitalism would inevitably collapse and give way to socialism. He argued that under capitalism workers would receive only a subsistence wage. Capitalists would extract the difference between what workers receive and what they produce as surplus value, a concept roughly equivalent to profit. As capitalists struggled to maintain surplus value, the degree and extent of exploitation of workers would rise. Capitalist systems would suffer through a series of crises in which firms cut back their output. The suffering of workers would increase, and the capitalist class would be weakened. Ultimately, workers would overthrow the market capitalist system and establish socialism in its place.

Marx's predictions about capitalist development have not come to fruition, but his ideas have been enormously influential. By the 1980s, roughly one-third of the world's people lived in economies built on the basis of his ideas.

The most important command socialist economy was the Soviet Union. In this economy, central planners determined what would be produced and at what price. Quotas were given to each state-owned firm. The system, which was emulated in most socialist nations, failed to deliver living standards on a par with those achieved by market economies. This failure ultimately brought down the system.

A very different approach to socialism was pioneered by Yugoslavia. State-owned firms were managed by their workers, who shared in their profits. Yugoslavia's economic system fell apart as the country broke up and suffered from ethnic strife and civil war.

As the governments of command socialist nations fell in 1989 and early in the 1990s, new governments launched efforts to achieve transition to market capitalism. We examined two cases of transition. China's gradual strategy has produced rapid growth, but in a politically repressive regime. As this book went to press, China continued to be one of the fastest growing economies in the world.

Russia's transition has been much more difficult. Although its growth rate has improved in the last decade, there is still concern over the coherence of its reform efforts and the sustainability of recent improvements

CONCEPT PROBLEMS

1. There is a gap between what workers receive and the value of what workers produce in a market capitalist system. Why? Does this constitute exploitation? Does it create the kinds of crises Marx anticipated? Why or why not?

2. What is meant by the labor theory of value? What are the shortcomings of the theory?

3. What would you say is the theory of value offered in this book? How does it differ from the labor theory of value?

4. In what ways does reliance on the labor theory of value create a problem for the allocation of natural resources?

5. What do you think would be the advantages of labor-managed firms of the kind that operated in the former Yugoslavia? The disadvantages?

6. Suppose you were the manager of a Soviet enterprise under the old command system. You have been given a quota and the promise of a big bonus if your firm meets it. How might your production choices differ from those of the management of a profit-maximizing firm in a market capitalist economy?

7. What are some government-operated enterprises in the United States? Do you see any parallels between the problems command economies faced with the production of goods and services and problems in the United States with state-run enterprises?

8. A Chinese firm operating as a state-owned enterprise had an incentive to produce the efficient level of output, even though some of its output was claimed by the state at state-determined prices. Why is that the case?

9. Given that market capitalist systems generate much higher standards of living than do command socialist systems, why do you think many Russian government officials have opposed the adoption of a market system?

10. How does widespread criminal activity sap economic growth?

ENDNOTES

1. While resources in Cuba were generally privately owned, the government had broad powers to dictate their use.

CHAPTER 21

Appendix A: Graphs in Economics

A glance through the pages of this book should convince you that there are a lot of graphs in economics. The language of graphs is one means of presenting economic ideas. If you are already familiar with graphs, you will have no difficulty with this aspect of your study. If you have never used graphs or have not used them in some time, this appendix will help you feel comfortable with the graphs you will encounter in this text.

1. HOW TO CONSTRUCT AND INTERPRET GRAPHS

LEARNING OBJECTIVES

1. Understand how graphs show the relationship between two or more variables and explain how a graph elucidates the nature of the relationship.
2. Define the slope of a curve.
3. Distinguish between a movement along a curve, a shift in a curve, and a rotation in a curve.

Much of the analysis in economics deals with relationships between variables. A variable is simply a quantity whose value can change. A **graph** is a pictorial representation of the relationship between two or more variables. The key to understanding graphs is knowing the rules that apply to their construction and interpretation. This section defines those rules and explains how to draw a graph.

graph

A pictorial representation of the relationship between two or more variables.

1.1 Drawing a Graph

To see how a graph is constructed from numerical data, we will consider a hypothetical example. Suppose a college campus has a ski club that organizes day-long bus trips to a ski area about 100 miles from the campus. The club leases the bus and charges $10 per passenger for a round trip to the ski area. In addition to the revenue the club collects from passengers, it also receives a grant of $200 from the school's student government for each day the bus trip is available. The club thus would receive $200 even if no passengers wanted to ride on a particular day.

The table in Figure 21.1 shows the relationship between two variables: the number of students who ride the bus on a particular day and the revenue the club receives from a trip. In the table, each combination is assigned a letter (A, B, etc.); we will use these letters when we transfer the information from the table to a graph.

FIGURE 21.1 Ski Club Revenues

The ski club receives $10 from each passenger riding its bus for a trip to and from the ski area plus a payment of $200 from the student government for each day the bus is available for these trips. The club's revenues from any single day thus equal $200 plus $10 times the number of passengers. The table relates various combinations of the number of passengers and club revenues.

Combination	Number of passengers	Club revenue
A	0	$200
B	10	300
C	20	400
D	30	500
E	40	600

We can illustrate the relationship shown in the table with a graph. The procedure for showing the relationship between two variables, like the ones in Figure 21.1, on a graph is illustrated in Figure 21.2. Let us look at the steps involved.

FIGURE 21.2 Plotting a Graph

Here we see how to show the information given in Figure 21.1 in a graph.

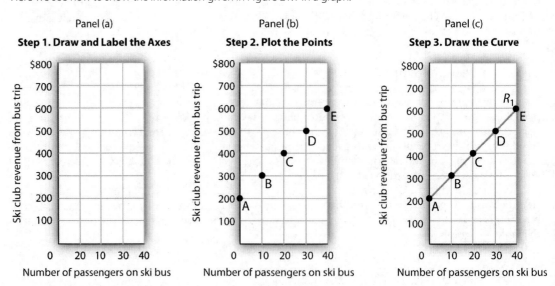

Step 1. Draw and Label the Axes

The two variables shown in the table are the number of passengers taking the bus on a particular day and the club's revenue from that trip. We begin our graph in Panel (a) of Figure 21.2 by drawing two axes to form a right angle. Each axis will represent a variable. The axes should be carefully labeled to reflect what is being measured on each axis.

It is customary to place the independent variable on the horizontal axis and the dependent variable on the vertical axis. Recall that, when two variables are related, the dependent variable is the one that changes in response to changes in the independent variable. Passengers generate revenue, so we can consider the number of passengers as the independent variable and the club's revenue as the dependent variable. The number of passengers thus goes on the horizontal axis; the club's revenue from a trip goes on the vertical axis. In some cases, the variables in a graph cannot be considered independent or dependent. In those cases, the variables may be placed on either axis; we will encounter such a case in the chapter that introduces the production possibilities model. In other cases, economists simply ignore the rule; we will encounter that case in the chapter that introduces the model of demand and supply. The rule that the independent variable goes on the horizontal axis and the dependent variable goes on the vertical usually holds, but not always.

The point at which the axes intersect is called the **origin** of the graph. Notice that in Figure 21.2 the origin has a value of zero for each variable.

In drawing a graph showing numeric values, we also need to put numbers on the axes. For the axes in Panel (a), we have chosen numbers that correspond to the values in the table. The number of passengers ranges up to 40 for a trip; club revenues from a trip range from $200 (the payment the club receives from student government) to $600. We have extended the vertical axis to $800 to allow some changes we will consider below. We have chosen intervals of 10 passengers on the horizontal axis and $100 on the vertical axis. The choice of particular intervals is mainly a matter of convenience in drawing and reading the graph; we have chosen the ones here because they correspond to the intervals given in the table.

We have drawn vertical lines from each of the values on the horizontal axis and horizontal lines from each of the values on the vertical axis. These lines, called gridlines, will help us in Step 2.

Step 2. Plot the Points

Each of the rows in the table in Figure 21.1 gives a combination of the number of passengers on the bus and club revenue from a particular trip. We can plot these values in our graph.

We begin with the first row, A, corresponding to zero passengers and club revenue of $200, the payment from student government. We read up from zero passengers on the horizontal axis to $200 on the vertical axis and mark point A. This point shows that zero passengers result in club revenues of $200.

The second combination, B, tells us that if 10 passengers ride the bus, the club receives $300 in revenue from the trip—$100 from the $10-per-passenger charge plus the $200 from student government. We start at 10 passengers on the horizontal axis and follow the gridline up. When we travel up in a graph, we are traveling with respect to values on the vertical axis. We travel up by $300 and mark point B.

Points in a graph have a special significance. They relate the values of the variables on the two axes to each other. Reading to the left from point B, we see that it shows $300 in club revenue. Reading down from point B, we see that it shows 10 passengers. Those values are, of course, the values given for combination B in the table.

We repeat this process to obtain points C, D, and E. Check to be sure that you see that each point corresponds to the values of the two variables given in the corresponding row of the table.

The graph in Panel (b) is called a scatter diagram. A **scatter diagram** shows individual points relating values of the variable on one axis to values of the variable on the other.

Step 3. Draw the Curve

The final step is to draw the curve that shows the relationship between the number of passengers who ride the bus and the club's revenues from the trip. The term "curve" is used for any line in a graph that shows a relationship between two variables.

We draw a line that passes through points A through E. Our curve shows club revenues; we shall call it R_1. Notice that R_1 is an upward-sloping straight line. Notice also that R_1 intersects the vertical axis at $200 (point A). The point at which a curve intersects an axis is called the **intercept** of the curve. We often refer to the vertical or horizontal intercept of a curve; such intercepts can play a special role in economic analysis. The vertical intercept in this case shows the revenue the club would receive on a day it offered the trip and no one rode the bus.

To check your understanding of these steps, we recommend that you try plotting the points and drawing R_1 for yourself in Panel (a). Better yet, draw the axes for yourself on a sheet of graph paper and plot the curve.

1.2   The Slope of a Curve

In this section, we will see how to compute the slope of a curve. The slopes of curves tell an important story: they show the rate at which one variable changes with respect to another.

origin

The point at which the axes of a graph intersect.

scatter diagram

A graph that shows individual points relating values of the variable on one axis to values of the variable on the other.

intercept

The point at which a curve intersects an axis.

slope

The ratio of the change in the value of the variable on the vertical axis to the change in the value of the variable on the horizontal axis measured between two points on the curve.

The **slope** of a curve equals the ratio of the change in the value of the variable on the vertical axis to the change in the value of the variable on the horizontal axis, measured between two points on the curve. You may have heard this called "the rise over the run." In equation form, we can write the definition of the slope as

EQUATION 21.1

$$\text{Slope} = \frac{\text{vertical change}}{\text{horizontal change}}$$

Equation 21.1 is the first equation in this text. Figure 21.3 provides a short review of working with equations. The material in this text relies much more heavily on graphs than on equations, but we will use equations from time to time. It is important that you understand how to use them.

FIGURE 21.3 Reading and Using Equations

Many equations in economics begin in the form of Equation 21.1, with the statement that one thing (in this case the slope) equals another (the vertical change divided by the horizontal change). In this example, the equation is written in words. Sometimes we use symbols in place of words. The basic idea though, is always the same: the term represented on the left side of the equals sign equals the term on the right side. In Equation 21.1 there are three variables: the slope, the vertical change, and the horizontal change. If we know the values of two of the three, we can compute the third. In the computation of slopes that follow, for example, we will use values for the two variables on the right side of the equation to compute the slope.

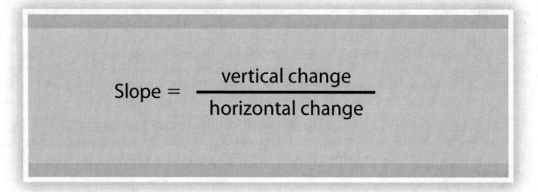

Figure 21.4 shows R_1 and the computation of its slope between points B and D. Point B corresponds to 10 passengers on the bus; point D corresponds to 30. The change in the horizontal axis when we go from B to D thus equals 20 passengers. Point B corresponds to club revenues of $300; point D corresponds to club revenues of $500. The change in the vertical axis equals $200. The slope thus equals $200/20 passengers, or $10/passenger.

FIGURE 21.4 Computing the Slope of a Curve

1. Select two points; we have selected points B and D.
2. The slope equals the vertical change divided by the horizontal change between the two points.
3. Between points B and D, the slope equals $200/20 passengers = $10/passenger.
4. The slope of this curve is the price per passenger. The fact that it is positive suggests a positive relationship between revenue per trip and the number of passengers riding the bus. Because the slope of this curve is $10/passenger between any two points on the curve, the relationship between club revenue per trip and the number of passengers is linear.

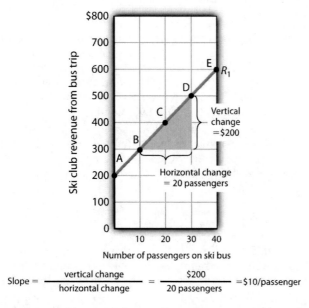

$$\text{Slope} = \frac{\text{vertical change}}{\text{horizontal change}} = \frac{\$200}{20 \text{ passengers}} = \$10/\text{passenger}$$

We have applied the definition of the slope of a curve to compute the slope of R_1 between points B and D. That same definition is given in Equation 21.1. Applying the equation, we have:

$$\text{Slope} = \frac{\text{vertical change}}{\text{horizontal change}} = \frac{\$200}{20 \text{ passengers}} = \$10 \big/ \text{ passenger}$$

The slope of this curve tells us the amount by which revenues rise with an increase in the number of passengers. It should come as no surprise that this amount equals the price per passenger. Adding a passenger adds $10 to the club's revenues.

Notice that we can compute the slope of R_1 between any two points on the curve and get the same value; the slope is constant. Consider, for example, points A and E. The vertical change between these points is $400 (we go from revenues of $200 at A to revenues of $600 at E). The horizontal change is 40 passengers (from zero passengers at A to 40 at E). The slope between A and E thus equals $400/(40 passengers) = $10/passenger. We get the same slope regardless of which pair of points we pick on R_1 to compute the slope. The slope of R_1 can be considered a constant, which suggests that it is a straight line. When the curve showing the relationship between two variables has a constant slope, we say there is a **linear relationship** between the variables. A **linear curve** is a curve with constant slope.

The fact that the slope of our curve equals $10/passenger tells us something else about the curve—$10/passenger is a positive, not a negative, value. A curve whose slope is positive is upward sloping. As we travel up and to the right along R_1, we travel in the direction of increasing values for both variables. A **positive relationship** between two variables is one in which both variables move in the same direction. Positive relationships are sometimes called direct relationships. There is a positive relationship between club revenues and passengers on the bus. We will look at a graph showing a negative relationship between two variables in the next section.

1.3   A Graph Showing a Negative Relationship

A **negative relationship** is one in which two variables move in opposite directions. A negative relationship is sometimes called an inverse relationship. The slope of a curve describing a negative relationship is always negative. A curve with a negative slope is always downward sloping.

As an example of a graph of a negative relationship, let us look at the impact of the cancellation of games by the National Basketball Association during the 1998–1999 labor dispute on the earnings of one player: Shaquille O'Neal. During the 1998–1999 season, O'Neal was the center for the Los Angeles Lakers.

linear relationship

Relationship that exists between two variables when the curve between them has a constant slope.

linear curve

A curve with constant slope.

positive relationship

Relationship that exists between two variables when both variables move in the same direction.

negative relationship

Relationship that exists between two variables when the variables move in opposite directions.

O'Neal's salary with the Lakers in 1998–1999 would have been about $17,220,000 had the 82 scheduled games of the regular season been played. But a contract dispute between owners and players resulted in the cancellation of 32 games. Mr. O'Neal's salary worked out to roughly $210,000 per game, so the labor dispute cost him well over $6 million. Presumably, he was able to eke out a living on his lower income, but the cancellation of games cost him a great deal.

We show the relationship between the number of games canceled and O'Neal's 1998–1999 basketball earnings graphically in Figure 21.5. Canceling games reduced his earnings, so the number of games canceled is the independent variable and goes on the horizontal axis. O'Neal's earnings are the dependent variable and go on the vertical axis. The graph assumes that his earnings would have been $17,220,000 had no games been canceled (point A, the vertical intercept). Assuming that his earnings fell by $210,000 per game canceled, his earnings for the season were reduced to $10,500,000 by the cancellation of 32 games (point B). We can draw a line between these two points to show the relationship between games canceled and O'Neal's 1998–1999 earnings from basketball. In this graph, we have inserted a break in the vertical axis near the origin. This allows us to expand the scale of the axis over the range from $10,000,000 to $18,000,000. It also prevents a large blank space between the origin and an income of $10,500,000—there are no values below this amount.

What is the slope of the curve in Figure 21.5? We have data for two points, A and B. At A, O'Neal's basketball salary would have been $17,220,000. At B, it is $10,500,000. The vertical change between points A and B equals -$6,720,000. The change in the horizontal axis is from zero games canceled at A to 32 games canceled at B. The slope is thus

$$\text{Slope} = \frac{\text{vertical change}}{\text{horizontal change}} = \frac{-\$6{,}720{,}000}{32 \text{ games}} = -\$210{,}000 \big/ \text{game}$$

Notice that this time the slope is negative, hence the downward-sloping curve. As we travel down and to the right along the curve, the number of games canceled rises and O'Neal's salary falls. In this case, the slope tells us the rate at which O'Neal lost income as games were canceled.

The slope of O'Neal's salary curve is also constant. That means there was a linear relationship between games canceled and his 1998–1999 basketball earnings.

1.4 Shifting a Curve

When we draw a graph showing the relationship between two variables, we make an important assumption. We assume that all other variables that might affect the relationship between the variables in our graph are unchanged. When one of those other variables changes, the relationship changes, and the curve showing that relationship shifts.

Consider, for example, the ski club that sponsors bus trips to the ski area. The graph we drew in Figure 21.2 shows the relationship between club revenues from a particular trip and the number of passengers on that trip, assuming that all other variables that might affect club revenues are unchanged. Let us change one. Suppose the school's student government increases the payment it makes to the club to $400 for each day the trip is available. The payment was $200 when we drew the original graph. Panel (a) of Figure 21.6 shows how the increase in the payment affects the table we had in Figure 21.1; Panel (b) shows how the curve shifts. Each of the new observations in the table has been labeled with a prime: A′, B′, etc. The curve R_1 shifts upward by $200 as a result of the increased payment. A **shift in a curve** implies new values of one variable at each value of the other variable. The new curve is labeled R_2. With 10 passengers, for example, the club's revenue was $300 at point B on R_1. With the increased payment from the student government, its revenue with 10 passengers rises to $500 at point B′ on R_2. We have a shift in the curve.

FIGURE 21.5 Canceling Games and Reducing Shaquille O'Neal's Earnings

If no games had been canceled during the 1998–1999 basketball season, Shaquille O'Neal would have earned $17,220,000 (point A). Assuming that his salary for the season fell by $210,000 for each game canceled, the cancellation of 32 games during the dispute between NBA players and owners reduced O'Neal's earnings to $10,500,000 (point B).

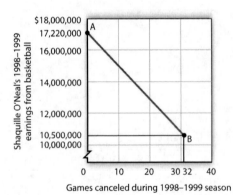

shift in a curve

Change in the graph of a relationship between two variables that implies new values of one variable at each value of the other variable.

FIGURE 21.6 Shifting a Curve: An Increase in Revenues

The table in Panel (a) shows the new level of revenues the ski club receives with varying numbers of passengers as a result of the increased payment from student government. The new curve is shown in dark purple in Panel (b). The old curve is shown in light purple.

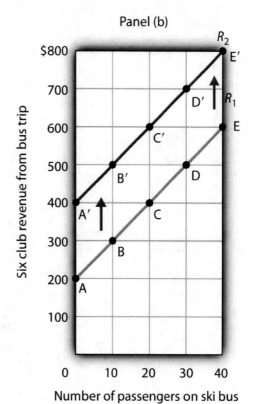

Panel (b)

Panel (a)

Combination	Number of passengers	Club revenue (with $400 payment from student government)
A'	0	$400
B'	10	500
C'	20	600
D'	30	700
E'	40	800

It is important to distinguish between shifts in curves and movements along curves. A **movement along a curve** is a change from one point on the curve to another that occurs when the dependent variable changes in response to a change in the independent variable. If, for example, the student government is paying the club $400 each day it makes the ski bus available and 20 passengers ride the bus, the club is operating at point C' on R_2. If the number of passengers increases to 30, the club will be at point D' on the curve. This is a movement along a curve; the curve itself does not shift.

Now suppose that, instead of increasing its payment, the student government eliminates its payments to the ski club for bus trips. The club's only revenue from a trip now comes from its $10/passenger charge. We have again changed one of the variables we were holding unchanged, so we get another shift in our revenue curve. The table in Panel (a) of Figure 21.7 shows how the reduction in the student government's payment affects club revenues. The new values are shown as combinations A" through E" on the new curve, R_3, in Panel (b). Once again we have a shift in a curve, this time from R_1 to R_3.

movement along a curve

Change from one point on the curve to another that occurs when the dependent variable changes in response to a change in the independent variable.

FIGURE 21.7 Shifting a Curve: A Reduction in Revenues

The table in Panel (a) shows the impact on ski club revenues of an elimination of support from the student government for ski bus trips. The club's only revenue now comes from the $10 it charges to each passenger. The new combinations are shown as A″ – E″. In Panel (b) we see that the original curve relating club revenue to the number of passengers has shifted down.

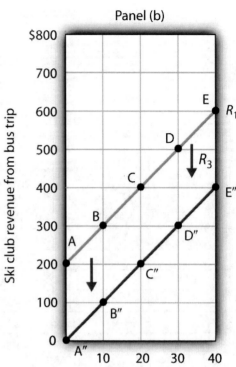

Panel (a)

Combination	Number of passengers	Club revenue (with no payment from student government)
A″	0	0
B″	10	100
C″	20	200
D″	30	300
E″	40	400

The shifts in Figure 21.6 and Figure 21.7 left the slopes of the revenue curves unchanged. That is because the slope in all these cases equals the price per ticket, and the ticket price remains unchanged. Next, we shall see how the slope of a curve changes when we rotate it about a single point.

1.5   Rotating a Curve

rotation of a curve

Change In a curve that occurs when its slope changes with one point on the curve fixed.

A **rotation of a curve** occurs when we change its slope, with one point on the curve fixed. Suppose, for example, the ski club changes the price of its bus rides to the ski area to $30 per trip, and the payment from the student government remains $200 for each day the trip is available. This means the club's revenues will remain $200 if it has no passengers on a particular trip. Revenue will, however, be different when the club has passengers. Because the slope of our revenue curve equals the price per ticket, the slope of the revenue curve changes.

Panel (a) of Figure 21.8 shows what happens to the original revenue curve, R_1, when the price per ticket is raised. Point A does not change; the club's revenue with zero passengers is unchanged. But with 10 passengers, the club's revenue would rise from $300 (point B on R_1) to $500 (point B′ on R_4). With 20 passengers, the club's revenue will now equal $800 (point C′ on R_4).

FIGURE 21.8 Rotating a Curve

A curve is said to rotate when a single point remains fixed while other points on the curve move; a rotation always changes the slope of a curve. Here an increase in the price per passenger to $30 would rotate the revenue curve from R_1 to R_4 in Panel (a). The slope of R_4 is $30 per passenger.

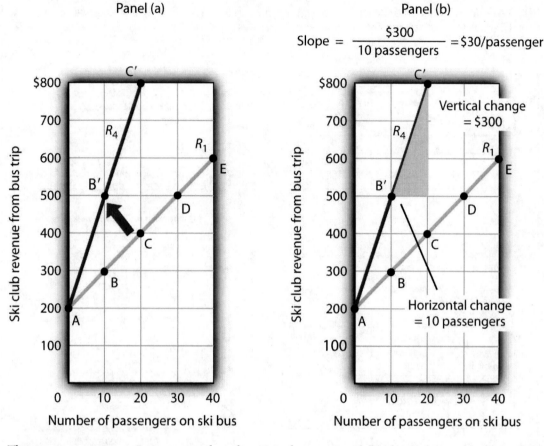

The new revenue curve R_4 is steeper than the original curve. Panel (b) shows the computation of the slope of the new curve between points B′ and C′. The slope increases to $30 per passenger—the new price of a ticket. The greater the slope of a positively sloped curve, the steeper it will be.

We have now seen how to draw a graph of a curve, how to compute its slope, and how to shift and rotate a curve. We have examined both positive and negative relationships. Our work so far has been with linear relationships. Next we will turn to nonlinear ones.

KEY TAKEAWAYS

- A graph shows a relationship between two or more variables.
- An upward-sloping curve suggests a positive relationship between two variables. A downward-sloping curve suggests a negative relationship between two variables.
- The slope of a curve is the ratio of the vertical change to the horizontal change between two points on the curve. A curve whose slope is constant suggests a linear relationship between two variables.
- A change from one point on the curve to another produces a movement along the curve in the graph. A shift in the curve implies new values of one variable at each value of the other variable. A rotation in the curve implies that one point remains fixed while the slope of the curve changes.

TRY IT!

The following table shows the relationship between the number of gallons of gasoline people in a community are willing and able to buy per week and the price per gallon. Plot these points in the grid provided and label each point with the letter associated with the combination. Notice that there are breaks in both the vertical and horizontal axes of the grid. Draw a line through the points you have plotted. Does your graph suggest a positive or a negative relationship? What is the slope between A and B? Between B and C? Between A and C? Is the relationship linear?

Combination	Price per gallon	Number of gallons (per week)
A	$1.00	1,000
B	1.20	900
C	1.40	800

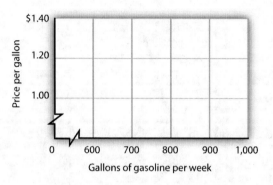

Now suppose you are given the following information about the relationship between price per gallon and the number of gallons per week gas stations in the community are willing to sell.

Combination	Price per gallon	Number of gallons (per week)
D	$1.00	800
E	1.20	900
F	1.40	1,000

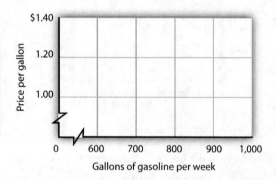

Plot these points in the grid provided and draw a curve through the points you have drawn. Does your graph suggest a positive or a negative relationship? What is the slope between D and E? Between E and F? Between D and F? Is this relationship linear?

ANSWER TO TRY IT!

Here is the first graph. The curve's downward slope tells us there is a negative relationship between price and the quantity of gasoline people are willing and able to buy. This curve, by the way, is a demand curve (the next one is a supply curve). We will study demand and supply soon; you will be using these curves a great deal. The slope between A and B is −0.002 (slope = vertical change/horizontal change = −0.20/100). The slope between B and C and between A and C is the same. That tells us the curve is linear, which, of course, we can see—it is a straight line.

Here is the supply curve. Its upward slope tells us there is a positive relationship between price per gallon and the number of gallons per week gas stations are willing to sell. The slope between D and E is 0.002 (slope equals vertical change/horizontal change = 0.20/100). Because the curve is linear, the slope is the same between any two points, for example, between E and F and between D and F.

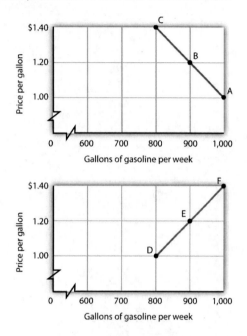

2. NONLINEAR RELATIONSHIPS AND GRAPHS WITHOUT NUMBERS

LEARNING OBJECTIVES

1. Understand nonlinear relationships and how they are illustrated with nonlinear curves.
2. Explain how to estimate the slope at any point on a nonlinear curve.
3. Explain how graphs without numbers can be used to understand the nature of relationships between two variables.

In this section we will extend our analysis of graphs in two ways: first, we will explore the nature of nonlinear relationships; then we will have a look at graphs drawn without numbers.

2.1 Graphs of Nonlinear Relationships

In the graphs we have examined so far, adding a unit to the independent variable on the horizontal axis always has the same effect on the dependent variable on the vertical axis. When we add a passenger riding the ski bus, the ski club's revenues always rise by the price of a ticket. The cancellation of one more game in the 1998–1999 basketball season would always reduce Shaquille O'Neal's earnings by $210,000. The slopes of the curves describing the relationships we have been discussing were constant; the relationships were linear.

Many relationships in economics are nonlinear. A **nonlinear relationship** between two variables is one for which the slope of the curve showing the relationship changes as the value of one of the variables changes. A **nonlinear curve** is a curve whose slope changes as the value of one of the variables changes.

Consider an example. Suppose Felicia Alvarez, the owner of a bakery, has recorded the relationship between her firm's daily output of bread and the number of bakers she employs. The relationship she has recorded is given in the table in Panel (a) of Figure 21.12. The corresponding points are plotted in Panel (b). Clearly, we cannot draw a straight line through these points. Instead, we shall have to draw a nonlinear curve like the one shown in Panel (c).

FIGURE 21.12 A Nonlinear Curve

The table in Panel (a) shows the relationship between the number of bakers Felicia Alvarez employs per day and the number of loaves of bread produced per day. This information is plotted in Panel (b). This is a nonlinear relationship; the curve connecting these points in Panel (c) (Loaves of bread produced) has a changing slope.

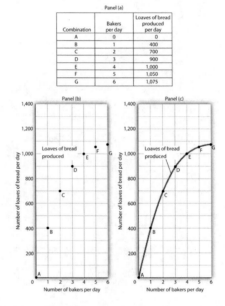

Combination	Bakers per day	Loaves of bread produced per day
A	0	0
B	1	400
C	2	700
D	3	900
E	4	1,000
F	5	1,050
G	6	1,075

Inspecting the curve for loaves of bread produced, we see that it is upward sloping, suggesting a positive relationship between the number of bakers and the output of bread. But we also see that the curve becomes flatter as we travel up and to the right along it; it is nonlinear and describes a nonlinear relationship.

How can we estimate the slope of a nonlinear curve? After all, the slope of such a curve changes as we travel along it. We can deal with this problem in two ways. One is to consider two points on the curve and to compute the slope between those two points. Another is to compute the slope of the curve at a single point.

When we compute the slope of a curve between two points, we are really computing the slope of a straight line drawn between those two points. In Figure 21.13, we have computed slopes between pairs of points A and B, C and D, and E and F on our curve for loaves of bread produced. These slopes equal 400 loaves/baker, 200 loaves/baker, and 50 loaves/baker, respectively. They are the slopes of the dashed-line segments shown. These dashed segments lie close to the curve, but they clearly are not on the curve. After all, the dashed segments are straight lines. Our curve relating the number of bakers to daily bread production is not a straight line; the relationship between the bakery's daily output of bread and the number of bakers is nonlinear.

FIGURE 21.13 Estimating Slopes for a Nonlinear Curve

We can estimate the slope of a nonlinear curve between two points. Here, slopes are computed between points A and B, C and D, and E and F. When we compute the slope of a nonlinear curve between two points, we are computing the slope of a straight line between those two points. Here the lines whose slopes are computed are the dashed lines between the pairs of points.

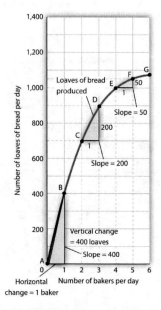

Every point on a nonlinear curve has a different slope. To get a precise measure of the slope of such a curve, we need to consider its slope at a single point. To do that, we draw a line tangent to the curve at that point. A **tangent line** is a straight line that touches, but does not intersect, a nonlinear curve at only one point. The slope of a tangent line equals the slope of the curve at the point at which the tangent line touches the curve.

Consider point D in Panel (a) of Figure 21.14. We have drawn a tangent line that just touches the curve showing bread production at this point. It passes through points labeled M and N. The vertical change between these points equals 300 loaves of bread; the horizontal change equals two bakers. The slope of the tangent line equals 150 loaves of bread/baker (300 loaves/2 bakers). The slope of our bread production curve at point D equals the slope of the line tangent to the curve at this point. In Panel (b), we have sketched lines tangent to the curve for loaves of bread produced at points B, D, and F. Notice that these tangent lines get successively flatter, suggesting again that the slope of the curve is falling as we travel up and to the right along it.

tangent line

A straight line that touches, but does not intersect, a nonlinear curve at only one point.

FIGURE 21.14 Tangent Lines and the Slopes of Nonlinear Curves

Because the slope of a nonlinear curve is different at every point on the curve, the precise way to compute slope is to draw a tangent line; the slope of the tangent line equals the slope of the curve at the point the tangent line touches the curve. In Panel (a), the slope of the tangent line is computed for us: it equals 150 loaves/baker. Generally, we will not have the information to compute slopes of tangent lines. We will use them as in Panel (b), to observe what happens to the slope of a nonlinear curve as we travel along it. We see here that the slope falls (the tangent lines become flatter) as the number of bakers rises.

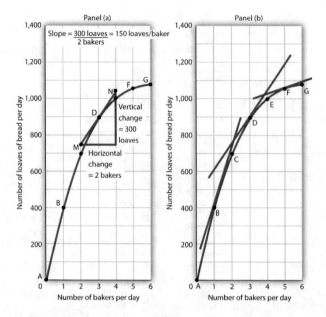

Notice that we have not been given the information we need to compute the slopes of the tangent lines that touch the curve for loaves of bread produced at points B and F. In this text, we will not have occasion to compute the slopes of tangent lines. Either they will be given or we will use them as we did here—to see what is happening to the slopes of nonlinear curves.

In the case of our curve for loaves of bread produced, the fact that the slope of the curve falls as we increase the number of bakers suggests a phenomenon that plays a central role in both microeconomic and macroeconomic analysis. As we add workers (in this case bakers), output (in this case loaves of bread) rises, but by smaller and smaller amounts. Another way to describe the relationship between the number of workers and the quantity of bread produced is to say that as the number of workers increases, the output increases at a decreasing rate. In Panel (b) of Figure 21.14 we express this idea with a graph, and we can gain this understanding by looking at the tangent lines, even though we do not have specific numbers. Indeed, much of our work with graphs will not require numbers at all.

We turn next to look at how we can use graphs to express ideas even when we do not have specific numbers.

2.2 Graphs Without Numbers

We know that a positive relationship between two variables can be shown with an upward-sloping curve in a graph. A negative or inverse relationship can be shown with a downward-sloping curve. Some relationships are linear and some are nonlinear. We illustrate a linear relationship with a curve whose slope is constant; a nonlinear relationship is illustrated with a curve whose slope changes. Using these basic ideas, we can illustrate hypotheses graphically even in cases in which we do not have numbers with which to locate specific points.

Consider first a hypothesis suggested by recent medical research: eating more fruits and vegetables each day increases life expectancy. We can show this idea graphically. Daily fruit and vegetable consumption (measured, say, in grams per day) is the independent variable; life expectancy (measured in years) is the dependent variable. Panel (a) of Figure 21.15 shows the hypothesis, which suggests a positive relationship between the two variables. Notice the vertical intercept on the curve we have drawn; it implies that even people who eat no fruit or vegetables can expect to live at least a while!

FIGURE 21.15 Graphs Without Numbers

We often use graphs without numbers to suggest the nature of relationships between variables. The graphs in the four panels correspond to the relationships described in the text.

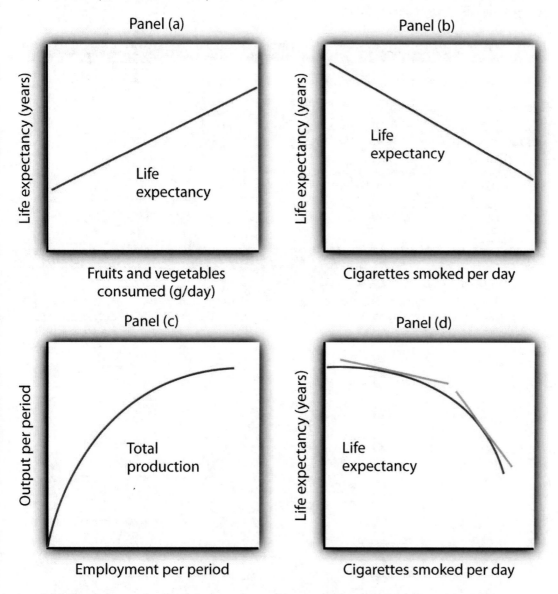

Panel (b) illustrates another hypothesis we hear often: smoking cigarettes reduces life expectancy. Here the number of cigarettes smoked per day is the independent variable; life expectancy is the dependent variable. The hypothesis suggests a negative relationship. Hence, we have a downward-sloping curve.

Now consider a general form of the hypothesis suggested by the example of Felicia Alvarez's bakery: increasing employment each period increases output each period, but by smaller and smaller amounts. As we saw in Figure 21.12, this hypothesis suggests a positive, nonlinear relationship. We have drawn a curve in Panel (c) of Figure 21.15 that looks very much like the curve for bread production in Figure 21.14. It is upward sloping, and its slope diminishes as employment rises.

Finally, consider a refined version of our smoking hypothesis. Suppose we assert that smoking cigarettes does reduce life expectancy and that increasing the number of cigarettes smoked per day reduces life expectancy by a larger and larger amount. Panel (d) shows this case. Again, our life expectancy curve slopes downward. But now it suggests that smoking only a few cigarettes per day reduces life expectancy only a little but that life expectancy falls by more and more as the number of cigarettes smoked per day increases.

We have sketched lines tangent to the curve in Panel (d). The slopes of these tangent lines are negative, suggesting the negative relationship between smoking and life expectancy. They also get steeper as the number of cigarettes smoked per day rises. Whether a curve is linear or nonlinear, a steeper curve is one for which the absolute value of the slope rises as the value of the variable on the horizontal axis rises. When we speak of the absolute value of a negative number such as −4, we ignore the minus sign and simply say that the absolute value is 4. The absolute value of −8, for example, is greater than the absolute value of −4, and a curve with a slope of −8 is steeper than a curve whose slope is −4.

Thus far our work has focused on graphs that show a relationship between variables. We turn finally to an examination of graphs and charts that show values of one or more variables, either over a period of time or at a single point in time.

KEY TAKEAWAYS

- The slope of a nonlinear curve changes as the value of one of the variables in the relationship shown by the curve changes.
- A nonlinear curve may show a positive or a negative relationship.
- The slope of a curve showing a nonlinear relationship may be estimated by computing the slope between two points on the curve. The slope at any point on such a curve equals the slope of a line drawn tangent to the curve at that point.
- We can illustrate hypotheses about the relationship between two variables graphically, even if we are not given numbers for the relationships. We need only draw and label the axes and then draw a curve consistent with the hypothesis.

TRY IT!

Consider the following curve drawn to show the relationship between two variables, A and B (we will be using a curve like this one in the next chapter). Explain whether the relationship between the two variables is positive or negative, linear or nonlinear. Sketch two lines tangent to the curve at different points on the curve, and explain what is happening to the slope of the curve.

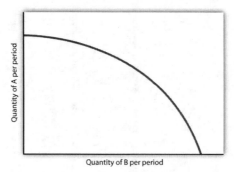

ANSWER TO TRY IT!

The relationship between variable A shown on the vertical axis and variable B shown on the horizontal axis is negative. This is sometimes referred to as an inverse relationship. Variables that give a straight line with a constant slope are said to have a linear relationship. In this case, however, the relationship is nonlinear. The slope changes all along the curve. In this case the slope becomes steeper as we move downward to the right along the curve, as shown by the two tangent lines that have been drawn. As the quantity of B increases, the quantity of A decreases at an increasing rate.

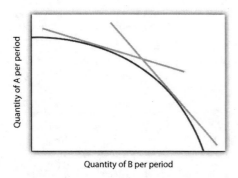

3. USING GRAPHS AND CHARTS TO SHOW VALUES OF VARIABLES

LEARNING OBJECTIVE

1. Understand and use time-series graphs, tables, pie charts, and bar charts to illustrate data and relationships among variables.

You often see pictures representing numerical information. These pictures may take the form of graphs that show how a particular variable has changed over time, or charts that show values of a particular variable at a single point in time. We will close our introduction to graphs by looking at both ways of conveying information.

3.1 Time-Series Graphs

One of the most common types of graphs used in economics is called a time-series graph. A **time-series graph** shows how the value of a particular variable or variables has changed over some period of time. One of the variables in a time-series graph is time itself. Time is typically placed on the horizontal axis in time-series graphs. The other axis can represent any variable whose value changes over time.

The table in Panel (a) of Figure 21.18 shows annual values of the unemployment rate, a measure of the percentage of workers who are looking for and available for work but are not working, in the United States from 1998 to 2007. The grid with which these values are plotted is given in Panel (b). Notice that the vertical axis is scaled from 3 to 8%, instead of beginning with zero. Time-series graphs are often presented with the vertical axis scaled over a certain range. The result is the same as introducing a break in the vertical axis, as we did in Figure 21.5

time-series graph

A graph that shows how the value of a particular variable or variables has changed over some period of time.

FIGURE 21.18 A Time-Series Graph

Panel (a) gives values of the U.S. unemployment rate from 1998 to 2008. These points are then plotted in Panel (b). To draw a time-series graph, we connect these points, as in Panel (c).

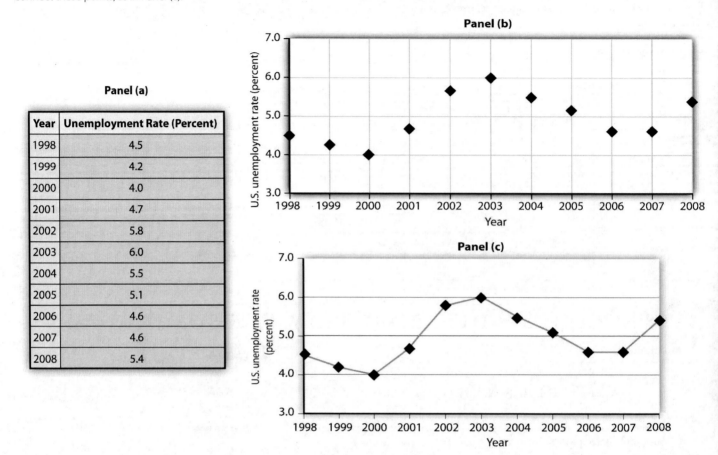

Panel (a)

Year	Unemployment Rate (Percent)
1998	4.5
1999	4.2
2000	4.0
2001	4.7
2002	5.8
2003	6.0
2004	5.5
2005	5.1
2006	4.6
2007	4.6
2008	5.4

The values for the U.S. unemployment rate are plotted in Panel (b) of Figure 21.18. The points plotted are then connected with a line in Panel (c).

Scaling the Vertical Axis in Time-Series Graphs

The scaling of the vertical axis in time-series graphs can give very different views of economic data. We can make a variable appear to change a great deal, or almost not at all, depending on how we scale the axis. For that reason, it is important to note carefully how the vertical axis in a time-series graph is scaled.

Consider, for example, the issue of whether an increase or decrease in income tax rates has a significant effect on federal government revenues. This became a big issue in 1993, when President Clinton proposed an increase in income tax rates. The measure was intended to boost federal revenues. Critics of the president's proposal argued that changes in tax rates have little or no effect on federal revenues. Higher tax rates, they said, would cause some people to scale back their income-earning efforts and thus produce only a small gain—or even a loss—in revenues. Op-ed essays in *The Wall Street Journal*, for example, often showed a graph very much like that presented in Panel (a) of Figure 21.19. It shows federal revenues as a percentage of gross domestic product (GDP), a measure of total income in the economy, since 1960. Various tax reductions and increases were enacted during that period, but Panel (a) appears to show they had little effect on federal revenues relative to total income.

FIGURE 21.19 Two Tales of Taxes and Income

A graph of federal revenues as a percentage of GDP emphasizes the stability of the relationship when plotted with the vertical axis scaled from 0 to 100, as in Panel (a). Scaling the vertical axis from 16 to 21%, as in Panel (b), stresses the short-term variability of the percentage and suggests that major tax rate changes have affected federal revenues.

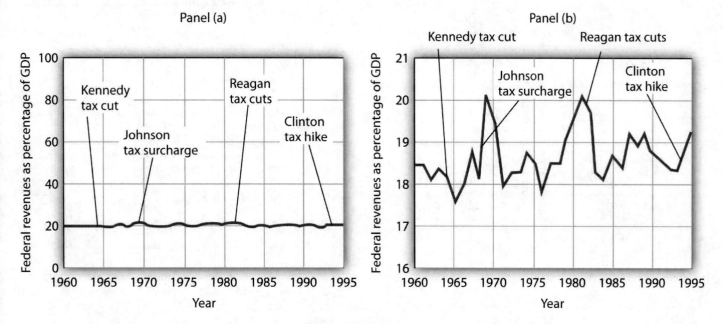

Laura Tyson, then President Clinton's chief economic adviser, charged that those graphs were misleading. In a *Wall Street Journal* piece, she noted the scaling of the vertical axis used by the president's critics. She argued that a more reasonable scaling of the axis shows that federal revenues tend to increase relative to total income in the economy and that cuts in taxes reduce the federal government's share. Her alternative version of these events does, indeed, suggest that federal receipts have tended to rise and fall with changes in tax policy, as shown in Panel (b) of Figure 21.19.

Which version is correct? Both are. Both graphs show the same data. It is certainly true that federal revenues, relative to economic activity, have been remarkably stable over the past several decades, as emphasized by the scaling in Panel (a). But it is also true that the federal share has varied between about 17 and 20%. And a small change in the federal share translates into a large amount of tax revenue.

It is easy to be misled by time-series graphs. Large changes can be made to appear trivial and trivial changes to appear large through an artful scaling of the axes. The best advice for a careful consumer of graphical information is to note carefully the range of values shown and then to decide whether the changes are really significant.

Testing Hypotheses with Time-Series Graphs

John Maynard Keynes, one of the most famous economists ever, proposed in 1936 a hypothesis about total spending for consumer goods in the economy. He suggested that this spending was positively related to the income households receive. One way to test such a hypothesis is to draw a time-series graph of both variables to see whether they do, in fact, tend to move together. Figure 21.20 shows the values of consumption spending and disposable income, which is after-tax income received by households. Annual values of consumption and disposable income are plotted for the period 1960–2007. Notice that both variables have tended to move quite closely together. The close relationship between consumption and disposable income is consistent with Keynes's hypothesis that there is a positive relationship between the two variables.

FIGURE 21.20 A Time-Series Graph of Disposable Income and Consumption

Plotted in a time-series graph, disposable income and consumption appear to move together. This is consistent with the hypothesis that the two are directly related.

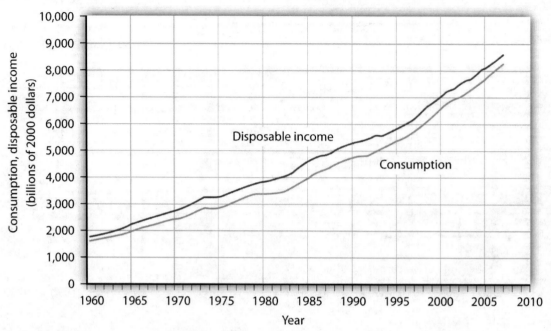

Source: Department of Commerce

The fact that two variables tend to move together in a time series does not by itself prove that there is a systematic relationship between the two. Figure 21.21 shows a time-series graph of monthly values in 1987 of the Dow Jones Industrial Average, an index that reflects the movement of the prices of common stock. Notice the steep decline in the index beginning in October, not unlike the steep decline in October 2008.

FIGURE 21.21 Stock Prices and a Mystery Variable

The movement of the monthly average of the Dow Jones Industrial Average, a widely reported index of stock values, corresponded closely to changes in a mystery variable, *X*. Did the mystery variable contribute to the crash?

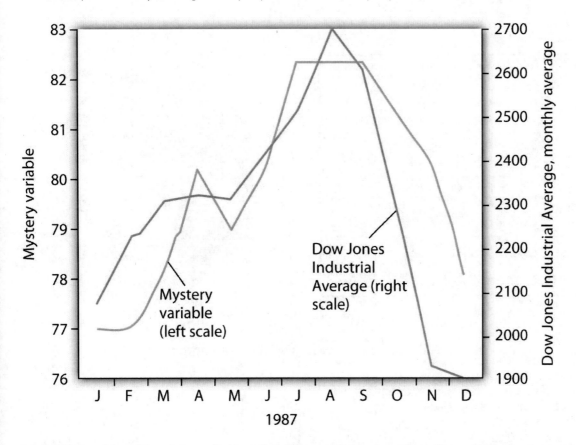

It would be useful, and certainly profitable, to be able to predict such declines. Figure 21.21 also shows the movement of monthly values of a "mystery variable," *X*, for the same period. The mystery variable and stock prices appear to move closely together. Was the plunge in the mystery variable in October responsible for the stock crash? The answer is: Not likely. The mystery value is monthly average temperatures in San Juan, Puerto Rico. Attributing the stock crash in 1987 to the weather in San Juan would be an example of the fallacy of false cause.

Notice that Figure 21.21 has two vertical axes. The left-hand axis shows values of temperature; the right-hand axis shows values for the Dow Jones Industrial Average. Two axes are used here because the two variables, San Juan temperature and the Dow Jones Industrial Average, are scaled in different units.

3.2 Descriptive Charts

We can use a table to show data. Consider, for example, the information compiled each year by the Higher Education Research Institute (HERI) at UCLA. HERI conducts a survey of first-year college students throughout the United States and asks what their intended academic majors are. The table in Panel (a) of Figure 21.22 shows the results of the 2007 survey. In the groupings given, economics is included among the social sciences.

FIGURE 21.22 Intended Academic Major Area, 2007 Survey of First-Year College Students

Panels (a), (b), and (c) show the results of a 2007 survey of first-year college students in which respondents were asked to state their intended academic major. All three panels present the same information. Panel (a) is an example of a table, Panel (b) is an example of a pie chart, and Panel (c) is an example of a horizontal bar chart.

Panel (a)

Intended Major	Percentage of First-Year College Students
Arts and Humanities	12.8
Biological sciences	8.6
Business	17.7
Education	9.2
Engineering	7.5
Other fields	7.2
Physical sciences	3.2
Professional	14.5
Social sciences	11.1
Technical	1.0
Undecided	7.0

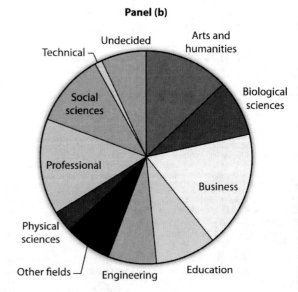

Panel (b)

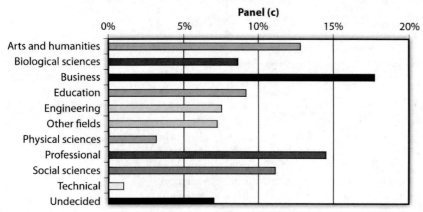

Panel (c)

Source: Higher Education Research Institute, 2007 Freshman Survey. Percentages shown are for broad academic areas, each of which includes several majors. For example, the social sciences include such majors as economics, political science, and sociology; business includes such majors as accounting, finance, and marketing; technical majors include electronics, data processing/ computers, and drafting.

Panels (b) and (c) of Figure 21.22 present the same information in two types of charts. Panel (b) is an example of a pie chart; Panel (c) gives the data in a bar chart. The bars in this chart are horizontal; they may also be drawn as vertical. Either type of graph may be used to provide a picture of numeric information.

KEY TAKEAWAYS

- A time-series graph shows changes in a variable over time; one axis is always measured in units of time.
- One use of time-series graphs is to plot the movement of two or more variables together to see if they tend to move together or not. The fact that two variables move together does not prove that changes in one of the variables cause changes in the other.
- Values of a variable may be illustrated using a table, a pie chart, or a bar chart.

TRY IT!

The table in Panel (a) shows a measure of the inflation rate, the percentage change in the average level of prices below. Panels (b) and (c) provide blank grids. We have already labeled the axes on the grids in Panels (b) and (c). It is up to you to plot the data in Panel (a) on the grids in Panels (b) and (c). Connect the points you have marked in the grid using straight lines between the points. What relationship do you observe? Has the inflation rate generally increased or decreased? What can you say about the trend of inflation over the course of the 1990s? Do you tend to get a different "interpretation" depending on whether you use Panel (b) or Panel (c) to guide you?

Panel (a)

Year	Inflation rate (percent)
1990	6.1
1991	3.1
1992	2.9
1993	2.7
1994	2.7
1995	2.5
1996	3.3
1997	1.7
1998	1.6

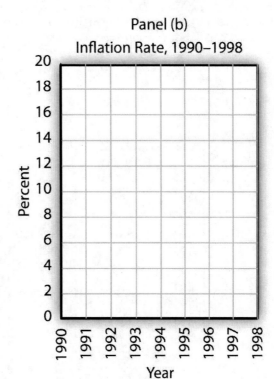

Panel (b)
Inflation Rate, 1990–1998

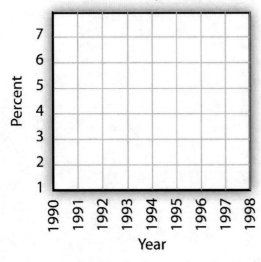

Panel (c)
Inflation Rate, 1990–1998

Here are the time-series graphs, Panels (b) and (c), for the information in Panel (a). The first thing you should notice is that both graphs show that the inflation rate generally declined throughout the 1990s (with the exception of 1996, when it increased). The generally downward direction of the curve suggests that the trend of inflation was downward. Notice that in this case we do not say negative, since in this instance it is not the slope of the line that matters. Rather, inflation itself is still positive (as indicated by the fact that all the points are above the origin) but is declining. Finally, comparing Panels (b) and (c) suggests that the general downward trend in the inflation rate is emphasized less in Panel (b) than in Panel (c). This impression would be emphasized even more if the numbers on the vertical axis were increased in Panel (b) from 20 to 100. Just as in Figure 21.19, it is possible to make large changes appear trivial by simply changing the scaling of the axes.

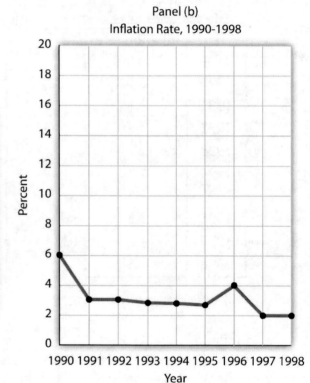

Panel (a)

Year	Inflation rate (percent)
1990	6.1
1991	3.1
1992	2.9
1993	2.7
1994	2.7
1995	2.5
1996	3.3
1997	1.7
1998	1.6

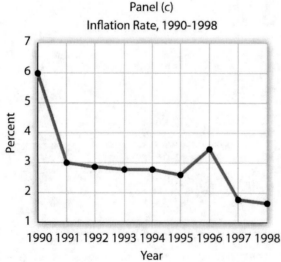

PROBLEMS

1. Panel (a) shows a graph of a positive relationship; Panel (b) shows a graph of a negative relationship. Decide whether each proposition below demonstrates a positive or negative relationship, and decide which graph you would expect to illustrate each proposition. In each statement, identify which variable is the independent variable and thus goes on the horizontal axis, and which variable is the dependent variable and goes on the vertical axis.

Panel (a)

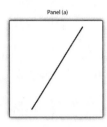

Panel (b)

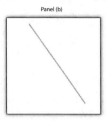

   a. An increase in national income in any one year increases the number of people killed in highway accidents.
   b. An increase in the poverty rate causes an increase in the crime rate.
   c. As the income received by households rises, they purchase fewer beans.
   d. As the income received by households rises, they spend more on home entertainment equipment.
   e. The warmer the day, the less soup people consume.

2. Suppose you have a graph showing the results of a survey asking people how many left and right shoes they owned. The results suggest that people with one left shoe had, on average, one right shoe. People with seven left shoes had, on average, seven right shoes. Put left shoes on the vertical axis and right shoes on the horizontal axis; plot the following observations:

Left shoes	1	2	3	4	5	6	7
Right shoes	1	2	3	4	5	6	7

   Is this relationship positive or negative? What is the slope of the curve?

3. Suppose your assistant inadvertently reversed the order of numbers for right shoe ownership in the survey above. You thus have the following table of observations:

Left shoes	1	2	3	4	5	6	7
Right shoes	7	6	5	4	3	2	1

   Is the relationship between these numbers positive or negative? What's implausible about that?

4. Suppose some of Ms. Alvarez's kitchen equipment breaks down. The following table gives the values of bread output that were shown in Figure 21.12 It also gives the new levels of bread output that Ms. Alvarez's bakers produce following the breakdown. Plot the two curves. What has happened?

	A	B	C	D	E	F	G
Bakers/day	0	1	2	3	4	5	6
Loaves/day	0	400	700	900	1,000	1,050	1,075
Loaves/day after breakdown	0	380	670	860	950	990	1,005

5. Steven Magee has suggested that there is a relationship between the number of lawyers per capita in a country and the country's rate of economic growth. The relationship is described with the following Magee curve.

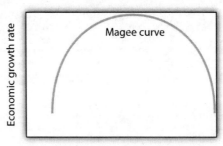

Lawyers per 1,000 population

What do you think is the argument made by the curve? What kinds of countries do you think are on the upward- sloping region of the curve? Where would you guess the United States is? Japan? Does the Magee curve seem plausible to you?

6. Draw graphs showing the likely relationship between each of the following pairs of variables. In each case, put the first variable mentioned on the horizontal axis and the second on the vertical axis.

   a. The amount of time a student spends studying economics and the grade he or she receives in the course

   b. Per capita income and total expenditures on health care

   c. Alcohol consumption by teenagers and academic performance

   d. Household income and the likelihood of being the victim of a violent crime

CHAPTER 22

Appendix B: Extensions of the Aggregate Expenditures Model

In this appendix, we will extend the aggregate expenditures model in two ways. First, we will express the model in general algebraic form and show how to solve it for the equilibrium level of real GDP. The advantage of using general algebraic expressions in place of the specific numbers that we used in the chapter is that we can then use the results to solve for any specific value that may pertain to a given economy. Second, we will show how the aggregate expenditures model can be used to analyze the impact of fiscal policies on the economy.

1. THE ALGEBRA OF EQUILIBRIUM

Suppose an economy can be represented by the following equations:

EQUATION 22.1

$$C = C_a + bY_d$$

EQUATION 22.2

$$T = T_a + tY$$

EQUATION 22.3

$$I_p = I_a$$

EQUATION 22.4

$$G = G_a$$

EQUATION 22.5

$$X_n = X_{n_a}$$

As in our specific example in the chapter, the consumption function given in Equation 22.1 has an autonomous component (C_a) and an induced component (bY_d), where b is the marginal propensity to consume (MPC). In the example in the chapter, C_a was $300 billion and the MPC, or b, was 0.8. Equation 22.2 shows that total taxes, T, include an autonomous component T_a (for example, property taxes, licenses, fees, and any other taxes that do not vary with the level of income) and an induced component that is a fraction of real GDP, Y. That fraction is the tax rate, t. Disposable personal income is just the difference between real GDP and total taxes:

EQUATION 22.6

$$Y_a = Y - T$$

In Equation 22.3, Equation 22.4, and Equation 22.5, I_a, G_a, and X_{n_a} are specific values for the other components of aggregate expenditures: investment (I_p), government purchases (G), and net exports (X_n). In this model, planned investments, government purchases, and net exports are all assumed to be autonomous. For this reason, we add the subscript "a" to each of them.

We use the equations that describe each of the components as aggregate expenditures to solve for the equilibrium level of real GDP. The equilibrium condition in the aggregate expenditures model requires that aggregate expenditures for a period equal real GDP in the period. We specify that condition algebraically:

EQUATION 22.7

$$Y = AE$$

Aggregate expenditures AE consist of consumption plus planned investment plus government purchases plus net exports. We thus replace the right-hand side of Equation 22.7 with those terms to get

EQUATION 22.8

$$Y = C + I_p + G + X_n$$

Consumption is given by Equation 22.1 and the other components of aggregate expenditures by Equation 22.3, Equation 22.4, and Equation 22.5. Inserting these equations into Equation 22.8, we have

EQUATION 22.9

$$Y = C_a + bY_d + I_a + G_a + X_{n_a}$$

We have one equation with two unknowns, Y and Y_d. We therefore need to express Y_d in terms of Y. From Equation 22.2 and Equation 22.6, we can write

$$Y_d = Y - (T_a + tY)$$

And remove the parentheses to obtain

EQUATION 22.10

$$Y_d = Y - T_a - tY$$

We then factor out the Y term on the right-hand side to get

EQUATION 22.11

$$Y_d = (1 - t)Y - T_a$$

We now substitute this expression for Y_d into Equation 22.9 to get

$$Y = C_a + b[(1 - t)Y - T_a] + I_a + G_a + X_{n_a}$$

EQUATION 22.12

$$Y = C_a - bT_a + b(1 - t)Y + I_a + G_a + X_{n_a}$$

The first two terms $(C_a - bT_a)$ show that the autonomous portion of consumption is reduced by the marginal propensity to consume times autonomous taxes. For example, suppose T_a is \$10 billion. If the marginal propensity to consume is 0.8, then consumption is \$8 billion less than it would have been if T_a were zero.

Combining the autonomous terms in Equation 22.12 in brackets, we have

EQUATION 22.13

$$Y = \left[C_a - b(T_a) + I_a + G_a + X_{n_a} \right] + b(1 - t)(Y)$$

Letting $\bar{A}$ stand for all the terms in brackets, we can simplify Equation 22.13:

EQUATION 22.14

$$Y = \bar{A} + b(1 - t)Y$$

The coefficient of real GDP (Y) on the right-hand side of Equation 22.14, $b(1 - t)$, gives the fraction of an additional dollar of real GDP that will be spent for consumption: it is the slope of the aggregate expenditures function for this representation of the economy. The aggregate expenditures function for the simplified economy that we presented in the chapter has a slope that was simply the marginal propensity to consume; there were no taxes in that model, and disposable personal income and real GDP were assumed to be the same. Notice that in using this more realistic aggregate expenditures function, the slope is less by a factor of $(1 - t)$.

We solve Equation 22.14 for Y:

$$Y - b(1 - t)(Y) = \bar{A}$$

$$Y[1 - b(1 - t)] = \bar{A}$$

EQUATION 22.15

$$Y = \frac{1}{1 - b(1 - t)}(\bar{A})$$

In Equation 22.15, $1/[1 - b(1 - t)]$ is the multiplier. Equilibrium real GDP is achieved at a level of income equal to the multiplier times the amount of autonomous spending. Notice that because the slope of the aggregate expenditures function is less than it would be in an economy without induced taxes, the value of the multiplier is also less, all other things the same. In this representation of the economy, the value of the multiplier depends on the marginal propensity to consume and on the tax rate. The higher the tax rate, the lower the multiplier; the lower the tax rate, the greater the multiplier.

For example, suppose the marginal propensity to consume is 0.8. If the tax rate were 0, then the multiplier would be 5. If the tax rate were 0.25, then the multiplier would be 2.5.

2.   THE AGGREGATE EXPENDITURES MODEL AND FISCAL POLICY

In this appendix, we use the aggregate expenditures model to explain the impact of fiscal policy on aggregate demand in more detail than was given in the chapter on government and fiscal policy. As we did in the chapter, we will look at the impact of various types of fiscal policy changes. The possibility of crowding out was discussed in the fiscal policy chapter and will not be repeated here.

2.1   Changes in Government Purchases

All other things unchanged, a change in government purchases shifts the aggregate expenditures curve by an amount equal to the change in government purchases. A $200-billion increase in government purchases, for example, shifts the aggregate expenditures curve upward by $200 billion. A $75-billion reduction in government purchases shifts the aggregate expenditures curve downward by that amount.

Panel (a) of Figure 22.1 shows an economy that is initially in equilibrium at an income of $7,000 billion. Suppose that the slope of the aggregate expenditures function (that is, $b[1 - t]$) is 0.6, so that the multiplier is 2.5. An increase of $200 billion in government purchases shifts the aggregate expenditures curve upward by that amount to AE_2. In the aggregate expenditures model, real GDP increases by an amount equal to the multiplier times the change in autonomous aggregate expenditures. Real GDP in that model thus rises by $500 billion to a level of $7,500 billion.

FIGURE 22.1 An Increase in Government Purchases

The economy shown here is initially in equilibrium at a real GDP of $7,000 billion and a price level of P_1. In Panel (a), an increase of $200 billion in the level of government purchases shifts the aggregate expenditures curve upward by that amount to AE_2, increasing the equilibrium level of income in the aggregate expenditures model by $500 billion. In Panel (b), the aggregate demand curve thus shifts to the right by $500 billion to AD_2. The equilibrium level of real GDP rises to $7,300 billion, while the price level rises to P_2.

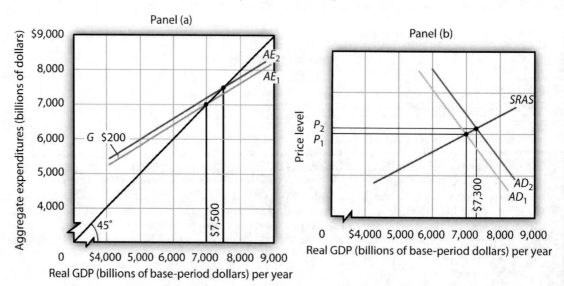

The aggregate expenditures model, of course, assumes a constant price level. To get a more complete picture of what happens, we use the model of aggregate demand and aggregate supply. In that model shown in Panel (b), the initial price level is P_1, and the initial equilibrium real GDP is $7,000 billion. That is the price level assumed to hold the aggregate expenditures model. The $200-billion increase in government purchases increases the total quantity of goods and services demanded, at a price level of P_1 by $500 billion. The aggregate demand curve thus shifts to the right by that amount to AD_2. The equilibrium level of real GDP, however, only rises to $7,300 billion, and the price level rises to P_2. Part of the impact of the increase in aggregate demand is absorbed by higher prices, preventing the full increase in real GDP predicted by the aggregate expenditures model.

A reduction in government purchases would have the opposite effect. All other things unchanged, aggregate expenditures would shift downward by an amount equal to the reduction in aggregate purchases. In the model of aggregate demand and aggregate supply, the aggregate demand curve would shift to the left by an amount equal to the initial change in autonomous aggregate expenditures times the multiplier. Real GDP and the price level would fall. The fall in real GDP is less than would occur if the price level stayed constant.

In the remainder of this appendix, we will focus on the shift in the aggregate expenditures curve. To determine what happens to equilibrium real GDP and the price level, we must look at the intersection of the new aggregate demand curve and the short-run aggregate supply curve, as we did in Panel (b) of Figure 22.1.

2.2   Change in Autonomous Taxes

A change in autonomous taxes shifts the aggregate expenditures in the opposite direction of the change in government purchases. If the autonomous taxes go up, for example, aggregate expenditures go down by a *fraction* of the change. Because the initial change in consumption is less than the change in taxes (because it is multiplied by the *MPC*, which is less than 1), the shift caused by a change in taxes is less than an equal change (in the opposite direction) in government purchases.

Now suppose that autonomous taxes fall by $200 billion and that the marginal propensity to consume is 0.8. Then the shift up in the aggregate expenditures curve is $160 billion (= 0.8 × $200). As we saw, a $200-billion increase in government purchases shifted the aggregate expenditures curve up by $200 billion. Assuming a multiplier of 2.5, the reduction in autonomous taxes causes equilibrium real GDP in the aggregate expenditures model to rise by $400 billion. This is less than the change of $500 billion caused by an equal (but opposite) change in government purchases. The impact of a $200-billion decrease in autonomous taxes is shown in Figure 22.2.

FIGURE 22.2   A Decrease in Autonomous Taxes

A decrease of $200 billion in autonomous taxes shifts the aggregate expenditures curve upward by the marginal propensity to consume of 0.8 times the changes in autonomous taxes of $200 billion, or $160 billion, to AE_2. The equilibrium level of income in the aggregate expenditures model increases by $400 billion to $7,400 billion. All figures are in billions of base-year dollars.

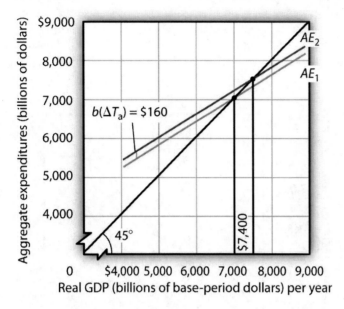

Similarly, an increase in autonomous taxes of, for example, $75 billion, would shift the aggregate expenditures curve downward by $60 billion (= 0.8 × $75) and cause the equilibrium level of real GDP to decrease by $150 billion (= 2.5 × $60).

2.3   Changes in Income Tax Rates

Changes in income tax *rates* produce an important complication that we have not encountered thus far. When government purchases or autonomous taxes changed, the aggregate expenditures curve shifted up or down. The new aggregate expenditures curve had the same slope as the old curve; the multiplier was the same before and after the change in government purchases or autonomous taxes. When income tax rates change, however, the aggregate expenditures curve will rotate, that is, its slope will change. As a result, the value of the multiplier itself will change.

We saw in the first section of this appendix that when taxes are related to income, the multiplier depends on both the marginal propensity to consume and the tax rate. An increase in income tax rates will make the aggregate expenditures curve flatter and reduce the multiplier. A higher income tax rate thus rotates the aggregate expenditures curve downward. Similarly, a lower income tax rate rotates the aggregate expenditures curve upward, making it steeper.

Suppose that an economy with an initial real GDP of $7,000 billion has an income tax rate of 0.25. To simplify, we will assume there are no autonomous taxes (that is, $T_a = 0$). So $T = tY$. Thus, disposable personal income Y_d is 75% of real GDP:

EQUATION 22.16

$$T = 0.25Y$$

EQUATION 22.17

$$Y_a = Y - T = 0.75Y$$

Suppose the marginal propensity to consume is 0.8. A $1 change in real GDP produces an increase in disposable personal income of $0.75, and that produces an increase in consumption of $0.60 (= 0.8 × 0.75 × $1). If the other components of aggregate expenditures are autonomous, then the multiplier is 2.5 (= 1 / [1 − 0.6]).

The impact of a tax rate change is illustrated in Figure 22.3. It shows the original aggregate expenditures curve AE_1 intersecting the 45-degree line at the income of $7,000 billion. The curve has a slope of 0.6. Now suppose that the tax rate is increased to 0.375. The higher tax rate will rotate this curve downward, making it flatter. The slope of the new aggregate expenditures curve AE_2 will be 0.5 (= 1 − 0.8[1 − 0.375]). The value of the multiplier thus falls from 2.5 to 2 (= 1 / [1 − 0.5]).

FIGURE 22.3 The Impact of an Increase in Income Tax Rates

An increase in the income tax rate rotates the aggregate expenditures curve downward by an amount equal to the initial change in consumption at the original equilibrium value of real GDP found in the aggregate expenditures model, $7,000 billion in this case, assuming no other change in aggregate expenditures. It reduces the slope of the aggregate expenditures curve and thus reduces the multiplier. Here, an increase in the income tax rate from 0.25 to 0.375 reduces the slope from 0.6 to 0.5; it thus reduces the multiplier from 2.5 to 2. The higher tax reduces consumption by $700 billion and reduces equilibrium real GDP in the aggregate expenditures model by $1,400 billion.

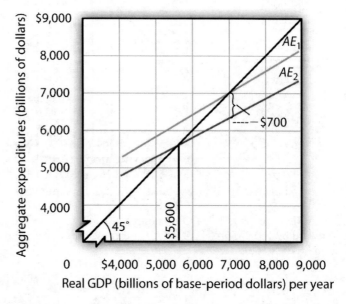

At the original level of income, $7,000 billion, tax collection equaled $1,750 billion (again, for this example, we assume $T_a = 0$, so $T = 0.25 \times \$7,000$). At the new tax rate and original level of income, they equal $2,625 billion (0.375 × $7,000 billion). Disposable personal income at a real GDP of $7,000 billion thus declines by $875 billion. With a marginal propensity to consume of 0.8, consumption drops by $700 billion (= 0.8 × $875 billion). The aggregate expenditures curve rotates down by this amount at the initial level of income of $7,000 billion, assuming no other changes in aggregate expenditures occur.

Before the tax rate increase, an additional $1 of real GDP induced $0.60 in additional consumption. At the new tax rate, an additional $1 of real GDP creates $0.625 in disposable personal income ($1 in income minus $0.375 in taxes). Given a marginal propensity to consume of 0.8, this $1 increase in real GDP increases consumption by only $0.50 (= [$1 × (0.8 × 0.625)]). The new aggregate expenditures curve, AE_2 in Figure 22.3, shows the end result of the tax rate change in the aggregate expenditures model. Its slope is 0.5. The equilibrium of the level of real GDP in the aggregate expenditures model falls to $5,600 billion from its original level of $7,000. The $1,400-billion reduction in equilibrium real GDP in the aggregate expenditures model is equal to the $700-billion initial reduction in consumption (at the original equilibrium level of real GDP) times the new multiplier of 2. The tax rate increase has reduced aggregate expenditures and reduced the multiplier impact of this change (from 2.5 to 2). The aggregate demand curve will shift to the left by $1,400 billion, the new multiplier times the initial change in aggregate expenditures.

In the model of aggregate demand and aggregate supply, a tax rate increase will shift the aggregate demand curve to the left by an amount equal to the initial change in aggregate expenditures induced by the tax rate boost times the *new* value of the multiplier. Similarly, a reduction in the income tax rate rotates the aggregate expenditures curve upward by an amount equal to the initial increase in consumption (at the original equilibrium level of real GDP found in the aggregate expenditures model) created by the lower tax rate. It also increases the value of the multiplier. Aggregate demand shifts to the right by an amount equal to the initial change in aggregate expenditures times the new multiplier.

3.   REVIEW AND PRACTICE

NUMERICAL PROBLEMS

1. Suppose an economy is characterized by the following equations. All figures are in billions of dollars.

    $C = 400 + \frac{2}{3}(Y_d)$

    $T = 300 + \frac{1}{4}(Y)$

    $G = 400$

    $I = 200$

    $X_n = 100$

    a. Solve for the equilibrium level of income.

    b. Now let G rise to 500. What happens to the solution?

    c. What is the multiplier?

2. Consider the following economy. All figures are in billions of dollars.

    $C = 180 + 0.8(Y_d)$

    $T = 100 + 0.25Y$

    $I = 300$

    $G = 400$

    $X_n = 200$

    a. Solve for the equilibrium level of real GDP.

    b. Now suppose investment falls to $200 billion. What happens to the equilibrium real GDP?

    c. What is the multiplier?

3. Suppose an economy has a consumption function $C = \$100 + \frac{2}{3} Y_d$. Autonomous taxes, T_a, equal 0, the income tax rate is 10%, and $Y_d = 0.9Y$. Government purchases, investment, and net exports each equal $100. Solve the following problems.

    a. Draw the aggregate expenditures curve, and find the equilibrium income for this economy in the aggregate expenditures model.

    b. Now suppose the tax rate rises to 25%, so $Y_d = 0.75Y$. Assume that government purchases, investments, and net exports are not affected by the change. Show the new aggregate expenditures curve and the new level of income in the aggregate expenditures model. Relate your answer to the multiplier effect of the tax change.

    c. Compare your result in the aggregate expenditures model to what the aggregate demand–aggregate supply model would show.

4. Suppose a program of federally funded public-works spending were introduced that was tied to the unemployment rate. Suppose the program were structured so that public-works spending would be $200 billion per year if the economy had an unemployment rate of 5% at the beginning of the fiscal year. Public-works spending would be increased by $20 billion for each percentage point by which the unemployment rate exceeded 5%. It would be reduced by $20 billion for every percentage point by which unemployment fell below 5%. If the unemployment rate were 8%, for example, public-works spending would be $260 billion. How would this program affect the slope of the aggregate expenditures curve?

Index

absolute income test
443-444, 450-452

aggregate demand
4, 161-192, 202, 208, 237-244, 249-257, 261-271, 276-280,
285-286, 293-307, 311-315, 322, 329-356, 360-370,
375-381, 387-399, 404-425, 430-432, 534-537

aggregate demand curve
161-187, 239, 243, 249-253, 262-271, 277, 293-307, 315,
322, 329-336, 340-343, 351-352, 361-366, 376-381, 389,
398-399, 412-417, 421-425, 432, 534-536

aggregate expenditures
307-337, 390, 531-537

aggregate expenditures function
317-325, 532-533

aggregate expenditures model
307-337, 390, 531-537

aggregate production function
197-202, 208-211, 340, 351-354

assets
27, 112, 139, 158, 163-165, 216-221, 225-227, 231-233,
240-246, 250-251, 264, 310-312, 349, 367-377, 381-382,
427, 481, 489

automatic stabilizer
293, 303

autonomous aggregate expenditures
315-336, 533-534

balance of payments
367, 371, 375

balance on capital account
369-373, 379-381

balance on current account
368-373, 379-381

balance sheet
220-221, 225-231

balanced budget
286-289

bank
5, 46-48, 111, 117, 131, 151-154, 161, 167, 175-176,
180-181, 216-241, 247-248, 252, 262, 267-275, 280-284,
359-360, 365, 374-381, 412-415, 429-433, 438, 456-457,
463-466, 470-471, 475-481, 485, 494-502

barter
214

base period
120-123

bond
137-139, 159, 230-231, 237-256, 262-265, 273, 277, 281,
298-299, 303, 312, 329, 344-347, 352-354, 370, 427

budget deficit
286-293, 298, 303-304

budget surplus
286-293, 426

business cycle
112-117, 132-137, 142, 196, 273, 287, 298, 428, 489

capacity utilization rate
348-349

capital
26-31, 37-39, 43-53, 64, 79-80, 93, 127, 139-149, 160-166,
171, 175, 198-210, 239, 278, 300-301, 306, 321, 332,
339-356, 363, 367-373, 379-381, 412, 417, 455-457, 463,
467, 474-483, 488-502

capital account
367-373, 379-381

capital account deficit
369

capital account surplus
367-370, 379-380

cash assistance
447-448, 458

central bank
48, 161, 167, 180-181, 218, 228-235, 262, 267-272,
280-284, 359-360, 374-381, 432, 481, 497

ceteris paribus
17-22, 58-60, 65-66

change in aggregate demand
162-167, 171, 185, 307, 322, 405, 413

change in demand
60-63, 72-77, 173, 238, 381

change in quantity demanded
59-66, 77

change in quantity supplied
69

change in short-run aggregate supply
168-171

change in supply
66-69, 74-77

**change in the aggregate quantity of goods
and services demanded**
162-163

**change in the aggregate quantity of goods
and services supplied**
168-171

check
4-5, 77, 150, 216, 222-223, 230-235, 244, 252, 474-477,
507

checkable deposits
216-235, 245

choice at the margin
13, 17

circular flow model
72, 79-81, 85, 93, 138-144, 156

classical economics
411, 420-421, 4

command socialist economy
45, 496-497, 5

commodity money
214-2

commodity standard system
3

comparative advantage
33-41, 46-53, 360-364, 380, 4

complements
61-63,

constant
17-19, 32, 60, 75, 79, 83, 113, 119, 123, 152, 171, 198, 2
275-282, 316, 323, 330-332, 348, 385-388, 403-4
472-474, 491, 498, 509-518, 5

consumer price index (CPI)
121, 125, 1

consumption function
307-316, 333-335, 362, 531, 5

contractionary policy
181-183, 261-269, 279-280, 297-302, 396, 417, 4.
425-4

corporate stock
93-95, 1

corporation
10, 16, 20, 29, 39, 48, 64, 70, 81, 93-97, 101, 105, 111, 1
227-230, 235, 367, 441, 451, 456, 490, 5

credit easing
271, 2

crowding in
3

crowding out
298-304, 5

currency
48, 153, 158, 165, 213-223, 230-241, 260-262, 359-3
367-381, 465, 480-4

currency board arrangements
3

current account
367-373, 379-3

current account deficit
368-372, 379-3

current account surplus
368-3

current income hypothesis
307, 311-3

cyclical unemployment
129-132, 397-4

deflation
118-125, 132-135, 259-262, 270-271, 284, 398-3

demand curve

58-65, 72-87, 93-104, 128, 161-187, 200-203, 239-257, 262-271, 277, 293-307, 315, 322, 329-336, 340-356, 361-366, 376-381, 389, 398-399, 412-417, 421-425, 432, 515, 534-536

demand curve for money

244-246, 254

demand for money

163, 244-254, 276-280, 429

demand schedule

58-63

demand shifter

58-63, 71, 162-164

demographic transition

472-477

dependency theory

478-483

dependent variable

19, 31, 506-507, 515-519, 529

deposit multiplier

219, 224-226, 230-233

depreciation

147-150, 156-158, 165, 209, 315, 332, 341-345, 349, 355-356, 378, 417

developing country

464-465, 480

diminishing marginal returns

197-198

direct tax

148

discount rate

230-231, 260-262, 266

discrimination

435-461, 470

disposable personal income

146-149, 156-157, 191, 293-296, 302, 307-325, 333-335, 531-536

dividends

80, 94, 349

economic development

55, 456, 463-485

economic growth

7, 40-55, 95, 111, 140, 191-212, 259-260, 300-301, 306, 340, 351-354, 376, 385, 397-404, 409, 426-428, 449, 464, 468-472, 478-484, 498, 503, 529

economic system

25-28, 38-40, 45-46, 50, 489-492, 502-503

economics

1-23, 49, 57, 68, 80, 85, 131, 136, 160-161, 184, 219, 233-236, 284, 292, 298-301, 398, 405-436, 442, 452-453, 461, 470, 485-488, 505-530

efficiency-wage theory

402

efficient production

37, 493

entrepreneur

28, 458

equation of exchange

273-283, 397, 418

equilibrium price

72-109, 175, 186-188, 239, 254-255, 376, 502

equilibrium quantity

72-98, 103, 107-109

excess reserves

221-224, 230-235

exchange rate

165, 219, 241-243, 250-256, 262-268, 281, 299-303, 359, 363-365, 369-382, 465-466, 480-481

expansion

113-115, 128, 132, 136, 142, 161, 176, 230, 238, 260, 268, 287, 296, 353, 365, 392, 421, 431, 499

expansionary policy

180-185, 261, 265-268, 280, 302, 395, 404-405, 416-417, 422-429

exponential growth

194-196, 212

exports

41, 112, 138-148, 156-171, 175-179, 185-188, 240-243, 250-256, 262-268, 281, 299-303, 314, 324-336, 342, 359-383, 412, 479-481, 531-532, 537

face value of a bond

238-239, 370

factor markets

72, 80-81

factors of production

25-31, 35-54, 68-69, 79-80, 93, 126, 139-143, 150, 157, 171, 175, 179, 198, 204-209, 343, 360, 367, 495-496, 502

fallacy of false cause

17-22, 525

federal funds market

230

federal funds rate

230-232, 243, 251-252, 259-262, 268-273, 280-281, 385, 429

fiat money

214-218

financial capital

27

financial intermediary

219

financial markets

112, 176, 206, 230-233, 237-262, 277, 367, 480

fiscal policy

181, 260, 271, 285-305, 327, 339, 378, 386-387, 391-398, 409-433, 481-483, 533

fixed exchange rate system

375-377

flow variable

138-139, 146

foreign exchange market

238-242, 250, 254, 299, 370, 379-381

fractional reserve banking system

219-220

free good

8-9

free-floating exchange rate system

374-377

frictional unemployment

129, 399-405

full employment

30, 36-37, 42, 128, 134, 161, 260-261, 328, 387-390, 402-405, 409-413, 417-418, 430-431

Gini coefficient

437-440

government purchases

98-101, 112, 138-146, 158-168, 173-181, 186, 275-278, 286-305, 314, 324-327, 333-336, 342-343, 360, 370, 387-390, 413, 421, 432, 531-537

graph

39, 46, 53, 59, 63, 70-72, 77, 86-87, 103-107, 116, 158, 162-163, 175, 185-186, 192, 202, 210, 251-256, 260, 267, 304-313, 335-336, 352, 378-381, 398, 423, 438, 459-460, 505-529

gross domestic income (GDI)

146

gross national product (GNP)

143, 149

gross private domestic investment

122, 138-140, 148, 158, 340-345, 354-356, 412

human capital

26-28, 43-51, 204-207, 301, 352, 455-457, 467, 477-483

hyperinflation

120, 247, 501

hypothesis

18-21, 267, 271-272, 307, 311-314, 333, 421, 427-428, 470, 518-524

impact lag

268, 273, 298-301, 426-428

implementation lag

268, 298-303, 418

implicit price deflator

122-126, 132-134, 161-162, 176, 274, 385-387, 391, 418, 425

import substitution

478-483

imports

51, 141-144, 148-149, 158-165, 240-243, 264, 329, 337, 361-373, 381-382, 480

independent variable

19, 506-511, 515-519, 529

Indirect taxes
148-150, 156-160

induced aggregate expenditures
314-316, 326

inefficient production
30, 37-38, 45, 53

inferior good
62-65

inflation
13, 22, 111, 118-126, 132-136, 155, 172, 182-183, 191-193, 197, 206-207, 215-216, 237, 247, 260-284, 297-300, 328, 376, 385-409, 418-419, 424-432, 438, 493-497, 501, 527-528

inflationary gap
178-185, 194, 251-253, 263-271, 293-298, 302-303, 328, 387, 395, 404, 411-413, 417-418, 422-424, 429-432

intercept
309, 323-328, 507-510, 518

interest rate
163-167, 185, 221, 230-232, 238-256, 261-270, 277, 299-302, 329-333, 346-355

interest rate effect
163-167, 185, 329-333

international finance
359-383

international trade effect
163, 167, 185, 329-333, 363-364

investment demand curve
346-356

Keynesian economics
410-431

labor
4, 10-15, 23-31, 37-39, 43-44, 49-51, 57, 68, 76-80, 90, 100-102, 119-134, 139, 143, 152, 157, 161, 167-186, 197-210, 266, 292, 340-351, 361-364, 392, 401-405, 419, 439-441, 448-460, 468-470, 474, 480-481, 487-498, 502-503, 509-510

labor force
127-134, 171, 200, 206, 210, 266, 292, 343, 392, 448-451, 457, 470

labor theory of value
488-493, 503

law
14-21, 34-38, 50-51, 59, 63-65, 83, 99-100, 110, 123, 133, 152, 206, 215-218, 229, 246, 254, 350, 427, 435, 444, 455, 474, 479, 496

law of demand
59, 63, 83, 123, 246, 474

law of increasing opportunity cost
34-38, 50-51

liabilities
220-221, 225, 229, 233, 296

linear curve
35, 509

linear relationship
509-513, 518-521

liquidity
216, 230-233, 244, 262, 266-272, 279, 314, 432

liquidity trap
262, 267-270, 279

loaned up
221-227, 235

long run
138, 168-169, 175-180, 184-186, 192-195, 201, 271-279, 283-284, 339-340, 353-356, 360, 364, 370, 380-382, 397-404, 411-414, 419-421, 425-431, 488-489

long-run aggregate supply (LRAS) curve
169

Lorenz curve
437-442, 459-460

M1
214-218, 233-234, 252, 282

M2
214-218, 233-234, 252, 274-277, 282, 398, 419-422, 426-427

macroeconomics
4-536

Malthusian trap
472-477, 483

managed float
374-377

margin
13-17, 21-22, 474

marginal propensity to consume
308-309, 313-325, 333-336, 531-536

marginal propensity to save
311-313, 323, 333-335

market capitalist economy
45, 487-489, 497-499, 503

markets
12-13, 18, 26, 57, 72-73, 79-85, 89-92, 97-98, 103-108, 112, 137-139, 152, 162-163, 168, 172, 176, 206, 214, 230-233, 237-262, 271-273, 277, 365-374, 441, 455, 460, 478-481, 489-493, 498

maturity date
238-239, 254-255

medium of exchange
213-219, 233-234

microeconomics
4, 12-16, 21-22, 65, 139, 160, 184

mixed economies
45, 50

model
4, 18, 25, 30-31, 35-42, 47-50, 57, 72-75, 79-108, 123, 128, 138-144, 156, 161, 166, 171-175, 184-186, 191-192, 197-209, 237, 241, 251, 256, 262, 271, 278-280, 296, 307-340, 351-356, 362, 389-402, 406, 410-414, 418-421, 425, 431-432, 452-455, 460, 478, 492-494, 507, 531-537

model of demand and supply
18, 57, 72-75, 80-90, 94-97, 102-108, 241, 5

monetarist school
416-4

monetary policy
111, 181, 219, 228-233, 248-286, 293, 297-303, 3 376-379, 385-387, 395-397, 405, 409-431, 4

money
9, 27, 70, 106, 112, 119-120, 125, 132, 139, 146, 1 213-264, 268-287, 306, 311-312, 329, 340, 346, 3 375-377, 386, 390, 397-430, 436, 443, 448, 463, 480, 4

money market
217, 237, 244-256, 262-264, 271, 2

money market equilibrium
248-2

money supply
213-237, 244, 248-256, 261-264, 268-283, 375-3 397-398, 406, 412-430, 4

movement along a curve
115, 505, 5

Multiplier
162, 166-167, 184, 188, 219, 224-226, 230-233, 262-2 268, 294-296, 302-306, 314, 320-336, 343, 348-3 363-364, 381, 479, 533-5

multiplier
162, 166-167, 184, 188, 219, 224-226, 230-233, 262-2 268, 294-296, 302-306, 314, 320-336, 343, 348-3 363-364, 381, 479, 533-5

national debt
286, 290-293, 302-304, 370, 378, 4

natural level of employment
126-132, 168-169, 175-178, 183-186, 194, 199-201, 3 364, 410-4

natural rate of unemployment
126-130, 183-185, 392, 399-405, 4

natural resources
26-28, 37, 45, 49-51, 79, 127, 139, 147, 171, 175, 198-2 343-346, 353, 492-496, 5

negative relationship
31, 162-163, 185, 239, 246, 346-347, 354, 363, 386, 4 509, 513-515, 519-520, 5

net exports
112, 138-148, 156-167, 175-179, 185-186, 242-24 250-256, 262-268, 281, 299-303, 314, 324-336, 34 359-383, 480, 531-532, 5

net worth
220, 2

new classical economics
420-421, 4.

new Keynesian economics
425-4

nominal GDP
113, 122-126, 132-134, 138, 151-156, 273-282, 37 419-422, 426-4.

nominal value
123, 418-4

noncash assistance
448-450

nonintervention policy
180-185

nonlinear curve
35, 515-520

nonlinear relationship
516-520

normal good
62-65, 246, 482

normative statement
19

open-market operations
229-234, 248-250, 261-268, 412

opportunity cost
8-17, 21-22, 26, 31-38, 50-53, 68, 105, 214, 346-347, 360, 474

origin
60, 163, 394, 445, 454, 507-510, 528

output per capita
192-197, 210

partnership
93, 464

peak
1, 114-116, 132, 136, 293

per capita real GNP or GDP
151-153

permanent income
307, 311-314, 333

permanent income hypothesis
307, 311-314, 333

personal consumption
122, 138-148, 156, 162, 308, 342-343

personal consumption expenditures price index
122

personal saving
310-313, 335

Phillips curve
386-404

Phillips phase
389-396, 404-406

planned investment
315-327, 336, 532

positive relationship
66, 239, 398, 482, 509, 513-518, 529

positive statement
19

potential output
161-162, 167-187, 192-203, 208-210, 262, 276, 282, 303, 340, 356, 382, 392-393, 397-399, 405, 410-426, 432, 472

poverty line
106-108, 191, 442-452, 458-463

poverty rate
443-450, 457-458, 463-464, 529

precautionary demand for money
244

price ceiling
99-100, 107-108

price floor
97-100, 107-109

price index
118-125, 132-136, 262, 273, 390, 405

product markets
80, 206, 441

production possibilities curve
30-53, 126, 140, 191-192, 196, 204, 343-344, 351-354, 360, 453-457

production possibilities model
25, 30-31, 35-40, 47-50, 192, 340, 478, 507

productivity
29-30, 51, 152, 160, 200-205, 340, 352, 372, 378, 402, 468-470, 474, 479, 483, 499-502

quantitative easing
270-271, 279

quantity demanded
18-19, 58-66, 72-77, 81-87, 97-100, 109, 163, 239, 244-246, 255-256

quantity supplied
65-87, 97-100, 104, 109, 128, 183, 239-241, 255, 367-368, 379, 500

quantity theory of money
273-276

quota
11, 360, 493, 503

rational expectations hypothesis
267, 271-272, 421, 427-428

real GDP
113-117, 122-126, 132-138, 151-188, 192-201, 205-213, 217, 237-257, 261, 265-307, 314-343, 351-356, 360-366, 375-376, 380-382, 389-397, 404-432, 468-473, 481, 502, 531-537

real value
120-125, 138, 163-164, 175, 329

recession
4-7, 111-117, 131-132, 136, 151, 161, 175-176, 181, 237, 260-262, 266-273, 285-287, 293-300, 311-313, 339-340, 356, 361, 365, 375-381, 385, 389, 393-396, 404-405, 410-412, 418, 422-430

recessionary gap
177-187, 194-197, 256, 260-270, 294, 300-303, 311, 359, 387, 392-396, 402-405, 410-426, 431-432

recognition lag
267, 273, 298, 302

recovery phase
389-396, 404-406

relative income test
443-444, 450-452

required reserve ratio
221-227, 232-235

required reserves
221-222, 227

reservation wage
400-401

reserves
220-237, 248, 267-270, 376-378, 412

retained earnings
94, 149, 315

rotation of a curve
512

rule of 72
192-196, 208, 212, 484

saving function
307-310, 333-335

scarce good
8

scarcity
8-12, 21-55

scatter diagram
507

scientific method
17-21

shift in a curve
505, 510-511

short run
168-179, 183-188, 206, 251, 256, 273-285, 299, 339-343, 351, 356, 361-364, 370, 380-382, 397-399, 412-421, 425-427, 481

short-run aggregate supply (SRAS) curve
171

shortage
74, 81-83, 87, 99-100, 108, 168, 181, 502

slope
30-38, 50-52, 59, 94, 162-165, 175, 186, 246, 308-310, 315-328, 333-337, 347, 363, 400, 505-521, 528-537

sole proprietorship
93

specialization
30, 38, 42, 47-50, 380

speculative demand for money
245-246

stabilization policy
180-185, 266, 271, 297, 386, 397, 419, 425, 432

stagflation phase
389-395, 404-406

sticky price
168, 172

ck market

89-96, 161-164, 176, 266, 280, 307, 374, 412, 432

stock variable

138-139

store of value

213-219, 233

structural unemployment

129-132, 397-405

substitutes

61-64, 84, 254

supply curve

65-87, 91-99, 103-108, 128, 168-187, 192, 197-211,
239-243, 247-254, 262-264, 271, 298-302, 306, 340,
352-354, 361-364, 376-379, 389-399, 404, 412-425,
431-432, 472, 515, 534

supply curve of money

248

supply schedule

65-69

supply shifter

65-71

supply-side economics

298-301

surplus

73-74, 81-83, 87, 97-102, 108-109, 141, 149, 160, 168,
286-293, 298-303, 367-370, 375, 379-380, 422, 426,
488-489, 503

surplus value

488-489, 503

tangent line

517-518

tariff

101, 360, 412

technology

25-31, 35, 43-51, 65-69, 76, 129, 171, 175-179, 186,
198-211, 343, 349, 354, 363-364, 379, 389, 401, 405, 477,
493-495

theory

1-4, 14, 18-21, 48, 89, 229, 260, 273-276, 284, 397,
402-405, 409-411, 420-424, 428-432, 461, 478-483,
488-493, 503

third-party payer

104-107

time-series graph

521-526

trade deficit

141, 370, 380

trade surplus

141

trade-weighted exchange rate

241, 381

transactions demand for money

244

transfer payment

287, 291-293, 367, 432, 4

transfer payments

141, 146-150, 158-160, 165, 181, 287-288, 292-3(
367-368, 381, 4.

trough

114-116, 132-136, 2

unemployment rate

13, 112-115, 127-134, 172, 183-185, 260-261, 28
385-406, 410, 417-418, 429, 521-522, 5.

unit of account

213-214, 218-219, 233-2

unplanned investment

315, 320, 3

utility

10, 26-

value added

142-146, 152, 1

variable

17-19, 31, 61, 68, 79, 138-139, 146, 172, 194, 198, 2(
276-278, 348, 415, 419, 479, 505-5

velocity

274-282, 397-399, 404-406, 419, 427-4.

wealth effect

163, 167, 185, 312, 329-3

welfare programs

207, 426, 442, 447-4